![bizmanualz logo]

Computer & IT
Policies and Procedures Manual

Easily Create Your IT Policy Manual to Manage
IT Security, IT Assets, and Software Development
Procedure Templates

Bizmanualz, Inc.

St. Louis, MO, USA

TRADEMARKS

Bizmanualz® is a Registered Trademark of Bizmanualz, Inc.

This publication is sold with the understanding that the publisher is not engaged in rendering legal, accounting, or other professional services. If legal advice or other expert assistance is required, the services of a competent professional should be sought. The Publisher cannot in any way guarantee that the forms, agreements, and statements in this manual are being used for the purpose intended and, therefore, assumes no responsibility for their proper and correct use.

Other Products from Bizmanualz, Inc.

ABR31M	Accounting Policies and Procedures Manual	ISBN 978-1-9315-9102-7
ABR41M	Human Resources Policies and Procedures Manual	ISBN 978-1-9315-9110-2
ABR42M	Finance Policies and Procedures Manual	ISBN 978-1-9315-9104-1
ABR33M	Disaster Recovery Policies and Procedures Manual	ISBN 978-1-9315-9113-3
ABR44M	Sales & Marketing Policies and Procedures Manual	ISBN 978-1-9315-9111-9
ABR32M	Security Planning Policies and Procedures Manual	ISBN 978-1-9315-9112-6
ABR211M	ISO 9001 QMS Policies and Procedures Manual	ISBN 978-1-9315-9115-7
ABR213M	ISO 22000 FSMS Policies and Procedures Manual	ISBN 978-1-9315-9116-4

IT Policies and Procedures
Table of Contents

PROCEDURES

IT Administration

IT Asset Management

IT Training & Support

IT Security & Disaster Recovery

Software Development
ITSW101-1 IT Project Plan
ITSW102-1 IT Project Development Database
ITSW102-2 IT Project Status Report
ITSW102-3 IT Project Team Review Checklist
ITSW102-4 IT Project Progress Review Checklist
ITSW104-1 Design Review Checklist
ITSW105-1 Work Product Review Checklist
ITSW106-1 Request For Document Change (RDC)
ITSW107-1 Software Project Test Script
ITSW107-2 Software Project Test Checklist
ITSW107-3 Software Project Test Problem Report
ITSW108-1 Design Change Request Form
ITSW109-1 Software License Agreement
ITSW109-2 Software Limited Warranty
ITSW109-3 Software Copyright Notice
ITSW111-1 Software Consulting Agreement
ITSW111-2 Statement Of Work
ITSW111-3 Software Consulting Customer Support Log
ITSW112-1 Software Training Evaluation Form

IT Policies and Procedures

Section 100

Introduction

Section 100
Introduction

Introduction

This section provides an introduction to the basic concepts of Information Technology (IT) – its structure, standards, security requirements, and definitions.

The IT field is constantly changing, so that no document can claim to capture every possible issue, policy, or procedure and still be current. The concepts discussed in this manual cover the common, basic elements of an IT Management System.

[This page intentionally left blank]

Contributors

CHRISTOPHER ANDERSON, MBA, CQA

Christopher Anderson is currently the Managing Director of Bizmanualz, Inc., responsible for leading services engagements and directing the development of all manual products and training materials. He has over 17 years of business management and quality process consulting experience working with small to large software and technology corporations.

As founder, CEO and President of Investorsoftware.com, an Internet catalog and e-commerce company, Chris oversaw the construction of the e-commerce website, LAN & WAN networks, firewalls, Internet marketing, and other IT systems that supported the company, including multiple Linux web, mail and e-commerce servers, Microsoft Windows 2000/NT domain controllers, PC and MAC systems, and digital copiers, faxes, and printers connected over a LAN. The LAN is connected to a dedicated high-speed internet line behind a firewall.

Mr. Anderson served as Vice President at Arc Tangent, a software publisher where he managed all operations, technical support, sales, accounting and administration. Software development was performed over a Novell LAN.

Prior to Arc Tangent, Mr. Anderson managed North American distribution sales for Interactive Systems, a UNIX operating system developer, publisher and services firm. Interactive Systems supported or developed UNIX multi-user systems, TCP/IP networking and X11 workstation solutions including VP/ix, Novell Ported Netware, Norton Utilities, Lotus 1-2-3, OSF Motif, Visix Looking Glass and variants of UNIX System releases for computer companies.

He has worked as a marketing analyst as Nixdorf Computer Corporation that provided integrated custom solutions for retail department stores, fire and police dispatch, large-scale data entry, and other markets.

As an electrical and computer engineer for McDonnell-Douglas Corporation (now Boeing), Mr. Anderson developed Tomahawk anti-ship missile simulation and analysis software on a high-end line of HP Unix workstations. He developed custom interfaces using FORTRAN and C, color graphics routines, and full screen edit and color windowing capabilities similar to Unix curses routines. He designed and implemented an automated source code management system using Unix's SCCS and INFORMIX SQL relational database and he was responsible for basic system administration, installation, and configuration of all systems.

He served as a Lieutenant and Aeronautical Engineering Duty Officer for the U.S. Navy, working for the Naval Air System Command. He is currently the Managing Director of Bizmanualz, Inc., and lead business process consultant and instructor for his company's "How to Create Well-Defined Processes" and "How to Align a System of People and Processes for Results" course.

Mr. Anderson holds a Master of Business Administration (MBA) degree from Pepperdine University and a Bachelor of Science degree in Electrical Engineering (BSEE) from Southern Illinois University-Carbondale.

STEPHEN FLICK, MBA, MIM, CQA, CMQ/OE, CSSGB

Steve was the Bizmanualz, Inc., Product Manager from 2005-2011. As such, Steve was responsible for developing new products and updating product inventory. Prior to that, he had over 20 years of information technology experience, working primarily with large corporations in the manufacturing and service sectors. Steve he has been a member of the Quality field for about a decade, mainly as a quality auditor and content developer/technical writer.

Steve has served a variety of organizations as a software designer, systems analyst, data analyst, and data warehouse subject matter expert. He has significant experience developing policy and procedure manuals, systems documentation, and training materials for Brown Group, General Metal Products, Amdocs, Charter Communications, CenturyLink, and others.

Steve holds a Master of Business Administration degree in marketing from Webster University and a Master of Information Management from Washington University of St. Louis. He is certified by the American Society for Quality (ASQ) and the International Register of Certificated Auditors (IRCA) as an ISO 9001 Quality Auditor.

Steve is currently a self-employed quality consultant (Q9C Quality Consulting, LLC, is his firm); he counts Bizmanualz, Inc., among his clients.

IT MANUAL INTRODUCTION
TABLE OF CONTENTS

[This page intentionally left blank]

Who Needs I.T. Policies and Procedures?

This introduction is meant to explain the basic concepts of information technology – its background, structure, standards, and definitions – and their effect on business process management. The need to review these concepts is greater now than it ever was and it will continue to be, as information technology solutions have become more robust, more specialized, and more varied with time. The rapid pace of technology change continues, in spite of predictions over a decade ago that "Moore's Law" had run its course.

The Recent Past

Only twenty years ago, small- to medium-sized businesses had a limited number of hardware and software choices. The de facto hardware standard was the IBM System/36 (which was followed by the System/38 and AS/400). The computer "network" in those days consisted of a number of "dumb" terminals, hard-wired to the mainframe or midrange computer. High-speed impact printers – perhaps one to a department, but often one to a building – were the order of the day.

Practically all data processing was done in "batch mode." Companies hired programmers to develop proprietary applications which, because of extremely limited processing and storage space (the System/36 5360 offered 128 to 512 Kb of main storage and 30 to 400 Mb of internal disk storage), were limited to processes that generated large volumes of data and were relatively simple to translate into computer code, such as accounting and inventory tracking.

Users did not immediately have direct access to raw data stored on the computer; instead, they received periodic reports, like monthly sales by region. By the mid-1980's, microcomputers were gaining wide acceptance. Processing power was increasing exponentially, even as the cost of processors was decreasing. Personal computers came into being, which meant users could process data on demand. They could take their monthly sales figures, for example, and perform detailed analyses in much less time. However, user still could not access raw data directly, which is what they really wanted.

Microcomputer applications were originally one of two types, spreadsheet or text (one of the first off-the-shelf spreadsheet applications was VisiCalc; WordStar was one of the earliest forms of word processing software). Gradually, improvements in applications, true computer networking capability, and the like came about because personal computer users needed and demanded changes.

As processors, applications, and operating systems improved, fewer computer users had to be technologically savvy to get work done. High-speed network backbones, client-server environments, and the coming of the Internet enabled greater amounts of data to be acquired and shared across boundaries than ever before. Unfortunately, changes in the technology have not automatically led to changes in the way users work with the data, or with one another. Connectivity has not guaranteed collaboration or unity of purpose.

Few companies acquired computers or applications with an eye to the long term. Acquiring information technologies, which began as as a departmental exercise – an attempt by users to "regain" control of "their" information – remained (and still remains) a fragmented process in many organizations. As the technology has changed, businesses have not often looked at what was best for the organization, as a whole. Little consideration is given to whether the company's business strategy is driving its IT capabilities, and not the other way around.

The Present

Some organizations have begun to recognize the benefits of the long-term, customer oriented approach to systems development. Decision makers are buying into the concepts long ago proposed by people like W. Edwards Deming and Joseph Juran. They are taking a look at their organizations, comparing what they are with what they would like to be, and are taking steps to get there, developing "The Strategic Plan." They are modeling business processes, looking at ways to improve those processes, and using that information to drive the technology.

The Future

The future begins today, with your purchase of this *Bizmanualz® Computer and Network Policies and Procedures Manual*. This manual is needed more now than ever. Information systems are more accessible than ever before. More people in the business world have grown up with computers, are more comfortable with them in every aspect of their lives, and are more reliant on technology to get them through every waking moment. The technology world is all about connectivity.

Unfortunately, these devices come with no instructions for incorporating them into the enterprise's long-range plans. Equipment user guides explain what the user's options are for that device, but they don't explain which options may result in sound IT or business practices. That is where this IT policy and procedure manual fits in. It gives your organization a framework upon which to build its own unique IT policies and procedures, laying the groundwork for process improvement and helping your company consistently deliver greater customer satisfaction.

Information Technology and Business Management

Yes, it's a technology-driven world and given the changes that have been brought about in the business world due to such drivers as the Sarbanes-Oxley Act in the U.S., COBIT, and international standards such as ISO 17799, companies will have to align their business processes with available technology. Perhaps you are waiting because technology is expensive. Well, the amazing thing is that it's getting cheaper all the time...a *lot* cheaper.

Technological Advancements

If you've got kids, you are probably aware of video game technology like the Sony PlayStation®. But have you ever stopped to look at what's under the hood of one of those boxes? In May, 2005, the latest incarnation of the PlayStation – the PS3® – was announced. This is a *powerful* gaming console! It uses the latest multi-core 3.2 GHz cell processor with full wireless, HDTV, and Bluetooth support that can process two high-definition (1080p) video streams at the same time!

The technical specifications of the PS3 far surpass most desktop PCs. The Pentium-4® chip in your desktop or laptop processes about two gigaflops, or two billion floating-point operations a second. The PS3 processes around two *tera*flops, which means it's about a *thousand times faster* than your PC. So, while you work all day on an average computer, your kids will be playing – that's right, playing – with a supercomputer that will retail for around $360.

This section is not about computing performance – flops are not the whole story. Besides, unlike a desktop PC, the PS3 is tuned primarily for high-definition *video* processing. Still, what could your business do with supercomputing power on your desktop for $360? You may have to think outside the box for the answer to that one. And that's one of the things your organizational leadership should be looking at in developing your strategy.

> "Information technology and business are becoming inextricably interwoven. I don't think anybody can talk meaningfully about one without talking about the other."
>
> *Bill Gates*

Technological performance is doubling every year, yet the cost of that performance is actually falling, the result being "more bang for your buck." The question is: How are you using this technology to release the growth in your business, improve your processes, and deliver better results?

It is not just about the information technologies organizations employ. It's the quality of the business processes and the associated information interactions delivered by the technology that are *really* important – *not* the technology infrastructure itself.

What we should really be talking about is information deployment – how you create, capture, deliver, use and measure your business information. Information deployment is the strategic differentiator that your business processes require. Information Technology is now a commodity. But your business processes are your business.

Information Deployment

Information Deployment is about the quality of the business processes and their associated information interactions that are delivered by way of the technology – the way a company creates, captures, delivers, uses, and measures its business information. Information Deployment is the strategic differentiator that business processes require.

Information Interactions

The quality of business processes and the associated information interactions that are delivered over the technology is really the focus in today's IT departments. Data processing has given way to business process management. Companies no longer just move data – they *enable* business processes.

Historically, we used manual systems to run a business like paper based orders (purchasing, sales, and production). Technology was introduced to automate – or to speed up – the paper shuffling. Productivity increased, job descriptions changed, and the new technology was accepted.

But now that all the numbers are in a computer system, more people want access to those numbers. People want new reports describing new relationships and the IT department has responded by developing more applications for more users. Instead of being proactive the IT department is reacting to demands.

Organizations focusing on just meeting users' needs with applications development are missing the boat. Certainly, applications (for HR, accounting, production, sales, and marketing, to name a few) will always need to be developed. But, if all the company is doing is developing applications, it is limiting the strategic value of the IT department. What is needed now is a way to rise above merely reacting to user demand. The IT department needs a new model, based on proactive approaches to user needs.

> "The number one benefit of information technology
> is that it empowers people to do what they want to do.
> It lets people be creative. It lets people be productive."
>
> *Steve Ballmer, CEO, Microsoft*

Information Usage

Applications development has always been about getting the right data in front of the right user using the right interface. Only now are we are finding that, in our ever-increasing complex world, how you create, capture, deliver, use, and measure your business information is even more critical than ever.

The Internet is a perfect example of how things are changing in the IT department. Users are now entering their own orders online, tracking their shipping and reviewing their account. As paper is eliminated from processes and as companies use principles of "Lean Thinking," they find inefficiencies in their old methods. The Internet is forcing organizations to rethink how they use Information Technology.

The Internet is forcing organizations to recognize and examine their core processes, to understand the customers of those processes and determine how to best use the available information. Only in this way can companies get ahead of users' demands. The more proactive an organization becomes, the less reactive it will be to demands for application changes.

IT as a Strategic Differentiator

In response, the IT department is now being asked to improve business processes. This is a strategic shift for organizations – requiring IT to take on new responsibilities, to be an integral part of Business Process Management. The new question is: How does the company build effective management systems and manage business processes?

Organizations that learn how to effectively deploy information will have found a valuable strategic differentiator. Information Technology is now a commodity – companies' business processes are their business. Those with the organizational leadership in place to take advantage of this new shift will beat out those who do not.

Business Process Management

Corporate strategy changes over time, but it always requires the alignment of people and processes in order to realize the mission of the organization.

In the past, the Information Technology (IT) department has delivered the systems. What is now required is for IT to move beyond the systems focus and coordinate with the people in the organization in what is called "Business Process Management" (BPM). IT is the medium that transforms ideas into intellectual property.

Process Flow and IT

BPM is the management of well-defined processes from beginning to end. These processes are broken into descriptions of activities and tasks that define a business workflow under varying business conditions, such as the steps needed to execute an accounts payable operation. Documenting workflow for a group of individuals is done using document maps or process maps. However, the IT department needs a lot more than a process map – they need to construct an information map, or what some might call a "Data Flow Diagram" (DFD).

Information Maps

The information map contains the flow of data from one process, activity, or task to another. As opposed to product flow, information flow (i.e., documents, records, or other data) must be described in detail in order for IT to implement the process. DFDs are used to illustrate the sources and uses of data, the data stores (databases), and, of course, the data flows. Information maps are used to describe your Information Deployment strategy.

Business Process Management Software (BPMS)

Information maps can get really complicated, really fast. So, how does an organization reduce the size and complexity of information maps? Use software. New BPM software tools have been developed that allow organizations to graphically define processes, describe information flows, and add detailed business rules used to process information.

Once all of this information is defined, BPM software can execute simulations using the company's definitions and show the results of the simulation. And that's not all – BPM software can convert a design into software programs that can be executed.

Next, the company adds process metrics (effectiveness criteria or key performance indicators), along with hooks into your existing applications, and the BPM software can monitor the results. Some BPM applications even interface with metrics databases that allow companies to benchmark their performance and compare it with industry standards.

BPMS is being used at many major corporations today. To move your company's IT department into the 21st century, you will need to implement some type of BPMS tool. The question is – which one?

For more information on BPM

Visit the following websites:

- Active Journal of Business Process Management
  (http://www.business-process-management.info/)

- The Resource for Business Process Management
  (http://www.bpm.com)

- BPM Institute
  (http://www.BPMinstitute.org)

- Business Process Management – the Third Wave
  (http://www.fairdene.com)

- Business Process Trends
  (http://www.bptrends.com/)

Accelerating Returns and Paradigm Shifts

The concept of *accelerating returns*, recently depicted in "Moore's Law," requires a basic understanding of paradigms and the implications of technology on the future of business processes. First what's Moore's Law?

Moore's Law

Gordon Moore, co-founder of Intel, observed that chip (integrated circuit) complexity, relative to minimum cost, would double every 24 months. This implies that we will be using 100 GHz personal computers by 2015, compared with 4 GHz today. At this rate of advancement, sometime in the next 20 years, we may approach the size of the atom as a fundamental barrier to future growth. Or will we?

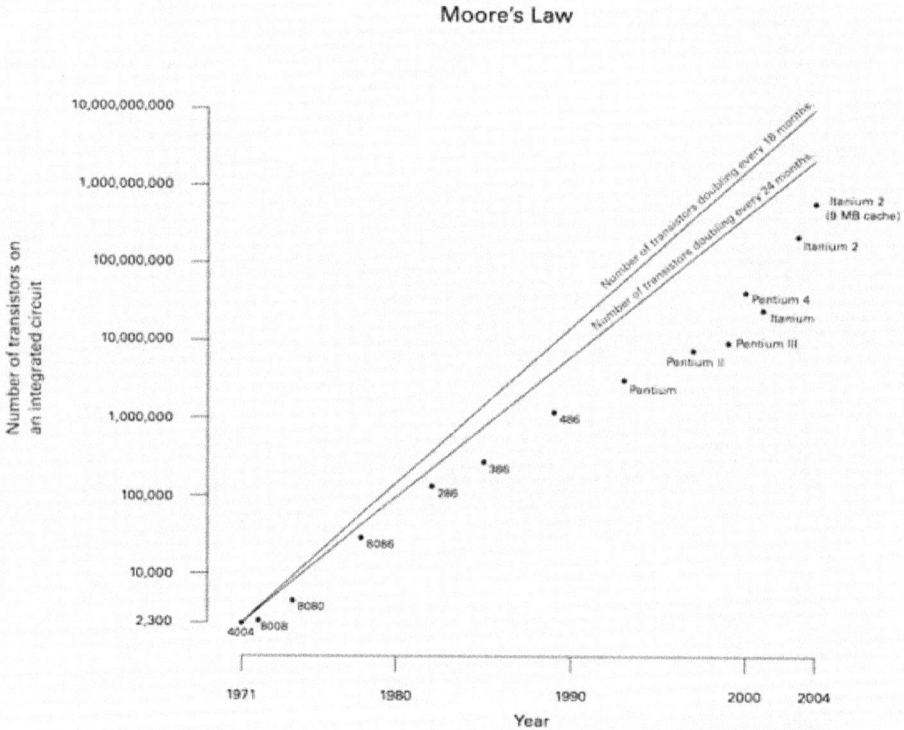

Figure 1 – Moore's Law

Paradigms

The belief that we cannot keep increasing the performance of computers because of a barrier like the atom is an example of a belief *paradigm*. Paradigms operate as filters of new information because they are deeply rooted in the rules of thought a person has learned from schools, books, culture, religion, friends, the workplace, and so forth.

These rules of thought – thought patterns, or paradigms – block our ability to see new information, no matter how valid or accurate it may be. In other words, you don't know what you don't know and for most people one has to believe it to see it. But paradigms can change – when they do, that is known as a *paradigm shift*.

Paradigm Shifts

Thomas Kuhn began using the term "paradigm shift" in his 1962 book, "The Structure of Scientific Revolutions". When you encounter something you do not understand – an object, event, or idea that doesn't fit into your well-established paradigm – what do you do? Do you ignore it or investigate the issue? If you throw it out, you maintain your old paradigm, perhaps noting the thing or event as an anomaly or error. What if the anomaly occurs again? Do you keep ignoring it, again and again? In the typical business environment, this can and does occur quite frequently.

Let's say a customer complains about a purchase. You might ignore the first complaint; after all, you may think no one has complained about that before. But another complaint like the first comes in, and then another. At some point, you can't ignore the complaints and you investigate them. What if you find nothing wrong?

You might say it is just user error and rationalize the fact that your engineers have studied the issue, your marketing people have done user studies and you know the product is right. Yet, another complaint comes in. Can so many users really be in error? So, what is going on?

Are you looking at the problem from your vendor's point of view? What does the customer see that is different? These are two different paradigms in conflict. In the role of the vendor, you see the designs, marketing, and company perspective based on what *you* want to see. But as the customer, you do not see the designs, and perhaps you interpret the vendor's marketing differently.

From your perspective, the product does not work. If you truly investigate the anomaly and try to understand what could cause the errors, you may find yourself faced with a paradigm conflict.

> "Finally, we shall place the Sun himself at the center
> of the Universe. All this is suggested by the systematic
> procession of events and the harmony of the whole Universe,
> if only we face the facts, as they say, `with both eyes open'."
>
> *Nicolas Copernicus, 16th century astronomer*

Your world view may need to change in order for you to "see" the customer's problem. This may introduce a crisis, in which you are not sure which view is right. If that is so, you are in the middle of a *paradigm shift*. If your company refuses to shift to the new paradigm, you will see business decline. On the other hand, if you make the shift, your company's business will continue to grow.

Accelerating Returns

Paradigms are critical for understanding how the concept of accelerating returns works. Moore thinks the atom will stop us from building more powerful transistors. But why are we constraining our thinking of a transistor to silicon? Could we build more powerful computers out of light and use optical transistors? Or, perhaps another technology will come along and replace optics.

The concept of accelerating returns states that knowledge increases exponentially, and so do the returns. In other words, we won't experience 100 years of progress in the 21st century – it will be more like 20,000 years of progress, at today's rate. The more ideas we develop now, the more new ideas we will be able to develop in the future.

Future Business Processes

The future for business process looks bright. Newer, more powerful technology will replace the old and knowledge will continue to increase. With increased knowledge comes a reduction in waste and cost. Nowhere has this been more evident than with computers. Computers, technology, and the Internet continue to drive down the cost of doing business, which in turn introduces new paradigms and, with it, new paradigm leaders.

Processes will continue to improve as quality methods and tools propagate from company to company. Competition will continue to increase, as those that have moved to a newer paradigm create and leverage new competitive advantages that old-paradigm companies fail to match.

Paradigms and accelerating returns suggest that nothing is impossible. If knowledge were linear, Moore might be right, but it's not. New technology comes along and solves problems we thought were impossible to solve. The *impossible* comes from sticking with a "can't-do" paradigm – the *possible* comes from pursuing a new "can-do" paradigm, which you may not be aware of...yet.

In the last 100 years, we have seen humans walk on the moon, the near-eradication of smallpox and polio, and toys being made out of supercomputers. Decades ago, it was thought that 10% waste was normal and "zero defects" was impossible. Today, 1% waste is normal and process improvement tools like "lean thinking" and "Six Sigma" have shown us it is possible to attain "zero defects". Does this mean all companies will eventually be producing with zero defects? We know anything is possible...if you change your paradigm.

Information Security and IT Standards

Computers and IT have become important parts of business operations, storing and circulating critical information between numerous business processes. Many business functions require the use of computer systems and networks, and businesses and computer networks are increasingly interconnected.

But how do you govern these systems and what standards do you choose? In other words, how much should you think about coordinating and securing the information that is so important to you and your business?

Information Security

Any information is susceptible to leakage or damage unless protected by a strong security system. Information stored in computers is no exception. With computers becoming ubiquitous and with them and servers and many systems connected by layers of networks, security is one of the key challenges for IT professionals today. We hear so much about identity theft, virus infections, and spyware hijacks. At various levels, all these activities put heavy burdens on your resources.

In order to preempt this threat and protect your information, you must have information security measures in place to maximize results. This means developing and implementing a set of controls through appropriate policies, procedures and processes. Besides meeting your organization's goals and objectives, these controls should also be aligned with other business processes in your organization.

IT Governance

This is where the issue of IT governance comes in. The executive summary of COBIT (which stands for "*C*ontrol *Ob*jectives for *I*nformation and Related *T*echnology") identifies IT governance as "a structure of relationships and processes to direct and control the enterprise in order to achieve the enterprise's goals by adding value while balancing risk versus the return or IT and its processes." In other words, IT governance is about balancing risk and return from your IT processes.

So, how do you approach IT governance? Businesses can either create their own structures and frameworks or adopt universally accepted best practices and standards that have been tried, tested, and improved by a large number of organizations and individuals. Implementing an IT quality standard has its own benefits.

> "The superior man, when resting in safety, does not forget
> that danger may come. When in state of security he does
> not forget the possibility of ruin. When all is orderly,
> he does not forget disorder may come"
>
> *Confucius*

IT Standards

Two main IT standards available today are COBIT and ISO 27002:2013. In its fifth edition[1], COBIT is a framework for managing IT risk. It was created by the Information Systems Audit and Control Association (ISACA) and the IT Governance Institute (ITGI). It consists of 34 high level objectives, covering 318 control objectives categorized in four areas—planning and organization, acquisition and implementation, delivery and support, and monitoring.

The six elements of COBIT are documented in separate volumes and include management guidelines, control objectives, COBIT framework, executive summary, audit guidelines, and an implementation toolset.

ISO 27002:2013 can be traced back to BS 7799, the British Standard for creating information security plans, originally published in 1995.

Benefits of IT Standards

Adopting an IT Standard does not, in itself, mean your organization is 100% secure. However, compliance with these established standards goes a long way in demonstrating that you take security issues very seriously. At the top level, four obvious benefits of IT standards stand out:

>	**Completeness** – Like any other internationally accepted standard, IT standards spare you from reinventing the wheel. Why spend the time and resource creating something that already exists and is proven to work?

>	**Compliance** – Using a widely regarded standard demonstrates that the organization practices industry norms and follows applicable laws and regulations.

>	**Credibility** – Having a standard in place reassures stakeholders of the company, including customers, suppliers, and employees by demonstrating that your organization is committed towards protecting valuable information.

>	**Confidence** – By minimizing risk of information leakage, IT standards lead to better knowledge management and more efficient use of IT assets and resources.

We have now looked at how to govern these systems and what standards to choose in order to coordinate and secure the information that is so important to your company's business.

---

[1] See http://www.isaca.org for the latest version of CObIT.

Information-Knowledge-Wisdom

Information defines your business – it represents not only your organization's experience, but its potential. Your use of technology to manage information could be a source of strategic advantage. But information is not enough – you need knowledge and wisdom to build an organization.

Data To Information

Today's IT departments and resources are required to handle enormous amounts of data. This is where some degree of standardization can help minimize inconsistencies, confusions and resulting risks. But all data is not equal in terms of importance or sensitivity. Data itself is not very useful. Think of this as the **"Know-nothing"** stage.

We must understand what the data is and how it relates to our needs. Once a relationship has been defined then the data becomes information. This is the **"Know-what"** stage.

Information To Knowledge

Information must be converted into knowledge by finding useful patterns within relationships. These patterns have the potential to represent knowledge once the patterns – and their implications – are understood. Knowledge allows us to predict; information by itself does not. This is the **"Know-how"** stage.

Knowledge To Wisdom

Wisdom arises when knowledge is transformed into insight or principles. In other words, once you understand the source of the patterns, you have found an eternal truth. This is the **"Know-why"** stage.

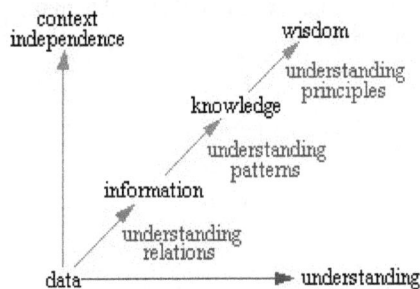

Figure 2 – Data to Wisdom

Company Policies and Procedures

Policies and procedures are written for a host of reasons, including decreasing training time, meeting compliance requirements, communicating effectiveness measures, simplifying access to information, and transferring knowledge.

Use of consistent, well-defined policies and procedures saves time by guiding users in converting raw data into meaningful information, transferring knowledge, and imparting the wisdom from past generations in order to take appropriate actions in not-so-obvious situations.

IT Policies and Procedures

Having formal computer and network policies and procedures in place enables an organization to assign responsibilities and provides definitions, guidelines and rules for employees. Your IT policies and procedures should cover all aspects of your information technology management, from computer usage and network security to IT asset management and training & support.

Policies and procedures allow managers to communicate the way things should be done – IT policies and procedures are no exception. Prewritten documents can speed up procedures development, which, in turn, speeds an IT department's path towards greater effectiveness and better, more consistent results.

Summary

We hope this introduction to your *Bizmanualz® IT Policy and Procedure Manual* increases your appreciation of the importance of establishing effective IT procedures. Your business is a continuously flowing stream of transactions. Like a net cast across that stream, effective IT policies and procedures help trap all of the data completely and accurately.

Once the data has been collected, the real benefit is in using the data to provide information, knowledge and wisdom – wisdom that will help the enterprise review the past, position the present, and chart the future.

bizmanualz

IT Policies and Procedures

Section 150

IT Glossary

Section 150

IT Glossary

INFORMATION TECHNOLOGY GLOSSARY

TERM	DEFINITION
Access control	A process or method of limiting access to system objects and resources to authorized principals; enforcement of specified authorization rules based on positive identification of users and the systems or data they are permitted to access; providing access to authorized users while denying access to unauthorized users.
Access control list (ACL)	A table that tells a computer operating system which access rights each user has to a particular system object, such as a file directory or individual file. Each object has a security attribute that identifies its access control list. The list has an entry for each system user with access privileges. The most common privileges include the ability to read a file (or all the files in a directory), to write to the file or files, and to execute the file (if it is an executable file, or program).
Active	When referring to business records, "active" records are those used in the conduct of current business. Active records are often referred to as "production" records.
Archive	Storing records offline (onto backup tapes, floppy disks, optical disks, etc.). Also, files containing data no longer in current use but kept in long-term storage (for possible future needs, such as fulfilling legal requirements or being in compliance).
Business continuity	Uninterrupted stability of systems and operational procedures; or, the degree to which an organization achieves uninterrupted stability.
Cold boot	Start a computer (CPU) from its powered-down (off) state; also referred to as a "hard boot".
Computer security incident response team (CSIRT)	A team of computer technicians whose purpose it is to respond to security incidents. Their response may vary according to the seriousness of the event, the risk of further or additional damage, and the type of coordination and notification required.
Designated approving authority (DAA)	A person empowered to act (e.g., indicate approval) on behalf of an IT system or subsystem.
Extranet	An intranet that is accessible to authorized outsiders; a collaborative network that uses Internet technology to link businesses with their suppliers, customers, or other businesses that share common goals.

TERM	DEFINITION
Gap analysis	1. The process of determining, documenting, and approving the variance between business requirements and system capabilities. 2. Determining and analyzing the difference between where you are (point A) and where you want to be (point B), to understand the root causes and figure out the best method of getting from point A to point B.
Internal user	An employee or contractor using Company IT assets in the course of performing a job (task) for the Company.
Internet	The international computer network of networks that connect government, academic and business institutions; the Internet (capitalized) refers specifically to the DARPA Internet and the TCP/IP protocols it uses.
Intranet	A private network contained within an enterprise; an organizational network that uses Web technologies for the sharing of information internally.
IT asset	Any computer hardware, software, or reference or other supporting material (in printed or other form), including rights and licenses, that is owned or controlled by the Company.
IT disaster	A sudden, significant event that may result in the loss or destruction of company information and/or loss of service on the company's IT network, or intranet.
Malware	Short for "malicious software"; malware is designed to damage, disrupt, or abuse an individual computer or an entire network and/or steal or corrupt an organization's most valuable and sensitive data. Viruses, worms, and Trojan horses are examples of malware.
Multi Router Traffic Grapher (MRTG)	A tool for monitoring traffic load on network-links. MRTG generates HTML pages containing graphical images, which provide a live visual representation of traffic.
Network attached storage (NAS)	Hard disk storage set up with its own network address rather than being attached to the department computer serving applications to a network's workstation users.
Network scan	Scanning a computer network (with specialized scanning software) to detect the presence or absence of computer hardware or software, check configurations, verify software versions, look for security patches, inspect for vulnerabilities, etc.

TERM	DEFINITION
Phishing	A type of security attack that relies on social engineering. The victim is tricked into revealing sensitive information, based on the human tendency to believe in the security of a brand name because they associate the brand name with trustworthiness.
Production environment	The database, equipment, documentation, and procedures used in support of live business operations; see "test environment".
RAID	Redundant Array of Independent Disks; a method of storing the same data in different places (thus, redundantly) on multiple hard disks.
Random sampling	A sampling technique whereby a group of subjects (a sample) is selected for study from a larger group (a population), each subject is chosen entirely by chance, and each member of the population has a known, but possibly non-equal, chance of being included in the sample. By using random sampling, the likelihood of bias should be reduced.
Reboot	Restart a computer, either by warm booting or cold booting.
Record	In IT, a record is a data structure aggregating several items of possibly different types. The items being aggregated are called fields and are usually identified or indexed by field labels.
Request for proposal (RFP)	A document that an enterprise sends to a vendor, inviting the vendor to submit a bid for hardware, software, services, or any combination of the three. An organization will typically issue several RFPs to obtain and evaluate competing bids.
Risk	Possibility of losing availability, integrity, or confidentiality of IT assets due to a specific threat. Also, the product of threat level and vulnerability level (threat x vulnerability = risk).
Risk assessment	The process by which risks are identified and their impact is determined.
Service level agreement (SLA)	A binding contract, formally specifying or quantifying a customer's expectations with regard to solutions and tolerances; a collection of service level requirements, negotiated and mutually agreed upon by the service provider and the consumer.
Smart card	Typically, a credit-card-sized device with a small, embedded computer chip. This card-computer can be programmed to perform tasks and store information. A smart card is inserted into a smart card reader (commonly called a card terminal), which makes the PC or other smart-card-enabled device available to the user. The smart card is being considered by some organizations as a substitute for password security.

TERM	DEFINITION
Social engineering	The act of obtaining or attempting to obtain otherwise secure data by tricking an individual into revealing secure information. Social engineering is successful because its victims innately want to trust other people and are naturally helpful. Also see "phishing".
Spam	Unsolicited commercial e-mail sent in bulk over the Internet. A frequent malware vector, spam puts a cost and a burden on recipients by clogging up network bandwidth, consuming disk space, and wasting employee time.
Spoofing	Forging an e-mail header to make it appear as if it came from somewhere or someone other than the actual source. The main protocol used in sending e-mail – SMTP – does not include a way to authenticate. There is an SMTP service extension (RFC 2554) that allows an SMTP client to negotiate a security level with a mail server. But if this precaution is not taken, anyone with the know-how can connect to the server and use it to send spoofed messages by altering the header information. Also see phishing, social engineering.
Statement of work (SOW)	A formal contract or agreement, signed by the client and the service provider, that states at a minimum the scope of work, deliverables, terms and conditions and commercial details. It typically also specifies service level agreement requirements, quality expectations, resource descriptions, and reward-penalty clauses.
Statistically significant	A finding (the observed difference between the means of two random samples, for example) is described as statistically significant when it can be demonstrated that the probability of obtaining such a difference by chance only is relatively low.
Storage area network (SAN)	A high-speed, special-purpose network or subnetwork connecting different kinds of IT storage devices with data servers on behalf of a large network of users.
Storage media	In computers, a storage medium is any technology (including devices and materials) used to place, keep, and retrieve data. The term "storage medium" usually refers to secondary storage, such as a hard disk or tape.

TERM	**DEFINITION**
Subscription service	A service whereby a software vendor offers support for its product, usually for a predetermined time period. For example, anti-virus vendors typically include a one-year subscription (for updates, notices, etc.) with the purchase of a product license. Many vendors also offer fee-based subscription services whereby subscribers automatically receive notifications, security bulletins, etc, related to their products for a set period of time.
System administration	Activities which directly support the operations and integrity of computing systems and their use and which manage their intricacies. These activities may include – but are not limited to – system installation, configuration, integration, maintenance, performance management, data management, security management, failure analysis and recovery, and user support.
Systems analysis	Work that involves applying analytical processes to the planning, design, and implementation of new and improved information systems to meet the business requirements of customer organizations; phase of the SDLC in which the current system is studied and alternative replacement systems are proposed.
Systems development life cycle (SDLC)	A method for developing information systems, made up of five main stages: analysis, design, development, implementation, and evaluation. Each stage is further comprised of several components (for example, the development stage includes programming, debugging, testing, and documenting).
Target	The ultimate goal or destination of an intentional security threat. Workstations, servers, and databases are typical threat targets.
Test environment	Where applications, systems, etc., are tested for accuracy, suitability, and performance prior to installation in a "live" or "production" environment.
Threat	Expression of intent to inflict evil, injury, or damage. A potential security violation. May be physical or electronic in nature.
Threat assessment	A process by which an organization identifies kinds of threats its IT network might be vulnerable to and where the network is most vulnerable.

TERM	DEFINITION
Threat model	Detailed description of a given threat and the type and degree of harm it may cause to any portion of an IT network. In other words, a threat model describes what the threat is, what it does, and how it does it.
Total cost of ownership (TCO)	The total price in money, time, and resources of owning and using resources; the purchase price of a product and its transportation cost, plus indirect handling, inspection, quality, rework, maintenance, and all other "follow-on" costs associated with the purchase, including costs of disposal.
Troubleshoot	Isolate the source of a problem and fix it; a process of elimination, whereby possible sources of the problem are investigated and eliminated, beginning with the most obvious or easiest problem to fix.
	In computer systems, the term *troubleshoot* is often used when the problem is thought to be *hardware*-related; if the problem is *software*-related, the term *debug* usually applies.
Vector	How a threat (virus, worm, etc.) reaches its target. For example, email is a common malware vector.
Vulnerability	Flaw or weakness in a system's design, implementation, or operation and management that may be exploited.
Warm boot	Restart a computer by way of its operating system (i.e., press "Control-Alt-Delete" to restart Windows OS). Warm booting normally returns a Windows computer to its initial state without shutting it off.

IT Policies and Procedures

Section 200

Manual Preparation

Section 200
Manual Preparation

Manual Preparation

For the Company Policies and Procedures Manual to be effective, it should be easily understood by all employees. Therefore, it has to be written clearly and concisely. The objectives of this Manual are to enable and encourage continual improvement within the organization, improve communication within the Company and with the Company's target market and channel partners, and increase customer satisfaction.

This section, "Manual Preparation", provides an introduction and guidance to help you develop and implement your Company's Policies and Procedures manual. ***Please read this entire section BEFORE you begin to modify your Manual.***

[This page intentionally left blank]

Manual Preparation
Table of Contents

SECTION 1 - INTRODUCTION

This prototype *Policies and Procedures Manual* was developed to assist organizations like yours in preparing their own policy and procedure manuals. As it is written in general terms, this document needs to be tailored to your Company's specific needs, requirements, and operations.

Bizmanualz Policies and Procedures manuals generally consist of eight sections:

100 – the Introduction

150 – a Glossary

200 – a Manual Preparation document (what you're now reading)

300 – a master Policy Manual

400 – a set of Procedures

500 – a Business or Departmental Guide

550 – Job Descriptions

600 – Index

The *Policy Manual* (section 300) is a policy manual template and is designed to work as a guide to the accompanying procedures (sections 400-4nn[1]). Note that Bizmanualz does not intend to imply that these are "best practices" or recommended for your Company's unique circumstances. They are designed to be used as a minimum documentation set for you to use in your effort to introduce controls to your Company's core functions – or improve existing ones – and thereby promote the concept of ***continual improvement***.

The language style and usage is generally representative of that practiced by companies based in the United States of America. In some cases, information presented in this manual will not apply to your business.

When you edit and construct a policy, it should be easy to read, to the point, and convey a message that is readily understood by both non-management and management employees.

When you have completed your Policy Manual and the Procedures, it is best that you have a team of managers from various departments review the entire set of

---

[1] In Bizmanualz Policies and Procedures manuals, Procedures are often broken into subsets (e.g., "400 Strategy procedures," "410 Tactics procedures").

documents, identify opportunities for improvement, and agree on changes needed before "finalizing" the documents.

This publication is sold and/or distributed with the understanding that the publisher is not engaged in rendering legal, accounting, or other professional services. Always seek the assistance of a qualified, competent legal advisor to review your "final" manual before you publish, even if it's only intended for internal use.

The corrected and finished product is then ready for distribution. However, it should never be considered final and complete. Building a Management System, described in your policies and procedures, is not a one-time event. The one constant in the business world is change. Therefore, your Company must look at its management systems as fluid. Revisions will be required from time to time if you are to keep your management systems current.

Top 10 Management Mistakes

As a busy executive, you face some extremely difficult challenges, like creating and dominating new markets and finding and keeping the best people. But do you find yourself spending too much time solving everyday problems and not enough time on strategy and growing your business?

If so, you may be making some of these mistakes:

1. You have a compelling *vision* for your company that projects a remarkable future <u>but</u> few of your employees have heard of it or can explain it in their own words.

2. You have a company *mission* that addresses your goals <u>yet</u> your operations fail to measure their progress towards your goals.

3. Your objectives focus on increasing *revenue* and *profitability* <u>while</u> your assets are performing poorly, generating negative cash flows, or encumbered by debt and unable to create a profit.

4. You talk a lot about your employees' *performance* (positive or negative) <u>without</u> noting what employee turnover or performance metrics are for your industry.

5. You spend a lot of time working IN your business on *tactics*, <u>yet</u> you fail to spend an adequate amount of time working ON your business, defining your *strategy*, performance metrics, and real resource needs.

6. You have regular *interactions with employees*, <u>yet</u> you fail to communicate the status of objectives, financials, or metrics.

7. You make resources available for *training*, <u>yet</u> you don't measure training in terms of achieving individual or Company goals.

8. You continually strive to improve your Company's performance, <u>yet</u> you don't compare your performance against external benchmarks for success.

9. You *believe* your customers, employees, and vendors all love your company, <u>yet</u> you don't have a process for monitoring and measuring their satisfaction.

10. You produce annual *forecasts* and **budgets**, <u>yet</u> you fail to achieve agreed-upon goals or learn from the experience to improve in the future.

Daily operational issues eat up much of a manager's time – too much for most managers. But with the purchase and use of this manual, you have the opportunity to correct all that and build a superior organization that keeps your best people, increases revenue, and increases margins.

You now have an opportunity to provide your organization with the methods, tools, and training to achieve superior results. Bizmanualz has helped companies all over the world build superior organizations with increased compliance, control, and customer satisfaction.

Manual Development Process

The manual development process consists of four phases: Discovery, Planning, Development, and Implementation. W. Edwards Deming, Ph.D., one of the leading experts on process improvement, called this the "Plan-Do-Study-Act" cycle. The Deming cycle is more commonly known as Plan-Do-Check-Act, or "PDCA."

The PDCA cycle consists of four main phases of continual process improvement. You should develop your manual in this manner to avoid mistakes that could occur later when you skip these steps. In other words, spending a little time on getting things right now is far better than spending a lot of time correcting mistakes later on.

Many people incorrectly believe they can save a lot of money by eliminating the Discovery and Planning steps and going directly into Development. If you start writing procedures without proper Discovery and Planning, though, you could find yourself in a lot of trouble before long. Without Discovery and Planning, expect project delays, cost overruns, scope creep, and a lot of rewrites.

The lack of prior organization and planning leads to a lack of cooperation, which then leads to frustration, anger, and indifference. Spend time in discovery and planning, and development and implementation will run a lot smoother. What you're trying to do is anticipate the future.

<u>Discovery</u>

Discovery starts by clearly identifying the project vision, mission, objectives and the action plan. It is considered part of the "Plan" phase in the PDCA cycle. In Discovery you are probably interpreting the results of a previous "Check" phase of some kind. You may have been dissatisfied with the results and, therefore, you are "Acting" on those results and preparing to "Plan" for the future.

You should include clear business objectives that include how customer needs are satisfied with agreed upon effectiveness criteria beyond compliance. Otherwise, the procedures look like administrative overhead and a waste of time to others, making it more difficult to get their buy-in and participation during implementation and training.

Once everyone agrees to the objectives and action plan then you can start management planning. The Discover phase takes about 2-4 weeks depending on how organized the executive management team is regarding mission, vision and objectives.

Does your project need a vision? You bet! Every project requires a vision of the future. All the employees involved will want to know how all of this work will improve their lives. You need to communicate a picture of "what's in it for them." If you can't explain it to them, all you have is a big wish that it turns out the way you planned. And it won't.

Planning

Planning starts with a "gap analysis" – a method of determining the difference between reality and your objectives. A Gap Analysis consists of an audit of your current processes, capabilities, and constraints, comparing them with the "ideal" state, and identifying the "gaps" that need to be filled.

You use the gap results, along with the objectives and action plans from Discovery to produce the management materials needed to control the project and set the budget/expectations. Other functions include creating a development team, assigning process owners for each process and deploying your effectiveness criteria to each process. This may take about 2-4 weeks.

This includes producing a:

- Project plan (activities, resources, dates, etc.);
- Project roles and responsibilities;
- Organization chart;
- Change & approval review structure;
- Status reports;
- Document control and format;
- Process maps identifying all process inputs and outputs;
- Compliance requirements; and
- Training, implementation, testing, and audit plans.

You should now be 1-2 months into the project. At this point, you should not yet have written a single procedure. Before that, everyone should understand the scope of the project, its relationship to the company objectives, what the future will look like, and what their roles are in development.

Development

Development starts by identifying a group of related processes and completing just that group. Follow the document control format, use the review structure, perform a walk through of the related processes, test for compliance and effectiveness, and move on to the next group until finished. It represents the "Do" phase of the PDCA cycle.

This takes two to four months, depending on the number of processes, compliance requirements, resource constraints, and the skill and knowledge of the project managers, leaders, writers and reviewers. If you have not done this before, plan on four months.

Development also includes creating all supporting documents such as job descriptions, forms, the training plan, and the collection of technical manuals, references, etc, for document and record control and later implementation.

Using a rule of thumb, you should plan on the Discovery, Planning, and Development phases taking as much as 50% of the total project time but consuming 80% of the project cost. You should try to include the time of all personnel working on the project in your project plan so you have a real picture of the costs involved. Frequently, it is a lot more than you imagine, at first.

You are now three to six months into the project and should have completed the procedure writing. You are now ready for a complete document review. You should not implement processes before the entire system is documented and reviewed; otherwise, you may find yourself rewriting and reimplementing and it will take longer to complete the development. Once you implement the system, you implement the concept of continual improvement.

Implementation

Implementation includes skills assessment, training to improve competencies, and auditing of the entire system against the objectives and compliance requirements. It represents the "Check" phase of the PDCA cycle. The length of time depends on number of employees, locations, and processes. It should take 3-6 months, or about 50% of the project time, to complete. You are working toward a stable system of processes and this takes time.

Training

Implementation starts with an assessment of employee skills and competencies to determine training gaps. Then training begins introducing the job descriptions, processes, procedures, and the relationship of people and tasks to objectives and effectiveness.

Once training is complete, you should use execute the processes as documented for 1-3 months. Procedure forms, logs, and other records should be used to collect data for measurement and analysis. All personnel should become accustomed to using the processes recently created. In fact, it is the collection of data which now becomes the most important part.

Collected data are used to:

- Determine if processes are in control;
- Identifying if a process can be improved; and
- Demonstrating to auditors and management that the organization is progressing towards achieving the objectives.

Auditing

Auditing is one of the most important steps in building business processes. Auditing provides management visibility into the ongoing progress towards objectives and the capabilities of the organization. Without auditing, management limits its predictive knowledge of the systems potential.

Management Review

You are now 6-12 months into the project and almost finished. The last step consists of analyzing what's been done, reviewing lessons learned, and looking for ways to improve performance, compliance, and effectiveness. This is typically done within a Management Review meeting held after the audit cycle has been completed.

Management holds the review meeting to discuss:

- The audit report documenting the findings of the audit team;
- Progress towards objectives;
- Results of customer satisfaction processes;
- Corrective actions to be taken to resolve "common cause" errors;
- Preventive action to be taken to resolve "special cause" errors; and
- Follow-up from previous meetings.

Rediscovery

The actions from the Management Review meeting lead into Rediscovery or the Discovery process for the next cycle. Rediscovery starts the process of continuous improvement all over again. It represents the "Act" phase of the PDCA cycle. The result is a new set of objectives and action plans for the next period and you now begin again. This phase overlaps with the discovery phase of the next year to chain together each period in a constant cause-effect cycle of improvement.

Using these four phases, you should complete the project in 6-12 months; spending less than six months or more than twelve indicates problems in scoping the project. If the organization is big and complex, the problem should be broken into smaller projects and focused on core processes, or outside contractors should be used to deploy the experience and bandwidth required to meet your schedule.

Staffing the project depends on the number of employees, locations, compliance requirements, and processes involved. You should consider at least one full-time project leader that drives the project, manages document controls, leads the audits, and reports to management on the overall effectiveness.

The project leader should be experienced in control methodologies and auditing. If your project leader is not experienced in these areas, you should look for training. Training is available to learn how to use quality tools, acquire auditing skills, and lead audit teams and programs.

Others are needed to create documents or perform audits. Obviously, there are a lot of variables to staffing requirements. It is difficult for one person to know everything about your business, build the system and then be responsible for auditing the processes. A solo person will lose their objectivity and they can not audit their own processes either.

Bizmanualz Training

Bizmanualz training courses are available for In-house training as well as on a customizable basis. A tailored in-house training program is one of the best options to meet your business objectives. Tailored programs are designed to specifically fit your organization's culture and circumstances, targeting the training to meet your specific needs.

A Training Advisor is available to discuss your organizational needs and plan a course designed around the outcomes you want to achieve. Stop by http://www.bizmanualz.com/ for a current schedule or call for more information.

Benefits of In-House Training

- <u>Save on Training Costs</u> – In-house training is more cost effective than public training if you have 5 of more delegates that require training.

- <u>Plan Around Your Schedule</u> – Training can be done at your convenience (i.e., dates and times that suit your organization).

- <u>Save on Travel Costs</u> – Training can be done at your location.

- <u>Customized to Your Needs</u> – Training courses can be tailored to the various roles within your organization.

- <u>Focused on Your Organization</u> – The trainer's time is dedicated to your organization.

<u>Onsite Training Classes for Your Place of Business</u>

Business Process Design
– Process Design & Consulting (2-4 days)
– Creating Well-Defined Processes (2 days)
– Aligning a System of People and Processes (3 days)

Quality Tools & Techniques
– Implementing Lean Thinking (2 days)
– Leading Lean Thinking in Your Organization (10 days)
– Statistical Process Control Workshop (2 days)
– Quality Tools Workshop (2 days)

ISO 9001 Quality Management
– ISO 9000 Series Internal QMS Auditor (2-3 days)
– ISO 9000 Series Auditor/Lead Auditor (5 days)
– Creating a Lean ISO 9000 QMS (1-2 days)

Technical Support

Thank you for your interest in our product. Please let us know how else we may be of service. We provide telephone support for the initial installation of the software without charge. Additional support is available for assistance on Microsoft Word usage, policies and procedures development, and other manual development questions.

Hours of Operation:	9am to 6 pm, Central US time
Phone:	314-863-5079
Fax:	314-863-6571
Sales:	800-466-9953
Web:	http://www.bizmanualz.com/
E-mail:	support@bizmanualz.com

Consulting and Advisory Services

We implement a full system approach to creating strategic growth for your company. We understand you want to increase sales, but our process goes a step further to ensure your revenue growth is built on quality management.

Whether you are trying to evaluate your business opportunities, implement strategic growth, or position your company for sale, our expert consultants can help you succeed. Contact us to find out more.

Value Proposition

Understanding the way your customers perceive your value is essential. We work with you to define your customer so you can tell your unique value story.

Lead Generation

Sell more! We help you create a visually compelling marketing plan that will bring customers to you who are ready to buy now.

Quality Management Planning

You could be saving hundreds of thousands of dollars. We work with you to cut the waste out of your organization and maximize your capacity.

Quality Training

An educated workforce is an efficient and empowered workforce. We create customized training classes for your staff to provide continual improvement.

Bizmanualz Consultants

A variety of in-house technical writers and consultants, as well as specialized professionals, are used to produce all of the policy and procedures content. These very same resources are also available on a project basis to utilize their business expertise to provide process implementation for your company.

Bizmanualz Engagements

A typical project consists of a full system engagement to create and maintain strategic growth. Projects of this type consist of identifying, developing and implementing management systems of business controls; increasing revenue through designing and testing a strategic or tactical value proposition and implementing lead-generation marketing techniques; as well as in-house or onsite training in many of these same industry standard techniques.

Implementation assistance, training, coaching, and/or mentoring are available to complete your project – call Bizmanualz today! Typical projects range from strategic marketing and sales planning, development, and support to more tactical ISO 9000 quality or Lean/Six-Sigma operations implementation to ensure you're delivering on your strategy.

Potential training, consulting and implementation engagements include:

- Strategic Planning, Goals and Objectives Implementation

- Sales and Marketing System Implementation and Support Through Value Proposition and Lead Generation Services
- ISO 9000 Quality Management Systems Certification, Business Process Design and Continuous Process Improvement
- General Policy and Procedure Development, Training, and Assistance

For a full explanation and examples of our consulting engagements, visit our consulting Web pages: http://www.Bizmanualz.com/consulting.

Benefits of Consulting

Over the past ten years thousands of CEOs, CFOs, and other executives worldwide have realized increased profits, compliance, and operating efficiencies from their business by using one of Bizmanualz® Policies and Procedures products or services.

Our consulting clients receive:

- A quality process designed to comply with accepted standards and regulations (e.g., ISO 9001, Sarbanes-Oxley);
- Demonstrable changes in quality improvement;
- An opportunity to compete for customers that require ISO certification; and
- An improved understanding of ISO and the quality process.

Why?

1. Using an objective third party such as Bizmanualz, Inc., to lead the process assists the Client in sidestepping internal political battles and power struggles resulting in keeping the focus on what's best for the organization.

2. Using an experienced third party such as Bizmanualz, Inc., to lead the process provides exposure to business process methodologies that allow the Client to keep the project on schedule, on budget, and on alignment with the project objectives.

3. Using a focused third party such as Bizmanualz, Inc., to lead the process ensures the result is not clouded with legal, accounting, or technical jargon; instead, it provides a foundation for real improvements in effectiveness, efficiency, and the bottom line.

Gap Analysis

The first step is a Gap Analysis, to determine gaps in performance or compliance. Bizmanualz, Inc., will arrange a mutually convenient date for your **Bizmanualz® Gap Analysis**.

During this assignment, Bizmanualz proposes two review meetings: one at the outset and the other at completion of the assignment, to review the effectiveness of the project and deliverables.

The analysis itself consists of five primary activities:

Activity 1   Pre-planning activity between the organization and Principal Consultant. The Principal Consultant will contact you to obtain background information used to become familiar with the engagement. Pre-planning occurs prior to the onsite visit and includes the collection of:

- An organization profile describing the business activities, locations, and number of employees at each location;
- Organization structure (chart) and employee data by function
- Current Quality Manual, if available; and
- Contact details identifying the employees available to support the gap analysis within the organization.

Activity 2   An introductory meeting with top management, facilitated by the Principal Consultant, outlining the methodology and deliverables. The introductory meeting will occur on the first morning of the engagement.

The aim of this meeting is to agree on the overall delivery plan and to review and determine the full requirements and scope of the project, allocate tasks and analyze and mitigate any project risks. There will also be an opportunity for questions and answers.

Activity 3   Data gathering activity involving interviews, data analysis, and observation with a cross-section of the organization's personnel. After the introductory meeting is concluded, the Principal Consultant will spend the rest of the first day collecting the data needed for the Gap Analysis Report.

NOTE: It is vitally important that the Client agrees to make available the data and/or personnel identified to support the engagement. Any delay caused by the Client may also cause a revaluation of the engagement sum, subject to client acceptance.

Activity 4   Production and distribution of the Gap Analysis Report and MS Project Plan. The Principal Consultant will produce a detailed report (see "Gap Analysis Product Specifications," below) that will be delivered to you, the Client, within five business days following Activity 3.

Activity 5   A concluding meeting with top management and the Principal Consultant. The Principal Consultant will lead a presentation and discussion of the Gap Analysis Report findings and recommendations.

The rest of the afternoon will be spent presenting the findings, answering questions about the findings, and discussing project implementation issues including agreement and finalization of the <u>MS Project Plan</u>.

Gap Analysis Product Specification

The primary purpose of the **Bizmanualz® Gap Analysis** is to identify, in practical and specific terms, the gaps that exist between your current management system and an ideal ("target") system.

You will receive a detailed report upon completion of the analysis, providing:

- A <u>Management System Plan</u> that identifies the strengths and weaknesses of the existing system and includes recommendations on how to proceed and address or close the identified gaps.
- A <u>Position Statement</u> on the degree to which the Client's management system meets the needs of the business and customers.
- A <u>Training Plan</u> that identifies the gaps, if any, in the Client's technical skills and knowledge that may prevent the Client from successfully transitioning to the ideal system. This Training Plan will also include recommendations on how to address training and development requirements.
- An <u>MS-Project Plan</u> outlining the phases, activities, and tasks the the Client must undertake in order to close the gaps and successfully implement a management system. This will also include generic timelines required to successfully implement the improved Management System.

New Requirements Resolution

Inevitably, during the development of proposed solutions, new requirements evolve. These requirements can either be listed and considered as part of a separate follow-on project or discussed and treated by an 'exception' mechanism, outlining the work involved, the timing, and any changes to the overall schedules and the costs involved.

Client Resource Requirements

In order to ensure that all activities are conducted in a timely fashion, the Client agrees to supply the following information and/or personnel prior to the start of and during the engagement:

- An organization profile describing the business activities, locations, and number of employees at each location;
- Current Scope and Objectives;
- The Client structure (chart), job descriptions, and employee data;
- Current policy and procedure manuals, if they exist; and
- Contact details identifying the Client's employees available to provide information required to support the gap analysis.

Engagement Process Description

Just like building a house, the best way to manage a development process is with well-thought-out and well-documented iterative phases. The ***Bizmanualz Management Architectural Process*** is Bizmanualz methodology for implementing the planning, design, development and optimization of your management system.

The process incorporates an objective appraisal of your management system to identify key performance metrics while incorporating a solid system of: project status reporting, appropriate delegation to less experienced personnel, and holding everyone accountable for their assigned tasks.

These are the primary elements behind any form of management conversion designed to get the right things done right.

The process incorporates critical features for success including:

- A simple-to-follow project management and monitoring methodology;
- A solid foundation based on business "best practices";
- Prompting and facilitating non-experts to create effective systems; and
- The ability to maximize the strengths and minimize the weaknesses of both technical and business people involved.

Management Architecture Process

The ***Bizmanualz Management Architectural Process*** has four phases:

1. Client Discovery & Assessment
   - Research Industry (research client)
   - Identify Needs (client objectives)
   - Industry Analysis (benchmarks)
   - Needs Analysis (standards, regulations, objectives)
   - Gap Analysis (objective appraisal, project definition)
   - Engagement Proposal (project scope, schedules, costs)

2. Project Management
   - Working Engagement Plan (actual schedules, costs)
   - Resource Staffing (work breakdown structure)
   - Process Communication (status reports, meetings, software)
   - Configuration Management (management controls)
   - Testing Sensitivity (test plan)

3. Process Design & Development
   - Process Requirements (constraints)
   - Process Definition (effectiveness criteria)
   - Process Mapping (inputs, outputs, action steps)
   - Draft individual processes
   - Test, discuss and review processes

4. Process Implementation & Conclusion
   - Publish Processes and Train Employees

o   Test and Optimize processes until objectives are achieved
o   Lessons learned and Recommendations
o   Project Performance Appraisal

Principal Consultants

A Principal Consultant (PC) provides experience in business process design, quality methodologies, communication, implementation, and training. Typical consultants have over 20 years of either accounting, sales, marketing, quality, and or business management experience working with small to large corporations.

It is standard company policy that all Managers/Consultants/Trainers shall be experienced professionals with advanced degrees, certification and training, and familiarity with business process design and the compliance standard for the projects implemented. A brief resumé or curriculum vitae (CV) of the consultants/trainers can be provided upon request, following order acceptance.

Subject Matter Experts

Subject matter experts (SMEs) provide the detailed technical knowledge that is often required to establish, implement, and continually improve the Management System. Their experience ranges from front-line to support to management to serving as adjunct professors, professors, and/or researchers at the college and university level.

Project Managers

Project Managers (PM) provide experience in project management, communication, implementation, and training. Bizmanualz PMs usually have an MBA and over 10 years of experience working with a variety of business projects from ISO quality and Sarbanes-Oxley to continuous process improvement. Project Managers use MS-Project for scheduling, MS-Word for engagement communication, and MS-Visio for process mapping.

Technical Writers

A Technical Writer provides the written communication expertise required to translate the SME and PC content into clear policy statements, procedure actions and understandable forms. A Technical Writer is utilized, as needed, to develop materials or train Client staff.

Technical writers usually have backgrounds in English, journalism, or quality or business communications. More experienced writers may have technical knowledge and experience in computer and software design, accounting, law, medical devices, chemistry, engineering, or other fields.

Bizmanualz Quality Management

The objective of Bizmanualz is to provide the highest quality services to its clients. In order to ensure this, we utilize an ISO 9001 Quality Management System, or QMS. The scope of the QMS covers all activities we will carry out during the life cycle of the projects. It has been designed to comply with the requirements of ISO 9001 and integrates techniques from Six-Sigma, Theory of Constraints, Lean Thinking, and other quality methodologies.

Project Management Methodology

The project management methodology's particular strengths are:

- A simple-to-follow project management and monitoring methodology with definition of the roles that are needed in a project.
- Involvement of The Client at all levels and in all aspects of the project from beginning to end including allowing non-technical business people to lead and manage the development of the project.
- A comprehensive set of plans, controls, and reviews relevant to the size and risk involved in the project.
- A solid foundation based on business "best practices" that facilitates non-experts to create effective systems.
- The ability to maximize the strengths and minimize the weaknesses of both technical and business people involved.

Meetings and Presentations

It is Bizmanualz philosophy to conserve the Client's time, communicate necessary information frequently, and use documentation to keep the process moving.

To accomplish this every meeting shall include:

- An agenda prepared and distributed before the meeting that contain a summary with action items and responsibilities for follow-up tasks from the previous meeting.
- A Principal Consultant responsible for moving the meeting along.
- Meetings notes prepared and distributed after the meeting that contain a summary with action items and responsibilities for follow-up tasks.

Progress Reports

Progress reports are generated at regular intervals throughout the engagement by the Project Manager to advise management and other personnel on the current status of the engagement.

Progress reports include:

- Key activities starting and project activities recently completed.
- Open items requiring resolution and Possible conflicts.
- Current project short term goals and new requirements identified.
- Comments, news and other information updates.
- Budget vs. Actual cost and activity summary.

References

A. American Marketing Association, 311 South Wacker Drive, Suite 5800, Chicago, IL 60606 (phone 800.262.1150) – ama.org/pages/default.aspx

B. National Association of Sales Professionals, 555 Friendly St., Bloomfield Hills, MI 48341 – http://www.nasp.com

SECTION 2 - USAGE INSTRUCTIONS

Once you have copied all the files into your computer, you are ready to edit or enter data into the included WORD files.

Editing Files

Word Processing (Text) Files

All files are written in Microsoft Word and stored as Word documents ("".doc"" or "".docx"" files). Graphics come from a variety of sources – there are picture files (in "".bmp"", "".jpg"", etc., format), screen captures, and MS-Visio. If you want to manipulate Visio files, you will need MS-Visio; you may, however, substitute with the file format of your choice. WordPerfect or Mac users should be able to load and use the Word files – consult your word processor's documentation for conversion instructions.

> **NOTE:** There may be compatibility issues if your copy of MS-Word predates Word 2000.

When you have loaded your word processing program, edit the manual's text files as you would any text file. Consider saving them under a new name immediately by changing the procedure number (from "MPnnnn", "MTnnnn", etc.) to one that conforms to your own numbering (indexing) system.

We also suggest you immediately create a new directory for your working files and preserve the original files that came with the CD-ROM.

File Properties and Style Formats

File Folders (Directories):
- Files are organized into various folders that are named by the groups that they represent. [ex. "200 Manual Preparation"].

Page Setup:
- Paper: Letter, 8-1/2 x 11" page size, portrait. (Use landscape as needed).
- Printer defaults: HP LaserJet 4 compatible.
- Mirror margins: One (1) inch inside, outside, left, and right. One-half (0.5) inch left/right gutter, to allow for binder holes. One-half (0.5) inch header and footer.

Header Settings:

- Manual name, left justified; Company name (in place of "Bizmanualz.com"), right justified.
- Font: Times New Roman, 10pt, normal, line below.

Footer Settings

- Filename, left justified; "page # of #", right justified.
- Font: Times New Roman, 10pt, normal, line above.

Section Headings

- Section # (soft return) then section name, set in a black bar with reversed type.
- Font: Arial, 24pt, bold, white on black fill.
- NOTE: Sections begin on odd-numbered (right hand) pages. Insert a spacing page with the words "[This page intentionally left blank]" (font: Times New Roman, 12pt, centered) at the end of any section ending on an odd page number.

Default Style Format Usage

Format	Used for	Font	Paragraph Setting
Normal	most manual-procedure text	Times New Roman, 12pt, regular	"0 pt" before, "6 pt" after, line=single
Heading 1	tab title pages	**Arial, 24pt, bold**	"18 pt" before, "6 pt" after, single line
Heading 2	procedure titles	**Arial, 12pt, bold, UPPERCASE**	"12 pt" before, "6 pt" after, single line
Heading 3	primary procedure components	**Arial, 12pt, bold, UPPERCASE**	"6 pt" before, "6 pt" after, single line

Other:

- Page breaks occur throughout the text to minimize orphan/widow occurrences, etc.
- Section breaks are inserted when, for instance, the document's layout is changed from "portrait" to "landscape", and vice versa (e.g., to accommodate certain forms).

SECTION 3 - THE POLICY MANUAL

This first step in building your Management System is the creation of a Policy Manual. This is a separate, distinct step from developing procedures. The purpose of the Policy Manual is to concisely state the Company's overall policies that drive its strategic and operational objectives.

More than likely, the input for your Policy Manual will come from your customers (and, to a lesser extent, from statutes, regulations, industry benchmarks, and guidelines, etc.). Concern for your customers' satisfaction will ultimately drive your business processes. Their requirements, needs, and future desires are the basis for implementing a management system in the first place.

At a minimum, your Policy Manual should address the products and services the Company provides and their associated Sales/Marketing processes. You may, however, wish to expand the scope of your manual to include other industry or sector specific requirements.

Each area covered by your Policy Manual should include, at a minimum, three parts – scope, policy, and responsibilities:

- The "Scope" portion should simply state the purpose of the functional area and indicate under what conditions the Manual applies;
- The "Policy" portion should state the company policy regarding the functional area; and
- The "Responsibility" portion should state who (by title or position, not by name) is responsible for the policy.

Nowhere is a format requirement specified for the Policy Manual. A sample manual is provided in this guide for your use as a template to create your own Policy Manual (see Tab 3). The Policy Manual's Table of Contents ensures that commonly-used elements are addressed and it provides an excellent starting point for building your management system.

Style and Format

1. Use a cover or title page.
2. Include a table of contents.
3. Put policy statements on a 8 1/2" x 11" page and print only on one side to make revisions easier.
4. Organize material by major headings, for easy reference.
5. Include an alphabetized index if your manual is lengthy and/or complex.
6. Avoid a detailed paragraph identification system of numbers and letters, as this will detract from your manual's readability and the message will be lost.
7. Write in simple, easy-to-understand statements to avoid confusion.

Sample administrative forms and instructions for their completion are included with many of the procedures in this manual. It is expected that you will use your existing forms instead of the forms we provide, where appropriate. Note that the forms included with this product are not designed to be all inclusive or to apply to every situation; rather, they are meant to be guidelines.

Considerations In Writing Your Manual

1. It is now common practice to use pronouns that are applicable to either sex or to use his or her, or the more personal and direct, "you." Social changes influence policies on topics concerning smoking, physical fitness, etc.

2. Have your manual reviewed by a qualified attorney, to ensure that your manual complies with applicable federal, state, and local laws, regulations, and statutes.

3. Define terms specific to your (type of) business in your manual. Definitions should be placed in each procedure, as appropriate; some terms are defined in individual procedures of this product. A glossary of terms (section 150) is included with some Policies and Procedures manuals, as well. We certainly recommend that you add a Glossary to your P&P manual, as it's especially helpful to new employees and contractors.

Revisions

Every organization is dynamic – in some state of change. This necessarily leads to changes to your policies from time to time. Revisions should be completed and sent to all personnel who hold a copy of the manual. The revision should have an effective date and should be distributed in advance of the effective date. When making a change to your manual, be cognizant of the impact that language might have on other policies. Finally, make sure there is a clear record of revisions made and that all employees have current information in a timely manner.

The Policy Manual includes a "Revision" section at the end, as does each procedure. It is important to keep this section – the revision log – up to date. It is the only way to ensure that distributed copies of your manual are current and approved.

Some companies, due to their size and specific business application, require expanded information. For this reason, Bizmanualz, Inc., offers additional business publications that include detailed, topic-specific manuals.

Each manual is intended to be a simple, "top-to-bottom" guide, addressing the minimum set of procedures for the administration and creation of a Management System. Most guidelines presented have immediate use and importance. However, by using the MS-Word documents, you can edit the samples and customize them to your company's individual needs.

- **ISO 9001 Quality Management System Policies and Procedures –** Includes a sample Quality Manual and easily editable quality policies and procedures. Also, it contains a guide to the ISO 9000 set of standards.

- **Accounting Policies and Procedures** – Includes sections on General and Administrative, Cash Management, Inventory & Asset Control, Revenue, and Purchasing.
- **Computer & Network (IT) Policies and Procedures** – Includes sections on Management Information Systems, Software Development, and Network Security.
- **ISO 22000 Food Safety Management System Policies and Procedures** - Includes a sample Food Safety Manual and easily adaptable policies and procedures, including guidance for developing a HACCP plan, standard operating procedures, and Good Practices.
- **Disaster Recovery Policies and Procedures** – Includes your Disaster Manual Preparation, Recovery Procedures, and a section on Coping with Workplace Violence.
- **Human Resources Policies and Procedures** – Includes Employee Handbook Preparation, sample HR policies and procedures, a Human Resources Legal Guide, a sample Employee Handbook, sample Job Descriptions, and sample Reports and Forms.
- **Security Planning Policies and Procedures** – This includes sample procedures for Security Operations and a special section on Embezzlement Prevention.

Bizmanualz, Inc., is committed to providing professional publications for those business owners and managers dedicated to the development and success of their companies. To this end, we will continue to publish useful business guides to assist you in your endeavors. To obtain the latest information on each of our products and services, visit our website, http://www.bizmanualz.com/.

Sources of Additional Information

With the help of the prewritten documentation in this publication, you should be able to produce an effective Management System. You may also wish to draw from other sources of information to develop a truly comprehensive program that meets the needs of your organization and your customers. Sources may include:

1. Industry or trade association publications;
2. Industry/sector consultants;
3. Your Company's legal, financial, and accounting counsel;
4. Other related company manuals and procedures;
5. Internal memos and records;
6. Equipment user manuals;
7. Customer surveys (formal or informal), proposals, or requirements;
8. Regulatory agencies or standards organizations (e.g., FDA, ISO); and
9. Small business advisory centers.

[This page intentionally left blank.]

SECTION 4 - EFFECTIVE COMMUNICATION

Communication – Addressing Your Audience

In order for your manual to be effective, it must be clearly written and easily understood by all employees in your organization. Remember – the <u>objective</u> of your Policies and Procedures Manual is to improve the efficiency and effectiveness of your Company. Therefore, the most important rule is that clarity and readability are more important than style, perfect grammar, and a large vocabulary.

While developing policy and procedure statements, you, the writer, must try to put yourself in the position of the user at all times. Some general guidelines for you to keep in mind are:

1. Explain new or unusual terms the first time they are used or in the "definitions" section of the procedure.
2. Avoid jargon wherever possible, especially when training new employees.
3. Avoid unneeded verbiage.
4. Avoid complex writing. If the writer's vocabulary is unusually large or if they write using complex sentence structures, the writing may be at too high a level for many of the users. Understanding is far more important than the correctness of the language.
5. Use active verbs instead of passive phrases.
6. Write the way you speak. Use words and phrases you would normally use in expressing the same thought orally.

Sexism in Writing

Webster's New Collegiate Dictionary defines "he" as used in the generic sense or when the sex of the person is unspecified. However, many people will not accept "he" being used when referring to people in general. There have been suggestions that the generic "he" be replaced with "he or she" and "him" with "him or her."

Another recent method that is gaining acceptance is the switch to a plural pronoun with a singular subject, such as "When someone orders their supplies, they will have to complete a ..."

Often it is more practical for the writer to use generic nouns or by recasting sentences to include positions or titles (i.e., Applicant, Manager, Accountant, Driver, etc.) to eliminate the need for most sexism in writing of policy and procedures.

Number Usage

Writing and development of procedures may often include the frequent usage of numbers in the writing. The following rules cover how numbers should be used in print.

1. Never begin a sentence with numbers. Write "Fifty states have been admitted to the union", not "50 states have been admitted..."
2. Spell numbers one through nine in word form; use the numeric form for 10 or greater.
3. Write compound numbers, such as fractions, in numeric form (e.g., 8-1/2 x 11").
4. When showing odds (ratios), use hyphens (e.g., "4-to-1").
5. For a number less than one in decimal format, place a zero to the left of the decimal point (e.g., "0.5 percent", not ".5 percent").
6. Write the year, decade, etc., in numeric form (e.g., "the 1990's"), rather than spell it out.
7. Spell out the percent sign ("%" as "percent" when embedding it in text; when listing several in a table, use the "%".
8. Indicate the time of day in numeric format (e.g., "12:00"), including "a.m." or "p.m."

Organizing Your Thoughts

To help the writer formulate and organize ideas for developing and writing policy and procedures, it may be useful to outline the material to be covered. Outlining is a fast and effective way to show a great amount of information in a concise, efficient manner with a minimum of writing.

To achieve well-written and easily understood policy and procedure statements that flow in a cohesive and logical form, your personnel should first outline their thoughts before beginning to write a procedure.

When outlining a policy and procedure, the following areas should be defined:

- What is the objective that the procedure is going to accomplish?
- What is the Company's policy on this matter?
- Who is affected?
- When is the policy/procedure appropriate?
- How is the objective to be accomplished? This should include outlining major areas in a step-by-step fashion in chronological order.

Outlining Technique

There are some basic standard rules for effective and consistent outlining. It may be helpful to briefly review a few of these that deal primarily with formatting. These rules concern indentation and numbering.

Standard outline formatting is as follows:

I.
    A.
        1.
        2.
            a.
            b.
    B.
II.

There should always be at least two of each type of character. For example, there should not be an I without a II, an A without a B, etc.

The four characters to mark each section level, Roman numerals, capital letters, Arabic numerals and lower case letters are followed by a period. Line up the periods vertically for each type of character. Thus, Roman numerals are shown:

    I.

    II.

Arabic numerals are lined up as follows:

    5.

  39.

By aligning the periods, the text is more visually pleasing. Indentation of section text should be uniform; two to five spaces (or 1/4 to 1/2 inch) for each change in type of line is common. The part of a single line carried to a second line should be indented the same number of spaces as the original part of the line (a "hanging indent").

Defining the Format and Organization of Your Manual

After reviewing the preliminary listing of procedures to be included in the manual and discussing with the personnel assigned to each section, you should be able to determine the estimated length and usage of your manual. With the guidelines presented in this publication and from your own organization's needs determine the format of your policy and procedures and how you will organize the manual into sections.

The format and appearance of your policy and procedures are just as important as the organization and content of the manual. A manual that is appealing to the eye and that emphasizes the importance of the procedures is more likely to be taken seriously and used on a regular basis by employees.

However, it is important to remember that the true objective of the manual is to disseminate information in a timely and efficient manner and <u>not</u> to "impress" the reader with intricate headings or fancy printing techniques.

The simplest format is often the best. A simple format also allows for the most time and cost effective manner for production and maintenance of the manual. Therefore, it may be best to avoid temptations such as, detailed corporate logos in headings, two sided copies, odd sized paper patterns, expensive and restrictive binding techniques, etc.

Design Features

No Manual or procedure within it should ever be regarded as "complete." The best manual is one that is geared to continual improvement over time and incorporates design features that make this kind of change possible. In this regard, the use of standard 8-1/2 x 11" paper, housed in a three-ring binder, is ideal.

The three-ring binder provides the benefits of allowing a place for procedures to be inserted while the manual is being developed and provides for easy updating through simple replacement of pages or superseded procedures. Further, as the organization grows, the use of standard three-ring binders allows additional copies of the manual to be produced on an as needed basis instead of having to be concerned with minimum production runs required for hard bound versions.

Production of procedures on a single-side, standard size paper medium provides for easy reproduction of the manual by high-speed copiers. Use of single-side printing also provides for easy updating of the manual with changes by allowing for one or two pages to be replaced without affecting the order or sequence of the manual. However, if the manual becomes too voluminous for ease of handling, it may be necessary to bind the manual by different sections or utilize two-sided printing to reduce paper volume.

A window type binder should be used to allow you to describe the contents of the manual on the spine, for locating sections quickly from a bookcase. The outside of the binder (front and spine) may be imprinted with the company's name and logo, to give the manual a more professional and authoritative appearance.

Divider tabs on heavy stock should be used to separate functional areas or departmental sections for ease in finding a specific procedure.

Style and Mechanics

The style and mechanics of writing include the paper, typestyle, and print quality.

Paper - Some organizations use color to differentiate manuals, forms, memos, etc. While color can create a pleasing appearance, it can complicate photocopying or printing. Some colors do not provide adequate contrast from the ink color for ease in reading. Nothing is better than black ink on white paper.

The grade of paper is not important, since the manual is designed for internal use only. Regular 20-pound paper is adequate for single-sided printing. A heavier weight (for greater opacity) may be necessary for two-sided printing.

Typestyle - Avoid unusual artwork or type styles that are difficult to read and/or reproduce over a long period of time. Strive for consistency in the overall appearance of the entire manual, regardless of what area or department originates the procedures, by selecting a common typewriter element or word processing typestyle font. 12-point Times New Roman and Arial are common typefaces in word processing software.

Avoid using small print, photocopy reductions, all-capital print, or fancy script styles whenever possible, as these are tiresome and difficult to read and, therefore, make it harder for the reader to comprehend the message.

Provide adequate margins on the printed page. Recommended margins are a one-inch (1") top and bottom margin with one-inch left and right mirror margins and a half-inch (1/2") gutter margin for punching holes.

Additional Sources

There are many excellent references available to technical writers, editors, and others developing policies and procedures. A sample of these is listed below:

- Alred, Gerald, Brusaw, Charles, and Oliu, Walter, Handbook of Technical Writing, 8th Edition, St. Martin's Press, 2006 (ISBN 0-312-35267-0)
- Campbell, Nancy, Writing Effective Policies and Procedures: A Step-by-Step Resource for Clear Communication, American Management Assn., 1998 (ISBN 0-814-47960-X)
- Hartman, Peter, Starting a Documentation Group: A Hands-On Guide, Clear Point Consultants Press, 1999 (ISBN 0-967-41790-2)
- Hackos, JoAnne, Managing Your Documentation Projects, Wiley Publishing, 1994 (ISBN 0-471-59099-1)
- Microsoft Corp. Editorial Style Board, Microsoft Manual of Style for Technical Publications, 3rd Edition, 2004 (ISBN 0-735-61746-5)
- Page, Stephen, Establishing a System of Policies and Procedures, Project Management Institute, 2002 (ISBN 1-929-06500-0)
- Page, Stephen, Achieving 100% Compliance of Policies and Procedures, Process Improvement Publications, 2002 (ISBN 1-929-06549-3)

[This page intentionally left blank]

SECTION 5 - PROCEDURES

Format

Procedures address the primary steps or tasks of an activity for a department or function and the personnel (generic titles or positions) responsible for accomplishing the procedure(s). These procedures can be organized on a departmental basis.

The procedures in this manual start with various designations (e.g., "AD," "PD") and may be used as a template to create your own procedures. The exact format, field names, and titles in this manual are not prescribed by any industry standard – consider much of the information in this manual recommendations, not requirements.

Heading Information

The following heading format is a compromise between simplicity and completeness. Heading information should be kept to the minimum necessary to accurately describe the procedure, identify the revision level, demonstrate authorization and be easy to produce. If you don't need all of the information called for in this format, simplify it. If you need more, add it.

A sample heading follows:

Document ID **HR1040**	Title **JOB DESCRIPTIONS**	Print Date **mm/dd/yyyy**
Revision **1.0**	Prepared By **Preparer's Name / Title**	Date Prepared **mm/dd/yyyy**
Effective Date **mm/dd/yyyy**	Reviewed By **Reviewer's Name / Title**	Date Reviewed **mm/dd/yyyy**
	Approved By **Final Approver's Name / Title**	Date Approved **mm/dd/yyyy**
Applicable standard: **ISO 9001, clause 6.2.2**		

The heading above provides the following information:

Document Number – For small manuals, an ID/numbering system may be unnecessary; the title alone may suffice for identification purposes. With larger manuals, however, it is best to use a simple alphanumeric numbering system to identify procedures for ordered storage and easy retrieval in electronic document management systems.

The first two or three character(s) of the ID are alphabetical characters that represent the subject matter covered in the section (e.g., "MP" for marketing planning, "AD" for administration). You are not obliged to use the Bizmanualz ID format – this is supposed to be your company's policies and procedures manual, after all.

The numbering system employed here is sequential, within sections. The purpose of initially assigning numbers by tens is that if a new procedure belongs between existing procedures, for whatever reason, the new procedure number can fall between existing procedure IDs, so existing procedures don't have to be renumbered *and* references to existing procedures within other procedures don't have to be changed, either.

Title – Keep document titles concise and descriptive. Titles are usually incorporated as part of the filename for the electronic version of the file.

Print Date – This is a "field function" feature of MS-Word. It is useful in quickly assessing the degree to which documents used in the operation are kept up to date.

Revision Level – Once a procedure is issued, it will be subject to changes and updates as the operation matures and improves. A revision code should be used to distinguish the current document from all previous versions and assist with purging obsolete procedures. Initial procedures are often issued with a revision level of zero (0 or 0.0). If a new procedure supersedes this prior procedure, the revision number will be incremented upward by one (1 or .1).

Prepared By – It is useful to identify the primary individual or department that developed the procedure, in the event questions arise during the approval process or subsequent to the issuance (implementation) of the procedure.

Date Prepared – Accompanies "Prepared By."

Effective Date - The actual date the procedure or revision will be implemented. Note the effective date is <u>not</u> the issue date of the original procedure. Dates should be *consistently* formatted throughout the Manual (e.g., "mm/dd/yyyy," "dd mm yyyy").

Reviewed By – Multiple review levels may not be needed for some simple procedures but in the majority of cases, a procedure can only be improved by having additional persons evaluate it. This field provides a record, if necessary, of additional review.

Date Reviewed – See "Reviewed By."

Approved By - After the procedure has been properly reviewed and authorized, the title page is initialed by an authorized individual (typically, this is someone in top management, like the chief financial officer or the product vice president). It is best to initial the approval section by hand rather than type it in; this clearly indicates the PROCEDURE has been authorized and distinguishes the final version from any draft versions that may still be in circulation. The "Approved by" identification should be placed directly underneath the "Prepared by" section.

Page Numbering - All pages should be numbered in "Page # of #" format, to quickly identify the order or placement of pages within a procedure. It is also useful when updating an existing procedure where only one or two pages will be replaced. In this product, the page number is placed in the footer of each page.

In addition to the page number, the footer of all Bizmanualz products includes the *document name*.

Introduction

Located directly below the title block, the ***introduction*** section provides information the reader needs to determine the Company policy covering this area, the purpose of the procedure, who is affected in what situation(s), and the definition of any new or unusual terms.

A sample Introduction section can appear as follows:

Policy:	It is the policy of Sample Company that all departments will prepare and maintain standardized operating policies and procedures that cover the performance of all major functions within their department.
Purpose:	This procedure outlines the steps involved in preparing, maintaining and approving standard operating policies and procedures in order to provide consistent, informative and effective procedures to the employees of Sample Company.
Scope:	This procedure applies to all policies and procedures used or written by all departments and individuals of Sample Company.
Responsibilities:	All Personnel are required to understand and use this procedure. Management is responsible for approving and/or maintaining the procedure.
Definitions:	Policy – Definite course or method of action to guide and determine present and future decisions; guide to decision making under a given set of circumstances within the framework of corporate objectives, goals, and management philosophies. Procedure – Particular way of accomplishing something; established way of doing things; series of steps followed in a definite regular order to ensure consistent and repetitive approach to actions.

A general description of the Introduction follows:

Policy - The policy should clearly indicate the company's or top management's requirements, beliefs, and/or protocol affecting this area.

Purpose - A brief description of the objective of the procedure, it should expand and clarify the Policy statement.

Scope - Describes the areas, functions, individuals, or departments affected by the procedure and in what situations the procedure applies.

Responsibilities - Identify who is responsible for implementing or maintaining the procedure or parts of the procedure, in generic titles or positions. For example, write "The Department Manager is responsible for...", *not* "John Doe is responsible for...".

Definitions - Describes any terms contained in the procedure that may be new or unusual to the reader.

The Body Of The Procedure

The body of the procedure includes a complete description of the policy and/or the procedure, the methods to be used, form names, cross references to other procedures related to it, etc.

Although the narrative information in the body can vary considerably in format, it is imperative that it clearly explains to the reader in an orderly fashion exactly how to accomplish the objective of the procedure.

For lengthy procedures, it may be useful to identify and segregate the steps or areas by a numbering system. For example, each procedural category would be identified with a step number, starting with "1.0" and a heading. All steps within the category would then be numbered sequentially (For example, "1.1," "1.2," "1.3"). The step number should be located at the left margin with the narrative indented.

In addition to the detailed steps for implementing the procedure, a well written procedure will include the following items:

Effectiveness Criteria - Describe any thresholds or standards that are used to evaluate the work product or results of the procedure. How will an employee know that the procedure was executed correctly?

References - List applicable documents, procedures, manuals, laws and regulations, validation studies, or other sources that were used to develop, refine, or influence the policy/procedure statement.

Records - Describe the records, minutes, reports, notes, forms, or other documents that are generated or used when implementing the procedure.

Revision History - Describe all revisions made to the procedure. Include a revision number, date of the revision, a short description of the changes made, and the source of the change request.[2]

Attachments

Any forms, diagrams, illustrations or other documents referenced in the body of the procedure should be attached and referenced as exhibits in the Records section using a sequential numbering system, (e.g., "Exhibit 1"). It may be useful to use copies of actual completed forms or documents partially or completely filled in, to illustrate to the reader how they are completed.

Once all comments have been received and a final version approved, the procedure should be printed in its final form. The procedure should then be authorized by the appropriate individual and released for production and distribution.

---

[2] By name or initials

Authorization

Origination of policies and procedures usually begins at the unit level by employees or department managers. Once a draft copy of a proposed procedure is developed it should be reviewed, corrected if necessary, and approved before being released as a corporate policy and procedure. The approval process generally consists of review for consistency and accuracy, compatibility/conflict with corporate policy or other procedures, and general readability.

The approval process can vary widely between companies, but it is recommended to keep approvals to a minimum. If too many people or managers of equal ranking are required to authorize a procedure, it can turn procedure development into a bureaucratic nightmare – considerably slowing release of policies and procedures, while adding little of value to the final version.

A method for gaining the input of others while streamlining the process and keeping authority at the functional or departmental level is to release draft copies of proposed procedures to a select number of individuals for comment. It should be made clear to these individuals that they should confine their suggestions to what they feel is really essential to the procedure's accuracy, readability, and usefulness.

Who should receive a draft copy depends mainly on the nature and content of the procedure. Sensitive issues or areas that deal with corporate exposure (such as personnel, intellectual property, or trade secrets) should be reviewed by top management including the president and possibly the Company's legal counsel.

Review of rudimentary procedures – ones that affect only a small unit within the company and are not likely to affect others on a day-to-day basis – should be a minimal process; however, it is advisable to have someone familiar with the area but separate or outside of the unit or department review the proposed procedure (e.g., the chief financial officer might review a proposed accounting SOP). This type of review serves three purposes:

First, what makes sense to the preparer directly involved in enforcing the policy or conformance to a procedure may not be understood when read for the first time by someone not as closely or frequently involved;

Second, a review by multiple department managers may prevent a conflict with a policy/procedure document still in the formative or discussion stage elsewhere in the Company of which the original preparer was unaware; and

Third, it allows the input of multiple individuals while allowing the department manager to maintain control of the integrity of the procedure and drive its completion and release in a timely manner.

Production And Distribution

Once a policy and procedure statement is authorized, it may be duplicated on standard white copy paper and three-hole-punched on the left margin. Multiple page procedures may be corner stapled to prevent losing pages until it is included in the manual.

The number of copies of the procedure should correlate to the number of manuals that have been distributed. It is generally advisable to designate one individual in the company to develop procedures, keep track of the number of manuals issued, and ensure that new or revised procedures are distributed to the appropriate personnel.

The Company's top management should decide which departments or positions will receive copies of the manual or, as an alternative, which sections of the manual may be distributed to specific functions or departments. However, if the manual is to serve as a communication tool, enough copies of the manual should be available to employees.

Since the manual contains many operating procedures that are vital to the company's business practices and methods, there should be some accountability for the manuals. Generally, one individual will maintain a list of the number of copies in circulation and the names of those to whom they have been assigned. When a supervisor or manager leaves the company, there should be a strong incentive to return their copy of the manual; some companies withhold final compensation until the manual has been returned.

However, one should avoid numbering each copy of a manual, unless absolutely necessary. Numbering implies confidentiality and some degree of importance, which may not be the case. Besides, the issuer must maintain a permanent record of the numbers cross-referenced to the recipients that can make personnel changes a tedious record-keeping task.

The Company may elect to produce, distribute, and control copies of its manual electronically. According to the laws of most countries, electronic production, distribution, and control of Company documents is allowed and even encouraged (see various Paperwork Reduction Acts, for instance). In all cases, a clear audit trail is required. The question of "Paper or electronic?" is one your Company has to resolve on its own.

Revising and Updating Procedures

As we've already pointed out, your policy and procedure manual is never complete. It should never stop changing or evolving, because the needs of the business, its customers' needs, the legal landscape, and the business climate *are continually changing*.

Encourage all your employees to initiate changes or revisions to existing policies and procedures, especially those that affect their area of responsibility. Such encouragement will greatly assist the Company in keeping its Policies and Procedures manual accurate, comprehensive, and up-to-date, because it gives employees a sense of purpose and a stake in the Company's well-being.

In addition to an ongoing review process for all policies and procedures, the entire manual should periodically undergo a complete audit. This audit might occur every six months, annually, or every other year, depending on the Company and the business environment. Your policies and procedures should also reflect changing conditions within and outside the company, so you should also strongly consider revising them on an "as needed" basis.

A new procedure should be issued if an existing one is to be modified in any way. The revised procedure should undergo the same approval process as the initial release and should be assigned a new revision number level to indicate that it supersedes the prior procedure. Superseded procedures should be purged from the manual immediately and discarded.

[This page intentionally left blank]

IT Policies and Procedures

Section 300

IT Policy Manual

Section 300

IT Policy Manual

IT Policy Manual

The IT manual establishes and states the policies governing The
Company's IT standards and practices. These policies define
management's arrangements for managing operations and activities in
accordance with computer industry practices. These top-level policies
represent the plans or protocols for achieving and maintaining the
confidentiality, integrity and availability of all IT Assets.

[This page intentionally left blank]

<Company Logo>

<Our Company, Inc.>

IT Policy Manual

mm dd yyyy

Approved By _____ Date: _____

President/CEO

This manual is intended for the sole use of Our Company, Inc., and parts may
be provided to outside parties for informational purposes only.

© 20nn Our Company, Inc.

The contents of this manual may not be reproduced or reprinted, in whole or
in part, without the express written permission of Our Company, Inc.

The following document contains a sample IT policy manual covering the common IT requirements and practices. This sample is intended only to provide an example of wording that might be used in an IT manual.

This sample wording can be helpful in generating ideas for developing a manual for your own company. However, IT policies should be drafted, as appropriate and necessary, in a way that accurately reflects Our Company's IT standards and requirements.

Information Technology Policy Manual

Table of Contents

TABLE OF FIGURES

LIST OF REFERENCED PROCEDURES

IT Administration

1. ITAD101 Information Technology Management
2. ITAD102 IT Records Management
3. ITAD103 IT Document Management
4. ITAD104 IT Device Naming Conventions
5. ITAD105 TCP/IP Implementation Standards
6. ITAD106 Network Infrastructure Standards
7. ITAD107 Computer and Internet Usage Policy
8. ITAD108 Email Policy
9. ITAD109 IT Outsourcing
10. ITAD110 IT Department Satisfaction
11. ITAD111 BYOD Policy

IT Asset Management

1. ITAM101 IT Asset Standards
2. ITAM102 IT Asset Management
3. ITAM103 IT Vendor Selection
4. ITAM104 IT Asset Assessment
5. ITAM105 IT Asset Installation Satisfaction

IT Training and Support

1. ITTS101 IT System Administration
2. ITTS102 IT Support Center
3. ITTS103 IT Server/Network Support
4. ITTS104 IT Troubleshooting
5. ITTS105 IT User-Staff Training Plan

IT Security and Disaster Recovery

1. ITSD101 IT Threat And Risk Assessment
2. ITSD102 IT Security Plan
3. ITSD103 IT Media Storage
4. ITSD104 IT Disaster Recovery
5. ITSD105 Computer Malware
6. ITSD106 IT Access Control
7. ITSD107 IT Security Audits
8. ITSD108 IT Incident Handling

Software Development

1. ITSW101 IT Project Definition
2. ITSW102 IT Project Management
3. ITSW103 Systems Analysis
4. ITSW104 Software Design
5. ITSW105 Software Programming
6. ITSW106 Software Documentation

7. ITSW107 Software Testing
8. ITSW108 Design Changes During Development
9. ITSW109 Software Releases and Updates
10. ITSW110 Software Support
11. ITSW111 Software Consulting Services
12. ITSW112 Software Training

1.0   PURPOSE

The purpose of this Information Technology (IT) manual is to define, develop, and document the information policies and procedures that support organizational goals and objectives.

The policies and procedures provide:

- A foundation for a system of internal controls;
- Guidance in current Computer and Network activities;
- Criteria for decisions on appropriate IT security; and
- IT officers with direction and guidance in connection with those IT policies, procedures, and reports that should be uniform throughout the Company.

Information security policies and procedures represent the foundation for The Company's information security program. Information security policies serve as overarching guidelines for the use, management, and implementation of information security throughout the organization.

Internal controls provide a system of checks and balances intended to identify irregularities, prevent waste, fraud and abuse from occurring, and assist in resolving discrepancies that are accidentally introduced in the operations of the business.

When consistently applied throughout the Company, these policies and procedures assure that the information assets are protected from a range of threats in order to ensure business continuity and maximize the return on investments of business interests.

All additional departmental or functional policies and procedures written should conform to and parallel the policies in this manual. All changes to policies and procedures are required to be reviewed to ensure that there are no conflicts with the policies stated in this IT Policy Manual.

[This page intentionally left blank]

2.0   SCOPE

The IT Policy Manual is an official directive of the President. It is published and maintained by the Chief Information Officer (CIO) as part of the general responsibility for Company IT policy assigned to the IT office.

The policies stated in this manual apply to all operations and activities at Our Company. The attendant IT procedures serve to define the operational steps and practices that should be followed in order to support the organization's approach to IT management as defined by the policy statements.

2.1   RESPONSIBILITY

<u>Department Managers</u>. It is the responsibility of all department managers to help implement and maintain the procedures required by this manual and to ensure all processes conform to these requirements.

<u>All Employees</u>. It is the responsibility of all employees to follow procedures that implement these policies and to help strive for continuous improvement in all activities and processes of Our Company.

<u>All Users</u>. The goal is to make the Manual as clear and useful as possible. All users are encouraged to contact the Company CIO with any suggestions for revising or improving the Manual.

2.2   EXCLUSIONS

2.2.1   Security Planning

Some IT-related security planning functions are included with the IT manual. Additional information on *physical* security planning information is included with ABR32, *Bizmanualz® Security Planning Policies and Procedures Manual*.

2.2.2   Disaster Recovery

Some IT-related disaster recovery functions are included with this IT manual. Additional information on *physical* disaster recovery is available in ABR33, *Bizmanualz® Disaster Recovery Policies and Procedures Manual*.

2.2.3   Accounting

Accounting functions are not included with this manual but are available in ABR31, *Bizmanualz® Accounting Policies and Procedures Manual*.

2.2.4   Human Resources

Human resources functions are not included with this manual but are available in ABR41 *Bizmanualz® Human Resources Policies and Procedures Manual*.

[This page intentionally left blank]

3.0   MANAGEMENT RESPONSIBILITY

The IT department is headed by the Chief Information Officer (CIO), who is responsible for all IT functions.

3.1   IT ORGANIZATION

The IT department is organized into three main responsibilities, or functions: Training and Support; Operations; and Software Development.

3.1.1   IT Department Organizational Chart

The company's organizational framework is the foundation for coordinating and administrating IT systems and services. A description of the roles and responsibilities applicable to the IT staff are provided. Responsibilities specific to certain procedures or tasks are presented in the related procedures.

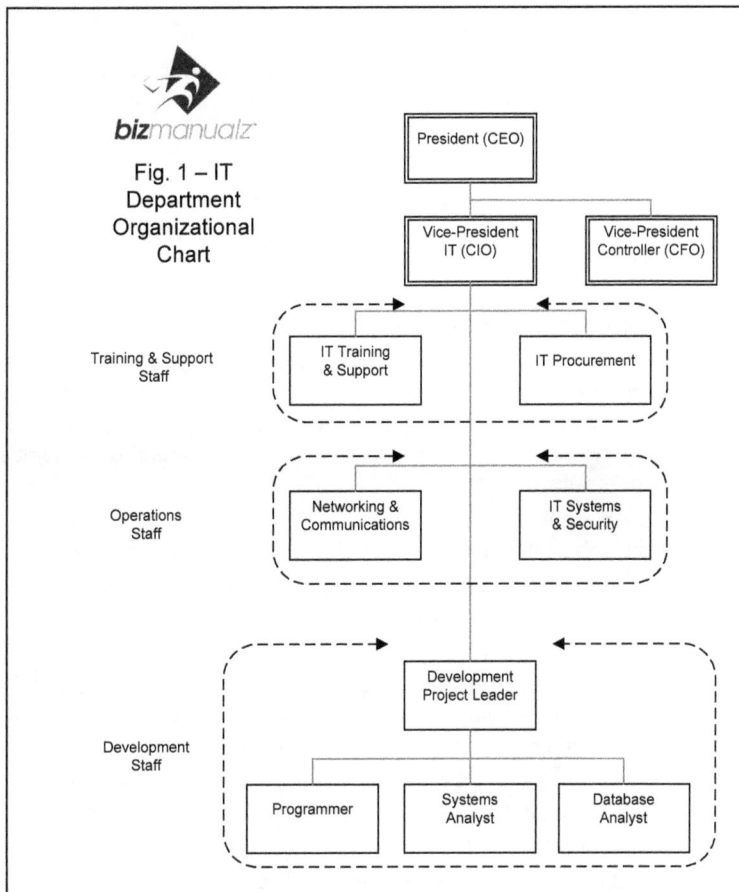

Fig. 1 – IT Department Organizational Chart

(Note: The actual Organization Chart may vary in detail, based on the size of the department or organization involved and the type of activity performed. In a smaller company, the CIO may be an IT Manager reporting to the CFO.)

3.1.2 CIO Responsibilities

The Chief Information Officer (CIO) provides the vision and leadership for developing and implementing Information Technology (IT) initiatives that improve cost effectiveness and service quality. The CIO directs the IT security and control functions to ensure the integrity of all information assets.

The CIO leads the company in implementing IT systems through strategies, plans, programs and services to support both distributed and centralized business operations. The CIO ensures appropriate technology is deployed to support the organizations objectives and reports on the results of operations. The CIO is accountable to the President and supervises the IT staff.

<u>Major Duties And Responsibilities:</u>

o   Develops and implements IT policies, coordination of processes and procedures, and the preparation of operating data and special reports as required.

o   Develops and maintains IT systems architecture defining standards and protocols for data exchange, communications, software, and interconnections.

o   Establishes, coordinates and administers as an integral part of management, an adequate plan for the control of operations including IT training, technical support, and software development, together with necessary controls and procedures to effectuate the plan.

o   Provides advice on evaluation, selection, implementation and maintenance of information systems, ensuring appropriate investment in strategic and operational systems. Negotiates all IT acquisition contracts, soliciting involvement and participation of other management team members as appropriate.

o   Ensures that enterprise information systems operate according to internal standards, external accrediting agency standards, and legal requirements.

o   In conjunction with the President, coordinates IT reviews and endorses strategic IT plans, budget proposals, and proposed changes.

o   Ensures appropriate training programs are in place to attract, retain and develop the key personnel required to support information services. Ensures all personnel are appropriately trained in the usage of all IT products and services in order to effectively carry out their job.

o   Assures protection for the information assets of the business through internal control, internal auditing, IT security, recovery procedures and assuring proper insurance coverage.

o   Develops and maintains a business IT recovery plan to ensure timely and effective restoration of IT services in the event of a disaster.

o   Provides advice on all technology matters to the President.

3.1.3 Training and Support

Training and Support responsibilities are focused on providing assistance to personnel in the field that use all of the computer hardware, software and IT services.

The Training and Support staff consists of the following positions:

o Training and Support Manager – Directs and organizes all general IT training activities for both the IT staff and company personnel. Prepares IT assessments and satisfaction surveys and reports. Reports directly to the CIO. Coordinates activities with all departments; works closely with IT Support

o Technical Support – Installs, tests, troubleshoots, and maintains hardware and software; implements and monitors PC standards and procedures; facilitates backup and recovery; maintains service logs security incident reports; coordinates vendor updates; provides technical guidance and training to end-users; monitors problem/change activities and coordinates the involvement of staff, clients, and vendors to ensure effective resolution of user problems. Reports directly to the Training and Support Manager. Assists in supervision of support staff. Works closely with IT Training, Development, and Operations.

o IT Procurement – Responsible for purchasing all IT tools, supplies and assets for the company including negotiating price, delivery and credit terms. Evaluates vendors and determines most cost-effective supplies inventory and reorder levels. Reports to the CIO. Coordinates activities with all departments; works closely with IT Operations.

3.1.4 Operations Staff Responsibilities

Operations staff responsibilities are focused on diligently maintaining the computer systems, software and hardware of the company to ensure the availability of disk space, response time, and information security.

The operations staff consists of the following positions:

o Network Communications – Designs and tests data communications networks; designs, configures, and implements LAN/WAN hardware, software, and ancillary services for network operating efficiency; assists in router installation, software upgrade, and connections to Internet and telecommunications; develops methods and criteria for network data collections and analysis; ensures network operating problems are resolved; maintains network security and sets up firewalls; maintains and monitors WAN networks; Reports directly to the CIO.

o IT Systems & Security – Installs, customizes, and maintains operating systems software; evaluates operating efficiency and analyzes performance and tuning; makes modifications to tuning parameters to improve performance; Implements and monitor policies and procedures for security and disaster recovery; implements and monitors security audit logs and access control practices to ensure adherence to policies and procedures. Reports directly to the CIO.

3.1.5 Development Responsibilities

The company focuses development staff responsibilities on creating, editing, and maintaining the custom software application in use.

The Development staff consists of the following positions:

- o **Project Leader** – Responsible for developing project management plans and coordinating the application development with the CIO and subordinates. Reports directly to CIO. Supervises programmer, system analyst, and database analyst. Works with training, technical support and operations.

- o **Programmer/Analyst** – Designs software applications writing in one or more commonly used programming languages or 4th generation languages appropriate for multi-user/multi-tasking environments; writes program documentation in accordance with published standards. Reports directly to the Project Leader.

- o **Systems Analyst** – Develops system proposals and cost-benefit analyses; designs application systems ensuring design specifications and documentation meet published standards; prepares illustrative output for review and approval; approves development of logical database design; prepares system flowcharts, logic, and data management descriptions; develops program and system specifications; conducts system tests. Works with users to define IT requirements. Reports directly to the Project Leader.

- o **Database Analyst** – Designs, develops, installs, and tests database systems; assures compatibility and efficiency of database applications through ongoing system monitoring and evaluation; prepares and updates data models and develops standards for updating the data dictionary; develops security requirements for all on-line applications. Reports directly to the Project Leader.

3.2   MANAGEMENT COMMITMENT

Top Management at Our Company shows its commitment to the IT management system through the development and implementation of this IT Policy Manual. Additionally, management commitment is demonstrated through the Company IT Policy, the specific objectives that are set and reviewed during Management Review Meetings, and by providing the resources required to meet our objectives for continually improving the effectiveness of our operations and IT system.

The management team consisting of the President and all department managers is chartered with ensuring our IT management system meets customer, as well as statutory and regulatory, requirements

3.3   MANAGEMENT IT POLICY

Our Company has established an IT Policy Manual that we feel is appropriate to our organization, meets the practices set forth by <u>IEEE</u> and <u>ISO</u> for information systems, and complies with all statutory and regulatory requirements. We accomplish this by adhering to our IT Management System and use operational methods as documented in our IT Policy Manual

This policy is communicated throughout the company. Department managers and supervisors are responsible for ensuring all employees understand the policy. To ensure our policy remains appropriate, it is reviewed at least annually at one of our Management Review meetings.

The Company IT Policy:

- We strive to continually improve the effectiveness of our IT Management System by monitoring our performance against our established objectives and through leadership that promotes employee involvement. This concept represents Our Company's commitment to quality IT and the increasing need to better serve our customers, shareholders, and employees.

- It is Company policy to safeguard and secure all information assets in accordance with industry-accepted standards and guidelines; for example, ISO/IEC 27002:2013, "Information Technology - Security Techniques - Code of Practice for Information Security Management", ISO/IEC 27001:2013, "Information technology - Security techniques - Information security management systems – Requirements", and ISO/IEC 27005:2011, "Information Technology Security Techniques Information Security Risk Management".

- It is Company policy to design and produce software that conforms to IEEE Standard #1058-1998, "Standards for Software Project Management Plans" and the data requirements of ISO/IEC 12207:2008, "Systems and Software Engineering - Software Life Cycle Processes".

3.4   PLANNING

3.4.1   IT Objectives

Our Company shall establish objectives on an annual basis. These objectives shall be measurable and consistent with the IT Policy, and reviewed at least annually at Management Review meetings.

3.4.2   IT System Planning

As part of annual strategic planning meetings, Our Company establishes strategic objectives and goals. These objectives are supported by specific measures that track performance against those objectives using the budgeting process. IT managers in turn set IT objectives with specific performance measures and targets that support the company objectives.

As situations arise that demand changes to the IT systems, either to meet objectives or because of changing business conditions, all changes will be reviewed by the management team to ensure the integrity of the IT systems are maintained.

3.5   RESPONSIBILITY, AUTHORITY, AND COMMUNICATION

3.5.1   Responsibility and Authority

Responsibilities and authorities at Our Company are defined in each Job Description. Job Descriptions are posted on the company intranet and are also used during annual performance reviews.

3.5.2   Management Representative

The President has appointed the CIO as the Management Representative with the responsibility and authority to:

a) Ensure that processes needed for IT Management are established, implemented and maintained.

b) Report to top management on the performance of the IT Systems and any need for improvement.

c) Ensure the promotion of awareness of IT requirements throughout the organization.

d) Serve as the liaison with external parties on matters relating to the IT Management System.

3.5.3   Internal Communication

In line with Our Company's policy of leadership through employee involvement, Our Company's personnel policies have been designed to establish and promote open communication throughout the organization.

The effectiveness of our IT Management System is evident through Internal Audit results, Management Reports, department satisfaction and departmental performance measures. Other than confidential information, company and departmental performance measures are posted on bulletin boards throughout Our Company. Internal Audit results are shared at departmental meetings, as appropriate.

3.5.4   Referenced Procedures:

ITAD101 – Information Technology Management
ITSD107 – IT Security Audits
ITSW102 – IT Project Management
ITAD110 – IT Department Satisfaction

3.6   MANAGEMENT REPORTING

3.6.1   General

The President and management team shall review the Company's IT Management Systems, on a semi-annual basis and more frequently if needed, to ensure its continuing suitability, adequacy and effectiveness. This review shall include assessing opportunities for improvement and the need for changes to the IT Management Systems, including the IT policy and objectives.

The CIO is responsible for maintaining records of management reviews.

3.6.2 Review Input

The CIO and IT managers provide the following information for Management Review meetings:

a) Results of audits
b) Department and employee feedback
c) Process performance
d) Follow-up actions from previous management reviews
e) Changes that could affect IT Management Systems
f) Recommendations for improvement

3.6.3 Review Output

Records shall include the output from the management review and shall include any decisions and actions related to:

a) Improvement of the effectiveness of IT Management Systems and its processes
b) Improvement of processes related to IT requirements
c) Resource needs

3.6.4 Referenced Procedures:

ITAD101 – Information Technology Management

3.7 BUSINESS CONDUCT

Unethical business conduct, actions or even the appearance of unethical behavior is unacceptable under any conditions. The reputation of the Company depends on each employee applying common sense in situations where specific rules of conduct are insufficient to provide clear direction. A strong sense of personal ethics, which should extend beyond compliance with applicable laws, is necessary to guide the behavior of all employees.

All employees should comply with the ethical standards of the Company as set forth in this manual. If a situation feels awkward or uncomfortable, employees should ask themselves:

- Is my action legal and ethical?
- Does my action comply with corporate policy?
- Is my action appropriate in the situation?
- Would my action be an embarrassment to the Company, if known?
- Does my action agree with my personal ethics or behavior?

Employees should be able to answer "yes" to all of these questions (except the fourth, of course) before taking action.

All Managers are responsible for the ethical business conduct and behavior of their employees. Managers should consider the appropriate courses of action in terms of both ethical and economic factors. Each decision should be based on the guidelines provided in this IT Manual as well as their own personal beliefs of what's right and wrong.

All employees are responsible for awareness of - and respect for - the intellectual property rights of others, for complying with the U.S. Digital Millennium Copyright Act of 1998, and for complying with privacy, trans-border data flow, and cryptographic regulations applicable to the Company's IT practices.

4.0   IT MANAGEMENT SYSTEM

4.1   OBJECTIVES

Through this manual and associated procedures and documents, Our Company has established, documented, and implemented an IT Management System. The system is designed to result in improving the effectiveness of our IT operations and in our ability to satisfy auditor requirements.

4.2   REQUIREMENTS

Maintenance of the IT Management System is the responsibility of the CIO, in conjunction with the IT Department.

4.2.1   Overview

The CIO maintains all documents that identify the sequence of IT processes and, in conjunction with the appropriate department managers, defines the interactions of the processes within the procedures defining these processes.

Processes for management activities, provision of resources, and measurement reporting are included. Procedures shall include the methods needed to ensure that the accountability and control of processes are effective.

Top Management will ensure the availability of resources to support the operation and monitoring of processes through regular interaction with department managers and through review activities at Management Review meetings.

Department Managers and the CIO will monitor, measure, and analyze processes and implement any actions necessary to achieve intended results and ensure continual improvement of processes. These results will also be monitored at Management Review meetings.

Any processes that are outsourced that may affect Our Company's conformity to requirements shall be controlled. The CIO and appropriate department manager(s) are responsible for defining the methods to control outsourced processes in procedures.

4.2.2   Internal Controls

Controls should be selected based on the cost of implementation relative to the reduction of risk and potential for loss, if and when a security breach occurs. Non-monetary factors, such as loss of reputation, should also be taken into account.

Internal controls, procedures, and practices ensure that:

- o   Risks are reduced to an acceptable level.
- o   All assets are safeguarded against waste, fraud, loss, unauthorized use or disclosure, and misappropriation.
- o   Programs are efficiently and effectively carried out in accordance with applicable laws and management policy.

4.2.3   Access Controls

Access to all IT assets should be properly controlled and recorded into the IT Management System in accordance with Company IT policies defined in this manual.

All transactions should be supported by documentary evidence, which becomes part of the IT records. Error transactions should be reviewed, resolved, and cleared in a timely fashion. Manually determined control should be reconciled with recorded results.

Access control should ensure that:

- o   Information access is authorized for effective use of media and application security.

- o   Personnel information is protected including defining and assigning access levels, guidelines for hiring/transfer/separation, and security awareness training.

- o   Rules for managing IT security are in place for regular testing, auditing and accreditation.

- o   Audit trails exist for detective and reactive response to system penetration, infection of systems and data due to malicious code, catastrophic system loss or a compromise of data integrity.

4.2.4   Audit Findings

Managers are to promptly evaluate findings and recommendations reported by auditors and then determine proper actions in response to audit findings and recommendations (e.g., develop corrective actions). Managers should complete, within established time frames, all actions that correct or otherwise resolve the matters brought to management's attention.

The audit resolution process begins when the results of an audit are reported to management, and is completed only after actions have been taken that correct identified deficiencies, produce improvements, or demonstrate the audit findings and recommendations are either invalid or do not warrant management actions.

4.3   TRANSACTIONS

All transactions recorded into the IT Management System should be properly authorized and accurately represent the activity occurring. The timing of the transaction should be in accordance with Company IT policies defined in this manual.

4.3.1   Authorization

Access to systems, transactions and other significant events are to be authorized and executed only by persons acting within the scope of their authority. It is the principal means of assuring that only valid transactions and other events are entered into. Modification or adjustment to previously recorded transactions requires authorization.

4.3.2 **Accuracy**

Transactions should be recorded in the IT system accurately. All transaction dates recorded in the Company IT system should accurately reflect the date the transaction occurred.

All transactions should be supported by documentary evidence, which becomes part of the IT records.

4.3.3 **Referenced Procedures:**

ITAD101 Information Technology Management
ITSD101 IT Threat And Risk Assessment
ITSD106 IT Access Control
ITSD107 IT Security Audits

4.4 DOCUMENTATION

This IT Manual and the associated procedures are intended to satisfy the documentation requirements for an IT Management System. Department managers and supervisors are responsible for identifying any additional documents needed to ensure the effective planning, operation and control of processes.

Procedures may vary in detail based on the size of the department or organization involved and the type of activity performed. Procedure developers shall consider this as well as the complexity of the processes and interactions, and the competence of the personnel involved.

The IT Management System utilizes standard forms and provides control and accountability over these forms. Supervisors should review posted IT transactions with source documents and processing documents. Documents may be any medium including: software programs, electronic text files, or hardcopy documents for example.

4.4.1 **IT Policy Manual**

This IT Policy Manual includes the scope of Our Company's IT Management system and sets forth management policy.

4.4.2 **Control of Documents**

All Documents required by the IT Management System shall be controlled. The Document Control Procedure defines the controls needed to:

a) Approve documents for adequacy prior to issue.
b) Review and update as necessary and re-approve documents.
c) Ensure that changes and the current revision status of documents are identified.
d) Ensure that relevant versions of applicable documents are available at points of use.
e) Ensure that documents remain legible and readily identifiable.
f) Ensure that documents of external origin are identified and their distribution controlled.

g) Prevent the unintended use of obsolete documents, and to apply suitable identification to them if they are retained for any purpose.

4.4.3 Control of Records

Procedures define appropriate records to be maintained in order to provide evidence of conformity to requirements and of the effective operation of the IT Management System. Records shall remain legible, readily identifiable and retrievable. The Files and Records Management Procedure defines the controls needed for the identification, storage, protection, retrieval, retention time, and disposition of records.

4.4.4 IT Transactions

All transactions and other significant events should be clearly documented, properly classified and readily available for examination.

This standard applies to:

- The entire process or life cycle of a transaction or event and includes the initiation and authorization
- All aspects of the transaction while in process
- Its final classification in summary records.

4.4.5 Software Coding

Formal change control is required for all production systems. All software libraries and other significant code should be clearly documented, properly classified and readily available for examination using a Source Code Control System (SCCS). The SCCS should be used to control all source code and software revisions.

Developers should document all code changes within the software. An appropriate comment should be made within the SCCS reflecting the changes made when code is checked-in and checked-out.

4.4.6 Referenced Procedures:

ITAD102 IT Records Management
ITAD103 IT Document Management
ITSW106 Software Documentation
ITSD107 IT Security Audits

4.5 SECURITY

Access to resources and records should be limited to authorized personnel only. Accountability for the custody and use of resources should be assigned and maintained as well.

Periodic comparisons should be made of the resources with the recorded accountability to determine whether the two agree. The frequency of the comparison shall be a function of the vulnerability of the asset.

Restrictions of access to resources shall also depend upon the vulnerability of the resource as well as the perceived risk of loss, both of which shall be periodically assessed.

4.5.1 Physical Security

Physical security measures should be adopted to protect the assets and employees of the Company from abuse, fraud, theft, or damage. Security procedures for the protection of assets and employees are addressed within the Company's Security Manual. See ABR32, *Bizmanualz® Security Planning Policies and Procedures Manual*.

4.5.2 Disaster Security

Disaster security measures should be adopted to enable the Company to continue the operations of the IT Management System with limited interruption. Disaster procedures for operations recovery are addressed within the Company's Disaster Manual. See ABR33, *Bizmanualz® Disaster Recovery Policies and Procedures Manual*.

4.5.3 Information Security

Information security policies and procedures represent the foundation upon which companies construct their information security program. Information security policies serve as overarching guidelines for the use, management, and implementation of information security throughout the organization.

4.5.4 Referenced Procedures:

ITSD101 IT Threat / Risk Assessment
ITSD102 IT Security Plan
ITSD104 IT Disaster Recovery
ITSD105 Computer Malware
ITSD106 IT Access Control
ITSD107 IT Security Audits
ITSD108 IT Incident Handling

[This page intentionally left blank]

5.0   PROCESSES AND CONTROLS

The following processes, controls, and procedures serve to define specific operational steps and practices to support the organization's approach to information security, operations, development, and support, as defined by the policy statements.

These processes and procedures include the IT objectives and requirements for our Company, the required verification, validation, and inspection activities specific to our Company and the criteria for software and hardware acceptance. The records needed to provide evidence that these processes meet all compliance requirements are defined in the procedures.

Consideration is given for the need to establish processes, documents, and obtain resources specific to information security to ensure the safety of all information

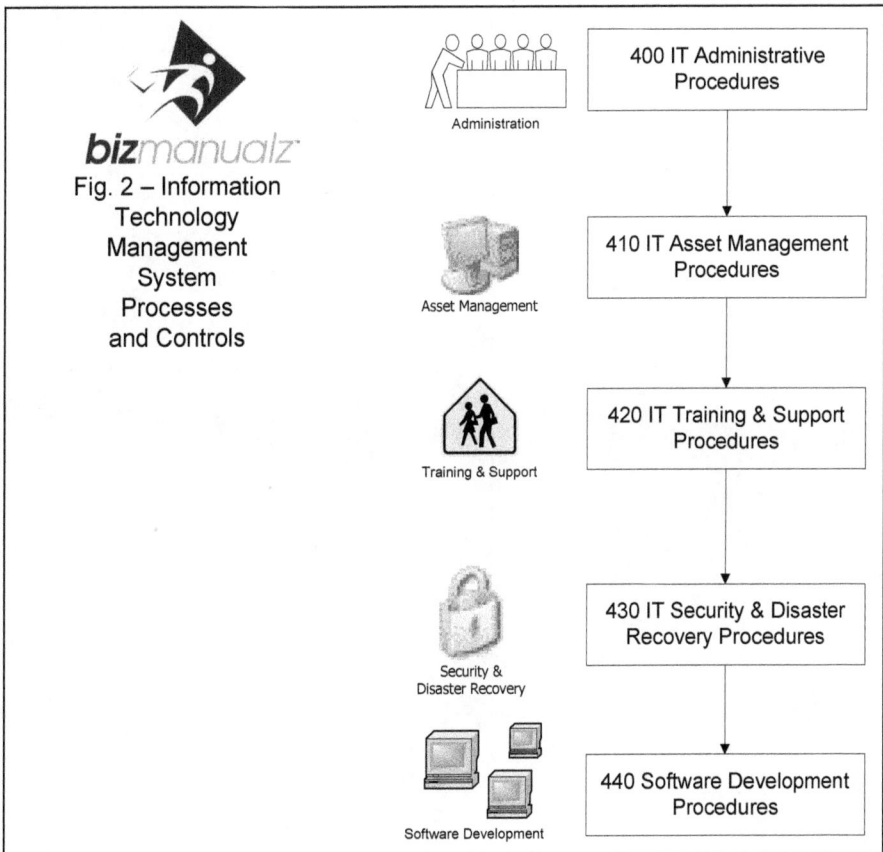

Fig. 2 – Information Technology Management System Processes and Controls

assets.

[This page intentionally left blank]

5.1   IT ADMINISTRATION

The IT Administrative procedures encompass a wide range of miscellaneous activities from the overall direction of IT Management, maintaining IT records and documentation, to network management standards and department satisfaction. The following IT Administrative procedures should be utilized to control the Company's miscellaneous IT activities.

Fig. 3 – IT Administrative Procedures

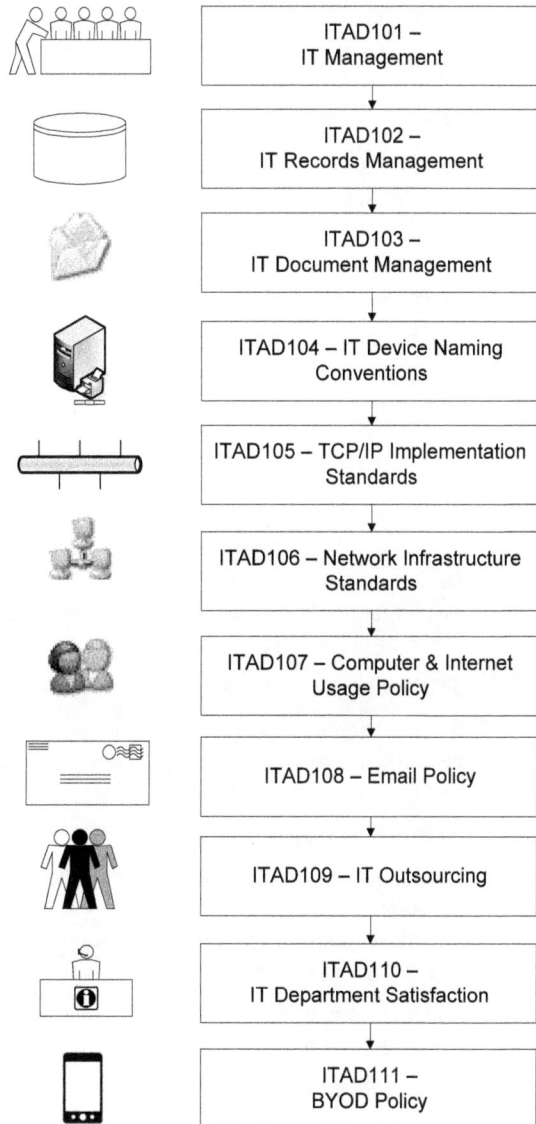

ITAD101 – IT Management

ITAD102 – IT Records Management

ITAD103 – IT Document Management

ITAD104 – IT Device Naming Conventions

ITAD105 – TCP/IP Implementation Standards

ITAD106 – Network Infrastructure Standards

ITAD107 – Computer & Internet Usage Policy

ITAD108 – Email Policy

ITAD109 – IT Outsourcing

ITAD110 – IT Department Satisfaction

ITAD111 – BYOD Policy

5.1.1 Information Technology Management

IT Management supports the Company's Strategic Plan through strategic planning and effective use of information technologies. Its goals include deployment of information technologies that increase overall Company productivity and performance, achieve greater efficiencies, and achieve positive returns on the investment in technology.

The Company should link Information Technology department goals and objectives to the Company's strategic vision, ultimately assuring that the Company meets customer requirements while undergoing continual improvement.

5.1.2 IT Records Management

The IT department organizes and manages Company records in a controlled, consistent, and effective manner while conforming to specified requirements and ensuring the safety, availability, confidentiality, and integrity of all electronic records.

5.1.3 IT Document Management

The IT department manages all electronic documents connected with official Company functions, storing them securely, ensuring their integrity, and allowing appropriate parties access to them. It is intended to provide methods and set forth responsibilities with regard to the control, storage, revision, retrieval, and disposal of documents.

5.1.4 IT Device Naming Conventions

All devices joined to the Company network are to be named in a way that facilitates management of network resources and delineates conventions for the assignment of host or device names for any equipment included with the Company IT infrastructure.

5.1.5 TCP/IP Implementation Standards

TCP/IP addresses are to be assigned in a way that facilitates management of the network and provide conventions for assigning TCP/IP addresses to equipment that is part of the Company IT infrastructure.

5.1.6 Network Management Standards

The Company network infrastructure shall be engineered and installed in accordance with appropriate industry standards and state and local building and electrical codes, to ensure safety, security, adequate capacity, and maximum efficiency.

Specific standards regarding the installation of the IT network infrastructure, such as cabling, routers, gateways, and other equipment, are spelled out.

5.1.7 Computer and Internet Usage Policy

Any employee using the Company IT network for any reason must adhere to strict guidelines regarding its use. Employees are being entrusted with the safety and security of Company information assets, not the least of which is Company information. A sound security policy for information and other IT assets will include the participation of every employee, at all times. Sound policy promotes information security.

5.1.8 Email Policy

Company email and the hardware and software that support it belong to the Company. Email can be a tool for promoting cooperation and collaboration between and among employees, clients, and suppliers. Any use of email on Company time while using Company assets should promote the Company's interests, as well as those of its customers and vendors.

5.1.9 IT Outsourcing

The Company must provide guidance to IT Management with regard to outsourcing IT functions or capabilities. This ensures that the customer's needs continue to be met while allowing the company to control costs, maintain its flexibility, and take advantage of specialized knowledge and expertise on an as-needed basis.

5.1.10 IT Department Satisfaction

The customers of the Company's IT department will most often be its internal user base. In order to enable greater productivity on the part of the user community and ensure the satisfaction of the Company's ultimate customers, the IT department must strive to improve service, enhance the users' satisfaction with IT products and services in general, and increase the user community's performance and productivity, supplying products and services that add value.

5.1.11 BYOD Policy

Company employees and contractors may use their personal electronic devices (e.g., smartphones, tablets) to conduct company business, provided they understand and agree with the policy, have been granted express permission to use their devices, and act in accordance with the policy.

5.1.12 Referenced Procedures:

ITAD101 Information Technology Management
ITAD102 IT Records Management
ITAD103 IT Document Management
ITAD104 IT Device Naming Conventions
ITAD105 TCP/IP Implementation Standards
ITAD106 Network Infrastructure Standards
ITAD107 Computer and Internet Usage Policy
ITAD108 Email Policy
ITAD109 IT Outsourcing
ITAD110 IT Department Satisfaction
ITAD111 BYOD Policy

[This page intentionally left blank]

5.2   ASSET MANAGEMENT

Adequate control over all IT assets – in this case, meaning the computer hardware and software the Company relies on, not only for conducting its day-to-day business, but for positioning itself for growth, which it achieves through increased customer satisfaction. The following procedures help the Company maintain control over its IT assets.

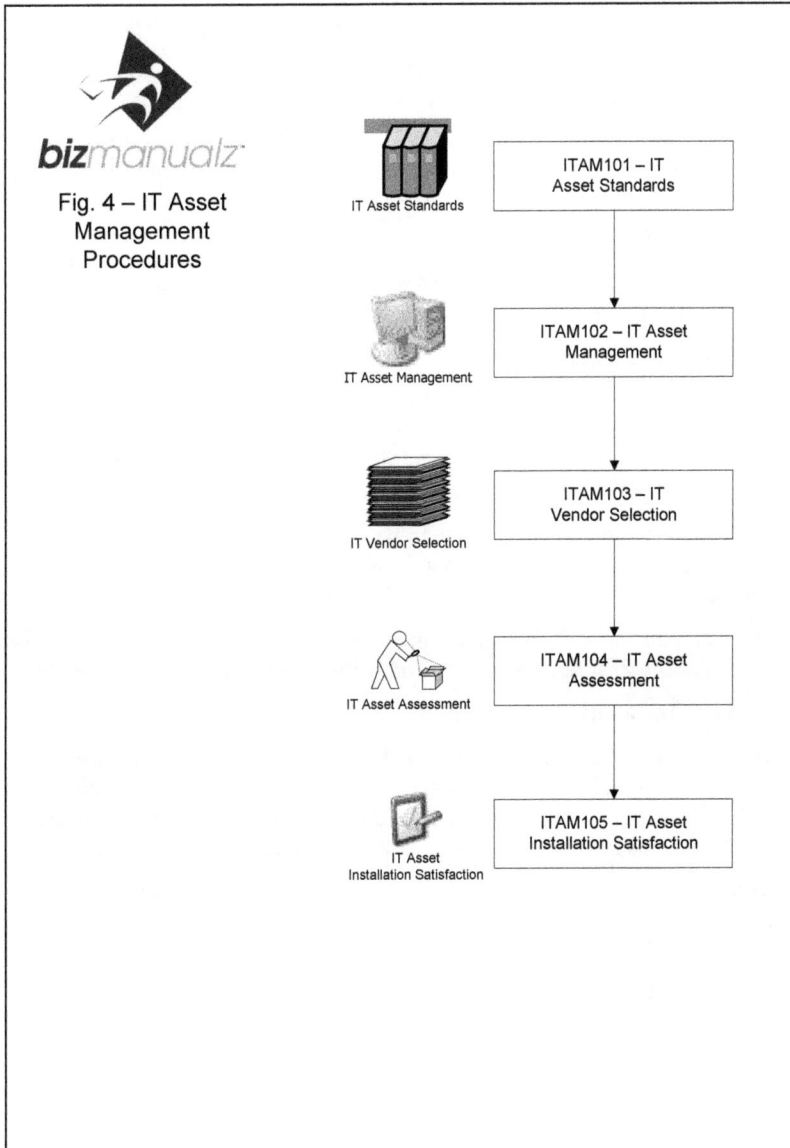

Fig. 4 – IT Asset Management Procedures

5.2.1   **IT Asset Standards**

Proper internal control should be maintained over all IT assets, at all times. The Company should identify and develop a set of IT asset standards that will allow it to minimize the complexity and cost of building and managing IT systems.

The Company should also be looking to the future at all times, knowing that whatever assets serve it (and its customers) well at this moment cannot continue to serve it indefinitely. The Company should expect its standards to change with business demands and should anticipate – even promote – change.

5.2.2   **IT Asset Management**

Proper IT asset management – from requisition to disposal – ensures a much greater likelihood that the Company will continue to meet customer requirements into the indefinite future by planning in an orderly fashion and mandating consistency throughout the enterprise.

5.2.3   **IT Vendor Selection**

The Company should establish and follow a set of guidelines for selecting IT vendors and maintaining vendor relationships.

5.2.4   **IT Asset Assessment**

The Company should review its IT assets on a regular basis to ensure their continuing ability to meet Company (and the customers') requirements, as well as to anticipate changing business conditions and assess the Company's ability to adapt by properly managing its IT assets.

The Company should ensure that only approved hardware and software (see IT Asset Standards) are used and that those are properly versioned, licensed, and adequately meet the users' (and Company) requirements.

The Company should also have a mechanism for adapting to changing business conditions, to ensure its hardware and software are not inadequate or obsolete.

5.2.5   **IT Asset Installation Satisfaction**

The Company should ensure that its internal users' requirements are being met, by measuring their level of satisfaction with the way the IT department conducts its business; in this case, not only whether an installation was performed, but whether the user's *perceived* (as well as actual) needs were satisfied.

5.2.6   **Referenced Procedures:**

ITAM101 IT Asset Standards
ITAM102 IT Asset Management
ITAM103 IT Vendor Selection
ITAM104 IT Asset Assessment
ITAM105 IT Asset Installation Satisfaction

5.3   IT TRAINING AND SUPPORT

Training and support are critical elements of information technology. In order to maintain the rapid pace of technological change the company shall plan for change and provide a framework for its employees' personal and professional growth.

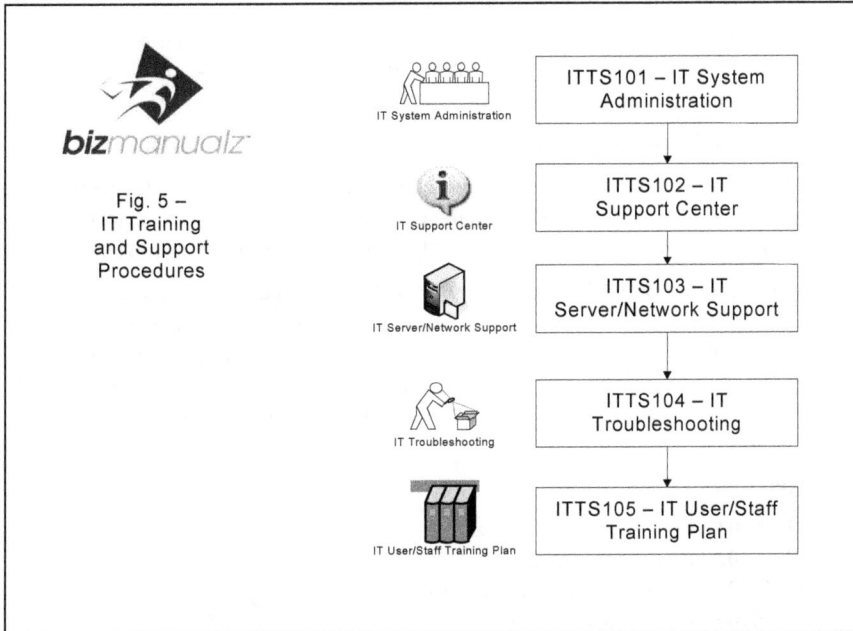

Fig. 5 –
IT Training
and Support
Procedures

IT System Administration — ITTS101 – IT System Administration

IT Support Center — ITTS102 – IT Support Center

IT Server/Network Support — ITTS103 – IT Server/Network Support

IT Troubleshooting — ITTS104 – IT Troubleshooting

IT User/Staff Training Plan — ITTS105 – IT User/Staff Training Plan

5.3.1   Systems Administration

The Company should have a central authority – a System Administrator (or "Sys Admin") – whose responsibility it is to oversee the day-to-day operation of all IT-based systems. The Sys Admin should be charged with administering the Company's IT systems in a manner that promotes the achievement of Company goals and objectives and provides for Company growth.

5.3.2   IT Support Center

The Company should operate an IT Support Center for the purpose of providing ongoing technology support (emergency and non-emergency) to all departments and IT users. Staffing, training, and logistic requirements for this support center should be identified and training provided in order that the support center satisfies user needs and maintains its effectiveness.

5.3.3 Server and Network Support

The Company should provide support for its servers and the network that enables sharing of data, ensuring a secure and effective environment.

5.3.4 Troubleshooting

The Company should develop and maintain guidelines for troubleshooting IT-related problems in order to ensure effectiveness, consistency, and continual improvement of the troubleshooting process.

The Company should seek to minimize disruptions, enhance employee productivity, and promote user satisfaction with the process and the people performing the service.

5.3.5 User-Staff Training Plan

The Company should determine adequate levels of competence for technical and non-technical personnel who use the Company's IT systems to perform work, then provide training or take other actions to satisfy training requirements.

The Company should provide personnel (IT personnel, in particular) with a learning path or guide, so that the employees in question build a skill set that benefits the Company and rewards the individual. An adequate training plan should aim to improve the Company's performance by reducing training/skill gaps, anticipating the Company's needs, and continually improving training availability and methods.

5.3.6 Referenced Procedures:

ITTS101 IT Systems Administration
ITTS102 IT Support Center
ITTS103 IT Server/Network Support
ITTS104 IT Troubleshooting
ITTS105 IT User-Staff Training Plan

5.4   IT SECURITY AND DISASTER RECOVERY

The Company should provide a safe, secure IT environment to serve its customers' requirements, ensure stability and continuity of the business, and promote confidence in its ability to not only continuously provide goods and/or services, but also to recover quickly from disaster and minimize disruption.

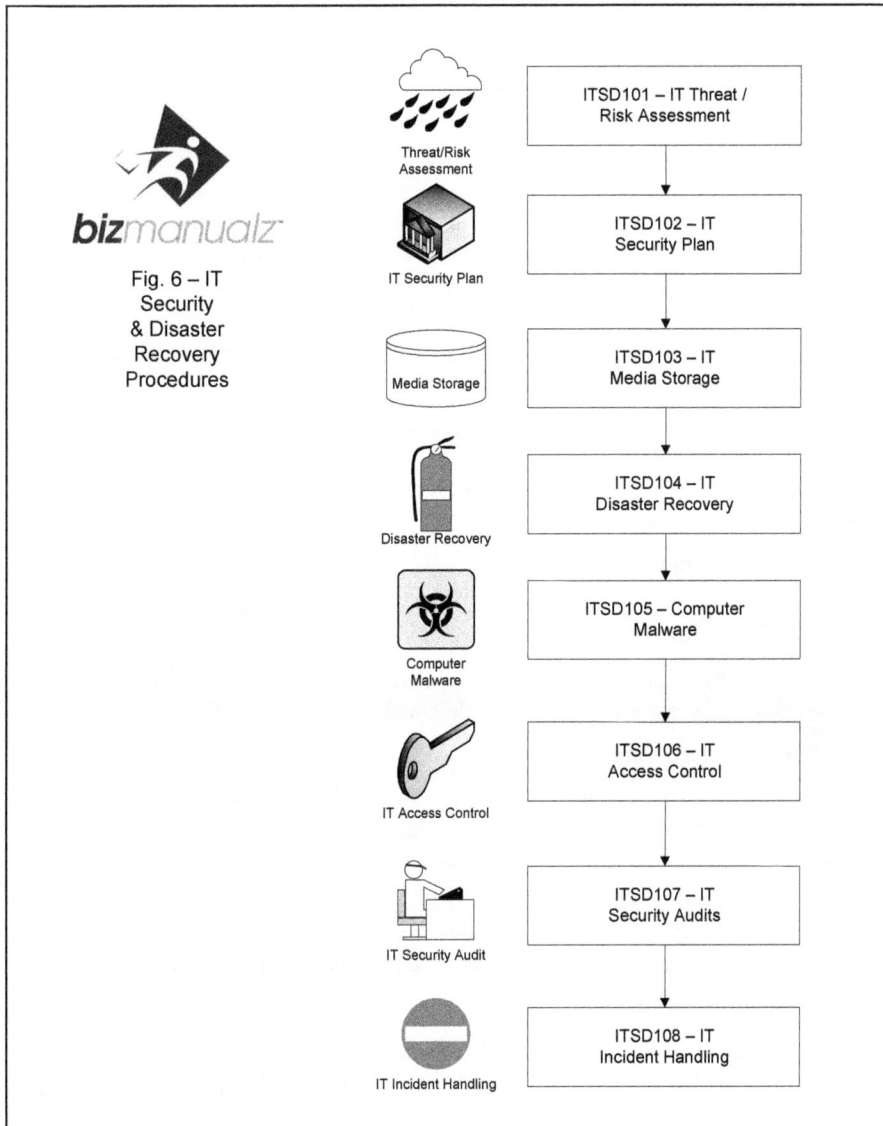

Fig. 6 – IT Security & Disaster Recovery Procedures

5.4.1   **IT Threat/Risk Assessment**

The Company should periodically evaluate its IT systems and network for threats and vulnerabilities, to protect its IT assets and reduce the Company's risk.

The Company should develop and follow a set of procedures for identifying threats to the Company's IT assets, assess those threats for probability and risk, and minimize the chances of loss or disruption.

5.4.2   **IT Security Plan**

The Company should develop and implement a plan to ensure the confidentiality and integrity of Company information while maintaining appropriate levels of accessibility.

The Company should set forth its own security requirements, which should be equal to or greater than security requirements prescribed by law and/or standards bodies (ISO, IEEE, etc.). The Company should also strive to keep its IT security plan current and active – continual improvement of the process is crucial to its success.

The Company should put in place all reasonable technological means (i.e., security software/hardware) to keep information and facilities secure.

Regardless of whatever technological means are available to the Company, it must ensure that its employees accept and understand the security plan and put it into practice on the jobs. Employees are a key part – if not the most important part – of the IT security plan.

5.4.3   **IT Media Storage**

The Company should establish controls and procedures for storage, protection, access, procurement, and destruction of Company data.

The Company should plan for cost-effective storage technologies that offer long asset life and scalability and ensure data integrity and availability.

5.4.4   **IT Disaster Recovery**

The Company should develop and implement a straightforward, workable plan to not only cope with the initial effects of a disaster, but to return the Company's IT operations to normal as quickly as possible.

The company should regularly test the IT disaster recovery plans. Every employee, regardless of his/her relation to the IT department, should be educated with regard to the IT disaster recovery plan and be prepared to play a part.

5.4.5   **Computer Malware**

To prevent data loss, corruption, or misuse of Company computing resources or information, the Company should develop and implement a plan for mitigating the risk posed by malware (*mal*icious soft*ware* – i.e., viruses, worms, spyware).

5.4.6 IT Access Control

The Company's requirements for controlling access should meet or exceed those set forth by standards bodies and by applicable laws.

The Company should control access to its information, to help ensure confidentiality and integrity of its data while making the data available to authorized parties.

5.4.7 IT Security Audits

The Company should, once it has implemented a security plan for IT, ensure that the plan is being effectively carried out in accordance with regulatory and Company requirements and meets or exceeds industry standards for information security.

The Company should have a qualified third party auditor conduct an audit of its IT security system on a regular basis, to ensure the plan's conformance to applicable standards and requirements and to promote continual improvement of the plan.

5.4.8 IT Incident Handling

An "IT incident" is an actual or suspected compromise of the Company's IT assets and/or operations. If an employee suspects Company assets are being misused or are under attack, that employee has an obligation to report that incident to IT Security.

When such an incident occurs, the Company should have a plan for dealing with (i.e., reporting, investigating, and resolving) the incident. This plan should help ensure the safety, confidentiality, availability, and integrity of Company information.

5.4.9 Referenced Procedures:

ITSD101 IT Threat / Risk Assessment
ITSD102 IT Security Plan
ITSD103 IT Media Storage
ITSD104 IT Disaster Recovery
ITSD105 Computer Malware
ITSD106 IT Access Control
ITSD107 IT Security Audits
ITSD108 IT Incident Handling

[This page intentionally left blank]

5.5   SOFTWARE DEVELOPMENT

Successful software products begin with careful planning and attention to detail. Documenting the organization's software policies and procedures provide a structure that streamlines development efforts and empowers employees. Documented policies and procedures eliminate guesswork, promote good working relationships, build quality standards into products/services, and simplify training for new employees.

The following sample policies and procedures document the functions performed by the software development organization.

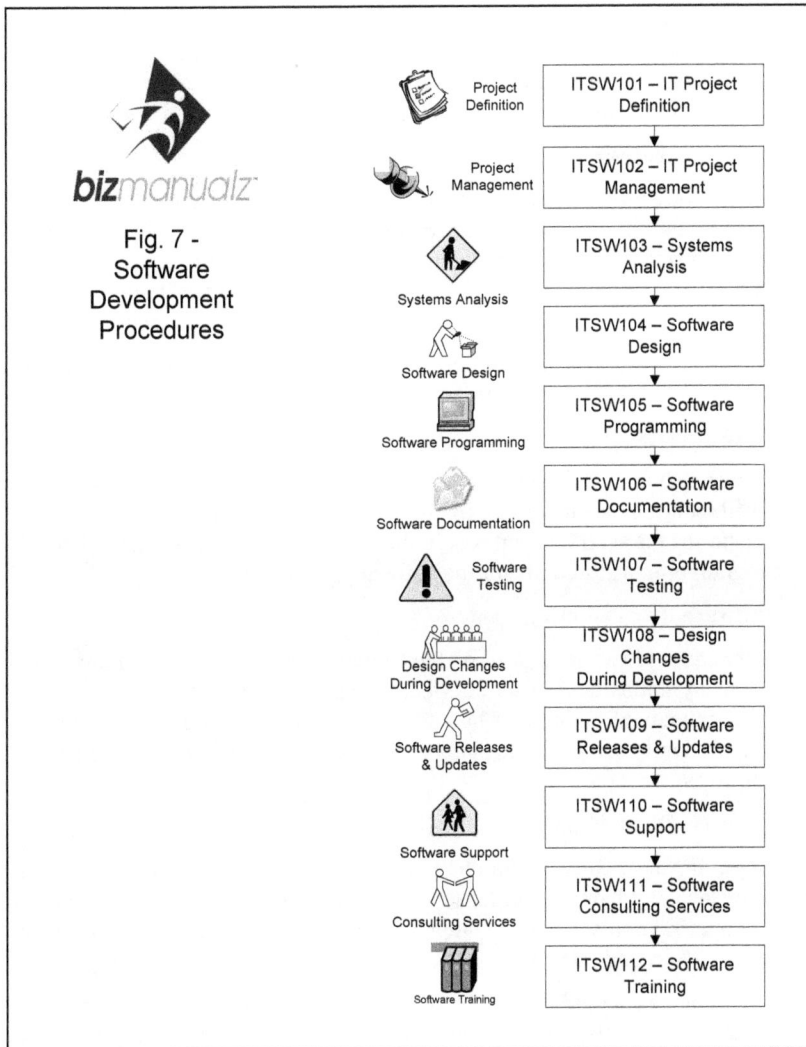

Fig. 7 - Software Development Procedures

Project Definition	ITSW101 – IT Project Definition
Project Management	ITSW102 – IT Project Management
Systems Analysis	ITSW103 – Systems Analysis
Software Design	ITSW104 – Software Design
Software Programming	ITSW105 – Software Programming
Software Documentation	ITSW106 – Software Documentation
Software Testing	ITSW107 – Software Testing
Design Changes During Development	ITSW108 – Design Changes During Development
Software Releases & Updates	ITSW109 – Software Releases & Updates
Software Support	ITSW110 – Software Support
Consulting Services	ITSW111 – Software Consulting Services
Software Training	ITSW112 – Software Training

5.5.1   IT Project Definition

A software development project begins with the project definition – explaining the purpose and scope of the project. The software developer must identify the goals and objectives of the project and determine the potential impact of the project on other projects, on the Company, and on the Company's customer base.

An IT Project Plan should be used as a framework for developing future IT projects. It should be reviewed prior to undertaking any project plan and should be continually reevaluated, in light of the Company's changing circumstances.

5.5.2   IT Project Management

All in-house software development projects should follow a defined project management procedure. This is to ensure that IT projects are clearly defined, well structured, efficiently and effectively managed, and are capable of producing the desired results, on time and within budget.

5.5.3   Systems Analysis

All software products developed by the organization must meet the needs of potential users. These users may be in-house or they may have contracted with the organization for software applications; in this case, the users' needs may be known and specific. In the case of software developed for an indeterminate number of users (i.e., an accounting or HR package), those needs are generalized.

The software developer must define the functions the system will perform, tell how those functions are interrelated, and describe how to test those functions.

5.5.4   Software Design

Software should be designed in a technically sound and efficient manner and fulfill requirements identified by the systems analyst. The software designer transforms the set of system requirements developed by the analyst into programming instructions for the software product.

5.5.5   Software Programming

Software products developed by the Company should, at a minimum, meet Company standards for user interface, program structure, system interface, toolset, and configuration. The job of the software programmer is to effectively and efficiently carry out the plans of the software designer, per Company standards.

5.5.6   Software Documentation

The Company's software products should be documented as thoroughly as practicable, with online help, user guides, and technical documentation, at a minimum. To this end, the Company should develop and implement standards for design, style, and content.

The Company should define the methods and responsibilities for controlling the revision, approval, and distribution of software reference and training materials.

5.5.7   Software Testing

All software products developed by the Company should undergo a series of tests – including acceptance tests, beta tests, and software release tests – before they are released to the customer or user community. Company-developed software must be tested free of errors in order to improve the likelihood of customer/user satisfaction.

5.5.8   Design Changes During Development

The Company should plan on design changes such that they are managed, controlled, and communicated effectively and efficiently.

The Company should expect that the user/customer will request product changes at some point in the software development process. The customer/client may come upon information only after such a project has begun – information that could have a significant impact on the project.

5.5.9   Software Releases and Updates

All of the Company's software releases and updates should be issued in a controlled manner to reduce difficulty and maintain consistency, quality, and versioning of its software products throughout the release and update sequence.

5.5.10   Software Support

The Company should ensure that their customers/users are able to install and operate software with as little effort and wasted time as possible.

The Company should provide a number of avenues for customers to ask questions, alert the Company to problems with its software, or request additional services.

The Company should continually solicit – and act on – feedback from customers/users in an effort to improve customer support.

5.5.11   Software Consulting Services

The Company should strive to engage its users proactively in a number of ways. Especially where the software product is complex, customers may need assistance through the life of the software, starting with installation. Users may require customization of the software.

5.5.12   Software Training

The Company should provide a sufficient level of training on the product, to ensure the users are actively learning to use the product by offering a range of training options. Ensuring that customers/users are able to effectively operate the Company's software helps to promote greater customer satisfaction.

The Company should actively seek feedback from the user on the training process.

5.5.13 **Referenced Procedures:**

ITSW101 IT Project Definition
ITSW102 IT Project Management
ITSW103 Systems Analysis
ITSW104 Software Design
ITSW105 Software Programming
ITSW106 Software Documentation
ITSW107 Software Testing
ITSW108 Design Changes During Development
ITSW109 Software Releases and Updates
ITSW110 Software Support
ITSW111 Software Consulting Services
ITSW112 Software Training

6.0   RESOURCE MANAGEMENT

6.1   PROVISION OF RESOURCES

During planning and budgeting processes and as needed throughout the year, the President, CIO and management team determine and ensure that the appropriate resources are available to implement and maintain the IT Management System and continually improve its effectiveness.

6.2   HUMAN RESOURCES

6.2.1   IT Staff

Managers and employees are to have personal and professional integrity and are to maintain a level of competence that allows them to accomplish their assigned duties, as well as understand the importance of developing and implementing good internal controls.

This requires managers and their staff to maintain and demonstrate at all times:

- o   Personal and professional integrity
- o   A level of skill necessary to help ensure effective performance
- o   An understanding of information security and internal controls sufficient to effectively discharge their responsibilities

IT staff shall be subject to a security clearance check before they are hired, transferred, or promoted. The level of checking shall depend on the relative sensitivity of the position. Any employee who was not subjected to such a clearance check when first hired should not be placed in a sensitive position until security clearance has been obtained.

6.2.2   Competence, Awareness, and Training

IT personnel shall be competent based on appropriate education, training, skills and experience. The minimum competencies required for each position at Our Company are defined in each position's Job Description. Human Resources, department managers and supervisors are responsible for ensuring job descriptions are current and adequate.

Where otherwise qualified personnel require additional training or other action to meet the minimum competency requirements, these needs are identified. The department provides task-specific training. General training or education is provided or coordinated by Human Resources. The department or Human Resources evaluate the effectiveness of training or other actions taken as appropriate.

The department generates records of task-specific training. Human Resources maintain records of all training and education, skills and experience in accordance with Human Resources Policies and Procedures and Computer and Network Policies and Procedures.

Department managers are responsible for ensuring their employees are aware of the relevance and importance of their activities and how they contribute to the achievement of the IT objectives.

6.2.3 Separation and Supervision of Duties

Key duties and responsibilities should be separated among individuals. Duties and responsibilities shall be assigned systematically to a number of individuals to ensure that effective checks and balances exist. Key duties include authorizing, approving, and recording transactions; issuing and receiving assets; and reviewing or auditing transactions.

A separation of duties should be maintained between the following functions:

o Data entry;
o Computer operation;
o Network management;
o System administration;
o Systems development and maintenance;
o Change management;
o Security administration; and
o Security audit.

Qualified and continuous supervision is to be provided to ensure that internal control objectives are achieved. This standard requires supervisors to continuously review and approve the assigned work of their staffs as well as provide the necessary guidance and training to ensure that errors, waste, and wrongful acts are minimized and that specific management directives are followed.

6.2.4 Cross-Training and Succession Planning

Cross-training and succession planning guidelines should be created to ensure backup for key personnel. Persons holding sensitive or key positions should take vacations (holidays) of at least a week in length, so that the Company can verify the effectiveness of its cross-training and prevent and detect fraudulent activity.

6.2.5 Referenced Procedures:

See ABR41 *Bizmanualz® Human Resources Policies and Procedures Manual*.

6.3 INFRASTRUCTURE

Our Company provides the infrastructure necessary to achieve conformity to IT standards and requirements. During the annual budgeting and strategic planning processes, buildings, workspace, hardware, software and associated utilities are evaluated and provided.

When new personnel are added, Human Resources coordinates activities to ensure appropriate process equipment including hardware and software, if required, and supporting services such as telephones etc., are available based on information provided on the Personnel Requisition.

6.4   WORK ENVIRONMENT

The management team, CIO and Office Manager determines and manages the work environment to ensure Our Company provides a safe and desirable place to work. They ensure the environment is appropriate for achieving conformity to product requirements.

IT MANUAL - REVISION HISTORY

Revision	Date	Description of Changes	Requested By
0	mm/dd/yyyy	Initial Release	

[This page intentionally left blank]

bizmanualz

IT Policies and Procedures

Section 400

IT Administration

Section 400

IT Administration

400 ITAD – IT Administration

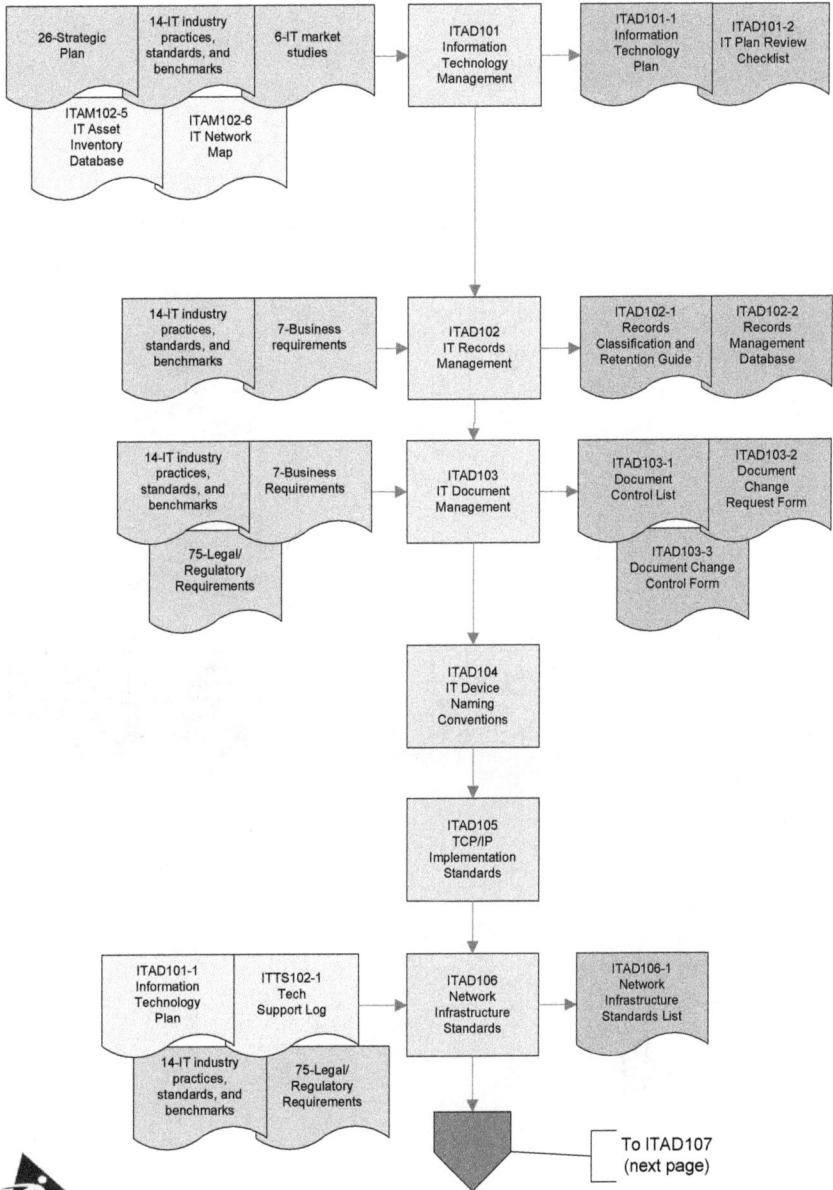

400 ITAD – IT Administration

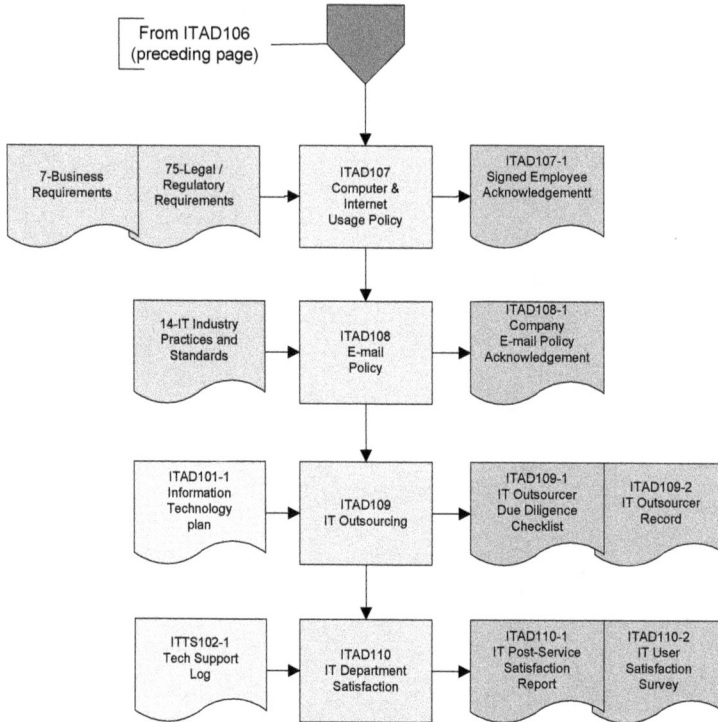

From ITAD106
(preceding page)

		ITAD107 Computer & Internet Usage Policy	ITAD107-1 Signed Employee Acknowledgementt
7-Business Requirements	75-Legal / Regulatory Requirements		

	ITAD108 E-mail Policy	ITAD108-1 Company E-mail Policy Acknowledgement
14-IT Industry Practices and Standards		

	ITAD109 IT Outsourcing	ITAD109-1 IT Outsourcer Due Diligence Checklist	ITAD109-2 IT Outsourcer Record
ITAD101-1 Information Technology plan			

	ITAD110 IT Department Satisfaction	ITAD110-1 IT Post-Service Satisfaction Report	ITAD110-2 IT User Satisfaction Survey
ITTS102-1 Tech Support Log			

bizmanualz®

Document ID **ITAD101**	Title **INFORMATION TECHNOLOGY MANAGEMENT**	Print Date **mm/dd/yyyy**
Revision **0.0**	Prepared By **Preparer's Name / Title**	Date Prepared **mm/dd/yyyy**
Effective Date **mm/dd/yyyy**	Reviewed By **Reviewer's Name / Title**	Date Reviewed **mm/dd/yyyy**
	Approved By **Final Approver's Name / Title**	Date Approved **mm/dd/yyyy**

Policy: To support the Company's business strategy through the productive use of information technology.

Purpose: To deploy information technologies that increase overall Company productivity and performance, achieve greater efficiencies, and achieve positive returns on the investment in technology.

To link the Information Technology Department's goals and objectives to the Company's strategic vision, assuring that the Company continues to meet customer requirements.

Scope: This applies to the Company's Information Technology department.

Responsibilities:

The Company's Board of Directors is responsible for approving the Company's Information Technology Plan and ensuring that Top Management effectively carries out the plan.

The Chief Executive Officer, or CEO, is responsible for conducting strategic planning and setting the strategic objectives for the Company.

Top Management is responsible for reviewing the Company's Strategic Plan with Information Technology Managers, developing a budget and other guidelines for Information Technology to follow in developing the Information Technology Plan, and for presenting the final Information Technology Plan to the Board of Directors for approval. Top Management will consist of the Company's chief executive officer and chief financial officer, at a minimum.

Information Technology Managers are responsible for developing the Information Technology Plan, reviewing the Plan with Top Management, overseeing implementation of the Plan, and periodically verifying that the Information Technology Plan continues to meet Company requirements.

Information Technology Staff are responsible for working with Information Technology Managers to carry out the Information Technology Plan.

Definitions: Information Technology asset – Any computer hardware, software, reference or other supporting material (in printed or other form), including rights and licenses, that is owned or controlled by the Company. Within the scope of this procedure, "asset", "Information Technology asset", "resource", and "Information Technology resource" are synonymous.

Risk – Possibility of loss or injury to the Company.

ROI – Return on Investment, calculated by dividing the expected results of committed resources by the resources committed to achieve the results. (ROI = Results/Resources.)

Procedure:

1.0   BUSINESS PLANNING

1.1   On an annual basis, the Company's CEO shall conduct strategic planning meetings with Top Management before the Information Technology Managers planning process. The CEO is responsible for seeing that strategic objectives for the Company are defined and measurable, as they will form the basis for Information Technology strategic objectives.

1.2   Within a month of the Company's strategic planning meeting, Top Management shall meet with Information Technology Managers to review the Company's Strategic Plan. Information Technology Managers shall develop an information technology plan, the main objective of which shall be to support the Company Strategic Plan. Information Technology Department objectives shall be specific and measurements shall be clearly defined.

1.3   Information Technology Managers shall develop a budget to determine the feasibility of projects included in the Plan. The Information Technology budget shall cover at least the coming fiscal year and should cover the coming FY and two following that (e.g., if this is FY07, the budget must address FY08 at a minimum and should include FY09 and FY10).

2.0   IT DEPARTMENT OBJECTIVE PLANNING

2.1   Information Technology Managers shall review relevant information to determine the Company's performance and productivity needs over the next five years. Sources of relevant information include:

- The Company's Strategic Plan and strategic objectives;

- The current Information Technology Plan and Information Technology department objectives;

- A SWOT analysis of IT;

- ITAM110-3 USER SATISFACTION SURVEY;

- ITAM102-5 IT ASSET INVENTORY DATABASE;

- ITAM102-6 IT NETWORK MAP;

- Information Technology industry standards, regulations, and practices changes; and

- Information Technology market studies, trends, opportunities and benchmarks.

2.2   Information Technology Managers shall determine the Information Technology Department Objectives as input to the Information Technology Plan. Information Technology Department Objectives shall incorporate an analysis of relevant information collected in order to achieve the Company's Strategic Objectives.

2.3   An Information Technology Steering Committee, consisting of Information Technology and Top Management and led by Information Technology Managers, shall be formed to evaluate the Information Technology Plan's suitability and performance.

2.4   Top Management shall review the proposed Information Technology Departmental objectives along with the budget requests. The review process may include adjustments to ensure objectives are relevant, challenging, and achievable. The review process also ensures resources are in the budget to support the objectives.

2.5   Information Technology Managers shall ensure that departmental objectives are communicated to employees on a need-to-know basis.

3.0   IT PLAN DEVELOPMENT

3.1   Information Technology Managers shall update the Information Technology Plan, which shall be a rolling five-year plan, using ITAD101-1 INFORMATION TECHNOLOGY PLAN as a guide. The Information Technology Plan includes the actual management process and content details.

3.2   The Information Technology Plan expands the technical details to include seven required sections:

- Mission statement. A good mission statement is a guiding principle that: mandates or constrains actions; applies to the entire organization; changes infrequently; sets a course for the foreseeable future; helps ensure compliance; reduces organizational risk; and will answer three key questions:

    a. Purpose – What are the opportunities/needs the Company will address?

    b. Business – How will (existing and emerging) information technologies address those opportunities/needs?

    c. Values – What principles/beliefs will guide the Information Technology Department's efforts?

- IT Departmental Goals and Objectives. The Information Technology Plan shall explain how information technologies are expected to help the Company achieve its strategic objectives in each area of the company, such as manufacturing, shipping, marketing, sales, accounting, and software support, among others. The Plan shall contain short- and long-range goals and objectives for the Information Technology Department and indicate how achievement will be measured.

- Risk. The risk each Information Technology goal and objective carries shall be identified and quantified (risk assessment); a qualitative or quantitative relationship between risks and benefits shall be established (risk evaluation);

and social, economic, and technological factors shall be considered with relevant risk assessments relating to potential hazards so as to analyze and compare regulatory and nonregulatory options and select the optimal response (risk management).

- <u>Timelines</u>. The Information Technology Plan shall project activities and deployment plans over a series of quarterly periods. Short, intermediate, and long-range (i.e., one-year, three-year, and five-year) milestones shall be prepared.

- <u>Resource and Budget Estimates</u>. The Information Technology Plan shall indicate resource (hardware, software, personnel, etc.) and fiscal budget estimates for every year of the Plan.

- <u>Roles and Responsibilities</u>. The Information Technology Plan shall identify who is responsible for implementing each aspect of the Plan.

- <u>Information Technology Plan Distribution List</u>. A list of personnel either named in the plan or that are required to support the plan's outcomes.

3.3   Information Technology Managers shall establish checkpoints for meeting with members of the Information Technology staff to review the Plan.

3.4   The Information Technology Steering Committee shall review the Information Technology Plan according to the following criteria:

- Improvement in overall productivity and performance of the Company;

- Achievement of greater efficiencies; and

- Realization of positive Returns On Investments (ROI) in technology.

3.5   The Information Technology Steering Committee shall present the final plan to the Board of Directors for approval prior to implementation.

4.0   IT PLAN IMPLEMENTATION

4.1   Information Technology Managers shall be responsible for distributing (communicating) the new Information Technology Plan to the appropriate personnel listed on the Information Technology Plan Distribution list and collecting the preceding Information Technology Plan.

4.2   Information Technology Managers shall ensure that resources are allocated and used in accordance with ITAM102 IT ASSET MANAGEMENT and that training is conducted according to ITTS101 IT USER-STAFF TRAINING PLAN and ITSW112 SOFTWARE TRAINING.

5.0   IT PLAN REVIEW

5.1   At established checkpoints in the Information Technology Plan, Information Technology Managers shall meet with members of the Information Technology staff to measure the Information Technology Plan's performance against expectations. ITAD101-2 IT PLAN REVIEW CHECKLIST shall be used as a guide.

5.2   At least twice per year (more often if deemed necessary), Information Technology Managers shall coordinate a meeting, to be attended by Top Management. The purpose of the meeting is to review the Information Technology Plan to ensure its continuing suitability, adequacy, and effectiveness. This review shall include assessing opportunities for improvement and the need for changes to the Information Technology Plan, including the Information Technology objectives.

- Information Technology Managers is responsible for ensuring minutes of the meeting are taken and for maintaining the minutes as an Information Technology Record, in accordance with ITAD102 – IT RECORDS MANAGEMENT. The meeting agenda will include the following reports from Information Technology Managers and appropriate Information Technology staff:

    a. Results of audits;

    b. User or customer feedback;

    c. Process performance and results of Information Technology Plan checkpoint reviews;

    d. Status of preventive and corrective actions;

    e. Follow-up actions from previous management reviews;

    f. Changes that could affect the Information Technology Plan; and

    g. Recommendations for improvement.

- The meeting minutes shall also include any decisions and actions related to:

    a. Improvement of the effectiveness of the Information Technology Plan and its processes;

    b. Technology improvements related to user requirements; and

    c. Resource needs.

5.3   Information Technology Managers shall submit the minutes of the Plan Review meeting to Top Management for approval.

6.0   IT PLAN UPDATE

6.1   After review of the Information Technology Plan, Information Technology Managers shall be responsible for implementing required updates.

6.2   Within three months of such updates, Top Management shall verify that updates to the Plan have been implemented and are providing the desired results.

6.3   Information Technology Managers shall maintain a complete record of any such update, for inclusion in the next formal Plan development (sections 2.0 and 3.0).

Forms:

- ITAD101-1 INFORMATION TECHNOLOGY PLAN
- ITAD101-2 IT PLAN REVIEW CHECKLIST

References:

A. CONTROL OBJECTIVES FOR INFORMATION AND RELATED TECHNOLOGY (COBIT)

COBIT is a process model developed to assist enterprises with the management of information technology resources. The process model focuses on developing suitable controls for each of the 34 Information Technology processes, raising the level of process maturity in information technology and satisfying the business expectations of Information Technology.

COBIT, issued by the Information Technology Governance Institute and now in its third edition, is increasingly accepted internationally as good practice for control over information, Information Technology, and related risks. COBIT's Management Guidelines component contains a framework responding to management's need for control and measurability of Information Technology by providing tools to assess and measure the enterprise's Information Technology capability for the 34 COBIT IT processes. The tools include:

- Performance measurement elements (outcome measures and performance drivers for all Information Technology processes)

- A list of critical success factors that provides succinct, nontechnical best practices for each Information Technology process

- Maturity models to assist in benchmarking and decision-making for capability improvements

Detailed information on COBIT may be found at http://www.isaca.org or at http://www.itgi.org/.

B. ISO INTERNATIONAL STANDARD 27002:2013 - INFORMATION TECHNOLOGY - SECURITY TECHNIQUES - CODE OF PRACTICE FOR INFORMATION SECURITY MANAGEMENT

ISO Standard 27002:2013 and its companion standards, ISO 27001:2013 and ISO 27005:2011, provide a comprehensive set of controls comprising best practices in the field of information security. The standard treats information as an asset which has value to an organization and, therefore, needs to be suitably protected. Information security protects information from a wide range of threats in order to ensure business continuity, minimize business damage, and maximize return on investments and business opportunities.

NOTE: ISO 27002 was formerly known as "ISO 17799" and before that, as BS 7799:2. For more, see http://www.iso.org/iso/home/store/catalogue_ics/catalogue_detail_ics.htm?csnumber=54533.

Additional Resources:

A. Microsoft's web site provides an outline for developing an "accessible information technology" plan, which can be adapted to a general Information Technology plan. See http://www.microsoft.com/enable/business/plan.aspx for details.

B. The Information Technology Governance Institute (ITGI) was established in 1998 in recognition of the increasing criticality of information technology to enterprise success. Effective IT governance helps ensure that Information Technology supports business goals, maximizes business investment in IT, and appropriately manages IT-related risks and opportunities.

   ITGI is a research think tank that exists to be the leading reference on Information Technology-enabled business systems governance for the global business community. More on the organization may be found at http://www.itgi.org/.

C. The Information Systems Audit and Control Association (ISACA)

   ISACA is a globally recognized organization for information governance, control, security, and audit professionals since its founding in 1967. ISACA's IT auditing and control standards are followed by practitioners worldwide and its research pinpoints professional issues important to its membership.

   To learn more about ISACA, go to http://www.isaca.org/pages.default.aspx.

Revision History:

Revision	Date	Description of Changes	Requested By
0.0	mm/dd/yyyy	Initial Release	

[This page intentionally left blank]

ITAD101-1 INFORMATION TECHNOLOGY PLAN

A. Mission Statement

The Information Technology Department's mission is:

- To support and promote the productive use of state-of-the-art information technology within the Company;

- To ensure that Company information technologies are secure, reliable, and minimize risk;

- To provide quality, cost-effective technologies that meet the needs of the Company and its customers; and

- To stay current with information technologies in order to identify and provide new products and services that will further Company goals and objectives.

B. Business Goals, Objectives, and Measures

One-year

-

Three-year

-

Five-year

-

Information Technology Goals, Objectives, and Measures

One-year

-

Three-year

-

Five-year

-

C. Risk Assessment and Evaluation

D. Timelines

E. IT Resource/Budget Estimates

Year one

-

Year two

-

Year three

-

Year four

-

Year five

-

F. Roles and Responsibilities

G. Distribution List

CEO	☐	Board of Directors	☐
CFO	☐	Other	☐
Information Technology Managers	☐	Other	☐

Approved:

_____ Date: _____

Chief Executive Officer

_____ Date: _____

Chief Financial Officer

_____ Date: _____

Chief Technology Officer

[This page intentionally left blank]

ITAD101-2 IT PLAN REVIEW CHECKLIST

Review Questions	Notes:
1.0 Business Goals, Objectives, and Measures Review	
• Do Information Technology projects deliver expected results?	
• What do end user surveys suggest about:	
o the quality of Information Technology service?	
o whether Information Technology is regarded as an enabler or as an inhibitor of change?	
• Are sufficient Information Technology resources, infrastructure and competencies available to meet strategic objectives?	
• What has been the average overrun of Information Technology operational budgets?	
o How often and by how much do Information Technology projects go over budget?	
o How does this influence the achieved vs. expected ROI?	
• Do Information Technology-related investments meet the ROI criteria of the enterprise?	
• How much of the Information Technology effort goes towards systems maintenance, patches or bug fixes versus enabling business improvements?	
o Is the ratio acceptable and representative for the Company's specific industry?	
• Are enterprise and Information Technology objectives maintaining alignment with each other?	
• Is the Company accurately measuring the Information Technology value delivered?	
o Are the assumptions reasonable?	
o How are intangible benefits verified?	
• Have the strategic initiatives requested by executive management affected Information Technology's criticality relative to maintenance and growth of the enterprise?	
o Are they appropriate?	

3.0 IT Risk Review	
• Is the enterprise clear on its technology risk position? (i.e., pioneer, early adopter, follower, or laggard).	
o Is the Company clear on its position of: risk avoidance versus risk taking?	
o Is the Company's risk position helping or holding back the Company from achieving its objectives?	
• Is there an up-to-date Information Technology risk register relevant to the enterprise?	
o What are the results of addressing those risks?	
2.0 Board of Directors Reviews	
• Is Information Technology a regular item on the board's agenda and, if so, is it addressed in a structured manner?	
• Does the board articulate and communicate the business objectives for Information Technology alignment?	
• Does the board review, and possibly approve, the Information Technology strategy?	
• Does the board have a clear view on the total Information Technology investment portfolio from a risk and return perspective?	
• Does the board receive regular progress reports on major Information Technology projects?	
• Is the board regularly briefed on those Information Technology risks to which the enterprise is exposed?	
• Is the board getting independent assurance on the achievement of Information Technology objectives and the containment of Information Technology risks?	

Document ID **ITAD102**	Title **IT RECORDS MANAGEMENT**	Print Date **mm/dd/yyyy**
Revision **0.0**	Prepared By **Preparer's Name / Title**	Date Prepared **mm/dd/yyyy**
Effective Date **mm/dd/yyyy**	Reviewed By **Reviewer's Name / Title**	Date Reviewed **mm/dd/yyyy**
	Approved By **Final Approver's Name / Title**	Date Approved **mm/dd/yyyy**

Policy: Organize and manage Information Technology records in a way that demonstrates controlled, consistent, and effective operations and conformance to specified requirements.

Purpose: To manage Information Technology records consistently and efficiently, ensuring safety, availability, accountability, and security of authorized access.

Scope: This procedure applies to all records managed by Information Technology, both in hard copy and electronic form.

Responsibilities:

Information Technology Managers is responsible for reviewing classification and retention of records, reviewing record obsolescence, conducting internal audits of the Records Management System, and ensuring that corrective actions prescribed by audits are taken.

The Information Technology Storage Librarian is responsible for maintaining Company records, maintaining a records log, and purging or physically destroying records.

The Tech Support Manager is responsible for updating storage medium and format of records when they are still required but in danger of becoming inaccessible.

Top Management is responsible for developing and approving a records classification and retention guide.

All Employees are responsible for ensuring records they generate and use are timely, accurate, and complete and are kept in the appropriate records store or database.

Definitions: Active – Currently in use; used in the conduct of current business. Active records are often referred to as "production" records.

Archive – Offline storage of records (onto backup tapes, floppy disks, optical disks, etc.); files containing data that are no longer in current use but are kept in long-term storage for possible future needs (to fulfill legal requirements, for instance).

Document – Information and its supporting medium (paper, magnetic, electronic, optical, photograph, or sample). A document is an object commonly found in office systems (a spreadsheet, word processing document, database, etc.), whereas a record is a document that provides evidence of a particular business activity.

Record – In Information Technology, a record is a data structure aggregating several items of possibly different types. The items being aggregated are called fields and are usually identified or indexed by field labels.

Generally, a record is data or information of any kind and in any form, created or received and accumulated by an organization in the course of conducting business and subsequently kept as "evidence of activity" through incorporation into a recordkeeping system.

Procedure:

1.0   IDENTIFICATION OF RECORDS

1.1   The Company requires documentation for every aspect of its business, to comply with regulations (see Reference A) and/or standards (see References B and C).

1.2   Each department or functional group within the Company is responsible for maintaining adequate records, to demonstrate and promote effective and efficient operations and to provide a clear audit trail.

1.3   The Information Technology Department shall use a standard classification scheme for all records.

- ITAD102-1 RECORDS CLASSIFICATION AND RETENTION GUIDE should provide a complete list of record types, stores, and retention periods. It shall be updated immediately upon adding a new record class or revising or dropping an existing record class.

- This classification scheme should be reviewed by Information Technology Managers on a regular basis to further ensure its consistency, currency, and usefulness.

2.0   RECORD GENERATION

2.1   The Information Technology Storage Librarian shall be responsible for maintaining all Company records in a safe and secure location and shall maintain a log (, index, catalog, etc.) of all records, indicating (at a minimum) the date of origin, the originator, record name, record ID, retention period, location, revision number, and revision date. ITAD102-2 RECORD MANAGEMENT DATABASE may be used as a guide.

2.2   Written records must be completed in ink to help ensure legibility and protect them from unauthorized change. Changes or corrections to written records should be made with a single line through the incorrect entry, dated and initialed by the person making the change. Correction fluid or tape must never be used. All employees making changes to written records must be authorized by their department managers, at a minimum.

2.3   Electronic records shall be maintained in a manner that prevents loss or alteration, ensures security, and optimizes record generation, maintenance, tracking, and retrieval, in accordance with ITSD103 Information Technology MEDIA STORAGE.

- Record access and update privileges shall be restricted, in accordance with ITSD106 Information Technology ACCESS CONTROL.

- Original records and any revisions must be kept for a specified total retention period, to be agreed upon by Top Management and Information Technology Managers and spelled out in ITAD102-1 RECORDS CLASSIFICATION AND RETENTION GUIDE. Records shall be differentiated by unique identifiers, unique version or revision ID's, and/or date of entry.

2.4 The total retention period for any record will be the sum of its active and archive periods.

- Every data store should have an "active" set and an "archive" counterpart to optimize search efficiency and make the most efficient use of space.

- Every record type must have an archival date, agreed upon by Information Technology Managers and management of the department producing that record.

- Every revision/update must reference, or point to, its predecessor, so that each record revision may be traced back to its original.

3.0   RECORD MANAGEMENT

3.1 The department or authority associated with a particular type of record (usually the entity generating that record) is responsible for ensuring that records are maintained in a manner that protects them from damage, deterioration, theft, or other loss.

- The department (authority) generating an electronic type of record is responsible for working with the Information Technology Department to ensure record safety.

3.2 Methods used to prevent loss of records in hard copy form may include storing in a controlled environment, strict access control, and auditing record stores.

- Electronic records must be protected from damage, deterioration, loss, or unauthorized change, in accordance with procedure ITSD103 Information Technology MEDIA STORAGE.

3.3 Active records (those that have not reached the end of their active retention period) must be stored in such a way that they are readily retrievable.

- Inactive Information Technology records – those that have reached the end of their active retention period but have not reached the end of their *total* retention period – should be *archived*. Archived records must be retrievable within a reasonable time frame; the Company is not required to make archived records readily available.

3.4 Unless otherwise indicated, the Information Technology Storage Librarian shall electronically purge or physically destroy records at the end of their total retention period. Management of the department responsible for generating records shall also be responsible for knowing which records are to be purged/destroyed and when.

If records must be kept beyond their total retention period, department management shall give a full explanation, in writing, why those records must be maintained beyond their normal retention period:

- It is aware of, and consents to, destruction of records; or

- It shall give a full explanation (justification) for why records must be retained.

4.0 TECHNOLOGY OBSOLESCENCE

4.1 Technology obsolescence is the result of technological evolution. As new media for storing digital information rapidly replace older media, devices, applications, etc., for reading these older media become unavailable. Newer versions of software constantly render older versions obsolete and the hardware required by this software also changes over time. Consequently, information which relies on obsolete technologies becomes inaccessible.

4.2 The Information Technology Storage Librarian shall periodically review the archived records log and submit a report to Information Technology Managers on all records archived prior to the last such review.

4.3 Information Technology Managers shall determine which archived records are still required and which are in danger of becoming inaccessible (need to be moved to a different medium, format, etc.). Information Technology Managers shall determine the method and resources needed to ensure continued accessibility of those records and shall delegate the task of updating those records to the Tech Support Manager.

4.4 The Tech Support Manager shall update archives, as needed, and report to Information Technology Managers and the Information Technology Storage Librarian when the task is complete. The Tech Support Manager shall supply information needed to update the archive log to the Information Technology Storage Librarian.

5.0 RECORDS AUDIT

5.1 Information Technology Managers (or its designee) shall conduct an internal audit of the Records Management System on an irregular basis, to ensure Company records continue to be accessible, have integrity, and continue to meet Company and legal requirements. A third-party audit of the Records Management System shall be conducted periodically (once every two years is recommended).

5.2 If any audit finds a nonconformity in the Records Management System, Information Technology Managers (or its designee) shall take corrective action and update the system accordingly. Within one month of taking corrective action, the auditor shall verify that the corrective action was taken, that it yielded the expected results, and that the system has been updated.

Forms:

- ITAD102-1 RECORDS CLASSIFICATION AND RETENTION GUIDE

- ITAD102-2 RECORDS MANAGEMENT DATABASE

References:

A. SARBANES-OXLEY ACT OF 2002

The Sarbanes-Oxley Act, passed by the U.S. Congress in 2002, is designed to prevent publicly-held companies that conduct business in the U.S.A. from manipulating, losing, or destroying records, regardless of the form those records take. It is crucial for such an organization to develop and execute a records management plan, to show it has an adequate internal control structure in place (and is thereby in compliance with the Act).

The Public Company Accounting Oversight Board (PCAOB) was created by the U.S. Congress to oversee and administer Sarbanes-Oxley.

B. ISO 15489-1:2001, INFORMATION AND DOCUMENTATION - RECORDS MANAGEMENT, PART 1-GENERAL and ISO 15489-2:2001 INFORMATION AND DOCUMENTATION - RECORDS MANAGEMENT, PART 2-GUIDELINES

ISO 15489 is the international standard for record management. There are two parts to the standard, ISO 15489-1:2001 and ISO/TR 15489-2:2001. Part 1 provides *guidance on managing records* of originating organizations, public or private, for internal and external clients. All the elements outlined in Part 1 are *recommended* to ensure that adequate records are created, captured, and managed.

Part 2 provides *procedures* that help ensure records are managed according to the principles and elements in Part 1.

D. ISO 9001:2008, QUALITY MANAGEMENT SYSTEMS-REQUIREMENTS

Clause 4.2.4 of ISO 9001 states, in part, that "(r)ecords shall be established and maintained to provide evidence of conformity to requirements and of the effective operation of the quality management system." It also requires that records remain legible, identifiable, and retrievable and it calls for the organization to establish a documented procedure to define record controls. This clause may, therefore, enable the organization to conform to the requirements of the Sarbanes-Oxley Act (SOX).

E. CONTROL OBJECTIVES FOR INFORMATION AND RELATED TECHNOLOGY (CObIT)

CObIT is a process model developed to assist enterprises with the management of information technology resources. The process model focuses on developing suitable controls for each of the Information Technology processes, raising the level of process maturity in information technology and satisfying the business expectations of Information Technology.

CObIT's Management Guidelines component contains a framework responding to management's need for control and measurability of Information Technology by providing tools to assess and measure the enterprise's Information Technology capability for the CObIT Information Technology processes. The tools include:

- Performance measurement elements (outcome measures and performance drivers for all Information Technology processes);
- A list of critical success factors that provides succinct, nontechnical best practices for each Information Technology process; and
- Maturity models to assist in benchmarking and decision-making for capability improvements.

Detailed information on CObIT may be found at http://www.isaca.org or at http://www.itgi.org/.

Revision History:

Revision	Date	Description of Changes	Requested By
0.0	mm/dd/yyyy	Initial Release	

ITAD102-1 RECORDS CLASSIFICATION AND RETENTION GUIDE

Record	File Location	Authority	Minimum Retention	Disposition
Management Review Minutes	President's Office	Information Technology Managers	3 years	Destroy
Training, education skills, and experience records	Personnel Files Department Files	Human Resources Dept. Mgrs.	Employment plus 3 years	Destroy
Quotation Review	Customer Service	Customer Service	1year	Destroy
Sales Order Review	Customer Files	Customer Service	3 years	Archive 7 years Destroy
Design Input	Project File	Software Engineering	Life of Product	Archive 7 yrs. Destroy
Design reviews	Project File	Software Engineering	Life of Product	Archive 7 yrs. Destroy
Design Verification	Project File	Software Engineering	Life of Product	Archive 7 yrs. Destroy
Design Validation	Project File	Software Engineering	Life of Product	Archive 7 yrs. Destroy
Design Change Reviews	Project File	Software Engineering	Life of Product	Archive 7 yrs. Destroy
Vendor Evaluations	Purchasing	Purchasing	5 years	Destroy
Purchase Orders	Purchasing	Purchasing	7 years	Destroy
Completed Work Orders	Quality Assurance	Quality Assurance	7 years	Destroy
Traceability Records	Quality Assurance	Quality Assurance	7 years	Destroy

ITAD102-1 RECORDS CLASSIFICATION AND RETENTION GUIDE

Record	File Location	Authority	Minimum Retention	Disposition
Calibration Records	Quality Assurance	Quality Assurance	7 years	Destroy
Internal Audit Records	Information Technology Managers	Information Technology Managers	3 years	Destroy
Inspection Records	Quality Assurance	Quality Assurance	7 years	Destroy
Product Release Records	Quality Assurance	Quality Assurance	7 years	Destroy
Nonconformance Reports	Quality Assurance	Quality Assurance	3 years	Destroy
Corrective Actions	Information Technology Managers	Information Technology Managers	5 years	Destroy
Preventive Actions	Information Technology Managers	Information Technology Managers	5 years	Destroy
Document Masters	Document Control	Quality Assurance	5 years	Destroy
User Complaints	Quality Assurance	Quality Assurance	3 years	Destroy
Design Plans	Project File	Software Engineering	Life of Product	Archive 7 yrs. Destroy
Process Validation Records	Quality Assurance	Quality Assurance	Life of Process	Destroy
User satisfaction surveys	Information Technology Managers	Information Technology Managers	5 years	Destroy

ITAD102-2 RECORDS MANAGEMENT DATABASE

Date	Record Id	Description	Dept Of Origination	Originated By	Origination Date	Revision ID	Revision Date	Revised By	Revising Dept	

Approval:

Originating
Department
Manager _____ Date _____

Information
Technology
Manager _____ Date _____

[This page intentionally left blank]

Document ID **ITAD103**	Title **IT DOCUMENT MANAGEMENT**	Print Date **mm/dd/yyyy**
Revision **0.0**	Prepared By **Preparer's Name / Title**	Date Prepared **mm/dd/yyyy**
Effective Date **mm/dd/yyyy**	Reviewed By **Reviewer's Name / Title**	Date Reviewed **mm/dd/yyyy**
	Approved By **Final Approver's Name / Title**	Date Approved **mm/dd/yyyy**

Policy: To enable any document connected with the Company's official functions to be managed, stored securely, and found at all times, regardless of its form (paper or electronic).

Purpose: To define methods and responsibilities for controlling documents and define methods for document storage, revision, availability (retrieval), and destruction.

Scope: This procedure applies to all documents required by the Company to conduct its business.

Responsibilities:

The Document Manager is responsible for developing and implementing the Document Management Plan, updating the Plan as needed, maintaining Company documents, controlling access to and distribution of such documents, managing document change, and communicating the Plan to employees.

All Employees are responsible for controlling Company documents in accordance with the Document Management Plan.

Information Technology Managers are responsible for reviewing and approving the Document Management Plan.

Department Managers are responsible for ensuring that current versions of all relevant documents are available at the point of use and that those documents are legible.

Definitions: Controlled Document – Any document for which distribution and status are to be kept current by the issuer, to ensure that authorized holders or users have the most up-to-date version available.

Document – Information and its supporting medium (paper, magnetic, electronic, optical, photograph, or sample). A document is an object commonly found in office systems (a spreadsheet, word processing document, database, etc.), whereas a record is a document that provides evidence of a particular business activity.

External Document: A document of external origin that provides information or direction for performing work. Examples of external documents are customer drawings, industry and governing body standards, vendor-supplied user manuals, and equipment manuals.

Record – In Information Technology, a record is a data structure aggregating several items of possibly different types. The items being aggregated are called fields and are usually identified or indexed by field labels.

Generally, a record is data or information of any kind and in any form, created or received and accumulated by an organization in the course of conducting business and subsequently kept as "evidence of activity" through incorporation into a recordkeeping system.

Procedure:

1.0 PLANNING DOCUMENT MANAGEMENT

1.1 To prepare the Company's Document Management Plan, The Document Manager shall review the following items:

- Information Technology Industry standards and best practices;
- Legal and regulatory requirements pertaining to document management; and
- The existing document management plan, if there is one.

1.2 The Document Manager shall use the preceding items to develop a Document Management Plan. The Plan shall be submitted to Information Technology Managers for review and approval.

1.3 Upon Information Technology Managers' approval of the Document Management Plan, the Document Manager shall implement the Plan, delegate duties as needed, and communicate the Plan to all employees.

2.0 DOCUMENT MANAGEMENT PLAN

2.1 Document Distribution

- The Document Manager shall maintain a master list of all controlled documents, ITAD103-1 - DOCUMENT CONTROL LIST. The document control list should include at a minimum the following information on each document:

  a. Document title;
  b. Unique ID;
  c. Date of issue;
  d. Current revision number and date; and
  e. Document location.

- The Document Manager shall keep Company documents in a secure location and control their availability and distribution.

  a. Hard-copy originals shall be in a secure storage area and control over copying and distribution shall be exercised.

  b. Electronic document location shall be identified within ITAD103-1. Access to electronic documents shall be in accordance with ITSD106 Information Technology ACCESS CONTROL.

- The Document Manager shall distribute hardcopy documents to locations specified within ITAD103-1 and shall remove and destroy any previous versions. Electronic document distribution shall be controlled in accordance with procedure ITSD106 Information Technology ACCESS CONTROL:

  a. Previous document versions shall be electronically archived, in accordance with Company requirements; and

  b. Previous versions shall be replaced by revised versions.

- Depending on the document's content and sensitivity (security) level, the Document Manager (with guidance from Information Technology Managers) shall restrict access to and distribution of Company documents, in accordance with procedure ITSD106 Information Technology ACCESS CONTROL.

- External documents are controlled primarily for distribution purposes. All external documents and revisions shall be added to ITAD103-1 as they are acquired.

2.2   Document Acceptance and Revision

- The Document Manager shall be responsible for coordinating with Department Managers to ensure all documents are periodically reviewed (annually, at a minimum), to ensure their continued suitability to Company requirements and to ensure timely updates.

- Anyone may submit a new document or recommend a revision to an existing document, in anticipation of or response to changing standards (see Reference A), legal requirements (see Additional Resource A), or business requirements.

  a. The requestor shall complete ITAD103-2 DOCUMENT CHANGE REQUEST FORM, indicating the nature of and reason for the change, and submit the Change Request Form with a copy of the recommended document (change) to the Document Manager.

  b. In the case of hard-copy documents, the requestor shall print a copy of the document, mark requested changes (if any) on the copy, and submit the document to the Document Manager for review.

  c. In the case of electronic documents, the requestor shall, at a minimum, prepare the document and/or detailed list of changes and e-mail a copy of the document (and changes) to the Document Manager.

  d. If document changes are extensive, a new document may be typed and submitted with a copy of the original.

- The Document Manager shall review original documents and/or change requests with Management of the affected department.

  a. Reviewers shall consider the reason for the change and determine if it is warranted (will it add value, will it add to or reduce complexity, etc.).

  b. Reviewers shall indicate their approval of the document or changes.

c. If the document/change is approved, a Document Change Number (DCN) shall be noted on ITAD103-3 DOCUMENT CHANGE CONTROL FORM. This form and a copy of the (changed) document, along with appropriate approvals, shall be submitted to the Document Manager for updating the document, indexing the revision, and updating the revision history.

d. If the document (change) request is denied, the requestor shall be notified of the reason(s) for denial.

- The Document Manager shall circulate the final document/revision in order to obtain the required approvals (signatures).

- When the required approvals have been obtained, the Document Manager shall update the master document list with the correct revision number, last review date, and other required information.

- In the case of hard-copy documents, the master document (revision) shall be stored with the master document list.

- Management of the affected department shall be formally notified of the new or revised document.

a. Hard copies shall be distributed to authorized personnel.

b. Electronic copies shall be made available through the Company Information Technology network, in accordance with ITSD106 IT ACCESS CONTROL.

2.3   Document Format

- All documents shall have a document name, ID, revision ID, and page number (in "page X of Y" format) on each page.

- All documents shall bear approval signatures on the first (or cover) page. Electronic documents shall bear approver names.

- Procedures and instructions may use this procedure document (ITAD103) as a template.

2.4   Temporary Changes

- Temporary changes shall be defined and controlled.

- Temporary changes may be developed in written form, on a hardcopy or electronic procedure template, or on a copy of an existing document, in contrasting color.

- Temporary changes shall be reviewed and approved by the Document Manager and the affected Department Manager(s), at a minimum.

a. On hard-copy documents, review and approval shall be indicated by signatures or by initials and date next to "red lines." Documents and changes shall be legible and identifiable.

b. On electronic documents, review and approval shall be indicated by appropriate notation in the document and the temporary status of the change shall be noted in the name of the document.

- Temporary change documents shall include the start and end date for the change period and the scope of applicability.

- Temporary changes to a document should not exceed two weeks; at the end of the change period, temporary changes shall be made permanent or removed.

3.0 DOCUMENT MANAGEMENT PLAN REVIEW

3.1   Information Technology Managers shall periodically (annually, at a minimum) review the Document Management System for continued applicability, effectiveness, and compliance.

3.2   A periodic audit of the Document Management System shall be conducted (once every two years, at a minimum) by a registered and qualified third party auditor.

4.0 DOCUMENT MANAGEMENT PLAN UPDATE

4.1   The Document Manager shall incorporate recommended updates into the Plan and communicate such changes to all employees.

4.2   Within a month of the Plan being updated, Information Technology Managers shall review the Plan to verify that updates have been implemented and are producing the desired results.

Forms:

- ITAD103-1 DOCUMENT CONTROL LIST
- ITAD103-2 DOCUMENT CHANGE REQUEST FORM
- ITAD103-3 DOCUMENT CHANGE CONTROL FORM

References:

A. ISO 9001:2008, QUALITY MANAGEMENT SYSTEMS-REQUIREMENTS

Clause 4.2.3 of ISO 9001 states that an organization's documents shall be controlled and the organization shall have a documented procedure in place that specifies document controls before an organization is in compliance with Quality Management System requirements.

B. ISO 27001:2013 INFORMATION TECHNOLOGY – SECURITY TECHNIQUES – INFORMATION SECURITY MANAGEMENT SYSTEMS – REQUIREMENTS

ISO 27001 states document requirements for an Information Security Management System (ISMS). It states general requirements for such documentation and that documents required by the ISMS shall be protected and controlled.

C. SARBANES-OXLEY ACT OF 2002

The Sarbanes-Oxley Act (or "SOX") passed by the U.S. Congress in 2002 is designed to prevent *publicly-held* companies from manipulating, losing, or destroying business-related documents. Section 404 of the Act requires company executives to attest to and ensure adequate internal controls and to periodically assess them. It is crucial for any organization wishing to be in compliance with SOX to develop and execute an effective document management plan.

D. CONTROL OBJECTIVES FOR INFORMATION AND RELATED TECHNOLOGY (CObIT)

CObIT is a process model developed to assist enterprises with the management of information technology resources. The process model focuses on developing suitable controls for each of the 34 Information Technology processes, raising the level of process maturity in information technology and satisfying the business expectations of Information Technology.

CObIT's Management Guidelines component contains a framework responding to management's need for control and measurability of Information Technology by providing tools to assess and measure the enterprise's Information Technology capability for the CObIT Information Technology processes. The tools include:

- Performance measurement elements (outcome measures and performance drivers for all Information Technology processes);
- A list of critical success factors that provides succinct, nontechnical best practices for each Information Technology process; and

- Maturity models to assist in benchmarking and decision-making for capability improvements.

Detailed information on CObIT may be found at http://www.isaca.org or http://www.itgi.org/.

Additional Resources:

A. Title 21, Code of Federal Regulations (21 CFR Part 11), "Electronic Records; Electronic Signatures".

Revision History:

Revision	Date	Description of Changes	Requested By
0	mm/dd/yyyy	Initial Release	

[This page intentionally left blank]

ITAD103-1 DOCUMENT CONTROL LIST

Document ID	Document Name	Internal/ External	Date of Issue (Receipt)	Dept. Owning	Originator	Approved By	Revision Number	Revision Date	Document Location	Distribute To

[This page intentionally left blank]

ITAD103-2 DOCUMENT CHANGE REQUEST FORM

Date:_____   RDC No.: _____

Originator: _____

Document Title and Publication Date: _____

Page and Chapter, or Paragraph Number: _____

Description of problem, opportunity, or other reason for request (define in detail): _____

_____

_____

_____

Solution Recommended: _____

_____

_____

_____

Date Action Required By: _____

Comments: _____

_____

_____

_____

_____

Department Manager Approval: _____

Recommended solution to problem or postponement/dissolution of request (attach all necessary documentation to support response): _____

_____

_____

_____

Approved By: _____   Date:_____

PROCEDURE FOR COMPLETING FORM

1) Complete top section of this form except for RDC number

2) Obtain Department Manager's approval

3) Forward original to Information Technology Managers who will assign a RDC number (Note: one copy will be returned to originator with RDC number assigned).

4) Information Technology Managers will take action and if appropriate will proceed with an RDC.

5) Information Technology Managers will send a copy to Originator upon resolution of request.

Distribution: Original - RDC File   Copy - Originator

[This page intentionally left blank]

ITAD103-3 DOCUMENT CHANGE CONTROL FORM

Date:_____

DCN#:_____

RDC#:_____

Doc. or Part No.	Description of Change, Documents affected and reason(s) for change(s)	Action Code(s)	Effective Date

Change Action Required

Make / Order New Document: _____

Current Document: ☐ Modify   ☐ Retain as is

Other: _____

Comments: _____
_____
_____
_____
_____

Authorization - Document Mgr.   **Authorization - Department Mgr.**

By:_____   By:_____

Date:_____   Date:_____

[This page intentionally left blank]

Document ID **ITAD104**	Title **IT DEVICE NAMING CONVENTIONS**	Print Date **mm/dd/yyyy**
Revision **0.0**	Prepared By **Preparer's Name / Title**	Date Prepared **mm/dd/yyyy**
Effective Date **mm/dd/yyyy**	Reviewed By **Reviewer's Name / Title**	Date Reviewed **mm/dd/yyyy**
	Approved By **Final Approver's Name / Title**	Date Approved **mm/dd/yyyy**

Policy: All devices attached to the Company network infrastructure shall be assigned names that facilitate easy management of network resources.

Purpose: To delineate specific conventions regarding the assignment of host or device names for equipment attached to (part of) the Company network infrastructure.

Scope: This set of conventions applies to all Company Local Area Networks (LAN) and all devices attached to those networks.

Responsibilities:

The Tech Support Manager is responsible for Information Technology asset (specifically, hardware and software) installation throughout the Company and as such, is responsible for ensuring installed assets are named according to the conventions spelled out in this document.

Definitions: Information Technology Asset – Any computer hardware, software, Information Technology-based Company information, related documentation, licenses, contracts or other agreements, etc. In the context of this document, Information Technology assets may be referred to as just "assets."

Procedure:

1.0 SERVER NAMING CONVENTIONS

1.1 Network file servers, web servers, print servers, mail servers, etc., shall be assigned names composed of a combination of the departmental abbreviation, function or role, and unique number. The pattern for this name shall be "<dept>-<role>-<number>" and the total number of letters and numbers, minus separators, shall not exceed 11. The unique number shall contain three digits and start with 001. The following names are examples of valid server names:

SALE-FILE-001

ADM-WEB-003

IT-NTWK-001

1.2 Servers located in small, remote offices shall be named using an abbreviation for the site name instead of the department name. For example:

CHI-SVR-001

DAL-SVR-006

DEN-SVR-004

2.0   NETWORK HOST NAMING CONVENTIONS

2.1   Workstation Naming Conventions

- Desktop computing resources shall be assigned names composed of a combination of the letters "DT", a departmental abbreviation, and a unique number. The total number of letters and numbers shall not exceed 10. The unique number shall contain three digits and start with 001. Examples are:

DTSALES001
DTADMIN002
DTENGRG005

- Laptop computers shall have no more than 10 characters in the name starting with the letters "LT." Following LT shall be the departmental code and a three-digit number starting with 001. For example:

LTSALES001
LTENGRG004
LTACCTG024

2.2   Printer Naming Conventions

- Printers are assigned names in order to make it easier for users to find and connect when required. Printer names will be constructed in such a manner that it is easy to determine the location and type of printer. Printer names shall not exceed 11 characters and shall follow the following convention:

<type>-<loc>-<letter>

For example the second of two HP Laserjet 4si printers in room 433 would be named.

lj4si-433-b

The single Laser Jet 4 in the Omaha satellite office would have the following name:

lj4-omh-a

3.0   MAINFRAME NAMING CONVENTIONS

3.1   Mainframes shall be assigned names according to the following format:

<system type>-<loc>

3.2   A number is not required since no site has multiple mainframe systems installed.
       For example, the AS/400 located in the Denver office would be named:

as400-den

4.0   INFRASTRUCTURE DEVICE NAMING CONVENTIONS

Infrastructure devices include all hardware that makes up the actual network. The
following table details the naming conventions for the applicable hardware:

Device Type	Naming Standard
Router	<site>-RTR-<number> la-rtr-1 den-rtr-3
Bridge	<site>-BR-<number> kc-br-3 chi-br-1
Concentrators and hubs	<site>-<wiring closet room no>-<number> chi-220-1 dal-1-1
Communications server	<site>-comm-<number> dal-comm-1 atl-comm-4
Modem banks, Modems, or CSU/DSUs	<site>-<type>-<number> dal-dsu-19 atl-mbnk-12

Forms:

- None.

References:

A. SARBANES-OXLEY ACT OF 2002

The Act, passed by the U.S. Congress in 2002, does not specify naming
conventions as a requirement. However, since the thrust of the Act is internal
control, developing and adhering to a set of naming conventions may be one way
of showing the Company is maintaining an adequate internal control structure.

Additional Resources:

- None.

Revision History:

Revision	Date	Description of Changes	Requested By
0	mm/dd/yyyy	Initial Release	

Document ID **ITAD105**	Title **TCP/IP IMPLEMENTATION STANDARDS**	Print Date **mm/dd/yyyy**
Revision **0.0**	Prepared By **Preparer's Name / Title**	Date Prepared **mm/dd/yyyy**
Effective Date **mm/dd/yyyy**	Reviewed By **Reviewer's Name / Title**	Date Reviewed **mm/dd/yyyy**
	Approved By **Final Approver's Name / Title**	Date Approved **mm/dd/yyyy**

Policy: All devices attached to the Company network infrastructure shall be assigned TCP/IP addresses that facilitate effective network management.

Purpose: To delineate specific conventions regarding the assignment of TCP/IP addresses for equipment attached to the Company network infrastructure.

Scope: This standard applies to all Company Wide Area Networks (WANs), Local Area Networks (LANs), and all devices attached to those networks.

Responsibilities:

The Network Manager is responsible for managing the Company TCP/IP addressing plan.

Remote Site LAN Administrators are responsible for coordinating TCP/IP addressing with the Network Manager.

Procedure:

1.0   TCP/IP ADDRESS

Transmission Control Protocol/Internet Protocol (TCP/IP) is the Company primary networking protocol. While other network protocols are in use on company networks, TCP/IP is particularly important since this is the primary protocol of the Internet. Access to any Internet resource, including the World Wide Web (WWW), must use this protocol.

Communication with the TCP/IP software suite depends upon the assignment of unique 32-Bit addresses. These addresses are expressed as a collection of decimal numbers separated by periods such as 132.159.121.16.

There are three classes of TCP/IP addresses:

- Class A addresses are assigned to networks with a very large number of hosts. Addresses in Class A range from 1.0.0.0 to 126.0.0.0 Each Class A address space can have up 17 million hosts.

- Class B addresses are assigned to medium-sized networks. Class B Addresses range from 128.1.0.0 to 191.254.254.0. Class B address ranges can have up to 65,000 hosts per network.

- Class C addresses are usually used for small LANs. Class C addresses range from 192.0.0.0 to 223.254.254.0. There are 2 million Class C networks with up to 254 hosts per network.

2.0   DYNAMIC HOST CONFIGURATION PROTOCOL (DHCP)

Each node on a TCP/IP network must have a unique IP Address. In previous years this process was accomplished manually and required a significant amount of recordkeeping and coordination to ensure duplicate IP Addresses were not assigned.

DHCP provides a means of automatically assigning IP addresses to network hosts. DHCP removes virtually all the record keeping requirements for managing an IP Address space since the DHCP server maintains a database of all assigned addresses.

All user workstations shall be assigned IP Addresses via DHCP. The only network devices that will not use DHCP are Network Infrastructure Devices (Routers and Hubs), File Servers and Network Printers – all other devices shall use DHCP.

3.0   NETWORK ADDRESS TRANSLATION (NAT)

TCP/IP addresses within the Company enterprise use the free subnet 172.16.0.0. This network address space is reserved by the Internet for private internal use only. Addresses from this subnet are not allowed to be directly connected to the Internet.

The Company enterprise is connected to the Internet through a security firewall. In addition to providing security, the firewall is configured to translate addresses from the 172.16.0.0 address space to legal Internet addresses.

4.0   SUBNET ADDRESSING STANDARDS

4.1   Headquarters Site

The Company headquarters site shall be assigned TCP/IP addresses in accordance with the following plan. All subnets use a class C subnet mask (255.255.255.0).

Subnet	Assignment
172.16.5.0	Main Network Backbone
172.16.10.0	Main Wing
172.16.11.0	Floor A East Wing
172.16.12.0	Floor A West Wing
172.16.13.0	Floor B East Wing
172.16.14.0	Floor B West Wing

4.2   Remote Site Subnet Assignments

The Company remote sites shall be assigned TCP/IP addresses in accordance with
the following plan. All large branch office subnets use a class C subnet mask
(255.255.255.0). The Class C subnet provides up to 254 addresses per subnet.
Remote Offices with more than 254 network hosts shall use multiple class C
subnets.

Virtually all Company satellite sites have networks with not more than 50 hosts.
These smaller satellite offices will be assigned subnet address spaces using the
subnet mask 255.255.255.192. This network mask provides for up to 62 network
addresses.

The following tables detail the Company branch and satellite office IP Address
subnet assignments.

Subnet	Subnet Mask	Remote Site
172.16.20.0	255.255.255.0	Atlanta
172.16.30.0	255.255.255.0	Boston
172.16.40.0	255.255.255.0	Chicago
172.16.50.0	255.255.255.0	Denver
172.16.60.0	255.255.255.0	Houston
172.16.65.0	255.255.255.192	Austin
172.16.65.64	255.255.255.192	San Antonio
172.16.65.128	255.255.255.192	El Paso
172.16.70.0	255.255.255.0	Kansas City
172.16.80.0	255.255.255.0	Los Angeles
172.16.90.0	255.255.255.0	Memphis
172.16.95.0	255.255.255.192	Little Rock
172.16.95.64	255.255.255.192	Nashville
172.16.100.0	255.255.255.0	New York
172.16.110.0	255.255.255.0	Portland
172.16.120.0	255.255.255.0	Seattle
172.16.130.0	255.255.255.0	Washington DC
172.16.135.0	255.255.255.192	Baltimore
172.16.135.64	255.255.255.192	Norfolk

5.0   WAN LINK ADDRESSING CONVENTIONS

All Company WAN Links shall be addressed with the smallest possible address
space in accordance with the following guidelines:

- The Subnet mask for all WAN Link addresses is: 255.255.255.252

- WAN Links shall be assigned addresses from 172.16.1.0 to 172.16.4.0

- The lowest numerical address in the subnet shall be assigned to the interface on central site end of the link. The highest numerical address in the subnet shall be assigned to the interface on the remote side of the WAN link.

5.1   Addressing Conventions

The following paragraphs detail the specific conventions for assignment of IP Address to hosts within a subnet.

5.2   Class C Sized Subnets

Network subnets assigned a Class C sized address space (254 address numbers) shall follow the following addressing guidelines.

Address Range	Host Type
001	Default Gateway
002 to 019	Network Infrastructure Devices
020 to 039	File Servers
040 to 059	Network Printers
060 to 249	DHCP Assignment Pool
250 to 251	Network Management Systems
252 to 254	Reserved for Network Administration Use

Domain name servers (DNS) shall always be assigned an address aaa.bbb.ccc.15. Should both a primary and secondary DNS be located on the same subnet then the secondary shall be assigned the next address: aaa.bbb.ccc.16.

5.3   Variably Sized Subnets

Variably sub netted address spaces are used in Company satellite sites. These remote sites normally have dramatically smaller host address requirements.

These sites have very limited network infrastructure and very few file server assets.

Network subnets assigned an address space of 128 addresses or less shall follow the following addressing guidelines.

Host Address	Host Type
1	Default Gateway
2	Hub
3	Terminal Server
4	File Server 1
5	File Server 2

6	Printer 1
7	Printer 2
8	Printer 3
9	Printer 4
10 to End	Workstations

For example; for the subnet 172.16.65.64 network host TCP/IP addresses would be assigned as follows:

IP Address	Host
172.16.65.65	Cisco 2501 Ethernet Interface
172.16.65.66	Stackable Hub
172.16.65.68	File Server
172.16.65.70	Printer #1
172.16.65.78	Workstation #4

Forms:

- None.

References:

A. SARBANES-OXLEY ACT OF 2002 (or "SOX")

In defining an "adequate internal control structure" – one of the most important requirements of SOX – the Act (U.S. law) does not specify information technology. By its ubiquity, however, IT is an integral part of internal controls. Having and adhering to standards gives evidence that internal controls are in place and the Company complies – in part, at least – with the Act.

Additional Resources:

A. None.

Revision History:

Revision	Date	Description of Changes	Requested By
0	mm/dd/yyyy	Initial Release	

Document ID **ITAD106**	Title **NETWORK INFRASTRUCTURE STANDARDS**	Print Date **mm/dd/yyyy**
Revision **0.0**	Prepared By **Preparer's Name / Title**	Date Prepared **mm/dd/yyyy**
Effective Date **mm/dd/yyyy**	Reviewed By **Reviewer's Name / Title**	Date Reviewed **mm/dd/yyyy**
	Approved By **Final Approver's Name / Title**	Date Approved **mm/dd/yyyy**

Policy: To ensure maximum safety, capacity, and efficiency, the Company network infrastructure shall be engineered and installed in accordance with appropriate industry standards and state and local building and electrical codes.

Purpose: To delineate specific standards regarding the installation of network infrastructure including cabling and equipment.

Scope: This standard applies to all Company Wide Area Networks (WAN) and Local Area Networks (LAN) and all infrastructure support devices attached to those networks.

Responsibilities:

The Network Manager is responsible for the design, installation, and management of the Company network infrastructure. The Network Manager will be responsible for the coordination of all aspects of the cable plant installation. In addition, the Network Manager will be the approval authority for the coordination of any additional adds, moves, or changes to the Company network infrastructure.

The LAN Administrator is responsible for the installation and operation of the LAN and WAN equipment and software installed within their LAN. The LAN Administrator will coordinate with the Telecommunications manager for all issues related to corporate WAN Links or other Telecommunications equipment such as telephones as associated systems. The LAN Administrator will coordinate all adds, moves, or other changes with the Network Manager.

The Telecommunications Manager, or Telecom Manager, is responsible for the installation of TCP/IP and operation of all Company WAN circuits and associated support equipment. The Telecom Manager provides direction to the LAN Administrator regarding operation, configuration and troubleshooting of all WAN equipment.

In addition, the Telecom Manager is responsible for the installation, operation, and troubleshooting of all Company voice, fax, and video communications systems.

The <u>Technology Support Manager</u>, or Tech Support Manager, is responsible for installing and maintaining network infrastructure in accordance with commonly accepted Network Infrastructure standards.

Procedure:

1.0 NETWORK INFRASTRUCTURE STANDARDS DEVELOPMENT

1.1 All Company network infrastructure standards shall conform to IEEE 802 standards, wherever applicable.

1.2 The Network Manager communicates the need for network infrastructure standards to Information Technology Management. They review the proposed standards with respect to:

- ITAD101-1 INFORMATION TECHNOLOGY PLAN;

- Industry standards, best practices, and benchmarks; and

- Applicable federal, state, and local regulations.

1.3 Once the need for standards has been recognized and formally agreed on, the Network Manager shall define the general content and scope of the future standards and present them to Information Technology Management.

1.4 Once agreement has been reached on the basic standard, the Network manager shall develop detailed standards specifications and present these to Information Technology Management.

1.5 When agreement on the detailed standards has been reached, Information Technology Management shall present the standards to Top Management for approval.

2.0 NETWORK INFRASTRUCTURE STANDARDS IMPLEMENTATION

2.1 Once approved by Top Management, network infrastructure standards shall be communicated by the Network Manager to the LAN Administrator, the Telecommunications Manager, and the Tech Support Manager personnel.

2.2 The Network Manager shall have primary responsibility for maintaining ITAD106-1 NETWORK INFRASTRUCTURE STANDARDS LIST.

3.0 NETWORK INFRASTRUCTURE STANDARDS REVIEW

3.1 At regular intervals (annually, at a minimum), the Network Manager shall review the current set of Company network infrastructure standards to verify that they continue to meet Company requirements. The Network Manager should review ITTS102-1 TECH SUPPORT LOG to determine if there are patterns or trends of Information Technology-related trouble that indicate outdated or incomplete standards.

3.2 If the Network Manager determines that infrastructure standards require updating, they shall meet with Information Technology Management to review their findings and required updates and determine to what extent ITAD101-1 INFORMATION TECHNOLOGY PLAN will be impacted.

If ITAD101-1 will be impacted by a change in standards, this issue shall be included in the next Technology Plan review, in accordance with procedure ITAD101, INFORMATION TECHNOLOGY PLAN.

Forms:

- ITAD106-1 NETWORK INFRASTRUCTURE STANDARDS LISTS

References:

A. INSTITUTE OF ELECTRICAL AND ELECTRONICS ENGINEERS (IEEE) STANDARD 802 STANDARD FOR LOCAL AND METROPOLITAN AREA NETWORKS

IEEE 802 is a family of standards that pertains to local area and metropolitan area networks; specifically, networks carrying variable-size packets. Services and protocols specified in these standards map to the lower two layers (Data Link and Physical) of the seven-layer OSI networking reference model. IEEE 802 subdivides the OSI Data Link Layer into sub-layers named Logical Link Control (LLC) and Media Access Control (MAC). One of the more familiar parts of the standard is 802.11, which pertains to wireless networks.

The IEEE 802 family of standards is maintained by the IEEE 802 LAN/MAN Standards Committee (LMSC). For more information on standard 802 or for copies, see http://standards.ieee.org/about/get, the IEEE Standards Association website.

Additional Resources:

None.

Revision History:

Revision	Date	Description of Changes	Requested By
0	mm/dd/yyyy	Initial Release	

ITAD106-1 NETWORK INFRASTRUCTURE STANDARDS LIST

1.0   CABLE PLANT STANDARDS

The Company network infrastructure is vital to company business operations. The following paragraphs detail the basic mandatory installation procedures that are intended to assure a high quality, dependable, network cable plant infrastructure.

The Company network infrastructure includes all local and wide area networks (LAN/WAN) and all associated equipment and software required for their continued operation and management. LAN infrastructure is red in a hierarchy composed of a Main Distribution Frame/Closet (MDF) and one or more Intermediate Distribution Frames/Closets (IDF). In some smaller locations the MDF and IDF are co-located or there may be no MDF and only and IDF is required.

There shall be as few IDF locations as possible, but at least one per floor. If possible, centrally locate the IDF.

Infrastructure connecting the MDF to the IDF locations will be regarded as part of the network backbone. The backbone is the main portion of the network and serves to distribute communication across the corporate infrastructure. The cable infrastructure from the IDF to individual network hosts, including user workstations, is referred to as the horizontal cable plant. Each portion of the cable plant has specific standards that must be followed to ensure reliable communication.

All installations shall be performed in accordance with ITAM102 – IT ASSET MANAGEMENT.

2.0   HORIZONTAL CABLE PLANT

The horizontal cable plant consists of all equipment and cabling found from the IDF to the network interface on a given network host.

3.0   TELECOMMUNICATIONS RACK

All equipment in an IDF shall be properly installed in an industry standard communications rack or enclosure. Equipment that cannot be directly mounted to the rack shall be installed on a rack mounted shelve. Equipment shelves shall not be excessively loaded. Equipment shall not be double stacked on equipment shelves.

The rack or enclosure shall be installed in a space or location that is not in the immediate vicinity of hot water heaters, hazardous equipment or material or equipment that could cause power fluctuations or electromagnetic interference (EMI) including heating and air-conditioning equipment, power transformers or distribution equipment.

The telecommunications closet or enclosure shall remain locked at all times. Only personnel from the Information Systems Department are authorized access to these spaces.

All cabling in the IDF/MDF will be dressed neatly with appropriate wire management (cable ties/wraps), as necessary, to protect and aesthetically manage the physical cabling.

a. Dedicated Communications Closet.

For installation locations with a large dedicated communications closet, the IDF shall be installed in an open Aluminum 19" telecommunications rack of at least seven feet in height.

The rack shall be solidly bolted to the floor with not less than four bolts. The rack shall be anchored sufficiently to comply with all local earthquake standards or other applicable building codes. The rack shall be fitted with a horizontal and vertical wire management system.

b. Small Telecommunications Closet

A wall mounted 19-inch telecommunications rack shall be used for locations with small telecommunications closets that preclude the installation of a traditional 19-inch rack.

To support the installation of telecommunications equipment a piece of industrial plywood shall be anchored to the wall of the closet. This plywood shall be not less than 0.75 inch in thickness and not less than 4 feet by 4 feet.

The wall-mounted rack shall be solidly anchored to the plywood.

c. No Telecommunications Closet

For locations without a suitable telecommunications closet, the IDF equipment shall be installed in an enclosed lockable Telecommunications Cabinet (freestanding or wall mounted as appropriate). The LAN Administrator shall control the keys and access to this cabinet.

4.0   POWER

The communications closet shall provide sufficient electrical power for all installed equipment. The available electrical load shall not be less than 150% of the required current for all installed equipment.

IDF racks or enclosures shall be electrically grounded in accordance with all applicable government (local, state and federal) laws.

The IDF shall be fitted with surge protected electrical power strips. The number of available outlets shall be 125% of number of outlets required by the installed equipment.

5.0   VENTILATION

Proper environmental controls are important to ensure the proper and continued operation of the Company network. All MDF/IDF locations shall have sufficient air conditioning to maintain continuous airflow and a temperature between 65 to 70 degrees Fahrenheit.

6.0   CABLE SPECIFICATIONS

6.1   All components proposed for the cable plant installation will meet or exceed all UL and EIA-TIA specifications, and will be installed along industry standard guidelines, within applicable OSHA, city, and federal fire code restrictions.

All Company cabling shall be installed in accordance with the guidelines contained in ANSI/EIA/TIA-568-1991 Commercial Building Telecommunications Wiring Standard and two associated bulletins:

- Additional Cable Specifications for Unshielded Twisted-Pair Cables EIA/TIA Technical System Bulletin TSB-36, Nov. 1991 (Transmission Characteristics of Category 3-5 UTP cables).

- Additional Transmission Specifications for UTP Connecting Hardware EIA/TIA Technical System Bulletin TSB-40A, Dec 1993 (Performance of Connectors and Patch Panels Above 20 MHz).

This standard defines a generic telecommunications wiring system for commercial buildings that will support a multiproduct, multivendor environment. It also provides direction for the design of telecommunications products for commercial enterprises. The purpose of this standard is to enable the planning and installation of building wiring with little knowledge of the telecommunications products that subsequently will be installed. This standard establishes performance and technical criteria for various wiring system configurations for interfacing and connecting their respective elements.

EIA/TIA Category Specification provides for the following cable transmission speeds with specifications. Note: prior to Jan94 UL and Anixter developed a LEVEL system, which has been dropped or harmonized with the CATEGORY system

Category 1 = No performance criteria

Category 2 = Rated to 1 MHz (used for telephone wiring)

Category 3 = Rated to 16 MHz (used for Ethernet 10Base-T)

Category 4 = Rated to 20 MHz (used for Token-Ring, 10Base-T)

Category 5 = Rated to 100 MHz (used for 100Base-T, 10Base-T)

All Company copper cabling (network and telephone) shall adhere to the standards for Category 5. Telephone cabling is normally cabled with Category 2. While more expensive, the use of Category 5 cable not only ensures maximum signal quality, but also ensures a growth path for future implementation of advanced technology such as ISDN.

EIA/TIA 568 specifies two different methods of installing cables. All company network cabling shall be installed in accordance with EIA/TIA 568A. EIA/TIA-568 defines 568A pinouts as follows:

Pair	Pin	Wire Color
3	1	White/Green
3	2	Green
2	3	White/Orange
1	4	Blue
1	5	White/Blue
2	6	Orange
4	7	White/Brown
4	8	Brown

6.2   Cable Plant Labeling

Color coded cable plant labels meeting the EIA/TIA 606 standard will be installed on all termination points including patch panels, punch blocks, and wall plates. In addition, color-coded labels shall be installed on each end of all installed cable, approximately 6" from each end.

Cable plant labels will be computer generated professionally and permanently affixed to each location, all reflecting the unique identification according to a pre-approved project labeling plan.

The color of label used on a cross connect field identifies field's function. The cabling administration standard (CSA T-528 & EIA-606) lists the colors and functions as:

- Blue - Horizontal voice cables

- Brown - Interbuilding backbone

- Gray - Second-level backbone

- Green - Network connections & auxiliary circuits

- Orange - Demarcation point, telephone cable from Central Office

- Purple - First-level backbone

- Red - Key-type telephone systems

- Silver or White - Horizontal data cables, computer, & PBX equipment

- Yellow - Auxiliary, maintenance, & security alarms

6.3   General Cable Installation Guidelines

- Each network drop location shall contain not less than two network ports and at least one telephone port.

- Each drop location shall be placed eighteen inches above floor level.

- Each drop location shall be at least 24 inches away from electrical outlets.

- Each end of a cable run shall have additional slack or service loop. There shall be no less than three and no more than ten feet of service loop at the IDF end of the horizontal cable run. There shall be at least 12 inches of service loop at the network node end of the horizontal run.

- All cabling will maintain bend radius, as prescribed by the EIA/TIA 568A standard.

- For locations with hollow gypsum walls (drywall), cable shall be routed inside the wall. Cables shall terminate in a flush-mounted wall plate.

- For locations with solid walls, such as concrete block or slab, cable shall be run inside approved wire molding. The color of the molding shall be as consistent as possible with the color of the wall. The wire molding shall be run in such as manner as to be as unobtrusive as possible.

- Cable run within the ceiling shall not be draped over ceiling tiles. All cable run through ceilings shall either utilize cable trays or hooks. The cable run shall be at close to the upper limit of the space between the false ceiling and the hard ceiling.

6.4   Vertical/Backbone Cable Plant

- Fiber Optic Cable

  Multi-mode (MM) Fiber

  Multi-mode fiber used in Company networks shall have a core diameter of 62.5 microns and cladding of 125 microns. Multi-mode fiber shall be used for backbone cable runs or for local area network connections that require reliable and secure communications at distances less than 2 km.

  Single Mode (SM) Fiber

  Single mode fiber has a very small core. Typical values are 5-10 microns. Single mode fiber has a much higher capacity and allows longer distances than multi-mode fiber. Single mode fiber has a maximum transmission distance of 40km. Single mode fiber shall typically be used for campus or wide area networks such as telephone company switch to switch connections and cable TV (CATV).

- Fiber Connectors

  There are several different types of fiber connectors. All fiber connections within the Company infrastructure shall use the following connector types.

FSD - Fixed Shroud Duplex. This type of connector shall only be used for FDDI connections

- SC - SC is the international standard. The SC connectors are recommended in SP-2840A. SC connectors shall be used on all multi-mode data fiber runs.

- ST - Keyed, bayonet-style connector. This type of connector shall be used on all single-mode fiber runs.

- SMA Shall not be used.

6.5   Cable Plant And Drop Location Numbering Scheme

To facilitate efficient management of the cable plant infrastructure all cables and drop locations shall be assigned a unique serial number. The serial number shall be constructed of three sets of alpha-numeric characters separated by a dash.

IDF-Panel-Port

IDF – The three character identifier for the IDF location

Panel – A character denoting the specific patch panel

Port – The port number on the patch panel

7.0   INFRASTRUCTURE TESTING

Proper cable plant testing, certification, and documentation are imperative for the successful operation of existing information systems, as well as the future planning and maintenance of the cable plant expansions.

7.1   Cable Plant Testing

Twisted pair testing and certification will be performed with a cable analyzer to obtain the following information:

* Cable Length	* Connectivity
* Cable Attenuation	* Category 5 Compliance
* NEXT (Near End Cross Talk)	* Ambient Noise Levels

Testing will be performed at 100 MHz ranges.

All information derived from the testing procedures will be included as part of an overall documentation.

7.2   Fiber Optic Cable Plant Testing

It will be the responsibility of cable installer (company or contractor) to assure that the quality and transmission integrity remains intact throughout the installation, from delivery of the fiber to the project site, until the fiber is tested in its completed stage.

To provide this assurance, as well as useful comparison documentation, the installer will certify the fiber optic cable in three separate stages.

<u>Pre-Installation Certification</u> – The initial check will test each fiber strand upon delivery to the project site and match the test results to the manufacture specifications sheets provided on the reels. This will be performed with an O.T.D.R. (Optical Time Domain Reflectometer) on the bare fibers on the reel.

This information will provide verification of the cable lengths and show that the integrity of the cable has not been compromised during shipping.

<u>Post- Installation</u> - The second fiber test procedure is performed after the installation and prior to termination of the fiber strands. This test will reveal damage to the fibers (if any) and provide accurate total lengths of each segment.

<u>Post-Termination</u> - The final certification will be performed after the fiber has been terminated and installed into the fiber panels, and the cable plant has been dressed for aesthetics and protection. This final certification will ensure that each connector mating does not exceed the tolerances prescribed by industry standard, and that no additional damage to the fiber segments has occurred during the dressout.

Actual OTDR printouts representing each of the test procedures at both industry accepted windows will be generated and retained.

7.3   Documentation

The LAN Administrator shall maintain a comprehensive cable plant documentation package for each LAN under their purview. The documentation package shall, at a minimum, contain the following information:

- Detailed "as-built" drawings and schematics of the cable plant

- Category 5 test results for each copper cable

- Test results for each fiber optic cable

- A table detailing the cable drop location/port number scheme.

[This page intentionally left blank]

Document ID **ITAD107**	Title **COMPUTER AND INTERNET USAGE POLICY**	Print Date **mm/dd/yyyy**
Revision **0.0**	Prepared By **Preparer's Name / Title**	Date Prepared **mm/dd/yyyy**
Effective Date **mm/dd/yyyy**	Reviewed By **Reviewer's Name / Title**	Date Reviewed **mm/dd/yyyy**
	Approved By **Final Approver's Name / Title**	Date Approved **mm/dd/yyyy**

Policy: All employees using the Company Information Technology network shall adhere to strict guidelines concerning appropriate use of network resources.

Purpose: To delineate policies and procedures for accessing the Company Information Technology network and/or accessing the Internet through the Company Information Technology network.

Scope: This policy applies to all employees with access to Internet and related services through the Company network infrastructure. Internet Related services include all services provided with the TCP/IP protocol, including but not limited to Electronic Mail (email), File Transfer Protocol (FTP), and World Wide Web (WWW) access.

Responsibilities:

All Employees are responsible for knowing and adhering to this usage policy.

The Information Technology Security Manager[1] is responsible for enforcement of this policy.

Definitions: Internet – The international computer network of networks that connect government, academic and business institutions; the Internet (capitalized) refers specifically to the DARPA Internet and the TCP/IP protocols it uses.

Intranet – A private network contained within an enterprise; a network within one organization, using Web technologies to share information internally.

Procedure:

1.0   ACCEPTABLE USE - COMPUTERS AND INTERNET

- Access to the Internet is specifically limited to activities in direct support of official Company business.

- In addition to access in support of specific work related duties, the Company Internet connection may be used for educational and research purposes.

---

[1] Also "IT Security Manager", "Information Security Manager", "InfoSec Manager"

- If any user has a question of what constitutes acceptable use he/she should check with their supervisor for additional guidance. Management or supervisory employees shall consult with the Information Services Manager for clarification of these guidelines.

2.0 INAPPROPRIATE USE - COMPUTERS AND INTERNET

- Internet access shall not be for any illegal or unlawful purpose. Examples of this are the transmission of violent, threatening, defrauding, pornographic, obscene, or otherwise illegal or unlawful materials

- Use of Company email or other messaging services shall be used for the conduct of Company business only. These services shall not be used to harass, intimidate or otherwise annoy another person.

- The Internet shall not be accessed for private, recreational, or any non-company-related activity.

- The Company's intranet or Internet connections shall not be used for commercial or political purposes.

- Employees shall not use Company network for personal gain such as selling access of a Company user login ID. Internet access through the Company network shall not be for or by performing unauthorized work for profit.

- Users shall not attempt to circumvent or subvert security measures on either the Company's network resources or any other system connected to or accessible through the Internet.

- Company employees shall not use Internet access for interception of network traffic for any purpose other than engaging in authorized network administration.

- Company users shall not make or use illegal copies of copyrighted material, store such material on Company equipment, or transmit such material over the Company network.

3.0 INTERNET AND EMAIL ETIQUETTE

- Company employees shall ensure all communication through Company email or messaging services is conducted in a professional manner. The use of suggestive, vulgar, or obscene language is prohibited.

- Company users shall not reveal private or personal information through email or messaging services without clear and specific written approval from management.

- Users should ensure that email messages are sent to only those users with a specific need to know. The transmission of email to large groups, use of email distribution lists, or sending messages with large file attachments (larger than 0.5 Mb) should be avoided.

- Email privacy cannot be guaranteed. For security reasons, messages transmitted through the Company email system or network infrastructure are the property of the Company and are, therefore, subject to inspection.

4.0 COMPUTER AND INTERNET USAGE - SECURITY

- Company users who identify or perceive an actual or suspected security problem shall immediately contact the Information Technology Security Manager, in accordance with procedure ITSD108 – IT INCIDENT HANDLING.

- Network users shall not reveal their account passwords to others or allow any other person, employee or not, to use their accounts. Similarly, users shall not use other employees' accounts.

- Any and all use of Information Technology assets is subject to monitoring by Information Technology Security.

- Access to Company network resources shall be revoked for any user identified as a security risk or who has a demonstrated history of security problems.

5.0 COMPUTER AND INTERNET USAGE - PENALTIES

Any user violating these policies or applicable local, state, or federal laws while using the Company network shall be subject to loss of network privileges and any other disciplinary actions deemed appropriate, possibly including termination and criminal / civil prosecution.

6.0 COMPUTER AND INTERNET USAGE - CONCLUSION

All terms and conditions as stated in this document are applicable to all users of the Company network and the Internet. These reflect an agreement of all parties and should be governed and interpreted in accordance with the laws of the country, state, municipality, etc., in which the Company is located.

7.0 USER COMPLIANCE WITH USAGE POLICY

The user signifies his or her understanding of the aforementioned policies and agrees to abide by them. The user also signifies understanding that violating these policies is, at the least, unethical and may even be a criminal offense, punishable by revocation of access privileges, disciplinary action (which may include termination), and/or court action that could result in a fine, imprisonment, or both.

Once the user signs form ITAD107-1, they shall deliver the signed original to Human Resources and retain or be given a copy for their personal records.

Forms:

- ITAD107-1 COMPANY COMPUTER AND INTERNET USAGE POLICY

References:

A. ISO 27002:2013, INFORMATION TECHNOLOGY - SECURITY TECHNIQUES - CODE OF PRACTICE FOR INFORMATION SECURITY MANAGEMENT

Clause 8.5.1(c) of ISO 27002 states that "(i)f necessary, special controls should be established to safeguard the confidentiality and integrity of data passing over public networks (i.e., the Internet) and to protect the connected systems...special controls may also be required to maintain the availability of the network services and computers connected."

ISO 27002 and its companion standards, ISO 27001 and ISO 27005, provide a comprehensive set of controls comprising best practices in the field of information security. The standard treats information as an asset which has value to an organization and, therefore, needs to be suitably protected. Information security protects information from a wide range of threats to ensure business continuity, minimize business damage, and maximize return on investments and opportunities.

NOTE: ISO 27002 was formerly known as "ISO 17799" and before that, BS 7799-2. For more information, see http://www.iso.org/iso/iso_catalogue/catalogue_tc/catalogue_detail.htm?csnumber=50297.

Additional Resources:

A. None.

Revision History:

Revision	Date	Description of Changes	Requested By
0	mm/dd/yyyy	Initial Release	

ITAD107-1 COMPANY COMPUTER AND INTERNET USAGE POLICY

Revision _____

Date _____

1.0   ACCEPTABLE USE - COMPUTERS AND INTERNET

- Access to the Internet is specifically limited to activities in direct support of official Company business.

- In addition to access in support of specific work related duties, the Company Internet connection may be used for educational and research purposes.

- If any user has a question of what constitutes acceptable use he/she should check with their supervisor for additional guidance. Management or supervisory employees shall consult with the Information Services Manager for clarification of these guidelines.

2.0   INAPPROPRIATE USE - COMPUTERS AND INTERNET

- Internet access shall not be for any illegal or unlawful purpose. Examples of this are the transmission of violent, threatening, defrauding, pornographic, obscene, or otherwise illegal or unlawful materials

- Use of Company email or other messaging services shall be used for the conduct of Company business only. These services shall not be used to harass, intimidate or otherwise annoy another person.

- The Internet shall not be accessed for private, recreational, or any non-company-related activity.

- The Company's intranet or Internet connections shall not be used for commercial or political purposes.

- Employees shall not use Company network for personal gain such as selling access of a Company user login ID. Internet access through the Company network shall not be for or by performing unauthorized work for profit.

- Users shall not attempt to circumvent or subvert security measures on either the Company's network resources or any other system connected to or accessible through the Internet.

- Company employees shall not use Internet access for interception of network traffic for any purpose other than engaging in authorized network administration.

- Company users shall not make or use illegal copies of copyrighted material, store such material on Company equipment, or transmit such material over the Company network.

3.0 INTERNET AND EMAIL ETIQUETTE

- Company employees shall ensure all communication through Company email or messaging services is conducted in a professional manner. The use of suggestive, vulgar, or obscene language is prohibited.

- Company users shall not reveal private or personal information through email or messaging services without clear and specific written approval from management.

- Users should ensure that email messages are sent to only those users with a specific need to know. The transmission of email to large groups, use of email distribution lists, or sending messages with large file attachments (attachments larger than 0.5 Mb) should be avoided.

- Email privacy cannot be guaranteed. For security reasons, messages transmitted through the Company email system or network infrastructure are the property of the Company and are, therefore, subject to inspection.

4.0 COMPUTER AND INTERNET USAGE - SECURITY

- Company users who identify or perceive an actual or suspected security problem shall immediately contact the Information Technology Security Manager, in accordance with procedure ITSD108, IT INCIDENT HANDLING.

- Network users shall not reveal their account passwords to others or allow any other person, employee or not, to use their accounts. Similarly, users shall not use other employees' accounts.

- Any and all use of Information Technology assets is subject to monitoring by Information Technology Security.

- Access to Company network resources shall be revoked for any user identified as a security risk or who has a demonstrated history of security problems.

5.0 COMPUTER AND INTERNET USAGE - PENALTIES

Any user violating these policies or applicable local, state, or federal laws while using the company network shall be subject to loss of network privileges and any other disciplinary actions deemed appropriate, possibly including termination and criminal and/or civil prosecution.

6.0 COMPUTER AND INTERNET USAGE - CONCLUSION

All terms and conditions as stated in this document are applicable to all users of the Company network and the Internet. These reflect an agreement of all parties and should be governed and interpreted in accordance with the laws of <State>.

7.0   USER COMPLIANCE

I understand and will abide by the Company computer, network, and Internet use policies. I further understand that any violation of this policy is considered unethical and may constitute a criminal offense. Should I commit any violation, my access privileges may be revoked and disciplinary action and/or appropriate legal actions may be taken.

User Signature _____ Date _____

[This page intentionally left blank]

Document ID **ITAD108**	Title **EMAIL POLICY**	Print Date **mm/dd/yyyy**
Revision **0.0**	Prepared By **Preparer's Name / Title**	Date Prepared **mm/dd/yyyy**
Effective Date **mm/dd/yyyy**	Reviewed By **Reviewer's Name / Title**	Date Reviewed **mm/dd/yyyy**
	Approved By **Final Approver's Name / Title**	Date Approved **mm/dd/yyyy**

Policy: The use of electronic mail (or email) shall be limited to support of the Company's business needs.

Purpose: To delineate specific standards regarding the use of email within the Company Information Technology network.

Scope: This policy applies to all Company personnel and computer systems.

Responsibilities:

All Employees are responsible for knowing, understanding, and adhering to the Company's email policy.

The Human Resources Manager is responsible for communicating the email policy to all new Employees and retaining employee policy acknowledgements.

Department Managers are responsible for communicating revisions to the email policy to employees in their respective departments.

Information Technology Managers are responsible for developing email policy and reviewing the policy (and any changes) with the Policy Committee.

The Information Technology Security Manager is responsible for monitoring email use and enforcing the Company email policy.

The Email Policy Committee is responsible for review and final approval of the Company email policy and any revisions.

Definitions: Email Policy Committee – A group comprised of Top Management, the Information Technology Security Manager, and Information Technology Managers and led by Information Technology Managers. The purpose of the Email Policy Committee is to develop, revise (as needed), and approve the Company's email policy.

Top Management – A group comprised of the Company's chief executive and chief financial officers, at a minimum.

Procedure:

1.0 EMAIL POLICY DEVELOPMENT

1.1 Information Technology Managers shall develop the Company email policy, which may be based on common business standards and practices and on legal/regulatory requirements (see Reference B).

1.2 Information Technology Managers shall present the policy to the Email Policy Committee for review.

1.3 The Email Policy Committee shall review the email policy, revise as needed, and signify its approval.

2.0 EMAIL POLICY IMPLEMENTATION

2.1 Upon approval of the email policy by the policy committee, Information Technology Managers shall communicate the policy to all department managers. Department managers shall, in turn, communicate the policy to all employees in their departments.

- The Human Resources Manager shall be responsible for communicating the Company email policy to all new employees.

- All employees shall receive a copy of ITAD108-1 COMPANY EMAIL POLICY ACKNOWLEDGEMENT. Upon reviewing the document, each employee shall sign and date their copy of the acknowledgement and return it to Human Resources. Employees should keep a copy of this document for themselves.

2.2 Email records shall be managed in accordance with ITAD102 IT RECORDS MANAGEMENT.

2.3 The Information Technology Security Manager shall be responsible for monitoring Company email and enforcing the email policy.

3.0 EMAIL POLICY REVIEW

3.1 At regular intervals (annually, at a minimum), Information Technology Managers shall review the Company's email policy, to see if it continues to meet Company requirements.

3.2 If the email policy does not conform to Company requirements, Information Technology Managers shall convene the policy committee for the purpose of implementing improvements to the policy.

4.0 EMAIL POLICY CHANGES

4.1 The Email Policy Committee shall periodically review the Company email policy, to verify that it continues to meet Company requirements.

4.2 Where the policy does not meet requirements, the Policy Committee shall revise the policy as needed and communicate the revised policy to all employees.

4.3   Within one month of such changes to the email policy, the Information Technology Security Manager shall verify that they are being implemented and that they are having the intended effect.

Forms:

- ITAD108-1 COMPANY EMAIL POLICY ACKNOWLEDGEMENT

References:

A. ISO 9001 QUALITY MANAGEMENT SYSTEMS-REQUIREMENTS, CLAUSE 4.2.4 (CONTROL OF RECORDS)

Clause 4.2.4 of this Standard states that "(r)ecords shall be established and maintained to provide evidence of conformity to requirements and of the effective operation of the quality management system. Records shall remain legible, readily identifiable, and retrievable. A documented procedure shall be established to define the controls needed for the identification, storage, protection, retrieval, retention time, and disposition of records."

B. SARBANES-OXLEY ACT OF 2002

The Sarbanes-Oxley Act ("SOX") passed by the U.S. Congress in 2002 is designed to prevent manipulation, loss, and/or destruction of publicly-held companies' records. According to a number of high-profile SOX-related cases, email is a company record and is subject to inspection and retention guidelines like any other Company document. Therefore, an organization has to have – and follow – an email policy to be in compliance with SOX.

Additional Resources:

A. ITAD103 IT DOCUMENT MANAGEMENT

Revision History:

Revision	Date	Description of Changes	Requested By
0	mm/dd/yyyy	Initial Release	

[This page intentionally left blank]

ITAD108-1 COMPANY EMAIL POLICY ACKNOWLEDGEMENT

Revision _____

Date _____

1.0   EMAIL AND THE COMPANY

All portions of the Company information infrastructure, including the information being transported by this infrastructure, are the property of the Company. This includes all email transmitted or received through the Company information infrastructure.

Since email is the property of the Company, all email accounts and the email stored by these accounts are subject to inspection at any time. Email is a powerful tool that can greatly enhance communication. The use of email within the following guidelines by Employees is encouraged.

2.0   GENERAL GUIDELINES

Employees shall follow the following general guidelines concerning the use of this company resource:

- Email is not private. Messages transmitted through the Company email system or network infrastructure are the property of the Company and are, therefore, subject to inspection at any time. Use of the Company email system automatically imply consent to search.

- Employees shall be required to retain emails related to essential, or mission-critical, projects. Emails that do not pertain to mission-critical projects or issues should be deleted when they are no longer needed.

- Because attachments to emails are a common method of attacking computers and systems and because attachments occasionally use a lot of bandwidth, sending a file as an email attachment or opening an email attachment is strongly discouraged.

- Use of Company email or messaging services shall be used for the conduct of Company business only. Company email shall not be used for private, recreational, or any other non-Company-related activity.

- Company email shall not be used for commercial or partisan political purposes.

- Employees shall ensure all communication through Company email or messaging services is conducted in a professional manner. The use of vulgar, obscene, lewd, or suggestive language is prohibited.

- Company users shall not reveal private or personal information by email without specific approval from management.

- Users should ensure that email messages are sent to only those users with a specific need to know. The transmission of email to large groups should be avoided.

- Company email shall not be used for any illegal or unlawful purposes. Examples of this are transmission of violent, threatening, defrauding, pornographic, obscene, or otherwise illegal or unlawful material.

- Company email services shall not be used to harass, intimidate, or otherwise annoy another person.

- The Company shall not be held liable for damages related to inappropriate use of email by Employees or their families.

- FAILURE TO FOLLOW ANY PART OF THIS POLICY WILL RESULT IN DISCIPLINARY ACTION, UP TO AND INCLUDING TERMINATION.

3.0   EMPLOYEE ACKNOWLEDGEMENT

I have reviewed the Company's email policy. By signing and dating this form, I attest to my understanding and acceptance of this policy. I understand that if I am found in violation of this policy, I may be subject to Company disciplinary action, up to and including termination, as well as civil and/or criminal prosecution.

Signature: _____ Date: _____

Print name: _____

Document ID	Title	Print Date
ITAD109	**IT OUTSOURCING**	**mm/dd/yyyy**
Revision	Prepared By	Date Prepared
0.0	**Preparer's Name / Title**	**mm/dd/yyyy**
Effective Date	Reviewed By	Date Reviewed
mm/dd/yyyy	**Reviewer's Name / Title**	**mm/dd/yyyy**
	Approved By	Date Approved
	Final Approver's Name / Title	**mm/dd/yyyy**

Policy: To provide Information Technology services that satisfy Company requirements while controlling costs, maintaining flexibility, and providing special expertise as needed.

Purpose: To provide guidance with respect to managing outsourcing of Information Technology functions. To ensure that outsourcing affords the best overall solution to an Information Technology problem, satisfying customer requirements while controlling costs and conforming to the Company's strategic goals and objectives.

Scope: This procedure may apply to any Information Technology function or process.

Responsibilities:

Information Technology Managers are responsible for managing the outsourcing proposal process, administering outsourcing contracts, overseeing outsourced projects and reporting to Top Management on their status, maintaining relationships with outsourcers, and evaluating outsourced services.

Financial Management is responsible for conducting the parts of the Due Diligence Investigation pertaining to financial matters.

Top Management is responsible for final approval of outsourcing contracts. Top Management should consist of the Company's chief executive officer and chief financial officer, at a minimum.

Definitions: Outsourcer – An outsourcing vendor; a business entity providing necessary services to the Company, allowing the Company to lower operating costs and gain flexibility while gaining special expertise on an as-needed basis.

Outsourcing – Seeking services (resources) outside the Company, typically to reduce costs, gain flexibility, and benefit from an outsourcer's expertise with respect to a given function or process.

Service Level Agreement (SLA) – A binding contract, formally specifying or quantifying a customer's expectations with regard to solutions and tolerances; a collection of service level requirements, negotiated and mutually agreed upon by the service provider and the consumer.

Procedure:

1.0   IDENTIFYING A CANDIDATE FUNCTION FOR OUTSOURCING

1.1   The Company may elect to outsource Information Technology functions in response to (or in anticipation of) changing business conditions or requirements, including – but not limited to – the following:

- Need to control costs;

- Improving service to the Company's customer base;

- Temporarily requiring access to skilled experts that do not currently exist within the Company;

- Concentrating Company resources on core services; and/or

- The function's relationship (relevance) to the Company's Strategic Plan.

1.2   In the case of a first-time outsourcer, the outsourced function should present a minimal risk of failure to the Company if it does not meet requirements or the outsourcer fails to live up to any of the Service Level Agreements in the contract.

1.3   Information Technology Managers shall periodically meet with Top Management (at least annually) to review the Company's Information Technology Outsourcing agreements and ensure that they support ITAD101-1 – INFORMATION TECHNOLOGY PLAN.

1.4   Responsibility for maintaining effective internal controls over financial reporting in conjunction with outsourced activities rests with the Company's chief financial officer, regardless of the Company's level of control over those outsourced activities. (See Reference A).

2.0   SELECTING AN IT OUTSOURCER

2.1   Information Technology Managers shall identify and select outsourcers in accordance with procedure ITAM103 – IT VENDOR SELECTION.

3.0   OUTSOURCER BILLINGS

3.1   Consider negotiating a "money-back" guarantee with the right to audit any bill for up to six months. Request that all fees that are proven to be unnecessary or excessive be returned.

3.2   All outsourcing arrangements contracted by the Company shall require itemized billings to include the following information:

- Start and end times and dates of each service transaction;

- Detailed description of services provided or work performed; and

- Distinct itemization for each individual performing a service.

3.3   Examine all internal discussions or conferences and note exactly who is working on the case and why. Ask for a justification for all individuals working on the project.

3.4   Consider alternatives such as contingent fees, fixed fees, and monthly retainers. All fees are negotiable.

4.0   ARBITRATION

4.1   Whenever practical, the Company should utilize arbitration to resolve disputes. Arbitration can significantly reduce the amount of time and legal fees to resolve a dispute. The major features of arbitration are:

- A written agreement to resolve disputes by the use of impartial arbitration. Such a provision can be inserted into a contract for the resolution of possible future disputes, or can be an agreement to submit to arbitration of an existing dispute.

- Under the rules of arbitration, the procedure is relatively simple and informal. Strict rules of evidence do not apply; there is no motion practice or formal discovery; no requirements for transcripts of the proceedings or for written opinions of the arbitrators. The rules are flexible and can be varied by mutual agreement of the parties.

- Impartial and knowledgeable neutrals serve as arbitrators. Arbitrators are selected for specific cases because of their knowledge of the subject matter. Based on that experience, arbitrators can render an award grounded on thoughtful and thorough analysis.

- Final and binding awards which are enforceable in a court. Court intervention and review is limited by applicable state or federal arbitration laws, and award enforcement is facilitated by these same laws.

4.2   The following standard clause should be inserted, whenever practical, into contracts, agreements, etc., to provide for the arbitration of possible future disputes:

> "Any controversy or claim arising out of or relating to this contract, or the breach thereof, shall be settled by arbitration in accordance with the Commercial [or applicable] Rules of the American Arbitration Association and judgment upon the award rendered by the arbitrator may be entered in any court having jurisdiction thereof."

Arbitration of existing disputes may be accomplished by mutual agreement of parties, using the following (or a similar) clause:

> "We, the undersigned parties, hereby agree to submit to arbitration under the Commercial [or applicable] Rules of the American Arbitration Association the following controversy.

> [Describe Briefly]

> We further agree that we will faithfully observe this agreement and the rules and that we will abide by and perform any award rendered by the arbitrator(s) and that a judgment of the court having jurisdiction may be entered upon the award."

5.0   OUTSOURCER RELATIONSHIP MANAGEMENT

5.1   The Company-outsourcer relationship shall be managed so as to meet the Company's needs and requirements, conform to Company budget requirements, and promote the Company's goals and objectives. This shall be done by Information Technology Managers or an appointed representative, whose responsibilities shall include:

- Developing and maintaining mutual understanding and trust;

- Communicating openly, clearly, and frequently;

- Monitoring and measuring project progress clearly and consistently; and

- Addressing issues promptly.

5.2   Information Technology Managers or its representative shall maintain an ITAD109-2 – IT OUTSOURCER RECORD on every Information Technology outsourcer and every outsourcer record shall be kept in an Information Technology Outsourcer file.

- Outsourcers shall be evaluated on an ongoing basis, at regular intervals, by Information Technology Managers. Outsourcers shall be evaluated on the basis of performance requirements (measured against Service Level Agreements) and conformance to Company standards and policies.

- Any outsourcer found not in compliance shall be handled in accordance with ITAM103 – IT VENDOR SELECTION.

Forms:

- ITAD109-1 IT OUTSOURCER DUE DILIGENCE CHECKLIST
- ITAD109-2 IT OUTSOURCER RECORD

References:

A. SARBANES-OXLEY ACT OF 2002

According to Sarbanes-Oxley (SOX), enacted by U.S. Congress in 2002, a **publicly-held** Company's responsibility for control of records does not stop "at the front door." Any activity performed by an outsourcer for the Company's benefit, as well as any result of that activity, is considered under the Company's control, regardless of where the activity takes place.

Additional Resources:

- Kaplan & Norton, "The Balanced Scorecard – Translating Strategy Into Action", HBS Press (1996).

Revision History:

Revision	Date	Description of Changes	Requested By
0	mm/dd/yyyy	Initial Release	

[This page intentionally left blank]

ITAD109-1 IT OUTSOURCER DUE DILIGENCE CHECKLIST

A. Company Information

1. Legal name of business.

2. Trade name or "Doing Business As" (DBA) name.

3. Type of business (sole proprietorship; partnership; corporation, subsidiary, or division, or nonprofit organization).

4. Complete address (street, city, state/province, zip code/postal code) and telephone number(s). NOTE: A post office box is <u>not</u> an acceptable address.

5. Years in business (credit risks increase for businesses in existence for less than five years).

6. Primary bank and name of commercial loan officer. Since money can be moved around easily, a reference does not mean much if an account has had significant balances for less than six months. A year is much better. If an applicant switched primary banks within the past year, find out why.

7. Trade References. Five references are better than the standard three. References will be contacted but should be expected to be favorable as people seldom give out "bad" references. Also, friends or relatives may be references.

B. Material Contracts & Agreements

1. List of banks or other lenders with whom outsourcer has a financial relationship (briefly describe relationship with lender - line of credit, etc.).

2. Credit agreements, debt instruments, security agreements, financial/performance guarantees, liens, leases or other agreements evidencing outstanding loans the outsourcer is or was a party to within the past 2-3 years.

3. All material correspondence between the outsourcer and lenders during the last three years, including compliance reports submitted by the outsourcer or its accountants.

4. List of major clients and locations.

5. Any other material contracts.

C. Litigation

1. Copies of <u>any</u> pleadings/correspondence for pending or prior lawsuits involving the outsourcer or its founders.

2. Summaries of disputes with suppliers, competitors, or customers.

3. Correspondence with the outsourcer's auditor or accountant regarding threatened or pending litigation, assessment, or claims.

4. A description of all contingent liabilities.

5. Decrees, orders, or judgments of courts or governmental agencies.

6. Settlement documentation.

D. Outsourcer Employees & Related Parties

1. A management organization chart and bios on top management.

2. Summary of any labor disputes.

3. Correspondence, memoranda, or notes concerning pending or threatened labor stoppages.

4. List of negotiations with any group seeking to become the bargaining unit for any employees.

5. All employment and consulting agreements, loan agreements, and documents relating to other transactions with officers, directors, key employees, and related parties.

6. Schedule of compensation paid to officers, directors, and key employees for the most recent fiscal year, showing salary, bonuses, and non-cash compensation (use of company vehicles, property, etc.) separately.

7. Summary of management incentives or other bonus plans not included in #6, above.

8. Summary of company-paid employee benefits.

9. Copies of pension, profit sharing, deferred compensation, and retirement plans.

10. Confidentiality agreements with all employees.

11. Descriptions of all transactions with related parties occurring during the last 3 years, as well as proposed transactions, and all related agreements.

E. Financial Information

1. Audited financial statements from the last 3 fiscal years.
2. Quarterly income statements for the last 2 fiscal years and the current year, to date.
3. Financial / operating budgets or projections.
4. Business plan and related documents.
5. A description of each change in accounting methods (or principles) during the last 3 fiscal years.
6. Documents relating to material write-downs or write-offs other than in the ordinary course.
7. Revenue, gross margin, and average selling price by product or service.
8. Management letters or special reports by auditors and outsourcer responses for the last 3 fiscal years.
9. Aging schedules for accounts receivable for the last 2 years.
10. Breakdown of general & administrative expenses for the last 2 years.
11. Copies of any valuations of the outsourcer's stock.

ITAD109-2 – IT OUTSOURCER RECORD

Outsourcer ID	
Outsourcer Name	
Outsourcer Main Address:	
Street	
City	
State	
Postal Code	
Country	
Outsourcer Contact Name	
Contact Phone	
Product Name	
Product/Service Description	
Contract Number	
Information Technology Project ID	
Project Description	
Project Start Date – Proposed	
Project Start Date – Actual	
Project End Date – Proposed	
Project End Date – Actual	
Project Revision Number	
Project Manager Employee ID	
Project Manager Name	
Outsourcer Rating For This Project (1=Lowest to 10=Highest)	

Comments (re, performance, adherence to Company policy, client satisfaction levels, etc.):

[This page intentionally left blank]

Document ID **ITAD110**	Title **IT DEPARTMENT SATISFACTION**	Print Date **mm/dd/yyyy**
Revision **0.0**	Prepared By **Preparer's Name / Title**	Date Prepared **mm/dd/yyyy**
Effective Date **mm/dd/yyyy**	Reviewed By **Reviewer's Name / Title**	Date Reviewed **mm/dd/yyyy**
	Approved By **Final Approver's Name / Title**	Date Approved **mm/dd/yyyy**

Policy: The Company shall continually strive to improve internal users' satisfaction with the Information Technology department.

Purpose: To improve service, enhance user satisfaction with Information Technology products and services in general, and increase the user community's performance and productivity by supplying products and services that add value to the Company.

Scope: This procedure applies to all Company Information Technology employees and Information Technology contractors or outsourcers.

Responsibilities:

The Quality Assurance Manager is responsible for reviewing reports on user satisfaction (from Information Technology Management and the Tech Support Manager) and recommending actions to improve user satisfaction.

The Tech Support Manager is responsible for maintaining a Tech Support Log, reporting on user satisfaction in the Log, and taking corrective actions related to user satisfaction.

Information Technology Department Managers are responsible for reviewing user satisfaction summaries and taking corrective actions in response to low user satisfaction.

Definitions: Information Technology Asset – Any computer hardware, software, Information Technology-based Company information, as well as related documentation, licenses, contracts or other agreements, etc. In the context of this document, "asset" is synonymous with "Information Technology asset."

Internal User – An employee or contractor using Company Information Technology assets in the course of performing a job (task) for the Company. In the context of this document, "user" is synonymous with "internal user."

Random Sampling – Technique whereby a group of subjects (a *sample*) is selected for study from a larger group (a *population*) entirely by chance. Each member of the population has a known, but possibly non-equal, chance of being included in the sample. By using random sampling, the likelihood of *sampling bias* is reduced.

Statistically Significant – A finding (the observed difference between the means of two random samples, for example) is described as statistically significant when it can be demonstrated that the probability of obtaining such a difference by chance only is relatively low.

Procedure:

1.0   DEPARTMENT SATISFACTION - GENERAL

The Tech Support Manager shall contact users at several points in the post-service process. These contacts are used to determine user satisfaction with Information Technology services and products. Information gathered will be used to make improvements in Information Technology operations, quality control, programming, product (application) design, etc.

2.0   DEPARTMENT SATISFACTION - POST-SERVICE FOLLOW-UP

2.1   The Tech Support Manager shall be responsible for contacting new users five to ten business days after an Information Technology asset has been serviced. An ITAD110-1 POST-SERVICE SATISFACTION REPORT should have the user's order information before making contact.

- Contact may be made by phone, e-mail, NetMeeting, or other avenues.

2.2   The contact should be made by Tech Support staff other than the person who performed the installation or other service. This contact should consist of an introduction of the Tech Support representative and the purpose of the contact. ITAD110-1 POST-SERVICE SATISFACTION REPORT provides a script for the person contacting.

The Tech Support representative should feel free to speak in a conversational style, substituting words or phrases in ITAD110-1 with those the representative feels the user will be more comfortable with. The length and format of the contact should be determined by the user and the representative should always respond appropriately, according to the needs of the person being contacted.

2.3   If any product was missing or not working properly or if the user is dissatisfied for any reason, the Tech Support representative should note the incident and take the necessary action to resolve the issue.

2.4   During the contact, the Tech Support representative shall verify the name of the individual or department that is using the product.

2.5   Upon completing the contact, the representative should ensure the completeness of ITAD110-1 POST-SERVICE SATISFACTION REPORT. If the representative encounters any unusual or informative items, requests, or comments by the user, this report should be copied to any interested parties (e.g., Sales, Engineering, Quality Control). The report should be forwarded to the Quality Assurance Manager for review and possible action.

3.0   DEPARTMENT SATISFACTION - USER SURVEY

3.1   On a monthly basis, the Tech Support Manager shall generate a statistically valid random sample of its clients (internal users). ITAD110-2 USER

SATISFACTION SURVEY should be prepared and addressed to each of the clients in the sample. The user(s) should have had sufficient time to use the equipment, experience any problems, and determine their degree of satisfaction with the product/service.

3.2   When a survey is returned, it is to be routed to the Quality Assurance Manager for analysis and inclusion in a summary report. The survey may be maintained by the QA Manager in a master chronological file for comparison with previous and subsequent user satisfaction data.

3.3   The Tech Support Manager is responsible for taking any corrective action or addressing user concerns. The Tech Support Manager shall contact the user and resolve the situation as quickly as possible and to the satisfaction of the user.

3.4   A copy of the User Satisfaction Survey Summary Report, prepared by the Quality Assurance Manager, shall be forwarded to all Information Technology Department managers for their review and possible corrective action.

4.0   DEPARTMENT SATISFACTION - USER SATISFACTION REVIEW

4.1   The QA Manager shall periodically (every six months, at a minimum) review User Satisfaction Survey Summary Reports to determine if the Information Technology Department is making progress with regard to user satisfaction levels. (If this review occurs every six months, the last six Satisfaction Reports shall be reviewed.)

4.2   The Tech Support Manager shall periodically review ITTS102-1 TECH SUPPORT LOG (monthly, at a minimum) for user satisfaction (dissatisfaction) remarks. Remarks should be measured, if possible, for trends and comparisons with historical records and industry standards. The Tech Support Manager shall summarize its findings and report them to the Quality Assurance Manager.

4.3   The QA Manager shall use information contained in the reports mentioned earlier (ITAD110-1, ITAD110-2, and ITTS102-1) to determine any change in user satisfaction levels and recommend possible actions to improve user satisfaction. The QA Manager shall report its findings to Information Technology Management and Top Management for their review.

- If user satisfaction levels are not improving or are declining, Top Management shall meet with management of the affected Information Technology departments and the QA Manager to recommend and schedule corrective actions.

Forms:

- ITAD110-1 IT POST-SERVICE SATISFACTION REPORT
- ITAD110-2 USER SATISFACTION SURVEY

References:

A. ISO 9001 QUALITY MANAGEMENT SYSTEMS- REQUIREMENTS, CLAUSE 8.2.1 (CUSTOMER SATISFACTION)

Clause 8.2.1 states, in part, "As one of the measurements of the performance of the quality management system, the organization shall monitor information relating to customer perception as to whether the organization has met customer requirements."

The intent of the satisfaction clause applies to internal users of information technologies as well as to external customers.

Additional Resources:

A. None.

Revision History:

Revision	Date	Description of Changes	Requested By
0	mm/dd/yyyy	Initial Release	

ITAD110-1 IT POST-SERVICE SATISFACTION REPORT

Person Contacting:_____   Date:_____

Major Products Installed:_____

Date Shipped:_____

User Name:_____   Telephone:_____

Contacted: ❐ Yes, Spoke with:_____

                    ❐ No, Left message with:_____

Telephone Conversation

Opening Message:

"Hi, I'm _____ with_____

we serviced your_____

on _____/_____/_____ and I'm following up to see if everything is OK since the service call."

"Have you been using (item) since the service call?"

_____

If so, "Is everything working properly?"_____

_____

If not, "Do you need assistance?"_____

_____

Are you satisfied with (item), overall?_____

_____

Initial User Feelings
❐ Very Happy
❐ Satisfied
❐ Unhappy
❐ Very Unhappy

	Completely	Mostly	No or Needs Improvement
1. Was Tech Support courteous, knowledgeable, and helpful?	❐	❐	❐
2. Were you satisfied with the ease of setup and/or the adequacy of instructions provided?	❐	❐	❐
3. How well does the product meet your needs?	❐	❐	❐
4. Overall, are you satisfied with the product?	❐	❐	❐
5. Would you feel comfortable recommending our services to your colleagues?	❐	❐	❐
6. Have you used our telephone or online support service?	❐ Yes	❐ No	
7. If yes, was the Tech Support representative friendly, knowledgeable and helpful?	❐	❐	❐
8. If yes, were your questions or problems resolved?	❐	❐	❐

Comments or Follow-up action:_____

_____

_____

_____

_____

_____

Copy To:

ITAD110-2 USER SATISFACTION SURVEY

Thank you for taking the time to provide feedback regarding the services provided by the Information Technology department. Your feedback is important to the continual improvement of Information Technology. Use the following quality and skill descriptions in your evaluation:

AREA	QUALITIES AND SKILLS EVALUATED
Service Orientation	Is courteous, congenial; responds in a timely manner; easily establishes rapport with users; is efficient, professional, and enthusiastic.
Results Orientation	Maintains focus; is persistent; shows strong commitment; is organized; has a 'can-do' attitude; takes initiative; shows pride in work; achieves goals; takes responsibility; is dependable.
Expertise	Demonstrates technical knowledge; has effective oral and written skills; is a good listener; is perceptive; maintains objectivity; is thorough, analytical, and decisive; shows insight.

Please use the following quality rating scale

Excellent:	Service significantly exceeded expectations
Very Good:	Service exceeded expectations
Good:	Service met expectations
Fair:	Service did not meet expectations
Poor:	Service significantly below expectations

(Note: If you rated a service Fair or Poor, please provide additional comments.)

1. USER ORIENTATION

Complete the following table by rating (excellent/very good/good/fair/poor) each of the services against the three attributes.

Service	Service Orientation	Results Orientation	Expertise
Business Applications: - Financial, H/R, Sales, Marketing, E-mail, Web Applications, etc.			
Desktop Support: - PC Hardware / Software, UNIX			
Network Support: - LAN/WAN, Phones/Voice mail, Web Access			
Technical Support: - Mainframe, UNIX, Win Servers, Web Servers, other servers			

2. GENERAL COMMENTS

Please provide your general comments in the following areas:

- Service Orientation:

- Results Orientation:

- Expertise:

What things do you feel the Information Technology department does well? What could we do *better*? What works and what does not work? (*Please* – be specific.)

3. CURRENT USAGE

This section helps the Information Technology department gain a better understanding of the service usage and support patterns of our customers, so please answer the following question.

How would you describe your reliance on information technology to perform your job? (Check only one.)

☐ Everything I do depends on information technology.

☐ Most of what I do depends on information technology.

☐ About half of what I do depends on information technology.

☐ Not much of what I do depends on information technology.

☐ Little, if any, of what I do depends on information technology.

Please indicate the most frequent contact you have with the Information Technology department in each of the following areas:

Contact Type	Daily	Weekly	Monthly	Quarterly	Annually
Reporting a service problem					
Requesting a new application project					
Requesting an application enhancement					
Adding a new user					
Requesting new network access					
Requesting service access					

4. FUTURE REQUIREMENTS

In your opinion, what specific areas should the Information Technology department focus on during the next year?
(Please be specific.)

5. OPTIONAL INFORMATION

Please provide the following information so that we can follow up with you:

Name: _____

E-mail address: _____

Department: _____

[This page intentionally left blank]

IT Policies and Procedures

Section 410

IT Asset Management

Section 410

IT Asset Management

410 ITAM – IT Asset Management

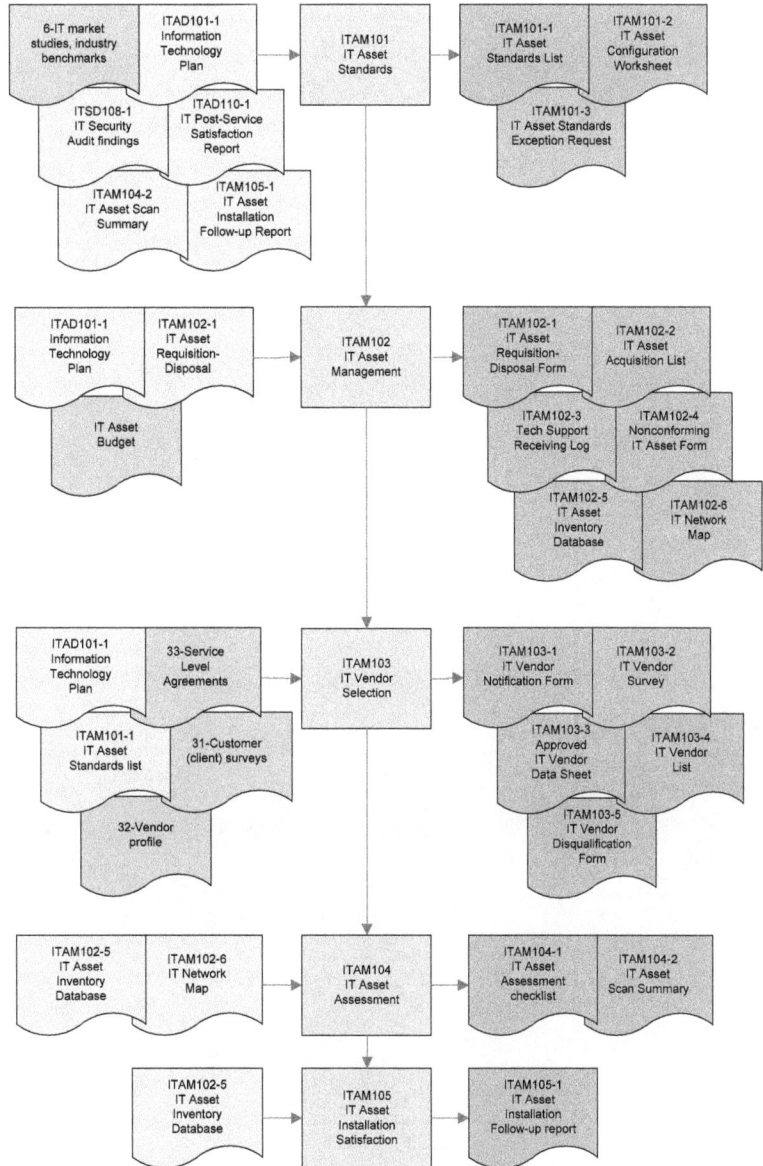

[This page intentionally left blank]

Document ID **ITAM101**	Title **IT ASSET STANDARDS**	Print Date **mm/dd/yyyy**
Revision **0.0**	Prepared By **Preparer's Name / Title**	Date Prepared **mm/dd/yyyy**
Effective Date **mm/dd/yyyy**	Reviewed By **Reviewer's Name / Title**	Date Reviewed **mm/dd/yyyy**
	Approved By **Final Approver's Name / Title**	Date Approved **mm/dd/yyyy**

Policy: The Company shall develop a set of IT asset standards to minimize the complexity and the cost of building and managing Information Technology systems.

Purpose: To specify and delineate minimum standards for Information Technology assets under the Company's control.

Scope: This standard shall apply to all company-controlled Information Technology assets.

Responsibilities:

Information Technology Managers are responsible for reviewing Information Technology asset standards.

The Information Technology Asset Manager is responsible for developing the Company's Information Technology asset standards, for reviewing such standards from time to time with Information Technology Managers, and for communicating these standards in an effective and timely manner to the Tech Support Manager.

The Tech Support Manager is responsible for implementing the Company's Information Technology asset standards.

The Human Resources Manager is responsible for communicating special employee requirements to the Information Technology Asset Manager.

Definitions: Information Technology Asset – Any computer hardware, software, Information Technology-based Company information, related documentation, licenses, contracts or other agreements, etc.

Procedure:

1.0   IT ASSET STANDARDS DEVELOPMENT

1.1   The Information Technology Asset Manager shall conduct a periodic assessment of Information Technology asset standards (at least once a year), in particular noting exceptions granted to determine if the exceptions should become part of the standards.

1.2   The Information Technology Asset Manager shall develop Company Information Technology asset standards, based on information that may be contained in:

- Information Technology market studies, industry benchmarking studies, human factor studies (ergonomics, etc.), and best practices (see References B and C);
- ITAD101-1 INFORMATION TECHNOLOGY PLAN;
- ITAM104-2 IT ASSET SCAN SUMMARY;
- ITAM105-1 IT ASSET INSTALLATION FOLLOW-UP REPORT;
- ITAD110-1 IT POST-SERVICE SATISFACTION REPORT;
- ITSD108-1 IT SECURITY AUDIT FINDINGS; and
- Asset standards exceptions (like ITAM 101-3) granted on the basis of special requirements.

1.3   Exceptions to the Information Technology asset standards may be required:

- To accommodate employee requirements (see Reference A for an example), in which case the Company's HR Department should provide the Information Technology Asset Manager with the information necessary to appropriately address those needs in the standards (see Reference D); or

- To further the Company's mission.

Exceptions may be requested using ITAM101-3 IT ASSET STANDARDS EXCEPTION REQUEST. Upon approval of Information Technology Managers, ITAM101-3 shall be submitted with ITAM102-1 IT ASSET REQUISITION/DISPOSAL FORM, in accordance with ITAM102 IT ASSET MANAGEMENT.

1.4   The Information Technology Asset Manager shall document proposed Information Technology asset standards on ITAM101-1 IT ASSET STANDARDS LIST.

1.5   The Information Technology Asset Manager shall review ITAM101-1 with Information Technology Managers. Information Technology Managers and the Information Technology Asset Manager shall indicate their acceptance of Information Technology asset standards by signing ITAM101-1.

1.6   The Information Technology Asset Manager shall keep the original ITAM101-1 and distribute copies to Information Technology Managers and to Tech Support, recalling any previous versions of ITAM101-1.

2.0   IT ASSET STANDARDS IMPLEMENTATION

2.1   Tech Support shall install, configure, repair, and replace Information Technology assets. In the course of performing such services, Tech Support shall ensure that the Company's Information Technology Asset Standards are met.

2.2   When configuring Information Technology assets for Company use, Tech Support shall record (or update) each Information Technology asset's configuration on ITAM101-2 IT ASSET CONFIGURATION WORKSHEET.

3.0   IT ASSET STANDARDS ASSESSMENT

3.1   The Information Technology Asset Manager shall conduct a periodic Information Technology asset scan, in accordance with ITAM104 IT ASSET ASSESSMENT, to determine if all assets on the Company Information Technology network conform to standards.

3.2   If an Information Technology asset is found not conforming to asset standards and an exception has not been granted, an investigation of the situation shall be conducted in accordance with procedure ITSD108 IT INCIDENT HANDLING.

Forms:

- ITAM101-1 IT ASSET STANDARDS LIST

- ITAM101-2 ASSET CONFIGURATION WORKSHEET

- ITAM101-3 IT ASSET STANDARDS EXCEPTION REQUEST

References:

A. AMERICANS WITH DISABILITIES ACT (ADA)

Title I of the ADA prohibits private employers, state/local governments, employment agencies, and labor unions from discriminating against qualified individuals with disabilities in their job application procedures, hiring, firing, advancement, compensation, job training, and other terms, conditions and privileges of employment.

A qualified employee or applicant with a disability is an individual who, with or without reasonable accommodation, can perform the essential functions of the job in question. Reasonable accommodation may include, but may not be limited to:

- Making existing facilities used by employees readily accessible to and usable by persons with disabilities;

- Job restructuring, modifying work schedules, reassignment to a vacant position; and

- Acquiring or modifying equipment or devices, adjusting modifying examinations, training materials, or policies, and providing qualified readers or interpreters.

An employer is required to make an accommodation to the known disability of a qualified applicant or employee if it would not impose an undue hardship on the operation of the employer's business. Undue hardship is defined as an action requiring significant difficulty or expense when considered in light of factors such as an employer's size, financial resources, and the nature and structure of its operation. An employer is not required to lower quality or production standards to make an accommodation nor is an employer obligated to provide personal use items, such as glasses or hearing aids.

B. INSTITUTE OF ELECTRICAL AND ELECTRONIC ENGINEERS COMPUTER SOCIETY (IEEECS) STANDARDS

The IEEE is a non-profit, technical professional association of more than 360,000 individual members in approximately 175 countries. The IEEE is a leading authority in technical areas ranging from computer engineering, biomedical technology, and telecommunications to electric power, aerospace, and consumer electronics. The IEEE Computer Society (IEEECS) is the branch of IEEE responsible for standards related to computers and computing.

The IEEE has nearly 900 active standards with 700 under development. The standards are too numerous and detailed to mention here; to learn about relevant IEEE or IEEECS standards, visit http://www.ieee.org/index.html or http://www.computer.org/portal/web/guest/home.

C. INTERNATIONAL ASSOCIATION OF INFORMATION TECHNOLOGY ASSET MANAGERS (IAITAM)

Starting in 1998, a group of software and hardware asset managers began meeting to discuss the need for a centralized organization devoted to expanding and codifying information and knowledge within the Information Technology Hardware & Software Asset Management fields. The research led to some specific needs for the newly created profession of Information Technology Asset Manager, including advanced training programs, easy access to vendor neutral answers and product reviews, and accurately monitoring Information Technology assets to prevent over-investment and underutilization.

For information on IAITAM, go to http://www.iaitam.org/.

D. BIZMANUALZ DOCUMENT #ABR41M – HUMAN RESOURCES POLICIES AND PROCEDURES MANUAL

This document provides guidance to companies looking to codify their Human Resources policies and procedures.

Additional Resources:

A. ISO/IEC 19770-1:2012, Information Technology - Software Asset Management - Part 1: Processes and Tiered Assessment of Conformance.

Revision History:

Revision	Date	Description of Changes	Requested By
0	mm/dd/yyyy	Initial Release	

[This page intentionally left blank]

ITAM101-1 IT ASSET STANDARDS LIST

1.0   WORKSTATIONS

Hardware

CPU	3rd Generation Intel® Core™ i5-3330 processor (up to 3.20 GHz)
Bus type	PCI
RAM	8 Gb DDR3 SDRAM @ 1600 MHz
Hard Drive (HDD)	1 TB 3.5" SATA, 7200 RPM
Removable device I/O ports	Four (4) USB 3.0 ports
Optical Drive	DVD+/-RW Tray Load Drive, 16X, SATA
Mouse	USB Optical Mouse MS111
Keyboard	KB113 USB Wired Entry Keyboard - US
Video card	Intel® HD Integrated Graphics
Monitor	20-inch HD Monitor with LED
Network Interface Card (NIC)	Integrated 10/100/1000 Ethernet

Software

Operating system	Microsoft (MS) Windows 7, 64-bit Pro
Office automation	
Word processing	MS Word 2013
Spreadsheet	MS Excel 2013
Presentation graphics	MS PowerPoint 2013
Personal database	MS Access 2013
Internet browser	Internet Explorer (IE) 9
E-mail	MS Outlook
Personal scheduling	MS Outlook
Anti-virus software	McAfee® Security Center

2.0   SERVERS

Hardware

CPU	Intel® Xeon® X3480, 3.06 GHz, 8M Cache, Turbo, HT
RAM	16GB Memory (4x4GB), 1333MHz, Dual Ranked RDIMM
HD Controller	PERC H700, Internal RAID Controller NVDIMM 512MB Cache
HD Configuration	RAID 10 - PERC6i/H200/H700 (SAS/SATA Cntrlr), 4 Hard Drives
Hard Drives (x4)	1TB 7.2K RPM SATA 3Gbps 3.5in Cabled
Power Supply (x2)	Dual, Redundant, 400W
Optical Drive	DVD-ROM
Removable device I/O ports	Two (2) USB 2.0 ports
Mouse	USB Optical Mouse MS111
Keyboard	KB113 USB Wired Entry Keyboard - US

Video card	Intel® HD Integrated Graphics
Monitor	20-inch HD Monitor with LED
Network Interface Card (x2)	Dual Intel PRO 1000PT 1GbE Single Port NIC, PCIe-1

<u>Software</u>

Operating system	Windows Server® 2012, Essentials Ed
Internet browser	Internet Explorer (IE) 9

3.0   NETWORK INFRASTRUCTURE

OSI Layer 2 data link protocol	10/100/1000 Ethernet (IEEE 802.3 Ethernet standard)
OSI Layer 3 network protocol	TCP/IP
UPS	Standby UPS for individual PC's; continuous UPS for servers
Firewalls	"Personal" firewall software installed on individual PC's, server(s), laptops, etc.
Routers	Cable/DSL Router; WAN - 1 x RJ-45 10/100/1000; LAN - 4 x RJ-45 10/100/1000; max transfer rate up to 1000 Mbps;
Switches	24 10/100/1000 Base-T auto-sensing Gigabit Ethernet switching ports; auto-negotiation for speed, duplex mode and flow control; auto MDI/MDIX; port mirroring (many-to-one); broadcast storm control; IEEE 802.1p tagging; port-based prioritization; four priority queues per port

4.0   PRINTERS

Type	Monochrome
Resolution	1200 x 1200 dpi
Connectors	USB, 10/100/1000 Ethernet
Compatibility	PS 3, PCL6, PCL 5e
PostScript support	PostScript level 3
Print capacity	500 sheets, 8.5 x 14"
Installed memory	64 Mb RAM, expandable to 256 Mb
Power	Energy Star compliant
Duplex print-capable	yes

5.0   PORTABLE IT ASSETS

Laptop Hardware

Laptops

CPU	3rd gen Intel® Core™ i5-3210M Processor (2.5GHz, 3M cache)
RAM	4GB DDR3 SDRAM at 1600MHz
Hard Drive (HD)	500GB 7200rpm
Removable device I/O ports	Four (4) USB 3.0 ports
Optical Drive	8X DVD+/-RW
Mouse	3-Button Wireless Mouse
Display	15.6" HD (1366x768) Anti-Glare WLED-backlit
AC Adapter	60-Watt with 6.5 ft Power Cord
Network Interface Card (NIC)	10/100/1000 Ethernet
Wireless	802.11g/n Single Band Wi-Fi
Battery	6-cell (60WH) Primary Lithium Ion Battery
Physical security	Secure storage locker; cable lock device
Carrying Case	17" Messenger

Laptop Software

Operating system	Microsoft (MS) Windows 7, 64-bit Pro
Office automation	
Word processing	MS Word 2013
Spreadsheet	MS Excel 2013
Presentation graphics	MS PowerPoint 2013
Personal database	MS Access 2013
Internet browser	Internet Explorer (IE) 9
E-mail	MS Outlook
Personal scheduling	MS Outlook
Anti-virus software	McAfee® Security Center

Others

_____

Approved:

IT Management: _____ Date: _____

IT Asset Mgr.: _____ Date: _____

[This page intentionally left blank]

ITAM101-2 IT ASSET CONFIGURATION WORKSHEET

A. System Identification

Component	Manufacturer	Model	Property Number	Serial Number
CPU				
Monitor				
Printer				
Other:				

B. Hardware Components

Component	Manufacturer	Model
CPU Unit		
Monitor		
Floppy Drive		
Mouse/Pointing Device		
Hard Drive 1		
Hard Drive 2		
Hard Drive 3		
CD-ROM Drive		
Tape Drive		
Video Card		
Sound Card		
Network Interface Card		
Disk Controller		
Modem		
Other		

C. Hardware Configuration

    1. CPU Type: _____   Clock Speed: _____

    2. System BIOS

        Manufacturer: _____   PNP: ❑ YES ❑ NO

        BIOS Date: _____   BIOS Revision: _____

    3. Memory

        RAM Type: _____   RAM Capacity: _____

4   Resource Assignments

Component	IRQ	Base I/O	Base Memory	DMA
COM1				
COM2				
MOUSE				
LPT1				
Disk Controller				
Video Controller				
Sound Card				
Network Interface				
Modem				
Other				

D. Software Configuration

Software	Vendor	Version/Revision	License ID
Operating System			
Word Processing			
Spreadsheet			
Presentation Graphics			
Database			
Electronic Mail			
Internet Browser			
Other			
Other			

E. Network Configuration

Resource	Primary IP Address	Secondary IP Address	Comments
DNS			
Gateway			
NIC/Machine IP		N/A	
WINS or Net Bios			

ITAM101-3 IT ASSET STANDARDS EXCEPTION REQUEST

Req # _____   Date: _____

Asset Description: _____

_____

_____

_____

_____

User ID: _____   Department: _____

Dept. Mgr.: _____

Reason for exception: _____

_____

_____

_____

_____

_____

_____

Approved:

HR Manager: _____ Date: _____

IT Management: _____ Date: _____

[This page intentionally left blank]

Document ID	Title	Print Date
ITAM102	**IT ASSET MANAGEMENT**	**mm/dd/yyyy**
Revision	Prepared By	Date Prepared
0.0	**Preparer's Name/Title**	**mm/dd/yyyy**
Effective Date	Reviewed By	Date Reviewed
mm/dd/yyyy	**Reviewer's Name/Title**	**mm/dd/yyyy**
	Approved By	Date Approved
	Final Approver's Name/Title	**mm/dd/yyyy**

Policy: Information Technology assets shall be managed in a manner consistent with the Company's business and technology requirements.

Purpose: Describe the actions taken for proper acquisition, installation, handling, tracking, and disposal of Information Technology assets to meet defined requirements for:

- Ensuring adherence to Company and industry standards;

- Ensuring consistency throughout the enterprise; and

- Conforming to or complying with customer, legal, and regulatory requirements.

Scope: This procedure applies to all Company Information Technology assets.

Responsibilities:

The Information Technology Asset Manager is responsible for tracking Information Technology assets through their acquisition, distribution, use, and disposal and for ensuring that all Information Technology assets conform to standards, in accordance with ITAM101 IT ASSET STANDARDS.

Information Technology Managers are responsible for approving acquisition or disposal of Information Technology assets and for reviewing this procedure with the Information Technology Asset Manager on a regular basis, to ensure its continued conformance to ITAD101-1 INFORMATION TECHNOLOGY PLAN.

The Tech Support Manager is responsible for logging, testing, accepting, installing, maintaining, and preparing for disposal of Information Technology assets. Tech Support is responsible for ordering and receiving software via the extranet. Tech Support is also responsible for updating the Information Technology Asset Inventory when any changes to Information Technology assets have been made.

The Purchasing Manager is responsible for ordering physical Information Technology assets.

Shipping/Receiving is responsible for receiving, distribution (to Tech Support), and final disposal of most physical Information Technology assets.

Financial Management is responsible for approving acquisition or disposal of Information Technology assets when their value is $5000 or greater. Finance is also responsible for ensuring corresponding updates to the appropriate financial documents.

Definitions: Information Technology Asset – Any computer hardware, software, Information Technology-based Company information, related documentation, licenses, contracts or other agreements, etc. In this context, "asset" and "Information Technology asset" are understood to be the same.

Nonconforming Information Technology asset - Any Information Technology asset that does not conform to Company requirements; Information Technology assets that don't work at all or don't work as expected are "nonconforming."

Procedure:

1.0   IT ASSET PLANNING

1.1   Certain activities/events may trigger acquisition and/or disposition of Information Technology assets, such as:

- Scheduled asset acquisitions, conducted in accordance with ITAD101-1 INFORMATION TECHNOLOGY PLAN; or

- Receiving an ITAM102-1 IT ASSET REQUISITION/ DISPOSAL FORM due to an unplanned event.

1.2   The Information Technology Asset Manager shall review each ITAM102-1 IT ASSET REQUISITION/ DISPOSAL FORM and from those prepare an ITAM102-2 IT ASSET ACQUISITION LIST, which shall be submitted to Information Technology Managers and Finance for budget approval.

2.0   IT ASSET ACQUISITION

2.1   Company personnel shall use ITAM102-1 IT ASSET REQUISITION/ DISPOSAL FORM to request new or replacement Information Technology assets. This form shall be approved by the appropriate department manager before being submitted to the Information Technology Asset Manager.

- The same form shall be used for assets being relocated within the Company or disposed of due to obsolescence.

2.2   The Information Technology Asset Manager should review the ITAM102-1 for correctness and completeness and shall ensure the requested assets are within the Information Technology asset budget.

- If there are issues preventing acquisition (i.e., budget constraints), the Asset Manager shall return ITAM102-1 to the requestor, with explanation. The Asset Manager shall keep a copy of the returned ITAM102-1.

2.3   If the value of the Information Technology asset being requested is less than $500, the Information Technology Asset Manager shall order the requested asset(s) without requiring further approval.

- If the value of the asset is at least $500 and less than $5000, ITAM102-1 shall require the approval of Information Technology Managers.

- If the value of the asset is $5000 or greater, ITAM102-1 shall require the approval of Finance.

2.4   If a purchase or lease agreement exists for the kind of asset being requested, that asset shall be ordered from the existing vendor, pursuant to the terms of the agreement.

- If such an agreement does not exist, the Information Technology Asset Manager may recommend entering into one, in accordance with procedure ITAM103 IT VENDOR SELECTION.

3.0   IT ASSET INSPECTION, ACCEPTANCE, & DISTRIBUTION

3.1   Physical assets shall be received by Shipping/Receiving and forwarded to Tech Support.

- Tech Support may receive non-physical assets, such as application software, directly from the vendor.

3.2   Tech Support shall log Information Technology assets in the "Received" section of ITAM102-3 TECH SUPPORT RECEIVING LOG as they are received.

3.3   Tech Support shall inspect and test assets for performance and capability prior to acceptance, if possible.

- When a nonconforming asset is identified, Tech Support shall report the nonconformity on ITAM102-4 NONCONFORMING IT ASSET FORM and forward a copy of the form to the Information Technology Asset Manager and to the Purchasing Manager.

- The Purchasing Manager shall contact the vendor for replacement of the nonconforming asset and dispose of the nonconforming asset in accordance with any purchase/lease agreement in place.

3.4   Tech Support shall indicate acceptance of Information Technology assets by:

- Signing and dating the TECH SUPPORT RECEIVING LOG on the "Accepted" line (Tech Support shall retain Receiving Logs on Information Technology assets for as long as those assets are in service);

- Placing a control tag, or asset ID tag, on larger assets (PC's, monitors, keyboards, etc.); and

- Forwarding the packing slip or invoice to the Purchasing Manager for payment.

3.5   Only Tech Support shall distribute and install Information Technology assets.

- In the case of assets designed for use by **individuals**, installation shall be scheduled primarily for the user's convenience.

- In the case of assets used by **multiple individuals** (network hardware/software, operating systems, common application software, etc.):

  a) Installations shall be scheduled at a date and time that will affect the least number of users;

  b) Ample advance notice shall be given to all affected users; and

  c) Tech Support shall mitigate risk by ensuring backup and/or redundancy of the affected systems/applications, in accordance with procedure ITSD102 IT SECURITY PLANNING.

- On installing hardware, Tech Support shall give each item a unique network identifier, in accordance with procedure ITAD104 IT DEVICE NAMING CONVENTIONS.

3.6   Tech Support shall update ITAM102-5 IT ASSET INVENTORY DATABASE and ITAM102-6 IT NETWORK MAP after installing assets.

4.0   IT ASSET DISPOSAL

4.1   Personnel shall request disposal of Information Technology assets by completing the bottom half of ITAM102-1 IT ASSET REQUISITION/DISPOSAL FORM and forwarding the form to the Information Technology Asset Manager.

4.2   The Information Technology Asset Manager shall direct Tech Support to dispose of Information Technology assets in accordance with procedure ITSD102 IT SECURITY AND DISASTER PLANNING.

4.3   All Information Technology assets shall be disposed of only through approved waste handlers or recyclers, in accordance with procedure ITAM103 IT VENDOR SELECTION, and in a manner that complies with applicable Federal, state, and local statutes and guidelines (See References "A" and "B"). Possible destinations for disposable Information Technology assets include:

- Reuse or reclamation by Tech Support;
- Returning to the vendor for failure of the asset to perform as expected or to conform to business requirements;
- Returning leased assets to the vendor at the time of lease expiration;
- Disposal of obsolete software versions in a manner approved by the vendor;
- Sending the purchased asset to a sanitary landfill; and
- Sending the purchased asset to an approved recycler.

4.4   Upon disposal of said assets, Asset Management shall update ITAM102-5 – IT ASSET INVENTORY DATABASE and ITAM102-6 IT NETWORK MAP.

5.0   IT ASSET VERIFICATION

5.1   The Information Technology Asset Manager shall conduct a periodic assessment of Information Technology assets to verify their status (i.e., in use/not in use), in accordance with procedure ITAM104 IT ASSET ASSESSMENT.

5.2   If an asset is not being used or is not being used as specified (for example, ITAM102-5 IT ASSET INVENTORY DATABASE and ITAM102-6 IT NETWORK MAP are not in agreement), the Information Technology Asset Manager shall take corrective action, which may include:

- Taking the asset out of service;

- Initiating an incident report, in accordance with ITSD109 IT INCIDENT HANDLING; and

- Updating ITAM102-5 and ITAM102-6.

Forms:

- ITAM102-1 IT ASSET REQUISITION/DISPOSAL FORM

- ITAM102-2 IT ASSET ACQUISITION LIST

- ITAM102-3 TECH SUPPORT RECEIVING LOG

- ITAM102-4 NONCONFORMING IT ASSET FORM

- ITAM102-5 IT ASSET INVENTORY DATABASE

- ITAM102-6 IT NETWORK MAP

References:

A. RESOURCE CONSERVATION & RECOVERY ACT (RCRA)

The RCRA, which amended the Solid Waste Disposal Act, established a regulatory structure for the management of solid and hazardous wastes. Disposal of physical Information Technology assets not only involves solid waste but often involves hazardous waste, too.

Subtitle C of the RCRA addresses *cradle-to-grave requirements for hazardous waste* and applies to any computer equipment (monitors, PC's, etc.) that contains a type and minimum (threshold) amount of hazardous material. The objective of Subtitle C is to ensure that hazardous waste is handled in a manner that protects human health and the environment.

The EPA may issue an administrative order to any person or company violating the RCRA; this order may impose a civil penalty and require compliance. Furthermore, the EPA may bring a civil action against persons failing to comply with any order issued under the Act. Visit http://www2.epa.gov/enforcement and http://www2.epa.gov/enforcement/criminal-enforcement for more detailed information on civil and criminal enforcement or visit the RCRA Online site at http://www.epa.gov/epawaste/infosources/online/index.htm.

B. CODE OF FEDERAL REGULATIONS, TITLE 40 – PROTECTION OF ENVIRONMENT, Rev July 1 2000 (40 CFR 260-299)

Title 40 of the CFR addresses enforcement of the RCRA (Reference A, above). Hazardous material is defined in Title 40 and disposal restrictions are spelled out; parts 260 through 299 pertain to generation and disposal of *hazardous* materials, sometimes found in computer equipment.

Hazardous waste generators are classified by generated amounts and requirements for each class are specified. There are requirements covering every step of the hazardous waste handling process, from generation to transport to treatment, storage, and disposal.

Enforcement of Title 40 is the responsibility of the EPA.

See http://www.gpo.gov/fdsys/pkg/CFR-2000-title40-vol1/content-detail.html for specific information.

Additional Resources:

A. "Software Asset Management", Microsoft Corp. (see http://www.microsoft.com/sam/en/ca/overview.aspx)

B. Economic Input-Output Life Cycle Assessment, Carnegie Mellon University (see http://www.eiolca.net/index.html)

C. IBM Global Asset Recovery Services (see http://www-03.ibm.com/financing/us/recovery/)

D. Carnegie-Mellon University, School of Engineering - "Green Design" web site (see http://www.cmu.edu/gdi/index.html)

Revision History:

Revision	Date	Description of Changes	Requested By
0	mm/dd/yyyy	Initial Release	

ITAM102-1 IT ASSET REQUISITION/DISPOSAL FORM

Requested by: _____   Date: _____

For department/employee: _____   Charge to: _____

Job Name: _____   Job No.: _____

Purpose / Use: _____

Standards exception granted: Y ☐ N ☐ (If "Y", form ITAM101-3 must be attached.)

ASSET REQUEST

Urgency: 1 – High   2 – Moderate   3 – Low   Date Needed: _____

Asset Description	Pchg. Dept. Use Only		
	Qty.	Unit Price	Extension

For Purchasing Department Use Only:

Asset Lease / Purchase (circle one)   Supplier Name / ID: _____

ASSET DISPOSAL

Asset ID Number	Asset Description	Location	Owner	Phone

Disposal Date: _____ Method: _____

Approved:

Dept. Manager: _____   Date: _____

IT Asset Manager: _____   Date: _____

IT Manager: _____   Date: _____

Finance Manager: _____   Date: _____

Disapproved (with explanation): _____

_____

[This page intentionally left blank]

ITAM102-2 IT ASSET ACQUISITION LIST

Asset Description	Qty.	Unit Price	Extension	Pchg-Lease Contract #

IT Asset Manager: _____   Date: _____

Requested by (date): _____

Budget Approval:

IT Manager: _____   Date: _____

Finance Manager: _____   Date: _____

[This page intentionally left blank]

ITAM102-3 TECH SUPPORT RECEIVING LOG

Received:

Asset Description	Asset Type	Serial Number	Vendor ID	Date Rec'd.

Accepted:

Name _____ Date _____

Approved:

Name _____ Date _____

[This page intentionally left blank]

ITAM102-4 NONCONFORMING IT ASSET FORM

Asset Description	Serial Number	Date Received	Vendor	Asset Class

Reasons For Rejection (detail defects):

_____

_____

_____

_____

_____

Approved:

IT Asset Manager _____   Date _____

IT Manager _____   Date _____

Finance Manager _____   Date _____

[This page intentionally left blank]

ITAM102-5 IT ASSET INVENTORY DATABASE

Asset ID	Asset Class	Asset Desc	Model Number	Serial Number	License Number	Copy _ Of _	Install Date	Expected Service Life (mos.)	Expiration Date	IP Address	Used By Dept.

[This page intentionally left blank]

ITAM102-6 IT NETWORK MAP

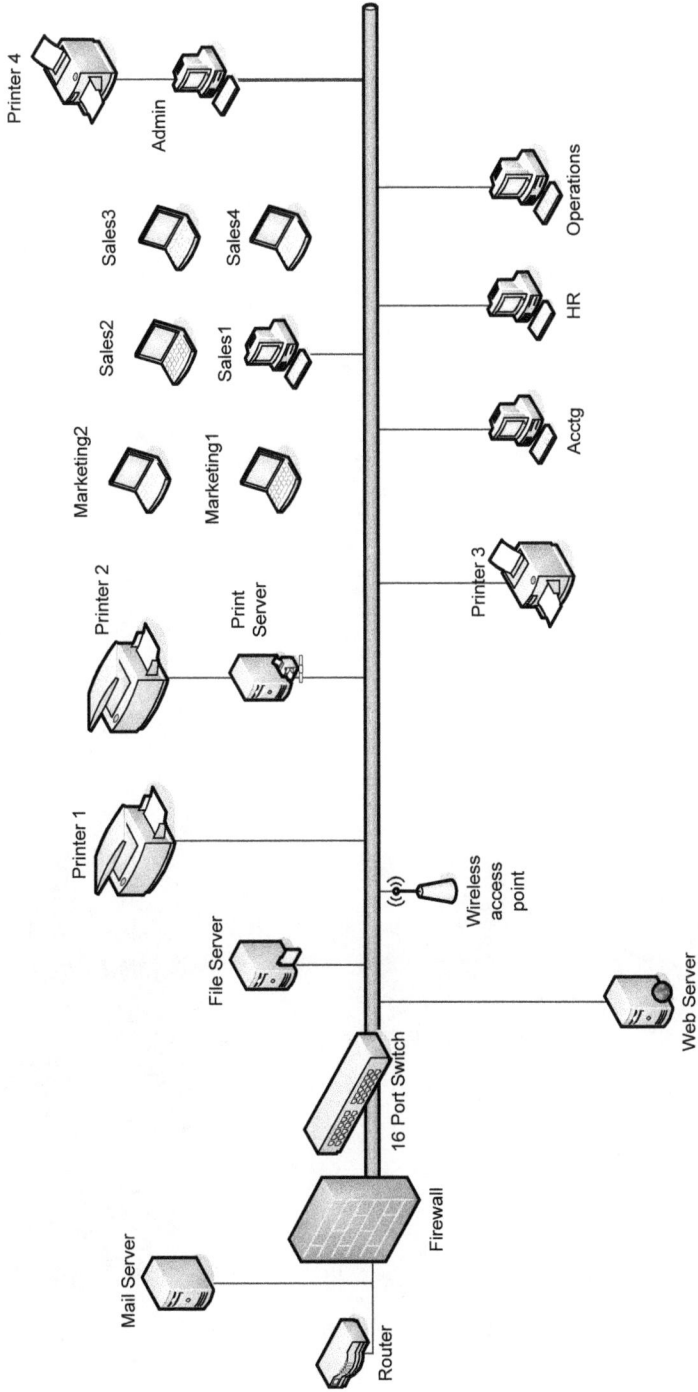

Printer 4

Admin

Sales3

Sales4

Operations

Sales2

Sales1

HR

Marketing2

Acctg

Marketing1

Printer 2

Print Server

Printer 3

Printer 1

File Server

Wireless access point

Web Server

16 Port Switch

Firewall

Mail Server

Router

[This page intentionally left blank]

Document ID **ITAM103**	Title **IT VENDOR SELECTION**	Print Date **mm/dd/yyyy**
Revision **0.0**	Prepared By **Preparer's Name / Title**	Date Prepared **mm/dd/yyyy**
Effective Date **mm/dd/yyyy**	Reviewed By **Reviewer's Name / Title**	Date Reviewed **mm/dd/yyyy**
	Approved By **Final Approver's Name / Title**	Date Approved **mm/dd/yyyy**

Policy: To ensure vendor performance capabilities are sufficient to meet Information Technology requirements.

Purpose: Provide methods for determining, documenting, and, where applicable, inspecting vendors for compliance with Company policies and purchase/lease requirements.

Scope: This procedure applies to all potential and current vendors of Information Technology products and services.

Responsibilities: The <u>Information Technology Asset Manager</u> is responsible for initial Information Technology vendor identification and collecting information regarding potential vendors. The Information Technology Asset Management is also responsible for maintaining vendor performance data for ongoing evaluations.

<u>Information Technology Managers</u> are responsible for final review and approval of new Information Technology vendors, as well as maintaining a file on current vendors.

<u>Financial Management</u> is responsible for evaluating potential vendors' financial information and for final vendor approval.

<u>Quality Management</u> is responsible for evaluating vendor quality systems, where appropriate, and for reporting vendor quality performance on a regular basis.

Definitions: <u>Request For Proposal (RFP)</u> – A document that an enterprise sends to a vendor, inviting the vendor to submit a bid for hardware, software, services, or any combination of the three. An organization will typically issue several RFPs to obtain and evaluate competing bids.

<u>Service Level Agreement (SLA)</u> – Contract between a service provider and an end user, stipulating and committing the provider to a required level of service. An SLA typically includes such features as support options, enforcement or penalty provisions for services not rendered, guaranteed system performance levels related to uptime/downtime, specific levels of customer support, what software or hardware will be provided, and product (and/or service) fees.

Procedure:

1.0   IT VENDOR EVALUATION

1.1   The Information Technology Asset Manager shall select Information Technology vendors in the following manner:

- Conduct vendor and market reviews.

- Request a full profile from the vendor, which should include:

  a. The vendor's history with firms similar to the Company in size, scope, and nature of business;

  b. The vendor's capabilities with regard to the Company's needs;

  c. Sales and marketing information; and

  d. Information on the company's financial strength.

- Obtain customer referrals – survey the vendor's current clients to determine their degree of satisfaction with the vendor and the product/service desired by the Company. If possible, visit one or more companies that have been using the vendor's product/service for a reasonable period of time. Investigate customer complaints against the vendor.

- Determine if the vendor is capable of conforming to minimum performance standards (vendor performance criteria):

  a. Ability to provide value to the Company through its product or service;

  b. Ability to meet Company requirements for quality and service;

  c. On-time delivery – 100% on-time (on-time is defined as "zero days early/ zero days late"); and

  d. Quality Rating (number of items accepted ÷ number of items received x 100). Quality Management must determine the Company's minimum acceptable quality rating and disqualify vendors that do not meet it. Exceptions to the Company's quality rating requirement may be granted (at the discretion of Quality Management) where the quantity of items received is small and the number of vendors is limited.

- For critical assets, or for asset purchases where the Company wishes to rely on the quality assurance of the vendor to reduce receiving inspection or testing requirements, an on-site vendor inspection shall be performed and approved.

  a. Quality Management will coordinate with the Information Technology Asset Manager to plan, arrange, and designate staff for vendor inspections.

  b. The Information Technology Asset Manager shall complete ITAM103-2 IT VENDOR SURVEY, noting approval/disapproval of the vendor's performance capability and quality assurance program, and submit this form to Quality Management and Information Technology Management for review.

- Check the vendor's certifications – ISO (see Reference A), Microsoft, Oracle, etc. – especially those that apply to the product or service under consideration. If all else between two vendors is equal, preference shall be given to the appropriately certified vendor.

- Conduct a security background check, to confirm the vendor's compliance with applicable legal and regulatory requirements.

- A vendor demonstration may be advisable if:

    a. The vendor is capable of demonstrating the capability/functionality of its product/service with regard to the Company's needs and concerns; and

    b. A client site visit either was not possible or did not adequately address the Company's needs and concerns.

1.2   Based on the criteria above, the Information Technology Asset Manager shall list a number of qualified vendors and submit the list to Finance for its review.

1.3   Finance shall request and evaluate financial information from vendors identified by the Information Technology Asset Manager.

- Cost is an important consideration, though the value added to the Company by the vendor's product or service over its useful life span should be the determining factor.

- Finance shall return the list of vendors to the Information Technology Asset Manager, indicating and ranking vendors that are best qualified, according to its criteria.

2.0   REQUEST FOR PROPOSAL

2.1   The Information Technology Asset Manager shall write a Request For Proposal (RFP), based on ITAD101 INFORMATION TECHNOLOGY PLAN and ITAM101 IT ASSET STANDARDS, to each qualified vendor.

- The Company's requirements, goals, and expectations shall be clearly communicated.

- The RFP shall include a request for proposed Service Level Agreements (SLA).

- The RFP shall clearly indicate a "required no later than" date, the Information Technology Asset Manager's contact information (office phone, e-mail address, etc.), and instruct the vendor to submit the proposal to the Company's Information Technology Asset Manager.

2.2   The RFP shall be submitted to Information Technology Managers for approval. The approved RFP shall then be submitted to the vendor(s).

3.0   IT VENDOR SELECTION

3.1   The Information Technology Asset Manager shall evaluate vendor proposals received by the due date, note (and attach) recommendations, and forward proposals and recommendations to Information Technology Managers and Finance.

3.2   Finance and Information Technology Managers shall evaluate vendor information and the accompanying recommendations, weigh all factors appropriately, and indicate their recommendation and approval of a vendor or vendors.

- ITAM103-1 IT VENDOR NOTIFICATION FORM shall be completed for all first time vendors. A copy of ITAM103-1 shall be sent to the vendor; the original shall be kept in a vendor file by the Information Technology Asset Manager.

3.3   The Information Technology Asset Manager shall maintain information on each vendor on a separate ITAM103-3 APPROVED IT VENDOR DATA SHEET; this shall be kept with the vendor's file.

3.4   The Information Technology Asset Manager shall maintain ITAM103-4 IT VENDOR LIST, listing vendors with which it has done business over the last five years, for reference purposes.

3.5   Information Technology Managers shall review the results of the security check and determine the level of vendor access to sensitive information. This security level shall be recorded on ITAM103-3 APPROVED IT VENDOR DATA SHEET.

4.0   IT VENDOR REVIEW

4.1   Quality Management shall periodically reevaluate Information Technology vendors (to be done at least annually), according to the Company's vendor performance criteria.

4.2   In the case of critical assets, Quality Management shall periodically request a vendor inspection, as described in Section 1.0.

4.3   If a vendor is found to be out of compliance, Quality Management shall submit a Corrective Action Request, in accordance with ITSD109 IT INCIDENT HANDLING.

- If a vendor does not respond to a Corrective Action Request or is unable to correct problems within a reasonable time frame, it may be disqualified.

  a. Quality Management shall submit a copy of ITAM103-5 IT VENDOR DISQUALIFICATION FORM to the disqualified vendor. The original shall be forwarded to the Information Technology Asset Manager, to be kept with the vendor file.

  b. The Information Technology Asset Manager shall update the disqualified vendor's entry in ITAM103-4 IT VENDOR LIST. Disqualified vendors shall be prohibited from doing business with the Company for one year from date of disqualification.

- If the vendor elects to take corrective action, Quality Management shall follow up with the vendor immediately and again within three months to verify that:

a. The corrective action has been taken; and

b. The corrective action continues to produce the desired results.

5.0 IT VENDOR FILES

5.1 A vendor file shall be prepared and maintained for each Information Technology vendor. This file shall be used for significant or ongoing purchasing or leasing. Each vendor file should include the following:

- Form ITAM103-1, IT VENDOR NOTIFICATION FORM;
- Form ITAM103-2, IT VENDOR SURVEY;
- Form ITAM103-3, APPROVED IT VENDOR DATA SHEET;
- Form ITAM103-5, IT VENDOR DISQUALIFICATION FORM, if applicable;
- Form REV103-1, CREDIT APPLICATION (see publication ABR31M, *Bizmanualz® Accounting Policies and Procedures Manual*, "Revenue Procedures");
- IRS W-9 Taxpayer Identification Certificate (PDF download available at http://www.irs.gov/pub/irs-pdf/fw9.pdf);
- Legal contracts, dealer or marketing agreements, etc.;
- Security, nondisclosure, service level, and other agreements; and
- Any other relevant correspondence or documentation.

5.2 The Company is required to file IRS Form 1099-MISC, "Miscellaneous Income", at the end of the calendar year for any *service* contractor (accountant, consultant, etc.) that is *not incorporated*.

To determine if Form 1099-MISC must be filed, refer to the IRS Form W-9, "Request for Taxpayer Identification Number Certificate," submitted by the vendor. All vendors must indicate their reporting status on Form W-9 and all vendors must submit Form W-9 before they can be engaged in business.

Forms:

- ITAM103-1 IT VENDOR NOTIFICATION FORM
- ITAM103-2 IT VENDOR SURVEY
- ITAM103-3 APPROVED IT VENDOR DATA SHEET
- ITAM103-4 IT VENDOR LIST
- ITAM103-5 IT VENDOR DISQUALIFICATION FORM

References:

A. ISO 9001:2008, "QUALITY MANAGEMENT SYSTEMS – REQUIREMENTS"

ISO 9001 describes what is needed for a company to establish and operate its own quality management system, or QMS.

Clause 6.1 of ISO 9001 states that an organization must determine and provide resources needed to implement and maintain a QMS and to enhance customer satisfaction. The organization should look for its vendors to promote quality and customer satisfaction. *Clause 6.2.2* says that an organization must determine competency requirements for its own employees; the organization should likewise require its vendors to provide qualified, competent staff.

Clause 7.5.1 says an organization must plan and execute production and service under controlled conditions. This means that the product/service has to be clearly described, there must be work instructions, workers must have suitable tools to do their job, and activities must be monitored and measured. Vendors likewise must conform to this part of the Standard.

Clause 7.5.3 says the product/service must be identified and all of its components must be traceable. The organization must also ensure that its *vendors* conform to identity and traceability requirements.

B. SARBANES-OXLEY ACT OF 2002

Sarbanes-Oxley, or SOX, requires that publicly-held organizations have proof of adequate internal controls with regard to financial information. Furthermore, if an organization contracts out (outsources) any work; it is liable for what the outsourcer does on its behalf. It is no longer enough to say that the outsourcer is bound by a contract to do the right thing, either. Companies wishing to comply with SOX will extend their own internal control structure to include their outsourcers.

Revision History:

Revision	Date	Description of Changes	Requested By
0.0	mm/dd/yyyy	Initial Release	

[This page intentionally left blank]

ITAM103-1 IT VENDOR NOTIFICATION FORM

Date:_____   **Anticipated Usage:**
                ☐ One Time Only_____
Prepared by (source):_____   ☐ Intermittent_____
                ☐ Ongoing_____

Contact Information:

Vendor Name: _____

Address: _____

Phone: (_____)_____   Fax: (_____)_____

Contact Person: _____

Products to be provided: a) _____

          b) _____

          c) _____

          d) _____

Vendor Certification:

Is vendor certified? ☐ Yes ☐ No By what bodies? _____

Has vendor applied for certification? ☐ Yes ☐ No Effective Date _____

Is certification current? ☐ Yes ☐ No Expiration date: _____

Payment Terms:_____

Estimated Annual Dollar Volume Expected with this Vendor:_____

Has vendor completed an IRS W-9, Request for Taxpayer Identification Number Certificate, and is it on file with the Company?   ☐ Yes ☐ No

Related Party Transactions:

Is vendor a relative or close friend of any employee of the Company? ☐Yes ☐ No

If yes, please describe relationship: _____

_____

Distribution: IT Asset Management (Vendor File)
       Accounts Payable

[This page intentionally left blank]

ITAM103-2 IT VENDOR SURVEY

Date:_____

Vendor Name: _____

Address: _____

_____

_____

Phone: (_____)_____   Fax: (_____)_____.

NOTICE: I (We) certify that the information contained in the attached survey form is accurate and complete as of the date indicated. Where trade secret or other proprietary information is involved, the person interviewed has initialed those responses not verified by the interviewer. All information obtained will be kept confidential. A corporate officer of the Company surveyed will review all responses made at the time of survey. This survey has been made with the permission of the Company surveyed

_____	_____	_____
Signature	Title	Location
_____	_____	_____
Signature	Title	Location

PART I - GENERAL INFORMATION

Annual Sales:	Years in Business:	Privately Owned:	Subsidiary Division:

Other Locations

_____

_____

Major Customers _____   Type of Contract _____

_____   _____

_____   _____

_____   _____

_ Not Available   _ Not Available

List Company
Management   Name   Title   Interviewed

_____   _____   _____

_____   _____   _____

_____   _____   _____

Product for which survey was performed (**Attach Labeling**):_____

_____

Total Employees_____Number of Supervisors_____Number of Production_____

Work Schedule Hours_____Number Shifts_____Days per Week_____

Are Training Programs for Personnel Utilized?   _ Yes _ No

FACILITY

Buildings on-site_____

Type:
    _ Single   _ Multistory _ Wood
    _ Brick   _ Block   _ Steel

Location In:
    _ Industrial Park _ Suburban
    _ Urban   _ Rural
    _ Equity Owned   _ Leased

Square Footage In:
    Production _____
    Administration _____
    Storage _____
    Engineering/R&D _____

List process capabilities and special production equipment essential to materials being procured:
    1)_____
    2)_____
    3)_____
    4)_____
    5)_____

Is there a document/process flow manual outlining all production steps, records, and controls from raw materials to finished product? (Required for some government contracts.)
    _ Yes   _ No

Does the Vendor have liability insurance?
    _ Yes   _ No
    Insured By_____

List operations managed by outside sources (subassembly, packaging, etc.)
    1)_____
    2)_____
    3)_____
    4)_____
    5)_____

Has the Vendor been inspected by any state or federal agency within the last two (2) years?
    _ Yes   _ No
    Name of Agencies:_____

Were recalls involved?
    _ Yes   _ No
    Comments_____
    _____

PART II - RAW MATERIALS

PURCHASING

Is Qualification Based On Written Specifications And Approval Of Vendor Sources?
    _ Yes   _ No

Are Reject/Accept Limits Shown?
    _ Yes   _ No

Is Approval Based on:
    _ Quality History _ Vendor
_ On-Site
    _ Own QC   _ Cards   _ Survey
    _ Certificate   _ Testing
    _ Other_____

Are specification changes reviewed and signed off by QC personnel?
    _ Yes   _ No

TESTING

Are written test procedures in use?
    _ Yes   _ No

Are Test Results On File?
    _ Yes   _ No

Is a Sampling Plan Used?
    _ 100% _ Mil Spec _ AQL _ Random
    _ Other_____

Do Test Results Indicate
    _ Quantity Sampled
    _ Method of Analysis
    _ Date/Signature of Analyst
    _ Sample Traceability

Is There A Retention Sample System For Raw Materials/Components?
    _ Yes   _ No

IN-PLANT CONTROL

Is Material Assigned Alphanumeric Or Identifying Mark For Each Incoming Lot?
    _ Yes   _ No

Is Material Visibly Marked As
    _ Sampled   _ Approved
    _ Rejected   _ Not Marked

Is an Inventory Log Or Record Kept?
    _ Yes   _ No

Is Storage Area Separate?
    _ Yes   _ No

Is Storage Area Segregated?
    _ Yes   _ No

Is a Stock Rotation (FIFO) System Used?

_ Yes   _ No

Is There Authorized Custodian Control?

_ Yes   _ No

Is General Housekeeping Neat And Orderly?

_ Yes   _ No

Rejected Materials Are:

Clearly Identified   _ Yes   _ No

Physically Segregated   _ Yes   _ No

PART III - PRODUCTION

MASTER PRODUCTION RECORDS

Is There A Single Controlled File Of Master Records For Each Product?

_ Yes   _ No

Are These Master Records Signed And Dated?

_ Yes   _ No

Double Signature _ Yes   _ No

Revision Dates   _ Yes   _ No

Are The Process, Assembly, Or Production Steps Fully Described:

In The Master Production Record?

_ Yes   _ No

In A Separate Document Or Record?

_ Yes   _ No

Does The Master Document Indicate:

QC Points For In-Process Production?

_ Yes   _ No

Type Of Test Or Inspection To Be Made?

_ Yes   _ No

Method Of Measurement?

_ Yes   _ No

Who Performs Test Or Inspection?

_ Yes   _ No

Level Of Accept/Reject (Limits)?

_ Yes   _ No

For Production, Processing, Subassembly, Or Packaging Done By Outside Sources, Are There:

Master Production Records?

_ Yes   _ No

QC Specifications And Methods Records?

_ Yes   _ No

Outside Sources Not Used?

_ Yes   _ No

PRODUCTION AREA

Is The Work Flow Organized?

_ Yes   _ No

Distinct Staging Area For Raw Materials Or Components Used In Production?

_ Yes   _ No

Production Or Assembly Lines Segregated?

_ Yes   _ No

Are General Housekeeping And Environmental Factors Adequate?

_ Yes   _ No

Are Written Procedures For Plant Sanitation Available?

_ Yes   _ No

PRODUCTION EQUIPMENT

Are Maintenance Or Service Records Available?

_ Yes   _ No

Are Calibration Records Kept On Periodic Basis?

_ Yes   _ No

Are There Means Of Readily Identifying Type, And Stage Of Processing Being Done, On The Equipment?

_ Yes   _ No

PRODUCTION RECORDS

Are Production Documents Collected / Filed?

_ Yes   _ No

Production Documents Kept _____(Years)

_ Complete History

_ Labeling Samples Included

_ Partial History

_ Traceability By Lot Or Serial#

PACKAGING

Are Finished Goods Packaging Operations Segregated?

_ Yes   _ No

Finished Goods Under Supervised Control?

_ Yes   _ No

Label Records Kept?

_ Yes   _ No

Pre-Label:

_ Count   _ Reconciliation

Are Finished Goods Properly Identified, Labeled, And Stored?

_ Yes   _ No

_ Prior To Release   _ After Release

REJECTED MATERIALS
Are There Written Procedures For Disposing Of Or Reworking Rejected Items?
_ Yes _ No
Are Rejected Products Held In Quarantine Pending Final Disposal?
_ Yes _ No
_ Held In Segregated Area
_ With Special Markings

RETENTION SAMPLES
Are Samples Of Finished Goods Retained?
_ Yes _ No
_ From Each Production Run
_ In A Separate Controlled Area
_ In The Same Container/Closure System In Which They Are Sold
_ In Containers Different From Unit As Sold
_ Kept For A Period Of ____ Years
_ Written Log or File

STERILE COMPONENTS (If Applicable)
Are There Procedures For Establishing And Maintaining Aseptic Conditions?
_ Yes _ No
Are There Methods For Routine Auditing Of Sterile Areas Used?
_ Yes _ No
Are There Procedures For Working In Sterile Areas?
_ Yes _ No
For Cleaning And Sterilization Of Equipment?
_ Yes _ No
For Bulk And Final Product Sterility Testing?
_ Yes _ No
Is Process Sterility For Each Run Documented In The Production Records?
_ Yes _ No
Are Sterile Processes Used?
_ Radiation   _ Steam   _ ETO
_ Filtration   _ Chemical
Other:_____
_____
_____
_____
_____

PART IV - QUALITY CONTROL / ASSURANCE

ORGANIZATION AND FUNCTION
Does The Quality Control-Inspection Group Report Directly To The Top, Independent Of Production, Marketing, Or Other Organization Groups Within The Production Company?
_ Yes _ No
Does The Quality Control-Inspection Group Have Full Authority To Withhold Shipment Or Further Production Of Rejected Items?
_ Yes _ No
Are The Quality Control Procedures:
Revised On A Periodic Basis?
_ Yes _ No
Does The Quality Control/Assurance-Inspection Group Have:
Education, Training Or Experience
_ Yes _ No
Understanding Of Their Function
_ Yes _ No

OPERATIONS
Are Stamps, Tags, Markers, Etc. Used To Verify Inspection Activity?
_ Yes _ No
Are The Markings Used Traceable To An Individual Inspector?
_ Yes _ No

PART V - CUSTOMER COMPLAINTS AND RECALL CAPABILITIES

Is There An Organized Complaint File System?
_ Yes _ No
Does Each Complaint State:
_ Nature Of Complaint
_ Response To Customer (Repair, Refund, Replace)
_ Further Corrective/Preventive Action By Vendor
Complaint Files Kept For _____ (Years)
Is There A Periodic Review Of Complaint Files For Trends?   _ Yes _ No
Is The Review File As A Written Summary?
_ Yes _ No

Is There A Group Or Individual Assigned To Handle Customer Inquiries And Follow Up On Complaints?

    _ Yes _ No

Are Product Defects Verified By Vendor Through Testing?

    _ Yes _ No]

Was Review Of Complaint Files For Survey Product Made?

    _ Yes _ No

Are Production Samples For QC Testing:

    Adequately Identified As To Source

       _ Yes _ No

    Recorded Somewhere At Time Of Sampling

       _ Yes _ No

    Entered On Filed Test Report

       _ Yes _ No

Written Sampling Plan Based On:

    _ 100% _ Mil. Spec _ AQL _ Random

    Other_____

Is The Product Used Tested Prior To Final Release?

    _ Yes _ No

Are Outside Sources Used For Production Testing?

    _ Yes _ No

    _ Under Formal Contract

    _ Used Test Protocols

    _ Written Procedures

    _ Copies In The Production File

    _ Facility Registered Or Licensed By Any Federal, State Or Professional Agency

    _ Outside Test Results Filed By Manufacturer

Is There A Formal Quality Assurance Program Involving Performance Testing Of The Product(S) After Release?

    _ Yes _ No

RECALL CAPABILITIES

Is There A Company Recall Plan?

    _ Yes _ No

    _ Shows How Decisions Are Made And By Whom

    _ How Recall Will Be Accomplished

    _ Instructions For Recovery And Accountability Of Recalled Product

Do Shipping Or Distribution Records On File Show:

    Customer/Distributor Name And Address?

       _ Yes _ No

    Date Of Shipments And Quantity Shipped?

       _ Yes _ No

    Lot Or Serial Number Of Product Shipped

       _ Yes _ No

Distribution Records Are Maintained _____ (Years)

Distribution Records Are Stored As:

    _ Computer Listing

    _ Microfilm/Microfiche

    _ Manual Card/Paper Files

PART VI - REGULATORY COMPLIANCE

Is The Plant Registered As A Device Manufacturer?

    _ Yes _ No

Are The Survey Product(s) Listed With Bureau Of Medical Devices?

    _ Yes _ No

Are All Necessary Approvals For Marketing Products Available?

    _ Yes _ No

Is There A File With Past And Current Labeling For Each Survey Product?

    _ Yes _ No

Is There A Formal Auditing Program Of The QC Operation? If So, Done By Whom

    _ Yes _ No

List of Attachments and Comments

_____

_____

_____

_____

_____

_____

[This page intentionally left blank]

ITAM103-3 APPROVED IT VENDOR DATA SHEET

1	Vendor ID	
2	Vendor Name	
3	Vendor Address	
4	Vendor Contact First Name	
5	Vendor Contact Last Name	
6	Vendor Contact Phone Number	
7	Vendor Contact Email Addr	
8	Vendor Part Number	
9	Item Description	
10	Item Serial Number	
11	Number Of Software Licenses, If Applicable	
12	Contract Status (Active / Inactive)?	
13	Contract Id	
14	Contract Start Date	
15	Contract End Date	
16	Terms Of Contract	
17	Service Level Agreement?	
18	Service Provider Id	
19	Service Provider Name	
20	Service Provider Address	
21	SP Contact First Name	
22	SP Contact Last Name	
23	SP Contact Phone Number	
24	SP Contact Email Addr	
25	Service Terms	
26	Security Clearance Level	

COMMENTS:

[This page intentionally left blank]

ITAM103-4 IT VENDOR LIST

1	Vendor ID	
2	Contract #	
3	Contract Expiration Date	
4	Asset Class	
5	Asset Description	
6	Vendor Status (Qualified / Disqualified)	
7	Status Effective Date	
8	Status Expiration Date	
9		
10		
11		
12		
13		
14		

COMMENTS:

[This page intentionally left blank]

ITAM103-5 IT VENDOR DISQUALIFICATION FORM

Date of disqualification: _____
Prepared by (source):_____

Contact Information:

Vendor Name: _____

Vendor ID: _____

Address:_____

Phone: (_____)_____   Fax: (_____)_____

Contact Person: _____

Reason for disqualification (attach supporting documentation): _____
_____
_____
_____
_____

Signed by: _____ (IT Management)

_____ (IT Asset Management)

_____ (Quality Management)

Distribution: IT Asset Management (Vendor File)
Disqualified Vendor

[This page intentionally left blank]

[This page intentionally left blank]

[This page intentionally left blank]

Document ID **ITAM104**	Title **IT ASSET ASSESSMENT**	Print Date **mm/dd/yyyy**
Revision **0.0**	Prepared By **Preparer's Name/Title**	Date Prepared **mm/dd/yyyy**
Effective Date **mm/dd/yyyy**	Reviewed By **Reviewer's Name/Title**	Date Reviewed **mm/dd/yyyy**
	Approved By **Final Approver's Name/Title**	Date Approved **mm/dd/yyyy**

Policy: The Company shall assess (evaluate) its Information Technology assets for conformance to Company requirements.

Purpose: To identify hardware and software (Information Technology assets) on the Company Information Technology network, determine if those assets are appropriate for the Company's needs, determine if these assets are properly licensed and versioned, and if they conform to Company standards.

Scope: All Information Technology assets that make up the Company's Information Technology system/network are subject to this procedure.

Responsibilities:

The Information Technology Asset Manager is responsible for supervising the Information Technology asset assessment program.

The Tech Support Manager is responsible for conducting complete, detailed, and objective Information Technology asset assessments, writing nonconformance reports, and reporting findings of Information Technology asset assessments.

Definitions: Network scan (or scan) – Scanning an Information Technology network (with specialized software) to confirm the presence or absence of computer hardware or software, check asset configurations, verify software versions, manage software licenses, track lease and warranty information, detect network vulnerabilities, etc. Commercial and open source software for conducting Information Technology asset scans is readily available; see Additional Resource A for guidance.

Information Technology Asset – Any computer hardware, software, Information Technology-based Company information, related documentation, licenses, contracts or other agreements, etc. In this context, Information Technology assets may be referred to as just "assets".

Nonconformance – A significant, material failure to conform to one or more requirements; also referred to as a "nonconformity". Moving a PC from one desk/user to another without the knowledge or permission of the Information Technology Asset Manager is one example of a nonconformance.

Procedure:

1.0   IT ASSET ASSESSMENT PLAN

1.1   Information Technology asset assessments shall be conducted at regular intervals. Assessments should be conducted annually, at a minimum. (See Reference A.)

- Information Technology asset assessments should also be conducted whenever a large turnover of assets (for example, a large number of PC leases expires in a short time frame) occurs.

1.2   Prior to an assessment, the Information Technology Asset Manager shall review ITAM104-1 IT ASSET ASSESSMENT CHECKLIST for possible modifications. This checklist shall be used by the Tech Support Manager as a guide to conducting Information Technology asset assessments.

2.0   IT ASSET SCAN

2.1   The Information Technology Asset Manager shall ensure that the Tech Support Manager has the current version of the following on hand prior to conducting a network scan:

- ITAM102-5 IT ASSET INVENTORY DATABASE;

- ITAM102-6 IT NETWORK MAP; and

- ITAM104-1 IT ASSET ASSESSMENT CHECKLIST.

2.2   the Tech Support Manager shall run a scan on the Company's Information Technology network to determine the status of all Information Technology assets on the network and compare the results with the documents listed in 2.1, looking for information such as:

- What Information Technology hardware is on the network and who are the registered "owners";

- Whether hardware is in use or not;

- What software is installed on each computer, whether it is the correct version, and whether it is a licensed copy; and/or

- Whether unapproved/unauthorized software has been installed on any PC.

2.3   If a nonconformance is found, the Tech Support Manager shall report it in accordance with procedure ITSD109 IT INCIDENT HANDLING.

3.0   DOCUMENTATION AND DISTRIBUTION

3.1   The Tech Support Manager shall consolidate and summarize asset scan results on ITAM104-2 IT ASSET SCAN SUMMARY.

3.2   The Tech Support Manager shall prepare and submit their findings – including forms ITAM104-1 and ITAM104-2 – to the Information Technology Asset Manager.

4.0   NONCONFORMANCE HANDLING

4.1   If a nonconformance is discovered in the course of an asset assessment, the Information Technology Asset Manager shall write a Corrective Action Request (CAR), in accordance with procedure ITSD109 IT INCIDENT HANDLING.

4.2   The CAR shall be submitted to the Manager of the department where the nonconformance occurred.

4.3   The Department Manager receiving the CAR shall submit a reply in accordance with procedure ITSD109 IT INCIDENT HANDLING.

4.4   If a corrective action was taken, the Information Technology Asset Manager should review the situation within three months to verify that the corrective action was effective.

5.0   IT ASSET RECORDS UPDATE

After the Information Technology asset assessment and subsequent corrective actions, The Information Technology Asset Manager shall ensure timely and accurate updates to ITAM102-5 IT ASSET INVENTORY DATABASE and ITAM102-6 IT NETWORK MAP. (See Reference B.)

Forms:

- ITAM104-1 IT ASSET ASSESSMENT CHECKLIST
- ITAM104-2 IT ASSET SCAN SUMMARY

References:

A. ISO STANDARD 27002:2013 – CODE OF PRACTICE FOR INFORMATION SECURITY MANAGEMENT, CLAUSE 8 ASSET MANAGEMENT

Clause 8 of the Standard is the Asset Management standard, which deals with asset accountability and information classification.

ISO Standard 27002:2011 and its companion standards, ISO 27001:2011 and ISO 27005:2008, provide a comprehensive set of controls comprising best practices in the field of information security.

ISO 27002 was formerly known to ISO as "17799" and may continue to be known that way in the business and Information Technology world for some time. See http://www.iso.org/iso/home/store/catalogue_ics/catalogue_detail_ics.htm

B. SARBANES-OXLEY ACT OF 2002

Sarbanes-Oxley, passed by the U.S. Congress in 2002, is designed to prevent manipulation, loss, or destruction of records within publicly-held companies doing business in the U.S. Because virtually all companies keep records electronically, Section 404 of the Act implies that "an adequate internal control structure" is Information Technology-based.

Therefore, regular scanning of the Company's Information Technology network, evidence of regular scanning, and keeping an up-to-date Information Technology asset inventory are all evidence of adequate internal controls.

Additional Resources:

A. There are many types of scans that may be conducted on a computer network – hardware scans, software scans, wireless and wired network scans, security scans, etc. System Center 2012 R2 Configuration Manager (http://www.microsoft.com/en-us/server-cloud/products/system-center/2012-r2-configuration-manager/default.aspx#fbid=Xd6tQVcmWsT) is one form of asset management software. Additional asset management software providers and their products may be found by searching the Internet.

Revision History:

Revision	Date	Description of Changes	Requested By
0	mm/dd/yyyy	Initial Release	

ITAM104-1 IT ASSET ASSESSMENT CHECKLIST

Assessment #: _____   Date: _____

Area Evaluated: _____

Dept. Mgr.: _____

Lead Assessor: _____

Assessor: _____

IT Asset Accountability   **Response and Comments**

1) Is every IT asset – hardware, software, and related documentation – accounted for?

2) Is an IT asset inventory maintained?

3) Is an IT asset classification scheme in place?

4) Does the inventory identify the owner and location of each asset?

5) Does the company have a clear set of standards for IT assets? Are the standards up to date? How often are they reviewed? Do they conform to industry standards and/or legal requirements?

6) Is the IT asset inventory reviewed regularly to see the company does not risk having obsolete IT assets in inventory?

7) Does every hardware asset conform to company standards? Are they clearly and properly identified?

8) Do all software assets conform to company standards? Are they clearly and properly identified?

9) Does the IT asset inventory thoroughly and accurately account for software versions and licenses?

10) Is there an IT network diagram? Is it accurate? Is it readily produced? When was it last reviewed? How frequently is it reviewed?

Tech Support Area   <u>**Response and Comments**</u>

1) Are workers organized and scheduled?

2) Are adequate working areas provided for tasks?

3) Are drawings and schematics organized,
   inventoried and readily accessible?

4) Are work instructions sufficient?

5) Are all items (new hardware/software, items
   being repaired, etc.) inventoried?

6) Is there any obvious disorganization?

   - Tools randomly scattered about?

   - Parts on benches disorganized?

   - Components or parts for other assemblies
     present?

7) Are work areas (benches) clean?

8) Are parts organized and stored efficiently? Are
   stores clearly marked?

9) Are staging areas organized?

Tech Support Equipment   <u>**Response and Comments**</u>

1) Are tools properly inventoried? Are records
   accurate and up-to-date?

2) Are tools properly stored when not in use?

3) Are tools in good working order?

4) Are tools requiring calibration being
   recalibrated on a regular basis? Are calibration
   records current?

Tech Support Records   <u>**Response and Comments**</u>

1) Are production records (installations, repairs,
   etc.) maintained? Are they complete and up-to-
   date? Are they readily accessible?

2) Are "work pending" and "work in process"
   records included with the above? Are they
   likewise complete and up-to-date? Are they
   also readily accessible?

User Complaints	**Response and Comments**

1) Is there a log of user complaints and concerns? Is it complete, up to date, organized, and readily accessible?

2) What is the level of detail in the log file? Are complaints/concerns classified clearly and logically?

3) Is this "complaint file" periodically reviewed for trends?

Authorization

Comments:_____

_____

_____

_____

Tech Support: _____   Date: _____

IT Asset Manager: _____   Date: _____

[This page intentionally left blank]

ITAM104-2 IT ASSET SCAN SUMMARY
(Attach results from scanning software to this sheet.)

Hardware scan results:

Software scan results:

Nonconformities (discrepancies) found:

Other comments:

Tech Support: _____ Date: _____

IT Asset Mgr.: _____ Date: _____

[This page intentionally left blank]

Document ID ITAM105	Title IT ASSET INSTALLATION SATISFACTION	Print Date mm/dd/yyyy
Revision 0.0	Prepared By Preparer's Name / Title	Date Prepared mm/dd/yyyy
Effective Date mm/dd/yyyy	Reviewed By Reviewer's Name / Title	Date Reviewed mm/dd/yyyy
	Approved By Final Approver's Name / Title	Date Approved mm/dd/yyyy

Policy: To improve internal users' satisfaction with Information Technology asset installation.

Purpose: By measuring and analyzing user satisfaction, Information Technology should be improving service and user satisfaction, thereby helping increase performance and productivity within the user community.

Scope: This procedure applies to all Company Information Technology employees and Information Technology contractors (outsourcers).

Responsibilities:

The Tech Support Manager is responsible for installing Information Technology assets and gathering satisfaction data from internal users after installations.

The Information Technology Asset Manager is responsible for analyzing user satisfaction data and presenting the analysis to Information Technology Managers.

Information Technology Managers are responsible for reviewing the user and recommending corrective and/or preventive actions.

Definitions: Information Technology Asset (IT asset) – Computer hardware, software, IT-based (i.e., electronic) Company information, related documentation, licenses, contracts or other agreements, etc. In the context of this document, "asset" is synonymous with "Information Technology asset".

Internal User – An employee or contractor using Company Information Technology assets in the course of performing a job for the Company. In the context of this document, the word "user" is synonymous with the term "internal user."

Procedure:

1.0   IT ASSET INSTALLATION SATISFACTION PLAN

1.1   Following installation of any Information Technology asset, the asset user shall be contacted for the purpose of determining the user's level of satisfaction with the installed hardware/software and with the installation process.

1.2   User satisfaction data shall be analyzed and the results of this analysis shall be used to correct and improve the asset installation process.

1.3   The process of measuring Information Technology user satisfaction shall be reevaluated on an ongoing basis, to continue to improve the process and to improve user satisfaction.

2.0   IT ASSET INSTALLATION FOLLOW-UP

2.1   Upon installing any Information Technology asset, data pertaining to the asset shall be recorded in ITAM102-5 IT ASSET INVENTORY DATABASE, in accordance with procedure ITAM102 IT ASSET MANAGEMENT.

2.2   The Tech Support Manager shall contact the asset user within five business days of installation. The user may be contacted by any of several methods (phone, e-mail, etc.).

2.3   The user shall be presented with a series of questions, covering the following topics:

- Reliability – Was the installation performed right the first time?

- Responsiveness – Was the asset installed promptly?

- Competence – Did the installer have the knowledge and skill required for the installation?

- Access – Was the Tech Support Manager accessible and approachable?

- Courtesy – Was the installer friendly, polite, considerate, and respectful of the user?

- Communication – Did the installer listen to the user? Did the installer communicate with the user in a way that the user understood?

- Credibility – Did the installer come across as trustworthy, believable, honest, and having the user's best interests at heart?

- Security – Is the user free from any sense of risk with regard to the installation?

2.4   the Tech Support Manager shall record the user's responses on ITAM105-1 – IT ASSET INSTALLATION FOLLOW-UP REPORT and forward this report to the Information Technology Asset Manager.

3.0   IT ASSET INSTALLATION SATISFACTION DATA REVIEW

3.1   The IT Asset Manager shall collect ITAM105-1 forms and add the information to an Installation Satisfaction Report file (or database).

3.2   The IT Asset Manager shall review the contents of the Installation Satisfaction Report file, analyze the information (identifying trends, anomalies, etc.), and report its findings to Information Technology Managers.

3.3   IT Managers shall review the Asset Manager's findings and may make recommendations regarding the findings (which may include corrective or preventive actions).

4.0   IT ASSET INSTALLATION – CORRECTIVE/PREVENTIVE ACTION

4.1   The IT Asset Manager shall initiate corrective or preventive action by writing a Corrective Action Request (CAR), in accordance with procedure ITSD109 IT INCIDENT HANDLING.

4.2   The IT Asset Manager shall submit a copy of the CAR to the Tech Support Manager and retain a copy.

4.3   Depending on the nature of the CAR, the Tech Support Manager or the IT Asset Manager may be required to take corrective action, in accordance with procedure ITSD109 IT INCIDENT HANDLING.

4.4   Upon taking corrective action, the responsible party shall note this on the CAR, return it to IT Managers, and submit a copy to the IT Asset Manager.

4.5   Within one month of a corrective action being taken, The IT Asset Manager shall verify that the appropriate action was taken, the desired effect was achieved, and the problem/nonconformance has not recurred.

5.0   IT ASSET INSTALLATION – ONGOING EVALUATION

5.1   The IT Asset Manager shall periodically review this process (annually, at a minimum), to ensure that it continues to address user satisfaction requirements.

5.2   The IT Asset Manager shall also review the process any time its effectiveness is called into question.

Forms:

- ITAM105-1 IT ASSET INSTALLATION FOLLOW-UP REPORT

References:

A. ISO 9001:2008 QUALITY MANAGEMENT SYSTEMS – REQUIREMENTS, CLAUSE 8.2.1 (CUSTOMER SATISFACTION)

Clause 8.2.1 states, in part, "As one of the measurements of the performance of the quality management system, the organization shall monitor information relating to customer perception as to whether the organization has met customer requirements."

The intent of this clause applies equally to internal users of information technologies, who should be regarded by the Information Technology Department as its customers.

Revision History:

Revision	Date	Description of Changes	Requested By
0.0	mm/dd/yyyy	Initial Release	

ITAM105-1 IT ASSET INSTALLATION FOLLOW-UP REPORT

Report ID: _____   Report Date: _____

User ID: _____

Asset Installed: _____

Asset Request Date: _____   Install Date: _____

Contact by: ❏ Phone   ❏ E-mail

_____

1. Was (asset) installed correctly the first time?   Y ❏ N ❏

    If N: How many attempts were required? (enter number)   _____

2. Was (asset) installed in a timely manner?   Y ❏ N ❏

    If N: When were you expecting installation? (enter date/time)   _____

3. Was it easy and convenient for you to schedule the installation?   Y ❏ N ❏

    If N, describe your concern(s) _____

    _____

If (Asset) Was Installed Where You Work:

4. Do you feel the installer had the knowledge and skills required to do

    The installation?   Y ❏ N ❏ N/A ❏

    If N, please explain: _____

    _____

5. Was the installer friendly, considerate, polite, and respectful?   Y ❏ N ❏ N/A ❏

    If N, please explain: _____

    _____

6. Did the installer communicate so that you understood him/her?   Y ❏ N ❏ N/A ❏

    If N, please explain: _____

    _____

7. If you expressed any concerns, did the installer listen, understand,

    and act on your concerns?   Y ❏ N ❏ N/A ❏

    If N, please explain: _____

    _____

8. Was the installer trustworthy and believable, in your opinion?   Y ❏ N ❏ N/A ❏

    If N, please explain: _____

    _____

9. Did the installer seem to place your interests before his/hers?   Y ❏ N ❏ N/A ❏

If N, please explain: _____

_____

For All Installations:

10. Do you have any doubts or concerns regarding the installation?   Y ☐ N ☐

    If Yes, please explain your concerns in some detail: _____

    _____

    _____

    _____

    _____

Additional Comments:

_____

_____

_____

_____

_____

_____

_____

_____

Thank you for your time.

Your input will help us improve the installation process.

IT Policies and Procedures

Section 420

IT Training & Support

Section 420
IT Training & Support

420 ITTS – IT Training & Support

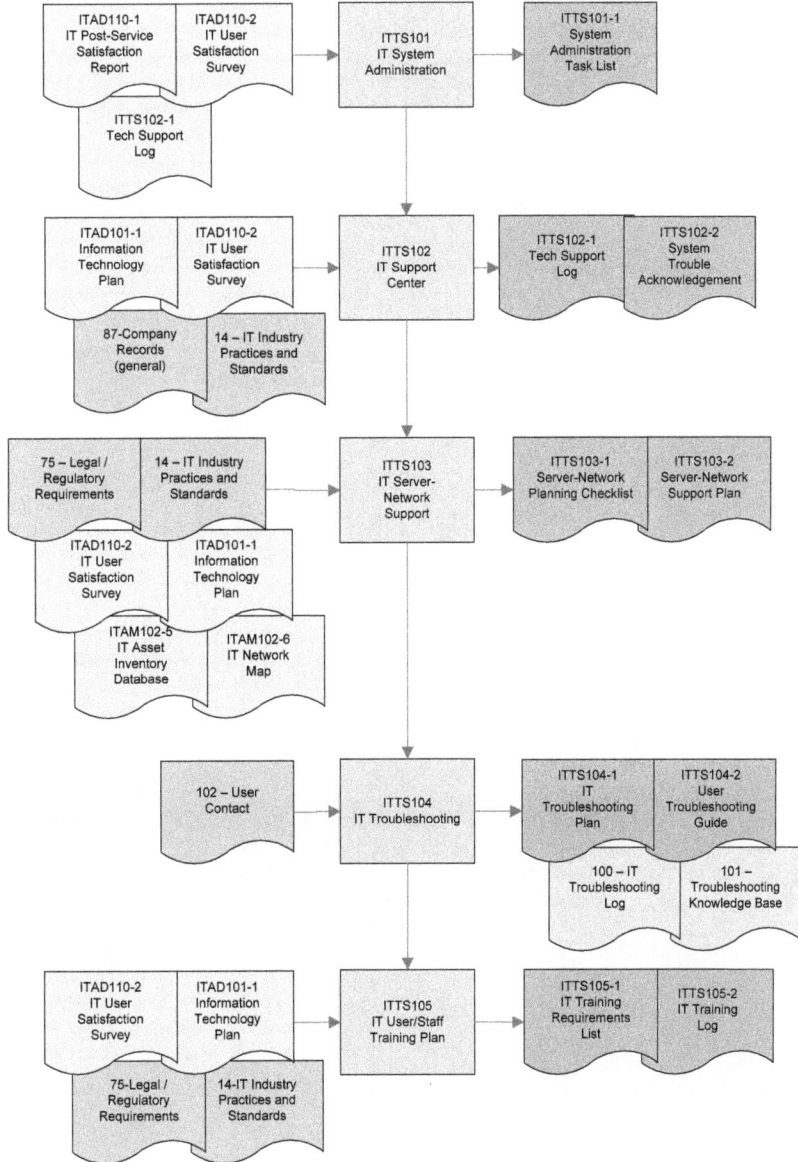

[This page intentionally left blank]

Document ID **ITTS101**	Title **IT SYSTEMS ADMINISTRATION**	Print Date **mm/dd/yyyy**
Revision **0.0**	Prepared By **Preparer's Name / Title**	Date Prepared **mm/dd/yyyy**
Effective Date **mm/dd/yyyy**	Reviewed By **Reviewer's Name / Title**	Date Reviewed **mm/dd/yyyy**
	Approved By **Final Approver's Name / Title**	Date Approved **mm/dd/yyyy**

Policy: To administer the Company's Information Technology systems in a way that promotes the achievement of Company goals and objectives.

Purpose: To delineate the System Administrator's tasks and responsibilities; to set up a mechanism for reviewing and updating sys admin responsibilities, as needed.

Scope: This procedure applies to all Company Information Technology systems.

Responsibilities:

The Information Technology Systems Administrator is responsible for managing the day-to-day operation of the Company's computer (Information Technology) systems.

Information Technology Managers are responsible for reviewing and approving the Company's System Administration Plan and ensuring its proper implementation.

Definitions: System Administrator – One whose primary job function is managing computer and network systems on behalf of another, such as an employer or client. Depending on the size of the organization, there may be several system administrators working on subsystems, reporting to an overall system administrator.

System administration – Activities that directly support the operation and integrity of computing systems, their use, and their intricacies. System administration activities may include but are not limited to: system installation, configuration, integration, maintenance, performance management, data management, security management, failure analysis and recovery, and user support. System administration is commonly known as "Sys Admin."

Procedure:

1.0   PLANNING SYSTEM ADMINISTRATION

1.1   The System Administrator shall conduct an assessment of the Company's current system administration (i.e., determine if it is doing the right things and how well it is doing them) by:

- Reviewing user satisfaction surveys (see ITAD110 IT DEPARTMENT SATISFACTION); and

- Reviewing system usage (reports based on various logs), to determine patterns, trends, and requirements.

1.2   The System Administrator shall determine the Company's requirements by reviewing, analyzing, and incorporating information from:

- Information Technology industry standards, best practices, and technology trends;

- Legal/regulatory issues pertaining to system administration; and

- Business issues, requirements, and trends.

1.3   The System Administrator shall develop a System Administration Plan and submit the Plan to Information Technology Managers for review and comments.

1.4   The System Administrator shall incorporate comments and suggestions from Information Technology Managers into the Plan and submit the revised Plan to Information Technology Managers for another review and final approval.

1.5   Upon final approval, the System Administrator shall implement the Plan.

2.0   SYSTEM ADMINISTRATION PLAN

2.1   The System Administrator shall manage the day-to-day operation of the Company's computer, or Information Technology, systems. The particular tasks for which the System Administrator is responsible shall be documented, using ITTS101-1 SYSTEM ADMINISTRATION TASK LIST as a guide.

2.2   The System Administrator shall regularly monitor, review, and report to Information Technology Managers on administration activities and on the status of the Company's Information Technology systems.

3.0   SYSTEM ADMINISTRATION PLAN REVIEW

3.1   The System Administrator shall periodically (monthly, at a minimum; weekly is advisable) review logs and other records generated in the course of implementing the Plan and report findings and observations to Information Technology Managers for review. Information Technology Managers shall review these findings and observations and recommend changes to the Plan, as needed.

3.2   Information Technology Managers should periodically (every six months is recommended) initiate a review of system administration, to determine if there is additional information not included in the periodic reports (referenced in 3.1) that may indicate or suggest that the Sys Admin Plan is or is not adequate.

3.3   A third-party audit of the System Administration Plan should be conducted at regular intervals (every two years, at a minimum). The auditor shall verify that the Plan is properly documented and implemented, that it meets Company requirements, and that it is continually monitored and measured for the purpose of improvement.

4.0   SYSTEM ADMINISTRATION PLAN UPDATE

4.1   The System Administrator shall revise the System Administration Plan, as directed, and notify the appropriate reviewer (auditor) that the Plan has been revised and implemented.

4.2   Within a month of the revised Plan being implemented, the third-party auditor or other reviewer shall verify that the revised Plan has been documented, implemented, and is yielding the expected results.

Forms:

- ITTS101-1 SYSTEM ADMINISTRATION TASK LIST

References:

None.

Additional Resources:

A. System Administrators' Group (SAGE) is a subgroup of the USENIX (or Advanced Computing Systems) Association and includes among its primary goals "to advance the status of computer system administration as a profession, establish standards of professional excellence and recognize those who attain them, develop guidelines for improving the technical and managerial capabilities of members of the profession, and promote activities that advance the state of the art of the community." Visit http://www.sage.org/ for more information.

B. Microsoft's TechNet provides some insight into the subject of system administration. One online document, "Service Management Functions – System Administration" – a good resource – is located at: http://technet.microsoft.com/library/cc506049.aspx.

C. The Sys Admin online journal (http://www.samag.com/) contains tips and advice for Unix and Linux system administrators.

Revision History:

Revision	Date	Description of Changes	Requested By
0	mm/dd/yyyy	Initial Release	

ITTS101-1 SYSTEM ADMINISTRATION TASK LIST

Administrative Task	Frequency
Print services	
• Set up printers (see ITAM101)	
• Administer printers, print servers	
System hardware	
• Installation/disposal (see ITAM101, ITAM102)	
• Configuration	
• Maintenance/repair (see ITTS103)	
System software	
• Install/uninstall (see ITAM101)	
• Configuration	
• Patches and other updates (see ITSD102, ITSD105)	
• License management (see ITSD102, ITTS102, ITTS103)	
System resources	
• Monitor system performance (see ITTS102, ITTS103)	
• Track resource usage; manage storage space (see ITSD102, ITSD103)	
• Data backup and recovery (see ITSD104)	
• Manage system processes	
• Manage operating systems	
User profiles (see ITSD106, ITSD107)	
System troubleshooting (see ITTS104)	
System accounting	
Change management	
Centralized/decentralized systems	
Data center	
• Databases	
• System hardware, software	
• Configuration, tuning	
Networks (see ITTS103)	
• Topology	
• Protocols	

Administrative Task	Frequency
• Hardware, software management	
User services	
• E-mail, messaging management	
• Password management (see ITSD106)	
• Other	
Scheduling system tasks	
Access control (see ITSD106)	
Security (see ITSD102)	
• Antivirus software management (see ITSD105)	
• Firewall management	
• Intrusion detection	
• Other	
System documentation (see ITAD103)	
Remote access	
• Methods	
• Standards	
• Hardware, configuration	

Document ID **ITTS102**	Title **IT SUPPORT CENTER**	Print Date **mm/dd/yyyy**
Revision **0.0**	Prepared By **Preparer's Name / Title**	Date Prepared **mm/dd/yyyy**
Effective Date **mm/dd/yyyy**	Reviewed By **Reviewer's Name / Title**	Date Reviewed **mm/dd/yyyy**
	Approved By **Final Approver's Name / Title**	Date Approved **mm/dd/yyyy**

Policy: The Company shall have an Information Technology Support Center, to provide ongoing emergency and non-emergency technology support to all departments and users.

Purpose: To identify staffing, training, and logistic requirements for an internal service/support center; to provide cost-effective staffing, training, and logistics for an effective support department.

Scope: This procedure applies, in particular, to the Information Technology Support Center. In general, all departments within the Company have technology needs, including:

Hardware support – Assistance with installation, usage, upgrades, or failures of all Information Technology related computer and communication equipment;

Software support – Assistance with technical questions on all operating systems, e-mail, applications, and database software; and

Telecommunications – Assistance with telephone, voice mail, pager, and all wireless equipment, including all setup, usage, and hardware difficulties.

Therefore this procedure, while not directly applicable to other departments, has a direct impact on the ability of every other department to do business in a manner that satisfies Company and customer requirements.

Responsibilities:

Information Technology Managers are responsible for developing Support Center goals, identifying needs, developing the Information Technology Support Plan, providing resources for the Information Technology Support Center, reviewing Support Center metrics with the Support Center Manager, and recommending changes to the Plan.

The Information Technology Support Center Manager is responsible for administering the Support Center budget and other recordkeeping, recording and analyzing Support Center metrics and reporting on such metrics and other Support Center activities to Information Technology Managers on a regular basis, managing a staff of (in-house or outsourced) Technical Support analysts, recommending improvements to Information

Technology Managers; and meeting or exceeding user expectations for the Support Center.

The <u>Tech Support Manager</u> is responsible for carrying out the daily operations of the Information Technology Support Center (i.e., delivering user support).

The <u>Technology Review Committee</u> is responsible for reviewing the Information Technology Support Plan, recommending revisions to the Plan, and for final approval of the Plan. The Technology Review Committee shall consist of Information Technology Managers (who shall chair the Committee) and management of the Company's functional departments or their representatives.

Definitions: <u>Technical Support (or "Tech Support")</u> – Provision of human resource and contract services for the installation, setup, and efficient operation of information technologies; also refers to personnel having responsibility for providing technical support.

<u>Help Desk</u> – Alternate name for technical support services.

Procedure:

1.0   IT SUPPORT CENTER OVERVIEW

1.1   Information Technology Managers shall determine the requirements for the Support Center by reviewing and analyzing such information as:

- Information Technology industry standards and best practices;

- Existing Company records – formal and informal – of instances where technical support was required, including descriptions, analyses, actions taken, personnel involved, dates, and outcomes; and

- ITAD110-2 – USER SATISFACTION SURVEY.

1.2   Information Technology Managers shall determine if the Company's needs are best met by operating and staffing the Support Center internally or by outsourcing, by:

- Measuring workload history and analyzing for trends; and

- Measuring and comparing the "total value" of each alternative to the Company.

1.3   Information Technology Managers shall develop an Information Technology Support Plan that integrates the Support Center into ITAD101-1 – INFORMATION TECHNOLOGY PLAN and ensures that the Support Center is accessible to the Company's computer network users. The Support Plan shall include guidelines and procedures for measuring response rates, priority levels, staffing requirements, customer satisfaction, and summary reports. Information Technology Managers shall submit the Information Technology Support Plan to the Technology Review Committee for input and approval.

1.4   When the Information Technology Support Plan has been approved, Information
        Technology Managers shall secure resources needed to implement the Plan on an
        ongoing basis, in accordance with ITAD109 IT OUTSOURCING.

2.0   IT SUPPORT CENTER OPERATIONS

2.1   Set up and maintain user accounts – As people enter the Company workforce, the
        Support Center will assign each new employee a unique identity within the
        Company's computer network and assign certain data and personnel access rights
        and privileges. Thereafter, the Support Center will ensure that user accounts are
        current.

2.2   User instruction/information – The Support Center should provide information on
        the Company's network and related services. The Support Center should ensure
        that new users are familiar with the current state of the network and the resources
        that are available by conducting brief introductory seminars and/or providing an
        introduction to network services in written form, in accordance with ITTS101 IT
        TRAINING PLAN. The Support Center should disseminate new and useful
        information on the computer network to all users as it becomes available or when
        needed.

2.3   Acquire and maintain computer equipment – The Support Center should install,
        relocate, or remove computer hardware (and related software) to/from the
        Company's computer network, in accordance with ITAM102 IT ASSET
        MANAGEMENT.

2.4   Provide software support – The Support Center should install and maintain all
        applications software users need to perform his/her job efficiently and effectively,
        ensuring that the latest version is installed, that a site license is available and
        updates (patches, etc.) are disseminated in a timely and orderly fashion; again, in
        accordance with ITAM102 IT ASSET MANAGEMENT.

2.5   Ad hoc problem solving – The Support Center operates a "help desk" to assist
        computer and network users at every level with any computer-related problems
        they may encounter. The help desk should categorize and prioritize user
        problems so that Support Center resources are assigned appropriately. The Help
        Desk contact shall:

- Identify, categorize, and assign an Incident ID or Trouble Ticket number
  and complete ITTS102-1 TECH SUPPORT LOG.

- Attempt to resolve the issue, in accordance with ITTS104 IT
  TROUBLESHOOTING. If the issue is resolved in this manner, close the
  entry in ITTS102-1; otherwise:

  a. Record **unresolved** user issues/problems on ITSD108-1 IT
     INCIDENT REPORT and forward to Information Technology
     Managers for resolution, in accordance with ITSD108 IT INCIDENT
     HANDLING.

  b. Acknowledge receipt of **unresolved** user issues/problems
     immediately, using ITTS102-2 SYSTEM TROUBLE REPORT

ACKNOWLEDGEMENT, submitting one copy each to the user and to Information Technology Managers.

2.6 The Information Technology Support Center Manager shall prepare a weekly report based on ITTS102-1 TECH SUPPORT LOG, listing Trouble Reports that occurred in the last week and categorizing by nature and severity. The weekly report shall be submitted to Information Technology Managers, which shall use to help allocate resources and plan the workload accordingly.

2.7 Load planning – The Support Center will monitor its activities and regularly report to Information Technology Managers. Information Technology Managers will analyze Support Center activity data to ensure continued, adequate support resources and adjust the Company's Technology Plan, as needed.

2.8 Training plans/goals for tech support personnel – Information Technology Managers will ensure that Support Center personnel are adequately trained to perform computer network support duties and that they maintain adequate training and certification levels. (See procedure ITTS101 IT TRAINING PLAN.)

3.0 IT SUPPORT REVIEW

3.1 Information Technology Managers shall periodically (at least monthly) review Tech Support Logs, user satisfaction surveys, and other sources of information, analyze the data on response times and satisfaction levels, and identify issues and trends. Information Technology Managers shall report its findings and observations to the Technology Review Committee. The Technology Review Committee shall review Information Technology Managers' findings and observations and possibly make change recommendations.

3.2 The Support Center shall be subjected to a periodic audit (once every two years, at a minimum), to verify that the Plan is clear and actionable and continues to meet Company requirements.

Forms:

- ITTS102-1 TECH SUPPORT LOG
- ITTS102-2 SYSTEM TROUBLE ACKNOWLEDGEMENT FORM

Additional Resources:

A. Help Desk Institute (HDI) (http://www.thinkhdi.com/).

B. Association of Support Professionals (ASP) (http:/www.asponline.com).

C. ITSW110 SOFTWARE SUPPORT

D. ITSD108 IT INCIDENT HANDLING

E. ITTS104 IT TROUBLESHOOTING

F. ITTS105 IT USER/STAFF TRAINING PLAN

Revision History:

Revision	Date	Description of Changes	Requested By
0	mm/dd/yyyy	Initial Release	

[This page intentionally left blank]

ITTS102-1 TECH SUPPORT LOG

Incident ID	Date-Time	Location	Problem Description	Problem Category	Severity Level	Problem Logged By (ID)	Problem Assigned To (ID)	Resolution	Resolved (Date)	Hours Logged	User Comments	Comment Code

[This page intentionally left blank]

ITTS102-2 SYSTEM TROUBLE ACKNOWLEDGEMENT FORM

A. INCIDENT ID: _____

B. USER IDENTIFICATION:

From: _____   Dept: _____

Phone: _____   Location: _____

C. SYSTEM IDENTIFICATION:

Property ID: _____ Serial Number: _____

D. PROBLEM CATEGORY:

Date Received: _____   Date problem first noted: _____

Type of Problem: (Check One)
     Hardware: _____   Software: _____   Security: _____ (See H. on back)

_____
_____
_____
_____
_____

E. DESCRIPTION OF PROBLEM:

_____
_____
_____
_____
_____
_____

F. EXPECTED TIME TO RESOLVE: _____

G. IF QUESTIONS, CONTACT: _____

H. SECURITY INCIDENT GUIDE:

a. A system alarm or similar indication from an intrusion detection tool

b. Suspicious entries in system or network accounting (e.g., a UNIX user obtains root access without going through the normal sequence necessary to obtain this access)

c. Accounting discrepancies (e.g., someone notices an 18-minute gap in the accounting log in which no entries whatsoever appear)

d. Unsuccessful logon attempts

e. Unexplained, new user accounts

f. Unexplained, new files or unfamiliar file names

g. Unexplained modifications to file lengths and/or dates, especially in system executable files

h. Unexplained attempts to write to system files or changes in system files

i. Unexplained modification or deletion of data

j. Denial of service or inability of one or more users to login to an account

k. System crash

l. Poor system performance

m. Unauthorized operation of a program or sniffer device to capture network traffic

n. "Door knob rattling" (e.g., use of attack scanners, remote requests for information about systems and/or users, or social engineering attempts)

o. Unusual time of usage (remember, more security incidents occur during non-working hours than any other time)

p. An indicated last time of usage of a user account that does not correspond to the actual last time of usage for that user

q. Unusual usage patterns (e.g., programs are being compiled in the account of a user who does not know how to program)

Observing one or more of these symptoms should prompt you to investigate events more closely. Work with other personnel at the Company that possess the appropriate technical and computer security knowledge to determine exactly what has occurred, if necessary.

Document ID **ITTS103**	Title **IT SERVER / NETWORK SUPPORT**	Print Date **mm/dd/yyyy**
Revision **0.0**	Prepared By **Preparer's Name / Title**	Date Prepared **mm/dd/yyyy**
Effective Date **mm/dd/yyyy**	Reviewed By **Reviewer's Name / Title**	Date Reviewed **mm/dd/yyyy**
	Approved By **Final Approver's Name / Title**	Date Approved **mm/dd/yyyy**

Policy: To ensure a secure Information Technology infrastructure, one that is properly maintained and is capable of performing in a manner that satisfies Company requirements.

Purpose: To ensure security and continuous availability of the Information Technology infrastructure; to provide around-the-clock support for the infrastructure and those who use it; to provide a framework for technical support of the Company's servers and network.

Scope: This procedure applies to all Company servers and to the Company's Information Technology network.

Responsibilities:

Information Technology Managers are responsible for assessing current support, conducting needs assessments, developing the Server / Network Support Plan, overseeing implementation of the Plan, monitoring the Plan's progress, and updating the Plan.

The Technology Review Committee is responsible for reviewing the Plan and any updates to it and for giving final approval to the Plan.

The Server/Network Support Team is responsible for maintaining the Company's servers and Information Technology network in accordance with the Plan and for reporting on server and network status.

Definitions: Multi Router Traffic Grapher (MRTG) – A tool for monitoring traffic load on network-links. MRTG generates HTML pages containing graphical images, which provide a live visual representation of this traffic.

Procedure:

1.0   SERVER / NETWORK SUPPORT PLANNING

1.1   Information Technology Managers shall conduct an assessment of the current server and network support capabilities by reviewing and analyzing the following, at a minimum:

- ITAM102-5 IT ASSET INVENTORY DATABASE;

- ITAM102-6 IT NETWORK MAP;

- ITTS103-1 SERVER/NETWORK PLANNING CHECKLIST; and

- Various server and network logs (activity, performance, etc.).

1.2 Information Technology Managers shall similarly conduct a needs assessment by reviewing and analyzing the following, at a minimum:

- ITAD101-1 INFORMATION TECHNOLOGY PLAN;

- Information Technology industry standards, best practices, and technology trends; and

- ITAD110-2 USER SATISFACTION SURVEY.

1.3 Information Technology Managers shall develop a gap analysis, to determine the Company's short- and long-term requirements with regard to resources, training, capacity, budget, etc.

1.4 Information Technology Managers shall develop the Server/Network Support Plan, including budget requirements, and submit it to the Technology Review Committee for review and recommendations.

1.5 Information Technology Managers shall incorporate recommended changes, if any, into the Plan and present the revised plan to the Committee for final approval. Information Technology Managers shall oversee implementation of the Plan and monitor, evaluate, and report on its progress.

2.0   SERVER / NETWORK SUPPORT PLAN

2.1 A Server and Network Support team shall be responsible for supporting servers and the Information Technology network infrastructure, in accordance with ITTS103-2 SERVER/NETWORK SUPPORT PLAN. Server and network support functions may reside entirely in-house and some or all functions may be outsourced, in accordance with ITAD109 IT OUTSOURCING.

2.2 The Server/Network Support team shall be responsible for:

- Server and network design;

- Testing, installation, and configuration of hardware and software;

- Daily operations (administration) of servers and the network; and

- Maintenance, repair, and service

in accordance with ITTS103-2 SERVER/NETWORK SUPPORT PLAN.

2.3 The Server/Network Support team shall regularly and frequently (weekly, at a minimum) submit a report to Information Technology Managers on the status of the Company servers and network, for review.

2.4 The Server/Network Support team shall manage servers and the network in accordance with Service Level Agreements set forth in the Plan.

3.0   SERVER/NETWORK SUPPORT PLAN REVIEW

3.1 The Server/Network Support Team shall periodically (monthly, at a minimum) review logs and other records generated in the course of managing the Company network and servers and report server and network statistics, as well as any findings and observations, to Information Technology Managers for review.

3.2   Information Technology Managers shall periodically review (quarterly, at a minimum) the Server/Network Support Plan to determine if the Plan is being properly implemented (adhered to) and if Plan management conforms to Company requirements. Information Technology Managers shall report its findings and recommendations to the Technology Review Committee.

3.3   A third-party audit of the Plan shall be conducted at regular intervals (at least once every two years), to verify that the Plan is properly documented and communicated to the appropriate parties; is being implemented in a manner that conforms to Company requirements; and is being monitored and measured, to determine if it is in need of change.

4.0   SERVER / NETWORK SUPPORT PLAN UPDATE

4.1   Information Technology Managers shall update (make revisions to) the Server/ Network Support Plan, as needed, and communicate the revised Plan to the Server/Network Support Team.

4.2   Within one month of implementing the revised Plan, the Technology Review Committee shall review server and network activity logs (and server/network related documentation, if necessary) of the last month to ensure that the revised Plan has been properly implemented and is yielding the desired results.

Forms:

- ITTS103-1 SERVER/NETWORK PLANNING CHECKLIST

- ITTS103-2 SERVER/NETWORK SUPPORT PLAN

References:

ISO 27002:2013, "INFORMATION TECHNOLOGY - CODE OF PRACTICE FOR INFORMATION SECURITY MANAGEMENT"

http://www.iso.org/iso/home/store/catalogue_ics/catalogue_detail.htm?csnumber=54533.

Additional Resources:

SARBANES-OXLEY ACT OF 2002

Sarbanes-Oxley, or SOX, passed by the U.S. Congress in 2002 was designed to create a new standard of corporate accountability and new penalties for corporate wrongdoing. SOX holds public companies' executive officers responsible for financial reporting, it mandates internal control processes, and it outlaws alteration or destruction of financial records. Because virtually all companies use Information Technology networks to share information (including sensitive financial data), effective network management is crucial to SOX compliance.

Revision History:

Revision	Date	Description of Changes	Requested By
0.0	mm/dd/yyyy	Initial Release	

ITTS103-1 SERVER/NETWORK PLANNING CHECKLIST

1. SERVERS

Does the Company currently have a server inventory?	
How often does the Company review server deployment?	
Server operating system choices are based on…? (List reasons.)	
As a percentage, how much of server administration time is allocated to routine server maintenance?	
How many servers does the Company currently have?	
What is the Company's employee-to-server ratio?	
Are all servers uniquely configured for a specific business function or are they multipurpose?	
Does the Company have a standard hardware and software build for new servers?	
Who supports Company servers?	
Does the Company have a server management plan?	
Does the Company have a roadmap for server deployment?	

2. INTERNAL NETWORK (LAN)

Does the Company periodically experience degraded internal network performance?	
If so, how often?	
Does the Company currently have an inventory or map of the Company's internal network?	
How often is the Company's network inventoried?	
Does the Company have a network management plan to clarify day-to-day operational responsibilities?	
How often does the Company review its network implementation?	
Does the Company have a roadmap for long-term planning of its internal network?	
How often does the Company engage in long-term network planning?	
Acquisition of hardware, software, or services for the internal network are based on…? (List reasons.)	
As a percentage, how much network administration time is allocated to routine LAN maintenance?	
Who supports the internal network?	
Does the Company use MRTG-based tools to analyze network performance?	

3. EXTERNAL NETWORK (WAN)

How does the Company currently connect to the Internet?	
How often does the Company experience degraded external network performance?	
Does the Company currently have an inventory or map of its external network configuration?	
How often does the Company review its inventory?	
If there is a network management plan, does it include external connections?	
How often does the Company review the external networking components of its network management plan?	
Does the Company have a roadmap for its external network?	
How often does the Company engage in updating its roadmap?	
Acquisition of hardware, software, or services related to the external network are based on…? (List reasons.)	
As a percentage, how much network administration time is allocated to routine maintenance of the WAN?	
Who supports the external network?	
Does the Company conduct bandwidth analysis to ensure its external connection is optimally utilized?	

ITTS103-2 SERVER/NETWORK SUPPORT PLAN

1.0 SERVER SUPPORT

1.1 Server planning and design	
• Network mapping	
• Load planning	
1.2 Server testing, installation, and configuration	
1.3 Operations / Administration	
• Monitor server usage (traffic), disk usage	
• Conduct performance testing (maintain performance logs), performance tuning (optimization)	
• Monitor server security (provide anti-malware defense, server backup, vulnerability tests, penetration tests, disaster recovery, etc.)	
• Provide server hardware and software license tracking	
• Server updates (hardware / software) – method, timing, frequency, testing & installation	
• Report on server traffic, disk usage, server-related incidents, etc.	
• Service Level Agreements (frequency, extent of reporting, conducting operations/admin tasks)	
1.4 Service / Maintenance / Repair	
• Help Desk (remote or local, remote/live/web-based support, extent of coverage, support logs, etc.)	
• Troubleshooting server(s)	
• Emergency support	
• Service level agreements (SLAs)	

2.0 NETWORK SUPPORT

2.1 Network planning and design	
• Network mapping	
• Load planning	
2.2 Network testing, installation, and configuration	
2.3 Operations (admin)	

• Create and manage network users, groups	
• Monitor network traffic (bandwidth usage, etc.)	
• Conduct network performance testing	
• Monitor network security (provide firewalls, disaster recovery, vulnerability testing, etc.)	
• Provide network hardware and related software license tracking	
• Network updates (hardware/software – method, timing, testing & installation)	
• Report on network traffic, usage, bottlenecks, network incidents, etc.	
• Service Level Agreements (frequency, extent of reporting, operations/admin tasks, etc.)	
2.4 Service / Maintenance / Repair	
• Help Desk	
• Troubleshooting	
• Emergency support	
• Service level agreements (SLAs)	

Approval

Technology Review Committee: _____ Date: _____

IT Management: _____ Date: _____

Support Team leader: _____ Date: _____

Document ID	Title	Print Date
ITTS104	**IT TROUBLESHOOTING**	**mm/dd/yyyy**
Revision	Prepared By	Date Prepared
0.0	**Preparer's Name / Title**	**mm/dd/yyyy**
Effective Date	Reviewed By	Date Reviewed
mm/dd/yyyy	**Reviewer's Name / Title**	**mm/dd/yyyy**
	Approved By	Date Approved
	Final Approver's Name / Title	**mm/dd/yyyy**

Policy: To minimize Information Technology system disruptions, enhancing productivity and promoting user satisfaction.

Purpose: To prescribe a procedure for troubleshooting Information Technology-related problems; to enable effectiveness, consistency, and continual improvement of the troubleshooting process.

Scope: This procedure applies to all Company Information Technology assets.

Responsibilities:

Information Technology Managers are responsible for evaluating the Information Technology Department's troubleshooting methods, approving the Information Technology Troubleshooting Plan, and periodically reviewing the Plan.

The Tech Support Manager is responsible for developing, communicating, and implementing the Plan.

The Tech Support Manager is responsible for acting on user requests for troubleshooting, knowing and consistently applying the Information Technology Troubleshooting Plan, and recording troubleshooting activities for the purpose of monitoring and improving the Plan.

Users are responsible for reporting problems to the Help Desk in a timely manner, reporting accurately and with as much detail as possible.

Definitions: Cold boot – Start a computer (CPU) from its powered-down (off) state; also referred to as a "hard boot".

Reboot – Restart a computer, either by warm booting or cold booting.

Troubleshoot - Isolate the source of a problem and fix it. Troubleshooting is a process of elimination, whereby possible sources of the problem are investigated and eliminated, beginning with the most obvious or easiest problem to fix. In computer systems, the term *troubleshoot* is often used when the problem is thought to be hardware-related; if the problem is software-related, the term *debug* is used.

Warm boot – Restart a computer by way of its operating system (i.e., "Control-Alt-Delete"). Warm booting returns a computer to its initial state without shutting it off.

Procedure:

1.0   IT TROUBLESHOOTING – PLANNING

1.1   Information Technology Managers (or its designee) shall review and evaluate the Information Technology Department's current troubleshooting methods and capabilities, comparing them with industry standards, best practices, and technology trends and performing a gap analysis. Information Technology Managers (or its designee) shall also review ITAD110-2 USER SATISFACTION SURVEY for indicators of user dissatisfaction with current troubleshooting methods and/or results.

1.2   The Tech Support Manager shall develop an Information Technology Troubleshooting Plan (using ITTS104-1 IT TROUBLESHOOTING PLAN as a guide) and submit the Plan to Information Technology Managers for review, comments, and possible revisions.

1.3   If Information Technology Managers requests revisions to the Plan, the Tech Support Manager shall revise the Plan and submit the revised Plan to Information Technology Managers for review and final approval.

1.4   Upon Information Technology Managers' approval, the Tech Support Manager shall ensure communication of the Plan to Tech Support personnel (and applicable parts of the Plan to all users) and shall oversee implementation of the Plan.

2.0   IT TROUBLESHOOTING PLAN

2.1   If a computer equipment problem is suspected, the user shall first attempt to correct or verify the problem, following ITTS104-2 USER TROUBLESHOOTING GUIDE, before contacting the Help Desk. The user may be able to conserve limited Help Desk resources. Furthermore, when it becomes necessary to contact the Help Desk, the user may greatly speed up problem resolution by providing detailed information.

2.2   If the user is unable to solve the problem by the User Troubleshooting Guide, he/she shall contact the Help Desk for assistance. The Tech Support Manager shall investigate and attempt to resolve the problem in accordance with ITTS104-1 IT TROUBLESHOOTING PLAN.

2.3   The Tech Support Manager shall record all troubleshooting occurrences in a Troubleshooting Log (ITSD108-3 IT SECURITY INCIDENT LOG may be used as a guide. Also, the Company may wish to combine the troubleshooting and security incident logs into one Help Desk log). The troubleshooting occurrence should also be entered into a "troubleshooting knowledge base" for future reference by the Tech Support (Help Desk) staff.

3.0   IT TROUBLESHOOTING PLAN REVIEW

3.1   The Tech Support Manager shall follow up on troubleshooting calls to determine users' satisfaction, in accordance with ITAD110 IT DEPARTMENT SATISFACTION. The Tech Support Manager should periodically review user satisfaction measures to help verify the Plan's effectiveness.

3.2   The Tech Support Manager shall periodically (monthly, at a minimum) review the Troubleshooting Log and other records generated in the course of troubleshooting problems and report its findings and observations to Information Technology Managers for review.

3.3   Information Technology Managers should periodically review the Plan with Tech Support personnel, to determine if the Plan is helping with problem resolution.

3.4   Information Technology Managers may direct the Tech Support Manager to revise the Plan, if it is ever determined that the Plan is not meeting requirements for response time, quality of response, or degree of improvement over time.

4.0   IT TROUBLESHOOTING PLAN UPDATE

4.1   The Tech Support Manager shall revise the Plan, as directed, test the revision(s) in a lab setting, and submit the revised Plan to Information Technology Managers for review and approval.

4.2   The Tech Support Manager shall communicate the revised Plan to Tech Support personnel and ensure its implementation.

4.3   Within two weeks of the Tech Support Manager implementing the revised Plan, Information Technology Managers (or its designee) shall review activity during the previous two weeks to ensure that the Plan is properly implemented and is yielding the desired results.

Forms:

- ITTS104-1 IT TROUBLESHOOTING PLAN
- ITTS104-2 USE TROUBLESHOOTING GUIDE

References:

- None.

Additional Resources:

- None.

Revision History:

Revision	Date	Description of Changes	Requested By
0	mm/dd/yyyy	Initial Release	

ITTS104-1 IT TROUBLESHOOTING PLAN

1.0   Problem discovery.

    1.1   The user implements the User Troubleshooting Guide prior to contacting the Help Desk.

    1.2   If the User Troubleshooting Guide has not provided a solution, the user escalates the problem by contacting the Help Desk (Tech Support).

2.0   The Help Desk enters the problem in the Troubleshooting Log.

3.0   The problem is assigned to a Tech Support person, who begins by isolating the problem.

    3.1   Check the Troubleshooting Knowledge Base for prior occurrence(s) of the problem.

    3.2   Evaluate the configuration of the problem unit.

    3.3   Perform other tests, as needed, to determine the root cause of the problem.

4.0   Identify possible solutions.

    4.1   Solution One

    4.2   Solution Two

5.0   Test possible solutions.

    5.1   Test Case One

    5.2   Test Case Two

6.0   Evaluate test results.

    6.1   Test Case One

    6.2   Test Case Two

7.0   Correct the problem.

8.0   Close the Troubleshooting Log.

9.0   Add the problem and solution to the Troubleshooting Knowledge Base.

[This page intentionally left blank]

ITTS104-2   USER TROUBLESHOOTING GUIDE

Before you contact the Help Desk (Tech Support):

- Make sure all components – monitor, CPU, and peripherals – are switched on and receiving power (see "Power Checklist"). If you call the Help Desk for assistance, make sure to tell the Tech Support analyst the results of your power check.

- See if all cables attached to the affected equipment are firmly connected. If you find any cable connections that seem loose, push them snugly into place (see "Equipment Connection Checklist").

- Save and close all open files, close all applications, and do a "warm reboot" of the computer. If a warm reboot does not resolve the problem, try a "cold reboot". If that does not resolve the problem, contact the Help Desk.

- If a keyboard, mouse, or monitor is not working properly, swap it out for one that is known to be functioning correctly on another computer. If the swapped equipment does not resolve the problem, contact the Help Desk.

- If you are having trouble printing, see if other computers using the same printer are experiencing the same printing problem. Check the Print Manager or a similar utility for the status of your print job. If your computer is networked to more than one printer, see if another printer will handle your job. Note the results of each type of test and contact the Help Desk with the details.

- Check to see if your computer is the only one in your subnetwork being affected by the problem. Knowing if the problem is an isolated case or affects other computers in the subnetwork will help Tech Support.

- Find out if any changes have been made to your computer since the last time it functioned properly (e.g., a software utility or a patch installed while you were out of the office). If hardware or software on your computer was altered or was added to or removed from your computer before the problem appeared, the Help Desk should have a record of this.

See: "Power Checklist" and "Equipment Connection Checklist" on the following pages.

POWER CHECKLIST

- Make sure all power cords are firmly in place on both ends.

- Check the power cord for damage.

- Make sure that each piece of equipment (including the power conditioning or UPS device) has its "power indicator" light on.

- Test the equipment and electrical outlet:

    a. Plug the suspect unit (monitor, CPU, UPS, etc.) into another electrical outlet that you have confirmed is working. If the unit works, the original outlet should be serviced. If the unit doesn't work after being plugged into the new outlet, report the problem to the Help Desk because the unit may need servicing.

    b. Plug another device, like a lamp, into the original electrical outlet. If the lamp works, the electrical outlet is not the problem. If the lamp does not work, the electrical outlet may be in need of repair and appropriate action should be taken.

    c. If the power cord to the CPU, monitor, etc., is removable, replace it with another removable power cord. If the unit works with a new power cord, your original power cord is damaged and should be replaced.

(Continued)

EQUIPMENT CONNECTION CHECKLIST

When you are experiencing problems with equipment, you should first check whether or not the connecting cables are securely plugged into the appropriate port. Connection confirmation procedures for specific devices are discussed below.

1. Keyboard and Mouse

    a. It is easy for keyboard and mouse cable plugs to work their way out of ports or sockets. When you check them, make sure they are securely plugged in. If you find that a mouse or keyboard plug is loose, plug it firmly into the port, reboot your computer and test the keyboard or mouse.

    b. If you continue to have problems, try replacing the current mouse or keyboard with one that you know works, and then reboot your computer. If the swapped-out device works then the original device needs to be permanently replaced and/or repaired. Report this to the Help Desk to initiate the repair process.

    c. If you have problems with the swapped-out mouse or keyboard, then call the Help Desk to report the incident because there may be a problem with your computer.

2. Monitor

    a. If you have monitor problems and the monitor is not integrated into the computer (such as in Apple iMacs), make sure the serial cable from the monitor to the computer is firmly connected to the computer. After you check the serial cable, make sure the monitor is securely plugged in. After you have reseated the serial cable, reboot your computer and monitor.

    b. If you continue to have problems, try replacing the current monitor with one that you know works and reboot your computer.

        •   If the swapped-out monitor works, the original monitor may need repair or replacement. Report this problem to the Help Desk.

        •   If you have problems with the swapped-out monitor as well, report this also to the Help Desk, as there may be a problem with your computer.

[This page intentionally left blank]

Document ID **ITTS105**	Title **IT USER-STAFF TRAINING PLAN**	Print Date **mm/dd/yyyy**
Revision **0.0**	Prepared By **Preparer's Name / Title**	Date Prepared **mm/dd/yyyy**
Effective Date **mm/dd/yyyy**	Reviewed By **Reviewer's Name / Title**	Date Reviewed **mm/dd/yyyy**
	Approved By **Final Approver's Name / Title**	Date Approved **mm/dd/yyyy**

Policy: To improve the Company's performance by reducing training/skill gaps, anticipating the Company's training/skill needs, and continually improving training availability and methods.

Purpose: Determine required competence levels for (a) non-technical personnel using the Company's computer systems to perform tasks and (b) Information Technology personnel; provide training or take other actions to satisfy training requirements and evaluate the effectiveness of actions taken; provide personnel (especially technical personnel) with a training path or guide, whereby courses build on one another and promote a skill set that benefits the individual and the Company.

Scope: This procedure applies to all employees who use the Company's Information Technology systems and network to perform their jobs.

Responsibilities:

Information Technology Managers, the Human Resources Manager, and the Information Technology Security Manager are jointly responsible for developing and administering the Information Technology Training Plan, ensuring that personnel have requisite training coming into various Information Technology positions or can get adequate training quickly, ensuring that all personnel have guidance and support for training and training plans, and ensuring that all personnel are updating their skill portfolios. They are also responsible for implementing changes to the Plan, as needed.

The Training Review Committee is responsible for reviewing and approving the Information Technology Training Plan and any changes to the Plan. The Committee shall, at a minimum, consist of the Company's chief executive and chief financial officers, in addition to the Human Resources Manager and Information Technology Managers - which shall jointly chair the Committee – and the Information Technology Security Manager.

Procedure:

1.0 PLANNING IT USER-STAFF TRAINING

1.1 The Human Resources Manager and Information Technology Managers shall jointly conduct a training needs assessment, which should include the following, at a minimum:

- Identifying Company positions using information technologies and determining skill and knowledge requirements (i.e., competency levels) for all such positions. Human Resources should have a list of skill and experience requirements, by position (if not, they must be developed before proceeding);

- Assessing current skill and knowledge levels of all employees using information technologies;

- Reviewing ITAD110-2 USER SATISFACTION SURVEY for training requests and requirements; and

- Determining future requirements by reviewing and analyzing such resources as the Company's Strategic Plan and Information Technology Plan, Information Technology standards and best practices, technology trends, and legal/regulatory requirements.

1.2   Information Technology Managers shall conduct a gap analysis, determining the difference between what the Company's knowledge and skills requirements are and will be (what are its short-term and long-term requirements) and what are the current capabilities and skills.

1.3   The Information Technology Security Manager shall review security training gaps (using such information as is contained in ITTS102-1 TECH SUPPORT LOG) and determine possible methods for closing those gaps, to ensure that all personnel are aware of and are playing an active, ongoing role in Information Technology security in the course of performing their normal duties.

1.4   Human Resources and Information Technology Managers shall jointly develop an Information Technology Training Plan, using the gap analyses mentioned in 1.2 and 1.3, above. The Plan shall include objectives, goals, and timelines, as well as estimates of resource and financial requirements for implementing the Plan. The Plan shall be submitted to the Training Review Committee for its review.

1.5   The Training Review Committee shall review the proposed Information Technology Training Plan. The review process may include adjustments to the Plan and budget to ensure training objectives are relevant, challenging, and achievable.

1.6   Information Technology Managers and the Human Resources Manager shall implement the Information Technology Training Plan. Information Technology Managers shall communicate the Plan to all employees. The Human Resources Manager shall be responsible for ensuring adequate technical training of every employee.

2.0   THE IT USER-STAFF TRAINING PLAN

2.1   Information Technology Managers shall develop and maintain a list of minimum technical skills and knowledge required to perform the primary duties of each Information Technology position (see ITTS105-1 ITS TRAINING REQUIREMENTS LIST). Information Technology Managers should include cross-training and succession planning guidelines, to ensure backup for key personnel.

There shall also be an Information Technology security awareness training requirement for every employee. All employees are to be made aware – and such awareness maintained – that they each are responsible for the security of Information Technology assets in the course of their normal work.

The Human Resources Department shall maintain a training record on each employee, indicating (at a minimum) the employee ID, the training (course) received, and when the employee was trained. ITTS105-2 IT TRAINING LOG may be used as a guide.

2.2   The Human Resources Department, in conjunction with Information Technology Managers, shall develop and maintain a training plan for each employee, so that an employee shall continue to acquire technical skills that meet the Company's short- and long-term requirements, in accordance with the Information Technology Plan.

2.3   The Human Resources Department shall ensure that all new employees (or employees new to a given position) receive the necessary technical and security training to perform their duties. Types of training, dates, times, and locations will be arranged for and communicated to employees.

2.4   Employees may receive ongoing technical and security training, depending on the requirements of the position, project requirements, and Company requirements. Employees or their supervisors may request technical training and ongoing technical training needs should be evaluated and training administered in accordance with ITAD105-1 INFORMATION TECHNOLOGY PLAN.

2.5   Training on the Company's proprietary software shall be administered in-house. Training on off-the-shelf software shall be administered by a qualified third party. Third-party training vendors shall be evaluated and selected in accordance with ITAM103 IT VENDOR SELECTION.

2.6   Training facilitator, facilities, dates, course durations, materials, and prerequisites for each course shall be arranged and communicated by the Human Resources Manager in advance of individual courses being offered.

2.7   Trainees shall be given an opportunity to evaluate courses. The Human Resources Manager shall be responsible for collecting evaluations and shall evaluate and report on course evaluations to the Training Review Committee on a quarterly basis.

3.0   IT USER-STAFF TRAINING PLAN EVALUATION (REVIEW)

3.1   Information Technology Managers and the Human Resources Manager shall review the Information Technology Training Plan and report their observations and findings to the Training Review Committee on an annual basis. The Training Review Committee shall review observations and findings with respect to ITAD105-1 INFORMATION TECHNOLOGY PLAN and recommend possible changes to the Information Technology Training Plan.

3.2   The Training Review Committee shall require an external audit of the Information Technology Training Plan to be conducted once every two years.

4.0   IT USER-STAFF TRAINING PLAN UPDATE

4.1   Where changes to the Information Technology Training Plan are required, Information Technology Managers and the Human Resources Manager shall update the Plan and communicate such changes to employees.

4.2   Within three months of the Plan being updated, the Training Review Committee shall review training records and employee evaluations to see whether updates have been implemented and if they are achieving the desired results.

Forms:

- ITTS105-1 ITS TRAINING REQUIREMENTS LIST
- ITTS105-2 ITS TRAINING LOG

References:

A. ISO 9001:2008 STANDARD – QMS REQUIREMENTS, CLAUSE 6.2.2 (COMPETENCE, AWARENESS, AND TRAINING)

This clause of the ISO standard states that an organization managing for quality improvement must determine required levels of competence for personnel, provide training or take other actions to satisfy required competence levels and evaluate effectiveness of such actions, ensure that its personnel are aware of the relevance and importance of their activities and how they contribute to the achievement of quality objectives, and maintain appropriate records of education, training, skills, and experience.

B. ISO/IEC 27002:2013 – INFORMATION TECHNOLOGY-CODE OF PRACTICE FOR INFORMATION SECURITY MANAGEMENT

For more, see http://www.iso.org/iso/catalogue_detail?csnumber=54533.

C. COBIT CONTROL OBJECTIVES, 5TH EDITION (2012)

Control Objective DS7, "Educate and Train Users", specifies control objectives for user education and training.

For more information on COBIT or the COBIT Control Objectives, visit http://www.isaca.org/ or http://www.itgi.org.

Additional Resources:

None.

Revision History:

Revision	Date	Description of Changes	Requested By
0	mm/dd/yyyy	Initial Release	

[This page intentionally left blank]

ITTS105-1 ITS TRAINING REQUIREMENTS LIST

Job Title	
Grade:	
Technical Requirements For This Job:	
Next Job Title In Normal Career Path:	
Next Job Grade:	
Technical Requirements For Next Job:	

Prescribed Career Path:

[This page intentionally left blank]

ITTS105-2 ITS TRAINING LOG

Employee Name: _____

Employee ID: _____ **Department:** _____

Employee Title / Grade: _____

COURSE ID	PREREQ COURSE ID	CERT. COURSE?	START DATE	END DATE	PASS / NO PASS

HR Management: _____ **Date:** _____

IT Management: _____ **Date:** _____

[This page intentionally left blank]

IT Policies and Procedures

Section 430

IT Security & Disaster Recovery

Section 430

IT Security & Disaster Recovery

430 ITSD – IT Security & Disaster Recovery

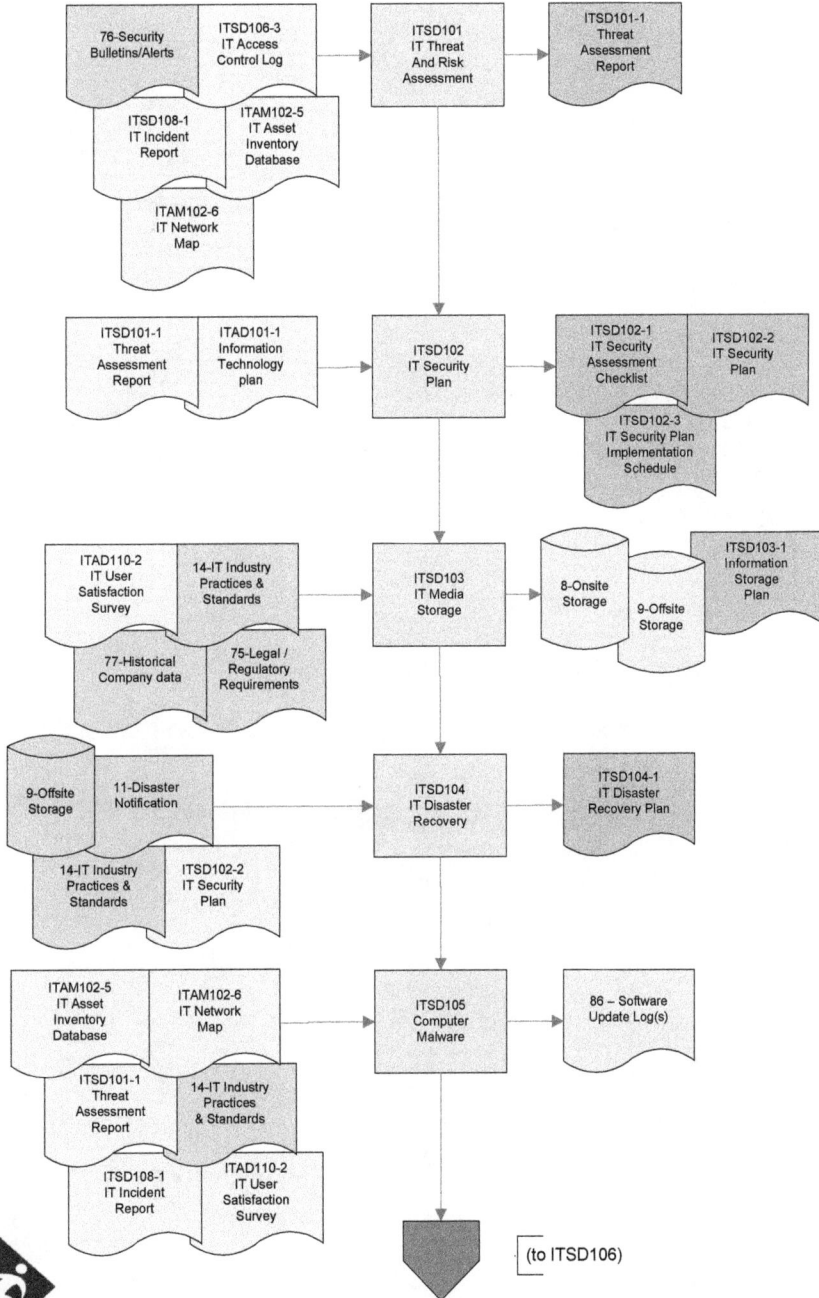

430 ITSD – IT Security & Disaster Recovery

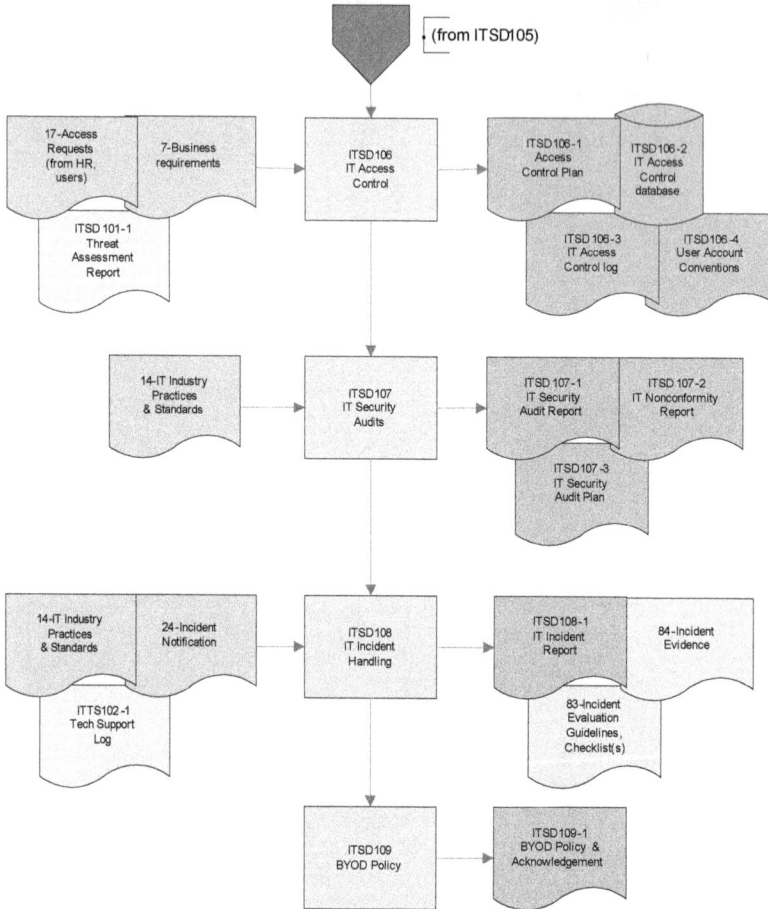

(from ITSD105)

17-Access Requests (from HR, users)	7-Business requirements	

ITSD106 IT Access Control

ITSD106-1 Access Control Plan	ITSD106-2 IT Access Control database

ITSD101-1 Threat Assessment Report

ITSD106-3 IT Access Control log	ITSD106-4 User Account Conventions

14-IT Industry Practices & Standards	ITSD107 IT Security Audits

ITSD107-1 IT Security Audit Report	ITSD107-2 IT Nonconformity Report

ITSD107-3 IT Security Audit Plan

14-IT Industry Practices & Standards	24-Incident Notification

ITSD108 IT Incident Handling

ITSD108-1 IT Incident Report	84-Incident Evidence

ITTS102-1 Tech Support Log

83-Incident Evaluation Guidelines, Checklist(s)

ITSD109 BYOD Policy

ITSD109-1 BYOD Policy & Acknowledgement

Document ID **ITSD101**	Title **IT THREAT AND RISK ASSESSMENT**	Print Date **mm/dd/yyyy**
Revision **0.0**	Prepared By **Preparer's Name / Title**	Date Prepared **mm/dd/yyyy**
Effective Date **mm/dd/yyyy**	Reviewed By **Reviewer's Name / Title**	Date Reviewed **mm/dd/yyyy**
	Approved By **Final Approver's Name / Title**	Date Approved **mm/dd/yyyy**

Policy: The Company shall regularly evaluate its Information Technology systems and network for threats and vulnerabilities in order to protect its Information Technology assets and reduce the Company's risk.

Purpose: To describe a procedure for identifying potential threats to the Company's information technology assets (Information Technology assets) and assessing threats on the basis of probability and risk.

Scope: This procedure applies to all Company Information Technology assets, including the Information Technology network.

Responsibilities:

The Information Technology Security Manager is responsible for conducting threat assessments of the Information Technology network and reporting on the results of such assessments. Also, the Information Technology Security Manager is responsible for continually monitoring threats and taking actions to mitigate risk to the Company's Information Technology assets.

Information Technology Managers are responsible for evaluating the results of a threat assessment, assessing the level of risk to various Information Technology assets, and recommending actions that mitigate risk.

Definitions: Risk – Possibility of losing availability, integrity, or confidentiality of Information Technology assets due to a specific threat; also, the product of threat level and vulnerability level.

Threat – Expression of intent to inflict evil, injury, or damage; potential violation of security.

Threat Assessment – A process by which types of threats an Information Technology network might be vulnerable to and where the network is most vulnerable are identified.

Vulnerability – Flaw or weakness in a system's design, implementation, or operation and management that could be exploited.

Procedure:

1.0   IT THREAT & RISK ASSESSMENT – INTRODUCTION

1.1   In order to prepare for threats to its Information Technology assets and infrastructure, the Company must be aware of the types of threats that exist, the likelihood that they will occur, their potential impact, and the risk these threats may pose to the Company.

1.2   Threats may be natural or manmade. Natural threats include floods, storms, and earthquakes. Manmade threats may be accidental or intentional. Examples of manmade threats include use of unauthorized hardware or software and having unauthorized access to Company systems.

   Intentional threats exist both outside the Company and within. According to one survey (see Additional Resource I), four-fifths of respondents believed the greatest threats to their organizations were internally-based.

1.3   The risk posed by any given threat is a function of the combined likelihood of the threat occurring and the impact it would have on the Company's assets (hardware, software, data, network/infrastructure, and personnel) if it were to occur. While risk to Company Information Technology assets cannot be completely eliminated, the Company must make all reasonable efforts to minimize risk. Those efforts should begin with assessing threats and risks.

2.0   IT THREAT ASSESSMENT PREPARATION

2.1   In advance of conducting a threat assessment of any of the Company's Information Technology systems, the Information Technology Security Manager shall establish a baseline for assessment, identifying systems to be assessed (accounting, HR, sales, etc.) and determining their interconnectivity with other systems. ITAM102-5 IT ASSET INVENTORY DATABASE and ITAM102-6 IT NETWORK MAP should be used as guides.

2.2   The Information Technology Security Manager should identify and describe threats that may target the Information Technology assets and systems under consideration by one or more of the following means:

   - Periodically (at least once a month) reviewing ITSD106-1 ACCESS CONTROL LOG for threat occurrences, such as unauthorized system access;

   - Reviewing Information Technology incidents for trends and/or patterns, in accordance with procedure ITSD110 IT INCIDENT HANDLING;

   - Reviewing any system test (test script, test procedures, expected results, etc.) for vulnerabilities testing;

   - Conducting penetration testing at irregular intervals, to verify the Information Technology network's ability to withstand intentional attempts at circumventing Information Technology security (see Additional Resource F).

2.3   The Information Technology Security Manager may acquire additional information for developing the assessment baseline by routinely reviewing threat alerts and bulletins from vendors, standards organizations, etc. Subscribing to one or more threat alert mailing lists is recommended (see Additional Resource G).

2.4   To determine if the Company needs to act on any given threat and to what extent it should act, the Information Technology Security Manager shall classify threats/ vulnerabilities should in the following manner:

- The **likelihood** of threats occurring, according to information provided by external sources (see Additional Resources B – D). Threat likelihood may be categorized as:

    a. Low – the threat is unlikely to occur. For example, the Company's three sites are all more than 500 miles from any ocean, so a hurricane or typhoon would not normally be a threat to the Company;

    b. Medium – the threat may occur. For example, one or more of the Company's sites is located in an earthquake zone, so an earthquake is likely to have an effect on the Company; and

    c. High – the threat is likely to occur. For example, if the Company does not require password access to computers or data stores, the likelihood is high that someone will eventually access and steal or compromise Company data.

- The **impact** of threats, in the absence of protection, and the possible or likely consequences of each. Threat impact may be classified as:

    a. Low – the threat may result in minimal loss of Company assets/resources;

    b. Medium – the threat may result in a significant loss of Company assets/ resources, harm the Company's mission or interests, or result in injury to an employee; and

    c. High – the threat may result in a very costly loss of Company assets/ resources, significantly harm the Company's mission, interests, or standing, or result in serious or fatal injury to an employee.

- An exposure rating or **risk assessment** shall be based on likelihood and impact ratings. A risk matrix is prescribed (Figure 1), with likelihood running from low to high along one axis and impact running from low to high on the other axis. The resulting exposure rating/risk assessment shall be used to prioritize threats (Figure 2).

    a. High-risk threats require the highest security levels and present the greatest need for immediate action, if existing security tools and techniques are inadequate.

    b. Low-risk threats may require little or no response on the part of the Information Technology Security Manager.

Impact	Low	Medium	High
High	Low	Medium	High
Medium	Low	Medium	Medium
Low	Low	Low	Low

(Likelihood, shown vertically along left axis)

Figure 1 – Risk Matrix

Risk Level	Description and Actions
High	Preventive actions are required and a preventive action plan shall be developed and implemented as soon as possible.
Medium	Preventive actions are required and a plan to incorporate those actions within a reasonable time frame shall be developed.
Low	IT Management should confer with managers of affected systems to determine if preventive action is required or if risk is acceptable.

Figure 2 – Threat Priority

3.0   IT THREAT/RISK ASSESSMENT

3.1   At regular intervals (once every six months, at least), the Information Technology Security Manager shall conduct a threat/vulnerability scan of the Information Technology network. This scan should be performed using commercially available software designed expressly for the purpose (see Additional Resource F).

3.2   The Information Technology Security Manager shall review scan results and analyze the findings in order to determine if the Company needs to act on them and to what extent.

3.3   The Information Technology Security Manager shall create ITSD101-1 THREAT ASSESSMENT REPORT, summarizing assessment findings and containing the following information, at a minimum:

- Systems reviewed;
- Number of threats found this period and last; and
- A summary of identified threats.

3.4   The Information Technology Security Manager shall submit ITSD101-1 to Information Technology Managers and the affected systems' management for their review. Information Technology Managers and management of the affected systems shall determine if preventive actions are required, in accordance with ITSD108 IT INCIDENT HANDLING.

4.0   IT THREAT/RISK MANAGEMENT REVIEW

4.1   The Information Technology Security Manager shall periodically review the risk assessment process to ensure its continued timeliness and applicability. Historical data from ITSD101-1 (i.e., number, nature, and severity of threats over time) shall help determine if risks are under control.

4.2   Any time a significant implementation, revision, etc., takes place, the Information Technology Security Manager shall review the risk assessment process, to ensure existing controls are applicable to such changes or if improved controls are required.

Forms:

• ITTS101-1 IT THREAT/RISK ASSESSMENT REPORT

References:

A. SARBANES-OXLEY ACT OF 2002

Threats to company information can come from within as well as from the outside, as incidents at Enron and WorldCom have shown. The Sarbanes-Oxley Act, passed by the U.S. Congress in 2002, was designed to prevent manipulation, loss, or destruction of publicly-held companies' records by requiring public companies to exercise adequate internal controls. Conducting regular threat assessments helps companies comply with the requirements of the Act and makes good business sense.

B. RISK IT FRAMEWORK FOR MANAGEMENT OF IT RELATED BUSINESS RISKS

Detailed information can be found at http://www.isaca.org/Knowledge-Center/Risk-IT-IT-Risk-Management/Pages/Risk-IT1.aspx.

C. HEALTH INSURANCE PORTABILITY & ACCOUNTABILITY ACT OF 1996 (HIPAA)

The Standards for Privacy of Individually Identifiable Health Information (the Privacy Rule) creates national standards to protect individuals' personal health information and gives patients increased access to their medical records. As required by the Health Insurance Portability and Accountability Act (HIPAA), passed by the U.S. Congress in 1996, the Privacy Rule covers health plans, health care clearinghouses, and those health care providers who conduct certain financial and administrative transactions electronically. Most covered entities (certain health care providers, health plans, and health care clearinghouses) must comply with the Privacy Rule by April 14, 2003. Small health plans have until April 14, 2004 to comply with the Rule.

D. NIST SPECIAL PUBLICATION #800-30, REV. 1 – GUIDE FOR CONDUCTING RISK ASSESSMENTS (SEPT. 2012)

This publication is available at http://csrc.nist.gov/publications/nistpubs/800-30-rev1/sp800_30_r1.pdf.

Additional Resources:

A. Microsoft TechNet provides a Security Risk Management Guide online that small businesses may find helpful. This guide can be found at http://technet.microsoft.com/en-us/library/cc163143.aspx.

B. SANS (SysAdmin-Audit-Network-Security) Institute – SANS is one of the largest sources for information security training and certification in the world. SANS develops, maintains, and makes available (at no cost) the largest collection of research documents about various aspects of information security and it operates the Internet's early warning system, the Internet Storm Center. Information on SANS is available at http://www.sans.org/about/.

C. The Institute of Internal Auditors (IIA) is another good source of information on tools and resources for managing security. The IIA's web site address is http://www.theiia.org/.

D. Klevinsky, Laliberte, and Gupta, <u>Hack I.T. – Security Through Penetration Testing</u>, Addison-Wesley, 2002.

E. Vulnerability scan tools are readily available via the Internet; one example is the Microsoft Baseline Security Analyzer (MBSA), which may be found at http://technet.microsoft.com/default.aspx. A list of other vendors and their scan tools may be found at the Network Computing web site (see http://www.nwc.com/showitem.jhtml?articleID=15000643).

F. Microsoft, SANS, ZDNet, and a number of other sources issue security (threat) alerts through public media and e-mail. Companies and individuals may usually subscribe to e-mail alerts at no cost to them. It is strongly recommended that the Company subscribe to at least one e-mail alert list.

G. Power, Richard, "1999 CSI/FBI Computer Crime and Security Survey," *Computer Security Issues & Trends*, Computer Security Institute, Winter, 1999.

Revision History:

Revision	Date	Description of Changes	Requested By
0	mm/dd/yyyy	Initial Release	

[This page intentionally left blank]

ITSD101-1 IT THREAT/RISK ASSESSMENT REPORT

Date: _____

Systems Reviewed: _____

_____

Threats found this period: _____

Description: _____

_____

_____

Threats found last period: _____

Description: _____

_____

_____

Threat Summary:

Risk Level	Number	Description
LOW		
MEDIUM		
HIGH		

IT Security Manager: _____

[This page intentionally left blank]

Document ID **ITSD102**	Title **IT SECURITY PLAN**	Print Date **mm/dd/yyyy**
Revision **0.0**	Prepared By **Preparer's Name / Title**	Date Prepared **mm/dd/yyyy**
Effective Date **mm/dd/yyyy**	Reviewed By **Reviewer's Name / Title**	Date Reviewed **mm/dd/yyyy**
	Approved By **Final Approver's Name / Title**	Date Approved **mm/dd/yyyy**

Policy: To protect the confidentiality and integrity of Company information while maintaining appropriate levels of accessibility.

Purpose: To provide an overview of the security requirements of the Company's Information Technology system and network, to describe the controls in place or planned for to meet those requirements, and to delineate responsibilities and expected behavior of all individuals who access the system.

Scope: This applies to all Information Technology assets and to all Company personnel.

Responsibilities:

The Information Technology Security Manager is responsible for preparing and developing the Information Technology Security Plan and implementation schedule, implementing the Plan and any updates, and monitoring and periodic reporting on the Plan.

Information Technology Managers are responsible for establishing and periodically convening the Security Review Committee, advising the Information Technology Security Manager regarding development of the Plan, coordinating with Human Resources Management to provide user training, and verifying implementation of updates to the Plan.

The Security Review Committee is responsible for periodic review and updates and for final approval of the Information Technology Security Plan.

Definitions: Security - The state of being free from danger or injury. The effort to create a secure computing platform, designed so that agents (users or programs) can only perform actions that have been allowed.

Procedure:

1.0   PREPARING THE IT SECURITY PLAN

1.1   The Information Technology Security Manager shall begin the planning process with an up-to-date inventory of Information Technology assets, in accordance with procedure ITAM104 IT ASSET ASSESSMENT.

1.2   The Information Technology Security Manager shall continue the planning process with an assessment of threats and risks to the Information Technology system/network, in accordance with procedure ITSD101 IT THREAT ASSESSMENT.

1.3   The Information Technology Security Manager shall conduct a security assessment of the Company's Information Technology network, using ITSD102-1 IT SECURITY ASSESSMENT CHECKLIST as a guide.

1.4   A Security Review Committee, consisting of Information Technology Managers, the Information Technology Security Manager, and management from the various Company departments (Human Resources, Accounting, Production, Sales, etc.), shall be established.

1.5   The Information Technology Security Manager shall evaluate findings and discuss recommendations to correct deficiencies and/or improve security with the Security Review Committee.

2.0   DEVELOPING THE IT SECURITY PLAN

2.1   The Information Technology Security Manager shall develop the Information Technology Security Plan with assistance from Information Technology Managers, using ITSD102-2 IT SECURITY PLAN as a guide.

2.2   The Information Technology Security Manager shall ensure that the plan is comprehensive and complete and shall present the Plan and an implementation schedule (see ITSD102-3 IT SECURITY PLAN IMPLEMENTATION SCHEDULE for guidance) to the Security Review Committee for its approval.

3.0   IMPLEMENTING THE IT SECURITY PLAN

3.1   All Information Technology systems shall be identified according to a standard format. Systems identification shall include, but not necessarily be limited to, the following:

- System name and ID;
- Responsible organization(s);
- Contact information;
- Operational status;
- Description & purpose;
- Interconnections and information sharing;
- Applicable regulations; and
- Information sensitivity.

3.2   Management controls for every system shall include, but not necessarily be limited to:

- Risk assessment and management;
- Review of security controls;
- Security planning throughout the system life cycle; and

- Processing authorization.

3.3   Operational controls for each system shall include, but not necessarily be limited to:

- Personnel security;
- Physical/environmental protections;
- Production and input/output controls;
- Contingency planning;
- Hardware/software maintenance controls;
- Integrity controls;
- System documentation;
- Security awareness and training; and
- Incident response.

3.4   Technical controls for each system shall include, but not necessarily be limited to:

- Identification and authentication of users;
- Access control; and
- Audit trails.

3.5   The Information Technology Security Manager shall communicate the Information Technology Security Plan to all affected persons, distributing the plan to all managers and supervisors, requiring managers and supervisors to communicate the Plan to their staff, and resolving any questions related to the Plan.

3.6   Information Technology Managers shall coordinate employee security training with Human Resources Management. Human Resources shall train all new users in Information Technology security within one week of their hiring and retrain all users in the Information Technology Security Plan at least once every two years.

4.0   IT SECURITY PLAN REVIEW

4.1   The Information Technology Security Manager shall routinely monitor and periodically report (once a quarter, depending on the size of the Company and its Information Technology network) to Information Technology Managers on the status of the Information Technology Security Plan.

- Any significant deviation from the Information Technology Security Plan shall require that Information Technology Managers convene the Security Review Committee to consider if changes to the Plan are required. (An example of significant deviation may be a change at the Information Technology Security Manager position, or a change in risk assessment or other security methodologies.)

4.2   Once the Security Plan is implemented, The Information Technology Security Manager shall conduct a periodic internal review of the Plan with the Security Review Committee. This review should take place at least annually and shall include an examination of:

- Current security conditions;

- Changes to the Plan, as recommended by The Information Technology Security Manager;

- User satisfaction, in accordance with ITAD110 IT DEPARTMENT SATISFACTION;

- Results of any internal or external audits, in accordance with ITSD107 IT SECURITY AUDITS; and

- Progress of the stated goals of the existing Plan.

4.3   At least once every three years, the Company shall participate in an external review (audit), to verify its compliance with the Information Technology Security Plan and help evaluate the Plan's effectiveness.

5.0   IT SECURITY PLAN UPDATE

5.1   After any review of the Information Technology Security Plan, the Information Technology Security Manager shall be responsible for implementing required updates.

5.2   Within three months of such updates, Information Technology Managers shall verify that the updates have been implemented and are providing the desired results.

Forms:

- ITSD102-1 IT SECURITY ASSESSMENT CHECKLIST
- ITSD102-2 IT SECURITY PLAN
- ITSD102-3 IT SECURITY PLAN IMPLEMENTATION SCHEDULE

References:

A. **ISO 27002:2013 – INFORMATION TECHNOLOGY - SECURITY TECHNIQUES - CODE OF PRACTICE FOR INFORMATION SECURITY CONTROL**

This ISO standard is part of a family of standards designed to provide a comprehensive set of information security controls and practices. For more, see http://www.iso.org/iso/catalogue_detail.htm?csnumber=54533.

B. **NATIONAL INSTITUTE OF STANDARDS AND TECHNOLOGY (NIST) SPECIAL PUBLICATION #800-18, REV. 1 – GUIDE FOR DEVELOPING SECURITY PLANS FOR INFORMATION TECHNOLOGY SYSTEMS (FEB., 2006)**

See http://csrc.nist.gov/ for details on NIST publications.

Additional Resources:

A. van der Walt, Charl, <u>Introduction To Security Policies, Part One: An Overview of Policies</u>, Symantec Corp. (created Aug., 2001; revised Nov., 2001). <u>http://www.symantec.com/connect/articles/introduction-security-policies-part-one-overview-policies</u>.

B. Rutgers Office of Information Technology, <u>Developing a Security Plan</u>, <u>http://rusecure.rutgers.edu/content/developing-security-plan</u>.

Revision History:

Revision	Date	Description of Changes	Requested By
0	mm/dd/yyyy	Initial Release	

[This page intentionally left blank]

ITSD102-1 IT SECURITY ASSESSMENT CHECKLIST

Hardware Risk:

Is there redundant hardware to allow work to continue in critical areas in the event of a hardware failure? When was this tested last?	
Does the UPS (uninterruptible power supply) notify someone when it goes into operation? When was it last tested?	
Is there a plan to have hardware replaced at regular intervals?	

Software Risk:

Do you have original disks to reinstall software if the hard drive fails?	
Is all software supported? If software is old or unsupported, what are your plans to replace it?	
Is locally developed software supported by an easy-to-reach developer?	
Do you have provisions to continue operation if central services software is not available?	

Environmental Risk:

Is your equipment located so that it is reasonably free from potential dangers (fire, water leaks, etc.)?	
Do UPSs protect all servers and workstations?	
Is the heating, cooling, and ventilation system (HVAC) keeping your equipment at the appropriate temperature and humidity?	

Network Failure:

Do you have physical and remote access to your network devices?	
Do you have the ability to continue to function in the event of a wide area network failure?	

Security Policy:

Does the Company have security policies, standards, and processes? Are they hard copy or electronic?	
Are they readily accessible?	
Do security standards identify all individuals responsible for implementing such standards and what their duties are?	
Do the standards identify steps to be taken if there is a physical and/or information security breach?	
Do the standards identify what physical and/or information are most important to protect?	
Are all employees aware of security processes?	
Are all employees aware of Company IT policies?	

Department Managers:

Is there a background and/or reference check on new employees?	
Are there clearly defined system security procedures for IT system administration?	
Are security-related duties clear to IT personnel?	
Is there an orientation course on good security practices for new employees?	
Do all security related IT duties appear in job descriptions?	
Are IT staff members aware of Company codes of conduct that relate to IT security-related positions?	
Do written procedures exist that explain how to perform all IT security related duties?	
Are IT personnel up to date on training for security related duties?	
Do personnel have sufficient authority to accomplish IT security related duties and policies?	
Are there available and competent personnel to back up IT security related duties in the event the regular IT Security Manager is unavailable?	
Are sufficient funds budgeted to cover IT security?	

Does the Company have a process to address incidents or compromises?	
Do employees sign nondisclosure agreements on the use of confidential material/research material?	
Has funding been provided to recycle old computers and operating systems?	
Does the IT staff know to review the security settings and policies?	
Does the IT staff know how to respond to security breaches?	
Does the IT staff know to use user level accounts when not providing administrative services?	
Are best security practices available?	
Can you ensure that any forms of media containing confidential and sensitive information are sanitized before disposal?	
Are you fully aware of your duties, responsibilities, and resources?	
Have you identified and secured systems that hold critical information or applications?	
Have you identified and secured documents designated as "critical?"	
Is equipment that is being disposed of stripped of data before disposal?	
Is appropriate documentation being completed?	

IT Management:

Does the technical staff know to review the security settings and policies?	
Does the technical staff know how to respond to security breaches?	
Does the technical staff know to use user level accounts when not providing administrative services?	
Can you ensure that any forms of media containing confidential and sensitive information are clean prior to disposal?	

Are you fully aware of your duties, responsibilities, and resources?	
Have you identified and secured systems that hold critical information or applications?	
Have you identified and secured documents designated as "critical?"	
Is equipment that is being disposed of stripped of data before disposal?	
Is appropriate documentation being completed?	

Department User:

Is staff instructed on basic workstation security?	
Are users aware that email attachments should not be opened as a regular practice on PCs?	
Are employees aware of the dangers attachments can bring?	
Does staff have written guidelines for protecting their workstations and storage media files?	

Accounts and Passwords:

Is there a policy for selecting strong passwords?	
Is the Company using software that enforces strong passwords?	
Is the IT Security Manager authorized to check for weak passwords?	
Are passwords changed? How often?	
Is the Company planning to use other forms of authentication other than passwords in the future?	
Does the Company have an account removal process?	
Does the Company have a method for identifying unauthorized users?	
Has Company staff received computer security awareness training?	
Is there a document establishing the identity and number of those having root access to departmental information?	

Is the identity of those having remote access to departmental information known?	
Are there written procedures for forgotten passwords?	
Are there written procedures for closing accounts when an employee terminates employment?	

Privacy and Confidential Data Storage:

Are backup files sent offsite to a physically secure location?	
Are files kept onsite in a secure location?	

Network and Configuration Security:

Does the Company have a network diagram that includes IP addresses, room numbers, and responsible parties?	
Is there an IT auditing standard in place?	
Are end users prevented from downloading and/or installing software? How?	
Are contents of system logs protected from unauthorized access, modification, and/or deletion? Is there a retention standard?	
Is the CD-ROM Autorun feature disabled on all workstations?	
Is password caching disabled on all workstations?	
Have "trusted workstations" (workstations with access to critical information) been identified for critical applications? Have special procedures been setup for these?	
Are the trusted workstations secured if used for other purposes?	
Are trusted workstations SSL, SSH, or VPN enabled?	
Are trusted workstations required to have complex passwords?	
Are workstations used by more than one employee secured? How?	

Are chat clients (ICQ, Yahoo Messenger, IM, etc.) managed (if allowed at departmental workstations) and if so, how are they managed?	
What security precautions are taken for dial-in modems?	
Will any clear-test passwords be embedded in SQL scripts for routine functions such as backup and recovery? If so, how will this data be protected?	
Are ActiveX, JavaScript, and Java disabled in web browsers and email programs for all workstations?	
Is remote control software (for example, PCAnywhere) permitted? If so, where? Explain how it is controlled.	
Is the "Administrator" account, and any equivalent accounts, on all workstations limited to the office technical support person? Is it password protected?	
Do administrators only use an administrative account when doing actual administration?	
Can users tell if files have been changed? (Is data integrity software in use?)	

Operating System(s):

Has the internal firewall been activated?	
Has the remote desktop and remote assistance been turned off?	

Web Servers:

Is the web server set to only accept traffic on port 80?	
Is the web server set to reject attempts to remotely administer it?	
Is the web server set to authenticate certain user traffic?	
Have the sample files, scripts, help and development files been removed?	

FTP:

Are all FTP servers set to authenticate users?	
Is this traffic encrypted/secured?	
Are all FTP directories set to either Read or Write but not to both?	

Email:

Is the email server set to scan mail and attachments for viruses?	
Is the email server set to reject attachments?	
Is the email server set NOT to act as a relay?	
Is web access to email secured?	
Are client connections from outside the subnet secured/encrypted?	

Network:

Does the department have an Internet Use Policy?	
Does the department have a network map/diagram?	
Does the department have an inventory of devices attached to the network?	
Are the room jacks mapped to a switch port?	
Is there a policy as to how network services are accessed by users?	

File Sharing:

Is file sharing permitted and secured on any workstation in the department? If so, how is it secured?	
Is file sharing "unbound" from TCP/IP transport (to prevent access from the Internet) while leaving it bound to NetBEUI for local transport?	

Disaster Planning:

Is there a written contingency plan to perform critical processing in the event that onsite workstations are unavailable?	
Do you have a plan to continue departmental business in the event that the Company's systems are down for an extended period?	
Do you have a partnership with vendors who can help in an emergency if your equipment is damaged due to disaster?	
Is the contingency plan periodically tested to verify it can be followed to resume critical processing?	

Backup and Recovery:

Are critical files regularly backed up?	
Do you store media off site?	
Is the environment of a selected off-site storage area (temperature, humidity, etc.) within the manufacturer's recommended range for the backup media?	
Are backup files periodically restored as a test to verify they are usable?	

Change Management:

Are records kept of systems changes?	
Is there a process for communication of systems changes?	
Does the Company have a configuration/asset control plan for all hardware and software products?	
Does the Company have a version control plan for software products?	
Does the Company have network and system diagrams of all system resources?	
Are only trained authorized individuals allowed to install computer equipment and software?	
Are maintenance records kept to indicate what repairs and/or diagnostics were performed and by whom?	

Patching:

Are software patches applied to all workstation software, especially operating system, web browser, word processing, spreadsheet, and database regularly? Checked how often?	
Have you created a plan for upgrades and set aside funding to enable you to keep software up to date?	

Software Licensing:

Is all software licensed to the Company?	
Is documentation available (licenses, purchase orders) if proof is necessary (e.g., a software audit is being conducted)?	

User Awareness Training:

Do you require new employees to read any Company documents?	
Does your staff know what's expected of them regarding security for the Company?	
Would you consider a security workshop for staff?	

Network and Host Based Security:

Intrusion Detection System (Network Based IDS)	
Does the Company have any way of telling that systems have been or are being compromised?	
Has penetration testing been done for the Company?	
Are any workstations running host-based IDSs?	
Host based firewall?	
Is critical data stored on every server protected from compromise?	
Can you monitor if anyone is accessing critical data?	
Is personal firewall software installed and in use? If so, on how many workstations? What are the settings?	
Do you have enough IT staff to manage individual firewalls on all desktops? Network firewall?	

Are settings password protected?	
How often are logs reviewed?	
Is there central monitoring of settings and logs?	

Antivirus Software:

Are all workstations running the latest version of antivirus software, scanning engine, and the virus signature file?	
Is staff aware that the majority of compromises are due to social engineering and the sharing of information?	
Are the monitors for trusted workstations positioned so that information cannot be viewed by anyone other than the intended viewer?	
Is staff aware that the information they handle may be of value to unintended parties?	
Are there guidelines for handling and storing confidential information and cards for one-time passwords?	

ITSD102-2 IT SECURITY PLAN

(From NIST Special Publication #800-18, Appendix C)

A. SYSTEM IDENTIFICATION

Date:

System Name/Title

- Unique Identifier and Name Given to the System

Responsible Organization

- List organization responsible for the system

Information Contact(s)

- Name of person(s) knowledgeable about, or the owner of, the system.

Name:

Title

Address:

Phone:

Assignment of Security Responsibility

- Name of person responsible for security of the system.

Name:

Title

Address:

Phone:

System Operational Status

If more than one status is selected, list which part of the system is covered under each status.

- Operational
- Under Development
- Undergoing a major modification

General Description/Purpose

- Describe the function or purpose of the system and the information processed.
- Describe the processing flow of the application from system input to system output.
- List user organizations (internal and external) and type of data and processing provided.
- List all applications supported by the general support system. Describe each application's functions and information processed.

System Environment

- Provide a general description of the technical system. Include any environmental or technical factors that raise special security concerns (dial-up lines, open network, etc.)
- Describe the primary computing platform(s) used and a description of the principal system components, including hardware, software, and communications resources.
- Include any security software protecting the system and information.

System Interconnection/Information Sharing

- List of interconnected systems and system identifiers (if appropriate).
- If connected to an external system not covered by a security plan, provide a short discussion of any security concerns that need to be considered for protection.
- It is required that written authorization (MOUs, MOAs) be obtained prior to connection with other systems and/or sharing sensitive data/information. It should detail the rules of behavior that must be maintained by the interconnecting systems. A description of these rules must be included with the security plan or discussed in this section.

Applicable Laws or Regulations Affecting the System

- List any laws or regulations that establish specific requirements for confidentiality, integrity, or availability of data/information in the system.

General Description of Information Sensitivity

- Describe, in general terms, the information handled by the system and the need for protective measures. Relate the information handled to each of the three basic protection requirements (confidentiality, integrity, and availability). For each of the three categories, indicate if the requirement is **High**, **Medium**, or **Low**.
- Include a statement of the estimated risk and magnitude of harm resulting from the loss, misuse, or unauthorized access to or modification of information in the system.

B. MANAGEMENT CONTROLS

Risk Assessment and Management

- Describe the risk assessment methodology used to identify the threats and vulnerabilities of the system. Include the date the review was conducted. If there is no system risk assessment, include a milestone date (month and year) for completion of the assessment.

Review of Security Controls

- List any independent security reviews conducted on the system in the last three years.
- Include information about the type of security evaluation performed, who performed the review, the purpose of the review, the findings, and the actions taken as a result.

Rules of Behavior

- A set of rules of behavior in writing must be established for each system. The rules of behavior should be made available to every user prior to receiving access to the system. It is recommended that the rules contain a signature page to acknowledge receipt.
- The rules of behavior should clearly delineate responsibilities and expected behavior of all individuals with access to the system. They should state the consequences of inconsistent behavior or noncompliance. They should also include appropriate limits on interconnections to other systems.
- Attach the rules of behavior for the system as an appendix and reference the appendix number in this section or insert the rules into this section.

Planning for Security in the Life Cycle

Determine which phase(s) of the life cycle the system or parts of the system are in. Describe how security has been handled in the life cycle phase(s) that the system is currently in.

Initiation Phase

- Reference the sensitivity assessment which is described in Section 3.7, Sensitivity of Information Handled.

Development/Acquisition Phase

- During the system design, were security requirements identified?
- Were the appropriate security controls with associated evaluation and test procedures developed before the procurement action?

- Did the solicitation documents (e.g., Request for Proposals) include security requirements and evaluation/test procedures?
- Did the requirements permit updating security requirements as new threats/vulnerabilities are identified and as new technologies are implemented?
- If this is a purchased commercial application or the application contains commercial, off-the-shelf components, were security requirements identified and included in the acquisition specifications?

Implementation Phase

- Were design reviews and systems tests run prior to placing the system in production? Were the tests documented? Has the system been certified?
- Have security controls been added since development?
- Has the application undergone a technical evaluation to ensure that it meets applicable federal laws, regulations, policies, guidelines, and standards?
- Include the date of the certification and accreditation. If the system is not authorized yet, include date when accreditation request will be made.

Operation/Maintenance Phase

- The security plan documents the security activities required in this phase.

Disposal Phase

- Describe in this section how information is moved to another system, archived, discarded, or destroyed. Discuss controls used to ensure the confidentiality of the information.
- Is sensitive data encrypted?
- How is information cleared and purged from the system?
- Is information or media purged, overwritten, degaussed or destroyed?

Authorize Processing

- Provide the date of authorization, name, and title of management official authorizing processing in the system.
- If not authorized, provide the name and title of manager requesting approval to operate and date of request.

C. OPERATIONAL CONTROLS

Personnel Security

- Have all positions been reviewed for sensitivity level?
- Have individuals received background screenings appropriate for the position to which they are assigned.

- Is user access restricted to the minimum necessary to perform the job?
- Is there a process for requesting, establishing, issuing, and closing user accounts?
- Are critical functions divided among different individuals (separation of duties)?
- What mechanisms are in place for holding users responsible for their actions?
- What are the friendly and unfriendly termination procedures?

Physical and Environmental Protection

- Discuss the physical protection for the system. Describe the area where processing takes place (e.g., locks on terminals, physical barriers around the building and processing area, etc.)
- Factors to address include physical access, fire safety, failure of supporting utilities, structural collapse, plumbing leaks, interception of data, and mobile and portable systems.

Production, Input/Output Controls

Describe the controls used for the marking, handling, processing, storage, and disposal of input and output information and media, as well as labeling and distribution procedures for the information and media. The controls used to monitor the installation of, and updates to, software should be listed. In this section, provide a synopsis of the procedures in place that support the system. Below is a sampling of topics that should be reported in this section.

- User support - Is there a help desk or group that offers advice?
- Procedures to ensure unauthorized individuals cannot read, copy, alter, or steal printed or electronic information
- Procedures for ensuring that only authorized users pick up, receive, or deliver input and output information and media
- Audit trails for receipt of sensitive inputs/outputs
- Procedures for restricting access to output products
- Procedures and controls used for transporting or mailing media or printed output
- Internal/external labeling for sensitivity (e.g., Privacy Act, Proprietary)
- External labeling with special handling instructions (e.g., log/inventory identifiers, controlled access, special storage instructions, release or destruction dates)
- Audit trails for inventory management
- Media storage vault or library-physical, environmental protection controls/procedures
- Procedures for sanitizing electronic media for reuse (e.g., overwriting or degaussing)
- Procedures for controlled storage, handling, or destruction of spoiled media or media that cannot be effectively sanitized for reuse
- Procedures for shredding or other destructive measures for hardcopy media when no longer required

Contingency Planning

Briefly describe the procedures (contingency plan) that would be followed to ensure the system continues to process all critical applications if a disaster were to occur. If a formal contingency plan has been completed, reference the plan. A copy of the contingency plan can be attached as an appendix.

- Any agreements of backup processing.
- Documented backup procedures in including frequency (daily, weekly, monthly) and scope (full, incremental, and differential backup).
- Location of stored backups and generations of backups kept.
- Are tested contingency/disaster recovery plans in place? How often are they tested?
- Are all employees trained in their roles and responsibilities relative to the emergency, disaster, and contingency plans?

Hardware and System Software Maintenance Controls

- Restriction/controls on those who perform maintenance and repair activities.
- Special procedures for performance of emergency repair and maintenance.
- Procedures used for items serviced through on-site and off-site maintenance (e.g., escort of maintenance personnel, sanitization of devices removed from the site).
- Procedures used for controlling remote maintenance services where diagnostic procedures or maintenance is performed through telecommunications arrangements.
- Version control that allows association of system components to the appropriate system version.
- Procedures for testing and/or approving system components (operating system, other system, utility, applications) prior to promotion to production.
- Impact analyses to determine the effect of proposed changes on existing security controls to include the required training for both technical and user communities associated with the change in hardware/software.
- Change identification, approval, and documentation procedures.
- Procedures for ensuring contingency plans and other associated documentation are updated to reflect system changes.
- Are test data "live" data or made-up data?
- Are there organizational policies against illegal use of copyrighted software or shareware?

Integrity Controls

- Is virus detection and elimination software installed? If so, are there procedures for updating virus signature files, automatic and/or manual virus scans, and virus eradication and reporting?
- Is reconciliation routines used by the system, i.e., checksums, hash totals, record counts? Include a description of the actions taken to resolve any discrepancies.
- Is password crackers/checkers used?
- Is integrity verification programs used by applications to look for evidence of data tampering, errors, and omissions?
- Are intrusion detection tools installed on the system?
- Is system performance monitoring used to analyze system performance logs in real time to look for availability problems, including active attacks, and system and network slowdowns and crashes?
- Is penetration testing performed on the system? If so, what procedures are in place to ensure they are conducted appropriately?
- Is message authentication used in the system to ensure that the sender of a message is known and that the message has not been altered during transmission?

Documentation

Documentation for a system includes descriptions of the hardware and software, policies, standards, procedures, and approvals related to automated information system security of the system to include backup and contingency activities, as well as descriptions of user and operator procedures.

- List the documentation maintained for the system (vendor documentation of hardware/software, functional requirements, security plan, program manuals, test results documents, standard operating procedures, emergency procedures, contingency plans, user rules/procedures, risk assessment, authorization for processing, verification reviews/site inspections).

Security Awareness & Training

- The awareness program for the system (posters, booklets, and trinkets)
- Type and frequency of general support system training provided to employees and contractor personnel (seminars, workshops, formal classroom, focus groups, role-based training, and on-the job training)
- The procedures for assuring that employees and contractor personnel have been provided adequate training

Incident Response Capability

- Are there procedures for reporting incidents handled either by system personnel or externally?
- Are there procedures for recognizing and handling incidents, i.e., what files and logs should be kept, who to contact, and when?

- Who receives and responds to alerts/advisories (e.g., vendor patches, exploited vulnerabilities)?
- What preventive measures are in place (i.e., intrusion detection tools, automated audit logs, penetration testing)?

D. TECHNICAL CONTROLS

Identification and Authentication

- Describe the method of user authentication (password, token, and biometrics).
- If a password system is used, provide the following specific information:
- Allowable character set;
- Password length (minimum, maximum);
- Password aging time frames and enforcement approach;
- Number of generations of expired passwords disallowed for use;
- Procedures for password changes;
- Procedures for handling lost passwords, and
- Procedures for handling password compromise.
- Procedures for training users and the materials covered.
- Indicate the frequency of password changes, describe how password changes are enforced (e.g., by the software or System Administrator), and identify who changes the passwords (the user, the system, or the System Administrator).
- Describe any biometrics controls used. Include a description of how the biometrics controls are implemented on the system.
- Describe any token controls used on this system and how they are implemented.
- Describe the level of enforcement of the access control mechanism (network, operating system, and application).
- Describe how the access control mechanism supports individual accountability and audit trails (e.g., passwords are associated with a user identifier that is assigned to a single individual).
- Describe the self-protection techniques for the user authentication mechanism (e.g., passwords are transmitted and stored with one-way encryption to prevent anyone [including the System Administrator] from reading the clear-text passwords, passwords are automatically generated, passwords are checked against a dictionary of disallowed passwords).
- State the number of invalid access attempts that may occur for a given user identifier or access location (terminal or port) and describe the actions taken when that limit is exceeded.
- Describe the procedures for verifying that all system-provided administrative default passwords have been changed.
- Describe the procedures for limiting access scripts with embedded passwords (e.g., scripts with embedded passwords are prohibited, scripts with embedded passwords are only allowed for batch applications).

- Describe any policies that provide for bypassing user authentication requirements, single-sign-on technologies (e.g., host-to-host, authentication servers, user-to-host identifier, and group user identifiers) and any compensating controls.
- If digital signatures are used, the technology must conform to FIPS 186, *Digital Signature Standard* and FIPS 180-1, *Secure Hash Standard* issued by NIST, unless a waiver has been granted. Describe any use of digital or electronic signatures.

Logical Access Controls

- Discuss the controls in place to authorize or restrict the activities of users and system personnel within the system. Describe hardware or software features that are designed to permit only authorized access to or within the system, to restrict users to authorized transactions and functions, and/or to detect unauthorized activities (i.e., access control lists (ACLs).
- How are access rights granted? Are privileges granted based on job function?
- Describe the system's capability to establish an ACL or register.
- Describe how users are restricted from accessing the operating system, other applications, or other system resources not needed in the performance of their duties.
- Describe controls to detect unauthorized transaction attempts by authorized and/or unauthorized users. Describe any restrictions to prevent user from accessing the system or applications outside of normal work hours or on weekends.
- Indicate after what period of user inactivity the system automatically blanks associated display screens and/or after what period of user inactivity the system automatically disconnects inactive users or requires the user to enter a unique password before reconnecting to the system or application.
- Indicate if encryption is used to prevent access to sensitive files as part of the system or application access control procedures.
- Describe the rationale for electing to use or not use warning banners and provide an example of the banners used. Where appropriate, state whether the Dept. of Justice, Computer Crime and Intellectual Properties Section, approved the warning banner.

Audit Trails

- Does the audit trail support accountability by providing a trace of user actions?
- Are audit trails designed and implemented to record appropriate information that can assist in intrusion detection?
- Does the audit trail include sufficient information to establish what events occurred and who (or what) caused them? (Type of event, when the event occurred, user id associated with the event, program or command used to initiate the event, etc.)
- Is access to online audit logs strictly enforced?

- Is the confidentiality of audit trail information protected if, for example, it records personal information about users?
- Describe how frequently audit trails are reviewed and whether there are guidelines.
- Does the appropriate system-level or application-level administrator review the audit trails following a known system or application software problem, a known violation of existing requirements by a user, or some unexplained system or user problem?

ITSD102-3 IT SECURITY PLAN IMPLEMENTATION SCHEDULE

Task	Completion Date
1. Draft Security Plan	_____
2. Submit Plan for review by other managers	_____
3. Edit Security Plan	_____
4. Finalize Security Plan	_____
5. Submit Plan to Board of Directors	_____
6. Revise as necessary	_____
7. Distribute Security Plan Memo to all personnel	_____
8. Distribute Security Plan to Management Staff	_____
9. Meet with Managers	_____
10. Establish means to accomplish security tasks and activities	_____
11. Establish Security Breach Committee	_____
12. Establish Proactive Security Committee	_____
13. Obtain and install required equipment	_____
14. Implement specific programs	_____
15. Evaluate Security Plan implementation	_____
16. Evaluate Security Program	
• Internal review	_____
• External audit	_____
17. Modify Security Program and Plan	
• Schedule Security Plan update	_____

IT Security Manager: _____ Date: _____

IT Management: _____ Date: _____

Security Review Committee: _____ Date: _____

[This page intentionally left blank]

Document ID **ITSD103**	Title **IT MEDIA STORAGE**	Print Date **mm/dd/yyyy**
Revision **0.0**	Prepared By **Preparer's Name / Title**	Date Prepared **mm/dd/yyyy**
Effective Date **mm/dd/yyyy**	Reviewed By **Reviewer's Name / Title**	Date Reviewed **mm/dd/yyyy**
	Approved By **Final Approver's Name / Title**	Date Approved **mm/dd/yyyy**

Policy: To ensure adequate protection and proper handling of Company data and Information Technology storage media.

Purpose: To establish controls and procedures for storage, protection, access, procurement and destruction of Company data, Information Technology storage media, and related software; to plan for cost-effective storage technologies that offer long asset life and scalability; and to ensure data integrity and availability.

Scope: This procedure applies to all Company data stored by the Information Technology Department, regardless of storage medium.

Responsibilities:

Information Technology Managers are responsible for developing and reviewing the Company's data storage plan.

The Information Technology Storage Librarian is responsible for implementing the Company data storage plan.

Definitions: Network-attached storage (NAS) – Hard disk storage set up with its own network address rather than being attached to the department computer serving applications to a network's workstation users.

RAID - Redundant Array of Independent Disks is a method of storing the same data in different places (thus, redundantly) on multiple hard disks.

Storage-area network (SAN) - A high-speed, special-purpose network or subnetwork connecting different kinds of Information Technology storage devices with data servers on behalf of a large network of users.

Storage media – In computers, a storage medium is any technology (including devices and materials) used to place, keep, and retrieve data. The term "storage medium" usually refers to secondary storage, such as that on a hard disk or tape.

Procedure:

1.0   IT STORAGE PLANNING

1.1   Information Technology Managers shall oversee development and implementation of an Information Storage Plan that:

- Ensures data availability, confidentiality, and integrity;

- Enables rapid and full recovery from natural or manmade disasters;

- Ensures Company compliance with industry standards and/or legal & regulatory requirements for data storage; and

- Allows efficient, cost-effective data management.

1.2   To develop the Company's Information Storage Plan, Information Technology Managers shall:

- Conduct a needs analysis – determine the Company's storage capacity and requirements by conducting a historical analysis of storage use and reviewing user satisfaction surveys, in accordance with ITAD110 IT DEPARTMENT SATISFACTION and ITAM102 IT ASSET MANAGEMENT;

- Research and benchmark Information Technology industry practices and standards; and

- Account for pertinent legal/regulatory requirements (see References A – D).

1.3   Information Technology Managers shall design the Information Storage Plan, with the assistance of the Information Technology Storage Librarian.

1.4   Information Technology Managers shall submit the Information Storage Plan to Top Management for its review and approval.

1.5   Upon approval of the Plan, Information Technology Managers shall communicate the Plan to the Information Technology Storage Librarian and shall arrange for training, as needed.

2.0   IT STORAGE PLAN

2.1   Data stores (databases, etc.) shall be uniquely identified, as shall their owners (departments/parties with primary responsibility for generating and updating information).

2.2   Data stores shall be identified as mission-critical or not and shall be assigned security levels, indicating whether access shall be restricted, in accordance with ITSD106 IT ACCESS CONTROL.

2.3   All data stores shall be backed up according to a set schedule and type. Data shall be retained and disposed of in accordance with ITAD102 IT RECORDS MANAGEMENT.

2.4   Backed-up data shall be subjected to a periodic recovery test, in accordance with ITSD104 IT DISASTER RECOVERY.

2.5   The Information Technology Storage Librarian shall be responsible for implementing the Information Storage Plan, monitoring storage use, and periodically submitting a status report on information storage to Information Technology Managers.

- The Information Technology Storage Librarian shall receive vendor training in the event of new storage technologies being implemented.

3.0   IT STORAGE PLAN REVIEW

3.1   Information Technology Managers shall periodically (annually, at a minimum) meet with the Information Technology Storage Librarian to review the Information Storage Plan and determine its continuing suitability and conformity to Company requirements and to ensure that data are retrievable and not in danger of loss due to technology changes.

The Information Technology Storage Librarian shall report on changes in Information Technology industry practices, standards, and technologies that have occurred since the most recent review, for possible incorporation into the Plan.

3.2   An external audit of the Company's Information Storage Plan and processes should be conducted no less than once every three years.

3.3   Information Technology Managers shall review the results of such audits and reviews, incorporate them into the Information Technology Storage Plan as needed, and communicate the changes to the Information Technology Storage Librarian.

4.0   UPDATING THE IT STORAGE PLAN

4.1   The Information Technology Storage Librarian shall implement required changes to the Information Technology Storage Plan.

4.2   Within a month of such changes being implemented, Information Technology Managers shall conduct a review with the Information Technology Storage Librarian to verify implementation of changes and verify that the desired results were achieved.

Forms:

- ITSD103-1 INFORMATION STORAGE PLAN

References:

A. NATIONAL ARCHIVES AND RECORDS ADMINISTRATION (NARA) RETENTION AND ACCESS REQUIREMENTS FOR RECORDS (36 CFR 1210.53)

Federal retention requirements for non-profits are specified in the Code of Federal Regulations (36 CFR 1210.53), which are published by the Office of the Federal Register, National Archives and Records Administration, and may be purchased from the U.S. Government Printing Office (GPO) in Washington, DC.

B. IRS PROCEDURE 98-25 – RECORDS RETENTION

The U.S. Tax Code requires that, except for farmers and wage-earners, anyone subject to income tax or any person required to file an information return with respect to income must keep such books and records, including inventories, as are sufficient to establish the amount of gross income, deductions, credits, or other matters reported. The books or records required by must be kept available at all times for inspection by authorized internal revenue officers or employees and must be retained so long as the contents thereof may become material in the administration of any internal revenue law.

Note: Section 6.01 requires taxpayers to maintain and make available documentation of the business processes that (1) create the retained records, (2) modify and maintain its records, (3) satisfy the requirements of section 5.01(2) of the procedure and verify the correctness of the taxpayer's return, and (4) evidence the authenticity and integrity of the taxpayer's records.

Section 6.02 sets forth four elements that the documentation required under section 6.01 must establish: (1) the flow of data through the system, (2) internal controls that ensure accurate processing, (3) internal controls that prevent unauthorized record changes, and (4) charts of account.

Section 6.03 sets forth six specific types of documentation for each retained file: (1) record formats, (2) field definitions, (3) file descriptions, (4) evidence that periodic checks are undertaken to ensure that data remains accessible, (5) evidence that the records reconcile to the taxpayer's books, and (6) evidence that the records reconcile to the taxpayer's return.

C. SARBANES-OXLEY ACT OF 2002

The Sarbanes-Oxley Act, enacted by the U.S. Congress in July 2002, created new standards for corporate accountability and new penalties for acts of wrongdoing. Sarbanes-Oxley, or SOX, holds corporate executive officers responsible for financial reporting, mandates internal control processes, and outlaws changing or destroying financial records. SOX also sets forth new records retention guidelines for corporations; in particular, section 802 of the Act pertains to criminal penalties for alteration or destruction of documents.

D. HEALTH INSURANCE PORTABILITY AND ACCOUNTABILITY ACT OF 1996 (HIPAA)

Regarding the subject of records storage, the Health Insurance Portability and Accountability Act (HIPAA), enacted by the U.S. Congress in 1996, does not specify storage requirements. The Act is, however, designed to allow patients access to their information, *however or wherever* it is stored.

E. ISO STANDARD 27002:2013 – INFORMATION TECHNOLOGY-CODE OF PRACTICE FOR INFORMATION SECURITY CONTROL, CLAUSE 12.1.3 (SAFEGUARDING OF ORGANIZATIONAL RECORDS)

For more, see http://www.iso.org/iso/iso_catalogue/catalogue_tc/catalogue_detail.htm?csnumber=50297.

Additional Resources:

A. The Storage Networking Industry Association (SNIA) is a registered 501-C6 non-profit trade association. See http://www.snia.org/home for more information on this organization.

B. American Institute of Certified Public Accountants (AICPA) Filing and Record Retention Procedures Guide. See http://www.aicpa.org for further information.

Revision History:

Revision	Date	Description of Changes	Requested By
0	mm/dd/yyyy	Initial Release	

[This page intentionally left blank]

ITSD103-1 INFORMATION STORAGE PLAN

Data store name:

Data store ID:

Department:

Responsible party / owner:

Key source of information
(information is mission-critical): ☐ Y ☐ N

Purpose: ☐ Daily usage   ☐ Archival   ☐ Backup & recovery

A. Security level (1=all may access / 5=restricted to owner, IT Security, auditors):

B. Backup schedule / frequency:

C. Backup type (full / partial / incremental):

D. Storage medium (disk, tape, SAN, NAS, etc.):
    • Expected useful life of medium:

E. Retention period:

F. Data disposal (archived data only)
    • Method of disposal:

G. Recovery testing (date):

IT Management: _____ Date: _____

IT Storage Librarian: _____ Date: _____

[This page intentionally left blank]

Document ID **ITSD104**	Title **IT DISASTER RECOVERY**	Print Date **mm/dd/yyyy**
Revision **0.0**	Prepared By **Preparer's Name / Title**	Date Prepared **mm/dd/yyyy**
Effective Date **mm/dd/yyyy**	Reviewed By **Reviewer's Name / Title**	Date Reviewed **mm/dd/yyyy**
	Approved By **Final Approver's Name / Title**	Date Approved **mm/dd/yyyy**

Policy: To ensure continuity of Company operations.

Purpose: To define recovery objectives and to specify a set of procedures for achieving those objectives.

Scope: This policy applies to all Company personnel and Information Technology systems, networks, and assets.

Responsibilities: The Information Technology Disaster Recovery Coordinator is responsible for chairing the Information Technology Disaster Recovery Planning Committee, coordinating Information Technology disaster response and recovery, reporting on disaster response and recovery, and updating the Recovery Plan.

The Information Technology Security Manager is responsible for conducting and/or supervising testing of the Information Technology Disaster Recovery Plan.

The Information Technology Disaster Recovery Planning Committee is responsible for developing and reviewing the Information Technology Disaster Recovery Plan.

The Information Technology Storage Librarian is responsible for backing up and restoring Company data.

The Tech Support Representative are responsible for various recovery tasks, such as installation and testing of replacement equipment, operations systems, applications software, communications, etc.

Top Management is responsible for final approval of the Information Technology Disaster Recovery Plan.

All employees are responsible for notifying the Information Technology Disaster Recovery Coordinator in the event of an actual or suspected disaster that may affect any part of the Company's Information Technology systems, infrastructure, or assets.

Definitions: Business continuity – The degree to which an organization may achieve uninterrupted stability of systems and operational procedures.

Information Technology disaster – A sudden, significant event that may result in the loss or destruction of Company information and/or loss of service on the Company's Information Technology network.

Procedure:

1.0 IT DISASTER RECOVERY PLANNING

1.1   The Company must assume a major disaster – environmental disaster, loss of utilities, large-scale equipment failure, a cyber attack, and so on – will befall it eventually. To be prepared for disaster – to best ensure the continuity of business, should a disaster occur – the Company shall develop an Information Technology Disaster Recovery Plan. The Information Technology Disaster Recovery Plan (DRP) shall be an integral part of the Company's overall DRP, just as information technology is an integral part of the Company. (See Reference A.)

The Company shall implement the Plan, educating employees in their roles and responsibilities; test the Plan, to see if it will ensure rapid and full recovery; and fix flaws identified in testing, to better ensure the Plan will work when it is most needed.

1.2   The Company shall establish an Information Technology Disaster Recovery Planning Committee (Information Technology DRPC), composed of key personnel from each functional area within the Company (HR, accounting, sales, etc.) and an Information Technology Disaster Recovery Coordinator, who shall chair the Committee.

1.3   The Information Technology Disaster Recovery Coordinator shall obtain and analyze information for development of the Information Technology Disaster Recovery Plan, such as:

- Conducting a risk assessment of each of the Company's Information Technology systems, in accordance with ITSD101 – IT THREAT/RISK ASSESSMENT;

- Determining the Information Technology Department's current state of readiness for disaster by running a recovery capability test, to establish a baseline;

- Gathering Information Technology industry information on best practices and technologies and identifying appropriate means of mitigating risk; and

- Identifying and assessing external resources and their capabilities.

1.4   The Information Technology DRPC shall meet to:

- Analyze and discuss the information obtained by the Information Technology Disaster Recovery Coordinator;

- Identify mission-critical systems and services, determining how long each business unit can survive without those systems/services in operation (conduct a business impact analysis);

- Establish recovery priorities;

- Develop the Information Technology Disaster Recovery Plan in accordance with ITSD102 IT SECURITY PLAN, using ITSD104-1 IT DISASTER RECOVERY PLAN as a guide.

- Submit to top management for final approval.

1.5   The Information Technology Disaster Recovery Coordinator shall:

- Ensure that the Information Technology Disaster Recovery Plan is documented and communicated to all employees; and

- Coordinate Information Technology disaster recovery training with the Human Resources Manager.

2.0   IT DISASTER RECOVERY PLAN

2.1   The Information Technology Storage Librarian shall ensure periodic backups of Company information stores (databases, etc.), in accordance with ITSD103 – IT MEDIA STORAGE.

2.2   The Information Technology Storage Librarian shall periodically conduct a test of all backed-up data for integrity and recovery speed; frequency and extent of such testing shall be determined by mission criticality of the information. The Storage Librarian shall submit a recovery test report to the Information Technology Disaster Recovery Coordinator for review and possible action.

2.3   In the event any employee knows of or suspects an Information Technology disaster, the employee shall contact the Information Technology Disaster Recovery Coordinator and the DRC shall begin the response and recovery process in accordance with the Plan.

3.0   IT DISASTER RECOVERY PLAN REVIEW

3.1   Subsequent to an actual disaster and recovery, the Information Technology Disaster Recovery Coordinator shall prepare a response and recovery report and submit it to the Information Technology Disaster Recovery Planning Committee for review. The Committee may recommend revisions to the Plan, based on the findings contained in the report.

3.2   The Information Technology Security Manager shall test Information Technology disaster response and recovery at least once every 12 months. The Information Technology Security Manager should also test response and recovery upon any changes to the Plan (see section 4.2).

3.3   The Information Technology DRPC shall review the Information Technology Disaster Recovery Plan on a regular basis (every two years, at a minimum) to determine if it continues to meet Company, customer, and legal/regulatory requirements.

3.4   The Information Technology Disaster Recovery Plan shall be periodically (at least once every three years) subjected to a third-party audit, to verify that the Plan is clear, sound, and continues to meet Company, customer, and legal/regulatory requirements.

4.0   IT DISASTER RECOVERY PLAN REVISION

4.1   After any review of the Information Technology Disaster Recovery Plan, the Information Technology Disaster Recovery Coordinator shall be responsible for updating the Plan.

4.2   Within one month of any such update, the Information Technology Security Manager shall verify that the update is capable of providing the desired results by conducting a response and recovery test.

Forms:

- ITSD104-1 DISASTER RECOVERY PLAN

References:

A. BIZMANUALZ® #ABR33M, "DISASTER RECOVERY POLICIES AND PROCEDURES"

This publication is a prototype, or template, for developing a *physical disaster recovery plan* suited to an organization's needs and requirements. Any Information Technology disaster recovery plan must be integrated into the organization's overall DRP, because Information Technology is an integral part of any organization and because Information Technology disasters may have a physical dimension to them (e.g., fire, flood).

B. THE PUBLIC COMPANY ACCOUNTING REFORM AND INVESTOR PROTECTION ACT OF 2002 (SARBANES-OXLEY, SOX)

While Sarbanes-Oxley (USA) does not specifically mention "disaster recovery", universal acceptance and use of information technologies and the requirements of SOX – that a public company demonstrate "adequate internal controls" and ensure integrity and timeliness of its financial records – imply that a disaster recovery plan is needed for an organization to maintain SOX compliance.

C. ISO/IEC 27002:2013, "INFORMATION TECHNOLOGY-CODE OF PRACTICE FOR INFORMATION SECURITY CONTROL (INFORMATION BACK-UP)"

For more, see http://www.iso.org/iso/catalogue_detail.htm?csnumber=54533.

D. HEALTH INSURANCE PORTABILITY AND ACCOUNTABILITY ACT OF 1996 (HIPAA)

HIPAA (US law) is designed primarily to allow patients access to their medical records and ensure privacy and portability of those records. The Act requires health care providers to have a "reasonable and appropriate" data backup plan, disaster recovery plan, and plan for operating in emergency mode.

E. EXPEDITED FUNDS AVAILABILITY ACT OF 1989 (EFA)

The EFAA (USA) requires that federally chartered financial institutions have a "business continuity plan" to ensure prompt availability of funds.

F. NIST SPECIAL PUBLICATION #800-53, REV. 4, "SECURITY AND PRIVACY CONTROLS FOR FEDERAL INFORMATION SYSTEMS AND ORGANIZATIONS"

This publication (last update – Apr., 2013) refers to contingency plan development, testing, update, and coordination. See details at http://nvlpubs.nist.gov/nistpubs/SpecialPublications/NIST.SP.800-53r4.pdf.

Additional Resources:

A. Business Software Alliance (BSA - http://www.bsa.org/)

B. The International Association of Emergency Managers (IAEM) is a non-profit educational organization dedicated to promoting the goals of saving lives and protecting property during emergencies and disasters. For more information, go to http://www.iaem.com/.

C. International Association of Emergency Managers (IAEM) – http://www.iaem.com.home/cfm.

D. Disaster Recovery Journal – http://www.drj.com/.

Revision History:

Revision	Date	Description of Changes	Requested By
0.0	mm/dd/yyyy	Initial Release	

ITSD104-1 IT DISASTER RECOVERY PLAN

Department: **Information Technology**

Address: _____

City: _____

State: _____ ZIP: _____

Phone: _____

FAX: _____

Department Leader: _____

Title _____

Assistant Department Leader: _____

Title _____

1.0   Maintaining contact with members of the Company's Disaster Recovery Team during a disaster is critical to a successful Department recovery effort. Usual business phone numbers are listed below; these numbers should be used for all primary contact with Team members.

Disaster Recovery Coordinator:

Primary   Name: _____

Office Phone: _____

Emergency Phone: _____

Cellular Phone: _____

Secondary   Name: _____

Office Phone: _____

Emergency Phone: _____

Cellular Phone: _____

Facilities / Equipment / Supplies / Transportation / Telecommunications:

Name: _____   Phone: _____

Emergency Phone: _____

Cellular Phone: _____

Other Department Leaders:

Name: _____   Phone: _____

Emergency Phone: _____

Cellular Phone: _____

Name: _____   Phone: _____

Emergency Phone: _____

Cellular Phone: _____

Name: _____   Phone: _____

Emergency Phone: _____

Cellular Phone: _____

Name: _____   Phone: _____
Emergency Phone: _____
Cellular Phone: _____

Name: _____   Phone: _____
Emergency Phone: _____
Cellular Phone: _____

2.0   In the event that normal phone lines are not functional, alternate communications may be available by public phones. The public phones most readily accessible by Department personnel are:
Public Phone #1 (area code & number): _____
        Location: _____
Public Phone #2: _____
        Location: _____
Public Phone #3: _____
        Location: _____

3.0   The company has established a hotline phone number for emergency use by all employees. Use of this special number is restricted to disaster recovery efforts and emergency notifications only, and is not to be used for any other purpose.
Disaster Recovery Hotline number (for employees only): _____
Security Alarm Company number: _____

4.0   The Department Leader or designate is to immediately take the following actions if a disaster occurs:
1. Assess any injury or damage to employees, clients, contractors, and facilities.
2. Temporarily close and secure the facility, if necessary.
3. Contact appropriate emergency services, if necessary.
4. Begin documenting the effects of the disaster and actions taken; secure all assets and records.
5. First attempt to contact the company's Disaster Recovery Team Coordinators or Chairpersons with a damage assessment and actions taken report, and act upon instructions received.
6. If all documented attempts to communicate with Coordinators and Chairpersons have failed, the Department Leader or designate is authorized to initiate reasonable and prudent responses necessary to minimize potential:
    • Injuries to employees, contractors, and clients;
    • Damage to facilities; and
    • Loss of assets and records.

5.0   The critical functions of the Information Technology Department, to be serviced before the performance of any other task, are:
    • Administrative operations;
    • Computer operations;
    • Network management;
    • Technical Support;

- Control (custody) of mission-critical Company records; and
- Security (physical and I.T.).

6.0   The accessory, or secondary, functions of the Information Technology Department are to be performed only after all critical functions have been addressed. Accessory functions of the Information Technology Department include:

- Information Technology project planning;
- Project management;
- System analysis and design;
- Software development;
- Software testing;
- Software documentation;
- Software release;
- Software support; and
- Software training.

7.0   Description of Department Leader's duties and responsibilities during a disaster:

1. Ultimately responsible for overall Department operations, including all personnel, clients, facilities, and Information Technology assets.
2. Department Security Officer, Department Compliance Officer, and Department Disaster Recovery Team Coordinator; interior and exterior Department physical security and appearance.
3. Ensure adequate supervision for all personnel and functions while absent from the company or unavailable for contact; operational quality control.
4. Respond to and comply with all regulations, policies, and procedures regarding Department operations; prepare reports as required.
5. Client (user) service and relations; resolving client complaints; approve unusual or unique transaction when no other person has immediate authority to do so; provide information to Company supervisor for media relations and all requests for interviews from the press, radio, and television.
6. Provide appropriate members of the Disaster Recovery Team with accurate and timely information updates regarding the Department's recovery efforts.
7. Other duties and responsibilities, as required.

8.0   Description of Assistant Department Leader's duties and responsibilities:

1. Perform all duties and responsibilities of the Department Leader in his/her absence or because of his/her unavailability.
2. Ensure dual custody requirements are maintained for all functions; maintain key, employee information log for dual custody assignments; enforce employee and functional security procedures, Department opening and closing procedures.
3. Manage day-to-day operational functions and directly supervise all staff personnel.
4. Other duties and responsibilities, as required.

9.0   If a disaster occurs during working hours, the staff will evacuate the facility and assemble at:

PRIMARY (name): _____

Location: _____

SECONDARY (name): _____

Location: _____

A diagram of the facility and designated emergency staging areas is located at the end of this section (Attachment 1).

10.0   If the Department is unable to function in its normal location, Department operations will immediately shift to these alternate sites:

PRIMARY: _____

Location: _____

Address: _____

City: _____

State: _____ ZIP: _____

Phone: _____

FAX: _____

SECONDARY: _____

Location: _____

Address: _____

City: _____

State: _____ ZIP: _____

Phone: _____

FAX: _____

11.0   Recovery shall proceed according to the following timeline:

Within **two hours** of an Information Technology disaster, The Information Technology Disaster Recovery Coordinator shall:

- Assess the damage;
- Ensure that Top Management and Information Technology Management have been notified;
- Determine if on-site recovery is feasible or if remote sites shall be utilized;
- Notify the Information Technology Security Manager and Tech Support of the problem; and
- Ensure that Company employees have been notified.

Within **four hours**, the Information Technology Disaster Recovery Coordinator shall:

- Notify the Company's Customer Support services;
- Notify offsite data storage facilities;
- Notify Information Technology Managers at the primary and secondary recovery sites;

- Confer with Tech Support, the LAN Administrator, and the Information Technology Security Manager to review the situation and assign and schedule recovery tasks; and
- Contact the Company's Information Technology equipment supplier, if replacement equipment is needed.

Within **eight hours**, the Information Technology Disaster Recovery Coordinator shall:

- Provide an updated assessment of the situation to Top Management, including a recovery schedule estimate;
- Alert software vendors to interim operations requirements;
- Ensure that recovery tasks are underway; and
- Establish a base of interim operations, if necessary.

Within **twenty-four hours**, the Information Technology Disaster Recovery Coordinator shall:

- If replacement equipment is unavailable, begin alternate production schedules from a remote base of operations; and
- Ensure that the Company's communications capabilities have been tested and verified.

Within **forty-eight hours**, the Information Technology Disaster Recovery Coordinator shall:

- Provide an updated assessment of the situation to Top Management,
- Notify Company departments of interim production schedules; and
- Reestablish a full production schedule, following the priorities set forth by the Information Technology Disaster Recovery Planning Committee.

On delivery of any replacement equipment, Tech Support shall:

- Notify the Information Technology Disaster Recovery Coordinator;
- Install and test software on the replacement equipment;
- Restore data on replacement equipment;
- Monitor restored operations; and
- Resume a full production schedule.

Within **five working days**, the Information Technology Disaster Recovery Coordinator shall:

- Provide an updated assessment of the situation to Top Management;
- Notify Company employees of resumption of normal production schedules; and
- Resume normal operations.

12.0   If the Department is still operable, this checklist describes the functions or sections upon which you will concentrate recovery efforts, and in what order. Before opening the Department:

a.   Assess safety considerations for employees and customers.

b. Coordinate with emergency services agencies, if necessary.

c. Conduct a damage assessment of the building and determine levels of operation and full restoration time for electricity, telephones, water, and computers.

d. Ensure all areas of responsibility are staffed.

e. Ensure adequate equipment and supplies are available.

f. Arrange for the safe relocation of all records and equipment, if necessary.

13.0   If it is safe to open the Department, reestablish:

- Employee, customer, facility, assets, and records security;
- Contact with Top Management;
- Corporate files and financial records;
- Personnel and fixed asset records;
- Accounting records;
- Sales records; and
- Other Company records.

14.0   The Department requires these logistical factors to be available to perform critical functions:
Square feet: _____
Maximum number of personnel (employees and contractors): _____
Maximum number of customers: _____
Special relocation needs in the event the facility is unable to support Department operations are:

_____

_____

15.0   A listing of all emergency services, personnel, and equipment available to this Department is located at the end of this procedure (Attachment 1). Additional guidelines to assist disaster recovery efforts for this Department are:
Written operations procedures: _____
Location stored: _____
Container description: _____

16.0   All service agreements and vendor information are available by contacting:

_____

_____

17.0   Additional office supplies, emergency equipment and survival supplies to assist disaster recovery efforts for this Department are:
Emergency medical supplies available:

_____

_____

Location stored:

_____

_____

Container description:

_____

_____

An appropriate supply of the following forms is to be maintained:

[This page intentionally left blank]

Attachment 1
FACILITY DIAGRAM AND EMERGENCY STAGING AREAS

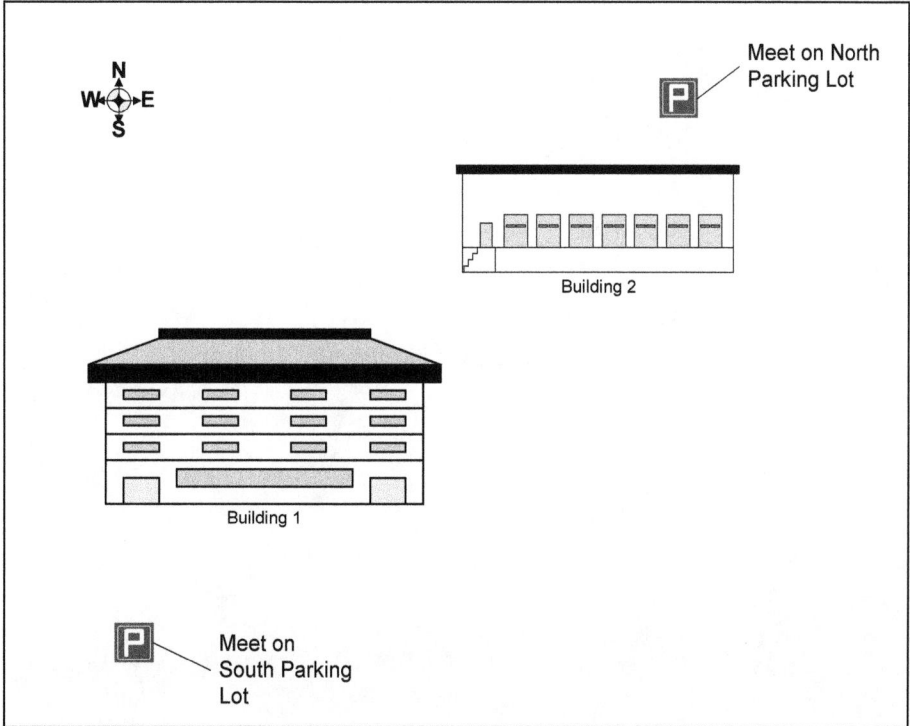

Meet on North
Parking Lot

Building 2

Building 1

Meet on
South Parking
Lot

[This page intentionally left blank]

Attachment 2
EMERGENCY SERVICES & AGENCIES LIST

EMERGENCY SERVICES

Name: Police Department

City:

County:

Emergency Phone: 911

Business Phone:

Name: Sheriff's Department

County:

Emergency Phone: 911

Business Phone:

Name: Fire Department

City:

County:

Emergency Phone: 911

Business Phone:

Name: Paramedic/Rescue #1

City:

County:

Emergency Phone: 911

Business Phone:

Name: Air Ambulance

County:

Emergency Phone:

Business Phone:

Name: Private Ambulance #1

County:

Emergency Phone:

Business Phone:

Name: Private Ambulance #2

County:

Emergency Phone:

Business Phone:

HOSPITAL / URGENT CARE FACILITY

Name: Hospital #1

Address:

City:

County:

Emergency Phone:

Business Phone:

Name: Hospital #2

Address:

City:

County:

Emergency Phone:

Business Phone:

Name: Hospital #3

Address:

City:

County:

Emergency Phone:

Business Phone:

Name: Urgent Care Facility #1

Address:

City:

County:

Emergency Phone:

Business Phone:

Name: Urgent Care Facility #2

Address:

City:

County:

Emergency Phone:

Business Phone:

EMERGENCY STAGING FACILITIES AND SHELTERS

Name: American Red Cross

Address:

City:

County:

Emergency Phone:

Business Phone:

Staging location:

Name: Community Center #1

Address:

City:

County:

Emergency Phone:

Business Phone:

Staging location:

Name: Community Center #2

Address:

City:

County:

Emergency Phone:

Business Phone:

Staging location:

Name: National Guard Center

Address:

City:

County:

Emergency Phone:

Business Phone:

Staging location:

Name: Veterans Memorial Building

Address:

City:

County:

Emergency Phone:

Business Phone:

Staging location:

DISASTER INFORMATION

Name: Medical Emergency Information Hotline

County:

Emergency Phone:

Name: Office of Emergency Services (City)

Address:

City:

County:

Emergency Phone:

Business Phone:

Staging location:

Name: Office of Emergency Services (County)

Address:

City:

County:

Emergency Phone:

Business Phone:

Staging location:

Name: Office of Emergency Services (State)

Address:

City:

County:

Emergency Phone:

Staging location:

COMMUNICATIONS

Name: Company for remote contact #1

Address:

Phone 1:

Phone 2:

FAX:

Name: Company for remote contact #2

Address:

Phone 1:

Phone 2:

FAX:

Name: Mobile telephone #1

Address:

Phone 1:

Phone 2:

Cellular access numbers:

Name: Mobile telephone #2

Address:

Phone 1:

Phone 2:

Cellular access numbers:

Name: Newspaper #1

City:

County:

Emergency Phone:

Business Phone:

FAX:

Name: Newspaper #2

City:

County:

Emergency Phone:

Business Phone:

FAX:

Name: Public telephone #1 (3 for each facility)

Address or location:

Phone:

Name: Public telephone #2 (3 for each facility)

Address or location:

Phone:

Name: Public telephone #3 (3 for each facility)

Address or location:

Phone:

Name: Radio Station #1

City:

County:

Emergency Phone:

Business Phone:

FAX:

Name: Radio Station #2

City:

County:

Emergency Phone:

Business Phone:

FAX:

Name: Television Station #1

City:

County:

Emergency Phone:

Business Phone:

FAX:

Name: Television Station #2

City:

County:

Emergency Phone:

Business Phone:

FAX:

SECURITY

Name: Alarm Company #1

City:

County:

Emergency Phone:

Business Phone:

Name: Alarm Company #2

City:

County:

Emergency Phone:

Business Phone:

Name: Guard Company #1

City:

County:

Emergency Phone:

Business Phone:

Name: Guard Company #2

City:

County:

Emergency Phone:

Business Phone:

TRANSPORTATION

Name: Airport/Municipal (City)

Address:

City:

County:

Emergency Phone:

Business Phone:

Name: Airport/Regional (County)

Address:

City:

County:

Emergency Phone:

Business Phone:

Name: Bus (City)

City:

County:

Emergency Phone:

Business Phone:

Name: Bus (County)

City:

County:

Emergency Phone:

Business Phone:

Name: Cab/Taxi #1

City:

County:

Emergency Phone:

Business Phone:

Name: Cab/Taxi #2

City:

County:

Emergency Phone:

Business Phone:

Name: Car Rental Agency #1

City:

County:

Emergency Phone:

Business Phone:

Name: Car Rental Agency #2

City:

County:

Emergency Phone:

Business Phone:

Name: Cash - Records Transport/Supplemental #1

City:

County:

Emergency Phone:

Business Phone:

Name: Cash - Records Transport/Supplemental #2

City:

County:

Emergency Phone:

Business Phone:

Name: Moving Company #1

City:

County:

Emergency Phone:

Business Phone:

Name: Moving Company #2

City:

County:

Emergency Phone:

Business Phone:

CITY / COUNTY OFFICES

Name: Administrative Offices (City)

City:

County:

Emergency Phone:

Business Phone:

Name: Administrative Offices (County)

City:

County:

Emergency Phone:

Business Phone:

Name: Air Quality Control Offices (County)

City:

County:

Emergency Phone:

Business Phone:

Name: Animal Control (City)

City:

County:

Emergency Phone:

Business Phone:

Name: Animal Control (County)

City:

County:

Emergency Phone:

Business Phone:

Name: Building Inspector (City)

City:

County:

Emergency Phone:

Business Phone:

Name: Building Inspector (County)

City:

County:

Emergency Phone:

Business Phone:

Name: Hazardous Materials Team (County)

City:

County:

Emergency Phone:

Business Phone:

Name: Health (City)

County:

Emergency Phone:

Business Phone:

Name: Health (County)

City:

County:

Emergency Phone:

Business Phone:

Name: Health and Safety Inspector (County)

City:

County:

Emergency Phone:

Business Phone:

Name: Mental Health (City)

City:

County:

Emergency Phone:

Business Phone:

Name: Mental Health (County)

City:

County:

Emergency Phone:

Business Phone:

Name: Parks and Recreation (City)

County:

Emergency Phone:

Business Phone:

Name: Parks and Recreation (County)

County:

Emergency Phone:

Business Phone:

Name: Public Information Office (City)

City:

County:

Emergency Phone:

Business Phone:

Name: Public Information Office (County)

City:

County:

Emergency Phone:

Business Phone:

Name: Public Works (City)

City:

County:

Emergency Phone:

Business Phone:

Name: Public Works (County)

City:

County:

Emergency Phone:

Business Phone:

Name: Schools Information (City)

City:

County:

Emergency Phone:

Business Phone:

Name: Schools Information (County)

City:

County:

Emergency Phone:

Business Phone:

Name: Transportation/Roads (City)

City:

County:

Emergency Phone:

Business Phone:

Name: Transportation/Roads (County)

City:

County:

Emergency Phone:

Business Phone:

FEDERAL OFFICES

Name: Department of Corporations

Address:

Emergency Phone:

Business Phone:

Name: Federal Bureau of Investigation

Address:

Emergency Phone:

Business Phone:

UTILITIES

Name: Electric

City:

County:

Emergency Phone:

Business Phone:

Name: Gas

City:

County:

Emergency Phone:

Business Phone:

Name: Sanitation/Sewer

City:

County:

Emergency Phone:

Business Phone:

Name: Telephone

City:

County:

Emergency Phone:

Business Phone:

Name: Water

City:

County:

Emergency Phone:

Business Phone:

CONTRACTORS / VENDORS

Name: Building/Reconstruction Contractor

City:

County:

Emergency Phone:

Business Phone:

Name: Electrical Contractor

City:

County:

Emergency Phone:

Business Phone:

Name: Glass Contractor

City:

County:

Emergency Phone:

Business Phone:

Name: Grounds keeping Contractor

City:

County:

Emergency Phone:

Business Phone:

Name: Hazardous Materials Response Contractor

City:

County:

Emergency Phone:

Business Phone:

Name: Health and Safety Contractor

City:

County:

Emergency Phone:

Business Phone:

Name: Janitorial Contractor

City:

County:

Emergency Phone:

Business Phone:

Name: Locksmith and Vault Contractor

City:

County:

Emergency Phone:

Business Phone:

Name: Office Supplies and Forms Contractor

City:

County:

Emergency Phone:

Business Phone:

Name: Plumbing Contractor

City:

County:

Emergency Phone:

Business Phone:

Name: Roofing Contractor

City:

County:

Emergency Phone:

Business Phone:

Name: Utility Contractor

City:

County:

Emergency Phone:

Business Phone:

<u>EQUIPMENT</u>

Name: Software vendor #1

City:

County:

Emergency Phone:

Business Phone:

Name: Software vendor #2

City:

County:

Emergency Phone:

Business Phone:

Name: Software vendor #3

City:

County:

Emergency Phone:

Business Phone:

Name: Software vendor #4

City:

County:

Emergency Phone:

Business Phone:

Name: Mainframe computer vendor

City:

County:

Emergency Phone:

Business Phone:

Name: Office equipment other than computers & peripherals

City:

County:

Emergency Phone:

Business Phone:

Name: Computer equipment (PC's, network hardware, peripherals) vendor #1

City:

County:

Emergency Phone:

Business Phone:

Name: Computer equipment (PC's, network hardware, peripherals) vendor #2

City:

County:

Emergency Phone:

Business Phone:

Name: Computer equipment (PC's, network hardware, peripherals) vendor #3

City:

County:

Emergency Phone:

Business Phone:

Name: Computer equipment (PC's, network hardware, peripherals) vendor #4

City:

County:

Emergency Phone:

Business Phone:

Document ID	Title	Print Date
ITSD105	**COMPUTER MALWARE**	**mm/dd/yyyy**
Revision	Prepared By	Date Prepared
0.0	**Preparer's Name / Title**	**mm/dd/yyyy**
Effective Date	Reviewed By	Date Reviewed
mm/dd/yyyy	**Reviewer's Name / Title**	**mm/dd/yyyy**
	Approved By	Date Approved
	Final Approver's Name / Title	**mm/dd/yyyy**

Policy: The Company shall protect its Information Technology assets from infection by malicious software, or malware.

Purpose: To prevent data loss, corruption, or misuse of Company computing resources or information that may occur when malware is introduced to the Company Information Technology network.

Scope: This policy applies to all Company personnel and to all computer hardware and software comprising the Company's Information Technology network.

Responsibilities:

The Information Technology Security Manager is responsible for implementing malware control procedures, training LAN Administrators and other Information Systems Department personnel, training users on computer malware control, and evaluating and updating appropriate computer malware detection software.

The LAN Administrator is responsible for coordinating actions required to prevent computer malware outbreaks, coordinating all actions required to eradicate the malware, and recovering data to the greatest extent possible.

The Tech Support Manager is responsible for installing and maintaining malware protection on Information Technology assets and for cleaning malware infections from Company applications, devices, etc.

Users are responsible for following the guidelines of this policy document and for immediately notifying the Information Technology Security Manager in the event a malware attack is suspected.

Definitions: Malware - Short for "malicious software", malware is designed to damage, disrupt, or abuse an individual computer or an entire network and/or steal or corrupt an organization's most valuable and sensitive data. Viruses, worms, and Trojan horses are examples of malware.

Spam or junk email – Unsolicited commercial email sent in bulk over the Internet. Spam puts a cost and a burden on recipients by clogging up network bandwidth, consuming disk space, and wasting employees' time. Spam is frequently a malware vector.

Subscription service – A service whereby a software vendor offers support for its product, usually for a predetermined time period. Anti-virus vendors typically include a one-year subscription (for updates, notices, etc.) with the purchase of a product license. Many vendors offer fee-based subscription services whereby subscribers automatically receive notifications, security bulletins, etc., for a set period of time.

Target – The ultimate destination for malware; that which the malware is designed to attack. Boot sectors, hard disk drives, email servers, and departmental (HR, accounting, etc.) servers are examples of malware targets.

Vector – How malware is carried to a computer, server, or system.

Procedure:

1.0   MALWARE DEFENSE PLANNING

1.1   How does malware typically work and what threats exist? Malware is commonly passed to a potential target through email. The person who receives the email opens an attachment, which unleashes the malware, which then spreads to other computers via a shared network. (Malware may attack by other means but this is a common method.) To lessen the potential for damage to the Company's Information Technology assets by malware, the Company should develop and implement a multifaceted approach to malware prevention.

1.2   To prepare the Company's Malware Defense Plan, The Information Technology Security Manager shall review the following items:

- ITSD101-2 IT THREAT ASSESSMENT REPORT;

- ITAM102-5 IT ASSET INVENTORY DATABASE;

- ITAM102-6 IT NETWORK MAP;

- Information Technology Industry standards and best practices;

- Anti-malware vendor web sites or portals; and

- Information Technology security alerts and bulletins (many of which are available for free and as a subscription service).

1.3   The Information Technology Security Manager shall use the preceding items (and possibly others) to develop a Malware Defense Plan. This Plan shall be submitted to Information Technology Management for review and approval.

1.4   Upon Information Technology Management's approval of the Malware Defense Plan, the Information Technology Security Manager shall implement the Plan, assign Plan responsibilities to members of the Tech Support Manager, and train (or supervise training of) Tech Support personnel.

The Information Technology Security Manager shall communicate the Plan to all employees except the Tech Support Manager and arrange employee training through the Human Resources department.

2.0   MALWARE DEFENSE PLAN

2.1   The Tech Support Manager shall install firewalls on all personal computers (workstations) and on all servers, in accordance with ITAM102 IT ASSET STANDARDS.

2.2   the Tech Support Manager shall ensure that operating systems, web browsers, email programs, and related software are configured for optimum security, also in accordance with ITAM102.

2.3   The Tech Support Manager shall install an anti-virus program on every PC and server (again, in accordance with ITAM102) and all anti-virus software shall be automatically updated through the use of a subscription service (updates should be automatically logged by the software).

- Additional anti-malware programs should be installed on all PC's and servers to protect against nuisances such as spyware and adware, which are potential malware vectors.

2.4   As vendors learn of vulnerabilities (bugs) in their software and repair them, they notify registered users, post bulletins on their web sites, and notify news media that these patches are available for download. Many vendors offer subscription services, through which the Company may be notified of security threats and related issues and obtain software patches.

The Company should subscribe to one or more notification services, in order to maintain its awareness of threats and to ensure all software is updated in a timely fashion.

2.5   The Tech Support Manager shall evaluate all software patches (for operating systems, browsers, email programs, applications, etc.) for relevance and criticality. If the patch is determined to be relevant (for example, an operating system security patch has more relevance - and is certainly more critical - than a foreign-language update of an application), the Tech Support Manager shall install the patch in a test environment and verify its effectiveness and compatibility with existing software before installing it in the production environment. Such updates shall be logged by the Tech Support Manager, if the software being patched does not automatically log activity.

2.6   All anti-malware protections shall be configured so as to prevent their being disabled by users. Only the Tech Support Manager staff, the Information Technology Security Manager, and members of the Information Technology Security staff shall be allowed to temporarily disable anti-malware measures (for example, disabling a local anti-virus program to install and configure an application locally).

- Users shall not be allowed to install software. Only the Tech Support Manager shall be allowed to install approved software, in accordance with ITAM101 IT ASSET STANDARDS.

2.7   The Company shall minimize malware risks by backing up critical information, in accordance with ITSD104 IT DISASTER RECOVERY.

2.8   All users shall be trained on the Malware Defense Plan at the outset. Users shall be retrained (updated) on the Plan at least once a year. The Human Resources Manager shall be responsible for Malware Defense Plan training.

- All users shall sign a statement at the end of training, indicating that they have received training, that they understand the Plan, and that they will conduct their business in accordance with the Plan.

3.0   MALWARE DEFENSE PLAN REVIEW

3.1   The Tech Support Manager shall periodically (once a week is recommended) review all anti-virus, firewall, and other relevant logs to determine if the software is up-to-date and is performing as expected. The Tech Support Manager shall report its findings to the Information Technology Security Manager for possible action.

3.2   The Information Technology Security Manager shall periodically (monthly, at a minimum) review user satisfaction data (see ITAD110-2 IT USER SATISFACTION SURVEY) and security incident information (see ITSD110-1 IT INCIDENT REPORT and ITSD101-1 IT THREAT ASSESSMENT REPORT) to determine incident trends and progress toward Company goals.

3.3   Information Technology Management shall periodically (annually, at a minimum) meet with the Information Technology Security Manager to review the Malware Defense Plan, to determine its continuing applicability and conformity to Company requirements.

3.4   A periodic (at least annual) audit of the Malware Defense Plan shall be conducted by an accredited auditor, to determine if the Plan is in use, if it is functioning as expected, and if it conforms to standards and requirements. Information Technology Management shall review the results of such audits and reviews with the Information Technology Security Manager and recommend changes to the Plan.

3.5   In the event that anti-malware measures do not prevent malware from infecting any part of the Company Information Technology network, that event shall be handled in accordance with ITSD110 IT INCIDENT HANDLING.

4.0   MALWARE DEFENSE PLAN UPDATE

4.1   The Information Technology Security Manager shall incorporate updates into the Malware Defense Plan and ensure communication of Plan changes to all employees.

4.2   Within a month of changes being made to the Malware Defense Plan, Information Technology Management shall conduct a review with the Information Technology Security Manager to verify that changes were implemented and the desired results are being achieved.

Forms:

- None.

References:

A. ISO/IEC 27002:2013 – INFORMATION TECHNOLOGY- CODE OF PRACTICE FOR INFORMATION SECURITY CONTROL

For more, see http://www.iso.org/iso/catalogue_detail.htm?csnumber=54533.

B. NIST SPECIAL PUBLICATION 800-83, REV. 1 (JULY, 2013) GUIDE TO MALWARE INCIDENT PREVENTION AND HANDLING FOR DESKTOPS AND LAPTOPS

This publication provides recommendations for improving an organization's malware incident prevention measures through several layers of controls. The guide gives extensive recommendations for enhancing an organization's existing incident response capability so that it is better prepared to handle malware incidents, particularly widespread ones.

The guide also focuses on providing practical strategies for detection, containment, eradication, and recovery from malware incidents in managed and non-managed environments. The recommendations in the publication address several forms of malware, as well as various malware transmission mechanisms, including removable media and network services such as email and Web browsing.

For details, see http://nvlpubs.nist.gov/nistpubs/SpecialPublications/NIST.SP.800-83r1.pdf.

Additional Resources:

A. "Microsoft Malware Defense Guide" – http://technet.microsoft.com/library/cc162791.

B. Search Security – http://searchsecurity.techtarget.com/.

C. Computer Security Institute – http://www.gocsi.com/.

D. Virus Bulletin – http://www.virusbtn.com/index.

E. Computer Security Resource Center, Computer Security Division, NIST (CSRC) – http://csrc.nist.gov/.

F. The SANS Institute – http://www.sans.org.

G. SecurityFocus.com (http://www.securityfocus.com/) facilitates discussions on security related topics, creates security awareness, and provides a comprehensive database of security knowledge and resources freely available to the public.

H. Microsoft Security Compliance Manager – http://technet.microsoft.com/library/cc677002.aspx.

Revision History:

Revision	Date	Description of Changes	Requested By
0	mm/dd/yyyy	Initial Release	

Document ID **ITSD106**	Title **IT ACCESS CONTROL**	Print Date **mm/dd/yyyy**
Revision **0.0**	Prepared By **Preparer's Name / Title**	Date Prepared **mm/dd/yyyy**
Effective Date **mm/dd/yyyy**	Reviewed By **Reviewer's Name / Title**	Date Reviewed **mm/dd/yyyy**
	Approved By **Final Approver's Name / Title**	Date Approved **mm/dd/yyyy**

Policy: The Company shall control access to its information to help ensure its confidentiality and integrity.

Purpose: To prevent unauthorized access to or use of Company information, to ensure its security, integrity, and availability to appropriate parties.

Scope: This applies to all Company information and to all storage and access methods.

Responsibilities:

The Human Resources Manager is responsible for reviewing requirements for access (with Information Technology Managers) and Access Control Plan user training.

Information Technology Managers are responsible for reviewing access requirements, convening the Security Review Committee to review the Plan, and verifying updates to the Plan.

The Information Technology Security Manager is responsible for developing an Access Control Plan, presenting the Plan to the Security Review Committee for review, communicating the Plan to Human Resources, monitoring the Plan, revising the Plan, as needed, and enforcing the Plan.

The Security Review Committee is responsible for reviewing and approving the Plan.

Users are responsible for knowing and following the Plan.

Definitions: Access control – Enforcement of specified authorization rules based on positive identification of users and the systems or data they are permitted to access (or, providing access to authorized users while denying access to unauthorized users).

Procedure:

1.0 PLANNING IT ACCESS CONTROL

1.1 Information Technology Managers shall, with the assistance of the Human Resources Manager, determine and evaluate the Company's position requirements for information access.

1.2   The Information Technology Security Manager shall determine the Company's current state of access control, to develop a baseline for the Access Control Plan.

1.3   Based on findings related to 1.1 and 1.2, the Information Technology Security Manager shall develop an Access Control Plan and submit it to Information Technology Managers for review and possible revision.

1.4   Information Technology Managers shall convene the Security Review Committee (see ITSD102 IT SECURITY PLAN) for review and final approval of the Access Control Plan.

1.5   The Information Technology Security Manager shall communicate the Plan to the HR Manager, who shall be responsible for training users on the Plan.

2.0   IT ACCESS CONTROL PLAN

2.1   The Access Control Plan shall contain the following, at a minimum:

- Business requirements for access regulation;

- Rules for managing user access;

- User responsibility guidelines;

- Access control and operating systems;

- Access control and applications; and

- Monitoring user access.

2.2   The Information Technology Security Manager shall be responsible for enforcing the Access Control Plan.

3.0   IT ACCESS CONTROL PLAN REVIEW

3.1   The Information Technology Security Manager shall monitor the Plan (are systems, databases, etc., being used appropriately by the right people) by reviewing access logs, security logs, etc., on a periodic basis (once a week is recommended). Findings of such reviews shall be reported to the Security Review Committee for its review and possible action.

3.2   The Security Review Committee shall periodically (annually, at a minimum) review the Access Control Plan for usability and applicability to Company and legal/regulatory requirements.

3.3   The SRC shall periodically (once every two years, at a minimum) authorize a third-party review of the Plan, to verify its conformance with requirements and to help evaluate the Plan's effectiveness.

3.4   Based on any findings, the Information Technology Security Manager may be required to revise the Plan. Any revision of the Plan shall be submitted to the Security Review Committee for its review and approval.

4.0   IT ACCESS CONTROL PLAN UPDATE

4.1   After any revision of the Access Control Plan, the Information Technology Security Manager shall implement required updates and communicate the revised

Plan to the HR Manager. The HR Manager shall be responsible for instructing employees on the revised Plan.

4.2   Within ten business days of any update to the Access Control Plan, Information Technology Managers shall verify that the update has been implemented and is providing the desired results.

Forms:

- ITSD106-1 IT ACCESS CONTROL PLAN
- ITSD106-2 IT USER ACCESS CONTROL DATABASE
- ITSD106-3 ACCESS CONTROL LOG
- ITSD106-4 USER ACCOUNT CONVENTIONS

References:

A. ISO 27002:2013 – INFORMATION TECHNOLOGY – CODE OF PRACTICE FOR INFORMATION SECURITY CONTROL

For more, see http://www.iso.org/iso/iso_catalogue/catalogue_tc/catalogue_detail.htm?csnumber=50297.

B. IEEE 802.1X – PORT-BASED NETWORK ACCESS CONTROL STANDARD

This IEEE standard is designed to enhance security of wireless local area networks on the IEEE 802.11 standard. 802.1x provides an authentication framework for wireless LANs which allows a user to be authenticated by a central authority.

C. GUIDE TO NIST INFORMATION SECURITY DOCUMENTS

This guide lists a number of NIST documents dealing with the subject of access control. See http://csrc.nist.gov/publications/CSD_DocsGuide.pdf.

Additional Resources:

A. Create Security Policies with Extended Port Access Control Lists for Windows Server 2012 R2 – http://technet.microsoft.com/en-us/library/dn375962.aspx.

Revision History:

Revision	Date	Description of Changes	Requested By
0	mm/dd/yyyy	Initial Release	

ITSD106-1 IT ACCESS CONTROL PLAN

1.0   Business Requirements For Regulating Access

    a. Every Information Technology user shall have a unique identifier and a system password assigned. See ITSD106-4 USER ACCOUNT CONVENTIONS for guidance.

    b. There shall be a system in place for authenticating and authorizing users beyond the login point. Access to applications, databases, etc., once a person is in the system must be controlled.

    c. Each user shall be given access to Information Technology resources based on position and department. Users shall be given the fewest privileges needed to perform their duties, as spelled out in their job descriptions.

    d. User activity shall be monitored frequently and reviewed for unusual, unauthorized, or illegal activity; current periods of inactivity, etc.

    e. User access may be suspended for:

- A number of consecutive failed logon attempts;
- Unauthorized or illegal activity; or
- An extended period of account inactivity.

Account suspension shall be conducted in accordance with ITSD110 Information Technology INCIDENT HANDLING.

    f. All users shall be made aware of access control policy and procedures. Users shall sign a statement to that effect and a record of that statement shall be kept by the Human Resources Department.

- All users shall review access control policy on an annual basis and shall sign a statement to the effect that they have reviewed the policy.

2.0   Management Of User Access

2.1   Users shall be formally registered at the time of their employment with the Company. Users shall be reregistered upon changing jobs within the company and deleted/unregistered upon leaving the Company or after a specific period (e.g., 30 days) of inactivity.

2.2   Access to Company information shall be granted on a need-to-know basis. Users shall be authorized according to minimum access requirements for their duties. Access may be "read only", "read/write", or "full access" and users may or may not be given administrative privileges for their computers and for certain data.

2.3   Password Control – also see ITSD106-4 USER ACCOUNT CONVENTIONS.

- Passwords must be eight characters or more in length.
- Passwords must contain a combination of alphabetic, numeric, and/or special characters.

- Default passwords must be changed upon initial login.

- Users shall change their passwords at least every sixty days. If a user password has not been changed in that time, a password change shall be forced on the user and the user shall be notified of the default password to be used at the next login.

- Passwords shall not be reused consecutively. There should be a system in place to keep a password history and prevent password reuse for several cycles (four or more is recommended).

- Accounts shall be automatically suspended upon three consecutive failed logon attempts. Users shall apply to the Information Technology Security Manager for a password reset.

- Systems shall identify and authenticate users before granting access.

2.4   The Information Technology Security Manager shall review all users' access rights/privileges on a regular basis (every 90 days, at a minimum).

3.0   User Responsibilities

3.1   Users must secure their equipment if it is to be unattended for any length of time. Screen locks should automatically activate after 15 minutes of inactivity (users may set screen locks to activate sooner and they should be allowed to activate screen locks immediately, if desired).

3.2   Users shall have direct access only to services and information that they have been specifically authorized to use. Unless expressly authorized, access to all resources and services is denied. The Information Technology Security Manager shall maintain an access control database for that purpose – see ITSD106-2 USER ACCESS CONTROL DATABASE for guidance.

3.3   All communications to external (i.e., Internet-based) resources by way of the Company Information Technology network shall be restricted to authorized users. Users shall apply for permission to access external resources and access shall be authorized on a case-by-case basis.

4.0   Operating Systems Access Control

4.1   Access to operating systems shall be limited to trusted, authorized users (for example, Tech Support staff).

4.2   Only authorized support personnel shall be authorized to access operating systems and utilities outside of normal business hours.

4.3   Access to operating systems and related utilities shall be logged and such logs shall be reviewed periodically (weekly, at a minimum) by the Information Technology Security Manager, who shall report unusual or suspect activity to Information Technology Managers.

4.4   Operating systems connections shall be terminated after 15 minutes of inactivity.

5.0   Application Access Control

5.1   Access to applications shall be limited to authorized users.

5.2   Access to applications shall be limited to normal business hours, with reasonable exceptions.

5.3   Application access shall be logged and those logs shall be reviewed by Information Technology Department Managers whose departments are responsible for developing, installing, and maintaining the applications.

5.4   Connections to applications should be terminated after a predetermined period of inactivity (15 minutes).

6.0   Monitoring System Access/Use

6.1   Instances of access and use of any Information Technology resource shall be automatically logged. ITSD106-3 ACCESS CONTROL LOG may be used for guidance.

6.2   Access control logs shall be retained in accordance with legal and regulatory requirements.

6.3   The Information Technology Security Manager shall periodically (once a week is recommended) review access control logs and present a status report to Information Technology Managers.

[This page intentionally left blank]

ITSD106-2 IT USER ACCESS CONTROL DATABASE

User ID	User Name	Department	Position	Password	Password Start Date	Resource 1	Access privilege	Resource 2	Access privilege	Resource 3	Access privilege

[This page intentionally left blank]

ITSD106-3 ACCESS CONTROL LOG

Access Date	Access Logon Time	Access Logoff Time	Equipment ID and Location	Access accepted-rejected	Data modification accepted-rejected	Nature of activity	

[This page intentionally left blank]

ITSD106-4 USER ACCOUNT CONVENTIONS

1.0   User Naming Conventions

Each Company employee granted access to the Information Technology network shall be assigned a unique user name or user ID. All user account names should be composed of eight or more alphanumeric characters and must follow a consistently applied pattern (for example, the first seven letters of the user's last name and first initial). Where users may share a pattern (for example, Ben and Bonnie Franklin), a character or number shall be substituted at the end of the second occurrence, to ensure that no two users have the same user name.

2.0   User Passwords

User passwords shall be a minimum of 6 alphanumeric characters. Passwords shall be set to expire every 90 days; users who wish to change their passwords more often shall not be prevented from doing so.

Users shall not continuously use the same password. The security subsystem of the network operating system or mainframe system shall be configured to remember at least the last five passwords.

When a new user account is created, the Information Technology Security Manager shall assign a temporary password. Security systems shall be set to force the new user to change his/her password upon logging in for the first time.

3.0   User Account Expirations

The Company corporate enterprise network supports a wide range of users. One user type is "Company employee." Employee user accounts shall not have an expiration date.

Users requiring temporary access, such as consultants or contractors whose tenure is finite, shall have an expiration date on their accounts. Extensions to temporary user accounts shall be coordinated with the departmental Systems Administrator and the HR Administrator.

4.0   Home Directories

Each user shall be assigned a home directory on a file server within their department.   User home directory names shall be the same as the user name. The user home directory shall have security permissions that allow the both the user and System Administrators full control over all contents in their home directories.

5.0   User Group Assignments

The access to resources on the network will be strictly limited to only those users with a specific business need. Security of specific file storage directories on network file servers will be managed by assigning appropriate access privileges to specific user groups. User groups are an administrative collection of users.

Users will be added to groups based on a number of criteria. Each department shall have an associated user group. Within each department, there may be any number of project specific user groups. Users may be members of multiple groups depending on their role in the Company and need for access to company resources. Users may also be members of groups within other departments if there is a specific business need.

6.0   Workstation Restrictions

In a high-security network where sensitive data is stored on a local computer, restrict which users can log on from that computer. For example, allow "UserA" to log onto the network only from a computer named "Computer1".

7.0   User Profiles

A user's computing environment is determined primarily by the user profile. Windows security, for example, requires a user profile for each account that has access to the system. The user profile contains all user-definable settings for the work environment of a computer running Windows, including display, regional, mouse, and sounds settings, and network and printer connections.

A user profile may be customized to restrict what users see in their interface and what tools they have available to use when they log on. For example, an administrator can remove the Administrative Tools folder to prevent a user from changing a configuration.

Document ID	Title	Print Date
ITSD107	**IT SECURITY AUDITS**	**mm/dd/yyyy**
Revision	Prepared By	Date Prepared
0.0	**Preparer's Name / Title**	**mm/dd/yyyy**
Effective Date	Reviewed By	Date Reviewed
mm/dd/yyyy	**Reviewer's Name / Title**	**mm/dd/yyyy**
	Approved By	Date Approved
	Final Approver's Name / Title	**mm/dd/yyyy**

Policy: To conduct periodic audits of Information Technology Security functions, processes, and procedures.

Purpose: To ensure that the Company's Information Technology security system conforms to legal, regulatory and Company requirements, that the system is effectively implemented and maintained, and that it performs as expected.

Scope: This applies to all Information Technology systems and assets.

Responsibilities:

Information Technology Managers are responsible for attending opening and closing meetings regarding the Information Technology Security audit, reviewing audit findings, and for final approval of the audit report.

The Audit Team Leader is responsible for: conducting and supervising the Information Technology Security audit; supervising audit team members, if any; conducting opening and closing meetings for the audit; preparing and presenting the final audit report.

The Information Technology Security Manager is responsible for reviewing findings of the Information Technology Security audit and overseeing corrective actions, if any.

Information Technology staff are responsible for complying with the Information Technology Security audit while in process and providing assistance to the security auditor, when needed.

Definitions: Audit criteria – Policies, practices, procedures, or requirements against which the auditor compares collected audit evidence about the subject matter.

Audit evidence – Records, statements of fact, and other information that are relevant to the audit criteria and verifiable.

Auditee – Party or parties whose processes, procedures, etc., are the subject of an audit.

Security audit – An examination of a computer system for security problems and vulnerabilities.

Procedure:

1.0   IT SECURITY AUDIT PLANNING

1.1   The Company shall conduct internal audits of its security management system at planned intervals (annually, at a minimum) to determine if its control objectives, controls, processes, and procedures conform to legal/regulatory and Company information security requirements; are effectively implemented and maintained; and perform as expected.

1.2   Information Technology Managers shall conduct an assessment of the existing Information Technology security system, in order to establish a baseline for auditing. Information Technology Managers shall report the results of this assessment to the Security Review Committee for review.

1.3   Information Technology Managers shall acquire and review additional pertinent information for Information Technology Security auditing, including applicable standards (see References A and B) and Information Technology industry standards and practices. This information shall also be shared with the Security Review Committee.

1.4   Information Technology Managers shall develop (or assign responsibility for development of) the Information Technology Security Audit Plan and submit the Plan to The Security Review Committee. The Security Review Committee shall review the Plan and may recommend changes.

1.5   Information Technology Managers shall incorporate changes into the Plan and submit it to the SRC for final review and approval.

1.6   The Plan shall serve as the basis for internal audits of Information Technology Security.

2.0   IT SECURITY AUDIT PLAN

2.1   Prior to conducting the audit, Information Technology Managers shall define the objectives, scope, and criteria of the audit; determine if the audit is feasible, and (if the audit is deemed feasible); appoint an audit team leader, who shall be required to meet minimum competency requirements for the position (see Reference B).

The audit team leader shall select an audit team, who shall be required to meet minimum competency requirements (Reference B), and shall establish contact with the Information Technology Security Manager.

2.2   The audit team leader shall conduct and/or supervise a review of Information Technology Security documentation.

2.3   The audit team leader shall prepare for onsite audit activity by preparing the audit plan (using ITSD107-3 IT SECURITY AUDIT PLAN as a guide) and assigning tasks to members of the audit team.

Audit team members shall prepare work documents, such as audit checklists, sampling plans, and forms for recording information (minutes of meetings, supporting evidence, audit findings, etc.).

2.4   The audit team shall conduct the onsite audit, which shall consist of:

- The audit team leader conducting an opening meeting with Information Technology Managers and the Information Technology Security Manager to confirm the audit plan (including roles and responsibilities of all parties), explain how audit activities will occur, confirm lines of communication during the audit, and provide the Auditee with an opportunity for feedback.

- Communication during the audit.

   a. The audit team should meet periodically to exchange information, assess the progress of the audit, and reassign work between members, if needed.

   b. The audit team leader should periodically (depends on the scope of the audit) communicate audit progress and any concerns to the Information Technology Security Manager.

   c. Evidence that suggests an immediate and significant risk should be reported to the Information Technology Security Manager immediately.

   d. Audit team members' concerns about issues outside the audit scope should be reported to the audit team member for possible communication to the Information Technology Security Manager.

- Audit team members shall collect, record, and verify information relevant to the objectives, scope, and criteria of the audit. Information may be acquired through interviews, observation of activities, and document reviews.

- Audit team members shall evaluate audit evidence against audit criteria and generate audit findings, which may indicate conformity or nonconformity with the criteria.

   a. Conformity with audit criteria should be summarized, indicating locations, functions, or processes that were audited.

   b. Nonconformities and supporting evidence should be recorded (ITSD107-2 IT NONCONFORMITY REPORT) and reviewed with the Information Technology Security Manager, to obtain acknowledgement of evidential accuracy and ensure that nonconformities are understood.

   c. The audit team shall meet as needed to review their findings.

- The audit team shall confer prior to conducting an audit closing meeting to:

   a. Review their findings against audit objectives;

   b. Come to an agreement on the audit conclusions;

   c. To prepare recommendations, if this is specified by the audit objectives; and

   d. To discuss audit follow-up, if it is included in the audit plan.

- The audit team leader shall conduct a closing meeting in order to formally present the audit team's findings and conclusions, to verify the understanding and obtain the acknowledgement of the Information Technology Security

Manager, and if nonconformities are found, to agree on a timeframe for the Information Technology Security Manager to present a corrective and preventive action plan.

2.5   The audit team shall prepare, approve, and distribute ITSD107-1 IT SECURITY AUDIT REPORT.

- The audit team leader shall be responsible for preparing ITSD107-1 and for its contents.

- The audit report should provide a complete, accurate, clear, and concise record of the audit and should include or refer to the following:

  a. Audit objectives and scope;

  b. Where and when the audit was conducted;

  c. Who took part in the audit;

  d. The audit criteria; and

  e. Audit findings and conclusions.

- The audit team leader and Information Technology Security Manager shall approve ITSD107-1, which shall then be distributed to persons designated by the Information Technology Security Manager.

3.0   IT SECURITY AUDIT REVIEW

3.1   The Information Technology Security Manager shall meet with Information Technology Managers to review ITSD107-1 (and ITSD107-2, if one has been generated) and plan to take corrective actions, if required.

3.2   If it has been decided to take corrective action, the Information Technology Security Manager shall submit a corrective action plan, including objectives, actions, and deadlines, to the audit team leader. If it has been decided not to take corrective action, the Information Technology Security Manager shall inform the audit team leader of this decision, with explanation.

4.0   IT SECURITY AUDIT – CORRECTIVE ACTION

4.1   The Information Technology Security Manager shall be responsible for taking corrective actions, if required. Corrective actions shall be taken within the period prescribed in audit and as agreed to by the Information Technology Security Manager.

4.2   The Information Technology Security Manager shall notify the audit team leader when corrective actions have been completed. The audit team leader shall verify that corrective actions have been taken and that they are having the desired effect.

Forms:

- ITSD107-1 IT SECURITY AUDIT REPORT
- ITSD107-2 IT NONCONFORMITY REPORT
- ITSD107-3 IT SECURITY AUDIT PLAN

References:

A. ISO/IEC 27001:2013 INFORMATION TECHNOLOGY – SECURITY TECHNIQUES – INFORMATION SECURITY MANAGEMENT SYSTEMS- REQUIREMENTS

Additional Resources:

A. SANS (SysAdmin-Audit-Network-Security) Institute, found at http://www.sans.org.

B. The Information Systems Audit and Control Association (ISACA), located at http://www.isaca.org/.

Revision History:

Revision	Date	Description of Changes	Requested By
0	mm/dd/yyyy	Initial Release	

[This page intentionally left blank]

ITSD107-1 IT SECURITY AUDIT REPORT

A. Audit Objectives

B. Audit Scope

C. Audit Client

   IT Security Manager

D. Audit Team (leader and members)

E. Dates And Locations Of Onsite Audit

F. Audit Criteria

G. Audit Findings

H. Audit Conclusions

Audit Team Leader: _____ Date: _____

IT Security Manager: _____ Date: _____

[This page intentionally left blank]

ITSD107-2 IT NONCONFORMITY REPORT

Date:

Auditor:

Area / System:

Description of nonconformity:

Supporting evidence:

[This page intentionally left blank]

ITSD107-3 IT SECURITY AUDIT PLAN

A. Audit Objectives:

B. Audit Criteria:

C. Audit Scope:

D. Dates and Locations of Audit:

E. Estimated Time and Duration of Onsite Audit Activities:

F. Roles and Responsibilities of Audit Team Members:

G. Resources Required to Conduct Audit:

H. Auditee Representative:

I. Audit Report Topics:

J. Logistical Arrangements (travel, etc.):

K. Confidentiality Matters:

L. Other:

[This page intentionally left blank]

Document ID **ITSD108**	Title **IT INCIDENT HANDLING**	Print Date **mm/dd/yyyy**
Revision **0.0**	Prepared By **Preparer's Name / Title**	Date Prepared **mm/dd/yyyy**
Effective Date **mm/dd/yyyy**	Reviewed By **Reviewer's Name / Title**	Date Reviewed **mm/dd/yyyy**
	Approved By **Final Approver's Name / Title**	Date Approved **mm/dd/yyyy**

Policy: To promptly report, investigate, and resolve all incidents that are or may be a threat to secure and effective Information Technology operations and the network.

Purpose: To detail policy and procedure for reporting any actual or suspected Information Technology security incident; to address security issues related to the safety, confidentiality, availability, and integrity of information maintained on the Company's Information Technology systems.

Scope: This policy applies to all Company remote data terminal sites, desktop and portable computers, data centers, and telecommunications facilities, as well as all data, software, hardware, and personnel involved in information technologies.

Responsibilities:

The Incident Response Handling Team is responsible for investigating actual or suspected Information Technology incidents, resolving such incidents, and reporting on incident responses.

The Help Desk is responsible for reporting potential security incidents to the Information Technology Security Manager.

The Human Resources Manager is responsible for facilitating training of the Incident Response Team.

Information Technology Managers are responsible for reviewing the Information Technology Incident, reports, and their handling.

The Information Technology Security Manager is responsible for developing the Information Technology Incident Handling Plan, building an Incident Response Team, assigning incidents to the IRT for resolution, reporting incidents and responses to the Security Review Committee, and updating the Information Technology Incident Handling Plan, as needed.

The Security Review Committee is responsible for periodic review and updates and final approval of Information Technology Incident Handling. The committee should consist of the Information Technology Security Manager, Information Technology Managers, Human Resources Manager, and a member of the Help Desk.

Definitions: Information Technology security incident – An actual or suspected occurrence of unauthorized (intentional or unintentional) use, loss, disclosure, modification, or destruction of Information Technology hardware, software, or information.

Procedure:

1.0   IT INCIDENT HANDLING PREPARATION

1.1   The Information Technology Security Manager shall gather information from outside sources on Information Technology industry standards and best practices (see Additional Resources and References) in order to review and analyze the Company's existing methods of dealing with Information Technology incidents.

1.2   The Information Technology Security Manager shall present observations and findings to the Security Review Committee for comment and approval.

1.3   The Information Technology Security Manager shall identify, recruit, and train technical support personnel for an Incident Response Handling Team.

- Minimum skill/experience requirements for Team members shall be established.

- The Incident Response Handling Team shall receive training as needed to meet or exceed skill requirements. The Information Technology Security Manager shall determine training requirements and arrange training with the Human Resources Manager.

2.0   IT INCIDENT HANDLING

2.1   Any employee who has evidence of an Information Technology security incident occurring or suspects such an incident may have occurred shall notify the Information Technology Help Desk, in accordance with procedure ITTS102 IT SUPPORT CENTER, and assign an Incident ID or Trouble Ticket Number in the ITTS102-1 TECH SUPPORT LOG.

2.2   The Help Desk contact shall open an ITSD108-1 IT INCIDENT REPORT and submit it to the Information Technology Manager to begin the investigation.

2.3   The Information Technology Manager shall evaluate the information contained on ITSD108-1, determine the potential for loss and the risk to the Company (in accordance with ITSD101 IT THREAT ASSESSMENT), and assign the incident to the Incident Response Handling Team.

2.4   The Incident Response Handling Team shall survey the incident scene, determine what information will be needed to evaluate the incident (logs, audit trails, etc.), and preserve and document evidence. The IRT shall examine and organize the evidence to facilitate analysis and reporting.

2.5   The Incident Response Handling Team shall analyze the incident evidence, develop and test hypotheses regarding the incident, develop a set of findings and conclusions, and resolve the incident.

2.6   The Incident Response Handling Team should perform a follow-up postmortem analysis, after an incident has been fully handled and all systems are restored to a normal mode of operation. The Team should discuss actions that were taken and the lessons learned. All existing procedures should be evaluated and modified, if necessary. All on-line copies of infected files, worm code, etc., should be removed from the system(s).

2.7   The Team should report its findings on the open ITSD108-1 IT INCIDENT REPORT (part 2) and then send it to the Information Technology Manager for review.

3.0   IT INCIDENT HANDLING REVIEW

3.1   The Information Technology Manager shall review all Incident Reports to ensure incidents are handled in a timely manner, users are satisfied with the results, and that the Company assets are protected from harm. Lessons learned, recommendations, and deficiencies should be presented to the Security Review Committee for discussion.

3.2   The Security Review Committee shall review the Information Technology Incident findings on a recurring basis to determine if Incident Response Handling and the company's security systems continue to meet Company requirements.

3.3   After any review of the Information Technology Incident Handling, the Information Technology Manager shall be responsible for making appropriate changes.

Forms:

- ITSD108-1 IT INCIDENT REPORT

References:

A. ISO/IEC 27002:2013 – INFORMATION TECHNOLOGY – SECURITY TECHNIQUES – INFORMATION SECURITY MANAGEMENT SYSTEMS – REQUIREMENTS

For more; see http://www.iso.org/iso//catalogue_detail.htm?csnumber=54533.

HEALTH INSURANCE PORTABILITY AND ACCOUNTABILITY ACT OF 1996 (HIPAA)

HIPAA requires the U.S. Secretary of Health and Human Services to adopt security standards for health information. These standards are known collectively as the HIPAA Security Rule, published in 2003. The Security Rule is largely comprised of administrative safeguards (section 164.308) that require documented policies and procedures for: management of day-to-day operations; conduct and access of workforce members to electronic protected health information (EPHI); and the selection, development, and use of security controls. One of these standards pertains to policies, procedures, and processes for reporting, responding to, and managing *security incidents*.

B. SARBANES-OXLEY ACT OF 2002

Since its enactment by the U.S. Congress, Sarbanes-Oxley (or SOX) has required public corporations to implement internal controls over financial recordkeeping and reporting. In this era where practically every company record is electronic, a Company must have adequate internal Information Technology controls to comply with the Act.

A service desk, or help desk, must ensure that problems are recorded, investigated, and responded to in a timely and effective manner. How an organization identifies, documents, and responds to events that fall outside of normal operations – which is the purpose of the help desk – may impact financial reporting. A properly run help desk may be evidence of SOX compliance.

C. NATIONAL INSTITUTE OF STANDARDS AND TECHNOLOGY (NIST) SPECIAL PUBLICATION #800-61 – COMPUTER SECURITY INCIDENT HANDLING GUIDE

D. NIST SPECIAL PUBLICATION #800-66 – INTRODUCTORY RESOURCE GUIDE FOR IMPLEMENTING HIPAA SECURITY RULE

(See http://csrc.nist.gov/ for a copy of documents "D" and "E," above.)

Additional Resources:

A. West-Brown, Moira J., and others, Handbook For Computer Security Incident Response Teams (CSIRTs), Software Engineering Institute, Carnegie Mellon University (2nd edition, 2003) – see (http://resources.sei.cmu.edu/library/asset-view.cfm?assetID=6305).

B. FIRST, The Forum of Incident Response and Security Teams (http://www.first.org/).

C. Internet Crime Complaint Center (IC3), a partnership between the Federal Bureau of Investigation (FBI) and the National White Collar Crime Center (NW3C) – see http://www.ic3.gov/default.aspx.

D. Bosworth, Kabay, & Whyne, Computer Security Handbook, 6th Ed. (Mar., 2014) – http://www.wiley.com/WileyCDA/WileyTitle/productCd-1118127064,subjectCdAC03.html .

Revision History:

Revision	Date	Description of Changes	Requested By
0.0	mm/dd/yyyy	Initial Release	

[This page is intentionally left blank]

ITSD108-1 IT INCIDENT REPORT

Date: _____   **Security Incident ID**: _____

From: Name: _____ Office Code: _____

Phone: _____

To: IT Security Manager

An IT security incident was detected / observed / discovered on
_____ (date/time) at _____ (location).

Priority (1=low, 5=high): _____

System Identification:

System Description: _____

Software Systems Involved: _____

Type of Security Incident:

The nature of this security incident was: (choose all that apply):

☐ Unauthorized access to computing resources
☐ Unauthorized disclosure or use of personal password
☐ Improper use of computing resources
☐ Alteration of data or computer systems
☐ Other: (Explain) _____

Sensitivity of Data:

☐ Not sensitive (routine correspondence, of little or no strategic value)
☐ Business Confidential / Proprietary Data
☐ Business Sensitive / Financial Data
☐ Business Sensitive / Personnel Data
☐ Business Sensitive / Other _____

Impact of Security Incident

The effect of the security violation included the following: (Check all that apply)

☐ Disclosure of data
☐ Destruction or modification of data or systems
☐ Denial of service
☐ Other: (Explain on separate sheet)

Personnel Involved: (List all involved personnel. Use additional sheets if required.)

Name	Office Code	Phone

Incident Description: (Describe incident in detail; use separate sheets, if needed.)

_____

_____

_____

_____

_____

_____

_____

_____

_____

_____

_____

_____

_____

_____

ITSD108-1 IT INCIDENT RESPONSE FORM (part 2)

Date Resolved: _____

Description of response to incident: _____

_____

_____

_____

_____

_____

_____

_____

_____

_____

_____

_____

_____

_____

Time, other resources needed to respond: _____

_____

_____

_____

Corrective action required: _____

_____

_____

_____

_____

Approved

_____   _____
                    IT Manager   Date

_____   _____
          Information Security Manager   Date

FOLLOW-UP ANALYSIS

Lessons Learned: _____

_____

_____

_____

_____

_____

_____

_____

_____

_____

_____

_____

_____

Observations/recommendations: _____

_____

_____

_____

_____

_____

_____

_____

_____

_____

_____

_____

_____

Document ID **ITSD109**	Title **BYOD POLICY**	Print Date **mm/dd/yyyy**
Revision **0.0**	Prepared By **Preparer's Name / Title**	Date Prepared **mm/dd/yyyy**
Effective Date **mm/dd/yyyy**	Reviewed By **Reviewer's Name / Title**	Date Reviewed **mm/dd/yyyy**
	Approved By **Final Approver's Name / Title**	Date Approved **mm/dd/yyyy**

Policy: Company employees and contractors may use their personal electronic devices (e.g., smartphones, tablets) for conducting company business, provided that they understand and agree with the "Bring Your Own Device" (BYOD) policy, have been granted express permission, and act in accordance with the policy.

Purpose: To communicate specific standards and guidelines regarding the use of personal devices to conduct company business.

Scope: This policy applies to all Company personnel and their personal electronic devices.

Responsibilities: All Employees are responsible for being aware of, understanding, and adhering to the Company's BYOD policy.

Department Managers are responsible for communicating BYOD policy updates to the employees in their respective departments.

The Human Resources Manager is responsible for communicating the BYOD policy to new employees and retaining employee policy acknowledgements.

The Information Security Manager monitors BYOD usage and enforces the BYOD policy.

The Information Technology Manager (IT Manager) is responsible for developing BYOD policy and for reviewing the policy and any changes to it with the Policy Committee. The IT Manager also oversees monitoring and enforcement of the BYOD policy.

The Policy Committee is responsible for review and final approval of the Company's BYOD policy and subsequent updates.

Definitions: BYOD – *B*ring *Y*our *O*wn *D*evice, or using one's personal mobile phone, PC, tablet, or other personal electronic device to conduct the Company's business.

Policy Committee – A group comprised of Top Management and the IT Manager. The purpose of the Policy Committee is to develop, review, approve, and revise the Company's BYOD policy, as needed.

Top Management – A group comprised of the Company's chief

executive and chief financial officer, at a minimum. In larger companies, top management may include department / functional managers (e.g., VP-Sales, CTO).

Procedure:

1.0   BYOD POLICY DEVELOPMENT

1.1   The Information Technology (IT) Manager shall develop the Company BYOD policy, which may be based on common business standards and practices and on legal/regulatory requirements (see Reference B).

It is important to understand the myriad considerations for a BYOD policy within this very dynamic technology space, in order to properly protect your corporate technology infrastructure. Don't take this step lightly. The BYOD Policy needs to take into account:

- The company's technology infrastructure;
- Roles and responsibilities of various support services;
- Education, use, and operation of BYOD devices;
- Security risks;
- Ethical and legal considerations;
- Applications that may run on BYOD devices; and
- IT asset management.

This is not a complete list of BYOD factors; the Company may have to consider additional issues.

1.2   The IT Manager shall present the policy to the Policy Committee for review.

1.3   The Policy Committee shall review the BYOD policy, revise as needed, and signify its approval.

2.0   BYOD POLICY IMPLEMENTATION

2.1   Upon final approval of the BYOD policy, the IT Manager shall communicate the policy to all department managers. Department managers shall, in turn, communicate the policy to all employees in their respective departments.

- The Human Resources Manager shall be responsible for communicating the Company BYOD policy to all *new employees*.

2.2   All employees shall receive a copy of ITSD109-1 COMPANY BYOD POLICY ACKNOWLEDGEMENT. Upon reviewing the document, each employee shall sign and date their copy of the acknowledgement and return it to Human Resources. Employees should keep a copy of this document for themselves.

2.3   The IT Department shall manage records and documents used or generated by BYOD devices in accordance with Company procedures ITAD102 IT RECORDS MANAGEMENT and ITAD103 IT DOCUMENT MANAGEMENT.

2.4   The Information Security Manager shall monitor Company email, text messages, etc., for the purpose of enforcing the BYOD policy, as well as security policies.

3.0   BYOD POLICY REVIEW

3.1   At regular intervals (annually, at a minimum), the IT Manager shall review the Company's BYOD policy to see if it continues to meet Company and other requirements (legal/regulatory, etc.).

3.2   If the BYOD policy does not adequately address Company and other requirements, the IT Managers shall convene the Policy Committee for the purpose of implementing revisions to the policy.

4.0   BYOD POLICY CHANGES

4.1   The Policy Committee shall periodically review the Company's BYOD policy, to verify that it continues to meet Company requirements. Implementation of the BYOD policy needs to be an iterative process, due to the changing nature of technology and how it impacts the Company and the general business environment.

4.2   Where the policy does not meet requirements, the Policy Committee shall revise the policy as needed and communicate the revised policy to the IT Manager, who is responsible for its implementation and distribution.

4.3   Within one month of such changes to the BYOD policy, the IT Manager shall verify that they have been implemented and are having the desired effect.

Forms/Records:

- ITSD109-1 BYOD POLICY & ACKNOWLEDGEMENT

References:

A. ISO 9001:2008, QUALITY MANAGEMENT SYSTEMS - REQUIREMENTS

Clause 4.2.4 of ISO 9001 states that the organization must establish and maintain records to provide *evidence of conformity to requirements*. Those requirements include legal and regulatory considerations, such as security and privacy. In addition, all records must remain legible, readily identifiable, and retrievable.

B. SARBANES-OXLEY ACT OF 2002

The Sarbanes-Oxley Act (or "SOX") is designed in part to prevent manipulation, loss, and/or destruction of publicly-held companies' records. Records used, stored, or generated by BYOD devices may be subject to inspection and retention guidelines. Therefore, it is important that publicly-held organizations consider implementing a BYOD policy to help ensure SOX compliance.

C. A TOOLKIT TO SUPPORT FEDERAL AGENCIES IMPLEMENTING BRING YOUR OWN DEVICE (BYOD) PROGRAMS

This is a product of the Digital Services Advisory Group and Federal Chief Information Officers' Council, intended to serve U.S. government agencies considering implementation of BYOD programs. This Toolkit provides key areas for consideration and examples of existing policies and best practices.

In addition to providing an overview of considerations for implementing BYOD, the BYOD Working Group members developed a small collection of case studies to highlight the successful efforts of BYOD pilots or programs at several government agencies. The Working Group also assembled examples of existing policies to help inform IT leaders who are planning to develop BYOD programs for their organizations.

For details, see http://www.whitehouse.gov/digitalgov/bring-your-own-device.

Additional Resources:

A. ITAD102 IT RECORDS MANAGEMENT

B. ITAD103 IT DOCUMENT MANAGEMENT

C. ITSD102 IT SECURITY PLAN

D. ITSD105 COMPUTER MALWARE

E. COBIT 5: A Business Framework for the Governance and Management of Enterprise IT, ISACA (2014) - http://www.isaca.org/cobit/pages/default.aspx.

Revision History:

Revision	Date	Description of Changes	Requested By
0.0	mm/dd/yyyy	Initial Release	

[This page intentionally left blank]

ITSD109-1 BYOD POLICY & ACKNOWLEDGEMENT

1.0   BYOD AND THE COMPANY

All portions of the Company information infrastructure, including the information being transported by this infrastructure, are the property of the Company. This includes all messages, documents, and data transmitted or received through the Company information infrastructure, which may be augmented by personal electronic devices

Since such messages, documents, and data are Company property, all BYOD-related accounts and any information used, exchanged, and stored by these accounts are subject to inspection at any time.

Personal portable devices are powerful tools that can greatly enhance communication and productivity. Use of personal devices, or BYOD, to conduct business within the following guidelines by Employees and contractors is encouraged. The Company reserves the right to revoke any employee's or contractor's BYOD privilege for cause.

In the context of this document, "personal electronic device," "personal device," and "BYOD device" are synonymous.

2.0   BYOD GUIDELINES

Employees shall follow the following general guidelines concerning the use of personal devices:

- All use of BYOD devices are subject to the companies Acceptable Use Policy.

- Text messages, email, and other forms of information transmission by BYOD devices are not private. Messages transmitted via BYOD devices are the property of the Company and are subject to inspection at any time. Use of a personal portable device to access Company information automatically implies consent to search.

- User will not download or transfer sensitive business data to their personal devices. Sensitive business data is defined as documents or data whose loss, misuse, or unauthorized access can adversely affect the privacy or welfare of an individual (personally identifiable information), the outcome of a charge/complaint/case, proprietary information, or agency financial operations.

- Users will password-protect their devices.
- The user agrees to maintain the original device operating system and keep the device current with security patches and updates released by the manufacturer. The user agrees not to "jail break" (i.e., install software that allows them to bypass standard built-in security features and controls) their device.

- User agrees that they will not share their device with other individuals or family members, due to the business use of the device.

- BYOD users shall be required to retain emails, text messages, etc., related to essential or mission-critical projects; such records should be transferred to

Company storage within two (2) business days. Messages or other transmissions that do not pertain to mission-critical projects or issues should be deleted when the Company no longer needs them.

- Because attachments to emails and messages are used to attack computers and systems – and because attachments occasionally use a lot of bandwidth – sending a file as an attachment and opening an attachment are discouraged.

- Personal devices shall not be used for commercial[1] or political purposes.

- Employees shall ensure all communication, whether through Company email, messaging services, or their personal devices, is conducted in a professional manner. The use of vulgar, obscene, lewd, or suggestive language or the use of language or tone that could reasonably be construed as harassment, intimidation, or threats is prohibited.

- Company users shall not reveal private or personal information via their personal devices without specific, written authorization from management.

- Users should ensure that any messages they send via their personal devices are sent only to users with a specific need to know. The transmission of messages to large groups via personal device should be avoided.

- Personal devices shall not be used for any illegal or unlawful purpose, including transmission of violent, threatening, defrauding, pornographic, obscene, or otherwise illegal or unlawful material.

- Personal devices shall not be used to harass, intimidate, or otherwise annoy anyone.

- The Company shall not be held liable for damages related to inappropriate use of personal devices by Employees, contractors, or their families.

- Failure to follow any part of this policy may result in disciplinary action, up to and including termination.

3.0   EMPLOYEE ACKNOWLEDGEMENT

I have reviewed the Company's BYOD policy. By signing and dating this form, I attest to my understanding and acceptance of this policy. Furthermore, I understand that if I am ever found violating this policy, I may be subject to Company disciplinary action, up to and including termination, as well as civil and/or criminal prosecution.

Signature: _____ Date: _____

Print name: _____

---

[1] Aside from those of the Company

IT Policies and Procedures

Section 440

IT Software Development

Section 440

IT Software Development

440 ITSW – Software Development

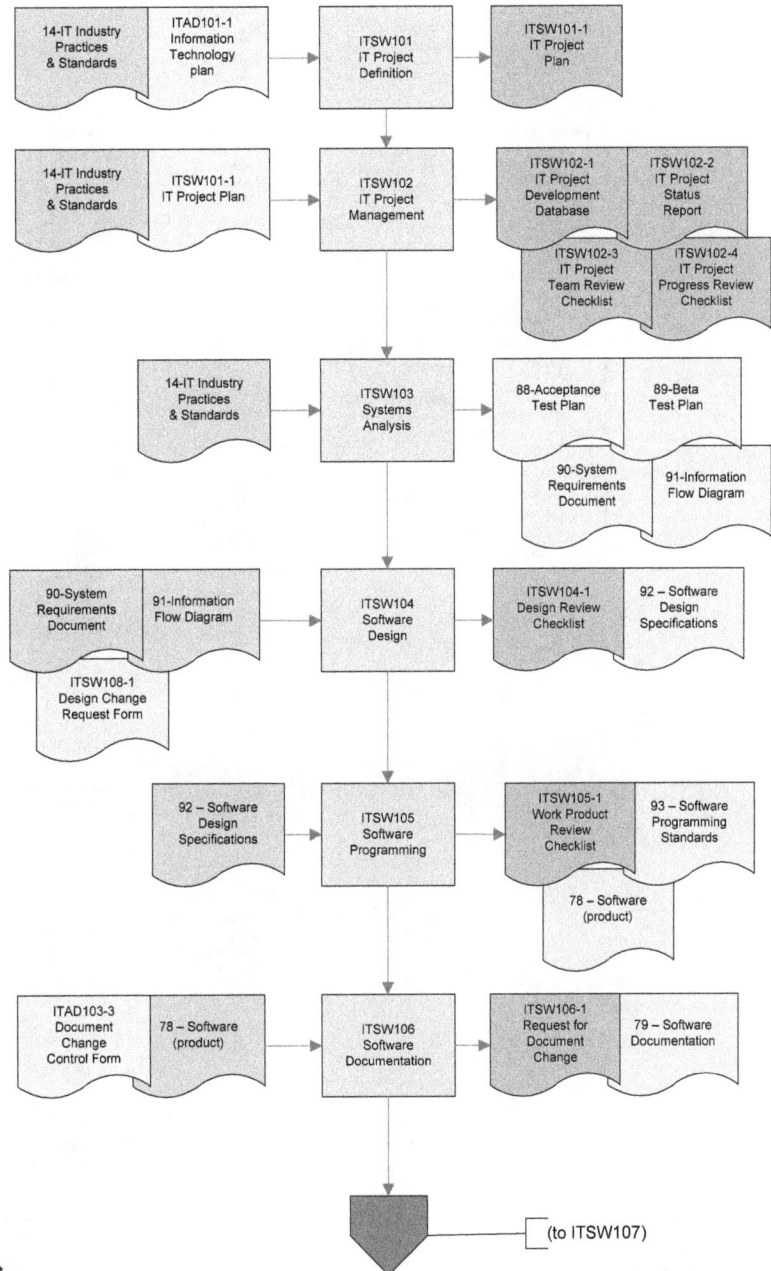

14-IT Industry Practices & Standards	ITAD101-1 Information Technology plan	ITSW101 iT Project Definition	ITSW101-1 IT Project Plan

14-IT Industry Practices & Standards	ITSW101-1 IT Project Plan	ITSW102 IT Project Management	ITSW102-1 IT Project Development Database / ITSW102-2 IT Project Status Report

ITSW102-3 IT Project Team Review Checklist / ITSW102-4 IT Project Progress Review Checklist

14-IT Industry Practices & Standards	ITSW103 Systems Analysis	88-Acceptance Test Plan / 89-Beta Test Plan

90-System Requirements Document / 91-Information Flow Diagram

90-System Requirements Document	91-Information Flow Diagram	ITSW104 Software Design	ITSW104-1 Design Review Checklist / 92 – Software Design Specifications

ITSW108-1 Design Change Request Form

92 – Software Design Specifications	ITSW105 Software Programming	ITSW105-1 Work Product Review Checklist / 93 – Software Programming Standards	

78 – Software (product)

ITAD103-3 Document Change Control Form	78 – Software (product)	ITSW106 Software Documentation	ITSW106-1 Request for Document Change / 79 – Software Documentation

(to ITSW107)

bizmanualz

440 ITSW – Software Development

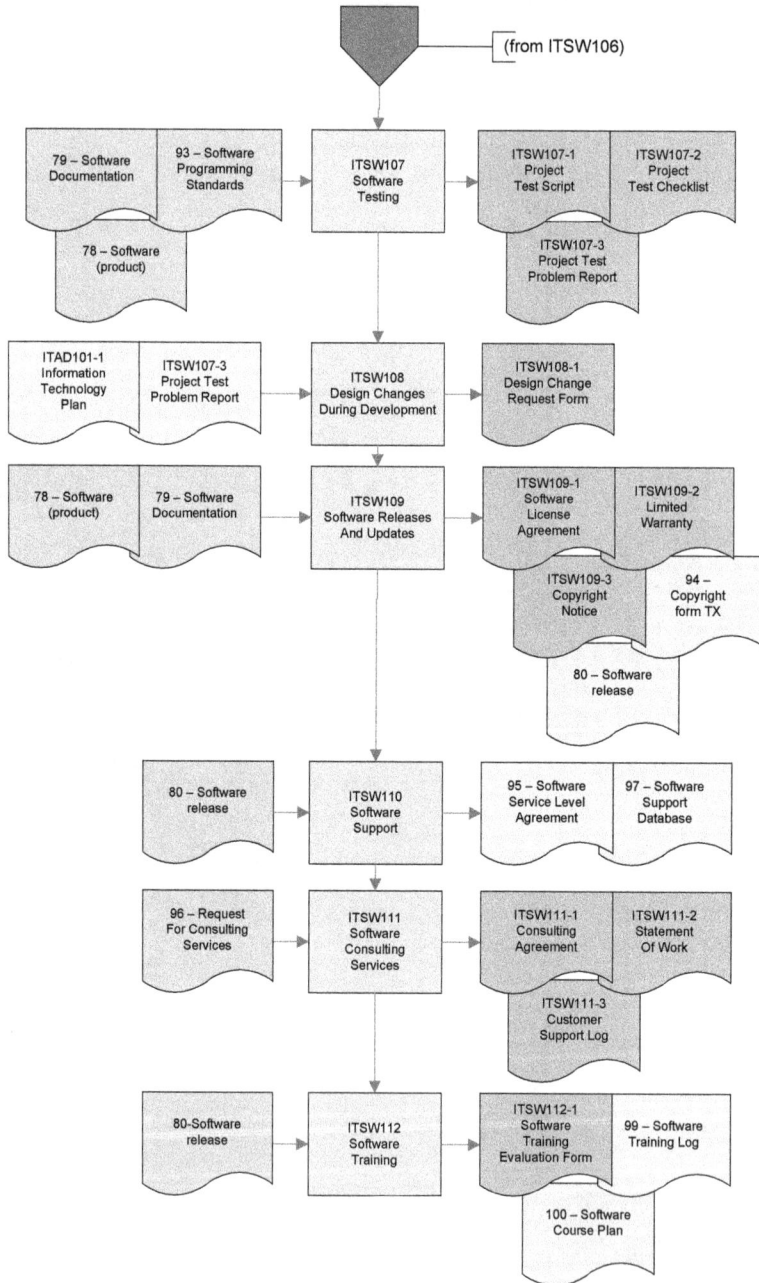

(from ITSW106)

79 – Software Documentation	93 – Software Programming Standards	**ITSW107** Software Testing	ITSW107-1 Project Test Script	ITSW107-2 Project Test Checklist
	78 – Software (product)		ITSW107-3 Project Test Problem Report	

ITAD101-1 Information Technology Plan	ITSW107-3 Project Test Problem Report	**ITSW108** Design Changes During Development	ITSW108-1 Design Change Request Form

78 – Software (product)	79 – Software Documentation	**ITSW109** Software Releases And Updates	ITSW109-1 Software License Agreement	ITSW109-2 Limited Warranty
			ITSW109-3 Copyright Notice	94 – Copyright form TX
			80 – Software release	

80 – Software release	**ITSW110** Software Support	95 – Software Service Level Agreement	97 – Software Support Database

96 – Request For Consulting Services	**ITSW111** Software Consulting Services	ITSW111-1 Consulting Agreement	ITSW111-2 Statement Of Work
		ITSW111-3 Customer Support Log	

80-Software release	**ITSW112** Software Training	ITSW112-1 Software Training Evaluation Form	99 – Software Training Log
		100 – Software Course Plan	

Document ID **ITSW101**	Title **IT PROJECT DEFINITION**	Print Date **mm/dd/yyyy**
Revision **0.0**	Prepared By **Preparer's Name / Title**	Date Prepared **mm/dd/yyyy**
Effective Date **mm/dd/yyyy**	Reviewed By **Reviewer's Name / Title**	Date Reviewed **mm/dd/yyyy**
	Approved By **Final Approver's Name / Title**	Date Approved **mm/dd/yyyy**

Policy: Every Information Technology project must be clearly defined in advance.

Purpose: To define the scope and purpose of an Information Technology project and determine its projected impact on - and potential risks to - the Company.

Scope: This applies to all software products and updates developed by the Company.

Responsibilities:

Information Technology Managers are responsible for conducting feasibility studies on proposed Information Technology projects, reviewing proposed projects with Top Management, and responding to User Management proposals.

The Information Technology Project Manager is responsible for creating, reviewing, and modifying project descriptions and creating project plans.

Top Management is responsible for reviewing project proposals with Information Technology Managers.

User Management is responsible for communicating its needs and requirements clearly when proposing an Information Technology project.

Definitions: Project definition – Stage in project planning that follows a project proposal; preliminary investigation of project's feasibility, suitability, etc.

Project plan – Stage in project planning that follows project definition; describing the details of a project definition based on a proposal that has been accepted.

Project proposal – User Management's formal, written proposal of a project for Information Technology. Typically followed by a request to Information Technology for a proposal, commonly known as an RFP.

Request For Proposal (RFP) – A formal user request to Information Technology for project estimates (time, other resources needed to deliver the project) and a description of project results.

Return on investment (ROI) - The annual financial benefit after an investment minus the cost of the investment; or, the total value gained after a solution has been deployed.

Procedure:

1.0   IT PROJECT NEEDS IDENTIFICATION

1.1   User Management shall gather information that identifies a need for a new software product or an enhancement to an existing product.

1.2   Such information should include:

- Customer feedback, surveys, and research about existing products;

- Competitive analysis;

- Market segmented needs analysis; and

- Changes in regulatory conditions or industry trends.

2.0   IT PROJECT DEFINITION

2.1   User Management shall state the problem or opportunity and how to address it in business terms in a document and submit this document to Information Technology Managers.

2.2   Information Technology Managers shall conduct a feasibility study of the situation, looking at issues such as:

- Will infrastructure created by this project be reusable?

- Can the project be developed using technology already on hand and in-house expertise?

- Can the project be developed with off-the-shelf software or will it require new applications?

- Will the project require additional hardware or user training?

- What are the estimated costs and the projected ROI?

2.3   Information Technology Managers shall review the proposed project with Top Management, evaluating it for fit with the Company's needs and objectives, stated in ITAD101-1 INFORMATION TECHNOLOGY PLAN.

- Information Technology Managers shall respond to User Management, explaining why the proposed project was accepted or rejected.

- If the project is accepted, Information Technology Managers shall present time and cost estimates and select a project manager.

2.4   The Information Technology Project Manager shall create a project definition identifying the problem, describing the resources required to solve the problem, and including a cost-benefit analysis. The project definition should include, at a minimum:

- The name and unique ID of the project;

- Names of the project originators;

- The name of the Information Technology Project Manager;

- A detailed description of the project;

- The projected impact of the project on other areas of the company, such as shipping, marketing, sales, and software support;

- An estimated start and finish date and the estimated time required to complete the project, in worker-months;

- The estimated cost of the project, including:

  a. People – a project may requires some or all of the following people, in addition to the Information Technology Project Manager: subject matter expert; systems analyst; software designer; programmer; technical writer; and/or quality assurance analyst;

  b. Hardware – new equipment or upgrades to existing equipment required for the project;

  c. Software – new software or upgrades to existing software required for the project;

  d. Office space and other logistical requirements; and

  e. An estimated project budget.

- Anticipated short- and long-term profits; and

- A cost analysis, to determine if the Company can afford the resources needed to develop the project.

3.0   IT PROJECT DEFINITION REVIEW

3.1   The Information Technology Project Manager shall review the project definition with Information Technology Managers. They shall discuss management's concerns and determine whether to go forward with the project. Concerns management might have may include:

- Are outside financing sources or partnerships feasible?

- How great is the market demand for the product?

- If the project cannot be completed on schedule, will it still be marketable?

3.2   The Information Technology Project Manager modifies the project definition to address management's concerns and then begins work on a detailed Information Technology Project Plan.

4.0   IT PROJECT PLAN

The Information Technology Project Manager shall create a project plan that describes in detail how the project will be accomplished; ITSW101-1 IT PROJECT PLAN may be used as a guide. The plan begins with the project definition and expands the technical details to include six required sections:

- Project Overview. Describes the purpose, scope, and objectives of the project as well as assumptions, constraints, risks, project deliverables, schedules, and budget. Any definitions, acronyms, and references should also be described.

- Project Organization. Defines the external interfaces, internal structures, and each person's roles and responsibilities on the project.

- Managerial Process Plans. Defines all of the management deliverables for the project from the start-up plan to the project closeout plan. Details include: project estimates, staffing, resources, training, scheduling, controls, reporting, tracking, risks, and project metrics. A lot of the managerial process revolves around the work breakdown structure which defines the principal activities in greater project management detail.

- Technical Process Plans. Describes the software processes, models, methods, tools, and techniques including definitions of infrastructure, product acceptance criteria and final deployment plans used for developing the work products or services for the project.

- Supporting Process Plans. Describes all other plans not included above that support the project including: configuration management, verification and validation, documentation, quality assurance, reviews and audits, problem resolution, subcontractor management, and process improvement.

- Additional Plans. Specify or reference any additional plans required to satisfy product requirements and contractual terms, which may include: plans for meeting safety, privacy, or security requirements, special facilities or equipment specification, product installation or integration plans, data conversion and system transition plans, and product training, support and maintenance plans.

Forms:

- ITSW101-1 IT PROJECT PLAN

References:

A. **ISO/IEC 12207:2008, "SYSTEMS AND SOFTWARE ENGINEERING – SOFTWARE LIFE CYCLE PROCESSES"**

B. **IEEE 12207-2008, "SYSTEMS AND SOFTWARE ENGINEERING – SOFTWARE LIFE CYCLE PROCESSES"**

This ISO standard describes the major component processes of a complete software life cycle and the high-level relations that govern their interaction. It establishes a software life cycle architecture based on two principles, modularity of processes and responsibility for processes. There are three process classes in the ISO software life cycle – primary, supporting, and organizational. Each life cycle process is made up of activities, and each activity is further subdivided into tasks. The standard is based on ISO quality management principles.

The IEEE version of 12207 is closely aligned with, but not the same as, its ISO counterpart. For more information, visit http://www.iso.org/iso/catalogue_detail.htm?csnumber=43447 or http://standards.ieee.org/findstds/standard/12207-2008.html.

C. IEEE #16326-2009, "SYSTEMS AND SOFTWARE ENGINEERING – LIFE CYCLE PROCESSES – PROJECT MANAGEMENT"

ITSW101-1 IT PROJECT PLAN is adapted from the IEEE standard for software project management, as well as from the data requirements of ISO/IEC 12207. For details, see http://standards.ieee.org/findstds/standard/16326-2009.html.

Additional Resources:

- IEEE Software and Systems Engineering Standards List – http://standards.ieee.org/findstds/standard/software_and_systems_engineering.html

Revision History:

Revision	Date	Description of Changes	Requested By
0.0	mm/dd/yyyy	Initial Release	

[This page intentionally left blank]

ITSW101-1 IT PROJECT PLAN

< ORGANIZATION >

< PROJECT NAME >

Document Revision
Date of Issue:

Approval Signatures

_____	_____
Prepared By Product Manager	Prepared By Project Manager
_____	_____
Approved By Executive in Charge	Reviewed By Quality Manager

Document Change Control

This section provides control for the development and distribution of revisions to the Project Charter up to the point of approval. The Project Charter does not change throughout the project life cycle, but rather is developed at the beginning of the project (immediately following project initiation approval, and in the earliest stages of project planning).

The Project Charter provides an ongoing reference for all project stakeholders. The table below includes the revision number (defined within your Documentation Plan Outline), the date of update/issue, a brief description of the context and/or scope of the changes in that revision, and the person responsible for authoring the changes.

Revision	Date	Description of Change	Author
0	mm/dd/yyyy		

Editor's Note:

ITSW101-1 IT PROJECT PLAN is adapted from the IEEE Standards for Software Project Management Plans, #1058-1998, and from the data requirements of ISO standard 12207 Software Life Cycle Processes. It is designed as a guide used to begin the project development plan. The plan should be dynamic, changing with project changes, but keeping the overall development plan well documented.

Table of Contents

1.0 PROJECT OVERVIEW

This section of the IT Project Management Plan provides an overview of the purpose, scope and objectives of the project for which the Plan has been written, the project assumptions and constraints, a list of project deliverables, a summary of the project schedule and budget, and the plan for evolving the IT Project Management Plan.

1.1 PURPOSE, SCOPE, AND OBJECTIVES

Describe the purpose, scope and objectives of the project. Explain how they fit within a broader vision of any overall program or product life cycle. Describe what is out of scope as well. Describe the business or system needs being satisfied by the project. Provide a reference to any requirements descriptions that drive this project.

- Define the purpose and scope of the project.

- Describe any considerations of scope or objectives to be excluded from the project or the deliverables.

- Ensure that the statement of scope is consistent with similar statements in the business case, the project charter and any other relevant system-level or business-level documents.

- Identify and describe the business or system needs to be satisfied by the project.

- Provide a concise summary of:
    - The project objectives;
    - The deliverables required to satisfy the project objectives; and
    - The methods by which satisfaction of the objectives will be determined.

- Describe the relationship of this project to other projects.

- If appropriate, describe how this project will be integrated with other projects or ongoing work processes.

- Provide a reference to the official statement of project requirements (e.g.: in the business case or the project charter).

1.2 ASSUMPTIONS, CONSTRAINTS, AND RISKS

Describe assumptions and any constraints on which the project is based. Include system dependencies that will affect this project.

- Describe the assumptions on which the project is based.

- Describe the imposed constraints and risks on the project such as:
    - Schedule;

- Budget;
- Resources;
- Quality;
- Software to be reused;
- Existing software to be incorporated;
- Technology to be used; and
- External interfaces.

1.3 PROJECT DELIVERABLES

List the deliverables or services to be provided by this project, or provide a reference to where such a list can be found. Include delivery dates, delivery locations, and quantities, as appropriate. It may be useful to portray these in a table.

- Identify and list the following, as required to satisfy the terms of the project charter or contract:
  - Project deliverables (either directly in this Plan, or by reference to an external document);
  - Delivery dates;
  - Delivery location; and
  - Quantities required.
- Specify the delivery media.
- Specify any special instructions for packaging and handling.

1.4 SCHEDULE AND BUDGET SUMMARY

Provide a summary of the schedule and budget, at the top level of the project work breakdown structure (or equivalent). Include all aspects of the project, including support functions, quality assurance, configuration management, and subcontracted work when treating the schedule and budget.

- Provide a summary of the schedule and budget for the IT project.
- Restrict the level of detail to an itemization of the major work activities and supporting processes (e.g., give only the top level of the work breakdown structure).

1.5 EVOLUTION OF THE PLAN

Describe how this plan will be completed, disseminated, and put under change control. Describe how both scheduled and unscheduled updates will be handled.

- Identify the compliance of this Plan to any standards.

  For example: The structure of this Project Plan is in compliance with the recommendations of IEEE Standard 1058-1998.

- Specify the plans for producing both scheduled and unscheduled updates to this Plan.

- Specify how the updates to this Plan shall be disseminated.

- Specify how the initial version of this Plan shall be placed under configuration management.

- Specify how changes to this Plan shall be controlled after its issue.

1.6   REFERENCES

Provide a list of all documents and other sources of information referenced in the plan.

- Identify each referenced document by title, report number, date, author, and publishing organization.

- Identify other referenced sources of information, such as electronic files, using unique identifiers such as path/name, date and version number.

- Include a reference for the authorizing document for this project, the Statement of Work or Marketing Requirements or Charter or whatever that might be for the organization.

- Identify and justify any deviations from the referenced standards or policies.

1.7   DEFINITIONS AND ACRONYMS

Define, or provide references to documents or annexes containing the definition of all terms and acronyms required to properly understand this Plan.

2.0   PROJECT ORGANIZATION

Describe the overall organization for the project including internal and external structures, roles, and responsibilities.

2.1   EXTERNAL INTERFACES

Describe the administrative and managerial interfaces between the project and the primary entities with which it interacts.

- Describe the organizational boundaries between the project and external entities.

- Identify, as applicable:

  − The parent organization;

  − The customer;

       –   Subcontracted organizations; and

       –   Other organizational entities that interact with the project.

- Use organizational charts or diagrams to depict the project's external interfaces.

2.2 INTERNAL STRUCTURE

Describe the internal management structure of the project, as well as how the project relates to the rest of the organization. Include employees and contract staffs that are managed as part of this project.

- Describe the interfaces among the units of the IT development team.

- Describe the interfaces between the project and organizational entities that provide supporting processes, such as configuration management, quality assurance, and verification and validation.

- Use organizational charts or diagrams to depict the lines of authority, responsibility and communication within the project.

2.3 ROLES AND RESPONSIBILITIES

Identify and state responsibilities assigned to each major role in the project, and identify the individuals who are responsible for those functions and activities.

- Identify and state the nature of each major work activity and supporting process.

- Identify the organizational units that are responsible for those processes and activities.

- Consider using a matrix of work activities and supporting processes vs. organizational units to depict project roles and responsibilities.

3.0 MANAGERIAL PROCESS PLANS

This section of the IT Project Management Plan specifies the project management processes for the project. It includes the plans for project start-up, risk management, project work, project tracking, and project close-out.

NOTE: This section may evolve over the lifetime of the project, and only a subset of them may be relevant; use elements accordingly. If there are documented processes that the project team is following, the plan may refer to the documented processes rather than reproduce them as part of this plan.

3.1 START-UP PLAN

Describe the effort required to begin the project. Provide estimates for staffing, resources, schedules, and training.

3.1.1 Estimates

Describe how the project effort, cost, and schedule will be estimated, including methods, tools, and techniques.

- Specify the estimated cost, schedule, and resource requirements for conducting the project, and specify the associated confidence levels for each estimate.

- Specify the methods, tools, and techniques used to estimate project cost, schedule and resource requirements;

- Specify the sources of estimate data and the basis of the estimation such as: analogy, rule of thumb, standard unit of size, cost model, historical database, etc.

- Specify the schedule for re-estimation, which might be regular, a periodic or event-driven (e.g., on project milestones).

3.1.2 Staffing

Describe how staffing will be done, along with the expected level of staffing by phase of the project, types of skills needed, and sources of staff (may be employees or contract personnel). Describe how the staff will be organized and supervised here, or include it in the section that describes the project internal structure.

- Specify the number of required staff, providing the following details:
  - Number of personnel by skill level;
  - Numbers and skill levels in each project phase; and
  - Duration of personnel requirement.

- Specify the sources of staff personnel (e.g.: internal transfer, new hire, contracted, etc.)

- Consider using resource Gantt charts, resource histograms, spreadsheets and tables to depict the staffing plan by skill level, by project phase, and by aggregations of skill levels and project phases.

3.1.3 Resource Acquisition

Identify (or refer to a location that contains a description of) the resources associated with each of the major work activities, as well as an overall summary of the resource loading for the project and how they will be acquired.

- Specify the plan for acquiring the resources and assets, in addition to personnel, needed to successfully complete the project.

- Describe the resource acquisition process.

- Specify the assignment of responsibility for all aspects of resource acquisition.

- Specify acquisition plans for equipment, computer hardware and software, training, service contracts, transportation, facilities, and administrative and janitorial services.

- Specify when in the project schedule the various acquisition activities will be required.

- Specify any constraints on acquiring the necessary resources.

- If necessary, expand this subsection to lower levels, to accommodate acquisition plans for various types of resources.

3.1.4 Project Staff Training

- Specify the training needed to ensure that necessary skill levels in sufficient numbers are available to successfully conduct the IT project.

- Specify the following training information:
  - The types of training to be provided;
  - Numbers of personnel to be trained;
  - Entry and exit criteria for training; and
  - The training method (e.g., lectures, consultations, mentoring, computer-assisted training, etc.).

- Identify training as needed in technical, managerial, and supporting activity skills.

3.2 WORK PLAN

Specify (or refer to a location that contains a list of) the work activities and their relationships, depicted in a work breakdown structure. Decompose the structure to a low enough level to facilitate sound estimating, tracking, and risk management. Work packages may be built for some or each of the elements of the work breakdown structure, detailing the approach, needed resources, duration, work products, acceptance criteria, predecessors, and successors.

3.2.1 Work Breakdown Structure

- Define a Work Breakdown Structure (WBS) to specify the various work activities to be performed in the IT project, and to depict the relationships among these work activities.

- Decompose the work activities to a level that exposes all project risk factors, and that allows accurate estimation of resource requirements and schedule duration for each work activity.

- Specify the following factors for each work activity:
  - Necessary resources;
  - Estimated duration;
  - Products or deliverables of the activity;
  - Acceptance criteria for the work activity products; and

    −   Predecessor and successor work activities.

- The level of decomposition internally within the WBS may vary depending on the quality of the requirements, familiarity of the work, applicable level of technology, etc.

3.2.2 Schedule Allocation

Specify (or refer to a location that contains) the schedule for the project, showing sequencing and relationships between activities, milestones, and any special constraints.

- Specify the scheduling relationships among the project work activities in a manner that depicts the time-sequencing constraints and illustrates opportunities for concurrent work activities.
- Identify the critical path in the schedule.
- Indicate any constraints on the scheduling of particular work activities, that are caused by external factors.
- Identify appropriate schedule milestones to assess the scope and quality of project work products and of project achievement status.
- Techniques for depicting schedule relationships may include milestone charts, activity lists, activity Gantt charts, activity networks, critical path networks and PERT charts.

3.2.3 Resource Allocation

Identify (or refer to a location that contains a description of) the resources associated with each of the major work activities, as well as an overall summary of the resource loading for the project.

- Provide a detailed itemization of the resources allocated to each major work activity in the project WBS.
- Specify the numbers and required skill levels of personnel for each work activity.
- Specify, as appropriate, the allocation of the following resources:
  - Personnel (by skill level);
  - Computing resources;
  - Software tools;
  - Special testing and simulation facilities; and
  - Administrative support.
- Use a separate line item for each type of resource for each work activity.

3.2.4 Budget Allocation

Show (or refer to a location that contains a description of) the budget allocated to each of the major work activities. Use the organization's standard cost categories such as personnel costs, travel, equipment, and administrative support.

- Provide a detailed breakdown of the necessary resource budgets for each of the major work activities in the WBS.
- Specify the estimated cost for activity personnel, and include as appropriate, the costs for the following items:
  - Travel;
  - Meetings;
  - Computing resources;
  - Software tools;
  - Special testing and simulation facilities; and
  - Administrative support.
- Use a separate line item for each type of resource in each activity budget.

3.3 PROJECT TRACKING PLAN

3.3.1 Requirements Management

Describe the process to be used for measuring, reporting, and controlling changes to the product requirements. Describe the techniques to be used for configuration management of the requirements, requirements traceability, impact analysis for proposed changes, and approving changes (such as a Change Control Board).

- Specify the process for measuring, reporting, and controlling changes to the project requirements.
- Specify the processes to be used in assessing the impact of requirements changes on product scope and quality, and the impacts of requirements changes on project schedule, budget, resources and risk factors.
- In the configuration management processes, specify change control procedures and the formation and use of a change control board.
- In the processes for requirements management, include traceability, prototyping and modeling, impact analysis, and reviews.

3.3.2 Schedule Control

Describe how progress will be monitored and controlled. Address how the schedule will be controlled (milestones, progress to plan on activities, corrective action upon serious deviation from the plan), when reporting will be done for both the project team and management, and what tools and methods will be used.

- Specify the schedule control activities by identifying the processes to be used for the following purposes:
  - To measure the progress of work completed at the major and minor project milestones;
  - To compare actual progress to planned progress; and
  - To implement corrective action when actual progress does not conform to planned progress.
- Specify the methods and tools that will be used to measure and control schedule progress.
- Identify the objective criteria that will be used to measure the scope and quality of work completed at each milestone, and hence to assess the achievement of each schedule milestone.

3.3.3 Budget Control

Describe how performance to budget will be monitored and controlled. Address how the actual cost will be tracked to the budgeted cost, how corrective actions will be implemented, at what intervals cost reporting will be done for both the project team and management, and what tools and techniques will be used. Include all costs of the project, including contract labor and support functions.

- Specify the budget control activities by identifying the processes to be used for the following purposes:
  - To measure the cost of work completed;
  - To compare the actual cost to the planned and budgeted costs; and
  - To implement corrective action when the actual cost does not conform to the budgeted cost.
- Specify when cost reporting will be done in the project schedule.
- Specify the methods and tools that will be used to track the project cost.
- Identify the schedule milestones and objective indicators that will be used to assess the scope and quality of the work completed at those milestones.
- Specify the use of a mechanism such as earned value tracking to report the budget and schedule plan, schedule progress, and the cost of work completed.

3.3.4 Quality Control

Describe the mechanisms that will be used to maintain quality control. [These may be described in detail in other plans or in the Supporting Process Plans of this document.]

- Specify the processes to be used to measure and control the quality of the work and the resulting work products.

- Specify the use of quality control processes such as quality assurance of conformance to work processes, verification and validation, joint reviews, audits, and process assessment.

3.3.5 Reporting

Describe how the progress of the project and other information needed by the project will be communicated to everyone associated with the project.

- Specify the reporting mechanisms, report formats and information flows to be used in communicating the status of requirements, schedule, budget, quality, and other desired or required status metrics within the project and to entities external to the project.

- Specify the methods, tools, and techniques of communication.

- Specify a frequency and detail of communications related to project management and metrics measurement that is consistent with the project scope, criticality, risk, and visibility.

3.3.6 Project Metrics

- Specify the methods, tools, and techniques to be used in collecting and retaining project metrics.

- Specify the following metrics process information:
  - Identification of the metrics to be collected;
  - Frequency of collection; and
  - Processes for validating, analyzing, and reporting the metrics.

3.4   RISK MANAGEMENT PLAN

Describe the process that will be used to identify, analyze, build mitigation and contingency plans, and manage the risks associated with the project. Describe mechanisms for tracking the specific risks, the mitigation plans, and any contingency plans.

Risk factors that should be considered when identifying the specific project risks include contractual risks, organization-related risks, technological risks, risks due to size and complexity of the product, risks in personnel acquisition and retention, risks in achieving customer acceptance of the product, and others specific to the context of the project.

- Specify the risk management plan for identifying, analyzing, and prioritizing project risk factors.

- Specify plans for assessing initial risk factors and for the ongoing identification, assessment, and mitigation of risk factors throughout the life cycle of the project.

- Describe the following:
  - Procedures for contingency planning;
  - Procedures for tracking the various risk factors;
  - Procedures for evaluating changes in the levels of the risk factors and responding to changes in the levels of the risk factors;
  - Risk management work activities;
  - Procedures and schedules for performing risk management work activities;
  - Risk documentation and reporting requirements;
  - Organizations and personnel responsible for performing specific risk management activities; and
  - Procedures for communicating risks and risk status among the various customer, project and subcontractor organizations.
- Identify and describe the applicable impact of any of the following risk factors:
  - Risks in the customer-project relationship;
  - Contractual risks;
  - Technological risks;
  - Risks caused by the size and complexity of the product;
  - Risks in the development and target environments;
  - Risks in personnel acquisition, skill levels, and retention;
  - Risks to schedule and budget; and
  - Risks in achieving customer acceptance of the deliverables.

3.5 PROJECT CLOSEOUT PLAN

Describe the plan for closing out this project. Identify the plans necessary to ensure orderly closeout of the IT project. Specify the following:

- A staff reassignment plan;
- A process for archiving project materials;
- A process for capturing project metrics in the business projects database;
- A process for post-mortem debriefings of project personnel;
- A plan for preparation of a final report to include lessons learned and an analysis of project objectives achieved;
- An examination of the initial cost/benefit analysis to see if objectives have been met; and

- Examine any performance measures intended to be impacted by the project.

4.0　TECHNICAL PROCESS PLANS

Describe the processes and approaches to be used for developing the work products or services for the project. The primary technical focus of the project may be one or more of the following:

- Acquisition – obtaining a system, product or service.
- Supply – providing a system, product, or service.
- Development – constructing a system or product.
- Operation – running a system or service for regular use.
- Maintenance – correcting, perfecting, or adapting a system.

4.1　PROCESS MODEL

Specify the life cycle model to be used for this project or refer to an organizational standard model that will be followed. If the project is tailoring an organization's standard life-cycle model, that tailoring should be described here.

- Define the relationships among major project work activities and supporting processes.
- Describe the flow of information and work products among activities and functions.
- Specify the timing of work products to be generated.
- Identify the reviews to be conducted.
- Specify the major milestones to be achieved.
- Define the baselines to be established.
- Identify the project deliverable to be completed.
- Specify the required approvals within the duration of the project.
- In the process model for the project, include project initiation and project termination activities.
- Use a combination of graphical and textual notations to describe the project process model.

4.2　METHODS, TOOLS, AND TECHNIQUES

Identify the methods to be used to develop the work products or services for the project.

- Specify the development methodologies, programming languages and other notations, and the processes, tools and techniques to be used to specify, design, build, test, integrate, document, deliver, modify and maintain the project deliverable and non-deliverable work products.

- Specify the technical standards, policies, and procedures governing development and/or modification of the work products.

4.3   INFRASTRUCTURE

Specify the plan for establishing and maintaining the development environment (hardware, operating system, network and software), and the policies, procedures, standards, and facilities required to conduct the IT project. These resources may include workstations, local area networks, software tools for analysis, design implementations, testing, and project management, desks, office space, and provisions for physical security, administrative personnel, and janitorial services.

4.4   PRODUCT ACCEPTANCE

Describe (or refer to a separate document that provides) the plan for acceptance of the project deliverables by the customer or acquirer of the product.

- Specify the plan for customer acceptance of the deliverables generated by the IT project and include the final approval process for product acceptance.

- Specify objective criteria for determining acceptability of the deliverables.

- Reference a formal agreement of the acceptance criteria signed by representatives of the IT organization and the customer.

- Specify any technical processes, methods, or tools required for deliverable acceptance, such as testing, demonstration, analysis, and inspection.

- Describe roles and responsibilities for reviewing the plan, generating the acceptance tests, running the tests, and reviewing results.

4.5   DEPLOYMENT PLAN

Describe (or refer to a separate document that provides) the plan for releasing and installing the project deliverables or deploying them to the acquirer or customer site. The plan may need to include hardware installation, telecommunications, or database infrastructure preparation, and other information, as well as describing the means of distributing the software.

- Describe (or refer to a separate document that provides) the plan for operating and maintaining the system after deployment.

- If this project develops a product that is packaged and shipped to customers for their installation, describe how the product will be prepared for release and shipment.

5.0 SUPPORTING PROCESS PLANS

Provide plans for the supporting processes here, or refer to the appropriate plans and where they can be found. In some cases, the organization's standard processes can provide the majority of the information and need not be reproduced in a plan.

5.1 CONFIGURATION MANAGEMENT

Specify or reference the configuration management plan for the IT project, providing the information identified in the following lines.

- Specify the methods that will be used to perform the following activities:
    - Configuration identification;
    - Configuration control;
    - Status accounting;
    - Evaluation; and
    - Release management.

- Specify the processes of configuration management including procedures for the following activities:
    - Initial base-lining of work products;
    - Logging and analysis of change requests;
    - Change control board procedures;
    - Tracking of changes in progress; and
    - Procedures for notification of concerned parties when baselines are established or changed.

- Identify the automated configuration management tools used to support the configuration management process.

5.2 VERIFICATION AND VALIDATION

Specify or reference the verification and validation plan for the IT project, providing the information identified in the following lines.

- Specify the scope, tools, techniques, and responsibilities for the verification and validation work activities.

- Specify the organizational relationships and degrees of independence between development activities and verification and validation activities.

- Specify the use of verification techniques such as traceability, milestone reviews, progress reviews, peer reviews, prototyping, simulation, and modeling.

- Specify the use of validation techniques such as testing, demonstration, analysis, and inspection.

- Identify the automated tools to be used in verification and validation.

5.3   DOCUMENTATION

Describe (or refer to the description of) the processes, techniques, and tools that will be used for generating the deliverable and non-deliverable work products for the project. Include the product deliverables described earlier in this plan, as well as the various supporting plans and other documentation used by the project team to conduct the project.

- Specify the organizational entities responsible for providing input information, and for generating and reviewing the project documentation.

- Specify the following information or object identification:
    - List of documents to be prepared;
    - Controlling template or standard for each document;
    - Who will prepare each document;
    - Who will review each document;
    - Due dates for review copies;
    - Due dates for initial baseline versions; and
    - A distribution list for review copies and baseline versions and quantities required.

Documents often found useful to perform the technical processes for developing software that satisfies the requirements include the following:

- User Requirements Specification – description of the problems to be solved, user needs to be served, in the words of the user.

- Software Requirements Specification – detailed technical descriptions of the product requirements, addressing functionality, quality attributes, interfaces, design constraints, and other information helpful to product design.

- Design Documentation – descriptions of major components of the product design, including architecture, process design, user interfaces, database design, and internal interface design.

- Test Documentation – test plans, test procedures, and test cases at all relevant levels of testing (unit, module, integration, system, acceptance, alpha, beta).

5.4   QUALITY ASSURANCE

Specify or reference the quality assurance plan for the IT project, containing the information identified in the following lines.

- Specify the plans for assuring that the IT project fulfills its commitments to the IT process and the IT product as specified in the requirements specification, the IT Project Management Plan, supporting plans and any standards, procedures, or guidelines to which the process or the product must adhere.

- As applicable, specify the quality assurance procedures to be used, such as analysis, inspection, review, audit, and assessment.

- Indicate the relationship among the quality assurance, verification and validation, review, audit, configuration management, system engineering, and assessment processes.

5.5   REVIEWS AND AUDITS

Describe the manner and methods used for all project reviews and audits.

- Specify the schedule, resources, processes, and procedures used in conducting project reviews and audits.

- Specify the plans for joint customer-project reviews, management progress reviews, developer peer reviews, quality assurance audits, and customer-conducted reviews and audits.

- List the external agencies that approve or regulate any project deliverable.

5.6   PROBLEM RESOLUTION

Describe the resources, methods, and tools to be used for reporting, analyzing, prioritizing, and handling project issues. Issues may include problems with staffing or managing the project, new risks that are detected, missing information, defects in work products, and other problems. Describe how the issues will be tracked and managed to closure.

- Indicate the roles of development, configuration management, the change control board, and verification and validation in problem resolution work activities.

- Provide for separate tracking of effort expended on problem reporting, analysis and resolution, so that rework can be tracked and process improvement accomplished.

Note: Work product defects in baselined work products should be handled by the configuration management change control process.

5.7   SUBCONTRACTOR MANAGEMENT

Specify or reference the plans for selecting and managing any subcontractors that may participate in or contribute to the IT project.

- Specify the criteria for selecting subcontractors.

- Generate a separate management plan for each subcontract, using a tailored version of this Project Plan, and include all items necessary to ensure successful completion of each subcontract as follows:

- Requirements management;

- Monitoring of technical progress;

- Schedule and budget control;

- Product acceptance criteria;

- Risk management procedures;

- Additional topics as needed to ensure successful completion of the subcontract; and

- A reference to the official subcontract and subcontractor/prime contractor points of contact.

5.8   PROCESS IMPROVEMENT

Specify the plans for periodically assessing the project, for determining areas for improvement, and for implementing the improvement plans. If this project carries a responsibility for defining, testing, or using some new organization process, describe how that is incorporated into the project's work. If this project is responsible for showing the impact to the business of using some new process, describe how that is included in the project's measurement plan.

- Ensure that the process improvement plan is closely related to the problem resolution plan.

- Include in the improvement plan a process to identify the project processes that can be improved without serious disruption to an ongoing project, and to identify the project processes that can best be improved by process improvement initiatives at the organizational level.

6.0   ADDITIONAL PLANS

Specify or reference any additional plans required to satisfy product requirements and contractual terms, which may include:

- Plans for assuring safety, privacy, and security requirements are met;

- Special facilities or equipment specification;

- Product installation plans;

- User training plans;

- Integration plans;

- Data conversion plans;

- System transition plans;

- Product support and maintenance plans; and

- Identify potential follow-up project plans which will use or supersede this project.

Document ID **ITSW102**	Title **IT PROJECT MANAGEMENT**	Print Date **mm/dd/yyyy**
Revision **0.0**	Prepared By **Preparer's Name / Title**	Date Prepared **mm/dd/yyyy**
Effective Date **mm/dd/yyyy**	Reviewed By **Reviewer's Name / Title**	Date Reviewed **mm/dd/yyyy**
	Approved By **Final Approver's Name / Title**	Date Approved **mm/dd/yyyy**

Policy: All in-house software development shall follow a defined project management procedure.

Purpose: To ensure that Information Technology projects are clearly defined, well structured, efficiently and effectively managed, and produce the desired results on time and within budget.

Scope: This procedure applies to all in-house software development projects.

Responsibilities:

The Information Technology Project Manager is responsible for ensuring that projects run smoothly, remain on schedule, and are completed on time.

Definitions: Quality Management System (QMS) – A formalized system that documents the structure, responsibilities, and procedures required to achieve effective quality management.

Procedure:

1.0   IT PROJECT SETUP

1.1   The Information Technology Project Manager should use the following tools:

- Company-wide standards that outline the look and feel of all software products;

- Industry standards and best-practices;

- A standard development method;

- Project scheduling software (for estimating timelines);

- A development database for storing all information about the project.

1.2   The Information Technology Project Manager shall select the members of the project development team, which should include one or more of the following people:

- Subject matter expert;

- Systems analyst;

- Software designer;

- Programmer;

- Technical writer; and

- Quality assurance analyst.

1.3   The Information Technology Project Manager shall set up e-mail and voice mail groups for the development team, which development team shall use to:

- Schedule meetings;

- Send updates and bulletins; and

- Pose suggestions, questions, and development issues to the rest of the group.

2.0   IT PROJECT SCHEDULE

2.1   The Information Technology Project Manager, with the assistance of the development team, shall create a preliminary development schedule from ITSW101-1 IT PROJECT PLAN, which shall indicate estimated duration and expected begin and end dates for each of the following tasks:

- Systems Analysis

    a. Create the system requirements specification.

    b. Create the acceptance test plan.

    c. Create the beta test plan.

- Software Design

    a. Create the software design specification.

    b. Create flow charts and process maps that define inputs, outputs, and process interactions.

- Programming

    a. Program the system.

    b. Unit test the system.

- Documentation

- Quality assurance

    a. Perform the acceptance test.

    b. Conduct the beta test.

- Production

    a. Configure the system for maintenance and support.

    b. Create release materials (such as disks and CDs) for shipping.

2.2   The Information Technology Project Manager shall review the proposed schedule with Information Technology Management. They shall discuss possible changes to the proposed project with respect to ITSW102-1 PROJECT DEVELOPMENT DATABASE and resolve possible scheduling conflicts with existing projects.

2.3   The Information Technology Project Manager shall discuss scheduling changes with the development team and revise the project schedule accordingly.

2.4   The Information Technology Project Manager shall enter the original project schedule into ITSW102-1 PROJECT DEVELOPMENT DATABASE so that at the end of the project, it can be evaluated in relation to the actual times spent on the project.

3.0   IT PROJECT CYCLE MANAGEMENT

3.1   Throughout the course of the project, the Information Technology Project Manager:

- Continually monitors progress on each major task;

- Resolves internal staff and scheduling conflicts;

- Keeps team members current on all changes;

- Updates and communicates the project schedule;

- Leads project meetings;

- Helps team members handle project-related requests from other departments and from management; and

- Periodically informs management of the progress on the project.

3.2   Throughout the course of the project, the Information Technology Project Manager should document the project status, as obtained above, at regular periodic intervals using ITSW102-2 IT PROJECT STATUS REPORT. The reporting cycle should be a function of the level of project activity but should not occur less often than once a month.

4.0   IT PROJECT REVIEW

4.1   After a project task is completed, the Information Technology Project Manager prints the outlines or charts that reflect actual time lines. The development team reviews the differences between the original estimates and the actual time required to complete each task.

4.2   ITSW102-3 IT PROJECT TEAM REVIEW CHECKLIST is reviewed before each meeting to determine of all pre-meeting steps have been accomplished. Important steps include:

- Determining the purpose of the review and communicating it to all required parties;

- Developing and distributing the agenda for the review;

- Determining the status of the review items including current action items, issues, risks; status of technical activities; and plans for next activities;

- Reviewing purpose and goals to determine achievement to date;

- Conducting a process review to identify improvements;

- Determining new items to be added to the agenda; and

- Preparing all handouts, charts, or presentation materials for each participant in the meeting.

4.3   A progress review is performed at important milestones indicated in the project plan. ITSW102-4 IT PROJECT PROGRESS REVIEW CHECKLIST is reviewed before each meeting to determine if all pre-meeting steps have been accomplished. Important steps include:

- Determining the purpose of the review and communicating it to all required parties;

- Developing and distributing the agenda for the review;

- Determining the status of the review items including current action items, issues, and risks, status of technical activities, and plans for next activities;

- Reviewing purpose and goals to determine achievement to date;

- Conducting a process review to identify improvements;

- Determining new items to be added to the agenda; and

- Preparing all handouts, charts, or presentation materials for each participant in the meeting.

4.4   The Information Technology Project Manager leads the progress review, documents each action item for resolution with the responsible party and a due date for completion, and schedules the next review.

4.5   The Information Technology Project Manager records the team's findings in the development database. These findings aid in estimating and scheduling future projects.

Forms:

- ITSW102-1 IT PROJECT DEVELOPMENT DATABASE

- ITSW102-2 IT PROJECT STATUS REPORT

- ITSW102-3 IT PROJECT TEAM REVIEW CHECKLIST

- ITSW102-4 IT PROJECT PROGRESS REVIEW CHECKLIST

References:

A. ISO 9001:2008, "QUALITY MANAGEMENT SYSTEMS - REQUIREMENTS"

ISO 9001 describes what a company needs to establish and operate its own quality management system, or QMS. A company's QMS should:
(a) demonstrate its ability to consistently provide products or services that meet customer and regulatory requirements; and (b) enable the company to enhance customer satisfaction by effectively applying the QMS, continually improving it, and assuring the company's continued conformity to customer, legal/regulatory, and other requirements.

B. ISO/IEC 12207:2008 – INFORMATION TECHNOLOGY-SOFTWARE LIFE-CYCLE PROCESSES

C. IEEE 12207-2008 – SYSTEMS AND SOFTWARE ENGINEERING – SOFTWARE LIFE CYCLE PROCESSES

This ISO standard describes the major component processes of a complete software life cycle and the high-level relations that govern their interaction. It establishes a software life cycle architecture based on two principles, modularity of processes and responsibility for processes. There are three process classes in the ISO software life cycle: primary, supporting, and organizational. Each life cycle process is made up of activities and each activity is subdivided into tasks. The standard is based on ISO quality management principles.

The IEEE version of 12207 is closely aligned with, though not a duplicate of, its ISO counterpart. For more information, visit http://www.iso.org and/or http://www.ieee.org/.

Additional Resources:

A. Software Project Survival Guide – http://www.construx.com/survivalguide/

B. Project Management Productivity Checklist – http://www.commercial-solutions.com/pages/checklists.html

C. Project Management Institute – http://www.pmi.org

Revision History:

Revision	Date	Description of Changes	Requested By
0	mm/dd/yyyy	Initial Release	

[This page intentionally left blank]

ITSW102-1 IT PROJECT DEVELOPMENT DATABASE[1]

Project ID	Proposed Start Date	Proposed End Date	Proposed Length (months)	Actual Start Date	Actual End Date	Actual Project Length	User Mgr (emp ID)	User Dept		

[1] This is only a suggested layout for a project development database; it is expected your company's will vary from this.

ITSW102 IT Project Management

[This page intentionally left blank]

ITSW102-2 IT PROJECT STATUS REPORT

General Information:

Agency name:	Date:
Contact Name:	Phone:
Project ID:	For the period beginning: and ending:
Name of the project:	
Project Start Date:	Current Phase:

Key Questions

1) Has the project scope of work changed?   Yes   No

2) Will upcoming target dates be missed?   Yes   No

3) Does the team have resource constraints?   Yes   No

4) Are there issues that require management attention? Yes   No

If any of the above questions is answered "yes," please provide an explanation of the "yes" answer.

Key Milestones for the Overall Project revised on <date>:

Milestone	Original Date	Revised Date	Actual Date

Milestones planned for this month and accomplished this month:

Milestone	Original Date	Revised Date	Actual Date

Accomplishments planned for this month but not completed:

Milestone/Item/Accomplishment	Original Date	Revised Date
1)		
2)		
3)		
4)		

For each item listed above, provide a corresponding explanation of the effect of this missed item on other target dates and provide the plan to recover from this missed item.

Items Planned for Next Month:

Milestone	Original Date	Revised Date

(Use a chart like the following to show actual expenditures compared to planned levels. Break the costs into other categories as appropriate.)

Year-to-Date Costs (000)

Fiscal Year 20__	Actual Costs to Date	Estimate to Complete	Total Estimated Costs	Total Planned Budget
Personnel Services				
Prof. & Outside Service				
Other Expenditures *				
Total Costs				

(Use a chart like the following if the project spans more than one fiscal year.)

Year-to-Date Costs (000)

Grand Total For Project	Actual Costs to Date	Estimate to Complete	Total Estimated Costs	Total Planned Budget
Personnel Services				
Prof. & Outside Service				
Other Expenditures *				
Total Costs				

* Other Expenditures include hardware, software, travel, training, support, etc.

Comments:_____

_____

_____

_____

_____

_____

_____

_____   _____

Project Leader   *Date*

Attach the current risk list.

For significant items that require management attention, attach a current issues / action item list.

[This page intentionally left blank]

ITSW102-3 IT PROJECT TEAM REVIEW CHECKLIST

ID	ITEMS TO BE CONSIDERED	RESPONSE
	TEAM REVIEWS	
1	Has the purpose of the review been determined and communicated?	
2	Has the agenda for the review been developed?	
3	Have the review items been prepared? Including: • Current action items, issues, risks • Status of technical activities • Plans for next activities	
4	Have action items been followed up as appropriate? Items such as the following should be included: • Due date assigned • Responsible party	
5	Have next tasks been assigned?	
6	Have purpose and goals been reviewed to determine success?	
7	Has process been reviewed to identify improvements?	
8	Other?	

[This page intentionally left blank]

ITSW102-4 IT PROJECT PROGRESS REVIEW CHECKLIST

ID	ITEMS TO BE CONSIDERED	RESPONSE
	PROGRESS REVIEWS	
1.	Has the purpose of the review been determined and communicated?	
2.	Has the information to be prepared and/or presented been identified?	
3.	Have assignments been made to gather, prepare and present the information for the review?	
4.	Have the participants for the review been identified and notified?	
5.	Have the logistics of the review been established?	
6.	Has the agenda for the review been prepared and distributed for comments? Have comments been resolved?	
7.	Has a review package been developed and distributed to the participants, with ample review time? The review package should include at least the following: <ul><li>Agenda identifying time allotted and responsible party</li><li>Current action item list, issues, and risks</li><li>Status of technical activities</li><li>Information on critical decisions to be made and possible alternatives</li><li>Plans for next activities</li></ul>	

ID	ITEMS TO BE CONSIDERED	RESPONSE
8.	Has the information for the review been prepared? Items such as the following should be included: • List of accomplishments in the last period • List of plans for the next period • Milestone progress reports (planned to actual) • Staffing profile (planned to actual) • Cost profile (planned to actual) • Size and Critical Computer Resources (if appropriate) • Risk Management Status • Action Item Status • Quality Assurance Status • Configuration Management Status • Requirements Management Status • Updated Cost-Benefit Analysis	
9.	Has the review been conducted?	
10.	Has agreement been obtained on next course of action?	
11.	Have assignments been given commensurate with next course of action?	
12.	Have action items been assigned?	
13.	Have minutes from the meeting been distributed?	
14.	Have purpose and goals been reviewed to determine success?	
15.	Has the process been reviewed to identify improvements?	
16.	Other?	

Document ID **ITSW103**	Title **SYSTEMS ANALYSIS**	Print Date **mm/dd/yyyy**
Revision **0.0**	Prepared By **Preparer's Name / Title**	Date Prepared **mm/dd/yyyy**
Effective Date **mm/dd/yyyy**	Reviewed By **Reviewer's Name / Title**	Date Reviewed **mm/dd/yyyy**
	Approved By **Final Approver's Name / Title**	Date Approved **mm/dd/yyyy**

Policy: All software products developed by the company must be designed to meet certain specific needs of potential users.

Purpose: To create:

- Documents that define the functions the system will perform;
- An acceptance test plan, which describes how to test those functions; and
- A beta test plan, which describes how to conduct a user test of those functions.

Scope: All software products and updates released by the company.

Responsibilities:

The Systems Analyst is responsible for developing and communicating the overall design approach that addresses the customer requirements, as well as producing the test plans.

Definitions: Systems analysis - Work that involves applying analytical processes to the planning, design, and implementation of new and improved information systems to meet the business requirements of customer organizations; phase of the SDLC in which the current system is studied and alternative replacement systems are proposed.

Systems development life cycle (SDLC) - A method for developing information systems, made up of five main stages: analysis, design, development, implementation, and evaluation. Each stage is further comprised of several components (for example, the development stage includes programming, debugging, testing, and documenting).

Procedure:

1.0   SYSTEMS ANALYSIS - INTRODUCTION

1.1   Systems analysis is a process of refinement. The analyst begins with a general model for a software product and gradually develops and refines it until it fulfills the requirements identified by users and subject matter experts. Good methods, patience, and attention to detail save time in the long run.

1.2   The Systems Analyst might use the following tools:

- A word processing program for typing text;

- A paint or draw program for creating graphics;

- A flow charting program or CASE tool for documenting process flows; and

- A central database for storing specifications, charts, and images.

    NOTE: If possible, scan sample documents to disk and store them with the specification files.

2.0   SYSTEMS ANALYSIS - REQUIREMENTS

2.1   The Systems Analyst interviews users and subject matter experts to determine the functions the software must perform.

2.2   The Systems Analyst researches how potential users are currently performing these functions.

    For example, if the software is a word processing system, the Systems Analyst researches how potential users are currently designing and creating documents. Research methods may include manual or paper systems, competing software systems, or industry standards the software must meet. See references A and B.

2.3   The Systems Analyst creates a document that specifies the functional requirements of the software.

2.4   The Systems Analyst reviews the requirements with users and subject matter experts and makes any necessary changes.

3.0   SYSTEMS ANALYSIS - INFORMATION FLOWS DOCUMENTATION

3.1   The Systems Analyst creates a high-level diagram that shows the information the software system manages and the way in which this information flows through the system. The diagram should contain all of the components required to support the information flows, including:

- Inputs;

- Outputs;

- Processes;

- Calculations; and

- Relations.

3.2   Large projects should be divided into subsystems with each subsystem individually designed. The Systems Analyst reviews the diagram with users and subject matter experts, and then makes any necessary changes.

3.3   The Systems Analyst writes a detailed description of each of the flows in the diagram, and of each input, output, process, calculation, and relation.

3.4   The Systems Analyst reviews the detail descriptions with users and subject matter experts, and then makes any necessary changes.

4.0   SYSTEMS ANALYSIS - ACCEPTANCE TEST PLAN

4.1   After defining and documenting the system requirements, the Systems Analyst creates an acceptance test plan. When programming for the project is complete, the Systems Analyst uses this test plan to verify that all elements of the software work as designed.

4.2   The Acceptance Test Plan includes:

- A list of the test team members, their titles, and their duties. Members of the test team typically include:

  a. Quality Assurance Manager;

  b. Systems Analyst;

  c. Software Designer;

  d. Users; and

  e. Subject Matter Experts.

- Instructions for setting up the software after it is released from development.

- Descriptions of the data required during the test. For example, a description of the data required to test an order entry database might include sample customers, parts, and orders.

- A step-by-step test procedure that specifies exactly what to do and what the expected results are.

5.0   SYSTEMS ANALYSIS - BETA TEST PLAN

5.1   In addition to the acceptance test plan, the Systems Analyst also creates a beta test plan. After the software has been programmed and tested internally, a selected group of users performs a beta test. The beta test plan explains how to coordinate the beta test.

5.2   The beta test plan describes how to:

- Select user sites – the sites selected should accurately represent the product's target market.

- Install the software at the beta sites. Specify any installation procedures that differ from those used for the official release. For example, the beta release might need to be installed manually, while the official release contains an automated installation procedure.

- Train beta testers on the software. For example, provide written training materials or on-site training for the beta testers.

- Support the beta release. Specify the individuals responsible for answering beta testers' questions. Include individuals from analysis, design, programming, and documentation.

- Report problems found during testing. Give each test site a packet that includes sample problem reporting forms and contact names and phone numbers.

6.0 SYSTEMS ANALYSIS - REVIEW

6.1 The Systems Analyst should present the systems analysis documents in a formal review to all interested people in the company, including:

- The Software Designer;

- Programmers;

- Technical Writers;

- Members of upper management; and

- Marketing and sales representatives.

6.2 Document ideas, comments and concerns for possible investigation. Plan on spending as much time as necessary to answer questions before turning the analysis over for software design. The more time spent in the early planning phases will help to create an easier coding specification and save time later in the software design phase.

Forms:

- None.

References:

A. ISO/IEC 12207:2008, "SYSTEMS AND SOFTWARE ENGINEERING – SOFTWARE LIFE CYCLE PROCESSES"

B. IEEE 12207-2008, "SYSTEMS AND SOFTWARE ENGINEERING – SOFTWARE LIFE CYCLE PROCESSES"

ISO 12207 describes the major component processes of a complete software life cycle and the high-level relations that govern their interaction. It establishes a software life cycle architecture based on two principles, modularity of processes and responsibility for processes. There are three process classes in the ISO software life cycle: primary; supporting; and organizational. Each life cycle process is made up of activities and each activity is subdivided into tasks. ISO 12207 is based on ISO quality management principles.

The IEEE version of 12207 is closely aligned with, but not an exact duplicate of, its ISO counterpart.

For more information, visit the ISO web site at http://www.iso.org or the IEEE web site at http://www.ieee.org/.

Revision History:

Revision	Date	Description of Changes	Requested By
0.0	mm/dd/yyyy	Initial Release	

[This page intentionally left blank]

Document ID **ITSW104**	Title **SOFTWARE DESIGN**	Print Date **mm/dd/yyyy**
Revision **0.0**	Prepared By **Preparer's Name / Title**	Date Prepared **mm/dd/yyyy**
Effective Date **mm/dd/yyyy**	Reviewed By **Reviewer's Name / Title**	Date Reviewed **mm/dd/yyyy**
	Approved By **Final Approver's Name / Title**	Date Approved **mm/dd/yyyy**

Policy: To design software in a technically sound and efficient manner and fulfill requirements identified by the systems analyst.

Purpose: To transform a set of system requirements (developed by the systems analyst) into programming instructions for a software product.

Scope: All software products and updates released by the company.

Responsibilities: The Software Designer is responsible for transforming system requirements developed by the systems analyst into programming instructions and then communicating the overall design approach.

Procedure:

1.0   SOFTWARE DESIGN – INTRODUCTION

1.1   The Software Designer transforms the system requirements and other design documents developed by the systems analyst (see ITSW103 SYSTEMS ANALYSIS) into instructions and specifications for programming a software product.

1.2   The Software Designer might use the following tools:

- A word processing program, for typing text;

- A paint or draw program, for creating graphics;

- A flow charting program, for documenting data flows;

- A source code control system, for controlling program revisions; and

- A central database, for storing specifications, charts, and images.

NOTE: If possible, scan sample documents to disk and store them with the specification files.

2.0   SOFTWARE DESIGN SPECIFICATION

2.1   The Software Designer shall write a description of the programming environment. The description should include instructions for:

- Locating the programming system (its directory/account structure);

- Accessing the programming system (startup, login);

- Applying for the required user codes;

- Locating programming libraries and tools;

- Checking components into and out of the software component library or source code control system[1];

- Assigning tasks to programmers;

- Reporting and tracking problems (or bugs); and

- Returning completed work to the designer.

2.2   The Software Designer shall create a general design of the software required to fulfill the system requirements developed by the systems analyst. To do this, the designer must:

- Fully address each process, calculation, relation, and flow defined in the system requirements;

- Design software components that leverage the strengths of the programming tools and run efficiently in the physical environment; and

- Incorporate internal and industry-accepted standards of design.

2.3   The Software Designer shall review the general design with the systems analyst and make any required changes.

2.4   The Software Designer shall write detailed programming instructions for each component in the design. The following table shows the types of components and instructions found in a typical database software design.

Programs	Forms	Reports	Menus	Database
program name	form name	report name	menu name	database name
description	description	description	description	description
screen layout	screen layout	screen layout	menu layout	table names
process logic	field edits	report layout		field names
messages	process logic	query logic		keys & indexing
	messages	process logic		format rules
		messages		edit rules
				update rules

2.5   The Software Designer shall create a catalog of messages used in the software. For each message, the Software Designer indicates the action the system users or administrators must take.

---

[1] For information about the software component library, see ITSW109 SOFTWARE RELEASES AND UPDATES procedure

2.6   The Software Designer shall review the detail design with the systems analyst and make any required changes.

3.0   SOFTWARE DESIGN REVIEW

3.1   The Software Designer should use ITSW104-1 DESIGN REVIEW CHECKLIST as a guide to preparation before presenting the software design documents in a formal review to everyone who will be working on the project, including:

- The project manager;

- The systems analyst;

- Programmers;

- Technical writers; and

- Quality assurance analysts.

3.2   The software design should be reviewed for compliance with overall design objectives, including:

- A clear understanding of the user environment, requirements, and system analyst specifications;

- Use of best practices in software design, including effective design strategies, modularity, performance, and extensibility; and

- Clear process flows, data integration, and data models.

3.3   Document ideas, comments, and concerns for possible investigation. Plan on spending as much time as necessary to answer any questions before turning the design over for programming. The more time spent in the early planning phases will help to create easier coding and save time later in the software programming phase.

3.4   Users may request design changes during this or any other phase of the software development life cycle; users shall submit change requests in accordance with ITSW108 DESIGN CHANGES DURING DEVELOPMENT.

Forms:

- ITSW104-1 DESIGN REVIEW CHECKLIST

References:

A. ISO/IEC 12207:2008 – SYSTEMS AND SOFTWARE ENGINEERING – SOFTWARE LIFE CYCLE PROCESSES

B. IEEE 12207-2008 – SYSTEMS AND SOFTWARE ENGINEERING – SOFTWARE LIFE CYCLE PROCESSES

This ISO standard describes the major component processes of a complete software life cycle and the high-level relations that govern their interaction. It establishes a software life cycle architecture based on two principles, modularity of processes and responsibility for processes. There are three process classes in the ISO software life cycle: primary (such as acquisition and operations); supporting (such as documentation and configuration management); and organizational (such as infrastructure and training). Each life cycle process is made up of activities, and each activity is further subdivided into tasks. The standard is based on ISO quality management principles.

The IEEE version of 12207 is closely aligned with, though not exactly the same as, its ISO counterpart. For more information, visit http://www.iso.org/iso/catalogue_detail.htm?csnumber=43447 and/or http://standards.ieee.org/findstds/standard/12207-2008.html.

Revision History:

Revision	Date	Description of Changes	Requested By
0.0	mm/dd/yyyy	Initial Release	

ITSW104-1 DESIGN REVIEW CHECKLIST

	DESIGN REVIEW	
ID	ITEMS TO BE CONSIDERED	RESPONSE
1	Have the work products to be reviewed been identified?	
2	Has the type of review been selected? Alternatives include: • Informal walk through by several team members • Technical review by project team members and stakeholders • Inspection by project team members(and perhaps others)	
3	Have the goals of the review been established?	
4	Has a moderator/facilitator been selected?	
5	Has a review package been developed and distributed to the participants with ample review time? The review package should include at least the following: • Work product to be reviewed • Related templates, guidelines, other background information • Forms with which to record defects, questions, issues	
6	Has the software design been reviewed for compliance with overall design objectives including: • A clear understanding of the user environment, requirements and system analyst specifications. • Use of "Best Practices" in software design including effective design strategies, modularity, performance and extensibility. • Clear process flows, data integration and data models.	
7	Have results of the review been used to update the work product?	
8	Have the goals of the review been reviewed to determine success?	
9	Has the process been reviewed to identify any improvements?	

[This page intentionally left blank]

Document ID	Title	Print Date
ITSW105	**SOFTWARE PROGRAMMING**	**mm/dd/yyyy**
Revision	Prepared By	Date Prepared
0.0	**Preparer's Name / Title**	**mm/dd/yyyy**
Effective Date	Reviewed By	Date Reviewed
mm/dd/yyyy	**Reviewer's Name / Title**	**mm/dd/yyyy**
	Approved By	Date Approved
	Final Approver's Name / Title	**mm/dd/yyyy**

Policy: All software products developed by the company must meet company standards for user interface, program structure, system interface, toolset, and configuration.

Purpose: To effectively and efficiently carry out the plans of the software designer.

Scope: All software products and updates released by the company.

Responsibilities:

The <u>Software Designer</u> is responsible for transforming the system requirements developed by the systems analyst into programming instructions and communicating the overall design approach to the team.

The <u>Software Programmer</u> is responsible for reviewing the programming instructions created by the software designer and using those instructions to design each software component.

Procedure:

1.0   PROGRAMMING STANDARDS

1.1   Members of the software development department should create basic programming standards, to be followed in programming all of the Company's software. The Company encourages all programmers to participate in setting these standards: welcoming programmers' input encourages teamwork and often makes programmers more willing to follow the standards.

1.2   Programming standards typically address:

- Conventions in the use of the programming tools;

- A locking strategy that defines how and when record locking is imposed;

- A strategy for handling messages in the various types of software components;

- Programming style guides for the various types of software components; and

- Strategies for dealing with inefficiencies and limits of the programming tools, software environment, or equipment.

1.3   Software Engineering Standards are used very early in the development of the project plan. See procedure ITSW101 PROJECT DEFINITION for additional information.

2.0   PROGRAMMING TASKS

2.1   The software designer divides the programming tasks among the members of the programming team and then conducts a series of meetings to introduce the design to each member of the team.

2.2   The software designer presents the software design to the entire programming team at an initial "kick-off" meeting. This meeting explains to the programmers the context for each programming task. For a large system, multiple meetings might require several sessions over the course of the programming effort.

2.3   The software designer explains each programming task with each programmer who has been assigned to it. This meeting clarifies the specifications to eliminate misunderstandings.

3.0   SOFTWARE DEVELOPMENT

3.1   The programmer reviews the programming instructions created by the software designer, and uses these instructions to design each software component.

3.2   If the programming instructions require the programmer to modify existing software components, the programmer checks those components out of the software component library. See ITSW109 SOFTWARE RELEASES AND UPDATES procedure for information about the software component library.

3.3   The programmer programs the software components. After completing each component, the programmer unit tests it to ensure that it:

- Complies with programming standards;

- Runs error free;

- Meets all the requirements listed in the software design specification; and

- The programmer corrects any errors the unit test identifies.

3.4   The programmer checks all new and modified software components into the software component library.

3.5   The software designer reviews and tests all software components to ensure that they comply with programming standards. Any variances shall be noted and steps 3.1 through 3.5 repeated until all variances are resolved.

4.0   PROGRAMMING REVIEWS

4.1   Throughout the project life cycle, the project team conducts team reviews of the work products being built. The types of reviews may vary from formal design reviews to informal code walk through, according to the plan set by the project team, to ensure best use of time spent on the review.

4.2   It is important to ensure that all people involved in the project understand the content of a given work product, and identify any changes needed in the work product before starting work on other work products that depend on it.

4.3   ITSW105-1 WORK PRODUCT REVIEW CHECKLIST contains items to consider when planning, conducting, and following up actions after a review. The project leader and/or Project Manager should review the work product, using ITSW105-1 as a guide.

Forms:

- ITSW105-1 WORK PRODUCT REVIEW CHECKLIST

References:

A. ISO/IEC 12207:2008 – SYSTEMS AND SOFTWARE ENGINEERING – SOFTWARE LIFE CYCLE PROCESSES

B. IEEE 12207-2008 – SYSTEMS AND SOFTWARE ENGINEERING – SOFTWARE LIFE CYCLE PROCESSES

This ISO standard describes the major component processes of a complete software life cycle and the high-level relations that govern their interaction. It establishes a software life cycle architecture based on two principles, modularity of processes and responsibility for processes. There are three process classes in the ISO software life cycle: primary (such as acquisition and operations); supporting (such as documentation and configuration management); and organizational (such as infrastructure and training). Each life cycle process is made up of activities, and each activity is further subdivided into tasks. The standard is based on ISO quality management principles.

The IEEE version of 12207 is more closely aligned with the ISO standard than it was in previous versions.

For more information, visit the ISO web site at http://www.iso.org/iso/catalogue_detail.htm?csnumber=43447 or the IEEE web site at http://standards.ieee.org/findstds/standard/12207-2008.html.

Revision History:

Revision	Date	Description of Changes	Requested By
0	mm/dd/yyyy	Initial Release	

ITSW105-1 WORK PRODUCT REVIEW CHECKLIST

WORK PRODUCT REVIEWS		
ID	**ITEMS TO BE CONSIDERED**	**RESPONSE**
1	Have the work products to be reviewed been identified?	
2	Has the type of review been selected? Alternatives include: • Informal walk through by several team members • Technical review by project team members and stakeholders • Inspection by project team members(and perhaps others)	
3	Have the goals of the review been established?	
4	Has a moderator/facilitator been selected?	
5	Has a review package been developed and distributed to the participants with ample review time? The review package should include at least the following: • Work product to be reviewed; • Related templates, guidelines, other background information; and • Forms with which to record defects, questions, issues.	
6	Have results of the review been used to update the work product?	
7	Have the goals of the review been reviewed to determine success?	
8	Has process been reviewed to identify any improvements?	

[This page intentionally left blank]

Document ID **ITSW106**	Title **SOFTWARE DOCUMENTATION**	Print Date **mm/dd/yyyy**
Revision **0.0**	Prepared By **Preparer's Name / Title**	Date Prepared **mm/dd/yyyy**
Effective Date **mm/dd/yyyy**	Reviewed By **Reviewer's Name / Title**	Date Reviewed **mm/dd/yyyy**
	Approved By **Final Approver's Name / Title**	Date Approved **mm/dd/yyyy**

Policy: All software products developed by the Company shall be documented with online help and user guides and all software documentation shall meet Company standards for design, style, and content.

Purpose: To define the methods and responsibilities for controlling the revision, approval, and distribution of documents used to provide software reference and training materials.

Scope: All software products and updates released by the company.

Responsibilities:

The Document Editor is responsible for reviewing software documentation for grammar, punctuation, understanding, and overall usability.

The Quality Assurance Manager is responsible for ensuring that software documentation meets quality requirements.

The Systems Analyst works with and educates the Technical Writer on the proper use of the software and reviewing all documentation for technical accuracy.

The Technical Writer is responsible for gathering information about the software that explains the use of the software to the target user using help files or manuals, and for developing, maintaining, and controlling documentation produced.

Definitions: Controlled Document – A document that provides information or direction for performance of work and that is within the scope of this procedure. Characteristics of control include such things as Revision Number (letter), signatures indicating review and approval, and controlled distribution.

Document – Information and its supporting medium. The medium can be paper, magnetic, electronic, optical computer disc, photograph, or sample.

External Document – A document of external origin that provides information or direction for the performance of activities within the scope of this procedure.

Procedure:

1.0   SOFTWARE ASSESSMENT

1.1   The Technical Writer gathers information about the software, the intended user and the users's environment. Methods of gathering information include:

- Studying the project defininition, design documents and any existing programming documentation;

- Running the software to learn how it works;

- Attending any available training sessions or product demonstrations on the software; and

- Interviewing the systems analyst.

1.2   The Technical Writer and Systems Analyst work together to create a list of the most common tasks, errors, pitfalls, and paths that a user can accomplish with the software. For example, some tasks you can accomplish with word processing software include: creating a document, formatting a document, or printing multiple documents.

2.0   SOFTWARE DOCUMENTATION PRODUCTION

2.1   The Technical Writer creates a preliminary outline (table of contents) based on the task list. The systems analyst edits and approves the table of contents.

2.2   The Technical Writer prepares a first draft of the documentation for review by the systems analyst.

2.3   The Systems Analyst edits the draft for comprehensiveness and clarity, ensuring that:

- All major tasks are documented as agreed;

- All important features and functions of the software are adequately explained;

- Tasks appear in a logical sequence; and

- Tasks are explained in terms that are familiar to a typical user.

2.4   The Editor edits the documentation, ensuring that it:

- Contains correct grammar, punctuation, and spelling;

- Adheres to the company's standard style and format rules; and

- Is clear and easy to read.

2.5   The Technical Writer rewrites the documentation, incorporating the Editor's changes and prepares the documentation for final review. Help files are created and a draft print master is prepared for the final review.

3.0   SOFTWARE DOCUMENTATION REVIEW

3.1   The Technical Writer should submit the final draft of the documentation to a formal review to everyone who will be working on the project, including:

- The Project Manager;

- The Systems Analyst;

- Programmers; and

- The Quality Assurance Manager.

3.2   The documentation should be reviewed for compliance with overall design objectives including:

- A clear understanding of the user environment, requirements and system analyst specifications; and

- Use of "Best Practices" in technical writing including effective design grammar, punctuation, spelling, style and format rules, and is clear and easy to read.

3.3   Document ideas, comments and concerns for possible investigation. Plan on spending as much time as necessary to answer any questions before releasing the documentation into production.

3.4   The Technical Writer rewrites the documentation, incorporating any final review changes.

4.0   SOFTWARE DOCUMENTATION RELEASE

4.1   Once the documentation passes the final review then it enters the production phase. Final masters are prepared and formatted for print, the web, technical support, training, and insertion as a help file within the software itself.

4.2   All final versions should then be entered into a revision control system to manage all future changes.

4.3   The Quality Assurance Manager is responsible for maintaining master lists of all controlled documents. Separate lists will be maintained of documents of internal origin and external origin. Examples of external documents include National or International Standards that may be used or referenced.

The master list for internal documents will contain the following information:

- Document Number;
- Document Title;
- Current Revision;
- Last Review Date; and
- Document Locations.

The master list for external documents will contain the following information:

- Document Number;
- Document Title;
- Issue Date or Revision (both if available); and
- Document Locations.

4.4   The Quality Assurance Manager distributes hardcopy documents to the locations listed on the Master List, and removes and destroys any old versions of procedures or instructions. The Systems Analyst distributes electronic versions of documents by moving the old revision to the OBSOLETE folder and moving the new revision to the RELEASED folder.

4.5   External documents are controlled only for distribution. All external standards should be purchased to ensure they are added to the External Document list and that new revisions are properly distributed.

5.0   SOFTWARE DOCUMENT REVISION

5.1   The Quality Assurance Manager is responsible for coordinating with the Technical Writer to review all procedures and instructions at least annually and update them as required to ensure documents remain current.

5.2   Anyone may submit a new document or changes to an existing document as necessary. To submit a change, the requestor completes ITSW106-1 REQUEST FOR DOCUMENT CHANGE (RDC), indicating the nature and reason for the change, and submits it to the Quality Assurance Manager for review, with a copy of the document with marks (red ink notes) indicating the required changes on the copy. If changes are extensive, a new document may be typed and submitted.

5.3   The Quality Assurance Manager reviews the request.

   • If the request is denied, the Quality Assurance Manager notifies the requestor the reason for the denial.

   • If the request is approved, the Quality Assurance Manager coordinates with the Systems Analyst and the Technical Writer to review all changes. Only the RDC needs to be submitted for approval.

5.4   If approved, the Quality Assurance Manager assigns a Document Change Number (DCN) on ITAD103-3 DOCUMENT CHANGE CONTROL FORM (see ITAD103 IT DOCUMENT MANAGEMENT) and submits the new or changed documents, along with the appropriate approvals, to the Technical Writer for typing and formatting. The Technical Writer updates the document, indexes the revision, and updates the revision history.

5.5   The Technical Writer notifies the reviewers indicated on the RDC via email when the document is available for review.

5.6   Reviewers indicate intended approval or submit comments via email. If comments are substantive, The Technical Writer incorporates the comments and contacts reviewers for re-review.

5.7   When all reviewers indicate intent to approve, The Technical Writer circulates the final documents to obtain signatures. And forwards all information to the Quality Assurance Manager for entery into the control system.

5.8   After the required approvals have been obtained, the Quality Assurance Manager updates the master list with the new revision number and last review date for changed documents or with all required information for new documents.

5.9   Sufficient copies are made for distribution to all locations indicated on the master list. The Quality Assurance Manager stamps "Controlled Copy" in red on each copy and distributes the controlled copies according to Section 4.0 above.

5.10   The master copy of the previous revision is pulled, marked "Obsolete" and filed in the historical files.

5.11   Because the electronic version will not show signatures, the current Master Copy is maintained as evidence of review and approval

6.0   SOFTWARE DOCUMENTATION PROCEDURE AND WORK INSTRUCTION FORMAT

6.1   Procedures and instruction should use this document as a template. If any of the headings are not applicable they may be deleted.

6.2   All procedures and instructions must have the Procedure Name, Revision Number, and Page Number in Page X of Y format on each page of the document.

6.3   All procedures and instructions must show approval signatures on the first page or cover page. Electronic versions may show the approver names typed. The master copy must contain the signatures however.

Forms:

- ITSW106-1 REQUEST FOR DOCUMENT CHANGE (RDC)

References:

A. ISO/IEC 12207:2008 – SYSTEMS AND SOFTWARE ENGINEERING – SOFTWARE LIFE CYCLE PROCESSES

B. IEEE 12207-2008 – SYSTEMS AND SOFTWARE ENGINEERING – SOFTWARE LIFE CYCLE PROCESSES

This ISO standard describes the major component processes of a complete software life cycle and the high-level relations that govern their interaction. It establishes a software life cycle architecture based on two principles, modularity of processes and responsibility for processes. There are three process classes in the ISO software life cycle: primary (such as acquisition and operations); supporting (such as documentation and configuration management); and organizational (such as infrastructure and training). Each life cycle process is made up of activities, and each activity is further subdivided into tasks. The standard is based on ISO quality management principles.

The IEEE version of 12207 is more closely aligned with the ISO standard than it was in previous versions.

For more information, visit the ISO web site at http://www.iso.org/iso/catalogue_detail.htm?csnumber=43447 or the IEEE web site at http://standards.ieee.org/findstds/standard/12207-2008.html.

Revision History:

Revision	Date	Description of Changes	Requested By
0	mm/dd/yyyy	Initial Release	

ITSW106-1 REQUEST FOR DOCUMENT CHANGE (RDC)

Date: _____   RDC No.: _____

Originator:_____

Document Title and Publication Date:_____

Page and Chapter, or Paragraph Number:_____

Description Of Problem, Opportunity Or Reason For Request (Define in Detail):

_____

_____

_____

Solution Recommended (if known) Date Action Required By:_____

_____

_____

_____

Comments:_____

_____

_____

_____

_____

Systems Analyst's Approval:_____

Recommended Solution To Problem or Postponement/Dissolution of Request
    (attach all necessary documentation to support response)_____

_____

_____

_____

Approved By:_____   Date:_____

PROCEDURE FOR COMPLETING FORM

1) Complete top section of this form except for RDC number
2) Obtain Systems Analyst's approval
3) Forward original to the Quality Assurance Manager who will assign a RDC number (Note: one copy will be returned to originator with RDC number assigned.
4) The Quality Assurance Manager will take action and if appropriate will proceed with an RDC.
5) The Quality Assurance Manager returns a copy to Originator upon resolution of request.
       Distribution: Original - RDC File   Copy 1 - Originator

[This page intentionally left blank]

Document ID **ITSW107**	Title **SOFTWARE TESTING**	Print Date **mm/dd/yyyy**
Revision **0.0**	Prepared By **Preparer's Name / Title**	Date Prepared **mm/dd/yyyy**
Effective Date **mm/dd/yyyy**	Reviewed By **Reviewer's Name / Title**	Date Reviewed **mm/dd/yyyy**
	Approved By **Final Approver's Name / Title**	Date Approved **mm/dd/yyyy**

Policy: All software products developed by the Company shall pass acceptance tests, beta tests, and software release tests before they are released to the customer or user community.

Purpose: To ensure that Company-developed software is error-free and is capable of consistently performing the tasks for which it was designed.

Scope: All software products and updates released by the company.

Responsibilities:

The Beta Test Coordinator is responsible for implementing, coordinating, and managing the beta testing with the beta test users.

The Quality Assurance Manager is responsible for administering and coordinating the tests indicated in accordance with the procedure found in the acceptance test plan.

The Software Designer is responsible for reviewing test problem reports and assigning problem reports to software programmers for resolution.

The Systems Analyst is responsible for creating test plans for completed software products.

Procedure:

1.0 SOFTWARE TESTING OVERVIEW

1.1 During software development, the Systems Analyst creates plans for testing the completed software product. For information on creating test plans, see ITSW103 SYSTEMS ANALYSIS.

1.2 After programming has been completed, the Quality Assurance Manager administers and coordinates the tests indicated in the test plan.

1.3 Each test conducted should include a test script or scripts with detailed instructions on what exactly to test, using ITSW107-1 PROJECT TEST SCRIPT as a guide. The tester should follow each procedure and note any irregularities discovered on the form.

1.4 ITSW107-2 PROJECT TEST CHECKLIST should be used to highlight specific test criteria.

1.5   The Quality Assurance Manager should maintain a central database of test problem reports, using ITSW107-3 PROJECT TEST PROBLEM REPORT as a guide.

2.0   SOFTWARE ACCEPTANCE TESTING

2.1   The Quality Assurance Manager tests the software in accordance with the procedure found in the acceptance test plan, in accordance with ITSW103 SYSTEMS ANALYSIS. The test must be completed error-free before the software is released to beta test.

2.2   The Quality Assurance Manager completes a problem report for each error encountered. If a problem prevents one or more components from being thoroughly tested, the Quality Assurance Manager:

- Discontinues testing the affected components.

- Immediately submits the problem report to the Systems Analyst for resolution.

2.3   The Systems Analyst and Software Designer review the test problem reports. They separate the reports into two groups, one for programming errors, and the other for design errors.

- To resolve a design error, the Project Manager, Systems Analyst and Software Designer perform the steps outlined in ITSW108 DESIGN CHANGES DURING DEVELOPMENT.

- To resolve a programming error, the Software Designer assigns the problem report to the responsible programmer. The programmer corrects the error and returns the updated software components to the Quality Assurance Manager for retesting.

2.4   After the acceptance test is complete, the Quality Assurance Manager releases the software to beta test.

3.0   SOFTWARE BETA TESTING

3.1   The Quality Assurance Manager appoints a Beta Test Coordinator responsible for implementing the beta test, in accordance with ITSW103 SYSTEMS ANALYSIS.

3.2   The Beta Test Coordinator contacts and schedules the beta test sites as early in the software development project as possible. The coordinator identifies the key contact at each site and promptly informs them of any changes in the project schedule.

3.3   The Beta Test Coordinator schedules training for the beta testers. The coordinator schedules this training as close as possible to the date on which the beta release will be installed. Properly coordinating training helps ensure that the information will be fresh in the minds of the users during the test.

3.4   The Beta Test Coordinator ensures that the testers get any additional help they might need to get ready to use the software. If necessary, an internal software consultant helps the testers install and implement the software.

3.5   To ensure that the testers continue to move forward with their testing, the Beta
        Test Coordinator contacts them weekly. The coordinator must be prepared to
        answer the testers' questions and address any problems they are having.

3.6   As the testers identify problems, The Beta Test Coordinator completes an
        ITSW107-3 PROJECT TEST PROBLEM REPORT for each error encountered.

3.7   The Systems Analyst and Software Designer review the beta test problem reports.
        They separate the reports into two groups, one for programming errors, and the
        other for design errors.

        • To resolve a design error, the Project Manager, Systems Analyst, and
          Software Designer perform the steps outlined in ITSW108 DESIGN
          CHANGES DURING DEVELOPMENT.

        • To resolve a programming error, the Software Designer assigns the problem
          report to the responsible programmer. Programmers should respond
          immediately to problems that prevent testers from using the system. Less
          severe problems can be fixed periodically, such as biweekly or monthly.

        • The programmer corrects the error, completes the resolution section of
          ITSW107-3 PROJECT TEST PROBLEM REPORT and returns the updated
          software components to the Beta Test Coordinator for retesting.

3.8   The Beta Test Coordinator sends updates to all beta sites. Beta testing continues
        as defined in the test plan until the Project Manager, Systems Analyst, and
        Quality Assurance Manager determine that sufficient beta testing has occurred.

3.9   After the beta test is complete, the Quality Assurance Manager releases the
        software for final release testing.

4.0   SOFTWARE FINAL RELEASE TESTING

4.1   When the software is fully tested and ready for release to sales and shipping, the
        Quality Assurance Manager tests to ensure that the software installation process
        functions without error.

4.2   If the software is an update to an existing software product, the quality assurance
        analyst must test the installation process for all versions of the software that the
        company supports.

4.3   After the final release test is complete, the Quality Assurance Manager releases
        the software for distribution, in accordance with ITSW109 SOFTWARE
        RELEASES AND UPDATES procedure.

Forms:

- ITSW107-1 SOFTWARE PROJECT TEST SCRIPT
- ITSW107-2 SOFTWARE PROJECT TEST CHECKLIST
- ITSW107-3 SOFTWARE PROJECT TEST PROBLEM REPORT

References:

A. IEEE STANDARD 829-2008 – STANDARD FOR SOFTWARE AND SYSTEM TEST DOCUMENTATION

This is the IEEE standard for documenting software testing, which specifies eight stages in the documentation process, each stage producing its own separate document:

- **Test Plan**: A detail of how the test will proceed, who will do the testing, what will be tested, in how much time the test will take place, and to what quality level the test will be performed.
- **Test Design Specification**: A detail of the test conditions and the expected outcome. This document also includes details of how a successful test will be recognized.
- **Test Case Specification**: A detail of the specific data that is necessary to run tests based on the conditions identified in the previous stage.
- **Test Procedure Specification**: A detail of how the tester will physically run the test, the physical set-up required, and the procedure steps that need to be followed.
- **Test Item Transmittal Report**: A detail of when specific tested items have been passed from one stage of testing to another.
- **Test Log**: A detail of what tests cases were run, who ran the tests, in what order they were run, and whether or not individual tests were passed or failed.
- **Test Incident Report**: A detail of the actual versus expected results of a test, when a test has failed, and anything indicating why the test failed.
- **Test Summary Report**: A detail of all the important information to come out of the testing procedure, including an assessment of how well the testing was performed, an assessment of the quality of the system, any incidents that occurred, and a record of what testing was done and how long it took to be used in future test planning. This final document is used to determine if the software being tested is viable enough to proceed to the next stage of development.

B. ISO/IEC 12207:2008 – SYSTEMS AND SOFTWARE ENGINEERING – SOFTWARE LIFE CYCLE PROCESSES

For detailed information, see
http://ieeexplore.ieee.org/xpl/articleDetails.jsp?arnumber=4578383.

C. IEEE 12207-2008 – SYSTEMS AND SOFTWARE ENGINEERING – SOFTWARE LIFE CYCLE PROCESSES

This ISO standard describes the major component processes of a complete software life cycle and the high-level relations that govern their interaction. It establishes a software life cycle architecture based on two principles, modularity of processes and responsibility for processes. There are three process classes in the ISO software life cycle: primary (such as acquisition and operations); supporting (such as documentation and configuration management); and organizational (such as infrastructure and training). Each life cycle process is made up of activities, and each activity is further subdivided into tasks. The standard is based on ISO quality management principles.

The IEEE version of 12207 is more closely aligned with the ISO standard than it was in previous versions.

For more information, visit the ISO web site at http://www.iso.org/iso/catalogue_detail.htm?csnumber=43447 or the IEEE web site at http://standards.ieee.org/findstds/standard/12207-2008.html.

Revision History:

Revision	Date	Description of Changes	Requested By
0	mm/dd/yyyy	Initial Release	

[This page intentionally left blank]

ITSW107-1 SOFTWARE PROJECT TEST SCRIPT

Test Case No. _____   Page ____ of ____

PROCEDURES	NOTES
LOGIN: 1. At Login Prompt, enter user name "Test" and press the "Enter" key 2. At Password Prompt, enter user password "Test1" and press the "Enter" key	[Sample text provided as an example]

[This page intentionally left blank]

ITSW107-2 SOFTWARE PROJECT TEST CHECKLIST

Test Case No. _____ Checklist No. _____ Page ___ of ___

No.	ITEM	YES	NO

[This page intentionally left blank]

ITSW107-3 SOFTWARE PROJECT TEST PROBLEM REPORT

Test Case No. _____   Test Date: _____

Test Phase (circle one):   Acceptance   Beta   Software Version: _____

PROBLEM DESCRIPTION	PROBLEM RESOLUTION

Problem Reported By: _____   **Date**: _____

Problem Status (circle one):   Open   Closed   On-Hold

Problem Reviewed By _____   **Date**: _____

[This page intentionally left blank]

Document ID **ITSW108**	Title **DESIGN CHANGES DURING DEVELOPMENT**	Print Date **mm/dd/yyyy**
Revision **0.0**	Prepared By **Preparer's Name / Title**	Date Prepared **mm/dd/yyyy**
Effective Date **mm/dd/yyyy**	Reviewed By **Reviewer's Name / Title**	Date Reviewed **mm/dd/yyyy**
	Approved By **Final Approver's Name / Title**	Date Approved **mm/dd/yyyy**

Policy: All design changes made to a software product during development shall be managed, controlled, and communicated efficiently and effectively.

Purpose: To ensure that design changes during development are handled efficiently and effectively.

Scope: All Company software development projects.

Responsibilities:

The <u>Project Manager</u> is responsible for reviewing design change requests/ proposals, to determine the appropriate actions to take, and for updating the project schedule accordingly.

The <u>Software Designer</u> is responsible for reviewing design changes and updated system requirements, determining the parts of the system affected by the change, and designing system changes to achieve the new requirements.

The <u>Systems Analyst</u> is responsible for reviewing design changes, determining the parts of the system affected by the changes, and updating the system requirements.

<u>User Management</u> is responsible for reviewing design specifications and, if necessary, submitting change requests in a timely and efficient manner.

Procedure:

1.0   DESIGN CHANGES - INTRODUCTION

Software systems typically are developed using a top-down design philosophy. Designing from the most general level (requirements) down to the most detailed (programming instructions) typically reduces the frequency with which design errors occur, and the amount of work required to recover from errors and design changes. The lower down in the development cycle that changes are made, the more complicated and time consuming those changes become.

2.0   DESIGN CHANGE REVIEW

2.1   Changes typically originate in the user area, though the software design team may initiate changes. A change request shall be submitted using ITSW108-1 DESIGN CHANGE REQUEST FORM. At a minimum, ITSW108-1 should capture the project name, project number, project manager's name, the name of the requestor, request date, resolution requested by date, description of and reason for change, impact on scope and/or deliverables, impact on time and cost, impact on resources and quality, change accepted or rejected, and sign-off signatures from those in charge.

2.2   The Project Manager shall consider changes with respect to problems noted on ITSW107-3 PROJECT TEST PROBLEM REPORT.

2.3   The Project Manager, Systems Analyst, and Software Designer shall review each proposed design change and determine what action to take. Questions to consider include:

- Do the benefits of the change outweigh its costs?

- Can the change be implemented in an acceptable amount of time?

- Is the change functionally necessary?

- Can the change be implemented in a subsequent release of the product?

2.4   Depending on the scope of the request, the Project Manager may be required to consult with IT Management and determine the impact of requested changes on ITAD101-1 INFORMATION TECHNOLOGY PLAN.

3.0   DESIGN CHANGE IMPLEMENTATION

3.1   When a design change is approved, the Software Designer shall identify all software components affected by the change. The programmer halts development work on those components.

3.2   The Software Designer shall estimate potential delays caused by the change, add this information to ITSW108-1, and forward ITSW108-1 to the project's Systems Analyst.

3.3   The Systems Analyst shall perform a new systems analysis on all parts of the system affected by the change and update project documentation, in accordance with ITSW103 SYSTEMS ANALYSIS. The Software Designer shall use the analysis to rework the design of the affected system components and update related project documentation, in accordance with ITSW104 SOFTWARE DESIGN.

3.4   The Project Manager shall rework the project schedule and submit ITSW108-1 to User Management for its approval.

3.5   If the requested changes are approved, the Project Manager shall notify all people affected by the change (such as managers, project team members, and the sales staff) of the design change and its impact on the project schedule.

Forms:

- ITSW108-1 DESIGN CHANGE REQUEST FORM

References:

A. **ISO/IEC 12207:2008 – SYSTEMS AND SOFTWARE ENGINEERING – SOFTWARE LIFE CYCLE PROCESSES**

B. **IEEE 12207-2008 – SYSTEMS AND SOFTWARE ENGINEERING – SOFTWARE LIFE CYCLE PROCESSES**

This ISO standard describes the major component processes of a complete software life cycle and the high-level relations that govern their interaction. It establishes a software life cycle architecture based on two principles, modularity of processes and responsibility for processes. There are three process classes in the ISO software life cycle: primary (such as acquisition and operations); supporting (such as documentation and configuration management); and organizational (such as infrastructure and training). Each life cycle process is made up of activities, and each activity is further subdivided into tasks. The standard is based on ISO quality management principles.

The IEEE version of 12207 is more closely aligned with the ISO standard than it was in previous versions.

For more information, visit the ISO web site at http://www.iso.org/iso/catalogue_detail.htm?csnumber=43447 or the IEEE web site at http://standards.ieee.org/findstds/standard/12207-2008.html.

Revision History:

Revision	Date	Description of Changes	Requested By
0	mm/dd/yyyy	Initial Release	

[This page intentionally left blank]

ITSW108-1 DESIGN CHANGE REQUEST FORM

Request Date: _____

Design Change ID: _____

Project Name and Number: _____

Project Manager: _____

Change Requestor: _____

Request Resolved By (date): _____

Description of Request (reason for change):

Anticipated Impact on Scope and/or Deliverables:

Anticipated Impact on Time and Project Cost:

Expected Impact on Resources and Quality:

Change Request: ☐ accepted   ☐ rejected

User Management: _____ Date: _____

IT Project Management: _____ Date: _____

[This page intentionally left blank]

Document ID **ITSW109**	Title **SOFTWARE RELEASES AND UPDATES**	Print Date **mm/dd/yyyy**
Revision **0.0**	Prepared By **Preparer's Name / Title**	Date Prepared **mm/dd/yyyy**
Effective Date **mm/dd/yyyy**	Reviewed By **Reviewer's Name / Title**	Date Reviewed **mm/dd/yyyy**
	Approved By **Final Approver's Name / Title**	Date Approved **mm/dd/yyyy**

Policy: All releases of Company software, including updates, shall be controlled to ensure correct, up-to-date versioning and configuration.

Purpose: To maintain consistency and quality of software products throughout all releases and updates.

Scope: All Company designed and developed software products and updates.

Responsibilities:

The Product Manager decides how many versions of a product the company will maintain and support.

Programmers use the software component library to control all changes, comment on the changes made, and indicate version numbers.

The Quality Assurance Manager manages the software library and releases software versions that successfully pass testing.

The Software Designer determines the specific software components that make up the final product release.

Definition: Software version – Consists of software components and corresponding documentation. Generally, a version is a checkpoint at which a particular thing or idea varies from its previous state or condition.

Software release – A software release refers to the creation and availability of a new version of a computer software product. Each time a software program is changed, the programmers and company doing the work decide on how to distribute the changes or the changed system or program to those people using it.

Procedure:

1.0   SOFTWARE RELEASES AND UPDATES - INTRODUCTION

1.1   After a software product has been developed and tested, the Software Designer must determine the specific software components that will make up the final product.

1.2   After a product is released and work on the next update has begun, all project team members must be able to determine which software components make up each version. Control of the software includes:

- Version control;

- Configuration control; and

- Release control.

2.0   SOFTWARE VERSION CONTROL STANDARDS

2.1   The company assigns a sequential version number to each release of a software product. For example, the first release of a product typically is called version 1.0. The next version is 1.1 or 1.01 if it is a minor release (containing mostly bug fixes) or 2.0 if it is a major release (containing major enhancements).

2.2   The company maintains a central software component library that contains all software and documentation components. Each component is identified as part of a particular software version. If a component that is included in one version of a product is changed in a subsequent version, the library contains a separate copy of that component for each version.

2.3   Programmers use the software component library to control all changes by:

- Checking in new components;

- Checking out existing components before modifying them; and

- Checking in updated components before they are tested.

2.4   Programmers must provide comments on the changes made and indicate a version number each time they check a component in.

2.5   The Quality Assurance Manager uses the library to flag components that successfully pass testing. A release should include only those components that have passed testing.

3.0   SOFTWARE CONFIGURATION CONTROL STANDARDS

3.1   The company should adopt a standard development and installation configuration for the software product. Standards should address:

- Platform integration. Specify the operating systems and networks with which the software is compatible. Standardize the method for configuring the software on each platform.

- Hardware integration. Specify the equipment (such as printers, monitors, and so on) with which the software is compatible. Standardize the method for configuring the software on each piece of equipment. Specify the minimum hardware requirements for the software.

- Software access. Develop standard methods for granting users access to all or parts of the software. Typical devices include:

    - Passwords;

    - User codes;

    - Access rights; and

    - Menus.

3.2   The release and installation programs include as much of the standard
        configuration as possible.

4.0   SOFTWARE RELEASE CONTROL STANDARDS

4.1   The company should adopt standards for:

*   Creating software releases, providing for two types of software release:

    a. A **full release**, which includes all software components required to install
        a version of the software. To create a full release, copy all software
        components for the version from the software component library to the
        release medium.

    b. An **update release**, which includes only those components required to
        update a previous version of the software to the current version. To create
        an update release, copy to the release medium only those software
        components that are required to update the oldest supported version to the
        current version.

*   Installing a software release.

*   Testing a release. The software designer defines the test plan that the quality
    assurance analyst uses to test that the release installs without error.

4.2   The process of installing the software should be as automated as possible. Use an
        installation program that:

*   Prompts the user for installation parameters and then automatically installs the
    software components. When prompting for parameters, the program should
    use the standard installation configuration as a default.

*   Makes the type of installation being performed transparent to the user. Users
    should use the same steps to install a full release as they do to install an
    update.

*   Creates a table that tracks the names and version numbers of all the
    company's products that are installed on the user's computer.

4.3   The Product Manager must decide how many versions of a product the company
        will maintain and support. Customers using older versions may not receive
        support.

4.4   The release process must allow for accumulative updates. For example, a user
        should be able to update from version 2.0 to 4.0 without installing all of the
        intermediate updates.

5.0   SOFTWARE LICENSE, WARRANTY, AND COPYRIGHT

5.1   License. The company sells each software product under ITSW109-1
        SOFTWARE LICENSE AGREEMENT, stating that the customer does not own
        the software but has a restricted right to use it under the terms of the agreement.

5.2   Limited Warranty. The company provides ITSW109-2 SOFTWARE LIMITED
        WARRANTY with the software, promising that for a specified period of time

(usually 90 days), the software will perform as the accompanying documentation says it will perform. The warranty applies only when the software is used as recommended.

5.3   Copyright. The company copyrights all software and documentation using a standard copyright message placed on all documentation and software programs. ITSW109-3 SOFTWARE COPYRIGHT NOTICE may be used as a guide. Copyrights should be filed with the U.S. Copyright Office within 90 days of each new release using US Copyright Office Form TX (see http://www.copyright.gov/forms/ for this and other Copyright Office forms). The first release should be noted as an original work and each subsequent release should be noted as a derivative work of the original release.

Forms:

- ITSW109-1 SOFTWARE LICENSE AGREEMENT
- ITSW109-2 SOFTWARE LIMITED WARRANTY
- ITSW109-3 SOFTWARE COPYRIGHT NOTICE

References:

A. ISO/IEC 12207:2008 – SYSTEMS AND SOFTWARE ENGINEERING – SOFTWARE LIFE CYCLE PROCESSES

B. IEEE/EIA 12207-2008 – SYSTEMS AND SOFTWARE ENGINEERING – SOFTWARE LIFE CYCLE PROCESSES

This ISO standard describes the major component processes of a complete software life cycle and the high-level relations that govern their interaction. It establishes a software life cycle architecture based on two principles, modularity of processes and responsibility for processes. There are three process classes in the ISO software life cycle: primary (such as acquisition and operations); supporting (such as documentation and configuration management); and organizational (such as infrastructure and training). Each life cycle process is made up of activities, and each activity is further subdivided into tasks. The standard is based on ISO quality management principles.

The IEEE version of 12207 is more closely aligned with the ISO standard than it was in previous versions.

For more information, visit the ISO web site at http://www.iso.org/iso/catalogue_detail.htm?csnumber=43447 or the IEEE web site at http://standards.ieee.org/findstds/standard/12207-2008.html.

Additional Resources:

A. U.S. Copyright Office, 101 Independence Avenue S.E., Washington, DC 20559-6000 / Phone: (202) 702-3000 / URL: http://www.copyright.gov/ File all copyright applications at the Library of Congress Electronic Copyright Office (eCO) website (https://eco.copyright.gov/eService_enu/start.swe).

Revision History:

Revision	Date	Description of Changes	Requested By
0	mm/dd/yyyy	Initial Release	

[This page intentionally left blank]

ITSW109-1 SOFTWARE LICENSE AGREEMENT

IMPORTANT: READ THIS FIRST.

The enclosed Agreement is a legal agreement between you (either an individual or entity), the end user, and Company. By opening the enclosed sealed disk package, you agree to be bound by the terms of the Agreement. The Agreement allows you to use the software included in this package, provided you agree to the terms of the Agreement.

If you do not agree to the terms of the Agreement, promptly return the unopened disk package, and the accompanying written materials and containers, to the place you obtained them. You will receive a full refund.

SOFTWARE LICENSE

1. GRANT OF LICENSE. Company grants to you the right to use one copy of the SOFTWARE PROGRAM X on a single computer. For the purposes of this section, "use" means loading the SOFTWARE into RAM, as well as installing it on a hard disk or other storage device (other than a network server). You may access the SOFTWARE from a hard disk, over a network, or any other method you choose, so long as you otherwise comply with this License Agreement.

2. COPYRIGHT. The software is owned by Company and is protected by United States copyright law and international treaty provisions. Therefore, you must treat the SOFTWARE like any other copyrighted material (such as a book) *except* that you either (a) make one copy of the SOFTWARE solely for backup or archival purposes, or (b) transfer the SOFTWARE to a single hard disk provided you keep the original solely for backup or archival purposes. You may not copy the written materials accompanying the SOFTWARE.

3. OTHER RESTRICTIONS. This License Agreement is your proof of license to exercise the rights granted herein and must be retained by you. You may not rent or lease the SOFTWARE, but you may permanently transfer your rights under this License Agreement provided that (a) you transfer this License Agreement, the SOFTWARE, and all accompanying written materials; (b) you retain no copies; and (c) the recipient agrees to the terms of this Agreement. You may not reverse engineer, decompile, or disassemble the SOFTWARE. If the SOFTWARE is an update, any transfer must include the update and all prior versions.

[This page intentionally left blank]

ITSW109-2 SOFTWARE LIMITED WARRANTY

WARRANTY. XYZ Company warrants that the SOFTWARE will perform substantially in accordance with the accompanying written materials for a period of ninety (90) days from the date of receipt. Any implied warranties on the SOFTWARE are limited to ninety (90) days. Some states do not allow limitations on duration of an implied warranty, so the above limitation may not apply to you.

CUSTOMER REMEDIES. XYZ Company's entire liability and your exclusive remedy shall be, at XYZ Company's option, either (a) return of the price paid, or (b) repair or replacement of the SOFTWARE that does not meet the Limited Warranty and that is returned to XYZ Company with a copy of your receipt. This Limited Warranty is void if failure of the SOFTWARE has resulted from accident, abuse, or misapplication. Any replacement SOFTWARE will be warranted for the remainder of the original warranty period or thirty (30) days, whichever is longer.

NO OTHER WARRANTIES. XYZ Company disclaims all other warranties, either express or implied, included but not limited to implied warranties of merchantability and fitness for a particular purpose, with respect to the SOFTWARE and the accompanying written materials. This limited warranty gives you specific legal rights. You may have others, which vary from state to state.

U.S. GOVERNMENT RESTRICTED RIGHTS

The SOFTWARE and documentation are provided with RESTRICTED RIGHTS. Use, duplication, or disclosure by the Government is subject to restrictions as set forth in subparagraph (c)(1)(ii) of The Rights in Technical Data and Computer Software clause at DFARS 252.227-7013 or subparagraphs (C)(1) and (2) of the Commercial Computer Software - Restricted Rights at 48 CFR 42.227-19, as applicable. Contractor/manufacturer is XYZ Company at 111 XYZ Avenue, Anytown, Anystate, USA.

This Agreement is governed by the laws of the State of Anystate.

[This page intentionally left blank]

ITSW109-3 SOFTWARE COPYRIGHT NOTICE

©Company 200_
All Rights Reserved
Printed in U.S.A.

[This page intentionally left blank]

Document ID	Title	Print Date
ITSW110	**SOFTWARE SUPPORT**	**mm/dd/yyyy**
Revision	Prepared By	Date Prepared
0.0	**Preparer's Name / Title**	**mm/dd/yyyy**
Effective Date	Reviewed By	Date Reviewed
mm/dd/yyyy	**Reviewer's Name / Title**	**mm/dd/yyyy**
	Approved By	Date Approved
	Final Approver's Name / Title	**mm/dd/yyyy**

Policy: The Company shall offer a complete range of support services to all customers who purchase Company-developed software, as well as to in-house users of Company-developed software.

Purpose: To ensure that customers can effectively install and operate the software they purchase from the company and to provide help for customers who have questions about or problems with the software they purchase from the company.

Scope: All software products and updates released by the Company.

Responsibilities:

The Product Manager is responsible for reviewing customer suggestions and determining which, if any, suggestions will be implemented.

Software Support Analysts are responsible for working with customers until their problems are resolved, surveying customers for feedback, and maintaining the software support database.

Software Trainers are responsible for developing training materials and provides training classes and instruction for customers.

Customer Consultants are responsible for developing custom solutions.

Definitions: Service Level Agreement (SLA) – A binding contract, formally specifying or quantifying a customer's expectations with regard to solutions and tolerances; a collection of service level requirements, negotiated and mutually agreed upon by the service provider and the consumer.

Procedure:

1.0   SOFTWARE SUPPORT OVERVIEW

To encourage customers to use their software to its full potential, the Company shall offer a full range of support services. Three general types of support services are:

- Emergency phone or email support;

- Customer training; and

- Customer consulting.

The Company may enter into a service level agreement (SLA) with individual customers, tailoring the agreement to each customer's requirements.

2.0   SOFTWARE SUPPORT SERVICES MANAGEMENT

2.1   To organize and manage support services, the software support department maintains a software support database of all support calls and support information. The table on the following page shows the type of information the software support database tracks.

2.2   On a rotating basis, members of the technical staff (Systems Analysts, Software Designers, and Programmers) help Software Support Analysts deal with complex problems.

SOFTWARE SUPPORT DATABASE

Section	Description	Information Tracked
Phone calls	Records of software support calls	• Customer name • Time and date of call • Name of software support analyst • Product name and version number • Description of the problem • Problem status • Problem resolution
Problem reports	Software bugs identified by customers or internal people	• Name of the person who reported the problem • Product name and version number • Description of problem • Date the problem was reported • Status of the problem (open, corrected, on hold, and so on) • Description of the problem's solution (reference the associated design document) • Date the problem was corrected • Version number of the release in which the problem is fixed • List of the software components affected by the fix • Names of all people who worked to correct the problem
Enhancement requests	Requests from customers to add features and functions to existing software products	The same type of information as for problem reports

Section	Description	Information Tracked
Training courses	Information about the software training courses the company offers	• Course name • Course description • Course outline • Course schedule • Names of qualified instructors • Equipment required • Suitable locations • Recommended class size
Course evaluations	Evaluation forms that students complete for each training class they attend	• Course name • Class date • Student's evaluation of the course content, materials, and instructor

2.3   On a monthly basis, Software Support Analysts contact randomly selected customers and survey them about the quality of the support they are receiving.

2.4   The Product Manager, Software Support Analysts, Client Consultants, and Software Trainers review customers' suggestions. This group determines which, if any, of the suggestions will be implemented.

3.0   FREE BASIC SOFTWARE SUPPORT SERVICES

3.1   The Company shall include the following documentation with each software product purchased:

* A self-guided tutorial;

* A user guide;

* An installation and implementation guide; and

* An annual newsletter.

3.2   The company provides e-mail, a website, and a telephone hotline for customers to call for software support.

3.3   Customers receive free support time for the first thirty days after the purchase date. Customers who need support after the first thirty days may pay an hourly usage fee or purchase an extended support agreement.

4.0   EXTENDED SOFTWARE SUPPORT SERVICES

4.1   Customers who need more than the basic support services may purchase the following additional services:

* Training classes (see ITSW112 SOFTWARE TRAINING);

* Unlimited phone support via a toll-free ("1-800") number;

- Newsletters that include articles, technical tips, product release information, class schedules, and company news;

- Implementation consulting (i.e., expert on-site help installing and implementing the software);

- Access to the company's internal experts, such as the software designer and systems analyst (which service may be particularly useful to advanced users, resellers, and business partners);

- Software customizations; and

- Access to internal system specifications or source code, for customers wanting to program their own software customizations. (Note: customers who purchase source code must either pay for support services on an hourly basis, or waive the right to purchase any support services.)

4.2   The Company sells support services both individually and packaged in groups, under the terms of an extended support agreement.

4.3   Purchasers of extended support agreements pay an annual fee to receive a specific set of support services. There are several levels of support agreements; the more expensive the agreement, the more services provide. To encourage customers to purchase extended support agreements, each agreement includes with it additional services or free items that are only available to agreement purchasers. For example, a typical extended support agreement includes:

- Free, unlimited phone support via a toll-free number;

- One introductory training class;

- Free product updates;

- Advance notice of product updates;

- Access to internal experts; and

- Quarterly newsletters.

5.0   USER GROUP SOFTWARE SUPPORT

5.1   The Company shall encourage customers to form regional product user groups, to allow customers to discuss problems and share solutions with each other.

5.2   The company provides user groups with:

- Advance notice of product releases and development plans; and

- Access to internal experts, who give presentations and product reviews.

6.0   PHONE/E-MAIL SOFTWARE SUPPORT SERVICES

Software support calls provide an opportunity to convey a positive company image to customers who are struggling with technical problems. Efficient, professional phone and email support is essential to good customer relations.

6.1   Assign Calls To Analysts

The software support department uses a phone call routing system to assign calls to Software Support Analysts on a first come, first served basis. The software support analyst enters each call into the phone calls section of the software support database. The analyst uses this database to track information about the call.

6.2   Determine The Nature Of The Call

The Software Support Analyst works with the customer until the customer's problem is resolved. In some cases, an analyst might need to consult someone more familiar or better qualified to handle the problem. However, the original analyst must still follow up with the customer and make sure that the customer is satisfied with the resolution of the problem.

Customer calls typically fall into one of the categories listed in the following table. For each call, the software support analyst performs the action described.

Type of Call	Category	Action
Request for help.	The customer made a mistake or needs help completing a task.	Help the customer figure out the cause of the problem and how to solve it.
Software problem report.	The customer has identified an error or deficiency in the software.	Enter the error into the problem reports section of the software support database. Refer to the phone call record in the description of the problem.
Request for enhancements.	The customer wants the software to perform in a way other than that in which it was designed.	Enter the enhancement into the enhancement requests section of the software support database. Refer to the phone call record in the description of the problem.

Forms:

- None.

References:

A. ISO/IEC 12207:2008 – SYSTEMS AND SOFTWARE ENGINEERING – SOFTWARE LIFE CYCLE PROCESSES

B. IEEE 12207-2008 – SYSTEMS AND SOFTWARE ENGINEERING – SOFTWARE LIFE CYCLE PROCESSES

This ISO standard describes the major component processes of a complete software life cycle and the high-level relations that govern their interaction. It establishes a software life cycle architecture based on two principles, modularity of processes and responsibility for processes. There are three process classes in the ISO software life cycle: primary (such as acquisition and operations); supporting (such as documentation and configuration management); and organizational (such as infrastructure and training). Each life cycle process is made up of activities and each activity is further subdivided into tasks.

The IEEE version of 12207 is more closely aligned with the ISO standard than it was in previous versions.

For more information, visit the ISO web site at http://www.iso.org/iso/catalogue_detail.htm?csnumber=43447 or the IEEE web site at http://standards.ieee.org/findstds/standard/12207-2008.html.

Additional Resources:

A. ITTS102 IT SUPPORT CENTER.

Revision History:

Revision	Date	Description of Changes	Requested By
0	mm/dd/yyyy	Initial Release	

Document ID **ITSW111**	Title **SOFTWARE CONSULTING SERVICES**	Print Date **mm/dd/yyyy**
Revision **0.0**	Prepared By **Preparer's Name / Title**	Date Prepared **mm/dd/yyyy**
Effective Date **mm/dd/yyyy**	Reviewed By **Reviewer's Name / Title**	Date Reviewed **mm/dd/yyyy**
	Approved By **Final Approver's Name / Title**	Date Approved **mm/dd/yyyy**

Policy: The Company shall offer consulting services to customers needing assistance installing or customizing software they purchase from the Company.

Purpose: To ensure that customers can effectively install and operate the software they purchase from the company; to ensure customer satisfaction with the Company's goods and/or support services.

Scope: All software products and updates released by the company.

Responsibilities:

Customer Software Consultants are responsible for developing custom solutions and recording their activities.

The Customer Consulting Manager is responsible for periodic reporting on consultants' activities and helping improve consulting services.

Definitions: Statement of Work (SOW) – A formal contract or agreement, signed by the client and the service provider, that states at a minimum the scope of work, deliverables, terms and conditions, and commercial details. It may also specify service level agreement requirements, quality expectations, resource descriptions, and reward-penalty clauses.

Service Level Agreement (SLA) – A binding contract, formally specifying or quantifying a customer's expectations with regard to solutions and tolerances; a collection of service level requirements, negotiated and mutually agreed upon by the service provider and the consumer.

Procedure:

1.0   SOFTWARE CONSULTING – INTRODUCTION

Customer consultants shall be made available to customers needing help implementing their software or wanting to modify the company's software to meet their unique requirements. Customer software consultants are experts in installing, implementing, customizing, and enhancing the company's products.

2.0   SOFTWARE CONSULTING – COST ESTIMATES

2.1   Customers shall be billed by the hour for consulting work. Before beginning a project, the customer software consultant shall estimate what the cost to the customer will be. The consultant shall also notifies the customer of potential cost overruns that may occur during the course of a project.

2.2   All work by customer software consultants shall be performed under the terms of ITSW111-1 CONSULTING AGREEMENT.

2.3   The customer and consultant shall agree on the exact scope of work to be performed. The scope of work shall be documented in ITSW111-2 STATEMENT OF WORK.

3.0   SOFTWARE CONSULTING - ENHANCEMENTS AND CUSTOMIZATIONS

3.1   To create an enhancement or customization, the Customer Consultant uses the standard development procedures for analysis, design, programming, documentation, test, and update. For very small projects, these procedures might require only one or two pages of written specifications. However, to guarantee a high-quality product, the consultant always follows the complete development cycle.

3.2   On the customer's system, all enhanced and customized software components must be kept separate from the base software. The Customer Consultant prefixes all modified and new components with the name or initials of the customer.

> For example, if the customer's initials are ASI, the component Print_PO becomes ASI_Print_PO on the customer's system.

3.3   Enhancements and customizations are the property of the customer unless otherwise stipulated by the consulting agreement.

3.4   The customer is responsible for integrating customizations and enhancements into updates to the base product. Customer Consultant are available (at an hourly rate) to help the customer perform such integration.

4.0   SOFTWARE CONSULTING - SOFTWARE PROBLEMS

4.1   If the customer reports a software problem, the customer software consultant shall enter the problem into ITSW111-3 CONSULTING LOG.

4.2   The consultant shall determine if the problem is:

- An error or deficiency in the base product; or

- A request for a new feature or enhancement; or

- An error or deficiency in the customized components of the product.

4.3   The consultant shall act to resolve the problem, updating the activity record in ITSW111-3, as needed.

5.0   SOFTWARE CONSULTING SERVICES REVIEW

5.1   The Customer Consulting Manager shall review, analyze, summarize, and report on consulting activity, as documented in ITSW111-3 CONSULTING LOG, and submit such a report to IT Management on a monthly basis, at a minimum.

5.2   IT Management may identify problems in and recommend revisions to the consulting process as a result of such reports.

5.3   When the consulting process has been changed, IT Management shall review the process within one month, to ensure that prescribed changes have been implemented and are yielding the desired results.

Forms:

- ITSW111-1 SOFTWARE CONSULTING AGREEMENT
- ITSW111-2 STATEMENT OF WORK
- ITSW111-3 SOFTWARE CONSULTING CUSTOMER SUPPORT LOG

References:

A. ISO/IEC 12207:2008 – SYSTEMS AND SOFTWARE ENGINEERING – SOFTWARE LIFE CYCLE PROCESSES

B. IEEE 12207-2008 – SYSTEMS AND SOFTWARE ENGINEERING – SOFTWARE LIFE CYCLE PROCESSES

This ISO standard describes the major component processes of a complete software life cycle and the high-level relations that govern their interaction. It establishes a software life cycle architecture based on two principles, modularity of processes and responsibility for processes. There are three process classes in the ISO software life cycle: primary (such as acquisition and operations); supporting (such as documentation and configuration management); and organizational (such as infrastructure and training). Each life cycle process is made up of activities, and each activity is further subdivided into tasks. The standard is based on ISO quality management principles.

The IEEE version of 12207 is more closely aligned with the ISO standard than it was in previous versions.

For more information, visit the ISO web site at http://www.iso.org/iso/catalogue_detail.htm?csnumber=43447 or the IEEE web site at http://standards.ieee.org/findstds/standard/12207-2008.html.

Additional Resources:

A. ITAD109 IT OUTSOURCING

Revision History:

Revision	Date	Description of Changes	Requested By
0	mm/dd/yyyy	Initial Release	

ITSW111-1 SOFTWARE CONSULTING AGREEMENT

This is an Agreement between CUSTOMER NAME, STREET ADDRESS, CITY, STATE ZIP, hereinafter referred to as "Customer" and SOFTWARE COMPANY, STREET ADDRESS, CITY, STATE ZIP, hereinafter referred to as "Consultant."

Customer and Consultant agree as follows:

1. Consultant will conduct the work as defined in the Description of Work, attached hereto as Exhibit A and hereinafter referred to as "Work." Such Work will be commenced and finished in accordance with the schedule set out in Exhibit A.

2. Consultant will invoice Customer and Customer will pay Consultant in accordance with the compensation, payment schedule and terms defined in Exhibit A.

3. Either party may terminate this Agreement at any time by giving the non-terminating party thirty (30) days written notice. Upon notice of termination of this Agreement, Consultant will conduct the Work to the date of termination in accordance with paragraph 1 and Customer will pay Consultant to the date of termination in accordance with paragraph 2.

4. Consultant will not use, except for Customer's Work, nor disclose to any third party, trade secrets or other confidential information derived from or developed for Customer, or any affiliate of Customer. Information is not subject to such restrictions if Consultant can show that (a) it was in its possession prior to its disclosure to Consultant by Customer; or (b) it is, or lawfully becomes, part of the public domain; or (c) it otherwise lawfully becomes available to Consultant from a source independent of Customer. A trade secret is any information, process, or idea that is not generally known in the industry, that Customer considers confidential, and that gives Customer a competitive advantage. Examples of trade secrets may include: computer program listings, source code and object code, all information relating to programs now existing or currently under development, and customer lists and records. Upon termination of the Agreement, Consultant will deliver to Customer all copies of all memoranda, drawings, tapes, discs, or any other material acquired by Consultant from Customer.

5. Consultant will not disclose to Customer any information deemed confidential by any third party and all information disclosed to Customer by Consultant under this Agreement will be deemed to be non-confidential insofar as Customer's use thereof is concerned. Consultant warrants that the possession, use, and/or disclosure by Customer of any information furnished by Consultant to Customer will not violate the proprietary rights of any third party. If, based upon its possession, use, and/or disclosure of such information, Customer is charged

Page 1

Software Consulting Agreement
Page 2

with violation of any proprietary rights of any third party, Consultant will defend and hold Customer harmless from losses or judgments arising out of such charge.

6.   Consultant is engaged as an independent contractor and not as an employee. Customer will have no control over the manner or method of performance of the subject matter of this Agreement. Consultant will serve in an advisory capacity only, shall have no right or power to bind Customer and shall not enter into any agreement with any third party on behalf of Customer.

7.   Consultant will not be liable for any lost profits or special, indirect or consequential damages which may result from Consultant's work under this Agreement. In the event Customer is dissatisfied with the work, Customer will, within a period of thirty (30) days of completion of the work, notify Consultant of any deficiencies and Consultant will attempt to remedy such deficiencies. Customer's compensation for any damages it may suffer as a result of the work can not exceed the amount Consultant received as payment for the work.

Consultant   Customer

By: _____   By: _____

Title   _____   Title   _____

Date: _____   Date: _____

ITSW111-2 STATEMENT OF WORK

Attached to and made a part of the consulting agreement between

SOFTWARE COMPANY and CUSTOMER NAME

Effective Date   MM-DD-YY

Compensation: $0.00 per hour

Duration: Enter begin/end dates for purchased time block. Possibly include
the maximum hours per week or for the entire time block.

Or,

This is an estimate of the number of hours required to complete
the work. Be advised that SOFTWARE COMPANY works strictly
on an hourly basis and that you will be charged for every hour
worked on the project. As a result, the actual cost may exceed
this estimate. We will make every effort to notify you as soon as
we are aware of potential overruns.

Estimate: 0.00 hours

Work Description: Description of the work to be performed including references to
specifications and other key documents.

Expenses: SOFTWARE COMPANY expects to be reimbursed for all travel
related expenses when working at locations other than CITY,
STATE. Travel expenses include airfare, hotel, per diem and
ground transportation.

[This page intentionally left blank]

ITSW111-3 SOFTWARE CONSULTING CUSTOMER SUPPORT LOG

Customer ID	Date of Contact	Problem Description	Problem Class	Urgency (1=high, 5=low)	Promised Date	Start Date	Date Resolved	Action Taken	Comments	

[This page intentionally left blank]

Document ID **ITSW112**	Title **SOFTWARE TRAINING**	Print Date **mm/dd/yyyy**
Revision **0.0**	Prepared By **Preparer's Name / Title**	Date Prepared **mm/dd/yyyy**
Effective Date **mm/dd/yyyy**	Reviewed By **Reviewer's Name / Title**	Date Reviewed **mm/dd/yyyy**
	Approved By **Final Approver's Name / Title**	Date Approved **mm/dd/yyyy**

Policy: To offer training on all software products developed by the Company.

Purpose: To ensure that customers and employees can effectively operate Company-developed software; to promote customer satisfaction with Company products and services.

Scope: All software products and updates released by the Company.

Responsibilities:

The Software Trainer is responsible for developing training materials and training classes, scheduling classes and facilities, developing training plans, and providing instruction.

The Tech Support Manager is responsible for setting up computer equipment to be used in software training.

The Training Manager is responsible for reviewing course evaluations and recommending changes to software courses.

The Training Assistant is responsible for entering courses, trainers, and schedules into the training course log (or database).

Maintenance is responsible for setting up non-computing equipment (tables, chairs, etc.) for training.

Procedure:

1.0   SOFTWARE TRAINING - INTRODUCTION

1.1   Customers are typically more satisfied with their software when they thoroughly understand its features and functions. Training classes help customers learn the software faster and more thoroughly than they could on their own.

1.2   Employees are more productive when they are fully trained in the Company's products; therefore, the Company shall encourage employees to become trained in the full software product line. At a minimum, employees must attend training classes for the products with which they work. (See ITTS105 IT USER-STAFF TRAINING PLAN.)

1.3   Internet and intranet web sites should be used to provide user training and tips (FAQ's, etc.), to reduce basic questions that may arise from a variety of technical skill amongst company personnel.

2.0   SOFTWARE TRAINING - STANDARD TRAINING COURSES

2.1   Trainers shall have extensive experience using the products they teach. Less experienced trainers must team-teach with those who have more extensive product knowledge.

2.2   Trainers shall design training courses for all software products developed by the Company. For each course, a trainer shall:

- Define course content and develop a course plan;

- Specify facilities and resources required to teach the course;

- Work with technical writers to develop training materials, in accordance with ITSW106 SOFTWARE DOCUMENTATION;

- Create demonstration data to be used in the class; and

- Design a course evaluation form to be issued at each class, for the purpose of improving course content and methods. ITSW112-1 SOFTWARE TRAINING EVALUATION FORM may be used as a guide.

2.3   A training assistant shall enter courses, trainers, and schedules into a training course log or database (ITTS105-2 IT TRAINING LOG may be used as a guide). Trainers shall use this log or database to schedule classes and track enrollment.

3.0   SOFTWARE TRAINING - CUSTOMIZED TRAINING COURSES

3.1   For customers who have highly customized software or atypical needs, the Company may offer training courses customized to match the customers' software and meet their specific needs. The company charges customers a specified hourly rate to develop a customized course.

3.2   For an additional fee, a trainer will teach a standard or customized course at the customer's site.

4.0   SOFTWARE TRAINING - TEACHING TRAINING COURSES

4.1   Training facilities maintenance staff shall set up the training facility and class-related equipment (desks, chairs, etc.). The Tech Support Manager shall set up computer equipment used for training.

4.2   The trainer shall install the training software and set up any needed props.

4.3   The trainer shall conduct classes at the appointed times and places.

- The trainer should have a backup who has course experience, course information, and a course roster, in the event the trainer is unable to fulfill his/her duties.

4.4   At the end of the class, the trainer shall ask students to evaluate the course. ITSW112-1 may be on paper or it may be online. In either case, course evaluations should be saved to a software support database, for periodic review and course improvements.

If the evaluation form is online, the trainer shall secure the database so that students have access to only the course evaluation form for the class they have attended.

4.5   The Training Manager shall review the completed course evaluations and determine which, if any, of the students' suggestions may be incorporated into the course material.

Forms:

- ITSW112-1 SOFTWARE TRAINING EVALUATION FORM

References:

A. ISO/IEC 12207:2008 – SYSTEMS AND SOFTWARE ENGINEERING – SOFTWARE LIFE CYCLE PROCESSES

B. IEEE 12207-2008 – SYSTEMS AND SOFTWARE ENGINEERING – SOFTWARE LIFE CYCLE PROCESSES

This ISO standard describes the major component processes of a complete software life cycle and the high-level relations that govern their interaction. It establishes a software life cycle architecture based on two principles, modularity of processes and responsibility for processes. There are three process classes in the ISO software life cycle: primary (such as acquisition and operations); supporting (such as documentation and configuration management); and organizational (such as infrastructure and training). Each life cycle process is made up of activities, and each activity is further subdivided into tasks. The standard is based on ISO quality management principles.

The IEEE version of 12207 is more closely aligned with the ISO standard than it was in previous versions.

For more information, visit the ISO web site at http://www.iso.org/iso/catalogue_detail.htm?csnumber=43447 or the IEEE web site at http://standards.ieee.org/findstds/standard/12207-2008.html.

Additional Resources:

A. ITTS105 IT USER-STAFF TRAINING PLAN.

B. Stackpole, Beth, "Five Mistakes IT Groups Make When Training End-Users", *CIO Magazine*, 13 March 2008.

C. International Association of IT Trainers (ITRAIN) – http://www.itrain.org/.

D. American Society for Training and Development (ASTD) – http://www.astd.org.

E. Association for Development, Advancement, and Professional Training (ADAPT) – http://adapttrain.org/.

Revision History:

Revision	Date	Description of Changes	Requested By
0	mm/dd/yyyy	Initial Release	

ITSW112-1 SOFTWARE TRAINING EVALUATION FORM

Session Name and ID: _____

Training Dates: _____

Instructor: _____

Rate Your Training Experience

(Rate the following from 1 to 5, one being "not at all useful" and five being "extremely useful".)

	1	2	3	4	5
Training session, overall:	□ 1	□ 2	□ 3	□ 4	□ 5
Facility:	□ 1	□ 2	□ 3	□ 4	□ 5
Course content:	□ 1	□ 2	□ 3	□ 4	□ 5
Trainer's knowledge:	□ 1	□ 2	□ 3	□ 4	□ 5
Trainer's interest in attendees:	□ 1	□ 2	□ 3	□ 4	□ 5
Trainer's instruction style:	□ 1	□ 2	□ 3	□ 4	□ 5
Exercises:	□ 1	□ 2	□ 3	□ 4	□ 5
Visual aids:	□ 1	□ 2	□ 3	□ 4	□ 5
Pace of session:	□ 1	□ 2	□ 3	□ 4	□ 5

Feedback

What did you like most about the training, or what did you find most useful?

What could be improved?

Was this session appropriate for your incoming skill and experience levels?

What skills did you learn that you could apply to your job now or in the near future?

Do you have suggestions for future training topics?

Instructor-related comments:

Other comments:

Optional

Your name: _____

Your e-mail address: _____

IT Policies and Procedures

Section 500

IT Security Guide

Section 500

IT Security Guide

IT Security Guide

Table of Contents

1.0 Why Information Security?

1.1 A Brief History of Information Security

Robbery is illegal, but people still find it prudent to lock doors and close windows in their homes: likewise we lock up information systems. Just as people lock their doors to prevent loss, organizations must be concerned about protecting valued resources, including confidential information contained in customer and employee records.

Before the widespread use of computers, managers were responsible for safeguarding paper records by keeping them locked in filing cabinets in a locked office. Maybe the manager held the only key; at most, a secretary was given a copy, in case of unforeseen problems. In the last forty or so years, however, most organizations have adopted technology as the primary means by which they organize and access information. Sharing information via computers and networks has proven to be a cost-effective way of getting things done. In fact, today's society relies upon computers now more than ever and will more than likely continue to increase its use of technology.

Although it may be fitting to discuss analogies between paper files in wooden cabinets and electronic files on hard drives or removable media, there are significant differences in the specific processes required to maintain appropriate security in the age of computer networking. With the flip of a switch, information can be damaged irreparably. With the careless turn of your head, a pocket-sized disk containing thousands of records can disappear. And, with connection to the World Wide Web (Internet), sensitive material can be shared with millions of users.

While these scenarios may seem foreboding and even scary, they are only part of the story, and in fact a small part, because by flipping a different switch, properly storing disks, and connecting the right wires, information stored on computers and networks can be secured more safely than any paper file in any administrator's filing cabinet, even a armored, fireproof cabinet locked with deadbolts and protected by armed guards.

The same technology that can be the source of so much concern when in the hands of untrained users can actually be used to protect information more securely than ever before imaginable if it is used wisely.

1.2 What Is At Risk?

Most people see the necessity of securing computer equipment. Machines cost money; therefore, they have intrinsic value to the company. But if you take a moment to consider why organizations are so willing to spend large amounts of money on their computer systems – to store, access, and transmit information – the value of that information becomes more apparent. After all, it makes no sense to spend significant amounts of a company's limited resources on equipment for processing information unless the information itself is of significant value. And because information has become so useful, it's not only the equipment that demands protection, but also the data. In the business community, information about customers, vendors, employees, and other resources is arguably of more value to the organization than its equipment. How could it be so?

For starters, company data represents years of investment in collection and maintenance activities and may be irreplaceable as an asset. What happens, for example, if a company "loses" last month's sales information? It's far more important to the company than simply being unable to generate the monthly sales report.

In the larger scheme, company information is considered confidential by its very nature; that is, certain types of sensitive information (in particular, financial and HR records) must, by law, be protected from all parties who do not have a verifiable need to know. Since the company is ultimately responsible for the integrity and security of its data, the organization and its management need to take active steps to ensure that valuable equipment and information are adequately protected.

If an organization fails to protect its confidential information using standards of due care and reasonable safeguards, it opens itself to a host of potential problems. Among these are allegations of negligence and incompetence, law suits charging computer malpractice, and forfeiture of insurance claims due to preventable losses.

In addition to the legal ramifications of privacy violations, the potentially priceless asset of public confidence is also at risk. Company boards of directors, shareholders, customers, and various governing bodies (the SEC, for example) look unfavorably upon institutions and staff who upset public confidence in the business sector, in general, and in the company, in particular. A company's customers, vendors, and even its own employees might justifiably lose confidence in the company if its records were accessed improperly, altered, stolen, or destroyed.

1.3   Why Company Executives Should Read These Guidelines

What makes the issue of information security more difficult, however, is that many managers do not have the technical expertise, nor do they have the time to develop, implement, and monitor information security policies and procedures within their organizations. Responsibility for both meeting the public's demands for accountability and securing sensitive information is inescapable for a company's top executives and middle managers.

Like it or not, it comes with the job. And, because top organizational executives are ultimately responsible for information security; they must develop a sufficient understanding of sound security strategies and how they can be realized through organizational policy.

The intent of this document is to provide basic guidance to decision makers by identifying factors that should be taken into consideration when they develop security strategies and policies. It is designed specifically to help employees as they walk the fine line between keeping data secure and available to authorized persons with legitimate needs. Because the technical methods for securing digital data lie outside the training and expertise of many executives, these guidelines are written in non-technical language.

Although a key recommendation of this document is that each company designate a technically competent staff person (or hire a consultant) to manage data security operations, executives and managers cannot disregard or delegate responsibility for security issues entirely. Operational *authority* can and should be delegated to employees or contractors, but the *responsibility* cannot be abdicated by top management. That is why executives need to develop a sufficient understanding of information security and its related issues; so they can judge whether their subordinates are acting competently and thoroughly, and can subsequently ascertain whether proposed policies and procedures will be effective and efficient. After all, each policy will be implemented over top executives' signatures.

This document *is*:

- Concerned primarily with information technology security as it relates to the privacy and confidentiality of organizational information;

- Designed for use by managers and staff at the department, division, and corporate levels;

- Organized so as to walk policymakers through the steps of developing and implementing sound security policy that is tailored to meet the needs of their individual organizations;

- Focused on both technical and procedural requirements (i.e., both computer-related and staff-related issues); and

- Presented as a set of recommended guidelines.

This document *is not*:

- An attempt to dictate policy (although it can and should serve as a guide to policymakers as they consider their options and needs);

- Focused on a high-end discussion of security issues that requires readers to have advanced knowledge of technology;

- Presented as a manual of technical solutions for securing systems; nor

- A source for specific software product recommendations.

1.4   A Final Word on Considering Security Issues

Security involves more than keeping intruders out of confidential files. While an organization must certainly be aware of hackers (unauthorized users who attempt to access a system and its information), it must more regularly deal with threats like failed hard drives, spilled coffee, and refrigerator magnets.

Most security concerns an organization must face are straightforward. For example, the phrase "mean time between failures" is quite common in the computer industry. For non-statisticians, it refers to when – not if – every computer disk you own will fail. Planning to deal with such an event is not simply an exercise in theory – it is inevitable that material will deteriorate.

Remember, however, that the goal of system security is not to put all of your organization's confidential records into an entry-proof vault that even authorized users have difficulty accessing. If that was the case, locking your door keys in the building you work at would be an effective security strategy for protecting the company – you could be fairly certain that no one else can get into the building if you, the business owner, were unable to do so.

Instead, the goal of security is to protect information and the system without unnecessarily limiting its utility. The system shouldn't be so secure that authorized users can't get to the data they need to do their jobs. After all, the only reason you bother to maintain such information in the first place is so that it can be used to better serve your customers.

At the same time, unauthorized access, especially to critical systems and sensitive information, must be prevented. Because of this contradiction, no system can be made 100% secure, but the ideal of developing and maintaining a trusted system is realistic, and should be the goal of every manager and executive.

To approach this goal, top-level decision makers must be involved in the organization's attempt to establish sound information security policy and procedures. Although at times the prospect of such an endeavor may seem daunting, especially to a person who doesn't have technical training, it must be undertaken. Simply by reading this document, you will be better prepared to grapple with general principles of security and those that are unique to your own situations.

However, despite the specific guidelines that follow throughout this document, policy makers must understand that in order to successfully institute security practices within an organization, the following overarching prerequisites must first be met:

- *Senior* management must provide consistent, visible and continuous strong support;

- A single, *empowered* staff member must be responsible for security initiatives (and have the time needed for testing, monitoring, and other activities designed to provide feedback on the system);

- Employees must be educated through *well-conceived training programs*; and

- *All* employees must participate at *all* times.

Committing to these requirements and educating yourself on the issues affecting information security are good first steps. Then developing and implementing a well-conceived set of safeguards that is customized to your organization's specific needs will increase the security of your system significantly.

1.5   Introductory Security Checklist

While it may be tempting to simply refer to the following checklist as your security plan, to do so would limit the effectiveness of the recommendations. They are most useful when incorporated within a larger plan to develop and implement security policy throughout an organization (see Bizmanualz document ABR 32M, "Security Planning and Procedures Manual" for additional guidance). Other chapters in this document also address ways to customize policy to meet an organization's specific needs – a concept that should not be ignored if you want to ensure the effectiveness of any given guideline.

Introductory Security Checklist

- Are top decision makers (company executives) aware that any and all information essential to the delivery of goods and/or services must be maintained in a secure manner?

- Have employees considered the implications of local, state, and federal laws and regulations that require certain types of information (payroll, HR, finance, etc.) to be protected from improper release?

- Has security been made a priority in the organization (as evidenced by top-level staff commitment to read this document and refer to these guidelines while planning the security of the organization's information system)?

- Has a single, empowered staff person – of significant rank (i.e., a company officer) – been appointed to manage the organization's security operation?

- Does the appointed security manager have the appropriate authority and requisite time to do the job properly?

- Are decision makers prepared to invest necessary resources in staff security training?

- Are all employees expected to participate in security initiatives at all times? Moreover, are they aware of this expectation?

[This page intentionally left blank]

2.0 Assessing Your Needs

2.1 Introduction to Risk Assessment

What would the damage be to a business if confidential information – its own or its clients' – was lost or misplaced? Would it cost the organization $5,000 to reenter the information? $20,000 (or $50,000 or $100,000) to reacquire information from the source? $250,000 to settle lawsuits? How about millions in future technology funding being withheld by wary board members, financial officers, or shareholders?

Estimating the toll of insufficient information security on a department, line of business, or even a single building is well beyond the scope of a single document. However, it is not outside the realm of issues responsible company executives should be considering within their own organizations. After all, if the organization's customers and stakeholders lost confidence in the organization's ability to protect confidential information, estimates of the most severe consequences might not be all that implausible--and a million-dollar issue deserves attention.

So, what could cause a multimillion dollar information leak? An intruder? A negligent or disgruntled employee? A technological snafu? A natural disaster?

How can such a catastrophe be prevented? In the case of a tornado, it can't – not with a high degree of certainty, anyway – but even the devastating effects of a tornado **can be minimized** through a well-conceived and properly implemented security policy. The first phase in more effectively securing your information and equipment begins with a process referred to as **risk assessment**.

Put simply, risk assessment involves identifying:

- *Assets* your organization possesses;
- Potential *threats* to those assets;
- Points in your organization where you may have *vulnerabilities* to those threats;
- Probabilities of threats striking an organizational vulnerability; and
- Cost estimates of losses should a potential threat be realized.

Such an endeavor may seem complicated on the surface, but it doesn't have to be. Risk assessment is a straightforward process and a most necessary step in decision-making. By evaluating risk, you are determining your needs so that you don't spend valuable resources on unnecessary safeguards while, at the same time, you don't leave yourself exposed to unprotected loss. Risk assessment forces an organization to consider the range of potential threats and vulnerabilities it faces.

What will your risk assessment tell you? Well, since risk assessment is a process and not a product, it depends on your specific situation. As stated above, it should identify your organization's assets, threats, vulnerabilities, probabilities of attack, and associated costs. How can that help you plan security? It tells you what you have, what it's worth, what to worry about, where you're weak, and why you should be concerned in the first place.

Say, for example, that you realize that the old building in which you store your staff records (an *asset*) was not constructed with fire-resistant materials in the way you would require for a newly built structure (a *vulnerability*). You also realize it's conceivable that a fire (a *threat*) could strike the site (a *probability* that, while low, is real, and could therefore be *estimated*). The question becomes whether you should introduce countermeasures to protect your staff records from a fire.

Knowing what you do about the asset, vulnerability, threat, and probability, the answer then depends upon the cost of replacing that lost asset. If yours is a small, single-site organization, it might be feasible for you to resurvey your staff to gather lost information at relatively little cost, in which case you could afford to risk the loss of staff records.

On the other, while it might be possible to resurvey staff in a large, multi-site organization, the associated costs would be much greater – so much so that despite the low probability of a fire damaging your *asset* (the records), you wouldn't want to accept the risk because it would be far too costly should the *threat* (the fire) actually strike. Thus, a small company could accept the threat of a fire, while a large company has to rebuild to meet fire-resistant standards. Right? Not quite.

While it may seem like a valid conclusion given the information presented, other issues must also be considered. One influencing factor might be that the building in question stores not only staff records, but also fiscal records, all of which are maintained on a state-of-the-art computer system. Suddenly the low cost of resurveying a few employees doesn't seem like an adequate solution because of the other costs you may incur if a fire damages the building.

Yet another consideration when evaluating the merit of protection plans is alternative solutions. Yes, rebuilding would be an effective way of protecting your records in the example above, but so might be installing a sprinkler system or training staff to use fire extinguishers.

There is also the option of keeping multiple copies of the information in different locations, or "offsite backup." That way, the only chance you have of losing your information would be if there was a combination of highly improbable fires that destroyed the primary site and each backup site. Supplement this with an insurance policy to replace your equipment, and you have yet another effective but less expensive security alternative to rebuilding.

It is precisely these types of thoughts that the risk assessment process should elicit. In fact, a properly executed risk assessment provides decision makers with a methodical approach to determining security strategies- an approach not based on a sales pitch or gut instinct, but on the concrete, context-specific findings of cost/benefit analysis. In a world of limited budgets, risk assessment provides an organization with the information it requires to accurately prioritize its needs. Options for meeting those needs can then be considered, ranked accordingly, and funded to reflect priority.

2.2   Commonly Asked Questions

Q. *Where do I begin to protect information and equipment?*
A. The answer to that question can be very straightforward if you know the answers to two related questions: (1) What information and equipment do you want to protect?; and (2) What do you want to protect it from? Drawing conclusions about these important issues can be accomplished most effectively by a systematic approach to determining your assets, threats, and vulnerabilities-a process referred to here as risk assessment. Risk assessment is a collaborative effort to identify potential threats to your organization's assets, estimate the likelihood of those threats being realized, and quantify the costs attributable to potential losses.

Q. *Why should I worry about all these details when I have far-reaching insurance policies to cover my losses?*
A. First of all, many insurance policies cover only tangible assets (e.g., equipment). As is emphasized throughout this document, information is often more valuable than the equipment used to access it. After performing a risk assessment, you will be in a better position to inquire about additional insurance policies to cover your information as well. You can then make sure that you have insured yourself against reasonably probable, high-cost losses because risk assessment will have helped you determine what they are more likely to be. Remember, as an executive you are the expert on your organization. It is your job to know where and why you need insurance coverage. Review all policies after performing your risk assessment; don't pay for insurance you don't need, and make sure that you have those policies you do need.

Q. *Even if my risk assessment identifies real threats and vulnerabilities, how can I possibly deal with them with such a small staff (not to mention budget)?*
A. The fewer the resources you have to put into protecting your organization, the more vital the risk assessment process becomes. Think about it. If you have unlimited security funding, then you may have enough resources to protect yourself against the entire spectrum of threats. Having said that, however, it should be noted that even the wealthiest organizations should perform a risk assessment to be sure that they have considered all of their potential threats. On the other hand, if funds are scarce, you need to perform a risk assessment to accurately prioritize your needs before allotting your limited resources. In this way, risk assessment provides you with the information needed to address your most pressing needs first and increase the effectiveness of those resources that are at your disposal, whatever they may be.

2.3   Components of Risk

What is a risk? For the purpose of information security and this document, a risk is any hazard or danger to which your information or equipment is subject. Storing an expensive computer within reach of an open window is risky. Allowing all employees to have access to computerized personnel files is also considered risky. But even if you now know what a risk is, the question of what is at risk still remains-and the answer is your assets.

Assets

An asset is often defined as real property. This being the case, it's likely that your organization's computer equipment is prominently listed on the balance sheets as an asset; a fitting designation considering the amount of money invested in the equipment. But recall that the only reason all those dollars were spent on technology in the first place was so that you could manipulate your organization's information more efficiently – information like customer data, support service data, employee health records, and organizational finances. The equipment is important only because it is the mechanism by which you access the files that are so essential to the operation of the enterprise – information is the real asset. Equipment is, of course, very valuable, but never forget that **the real asset is the information.**

Threats

Although you may think more threats come from outside the organization, internal threats (e.g., authorized users who are accident-prone, negligent, or criminal) are far more likely to breach system security than external threats.

It is estimated that as much as 67 percent of networked computers are infected with one form of a virus or another in a given year. Even accounting for the growing prevalence of virus threats, more than half of all reported system damage is caused by unintentional employee action; in most cases simple negligence. Any such action, actor, or event that contributes to risk is referred to as a *threat*.

Examples of Threats to an Organization's Assets

Natural Threats

- Lightning
- Flood
- Forest Fire
- Dirt/sand
- Tornado
- Earthquake
- Humidity
- Rain/Water Damage
- Hurricane
- Snow/Ice Storm
- High Temperatures
- Time (Aging Media)

Manmade Threats (Intentional)

- Theft
- Hacking
- Computer Viruses
- Vandalism
- File Sabotage
- Unauthorized Copying

- Arson
- Wire Taps

Manmade Threats (Unintentional)

- Equipment Failure
- Spilled Beverages
- Secondhand smoke
- Computer Viruses
- Lost Documentation
- Power Fluctuations
- User Error
- Heating Units
- Lost Encryption Keys
- Magnetic Fields (Static Discharge)
- Air Conditioning Ducts
- Programmer Error
- Aging Facilities
- Mishandled Equipment (Breakage)

As you consider types of potential threats, notice the secondary distinction that becomes relevant in the manmade category between intentional and unintentional threats. Intentional manmade threats are a source of particular resentment for many people. After all, why should an organization have to spend its valuable resources on keeping users from willfully causing damage? The same question can be asked about the need for uninsured motorist insurance, but the results will be the same. You have to be able to account for people who are unwilling to play by the rules!

Deliberate unauthorized assaults on a system can make sense to potential intruders when two conditions are met:

1. The intruder can benefit substantially from the act (i.e., something of value can be gained or a personal need (revenge, control, etc.) may be satisfied).

2. The act requires relatively little effort, in comparison with the potential gains.

The message is clear: Know the potential value of your information and make penetration more difficult than it's worth.

Vulnerabilities

Vulnerabilities refer to points within a system that are open to attack or damage. What type of attack? That depends on the threat. Vulnerabilities are the mechanisms by which threats access your system. Think of a thief (a threat), for example, who is ready to strike your building (which houses your assets). An open back window through which that thief might enter the premises is a *vulnerability*.

Countermeasures

A countermeasure is a step planned and taken in opposition to another act or potential act. While ultimately aimed at rebuffing threats, countermeasures are often deployed strategically at points of vulnerability, as is the case when a lock (a countermeasure) is installed on a back window through which a thief may try to enter your building (see vulnerabilities above). Countermeasures are often designed to serve one of the following functions.

- Prevention   For example, by initiating backup procedures, threats are prevented from damaging your lone copy of information in a single event.

- Deterrence   For example, by training users about the legal consequences of unacceptable use, potential threats who might otherwise consider destructive activities may be deterred.

- Containment   For example, by segmenting each separate type of information in your system, even active threats can be limited to the record areas they can find and enter.

- Detection   For example, by reviewing records of user activity, commonly referred to as audit trails, unwelcome activity can be uncovered.

- Recovery   For example, by preparing and testing a contingency plan, "lost" systems and "damaged" information can be salvaged (or at least losses and damage can be minimized).

2.4   Dealing with Risk

Options for dealing with risk:

- *Counter it* (an informed decision)

- *Accept it* (also an informed decision)

- *Ignore it* (an uninformed decision and a poor strategy)

Creating a risk-free environment is unrealistic, but instituting a "trusted system" (i.e., one that while not perfect is trustworthy) is possible. The reason for this limitation is that you simply cannot counter all risk. In actuality, countering risk is only one of three potential ways in which to deal with threats and vulnerabilities. Although it may seem counter-intuitive based on the stated purpose of this document, risk can also be accepted (sometimes a very practical strategy) or ignored (not a good plan under any circumstances).

Under what conditions could accepting risk make sense? Well, it is theoretically possible that an asteroid could smash into the earth and land, of all places, on your office. The risk is real, albeit small, and can be estimated as such. Should you build a concrete vault miles beneath the surface of the earth to store backup files of your records, or should you accept the risk of an asteroid strike and figure that your system will be the last of your worries should the event actually occur?

Your risk assessment (see Steps 1-8 below) and common sense will probably tell you that you can safely afford to accept the residual risk of asteroid strikes. You do not have to counter any and every risk conceivable – only those it makes sense to address based on the results of your risk assessment.

On the other hand, ignoring risk is not a good strategy (although it is an all too common practice). Risks are everywhere. If you choose not to perform a risk assessment and simply ignore the risks, you just won't be prepared for them. Thus, despite the fact that it is possible to handle risk in any of the three ways – counter it, accept it, or ignore it – only the first two are reliable strategies and both depend on the results of an accurate risk assessment.

While potential risks should never be ignored, it only makes sense for an organization to focus its attention on those risks that are most likely to affect the system.

2.5   Guidelines for Risk Assessment

A properly conceived and implemented risk assessment should:

- Provide the basis for deciding whether countermeasures are needed.

- Ensure that countermeasures counter actual risk.

- Save money that might have been wasted on unnecessary countermeasures.

- Determine whether residual risk (that risk which remains after countermeasures have been introduced) is acceptable.

Risk Assessment Outline

   A Team Effort

   First Things First

   Take stock in what you have and what it's worth
   Step 1 - Identify sensitive information and critical systems
   Step 2 - Estimate the value of system components

   Identify your potential threats and vulnerabilities
   Step 3 - Identify threats
   Step 4 - Identify vulnerabilities
   Step 5 - Estimate the likelihood of a potential penetration becoming an actual
         penetration
   Think through your defensive options
   Step 6 - Identify countermeasures for perceived threats and vulnerabilities
   Step 7 - Estimate costs of implementing countermeasures

   Make informed decisions
   Step 8 - Select suitable countermeasures for implementation

A Team Effort

If top executives in an organization don't actively participate and visibly demonstrate their commitment to the security effort, no one else will.

The process of risk assessment should be initiated and led by the top executives in an organization, but feedback from all levels and job categories is required. At a minimum, information collectors, data providers, data entry staff, and data processors and managers should be involved in the early stages of risk assessment. In short, more people involved in the brainstorming process results in more ideas being generated.

While it is never too late to do the right thing, postponing risk assessment invites undue peril and unnecessary liability.

First Things First

Risk Assessment is a prerequisite for any serious attempt to implement a security policy within an organization. It's a step that simply cannot be ignored. After all, unless the organization's needs are first accurately assessed, there is no way of knowing whether financial and staff resources are being wisely invested in security initiatives.

Take stock of what you have and what it's worth

Only careful and collaborative efforts will yield worthwhile results. Be inclusive, exhaustive, and realistic when documenting your assets.

Step 1 - Identify sensitive information and critical systems: The goal here is to make a distinction between general information and systems (i.e., information and systems that are helpful to your organization) and sensitive information and critical systems (i.e., information and systems that are private and/or mission critical).

For example, the computer that houses the "HELP" file for your organization's word processing software is a general support component. While it is most helpful to have access to user HELP when facing a word processing problem, the files themselves are not vital to running a business. Conversely, the software that manages production scheduling is vital to the company's mission: if it isn't available and working properly, shift managers could find themselves with fully staffed and stocked production lines and no idea of what to build and when. That makes the scheduling system "critical."

Sensitive information is that information which if lost or compromised might negatively affect the owner of the information or require substantial resources to recreate. An example of sensitive information would be employee records.

Critical systems are those systems or system components (hardware or software) that if lost or compromised would jeopardize the ability of the system to continue processing. An example of a critical system might be the cabling that links your administrative and instructional computer networks.

Brainstorming is a group activity that requires openness and creativity. Don't try to edit the list as ideas are put forward. Capture everyone's thoughts first, and then prioritize to identify the information and systems that are mission critical.

The primary deliverable from Step 1 is a list of all sensitive information and every critical system your organization depends on. To leave out a component because you didn't think broadly enough leaves the organization vulnerable.

Step 2 - Estimate the value of system components: Estimating the value of your information system is not always simple, but the task is made more manageable by focusing on the word "estimate." After all, it may very well be impossible, or at least impractical, to try to derive a precise dollar value for some assets (especially information assets). Instead, try to calculate a reasonable approximation of the replacement cost of each component of the system-both equipment and information. Be sure to consider the following factors when making your estimate:

- Direct replacement costs of hardware, software, and peripherals (Would there be installation costs? Consultant fees? Necessary upgrades?)

- Replacement costs of stored information (Would reentering data be necessary? Resurveying?)

- Costs associated with the disruption of service or other activities (Would you have to pay employees overtime during the recovery period? What about hiring temporary staffing to help make up for missed time?)

- Indirect but real costs associated with a loss of public confidence (Would it impede current or future business? What would be the effect on investment in the business?)

- Legislative and regulatory fines and penalties

Again, keep in mind that while the costs of hardware and software tend to be more readily measurable, information costs are very real as well. You may not be able to call a vendor and say "What is my information worth?" the way you can call your equipment sales representative, but you still have to ask yourself "What is it worth to my organization?" Estimates of these costs, no matter how rough, give you a more accurate sense of the true value of important information assets.

One common mistake in this process that can lead to serious flaws in assessment results is when you focus on only the sensitive and critical segments (as identified in Step 1) when estimating the value of an information system. While identifying sensitive information and critical systems is necessary for setting priorities, all information has value and requires attention in this step. If it doesn't, the information's overall utility should be reconsidered. After all, if it isn't valuable enough to recover or rekey upon being damaged (which requires a cost that can be estimated), what purpose could it possibly be serving?

If information isn't valuable enough to warrant consideration of its protection and recovery, can it be valuable enough to warrant precious disk space in the first place?

Identify your potential threats and vulnerabilities
How do you identify threats and vulnerabilities? In a word: Brainstorm! No idea about potential threats or vulnerabilities is unimportant. However, keep in mind that management has a very limited perspective on information and system use. Maximize the resources at your disposal by including representatives from all organizational levels and functions in the brainstorming effort. After all, you don't want to leave out site security when they might be the only people on duty to protect equipment and information after hours. Always keep an open mind to what your users have to say.

Step 3 - Identify threats: What actors, actions, or events threaten your system? Refer to the examples on page 14 and 15 before creating an exhaustive list through a collaborative brainstorming process. Be sure to consider the following types of threats:

- Natural (e.g., fire, flood, lightning, and humidity)

- Manmade unintentional (e.g., negligence and accidents)

- Manmade intentional (e.g., hackers and viruses)

Step 4 - Identify vulnerabilities: Where is your system susceptible? Consider vulnerabilities to natural threats and both intentional and unintentional manmade threats as identified in Step 3. Also look at other examples of threats, as listed on page 15, to see if any new ideas are triggered. After this initial brainstorming, organize the list of vulnerabilities you've generated into categories such as the following and then once again see if additional thoughts come to mind:

- Physical concerns (e.g., room access, building construction, and climate)

- Hardware- and software-related issues (e.g., equipment, programs, and compatibility)

- Media concerns (e.g., disks, tapes, hard drives, and print copies)

- Communications (e.g., access points and encryption)

- Human concerns (e.g., personnel and office behavior)

Where is your office vulnerable?

- A door is propped open and doesn't have a lock (see chapter 5.0).

- A cup of coffee is set on a computer case (see chapter 5.0).

- A computer monitor sits within plain sight and easy reach of a window (see chapter 5.0).

- Wiring is in the way of foot traffic (see chapter 5.0).

- Equipment is plugged into wall sockets without a surge protector (see chapter 5.0).

- Outlets are overloaded (see chapter 5.0).

- Backup files are stored in the same room as the original files (see chapter 6.0).

- Floppy disks are shared haphazardly and are not labeled (see chapter 6.0).

- Someone's password is written and posted on their monitor (see chapter 8.0).

- A computer is logged on but has been left unattended (see chapter 8.0).

Step 5 - Estimate the likelihood of a potential penetration becoming an actual penetration: What is the likelihood (probability) of a threat taking advantage of a vulnerability? As difficult as answering such a question might appear to be, you don't have to be able to predict the future in order to generate reasonable probabilities of future events. Do your research – use history to support your estimates. For example, for an institution located along the Mississippi River, earthquakes and floods are within the realm of possibility. Historical data will tell you the site is more susceptible to floods. Using flood data compiled by the National Weather Service, you can estimate the likelihood of the next 100-year flood. Similarly, by researching earthquake data, you can estimate the likelihood of an earthquake.

Think through your defensive options.

For recommended countermeasure options, see chapters 5.0 - 9.0.

Step 6 - Identify countermeasures for perceived threats and vulnerabilities: This step parallels Steps 3 and 4, in that its purpose is to generate an exhaustive list of ideas; this time, potential solutions to the concerns caused by your identified threats and vulnerabilities. When considering options, be sure to keep in mind that many threats and vulnerabilities can be addressed by more than one countermeasure. A potential thief, for example, could be thwarted by better locks, video cameras and other electronic surveillance, or even trained security patrol officers. Step 6 focuses on generating a list of such options for each perceived threat and vulnerability, not in selecting what appears to be the preferred option. That is attempted only after an exhaustive list is finalized and costs/benefits are considered. Issues to consider when brainstorming potential countermeasures include:

- **Physical security equipment and procedures**
  Location and environmental strategies such as climate monitors, required building specifications, and regulations governing room access and food and beverage use.

- **Information security practices**
  Storage and use regulations such as labeling and write-protecting files.

- **Software security techniques**
  Purchasing and programming concerns such as copyright infringements and proper documentation.

- **User access controls**
  Data and system access issues, including login and password protection.

- **Networking security initiatives**
  Connectivity issues like firewalls and encryption strategies.

Estimates should account for both start-up and maintenance costs.

Step 7 - Estimate costs of implementing countermeasures: This step entails determining the costs associated with countermeasures identified in Step 6. Remember that the vast majority of costs are twofold: initial and ongoing. Be certain to consider all of the following factors:

- Both money and time for research, development, procurement, installation, and maintenance of security features.

- Staff training time-the costs are real and absolutely necessary.

- Countermeasures already available to the organization that may require less investment to institute (e.g., if your accounting office currently uses certain security procedures, there may be fewer training costs because you already have a core of people who can share their expertise).

Make informed decisions

Step 8 - Select suitable countermeasures for implementation: In Step 8, it's finally time to decide which countermeasures make the most sense to implement. Remember that there will probably be more than one countermeasure that can protect your system from any given threat or vulnerability, so you have some choices. Your job is to determine which strategy makes the most sense from a cost/benefit perspective. This can be accomplished by comparing your estimated costs of potential losses for a given period of time (Steps 2-5) with actual security costs that would be incurred when preventing such a loss for the same period of time (Step 7).

A desired level of risk reduction is achieved when further reduction would cost more than the benefits gained.

One way to decrease your actual security costs is to keep in mind that a single countermeasure can actually serve as a solution to multiple threats and vulnerabilities. An example of this is when security officers who protect your most sensitive areas serve as a countermeasure to both external intruders and potentially misguided staff. Such a compromise solution is really no compromise at all-two potential threats are being countered for the price of one. In effect, you're getting twice the protection for the cost of a single countermeasure!

2.6   Closing Thoughts on Risk Assessment

Once you determine your needs and priorities through the above eight steps, you can then make security decisions based on concrete information. Sales pitches from vendors and gut instinct on the part of well-intentioned, but perhaps uninformed, staff need no longer serve as reasons for making security policy decisions.

It should be emphasized that **decision makers must be involved in the entire process of risk assessment**. Should they rely simply upon cost/benefit analysis without being aware of other important factors that might have been uncovered in the process, they cannot make a completely informed decision.

As discussed throughout this document, confidential records may need to be protected regardless of cost/benefit analysis, because of the various laws that mandate protection of company records (i.e., Sarbanes-Oxley). Not knowing this important fact could lead to disastrous results for the organization.

2.7   Risk Assessment Checklist

While it may be tempting to simply refer to the following checklist as your security plan, to do so would limit the effectiveness of the recommendations. They are most useful when initiated as part of a larger plan to develop and implement security policy throughout an organization. Other chapters in this document also address ways to customize policy to meet an organization's specific needs—a concept that should not be ignored if you want to maximize the effectiveness of any given guideline.

Risk Assessment Checklist

- Is the process of risk assessment being championed by a top-level decision-maker?

- Is feedback being elicited from representatives of all user areas?

- Have sensitive information and critical systems been identified (Step 1)?

- Has the value of all system components (not just sensitive information and critical systems) been estimated (Step 2)?

- Has an exhaustive list of potential threats been generated (Step 3)?

- Has an exhaustive list of vulnerabilities been generated (Step 4)?

- Has the likelihood of a potential penetration becoming an actual penetration been estimated (Step 5)?

- Has an exhaustive list of countermeasures to identified threats and vulnerabilities been generated (Step 6)?

- Have the costs of implementing identified countermeasures been estimated (Step 7)?

- Have suitable countermeasures been selected for implementation (Step 8)?

[This page intentionally left blank]

3.0   Security Policy: Development and Implementation

3.1   Why Do You Need a Security Policy?

Who is responsible for securing an organization's information? The Research and Evaluation department? The Information Technology, or IT, staff? Wrong both times. Ultimately, it is not only individual employees or departments that are responsible for the security of confidential information but also senior management. It is incumbent upon top management, charged with protecting the organization's best interests, to ensure that an appropriate and effective security policy is developed and implemented throughout the organization.

While policies themselves don't solve problems – in fact, they can actually complicate things, unless they are clearly written and observed – they are a way of ensuring that the organization focuses on its objectives. Security policy refers to *clear, comprehensive*, and *well-defined* plans, rules, and practices that regulate access to an organization's system and the information included in it. Good policy protects not only information and systems but also individual employees and the organization as a whole. It also serves as a clear statement to the outside world that the organization is committed to security.

3.2   Commonly Asked Questions

Q. What does this document have to offer that experienced policy makers don't already know?
A. Experienced policy makers certainly bring a great deal of skill to security policy development. But in many ways, security policy is different from more traditional policy. It requires policy makers to think like data entry clerks, MIS staff, research and evaluation specialists, legal counsel, administrators, and so on. Many of the procedural guidelines included here will already be appreciated by seasoned policy makers but this document tailors the information so that it can be more readily applied to the specific concerns of information and system security – an area of expertise not always held by executives and policy makers.

Q. Isn't policy written at the corporate level?
A. Yes, but not exclusively. Whoever is in charge of a site must be concerned about protecting sensitive information and critical systems that can be accessed from within that site. This concern is articulated through security policies that are designed to regulate access and protect information and systems as circumstances specifically warrant.

Q. Shouldn't expert technology consultants be hired to do the job?
A. Certainly there are roles for expert consultants when instituting security policy. They could be hired as general technical support or they might be useful in offering advice about countermeasures (e.g., a password system). But generally speaking, company executives and their employees need to accept responsibility for protecting their system because they own it. They are the people who know it best and they will be the ones who have to implement adopted security policy. Outside contractors, while certainly capable of lending expertise to the process, cannot take the place of committed and informed staff.

3.3   How to Develop Policy

Security policy must be based on the results of a risk assessment, as described in chapter 2.0. Findings from a risk assessment provide policymakers with an accurate picture of the security needs specific to their organization. This information is imperative because proper policy development requires decision makers to:

- Identify sensitive information and critical systems;

- Incorporate local, state, and federal laws, as well as relevant ethical standards;

- Define institutional security goals and objectives;

- Set a course for accomplishing those goals and objectives; and

- Ensure that necessary mechanisms for accomplishing the goals and objectives are in place.

In this way, legal and regulatory concerns, organizational characteristics, contractual requirements, environmental issues, and user input can all be incorporated into policy development. Effective security policy integrates these and other considerations into a clear set of goals and objectives that direct staff as they perform their required duties.

The Logic of Well-Planned Policy

If Organizational needs define policy and Policy guides personnel and technology decisions, then personnel and technology serve organizational needs.

If employees have minimal input in policy development, they may show minimal interest in policy implementation.

Getting Perspective

Final approval of policy is the responsibility of senior management, but contributing to the development of policy should be an organization-wide activity. While every employee doesn't necessarily need to attend each security policy planning session, executives should include representatives from all job levels and functions in the information gathering phase (just as in the case of brainstorming during risk assessment). Non-administrative employees often have a unique perspective to share with policymakers that simply cannot be acquired by any other means. Meeting with staff on a frequent basis to learn about significant issues that affect their work is a big step toward *ensuring that there is buy-in at all levels* of the organization.

While it makes sense to get as much input from potential users as is possible, it is also essential that voices from outside the organization be heard during the information gathering stages of policy development. Why? Because decision makers need to be informed of security arrangements that other organizations are making that potentially impact them and the policies they will be developing. If, for example, every company supplier but one commits to encryption software to protect messages sent over the Internet, the lone supplier that doesn't have the encryption key is going to have a very difficult time communicating with the company and with other suppliers. The point is that just as security planning demands coordination internally, it often requires it externally as well—a recommendation that should not be overlooked, especially by those organizations that practice site-based management.

Creating consortia, cooperatives, and other types of associations enables organizations to pool resources and share expenses as they endeavor to devise and implement security strategies.

What to Include

Specific security needs are defined by an organization's risk assessment. Irrespective of those findings, the following general questions should be addressed clearly and concisely in any security policy.

- What is the reason for the policy?
- Who developed the policy?
- Who approved the policy?
- Whose authority sustains the policy?
- Which laws or regulations, if any, is the policy based on?
- Who will enforce the policy?
- How will the policy be enforced?
- Whom does the policy affect?
- What information assets must be protected?
- What are users actually required to do?
- How should security breaches and violations be reported?
- What is the effective date and expiration date of the policy?

Writing with Proper Tone

Policy should be written in a way that makes sense to its intended audience. After all, guidelines that aren't implemented foreshadow objectives that won't be met. Tips for reader-friendly policy include:

- Be concise; focus on expectations and consequences, but explain the underlying rationale when appropriate;

- Don't water down the message; tell don't ask. Don't propose, suggest, or insinuate unless that is specifically what you mean to do;

- Use simple, straightforward language;

- Define any term that could potentially confuse a reader; no need to make things difficult; and

- Be creative; the presentation should never interfere with content. Checklists and reference cards increase utility.

Rewrite formal policy into a reader-friendly version that is distributed to staff.

Another hint for ensuring appropriate tone is to word policy in a way that makes sense to both developers and users before giving the draft to legal counsel. The purpose for this is to keep clear and meaningful points from being transformed into incomprehensible legal jargon. If the official policy does eventually get transformed into something particularly formal, consider rewriting a distributable version designed specifically for reader-friendliness.

Read chapters 5.0 – 9.0 for specific security guidelines to support your policies.

3.4   From Board Room to Break Room: Implementing Security Policy

This document presents a great deal of information for policymakers to consider. The role of an effective administrator, however, is to absorb these recommendations and distill the results into a meaningful and manageable set of employee regulations that fit his or her organization. These rules then serve as the mechanisms for implementing policy goals and objectives throughout the workplace. Although it might be tempting (and certainly possible) to create an exhaustive inventory of "do's and don'ts," formulating a short list of sensible rules that can realistically be implemented is undoubtedly a better strategy.

How can policy implementation be made realistic? Aside from keeping regulations clear, concise, and understandable, try to make them as easy as possible for staff to fulfill. By keeping things as simple as possible, employee participation becomes a realistic objective. Specific actions that increase the likelihood of your policies actually being followed in the work environment include:

- *Assign an empowered and committed manager to be accountable for security:* Someone must make security a day-to-day priority. This designated staff member must be authorized to both reward and reprimand employees, as necessary, at all levels of the organization (see chapter 4.0).

- *Institute staff training that is tailored to meet the requirements of security policy and the needs of your staff.* Most computer users have never been trained to properly use technology; and what little training they do have was probably aimed at overcoming their fears and teaching them how to turn on their machines. At most, they may have learned how to use a particular piece of software for a specific application. Thus, the majority of your employees have little understanding of security issues, and there is no reason to expect that to change unless the organization does its part to correct the situation. Reluctance on the part of the organization to adequately prepare staff for making security policy a part of the work environment makes the rest of the effort an exercise in the theoretical—and theory won't protect a system from threats that are all too real (see chapter 10.0).

- *Communicate organizational needs and expectations to employees in both initial and ongoing ways:* Make a serious attempt at getting the word out, but don't be overly serious in its presentation. As in any marketing campaign, creativity and consistency will be rewarded by audience responsiveness. The following examples are recommended as effective strategies for communicating security expectations:

  a. Hold security refresher workshops.

  b. Create an infrastructure for employee support (e.g., a Help Desk that is staffed with competent and readily available advisors).

  c. Frequently and publicly acknowledge and reinforce positive behavior.

  d. Develop and distribute reference materials (e.g., checklists, brochures, and summaries that are succinct and reader-friendly).

    e. Update the employee handbook to reflect security procedures.

    f. Keep security reminders visible throughout the workplace (e.g., posters, FYI memos, and email broadcasts).

- *Enforce security regulations equally at all levels of the organization:* Each individual in the system must understand that he or she is personally accountable for security. Bosses have to say "get with the system," mean it, and prove it by doing so themselves. If the rules don't apply to everyone, then they apply to no one. This is not simply an egalitarian issue. If the system is not secure from top to bottom, then, by definition, it is not secure.

Expecting every employee to become a security expert is unrealistic. Instead, break down recommended security practices into manageable pieces that are tailored to meet individual job duties. A single short and well-focused message each week will be better received than a monthly information overload.

If your institution has several types of work environments or levels of users, consider writing separate security regulations, all of which support broader policy, for each user group. Each policy can then be tailored to the specific needs of the particular environment or user type. To increase involvement and acceptance, have staff contribute to the development of their own policy guidelines and procedures. For completeness and consistency across the institution, each user group may require the services of an expert security coordinator while developing its own subset of guidelines.

Personnel Issues

One aim of successful security policy is that it should limit the need for trust in the system. While this may seem like a terribly cynical philosophy, it actually serves to protect both the organization's employees and the organization itself. But before the benefits of security can be realized, staff must be properly informed of their roles, responsibilities, and organizational expectations.

- Employees *must* be told *in writing*:

    a. What is and is not acceptable use of equipment.

    b. What the penalties for violating regulations will be.

    c. That their information system activities can and will be monitored.

    d. That security will be a part of performance reviews (users who do their share should be rewarded, while those who lag behind may be reprimanded or retrained).

- Employees *should* be continually reminded that:

    a. Organizational resources (computers, servers, data, etc.) belong to the organization.

    b. They should not expect privacy of information stored on or transmitted with the organization's equipment or software. This includes email and text messaging.

    c. Their personal electronic devices (smartphones, etc.) cannot be used for conducting company business unless certain conditions – proper authorization, training, approved security, etc. – are met.

- Employees shall be ***required to sign a Security Agreement***, acknowledging that they are aware of their responsibilities and that they will comply with security policy. This requires that they:

    a. Have ample opportunity to read and review all policies and regulations for which they will be held accountable.

    b. Be provided an appropriate forum for clarifying questions or concerns they may have about the organization's expectations.

    c. Not be given access to the system until a signed agreement is accounted for and maintained in a safe place.

All new employees should be expected to meet the organization's security requirements and procedures as a part of their job description. Once hired, new employees should be informed of and trained in security policy as a part of their orientation, to impress the importance of security upon them.

Outside organizations should be expected to guarantee via binding agreements that they and their employees will use and secure shared information in compliance with the company's requirements.

A Special Note on Contractors (Outsourcers)

Outsiders (e.g., repair technicians, consultants, and temporary help) and outside organizations (e.g., other departments, businesses, and contractors) with access to your system should sign agreements that require them to respect and maintain the confidentiality of your information, but signing the dotted line "don't necessarily make it so," as the saying goes.

Be careful not to share more about your security operation with outsiders than is absolutely necessary. Even apparently harmless warnings about what to expect of your defenses can give a skilled – or unskilled – intruder an edge in tampering with your system. Limit security briefings to those levels required to (1) keep them from breaching your defenses, (2) impress upon them that you are serious about protecting your system assets, and (3) ensure that they handle your assets in a secure manner.

Having said this, sharing general news with business partners about your organization's commitment to securing confidential information can instill a feeling of confidence throughout your organization and client community.

3.5   Closing Thoughts on Policy

The incredible pace of technological innovations requires that all security policies be reviewed on a frequent basis. How frequently? That depends on your organization's needs and technological savvy. Generally speaking, however, each new technological change has the potential to necessitate a corresponding policy change. ***Review all organizational policies***, security or otherwise, ***annually, at a minimum***.

3.6   Policy Development and Implementation Checklist

While it may be tempting to refer to the following checklist as your security plan, to do so would limit the effectiveness of the recommendations. They are most useful when initiated as part of a larger plan to develop and implement security policy throughout an organization. Other chapters in this document also address ways to customize policy to your organization's specific needs, a concept that should not be ignored if you want to maximize the effectiveness of any given guideline.

Policy Development and Implementation Checklist

- Are the findings of the organization's risk assessment (see chapter 2.0) available?

- Have employees representing a range of job levels and functions been included in the security policy development process?

- Have security-related practices, agreements, and arrangements in other organizations been reviewed to ensure that organizational policy is in line with those in comparable institutions and potential or actual trading partners?

- Has appropriate and meaningful support/reference information been provided within the policy itself (see checklist under "What to Include")?

- Has policy been written in a way that can be understood and appreciated by employees?

- Have policy goals and objectives been translated into organizational security regulations that are designed to modify employees' behavior?

- Has an empowered and committed administrator been specifically assigned to be accountable for security (see chapter 4.0)?

- Have employees received security training specifically tailored to their needs (see chapter 10.0)?

- Have organizational needs and expectations been communicated to employees in both initial and ongoing ways (see examples of recommended strategies in 3.4, page 28)?

- Are security regulations enforced equally at all levels of the organization?

- Have employees been informed of their security roles and responsibilities in writing?

- Have security issues been included as a part of employee performance reviews?

- Is adequate time provided for reading and reviewing Security Agreements before employees and outsiders are required to sign and submit them?

- Is an appropriate forum provided for clarifying concerns and answering questions about Security Agreements before employees and outsiders are required to sign and submit them?

- Are all new employees trained on their security roles, responsibilities, and expectations?

- Are outsiders (e.g., repair technicians) and outside organizations required to sign Security Agreements to acknowledge that they are aware of their responsibilities and will abide by the organization's security rules?

- Has news of the organization's commitment to security been shared with the general public as appropriate?

- Are security policies reviewed annually at a minimum?

4.0 Security Management

4.1 Introduction to Security Management

Because system security is the aggregate of individual component security, "system boundaries" must encompass individual users and their workstations. But because personal computers are just that (personal), employee behavior can't always be dictated without potentially hampering workers' overall productivity. Recall that security policy becomes ineffective if it's so restrictive that legitimate user access is threatened. Thus, a key to successful security implementation is finding a reasonable balance between system protection and user autonomy and convenience. The person responsible for finding that balance and actively promoting organizational security is the security manager.

Security management consists of nurturing a security-conscious organizational culture, developing tangible procedures to support security, and managing the myriad of pieces that make up the system. The security manager ensures that administration and employees are aware of their security roles, support security efforts, and are willing to tolerate the minor inconveniences that are inevitably a part of system change and improvement. After all, if personnel circumvent security procedures (e.g., write down passwords, share accounts, and disable virus-checking software), they put the entire system at risk.

Effective system security depends on creating a workplace environment and organizational structure where management understands and fully supports security efforts, and users are encouraged to exercise caution. The security manager leads this effort.

A security manager must:

1. Communicate to employees that protecting the system is not only in the organization's interests, but also in the best interest of users.

2. Increase employee awareness of security issues.

3. Provide for appropriate employee security training.

4. Monitor user activity to assess security implementation.

4.2 Commonly Asked Questions

Q. Can an organization make do without hiring a security manager?
A. Yes, but while a security manager doesn't always need to be hired (especially in smaller organizations), someone must perform the functions of security management all the same. Many organizations prefer to hire a systems administrator and include security management as one of his or her primary duties. This is an acceptable strategy as long as the administrator has sufficient time to dedicate to security management. If, however, routine administrative functions take up a considerable part of an administrator's work day, the organization will be better served by having someone who is able to focus on system security.

Q. Wouldn't assigning an executive to the security manager role show commitment to system security?

A. Not necessarily. Although executives have sufficient authority to be effective security managers, it is quite possible that they do not possess the technical expertise necessary for the job. Security managers are responsible for seeing that all aspects of system security are operational – a task that requires significant technical competence.

A secondary but important consideration is that managing system security can demand a great deal of time – time that policy makers and other top administrators may be unable to devote, given their essential duties. While it is imperative that top administrators are actively committed to security effectiveness, in most cases it makes sense that the day-to-day administration of system security be assigned to a security/systems professional.

Q. Where does the security manager fit into the organizational hierarchy?

A. Just as the title implies, security managers and system administrators are most often considered to serve in a management capacity. The important tasks of developing security regulations, training employees, and monitoring implementation require that the security manager be vested with substantial authority. While the security manager is not to be confused with an executive, he or she is the system "boss." If the security manager is not able to confidently address security miscues at even the highest levels of the organizational hierarchy, protecting system resources adequately is impossible.

4.3   Nurturing Support within the Organization

Even when an organization is committed to improving its information security, security managers often find themselves having to work harder than should be necessary to remind employees of the importance of each step in the security process. Fielding questions about the necessity of sometimes burdensome procedures or the expense of technical and training initiatives is an inevitable but important part of the security manager's job. Make no mistake about it, the security manager must not only administer security policy but must also champion it.

Gaining Management Support

Support for security at the managerial level is essential because security planning must be aligned within the context of broader company objectives and strategy. Management must make sure that the organization's business plans are adequately considered and that security policy conforms to existing rules, regulations, and laws to which the organization is subject. Management must ensure that adequate funding is budgeted. After all, every dollar that is invested in security, as necessary as it surely is, takes a dollar away from some other activity.

Security must be a joint effort among decision makers, technical employees, and all other personnel. While technical support personnel may have the best understanding of the ramifications of given technology initiatives, users implement policies and management enforces them. Policies that are neither implemented nor enforced are worthless. Real security requires strong, visible, and continued support from senior management as a group, as well as personal accountability and exemplary behavior from individual managers. If management ignores or circumvents security procedures, others will do likewise.

Management can encourage an atmosphere of security or they can undermine it. Their behavior will in large part determine whether employees are meticulous or careless about security. Employees have an ethical responsibility to maintain the security of confidential information entrusted to them, but they will not accept this responsibility without management support.

Ensuring User Support

Computers and networks are valuable tools to their users. Many people rely on them every day to do their jobs. When computer resources are not available, fulfilling job requirements can become considerably more difficult or impossible. One important role a security manager plays is communicating to employees that protecting the system is in their best interests, as well as those of the organization.

4.4   Planning for the Unexpected

Traditional computer security frequently relies heavily upon protecting systems from attack and minimizing the likelihood of software and equipment failure, but little attention is usually paid to how to handle an attack or failure once it actually occurs. The result is that when a problem does occur, many decisions are made in haste. Often, such decisions reflect this lack of forethought and don't contribute to tracking down the source of the incident, collecting evidence to be used in prosecution efforts, protecting the valuable information contained on the system, or preparing for system recovery.

A good policy whenever security is threatened, whether a disk crash, an external intruder attack, or natural disaster, is to have planned for potential adverse events in advance. The only way to be sure that you have planned in advance for such troubles is to plan now. You can never predict exactly when a security breach will happen. It could happen in a year, a month, or this afternoon. Planning for emergencies beforehand goes beyond "good policy." There is no substitute for security breach response planning and other more overarching contingency planning.

Security Breach Response Planning

There are three common responses to an attack on an information system: "protect and proceed," "pursue and prosecute," and "panic and pray." Either of the first two strategies, while clearly opposite in design, can be appropriate. The best approach depends on the nature of the security breach and the philosophy of the organization. The third approach, "panic and pray," is never an effective response. In fact, the entire rationale for contingency planning is to minimize the need for panic and prayer in the event of a security incident.

Protect and Proceed. If management fears that the site is particularly vulnerable to attack, it may choose a "protect and proceed" strategy. Upon detection of an attack, attempts are made to actively interfere with the intruder's penetration, prevent further encroachment, and begin immediate damage assessment and recovery. This process may involve shutting down facilities, closing off access to the network, or other drastic measures. The drawback is that unless the intruder is identified directly, he, she, or it may come back into the site via a different path, or may attack another site.

Pursue and Prosecute. This alternative to the "protect and proceed" approach adopts the opposite philosophy and goals. Here, the primary goal is to allow intruders to continue to access the system until they can be identified and have evidence of their unauthorized activities gathered against them. While this approach is endorsed by law enforcement agencies and prosecutors because of the evidence it can provide, the major drawback is that the system and its information remain open to potential damage while the organization is trying to identify the source and collect its evidence.

Prosecution is not the only possible outcome when an intruder is identified. If the culprit is an employee, the organization may choose to take internal disciplinary action.

Careful consideration must be given to both of these security breach response philosophies by site management. It is imperative that forethought and planning take place before a problem occurs, or employees may not know how to respond in the event of a real emergency.

In fact, the strategy eventually adopted might even be one of "it depends upon the circumstances." For example, an organization might be willing to accept the additional risks of allowing an intruder to access "honey pot" records (false and/or non-sensitive information) while he or she is incriminating himself (or herself) and being identified.

On the other hand, the organization might decide that threats that could access confidential employee records or other sensitive information must be thwarted immediately because the potential cost of disclosure is not worth the benefit of capturing the intruder. Regardless of the approach selected, the pros and cons must be examined thoroughly by policymakers and users must be made aware of their responsibilities.

Another decision that management must make concerns any distinctions it chooses to make about different types of unauthorized users. Sites may find it helpful to define who it considers to be "insiders" and "outsiders" by referring to administrative, legal, or political boundaries. These boundaries imply what type of action should be taken to reprimand an offending party, from written censure to pressing legal charges. Security plans need to spell out these options and how an appropriate response will be determined if someone is caught behaving in an unauthorized manner.

Security plans should also include procedures for interaction with outside organizations, including law enforcement agencies and other security support sites. The procedures must identify the party authorized to make such contact (including backup authorities) and how it should be handled.

Contingency Planning

Hard drives will crash, electrical surges will zap data, and files will be erased accidentally. General system security (chapters 5.0 – 9.0) is designed and implemented to protect an organization from these disturbing events. But as valuable as locks, virus scanners, disk labels, and passwords can be, if a fire, flood, or sophisticated intruder knocks at your door uninvited, be prepared for trouble. Make no mistake about the term "contingency planning" – events that could happen will happen. It's just a matter of when.

Contingency planning does not protect the organization from a threat but, instead, explicitly details what is to happen if and when there is a penetration or the system goes down. It prepares the organization for recovery from a breach in security as quickly and efficiently as possible. In fact, another term for contingency-type planning is recovery planning. Planning for recovery from loss or downtime is not pessimistic as much as it is realistic.

Contingency planning can be complex and detailed. After all, it amounts to a blueprint for jump-starting the most important (or as some like to say, "mission-critical") aspects of the organization from scratch; perhaps, at another site and possibly during or, at best, immediately after a catastrophe has struck. The following outline includes recommended steps and considerations for effectively and completely preparing a contingency plan. As with all other guidelines offered in this document, each organization (and its security manager and policymakers) will need to consider these recommendations and customize them to meet their unique needs.

When building the contingency planning team, include:

- Key policymakers;
- The security manager;
- Departmental management;
- Technical support;
- End users;
- Other representative employees;
- Local authorities; and
- Key outside contacts (e.g., contractors and suppliers).

You will need:

- An exhaustive list of critical activities performed within the organization (which you should have done at the risk assessment stage);
- An accurate estimate of the minimum space and equipment necessary for restoring essential operations;
- A time frame for starting initial operations after a security incident; and
- A list of key personnel and their responsibilities.

Contingency planning should be as specific as possible. (Example: If threat "a" happens, the organization's response is "b"; if "c" happens, its response is "d".)

Perform and/or delegate the following duties as part of contingency planning:

- Create an inventory of all assets, including information (data), software, hardware, documentation and supplies. Include item by item, the manufacturer's name, model, serial number, and other supporting evidence. Make a video scan of your facility, including close-ups. Keep it up-to-date and don't forget peripherals.

- Set up reciprocal agreements with other company sites (or for small organizations, agreements with suppliers or other noncompeting firms) to share equipment in the event of an emergency at one site. Organizations may also contract with vendors whose purpose is to provide backup facilities. The key is to have compatible hardware/software requirements (e.g., Mac-to-Mac or Windows-to-Windows).

- Make plans to procure hardware, software, and other equipment as necessary to ensure that mission-critical activities are resumed with minimal delay. Keep in mind that old equipment that you have replaced may no longer ideally meet your needs, but might suffice in a pinch if it still meets your minimum requirements.

- Establish contractual agreements with "hot" and "cold" backup sites as appropriate.

    a. A "hot" site is an offsite facility that includes computers, backed up data, etc. (everything necessary for resuming operations)

    b. A "cold" site is an offsite facility that includes everything necessary for resuming operations with the exception of actual computers (if some delay is acceptable, then the expense can be incurred when and only when necessary)

- Identify alternative meeting and start-up locations to be used in case regular facilities are damaged or destroyed.

- Prepare directions to all off-site locations (if and when moving off-site is actually required).

- Establish procedures for obtaining off-site backup records (i.e., who, what, where, how, and under whose direction).

- Gather and safeguard contact information and procedures for communicating with key personnel, suppliers, and other important contacts.

- Arrange with manufacturers to provide priority delivery of emergency orders.

- Locate support resources that might be needed (e.g., equipment repair, trucking, and cleaning companies).

- Establish emergency agreements with data recovery specialists.

- Arrange for uninterrupted site security with local police and fire departments.

Specify the following within the contingency plan:

- Individual roles and responsibilities- by name and job title so that everyone knows exactly what needs to be done.

- Actions to be taken in advance of an occurrence or undesirable event.

- Actions to be taken at the onset of an undesirable event to limit damage, loss, and compromise.

- Actions to be taken to restore critical functions.

- Actions to be taken to reestablish normal operations.

Test the plan:

- Test the plan frequently and completely.

- Analyze test results to determine further needs (e.g., more training and better backup storage).

Periodically try to restore files that have been backed up (be sure to make secondary backups so that you are not risking your only backup copy of the data, but otherwise make the process identical to a real emergency). Deal with damage appropriately:

- If a disaster actually occurs, document all costs (even interim assessment costs) and videotape the damage (to serve as proof of loss).

- Don't do anything about water damage to technical equipment except immediately contact professional recovery technicians.

- Be prepared to overcome downtime on your own- insurance settlements can take time to be resolved. Once settled, rebuilding, repurchasing, and reinstalling can take even more time, so don't expect that anything short of being completely prepared will get your office rolling again in a reasonable amount of time.

Give consideration to other significant issues:

- Don't make the plan unnecessarily complicated.

- Make one individual responsible for maintaining the plan, but have it structured so that others are authorized and prepared to implement it if needed.

- Keep the plan in a secure but convenient location (multiple locations for multiple users) so that it can be accessed as needed.

- Update the plan regularly and whenever changes are made to your system.

- Recognize that people *always* come before equipment, information, or mission.

4.5   Testing and Review

Most organizations undergo some sort of financial auditing as a regular part of their fiscal life. Likewise, security audits are an important part of running any computing environment. A complete security audit should include an examination of any policies that affect or are affected by system security, as well as a thorough test of each mechanism that is in place to enforce said policies. After all, a plan isn't much good if it can't be implemented; and the only way to really be sure that security policies and mechanisms are being implemented properly is through extensive testing (or during a real emergency, at which point it is too late to correct shortcomings).

Keep in mind that there are limits to reasonable testing. The purpose of testing is to verify that security procedures are being implemented properly and meet critical policy goals, not to prove the absoluteness of every aspect of the system and policy.

Although security drills can't be scheduled every day of the week without seriously affecting office productivity (and probably morale), they should be conducted as frequently as is necessary to determine that security procedures are being implemented effectively. What kind of drills? Well, if your risk assessment (see chapter 2.0) identifies a particular type of natural disaster as a primary threat to your organization, then a drill based on that scenario could be constructed (e.g., a test to verify your backup and recovery mechanisms after an earthquake). On the other hand, if your greatest threat is from external intruders attempting to penetrate your system, a drill might be conducted that simulates a hacker attack in order to observe access countermeasures in action.

Although security can't be tested each day, testing must be performed frequently enough to verify the effectiveness of security initiatives.

If full-fledged security drills prove to be too time-consuming and disruptive to normal operations to be implemented on a large scale, consider testing individual features of the security system one at a time. Backup procedures can be examined to make sure that data can be recovered from storage tapes. Log files can be checked to make sure that information that is supposed to be maintained has been done so accurately. And other features of the system can be evaluated and analyzed as well. When a security drill is performed, great care should be given to devising the test. It is important to clearly identify what is being tested, how the test will be conducted, and what results are to be expected. All aspects of this process should be documented and included in, or as an adjunct to, the security policy.

Who performs security audits and drills?

- The organization's security professional(s);

- Employee teams (peer reviewers from within the organization);

- External reviewer teams (from cooperatives, consortia, or other partner organizations); and/or

- Hired external expert security consultants.

4.6   Implementation and Day-to-Day Maintenance

Security is more than keeping hackers and other trouble-makers out of your system. It involves a host of internal practices that serve to protect information in the case of system or disk failure. Some of the main activities security managers engage in on a day-to-day basis include administering backup and virus protection mechanisms, staying abreast of software updates, managing user accounts, and monitoring system activity.

Backups

Recommended practices concerning backup procedures are included in chapter 6.0.

It is almost impossible to over-emphasize the need for a good backup strategy. System backups not only protect the organization in the event of hardware failure or accidental deletions, but they also protect employees against unauthorized or accidental changes made to file contents. If an error is ever made (and we all know that they are), having the option of accessing an unaltered backup can be very appealing.

Reaching into those archives is a viable strategy only when backup files have been made properly. A backup of a file that contains the errors and/or viruses you are trying to eliminate usually isn't very helpful. Similarly, backup files need to be created at appropriate intervals and themselves must be well protected from damage and destruction.

Which type of backup strategy makes sense for your organization? That depends on the types and number of files in the system, the level of technical expertise within the organization, and the organization's commitment to security- information that can be found in the results of a well-executed risk assessment (see chapter 2.0). Even after needs unique to the organization have been identified, however, there are several more overarching issues that need to be considered before establishing backup plans:

- What amount of exposure to data loss can your organization comfortably tolerate?

- How old is your equipment? How reliable is it?

- What is the nature of your workplace? Do you process new data everyday?

To further evaluate the type of backup strategy that will best meet your organization's needs, also weigh the following factors:

- The time and effort required to make changes to the files: If changes to the file take only a little time, backing up those changes may not be imperative. If the changes require a great deal of work (e.g., entering data collected from a long form), don't risk that effort and instead back it up frequently.

- The time and effort required to back up files: If the actual backing up process requires little effort, why put it off? If it is time consuming, be more aware of proper timing.

- The value of the data: If the data are particularly valuable, back them up more often. If not, frequent backup may be less necessary.

- The rate of file change: If a document changes rapidly (e.g., because of the operator's speed in data entry), more frequent backup is probably needed.

You may choose a combination of complete and partial backup routines. However, when initiating any system, a complete backup should first be done to serve as a reference point.

In general, there are three types of backup strategies:

- A *complete* backup - backing up your *entire* hard drive. The advantage of this strategy is its completeness; you will get a snapshot of all your hard disk's contents.

- A *partial* backup - only backing up *selected* directories. This is useful and efficient if your work is concentrated in a specific area of your hard disk.

- An *incremental* backup - backing up *only* those files that have been *changed* since the last backup. It means using backup software to scan the files to see if they have been changed since the last backup cycle. If so, the file is saved; if not, the previous backup is maintained.

Above all, devise a backup strategy that is realistic for your organization's setting.

So, how are all of these factors integrated into an effective strategy for meeting an organization's needs? The answer is simple: use the information available in order to devise a backup plan that is most likely to be implemented. Whatever the solution might be, be creative enough to develop the strategy that is most likely to ensure that your data gets backed up. It is imperative to establish realistic policies based on your agency's environment.

In any case, set a backup schedule that fits your agency's needs and work style and stick with it. Here are a few examples of common backup routines:

- Twice daily: partial at noon, full at end of day.
- Once daily: full backup at end of day.
- Three times weekly: full backup at end of every other day.
- Twice weekly (i.e., full backup on Tuesday, partial on Thursday).
- Weekly full backup.
- Monthly full backup

A last major planning issue to consider is what to do with backup files once they have been created. The choice of backup location depends on the agency's needs, resources, and ability to secure its physical structure. Any single option, or mixture of options, can be chosen as long as they meet the site's needs and have a realistic chance of being implemented. Backup storage options include:

Option A: In the same room - great for easily recovering files after data loss, but bad if a threat gets in the room.

Option B: In the same building - less convenient for correcting mistakes, but physical separation increases security as a single event is less likely to damage everything

Option C: In a secure offsite location - while not convenient for quick data recovery, this is excellent for protection, especially if maintained in a secure facility.

Option C, "In a secure offsite location," is the best option from purely a security perspective. See chapter 5.0 for recommendations on securing a location.

Like all security decisions, selecting a location for off-site storage facilities should be based on risk assessment findings. If, for example, risk assessment shows that an earthquake is the threat of chief concern, locating an off-site storage facility 100 miles away but along the same fault line makes little sense. Similarly, if risk assessment identifies flood as a paramount threat, the location of off-site storage should be outside the same flood plain.

See chapter 6.0 for more specific guidelines about combating viruses and other rogue programming.

Virus Protection

Every PC, iPad, server, and mobile phone is connected to a network in some way and is, therefore, vulnerable to computer viruses, worms, Trojan horses, and other malware. It is the IT Security Manager's duty to develop and monitor procedures for preventing viruses and other rogue programs from infiltrating the system.

As a rule of thumb, no device from outside (including brand name, shrink-wrapped software) should ever be used on the enterprise network or any part of it without first having been scanned by an up-to-date antivirus program.

Software Updates

It goes without saying that computer systems have bugs. Even operating systems, upon which we depend for so much of the protection of our information, have bugs. Because of this, software publishers release updates on a frequent basis. Often these updates are security patches. It is important that whenever bugs are identified, the system manager takes all action possible to remedy them as soon as possible in order to minimize exposure.

A corollary to the "bug problem" deals with the source for obtaining upgrades to software. Many computer systems and software packages come with support from the manufacturer or supplier. Remedies that come directly from such a source tend to be trustworthy and can usually be implemented fairly quickly after receipt (and proper testing, no matter the source). Other sources, such as software posted on Internet sites, must be scrutinized more closely. As a general rule, trust manufacturer upgrades more than those that are posted on the Internet.

Effective security demands "checks and balances" so that every user, including the system administrator and security manager, is accountable for system activity—no one should be able to print his or her own paycheck without being monitored.

User Account Management

As stated throughout this chapter, a single person needs to have primary responsibility for an information system. For this person, the security manager or systems administrator, to effectively supervise the system, he or she needs to have access to all system components and files- access that is commonly referred to as "system administrator privileges." It is generally considered to be good practice to share system administrator access privileges with someone other than the system administrator, if for no other reason than to have emergency system access should the administrator ever become unavailable. But, having said this, such total access also requires total accountability, and should be limited to the fewest number of employees as is necessary to keep the system secure- after all, each person with total system access has the ability to override any and all security features.

Users other than the system manager (and an accountable replacement in case of emergency) should be given access to the system based solely on their job needs. Restricting user access minimizes the opportunities for accidents and other possibly inappropriate actions (see chapter 8.0). Through the use of user accounts, each authorized user is identified before accessing the system, and any action that is made by that user is classified as such.

Users should be given access only to files and systems that they need to do their jobs, and nothing more.

System Use Monitoring

System monitoring can be done by either the security manager or by software designed specifically for that purpose. Monitoring a system involves looking at all aspects of the system, identifying patterns of regular use, and searching for anything unusual. Most operating systems store information about system use in special files referred to as log files. Examination of these log files on a regular basis is often the first line of defense in detecting unauthorized use of the system.

System managers should:

- Compare lists of currently logged-in users with their login histories. Most users log in and out at roughly the same time each day. An account logged in outside the "normal" time for the account may be a sign of unauthorized activity and warrants investigation and explanation.

- Check system logs for unusual error messages. For example, a large number of failed login attempts in a short period of time may indicate that someone is trying to guess passwords.

While the security manager is responsible for monitoring user activity, doing so becomes much more feasible when working with and not against employees.

The task of systems monitoring is not as daunting as it may seem. Security managers can execute many monitoring tasks periodically throughout the day during even the briefest of free moments (e.g., while waiting on hold on the telephone). By executing the commands frequently, the manager will rapidly become familiar with seeing "normal" activities and become better able to spot things that are out of the ordinary.

The single most important thing about monitoring system use is that it be done regularly. Picking one day out of the month to monitor the system is not a solid security strategy, since a breach can take place in a matter of hours or even minutes. Only by maintaining a constant vigil can you expect to detect security violations in time to react to them—hence one appeal of monitoring software that, unlike even the most dedicated of administrators, is able to work 24 hours and seven days a week.

Despite the advantages that regular system monitoring provides, some intruders will be aware of the standard login mechanisms used by systems they are attacking and will actively attempt to evade these mechanisms. Thus, while regular monitoring is useful in detecting intruders, it does not guarantee that your system is secure and should not be considered an infallible method of detecting unauthorized use.

A Final (But Very Important) Question: *How does a security manager verify that the system for which he or she is responsible is actually secure?*

- Read this document and follow the security guidelines as outlined in the checklists at the end of each chapter.

- Practice, drill, and test each and every security measure being implemented.

4.7   Security Management Checklist

While it may be tempting to simply refer to the following checklist as your security plan, to do so would limit the effectiveness of the recommendations. They are most useful when initiated as part of a larger plan to develop and implement security policy throughout an organization. Other chapters in this document also address ways to customize policy to your organization's specific needs—a concept that should not be ignored if you want to maximize the effectiveness of any given guideline.

Security Management Checklist

- Has it been communicated to all employees that protecting the system is in everyone's best interests?

- Has an effort been made to increase employee awareness of security issues?

- Has appropriate employee security training been provided?

- Are security activities regularly monitored?

- Has management support been developed?

- Has user support been achieved?

- Has a security breach response plan been developed?

- Have contingency plans been developed to deal with significant and probable threats?

- Are response and contingency plans frequently and exhaustively tested?

- Has a backup plan been developed and implemented?

- Is a virus protection system in place?

- Are software updates tracked?

- Are user accounts managed appropriately?

- Is system use monitored appropriately?

[This page intentionally left blank]

5.0   Protecting Your System: Physical Security

5.1   Introduction to Physical Security

Most people think about locks, bars, alarms, and uniformed guards when they think about security. While these countermeasures are by no means the only precautions that need to be considered when trying to secure an information system, they are a perfectly logical place to begin. Physical security is a vital part of any security plan and is fundamental to all security efforts; without it information security, software security, user access security, and network security (see chapters 6.0 - 9.0) are considerably more difficult, if not impossible, to initiate. Physical security refers to the protection of building sites and equipment (and all information and software contained therein) from theft, vandalism, natural disaster, manmade catastrophes, and accidental damage (e.g., from electrical surges, extreme temperatures, and spilled coffee). It requires solid building construction, suitable emergency preparedness, reliable power supplies, adequate climate control, and appropriate protection from intruders.

5.2   Commonly Asked Questions

Q. How can I implement adequate site security when I am stuck in an old and decrepit facility?
A. Securing your site is usually the result of a series of compromises; what you need versus what you can afford and implement. Ideally, old and unusable buildings are replaced by modern and more serviceable facilities, but that is not always the case in the real world. If you find yourself in this situation, use the risk assessment process described in chapter 2.0 to identify your vulnerabilities and become aware of your preferred security solutions. Implement those solutions that you can, with the understanding that any steps you take make your system that much more secure than it had been. When it comes time to argue for new facilities, documenting those vulnerabilities that were not addressed earlier should contribute to your evidence of need.

Q. Even if we wanted to implement these physical security guidelines, how would we go about doing so?
A. Deciding which recommendations to adopt is the most important step. Your risk assessment results should arm you with the information required to make sound decisions. Your findings might even show that not every guideline is required to meet the specific needs of your site (and there will certainly be some variation based on need priorities). Once decided on, however, actually initiating a strategy is often as simple as raising employee awareness and insisting on adherence to regulations.

Some strategies might require basic "handyman" skills to install simple equipment (e.g., key locks, fire extinguishers, and surge protectors), while others definitely demand the services of consultants or contractors with special expertise (e.g., window bars, automatic fire equipment, and alarm systems). In any case, if the organization determines that it is necessary and feasible to implement a given security strategy, installing equipment should not require effort beyond routine procedures for completing internal work orders and hiring reputable contractors. Determining countermeasures often requires creativity: don't limit yourself to traditional solutions.

Q. What if my budget won't allow for hiring full-time security guards?
A. Hiring full-time guards is only one of many options for dealing with security monitoring activities; part-time employees on watch during particularly critical periods is another. So are video cameras and the use of other employees (from managers to receptionists) who are trained to monitor security as a part of their duties. The point is that by brainstorming a range of possible countermeasure solutions you can come up with several effective ways to monitor your workplace. The key is that the function is being performed. How it is done is secondary--and completely up to the organization and its unique requirements.

Guidelines for security policy development can be found in chapter 3.0.

5.3   Policy Issues

Physical security requires that building sites be safeguarded in a way that minimizes the risk of resource theft and destruction. To accomplish this, decision makers must be concerned about building construction, room assignments, emergency procedures, laws and regulations regarding equipment placement and use, power supplies, product handling, and relationships with outside contractors and agencies.

The physical plant must be satisfactorily secured to prevent those people who are not authorized from entering the site and using the equipment. A building does not need to feel like a fort to be safe. Well-conceived plans to secure a building can be initiated without unduly burdening your employees. After all, if they require access, they will have it; as long as they are aware of, and abide by, the organization's stated security policies and guidelines (see chapter 3.0). The only way to ensure this is to demand that before any person is given access to your system, they have first signed and returned a valid Security Agreement. This necessary security policy is too important to permit exceptions.

Physical Threats (Examples)

Examples of physical **threats** include:

- Natural events (e.g., floods, earthquakes, and tornados)
- Other environmental conditions (e.g., extreme temperatures, high humidity, heavy rains, and lightning)
- Intentional acts of destruction (e.g., theft, vandalism, and arson)
- Unintentionally destructive acts (e.g., spilled drinks, overloaded electrical outlets, and bad plumbing)

Physical Security Countermeasures

The following countermeasures address physical security concerns that could affect your site(s) and equipment. These strategies are recommended when risk assessment identifies or confirms the need to counter potential breaches in the physical security of your system.

Countermeasures come in a variety of sizes, shapes, and levels of complexity. This document endeavors to describe a range of strategies that are potentially applicable to life in organizations. In an effort to maintain this focus, countermeasures that are *unlikely* to be applied are *not* included here. If, after risk assessment, your security team determines that your organization requires high-end countermeasures (like retinal scanners or voice analyzers), you will need to refer to other security references and perhaps even need to hire a reliable technical consultant.

Create a Secure Environment: Building and Room Construction

- *Don't arouse unnecessary interest in your critical facilities:* A secure room should have "low" visibility (e.g., there should not be signs in front of the building and scattered throughout the hallways, announcing "expensive equipment and sensitive information this way").

- *Maximize structural protection:* A secure room should have full height, fireproof walls and ceilings.

- *Minimize external access (doors):* A secure room should only have one or two doors--they should be solid, fireproof, lockable, and observable by assigned security personnel. Doors to a secure room should *never* be propped open.

- *Minimize external access (windows):* A secure room should not have excessively large windows. All windows should have locks.

- *Maintain locking devices responsibly:* Locking doors and windows can be an effective security strategy as long as appropriate authorities maintain the keys and combinations responsibly. If there is a breach, each compromised lock should be changed.

- *Investigate options other than traditional keyhole locks for securing areas as is reasonable:* Based on the findings from your risk assessment (see chapter 2.0), consider alternative physical security strategies such as window bars, anti-theft cabling (i.e., an alarm sounds when any piece of equipment is disconnected from the system), magnetic key cards, and motion detectors. Recognize that some countermeasures may not be feasible due to the constraints of an existing facility.

- *Be prepared for fire emergencies:* In an ideal world, a secure room should be protected from fire by an automatic fire-fighting system. Note that water can damage electronic equipment, so carbon dioxide systems or halogen agents are recommended. If implemented, employees must be trained to use gas masks and other protective equipment. Manual fire fighting equipment (i.e., dry chemical fire extinguishers) should also be readily available and employees should be properly trained in their use.

- *Maintain a reasonable climate within the room:* A good rule of thumb is that if people are comfortable, then equipment is usually comfortable—but even if people have gone home for the night, room temperature and humidity cannot be allowed to reach extremes (i.e., it should be kept between 50 and 80 degrees Fahrenheit and 20 and 80 percent humidity). Note that it's not freezing temperatures that damage disks, but the condensation that forms when they thaw out.

- *Be particularly careful with non-essential materials in a secure computer room:* Technically, this guideline should read "no eating, drinking, or smoking near computers," but it is quite probably impossible to convince employees to implement such a regulation. Other non-essential materials that can cause problems in a secure environment and, therefore, should be eliminated include curtains, reams of paper, and other flammables. Locking critical equipment in a secure closet can be an excellent security strategy if risk assessment findings establish that it is warranted.

Guard Equipment:

- *Keep critical systems separate from general systems:* Prioritize equipment based on its criticality and its role in processing sensitive information (see chapter 2.0). Store it in secured areas based on those priorities.

- *House computer equipment wisely:* Equipment should not be able to be seen or reached from window and door openings, nor should it be housed near radiators, heating vents, air conditioners, or other duct work. Workstations that do not routinely display sensitive information should always be stored in open, visible spaces to prevent covert use.

- *Protect cabling, plugs, and other wires from foot traffic:* Tripping over loose wires is dangerous to both personnel and equipment.

- *Keep a record of your equipment:* Maintain up-to-date logs of equipment manufacturers, models, and serial numbers in a secure location. Be sure to include a list of all attached peripheral equipment. Consider videotaping the equipment (including close-up shots) as well. Such clear evidence of ownership can be helpful when dealing with insurance companies.

- *Maintain and repair equipment:* Have plans in place for emergency repair of critical equipment. Either have a trained repair technician on staff or make arrangements with someone who has ready access to the site when repair work is needed. If funds allow, consider setting up maintenance contracts for your critical equipment. Local computer suppliers often offer service contracts for equipment they sell, and many workstation and mainframe vendors also provide such services. Once you've set up the contract, be sure that contact information is readily available. Technical support telephone numbers, maintenance contract numbers, customer identification numbers, equipment serial numbers, and mail-in information should be posted or kept in a log book near the system for easy reference. Remember that computer repair technicians may be in a position to access your confidential information, so make sure that they know and follow your policies regarding outside employees and contractors who access your system.

Rebuff Theft:

- *Identify your equipment as yours in an overt way:* Mark your equipment in an obvious, permanent, and easily identifiable way. Use bright (even fluorescent) paint on keyboards, monitor backs and sides, and computer bodies. It may decrease the resale value of the components, but thieves cannot remove these types of identifiers as easily as they can adhesive labels.

- *Identify your equipment as yours in a covert way:* Label the inside of equipment with the organization's name and contact information to serve as powerful evidence of ownership.

- *Make unauthorized tampering with equipment difficult:* Replace regular body case screws with hex socket or torx screws or comparable devices that require a special tool to open them.

- *Limit and monitor access to equipment areas:* Keep an up-to-date list of personnel authorized to access sensitive areas. Never allow equipment to be moved or serviced unless the task is pre-authorized and the service personnel can produce an authentic work order and verify who they are. Require picture or other forms of identification if necessary. Logs of all such activity should be maintained. Staff should be trained to always err on the cautious side (and the organization must support such caution even when it proves to be inconvenient).

Attend to Portable Equipment:

- ***Never leave a laptop computer, tablet, or other readily portable device unattended!*** Small, expensive things often disappear very quickly – even more so from public places and vehicles. While the X-ray conveyor belt is the preferred way of transporting a laptop through airport security (compared to subjecting the computer to the magnetic fields of walk-through or wand scanners), it is also a prime place for theft. Thieves love to "inadvertently" pick up the wrong bag and disappear while passengers are fumbling through their pockets to find the loose coins that keep setting off the metal detectors. ***Never take your eyes off your portable devices and never let them get beyond your reach!*** Require laptop users to read the recommended travel guidelines that should come with equipment documentation.

- *Store laptop computers wisely:* Secure laptops in a hotel safe rather than a hotel room, in a hotel room rather than a car, and in a car trunk rather than the back seat.

- *Stow laptop computers appropriately:* Just because a car trunk is safer than the back seat doesn't mean that the laptop won't be damaged by an unsecured tire jack. Even if the machine isn't stolen, it can be ruined all the same. Stow the laptop and its battery safely!

- *Don't leave a laptop computer in a car trunk overnight or for long periods of time:* In cold weather, condensation can form and damage the machine. In warm weather, high temperatures (amplified by the confined space) can also damage hard drives.

Regulate Power Supplies:

- *Be prepared for fluctuations in the electrical power supply.* Either (1) plug all electrical equipment into surge suppressors or electrical power filters or (2) use an uninterruptible power source (UPS) to serve as an auxiliary electrical supply in the event of a power outage.

- *Pay attention to the manufacturer's recommendations for storing portable computer batteries*: Laptop and mobile phone batteries carry live charges and are capable of igniting a fire by discharging if handled improperly.

- *Protect power supplies from environmental threats:* Consider having a professional electrician design or redesign your electrical system to better withstand fires, floods, and other natural and manmade disasters.

- *Select outlet use carefully:* Although little thought generally goes into plugging equipment into an outlet, machines that draw heavily from a power source can affect, and be affected by, smaller equipment that draws energy from the same outlet.

- *Guard against the negative effects of static electricity in the office place:* Install anti-static carpeting and anti-static pads, use anti-static sprays, and encourage employees to use grounding straps or discharge static electricity elsewhere before using, modifying, or repairing computer equipment.

Protect Output:

- *Keep photocopiers, fax machines, and scanners in public view:* These types of equipment are very powerful tools for disseminating information--so powerful, in fact, that their use must be monitored.

- *Assign printers to users with similar security clearances:* You don't want employees looking at sensitive financial information (e.g., employee salaries) or confidential employee information (like SSN's) while they're waiting for their documents to print. It is better to dedicate a printer to the Director of Finance than to have sensitive data scattered around a general use printer. Don't hesitate to put printers in locked rooms, if that is what circumstances dictate.

- *Label printed information appropriately:* Confidential printouts should be clearly identified as such.

- *Demand suitable security procedures of common carriers when shipping/receiving confidential information:* Mail, delivery, messenger, and courier services should be required to meet your organization's security standards when handling your confidential information.

- *Dispose of confidential waste adequately:* Print copies of confidential information should not be placed in common dumpsters unless shredded. (Comparable requirements for discarding electronic copies of confidential information can be found in chapter 6.0.)

5.4   Physical Security Checklist

While it may be tempting to simply refer to the following checklist as your security plan, to do so would limit the effectiveness of the recommendations. They are most useful when initiated as part of a larger plan to develop and implement security policy throughout an organization. Other chapters in this document also address ways to customize policy to your organization's specific needs – a concept that should not be ignored if you want to maximize the effectiveness of any given guideline.

Physical Security Checklist

Create a Secure Environment: Building and Room Construction

- Does each secure room or facility have low visibility (e.g., no unnecessary signs)?
- Has the room or facility been constructed with full-height walls?
- Has the room or facility been constructed with a fireproof ceiling?
- Are there two or fewer doorways?
- Are doors solid and fireproof?
- Are doors equipped with locks?
- Are window openings to secure areas kept as small as possible?
- Are windows equipped with locks?
- Are keys and combinations to door and window locks secured responsibly?
- Have alternatives to traditional lock and key security measures (e.g., bars, anti-theft cabling, magnetic key cards, and motion detectors) been considered?
- Have both automatic and manual fire-fighting equipment been properly installed and regularly inspected?
- Are personnel properly trained for fire emergencies?
- Are acceptable room temperatures always maintained (i.e., between 50 and 80 degrees Fahrenheit)?
- Are acceptable humidity ranges always maintained (i.e., between 20 and 80 percent)?
- Are eating, drinking, and smoking regulations in place and enforced?
- Has all non-essential, potentially flammable, material (e.g., curtains and stacks of computer paper) been removed from secure areas?

Guard Equipment

- Has equipment been identified as critical or general use, and segregated appropriately?
- Is equipment housed out of sight and reach from doors and windows, and away from radiators, heating vents, air conditioners, and other duct work?
- Are plugs, cabling, and other wires protected from foot traffic?
- Are up-to-date records of all equipment brand names, model names, and serial numbers kept in a secure location?
- Have qualified technicians (staff or vendors) been identified to repair critical equipment if and when it fails?

- Has contact information for repair technicians (e.g., telephone numbers, customer numbers, maintenance contract numbers) been stored in a secure but accessible place?

- Are repair workers and outside technicians required to adhere to the organization's security policies concerning sensitive information?

Rebuff Theft

- Has all equipment been labeled in a way that clearly - and permanently - identifies its owner (i.e., the company name)?

- Has all equipment been labeled in a way that only authorized employees would know to what to look for and where (i.e., infrared marker or microengraving inside the cover)?

- Have steps been taken to make it difficult for unauthorized people to tamper with equipment (e.g., by replacing slotted or Phillips-head case screws with hex socket or Torx screws)?

- Have security personnel been provided up-to-date lists of personnel and their respective access authority?

- Are security personnel required to verify identification of unknown people before permitting access to facilities?

- Are security staffers required to maintain a log of all equipment taken in and out of secure areas?

Attend to Portable Equipment and Computers

- Do users know not to leave laptops and other portable equipment unattended outside of the office?

- Do users know and follow proper transportation and storage procedures for laptops and other portable equipment?

Regulate Power Supplies

- Are surge protectors or other current filters/conditioners used with all equipment?

- Are uninterruptible power supplies (UPSs) in place for critical systems and equipment?

- Have power supplies been "insulated" from environmental threats by a professional electrician?

- Has consideration been given to the use of electrical outlets so as to avoid overloading?

- Are the negative effects of static electricity minimized through the use of anti-static carpeting, pads, and sprays as necessary?

Protect Output

- Are photocopiers, fax machines, and scanners kept in open view?

- Are printers assigned to users with similar security clearances?

- Is every printed copy of confidential information labeled "confidential"?

- Are outside delivery services required to adhere to security practices when transporting sensitive information?

- Are all paper copies of sensitive information shredded before being discarded?

[This page intentionally left blank]

6.0   Protecting Your System: Information Security

The terms "data" and "information" are often used synonymously when, in reality, information refers to "data that have meaning". In other words, "27 percent" is not information in and of itself. Only if it's in context does it become information (i.e., "sales were up 27% from last year") and only then does it have value.

6.1   Introduction to Information Security

As stated throughout this document, one of an organization's most valuable assets is its information. Local, state, and federal laws require that certain types of information (e.g., individual payroll records) be protected from unauthorized release. This facet of information security is often referred to as protecting confidentiality. While confidentiality is sometimes mandated by law, common sense and good practice suggest that even non-confidential information in a system should be protected as well - not necessarily from unauthorized release as much as from unauthorized modification and unacceptable influences on its accessibility.

Components of Information Security

- **Confidentiality:** Preventing unauthorized disclosure and use of information.

- **Integrity:** Preventing unauthorized creation, modification, or deletion of information.

- **Availability:** Preventing unauthorized delay or denial of information.

6.2   Commonly Asked Questions

Q. If an organization maintains physical, software, and user access security, isn't information security addressed by default?
A. Yes and no. Information backups and their storage are surely safer when the building is secure, software is used properly, and unauthorized users are effectively restricted. However, these security features are meaningless if the information that is being backed up and stored wasn't maintained in a sound way in the first place. While there is no doubt that physical, software, and user access security strategies all contribute to protecting information, ignoring those initiatives that are aimed directly at securing information is not a wise plan. While encryption prevents others from reading your information, encrypted files can still be damaged or destroyed so that they are no longer of any use to you.

Q. Isn't there software that can protect my information?
A. Yes, a variety of software products can help your organization in its effort to secure its information and system, but only a thorough, well-conceived, and committed effort to develop and implement an overarching security plan will prove effective in the long run.

Q. Doesn't it make sense to encrypt all information?
A. Not necessarily. Encryption and decryption are time consuming. If information is confidential, additional time for encrypting and decrypting makes sense but if information isn't confidential, why slow down processing speed for an unnecessary step? While encryption is a good practice for sensitive information or information that is

transmitted over unsecured lines, it is not a complete security strategy in itself. Encrypting information protects files from breaches in confidentiality, but the risks of unauthorized or accidental modification (including destruction) and/or denial of use are still real.

Guidelines for security policy development can be found in chapter 3.0.

6.3   Policy Issues

Perhaps more than any other aspect of system security, protecting information requires specific procedural and behavioral activities. Information security requires that data files be properly created, labeled, stored, and backed up. If you consider the number of files that each employee uses, these tasks clearly constitute a significant undertaking. Policymakers can positively affect this effort by conducting an accurate risk assessment (including properly identifying sensitive information maintained in the system). They should also provide organizational support to the security manager as he or she implements and monitors security regulations. The security manager must be given the authority and budget necessary for training staff and enforcing information security procedures at all levels of the organization.

A final consideration for policymakers is information retention and disposal. All information has a finite life cycle, and policymakers should make sure that mechanisms are in place to ensure that information that is no longer of use is disposed of properly.

6.4   Information Threats

As discussed more completely in chapter 2.0, a threat is any action, actor, or event that contributes to risk. Examples of information threats include:

- Natural events (e.g., lightning strikes, aging and dirty media)

- Intentional acts of destruction (e.g., hacking and viruses)

- Unintentionally destructive acts (e.g., accidental downloading of computer viruses, programming errors, and unwise use of magnetic materials in the office)

6.5   Information Security Countermeasures

The following countermeasures address information security concerns that could affect your site(s). These strategies are recommended when risk assessment identifies or confirms the need to counter potential breaches in your system's information security.

Transmit Information Securely (including email):

- *Use email only for routine office communication:* Never send sensitive information as email. If email absolutely must be used, encrypt the file and send it as an attachment rather than in the text of the email message.

- *Encrypt everything before it leaves your workstation:* Even your password needs to be encrypted before leaving the workstation on its way to the network server-otherwise it could be intercepted as it travels network connections.

- *Physically protect your data encryption devices and keys:* Store them away from the computer but remember where you put them. Use the same common-sense principles of protection you give your bank card's personal identification number (PIN).

- *Inform employees that all messages sent with or over the organization's computers belong to the organization:* This is a nice way of saying that everything in the office is subject to monitoring.

- *Use dial-up communication only when necessary:* Do so only after the line has been satisfactorily evaluated for security. Do not publicly list dial-up communication telephone numbers.

- *Confirm that outside networks from which there are dial-ins satisfy your security requirements:* Install automatic terminal identification, dial-back, and encryption features (technical schemes that protect transmissions to and from off-site users).

- *Verify the receiver's authenticity before sending information anywhere:* Ensure that users on the receiving end are who they represent themselves to be by verifying:

    a. *Something they should know* (i.e., a password or encryption key). This is the least expensive measure but also the least secure.

    b. *Something they should have*—e.g., an electronic keycard or smart card.

    c. *Something they are*—biometrics like fingerprinting, voice recognition, and retinal scans; these strategies are more expensive but also more secure.

Consider setting up pre-arranged transmission times with regular information trading partners: If you know to expect transmissions from your trading partners at specific times and suddenly find yourself receiving a message at a different time, you'll know to scrutinize that message more closely. Is it really your trading partner sending the message? Why has the pre-arranged time been ignored? Has the message been intercepted and consequently knocked off schedule?

Maintain security when shipping and receiving materials: When sending sensitive information through the mail, or by messenger or courier, require that all outside service providers meet or exceed your security requirements.

Select only those countermeasures that meet perceived needs as identified during risk assessment and support security policy.

Present Information for Use in a Secure and Protected Way:

- *Practice "views" and "table-design" applications*: A "view" selects only certain fields within a table of information for display, based on the user's access rights. Other table fields are excluded from the user's view and are thus protected from use. For example, although an employee record system may contain a range of information about each individual, departmental managers can view only information related to their work and accounting staff can view only information related to their work. This type of system maintains information much more securely than traditional paper systems, while at the same time increasing statistical utility and accountability options.

- *Use "key identifiers" to link segregated information:* If record information is maintained in a segregated manner for security purposes (for example, keep accounting information in a different database – or even a different domain – than customer information), a common file identifier (a primary key on one file and a secondary key on a related file) can be used to match records without unnecessarily divulging identities and compromising confidentiality.

Back up information appropriately (chapter 4.0):

- *Back up not only information, but also the programs you use to access information:* Back up operating system utilities so that you retain access to them even if your hard drive goes down. Also maintain current copies of critical application software and documentation as securely as if they were sensitive data.

  Caution! Some proprietary software providers may limit an organization's legal right to make copies of programs, but most allow for responsible backup procedures. Check with your software provider.

- *Consider using backup software that includes an encryption option when backing up sensitive information:* Encryption provides additional security that is well worth the extra effort, since it ensures that even if unauthorized users access your backup files, they still can't break confidentiality without also having access to your encryption key. If you adopt this recommendation, be sure to change your encryption key regularly.

- *Verify that your backups are written to the disk or tape accurately:* Choose a backup program that has a verification feature.

- *Rotate backup tapes:* Although backup tapes are usually quite reliable, they tend to lose data over time when under constant use. Retire tapes after two to three months of regular use (e.g., about 60 uses) to a backup activity that requires less regular use (e.g., program backups). Also note that routine tape drive cleaning can result in longer tape life.

- *Maintain a log of all backup dates, locations, and responsible personnel:* Accountability is an excellent motivator for getting things done properly. Remember to store the logs securely.

- *Avoid excessive back up:* Too many backup files can confuse users and thereby increase the possibility of exposing sensitive information. Clear hard drives, servers, and other storage media that contain old backup files to save space once you have properly secured (and verified) the last complete and partial backup.

- *Test your backup system:* This point has been made numerous times throughout this document but it truly cannot be overemphasized!

- *Check for storage medium/format obsolescence:* Backed up data are useless if in the time since they were stored, the media and equipment used to back them up has become unavailable.

- *Consider using cloud storage:* This can alleviate the risk of having all data backed up in-house but it poses other security risks (data integrity, security, and accessibility).

Many organizations prefer that users *back up only their own data files* - leaving software and operating system backups in the responsible hands of the security manager or system administrator.

Store Information Properly (chapter 5.0):

- *Apply recommended storage principles as found in this document to both original and backup files alike:* Backup files require the same levels of security as do the master files (e.g., if the original file is confidential, so is its backup).

- *Clearly label disks, tapes, containers, cabinets, and other storage devices:* Contents and sensitivity should be prominently marked so that there is less chance of mistaken identity.

- *Segregate sensitive information:* Never store sensitive information in such a way that it commingles with other data on floppy disks or other removable data storage media.

- *Restrict handling of sensitive information to authorized personnel:* Information, programs, and other data should be entered into, or exported from, the system only through acceptable channels and by staff with appropriate clearance.

- *Write-protect important files:* Write-protection limits accidental or malicious modification of files. Note that while write-protection is effective against some viruses, it is by no means adequate virus protection in itself.

- *Communicate clearly and immediately about security concerns:* Train staff to promptly notify the system administrator/security manager when data are – or are suspected of being – lost or damaged.

- *Create a media library if possible:* Storing backups and sensitive material in a single location allows for security to be concentrated (and perhaps even intensified). Note, however, that an on-site media library is not a substitute for off-site backup protection.

Dispose of Information in a Timely and Thorough Manner:

- *Institute a specific information retention and disposal policy as determined by the organization's needs and legal requirements:* All data have a finite life cycle. Consult local, federal, and state regulations for guidance before implementing the following:

- Establish a realistic retention policy.

- Mark files to indicate the contents, their expected life cycle, and appropriate destruction dates.

- Do not simply erase or reformat media, but overwrite it with random binary code. Sophisticated users can still access information even after it has been erased or reformatted, whereas overwriting actually replaces the discarded information.

- Consider degaussing (erasing information on a magnetic media by introducing it to a stronger magnetic field) as an option.

- Burn, shred, or otherwise physically destroy storage media (e.g., paper) that cannot be effectively overwritten or degaussed.

- *Clean tapes, disks, and hard drives that have stored sensitive data before reassigning them:* Never share disks that have held sensitive data unless they have been properly cleaned. Also remember to clean magnetic storage media before returning it to a vendor for trade-ins or disposal.

Retaining data beyond its useful life exposes the organization to unnecessary risk. Even if a vendor replaces a hard drive, require that the old one be returned so that you can verify that it has been cleaned and disposed of properly.

6.6   Information Security Checklist

While it may be tempting to refer to the following checklist as your security plan, to do so would limit the effectiveness of the recommendations. They are most useful when initiated as part of a larger plan to develop and implement security policy throughout an organization. Other chapters in this document also address ways to customize policy to your organization's specific needs-a concept that should not be ignored if you want to maximize the effectiveness of any given guideline.

Information Security Checklist

Transmit Information Securely (including email)

- Is email used for only the most routine of non-sensitive office communication?

- Is everything, including passwords, encrypted before leaving user workstations?

- Are encryption keys properly secured?

- Have policy goals and objectives been translated into organizational security regulations that are designed to modify staff behavior?

- Is dial-up communication avoided as much as is possible?

- Are outside networks required to meet your security expectations?

- Is the identity of information recipients verified before transmission?

- Have times for information transmission been pre-arranged with regular trading partners?

- Are security issues considered and addressed before shipping sensitive materials?

Present Information for Use in a Secure and Protected Way

- Are "views" and "table-design" applications being practiced?

- Are "key identifiers" used when linking segregated records?

Backup Information Appropriately

- Are programs that are used to access information backed up?

- Does backup software include an encryption option that is used?

- Does backup software include a verification feature that is used?

- Are backup tapes retired after a reasonable amount of use?

- Is a log of all backup dates, locations, and responsible personnel kept and maintained securely?

- Are storage media and formats checked for obsolescence?

- Is an effort made to avoid excessive back up (i.e., are old backups removed to avoid "clutter")?

- Does the backup system pass regularly administered tests of its effectiveness?

Store Information Properly

- Are recommended storage principles applied to master files and their backups alike?

- Are disks, tapes, containers, cabinets, and other storage devices clearly labeled?

- Is sensitive information segregated (i.e., is it maintained separately from normal use information at all times)?

- Is the handling of sensitive information restricted to authorized personnel?

- Are important files write-protected?

- Do employees know to communicate security concerns immediately?

- Has a secure media library been created as is possible?

Dispose of Information in a Timely and Thorough Manner

- Has an information retention and disposal policy been implemented?

- Are magnetic media that contain sensitive information properly cleaned before reuse or disposal?

[This page intentionally left blank]

7.0 Protecting Your System: Software Security

7.1 Introduction to Software Security

Saying that software is an integral part of your computer system is like saying that the steering wheel is an integral part of an automobile. It's an understatement if ever there was one. All the technological and mechanical muscle in the world is virtually useless without a way of controlling it—and software is precisely the means by which users control what they are doing on a computer system. Application software affects all areas of computing. It defines the concepts of word processing and spreadsheets, and allows for email and other forms of electronic communication that have recently become so prevalent. Its security, therefore, is essential to the overall security of your information and system.

7.2 Commonly Asked Questions

Q. Doesn't software come with its own security?
A. Many types of software include security components within their programming, but, generally speaking, these safeguards are fairly simple in nature. In most cases, they can be circumvented easily by skilled intruders. Effective software security requires a number of well planned practices in software procurement, development, and use that must be realized through staff activity and organizational commitment.

Q. Isn't software security starting to get too technical for policy makers?
A. Not necessarily. Effective software security can demand technical knowledge and experience, but policymakers can overcome these concerns by including technical support staff in the policy development process.

Q. How can an organization overcome programming errors and viruses?
A. Any new or modified software has the potential to have programming errors. In fact, errors are a normal part of the product refinement process. Viruses, while not a normal part of any healthy process, have also become far from uncommon. But a rigorous pre-implementation testing routine (developed in coordination with technical staff) can diagnose these problems before they damage the organization's system or information. It is imperative that such testing be done on dedicated computers that are not connected to the organization's network and with dummy data in order to minimize risk.

7.3 Policy Issues

Software security requires policies on software management, acquisition and development, and pre-implementation training. Unlike many personnel aspects of system security, appropriate software use requires that products and equipment match in a range of technical specifications. Policymakers may, therefore, choose to pay close attention to the advice of technical staff when considering software issues and generating policy. Software users (virtually anyone who turns on a computer) should also be surveyed about the types of software required to perform their jobs, the ways in which those pieces of software are used, and the kinds and amount of training that are necessary to properly prepare staff to meet their job requirements.

7.4   Software Threats (Examples)

As discussed more completely in chapter 2.0, a threat is any action, actor, or event that contributes to risk.

Examples of software threats include:

- Natural events (e.g., aging and dirty media)

- Intentional acts of destruction (e.g., hacking, creation of computer viruses, and copyright infringement)

- Unintentionally destructive acts (e.g., accidental downloading of computer viruses, losing instructions, and programming errors)

7.5   Software Security Countermeasures

Test backup files periodically, to ensure that they can be restored and that data integrity is maintained.

Coordinate (and Centralize) the Organization's Software Management:

- Centrally control all critical system software: (1) Know what programs are being added, deleted, and changed in your system; (2) control all additions, deletions, and modifications; and (3) take all necessary steps to ensure that new and old software work together appropriately (i.e., that they interface).

- *Initiate formal testing and certification procedures for new/modified software:* Require that any new or modified software be tested rigorously and certified as fully operational before releasing it for general use.

- *Maintain an off-site location for critical backup copies* (see chapter 6.0): Backups of any and all software, databases, and information that serve critical functions should reside in a secure off-site location and be readily accessible when and if needed. Backups require the same level of protection as master files (i.e., if the files are designated as confidential, treat the backups as confidential as well). Periodically check that the backups function as expected so that there are no surprises if and when they are really needed.

- *Secure master copies of software and associated documentation:* If master copies and/or their instructions are lost, an entire system can be put in jeopardy. But while documentation must be protected, it must also be kept available to users who have legitimate questions about proper use of the software.

- *Never lend or give proprietary software to unlicensed users:* By definition, proprietary software means that it isn't yours to give—someone else makes their living by selling it.

- *Tolerate nothing but licensed and organizationally approved software on workplace equipment:* Games are fun and software from home can sometimes be useful, but they have no place on organizational equipment unless explicitly authorized.

- *Monitor software use (and hard drive inventories) to counter possible copyright infringements:* Unlicensed software on organizational equipment puts the entire organization at risk for fines and other penalties stemming from copyright violations. Software inventories should include the name of the manufacturer, version number, assigned computer (as applicable), and function.

- *Permit only authorized personnel to install software:* In this way you know exactly what software is being introduced to your system and that it is being installed properly.

- *Train employees on software use and security policies:* The best designed software for accessing and manipulating information is useless if employees are unable to use it properly.

Regulate Software Acquisition and Development:

- *Define security needs before purchasing or developing new software*: After identifying your needs through a risk assessment (see chapter 2.0), the findings should be used as part of the criteria by which you select appropriate software products.

- *Require written authorization before anyone tampers with software*: Any changes to software requires a paper trail of what, why, and under whose auspices software was modified.

- *Conduct design reviews throughout the development process*: Continued feedback from expected users during development ensures that the product will satisfy functional specifications and security requirements.

- *Modify archived copies of software (not the copy that is up and running on the system)*: By doing so, you can be sure that you are not putting active applications and files at risk. Once the modified copy passes testing and is certified as operational, then and only then should it be loaded onto the system for use with "live" data.

- *Require that all software developed or modified by a programmer be reviewed by a second, independent programmer:* This review should verify that all code is appropriate and correct.

- *Maintain master files of all developed software independent of the programmer*: Software belongs to the organization, not the programmer. By controlling all original copies, the organization clearly guarantees this ownership.

- *Require documentation for all new or revised programming*: Requisite documentation includes the name of the developer, the name of the programming language, the development date, the revision number, and the location of the master copy (i.e., the source code).

- *Verify authenticity of public programs*: If software downloaded from the Internet must be used with sensitive information, be sure that it has not been tampered with by checking for a digital signature to verify its authenticity.

While the vast majority of employees are trustworthy, they are not immune to accidents or other events that could keep them from showing up for work some day. The organization is entitled to, and should, keep updated copies of everyone's work files.

Because new products are bound to have imperfections, software's cutting edge is often referred to (only half jokingly) as its "bleeding edge." For that reason, use of "cutting edge" software for mission-critical activities should be avoided.

Thoroughly Test Newly Acquired and Developed Software:

- *Specifically search for common types of computer viruses*: Have technical employees check for common viruses such as Trojan Horses and worms.

- *Verify that all software user functions are working properly before putting the software into operation*: Check that new software meets anticipated user needs, current system requirements, and all organizational security standards. This recommendation is also applicable when upgrading software.

- *Back up old files before installing new software and software upgrades*: Don't risk the latest copies of your files/records until you're certain that your new versions are up and running properly.

- *Never test application software with "live" data!* Don't risk losing real information if the software doesn't pass the test. Instead, verify software integrity with dummy files and/or copies of non-sensitive files.

- *Test on independent machines*: Initial software testing should never occur on computers that are connected to the system. By maintaining a separate test environment, the entire system is not at risk if the software malfunctions.

- *Run existing and upgraded versions of software in parallel during final testing phases*: By running the old software at the same time as the new and improved software, you can verify that the new versions generate the same or better results than the existing system.

7.6   Software Security Checklist

While it may be tempting to simply refer to the following checklist as your security plan, to do so would limit the effectiveness of the recommendations. They are most useful when initiated as part of a larger plan to develop and implement security policy within and throughout an organization. Other chapters in this document also address ways to customize policy to your organization's specific needs--a concept that should not be ignored if you want to maximize the effectiveness of any given guideline.

Software Security Checklist

Coordinate (and Centralize) Software Management

- Is critical system software controlled by central administration?

- Has a formal testing and certification procedure for new/modified software been developed and initiated?

- Are backups of critical software and information maintained in secure facilities at an off-site location?

- Have all master copies of software been properly secured?

- Has all software documentation been secured appropriately?
- Does the organization expressly forbid lending or giving proprietary software to unlicensed users?
- Does workplace equipment store and use only licensed and organizationally-approved software?
- Are software use and hard drive inventories monitored for copyright violations?
- Is installation of software limited to authorized personnel?
- Are employees adequately trained in software use and security?

Regulate Software Acquisition and Development

- Are risk assessment findings considered before purchasing and developing new software?
- Is written authorization required before any software is modified?
- Is software design reviewed throughout the development process?
- Are active applications and files (i.e., those actively running on the system) properly shielded from experimental/developmental software?
- Is all software that is created or modified by a programmer subjected to review by a second programmer?
- Are all master copies of internally developed software maintained by the organization and not the programmer?
- Is suitable documentation prepared for all newly developed software?
- Has all public software accessed via the Internet been verified for authenticity?

Thoroughly Test Newly Acquired and Developed Software

- Are common types of viruses searched for specifically during new software testing?
- Have all user functions been verified before new software is put into operation?
- Are all files backed up before installing and upgrading software?
- Are "live" data protected from new application testing?
- Is new application testing done on non-networked computers?
- Has old and new software been run in parallel to compare results?

[This page intentionally left blank]

8.0 Protecting Your System: User Access Security

8.1 Introduction to User Access Security

User access security refers to the collective procedures by which authorized users access a computer system and unauthorized users are kept from doing so. To make this distinction a little more realistic, understand that user access security limits even authorized users to those parts of the system that they are explicitly permitted to use (which, in turn, is based on their need-to-know). After all, there is no reason for someone in Payroll to be given clearance to confidential customer records.

While there is no question an organization has the right to protect its computing and information resources through user access security activities, users (whether authorized or not) have rights as well. Reasonable efforts must be made to inform all users, even uninvited hackers, that the system is being monitored and that unauthorized activity will be punished and/or prosecuted as deemed appropriate. If such an effort is not made, the organization may be invading the privacy rights of its intruders!

An excellent way of properly informing users of monitoring activities is through the opening screen that is presented to them. By reading a warning like the one that follows, users implicitly accept both the conditions of monitoring and punishment when they proceed to the next screen. Thus, the first screen any user sees when logging into a secure computer system should be something to the following effect:

Some believe you should never include the word "Welcome" as a part of the login process, because it implies that whoever is reading the word is *invited* to access the system. Instead, they feel it is better to use a greeting similar to the following:

WARNING!

This is a restricted network. Use of this network is monitored at all times and requires explicit permission from the network administrator. If you do not have this permission in writing, you are violating the regulations of this network and can and will be prosecuted to the full extent of the law. By continuing into this system, you are acknowledging that you are aware of and agree to these terms.

8.2 Commonly Asked Questions

Q. Is it possible to have a secure system if you have employees who telecommute or work otherwise non-traditional schedules?
A. Yes. While particular countermeasures might need to be adjusted to accommodate non-traditional schedules (e.g., the practice of limiting users to acceptable login times and locations), a system with telecommuters, frequent travelers, and other remote access users can still be secure. Doing so may require policymakers to think more creatively, but each security guideline needs to be customized to meet the organization's needs anyway (see chapter 2.0).

Q. Is the use of passwords an effective strategy for securing a system?
A. Just because password systems are the most prevalent authentication strategy currently being practiced doesn't mean that they have become any less effective. In fact, the reason for their popularity is precisely because they can be so useful in restricting system access. The major concern about password systems is not their technical integrity, but the degree to which (like many strategies) they rely upon proper implementation by users. While there are certainly more effective, (and more expensive) ways of restricting user access, if risk analysis determines that a password system meets organizational needs and is most cost-effective, you can feel confident about password protection as long as users are implementing the system properly—which, in turn, demands appropriate employee training (see chapter 10.0).

Q. Are all of these precautions necessary if an organization trusts its staff?
A. Absolutely. While the vast majority of system users are probably trustworthy, it doesn't mean that they're above having occasional computing accidents. After all, most system problems are the result of human mistake. By instituting security procedures, the organization protects not only the system and its information, but also each user who could at some point unintentionally damage a valued file. By knowing that "their" information is maintained in a secure fashion, employees will feel more comfortable and confident about their computing activities.

Initiating security procedures also benefits users by helping them protect their own files, decreasing the likelihood of their improperly releasing confidential information, and educating them in appropriate and inappropriate behavior.

8.3   Policy Issues

User access security demands that all persons (or systems) who engage network resources be required to identify themselves and prove that they are, in fact, who they claim to be. Users are subsequently limited to access to those files that they absolutely need to meet their job requirements, and no more.

To accomplish this, decision makers must establish policies regulating user account systems, user authentication practices, login procedures, physical security requirements, and remote access mechanisms. In addition, decision makers must consider the ubiquity of personal devices (e.g., tablets, smartphones); they should give thought to developing a "Bring your own device", or BYOD, policy.

Guidelines for security policy development can be found in chapter 3.0.

8.4   User Access Threats (Examples)

As discussed in chapter 2.0, a threat is any action, actor, or event that contributes to risk

Examples of user access threats include intentional acts (e.g., shared user accounts, hacking, and user spoofing, or impersonating) and unintentional acts (e.g., delayed termination of inactive accounts, unprotected passwords, and mismanaged remote access equipment).

8.5   User Access Security Countermeasures

The following countermeasures address user access security concerns that could affect your site(s) and equipment. These strategies are recommended when risk assessment identifies or confirms the need to counter potential user access breaches in your security system.

Implement a Program in Which Every User Accesses the System by Means of an Individual Account:

- *Limit user access to only those files they need to do their jobs:* Providing access that is not needed greatly contributes to risk without a corresponding increase in benefit. Why bother?

- *Avoid shared accounts*: Individual activity cannot be differentiated unless there are individual accounts.

- *Secure the user account name list*: Because of its importance to system security, the user account list should be considered to be confidential and should never be made public. Consider storing it as an encrypted file.

- *Monitor account activities*: Keep a record of all system use (many systems perform this function through an audit trail feature).

- *Terminate dormant accounts after a pre-set period of inactivity (e.g., 30 days)*: Legitimate users can always reapply and reestablish their accounts.

See chapter 9.0 for guidelines for authenticating messages transmitted over outside networks.

Countermeasures such as biometrics (fingerprints, retinal scans, etc.) and "smart cards" exceed most current requirements. Yet, while they may be prohibitively expensive for most small companies, any organization should consider implementing such methods eventually, as they promise far greater security than conventional methods.

Require Users to "Authenticate" Themselves in Order to Access Their Accounts (i.e., make sure they prove they are who they represent themselves to be):

- *Select an authentication system*: The right choice for an authentication system depends on the needs of the organization and its system, and should be based on the findings of a risk assessment (see chapter 2.0). Note that the following options progress from least secure to most secure; accordingly, they progress from least expensive to most expensive:

    a. Something the user knows (e.g., a password--see below);

    b. Something the user has (e.g., an electronic key card or "smart card"); and

    c. Something the user is (e.g., biometrics).

There are tradeoffs associated with making passwords more difficult to remember than a pet's name or a person's initials (employees are more likely to write down password reminders, for instance). The costs and benefits of these tradeoffs should be considered in the organization's risk assessment (see chapter 2.0).

Passwords

Because passwords are the most common method of user authentication, they deserve special attention:

- Require that passwords be at least six characters in length (although eight to ten are preferable);

- Prohibit the use of passwords that are words, names, dates, or other commonly expected formats;

- Forbid the use of passwords that reflect or identify the account owner (e.g., no birthdates, initials, or names of pets); and

- Require a mix of characters (i.e., letters and numbers - upper/lower case if the system is case sensitive - and special characters, if permitted).

Password maintenance:

- Require the system administrator to change all pre-set passwords that are built into software (e.g., administrator, demo, and root).

- Systematically require passwords to be changed at pre-set intervals (e.g., once per month).

- Maintain zero-tolerance for password sharing.

- Forbid unsecured storage of personal passwords (e.g., they should not be written on a Post-It™ note and taped to the side of a monitor).

- Never send a password as a part of an email message.

- Warn users not to type their password when someone may be watching.

- Mask (or otherwise obscure) password display on the monitor when users type it in.

- Remind users that it is easy to change passwords if they think that theirs may have been compromised.

- Maintain an encrypted history of passwords to make sure that users are not simply recycling old passwords when they should be changing them.

- Monitor the workplace to ensure that all regulations are being followed.

The security manager must be open to the concerns of system users. Security is a two-way street on which both users and security personnel have legitimate needs.

Remember to customize countermeasures to meet organizational and user needs.

Some intruders employ "password dictionaries" that, quite literally, try to match passwords one word at a time for thousands and thousands of attempts. This is also known as a brute force attack; and while it is one of the oldest and slowest methods, it works often enough that the practice is still in wide use.

Establish Standard Account and Authentication Procedures (known as login procedures):

- *Limit users to acceptable login times*: There is no reason for an average day-shift employee to be able to access the system in the middle of the night.

- *Limit users to acceptable login locations*: There is no reason for an average employee with a terminal on his or her desk to access the system from his or her supervisor's desk.

- *Set reasonable limits to the number of allowable login attempts*: Enable the system to assume that anyone who can't enter a password correctly after three attempts may not be who they say they are. Allow users more than one or two attempts or else they might make mistakes simply because they are worried about getting shut out. After three incorrect attempts, the account should be suspended (to prevent an intruder from simply calling back and trying three more times). Legitimate users can always have their accounts reopened by contacting the security manager.

- *Require employees to log off the system and turn off the computer*: The last important step of logging on properly is logging off properly. Users should be required to log off every time they leave their workstations (e.g., for lunch, breaks, and meetings). After all, an unauthorized user has free rein to an authorized user's access when a computer is left unattended and logged into the system.

Recognize that Routine Physical Security Plays an Important Role in User Access Management (see chapter 5.0):

- *Protect every access node in the system*: An "access node" is a point on a network through which you can access the system. If even one such point is left unsecured, then the entire system is at risk. A good example of frequently forgotten access nodes are modular network plugs that are often built into conference rooms (into which portable computers can be plugged). If unauthorized users can get to such a node with a laptop, they are in position to attack the system.

- *Protect cables and wires as if they were access nodes*: If a sophisticated intruder can access a span of cable that is used as a connector between pieces of equipment, he or she may be able to access the entire system. Physically accessing the wiring is referred to as "tapping the line." High-end equipment can monitor electrical emanations (known as Radio Frequency Interference) from wiring without even physically touching the cable.

- *Disconnect floppy drives from servers:* A sophisticated intruder can boot-up (the technical term for "starting the system") from an external disk drive.

- *Install screen savers (with mandatory locking features):* Prevent information from being read by anyone who happens to be walking past the display monitor.

See chapter 9.0 for more information about securing connections to outside networks, including the Internet.

Pay particular attention to Remote Access Systems (i.e., when someone, including an authorized user, accesses your system from offsite via a modem):

- *Consider requiring pre-approval for remote access privileges*: An identified subset of employees to monitor is more manageable than every random person who calls into the system.

- *Remind employees that remote access is particularly subject to monitoring activities*: Increased risk requires increased vigilance.

- *Set modems to answer only after several rings*: An authorized user will know that he has dialed a "slow" modem and will therefore be willing to wait. A random-dialer looking to bump into modems may be less likely to be so patient.

- *Use a "call back" communication strategy with remote access users*: Once users call in and properly identify themselves, the connection is dropped and the system then calls back the authorized users at a pre-approved access location.

- *Use software that requires "message authentication" in addition to "user authentication"*: Even if a user can provide the right password, each message sent and received must have its delivery verified to ensure that an unauthorized user didn't interrupt the transmission.

- *Never transmit sensitive information over public telephone lines unless the transmission has first been encrypted*: Unless a line can be verified as secure, it must be considered to be susceptible to tampering.

- *Investigate security features of external networks to which the system connects*: The Internet and other networks are not just things your employees can access and browse--they are two-way lines of communication. If security cannot be verified, then additional precautions must be taken (e.g., gateways and firewalls).

- *Install firewalls on your system at external access points*: A firewall is by far the most common way to secure the connection between your network and outside networks. It works by allowing only trusted (authenticated) messages to pass into your internal network from the outside (see also chapter 9.0).

- *Never list dial-in communication numbers publicly*: Why advertise what authorized users should already know?

- *Disable modems when not in use*: No need to provide a viable line of access to and from the system unless it's necessary.

- *Never leave a modem on automatic answer mode*: Such a practice opens the door to unauthorized and unsupervised system access.

- *Permit modem use only from secure locations*: Never allow a modem to be connected to a system machine that is not itself protected by a firewall or gateway.

- *Grant Internet access only to those employees who need it to perform their jobs*: A staff researcher or salesperson might need the Internet for legitimate learning purposes, but a records clerk probably does not.

- *Remind employees that the Internet (and all system activity for that matter) is for approved use only*: There are countless Internet sites and activities that have no positive influence on the business environment; therefore, they have no place on the system.

- *Require all users to sign Appropriate Use Agreements before receiving access to the system*: Signed Security Agreements (see chapter 3.0) verify that users have been informed of their responsibilities and understand that they will be held accountable for their actions.

8.6   User Access Security Checklist

While it may be tempting to refer to the following checklist as your security plan, to do so would limit the effectiveness of the recommendations. They are most useful when initiated as part of a larger plan to develop and implement security policy throughout an organization. Other chapters in this document also address ways to customize policy to your organization's specific needs—a concept that should not be ignored if you want to maximize the effectiveness of any given guideline.

User Access Security Checklist

Design an Appropriate Opening Screen That Users Must Visit Before Accessing the System

- Is the opening screen clear and specific about the organization's expectations of the user?

- Does the opening screen require the user to accept the conditions of monitoring and punishment before proceeding?

Implement a User Account System

- Is file access limited to that information users need to do their jobs?

- Are shared accounts explicitly prohibited?

- Is the list of user accounts and names maintained securely?

- Is account activity properly monitored?

- Are dormant accounts terminated after pre-set periods of inactivity?

Require Users to Authenticate Themselves

- Has an appropriate authentication system been selected based on risk assessment findings?

- Are passwords required to be at least six characters in length?

- Are names, dates, and other commonly anticipated password formats disallowed?

- Are passwords that reflect or identify the user forbidden (e.g., initials and pet names)?

- Is a mix of letters and numbers, and upper and lower cases required?

- Is the use of non-words and random characters encouraged?

- Has the system administrator changed all pre-set and packaged passwords?

- Are passwords required to be changed at regular intervals?

- Is password sharing expressly forbidden?

- Are password reminders stored securely by personnel?

- Have users been warned to never send their password as a part of an email message?

- Have users been warned not to type in their passwords when someone may be watching?

- Are password characters masked on display screens?

- Have users been told that they can, and should, change their password if they think it might be compromised?

- Is a history of user passwords maintained securely and reviewed routinely to ensure that users are not recycling passwords?

- Is the workplace appropriately monitored for adherence to security regulations?

Establish Standard Login Procedures

- Is each user limited to acceptable times for logging into the system?

- Is each user limited to acceptable places for logging into the system?

- Is there a limit to the number of times a user can attempt to log in incorrectly?

- Do employees know to log off and turn off computers?

Recognize the Importance of Physical Security

- Have all system access points (nodes) been secured?

- Has all cabling and wiring been secured?

- Have floppy drives been disconnected from servers?

- Are lockable screen savers installed and in use?

Pay Attention to Remote Access and Modem Use

- Is pre-approval required for remote access capabilities?

- Are employees aware that remote access is monitored? Is it?

- Are modems set to answer only after several rings?

- Is a call-back system in place?

- Is message authentication required in addition to user authentication?

- Is sensitive information prohibited from being transmitted over public lines unless the files are first encrypted?

- Is the organization aware of security features used by outside networks to which it connects? Are they acceptable?

- Are firewalls in use as needed?

- Are dial-in communication numbers protected from outsiders?

- Are modems disabled when not in use?

- Are modems always kept off automatic answer modes?

- Are modems only installed on computers in secure locations?

- Is Internet access granted to only those users who need it?

- Have all users been reminded that system use is only for approved activities?

- Are users required to sign Appropriate Use Agreements (see chapter 3.0) before receiving access to the system?

[This page intentionally left blank]

9.0 Protecting Your System: Network (Internet) Security

Any connection of two or more computers constitutes a network. The Internet is simply a worldwide connection of computers and networks.

9.1 Introduction to Network Security

Network security, especially as it relates to the biggest network of all - the Internet - has emerged as one of today's highest-profile information security issues. Many organizations have already connected their computing resources into a single network; others are in the process of doing so. The next step for these organizations is to weigh the costs and benefits of opening a connection between their private networks (with their trusted users) and the unknown users and networks that compose the Internet.

If, like many readers will, you have turned to this Network and Internet chapter first because it is your highest priority, be reminded that the information included in the other chapters of this document cannot be ignored. To reduce redundancy, security strategies from chapters 1.0 thru 8.0 and 10.0 that apply to Network and Internet security are not repeated in this chapter.

Discussions about Internet security can get technical. But while this issue is not for the faint of heart, it can and must be addressed before going online. While employment sanctions and denial of access privileges are enforceable deterrents for internal users, they are not options for external Internet users.

9.2 Commonly Asked Questions

Q. What is the Internet?
A. The Internet is simply a worldwide connection of computers and networks. That is why this chapter is titled Network Security – because the Internet is a very large network. If your organization has its own network (which can be called an Intranet), you are basically working with a scale model of the Internet.

Q. Wouldn't an internal network be safer if it was never connected to an external network like the Internet in the first place?
A. Yes, just as a person would be better protected from automobile accidents if he or she walked everywhere instead of driving. If walking (or avoiding external networks) meets your transportation (or computing and communication) needs, then it is a fine strategy. However, if an organization wants to take full advantage of its equipment's powerful communication capabilities, isolating itself from outside networks is a very poor plan. Instead, it would be better to connect with those networks that benefit the organization (including the Internet, if that is the case) and then invest in – and implement – those protection strategies necessary to provide adequate security.

Q. Why is there so much anxiety over connecting to the Internet?
A. Internet access opens lines of communication with the world but while this is a powerful tool, the admonition to "beware of strangers" certainly applies. The major concern about being connected to the Internet is one of trust. Internet users and machines are not known to your network, don't fall within your policy and management jurisdiction, and may not share your opinions on appropriate use.

When you don't know who is accessing your network, you also don't know their intentions or level of technical expertise--thus, choosing to connect to the Internet has a significant impact on an organization's risk assessment (see chapter 2.0).

Be realistic. Recognize that as beneficial as the Internet can be for communicating and gathering resources, not everyone on it has your company's best interests in mind.

9.3   Policy Issues

Guidelines for security policy development can be found in chapter 3.0.

Connecting to the Internet doesn't necessarily raise its own security policy issues as much as it focuses attention on the necessity of implementing security strategies properly. Internet security goals fall within two major domains. The first centers around protecting your networks, information, and other assets from outside users who enter your network from the Internet. The second deals with safeguarding information as it is being transmitted over the Internet.

Although it is not within the scope of this document to address in sufficient detail, policy makers must consider what information can and cannot be posted to the Internet on the company's web page (portal).

9.4   Network Threats (Examples)

As discussed more completely in chapter 2.0, a threat is any action, actor, or event that contributes to risk.

Examples of network threats include intentional acts of destruction (e.g., address spoofing and masquerading) and unintentionally destructive acts (e.g., accidental downloading of computer viruses and improper release of information)

If your brand-name operating systems, hardware, or software have any known security weakness built in, someone on the Internet will know about it. The Computer Emergency Response Team (CERT) Web site and comparable sites monitor weaknesses in computer software and post corrections. You should watch these sites – hackers do.

9.5   Network Security Countermeasures

A countermeasure is a step planned and taken in opposition to another act or potential act. Select only those countermeasures that meet perceived needs as identified during risk assessment (chapter 2.0) and that support security policy (chapter 3.0).

Because the Internet is relatively new, it isn't surprising that its standards are still being established and agreed upon. Consequently, it also shouldn't be surprising that its existing mechanisms for governing information exchanges are varied, not uniformly implemented, and, in many cases, not interoperable. Thus, it is only fair to admit that although the following countermeasures will greatly increase Internet security, more sophisticated and robust solutions remain on the horizon.

The following countermeasures address network security concerns that could affect your site(s) and equipment. These strategies are recommended when risk assessment identifies or confirms the need to counter breaches in the security of your network.

Many of these countermeasures get very technical very quickly. Non-experts need appreciate only the concepts and collaborate with technical staff, to ensure that appropriate solutions are properly implemented.

Digital signatures, time stamps, sequence numbers, and digital certificates are simply more examples of "authentication" procedures as discussed in chapter 8.0.

Keep in mind that monitoring "authentication" procedures is accomplished by software. Once the systems are established, the user need only read the warning that the transmission did not maintain its integrity.

Protect Your Network from Outsiders:

- *Implement applicable security recommendations as raised in previous chapters:* Solid defense against external Internet threats includes the proper implementation of relatively straightforward security measures like encryption software, virus scanners, remote access regulations, and passwords (chapters 6.0 - 9.0).

- *Isolate your network through the use of a firewall:* Installing a firewall enables the organization to decide which types of messages should be allowed into the system from external sources (e.g., "nothing with identifiable virus coding" and "nothing with decryptor coding structures"). The actual installation and operation of the complex features requires expert technical assistance, but policymakers can make informed decisions about product features all the same.

- *Locate equipment and information that is intended for external users outside the firewall:* If an organization's Web server is intended to provide information and services to the public, it should not be located on the private side of the firewall. Nor should it be able to access confidential information that resides inside the firewall. This way, if the public Web server should ever be compromised, confidential information is still protected.

Protect Transmissions Sent over the Internet:

- *Use Secure Sockets Layer (SSL) Servers to secure financial and information transactions made with a Web browser*: In a secure Web session, your Web browser generates a random encryption key and sends it to the Web site host to be matched with its public encryption key. Your browser and the Web site then encrypt and decrypt all transmissions.

- *Authenticate messages through the use of digital signatures:* A digital signature amounts to a "fingerprint" of a message. It depicts the message such that if the message were to be altered in any way, the "fingerprint" would reflect it--thus making it possible to detect counterfeits. The converse, of course, is that if the "fingerprint" does not change during transmission, you can be confident that the message was not altered.

- *Authenticate messages through the use of time stamps or sequence numbers:* Another way to recognize when messages have been modified is to challenge the "freshness" of the message. This is done by embedding time stamps, sequence numbers, or random numbers in the message to indicate precisely when and in what order the message was sent. If a received message's time and sequence are not consistent, you will be alerted that someone may have tampered with the transmission.

- *Authenticate message "receivers" through the use of digital certificates:* By requiring an authentication agent or digital certificate, you force the person on the other end of the transmission to prove his or her identity. In the digital world, trusted third parties can serve as certificate authorities – entities that verify who a user is for you. In this way, digital certificates are analogous to a state-issued driver's license. If you trust the party that issues the certificate (e.g., the state or the certificate authority), you don't need to try to verify who the user is yourself.

- *Encrypt all messages sent over the Internet* (see chapter 6.0). As more and more messages are sent over larger and larger networks, information becomes increasingly vulnerable to assault. Encryption has become a leading tool to combat this vulnerability. Like other countermeasures, it can be very effective if used properly and regularly.

"Encryption" is a term used for the transformation of information into a format that is unreadable without the appropriate key for decryption. The term "key" refers to a mathematical equation used to code (encrypt) information.

More Than You Need to Know about How Messages Are Encrypted

The process of encrypting and decrypting files depends on which encryption model your security solution employs. Encryption models vary in the number and size of the key(s) they use. As a general rule, the larger the key, the tougher it is to crack. There are two major types of encryption keys currently in use:

- In a Single Key Encryption System, parties exchange a key known only to themselves, and use that key to encrypt and decrypt messages. The fundamental premise of this system is that parties must securely communicate the secret key to each other in order to encrypt and decrypt messages.

- The Public/Private Key Encryption System is based on a pair of mathematically related keys--a public key and a private key. Each key can decrypt information encrypted by the other. Your public key is used by anyone who wishes to send you an encrypted message or to verify your digital signature. Your private key is known only to you and is used to decrypt messages sent to you through the public key, or to digitally sign messages you are sending. This model allows for a much larger number of users than single key encryption because you need not have a separate key sent secretly to every trading partner.

Consensus appears to be moving the Internet toward a public/private key system in which third-party organizations that are entrusted as certificate authorities provide key management. Key management refers to the secure administration of encryption keys so that they become available to users only when and where they are required. This system is often referred to as the Public Key Infrastructure.

Policymakers need not worry about the security of the entire Internet if they can be confident of the security of their connection to it.

9.6   Closing Thoughts on Network Security

The Internet simply is not secure unless you make it so. Luckily, basic Internet security is not beyond a non-technical person's ability to understand. By collaborating with technical support staff (or outside consultants if necessary), managers can ensure that the near limitless amount of information and resources that exist on the Internet are available to system users without jeopardizing system integrity.

It should also be noted that network configurations are constantly changing. Many organizations are now relying upon Intranets for their internal communications. All security recommendations for the Internet can also be applied to Intranet applications.

9.7   Network Security Checklist

While it may be tempting to refer to the following checklist as your security plan, to do so would limit the effectiveness of the recommendations. They are most useful when initiated as part of a larger plan to develop and implement security policy within and throughout an organization. Other chapters in this document also address ways to customize policy to your organization's specific needs--a concept that should not be ignored if you want to maximize the effectiveness of any given guideline.

Network Security Checklist

Protect Your Network from Outsiders

- Have you fully implemented applicable security strategies as recommended in previous chapters?

- Has your network been isolated from the outside (e.g., the Internet) through the use of a firewall?

- Is equipment and information that is intended for "external" use logically located outside of your firewall?

Protect Transmissions Sent over the Internet

- Is a Secure Sockets Layer (SSL) used to secure financial and information transactions made with a Web browser?

- Are messages authenticated via digital signatures?

- Are messages authenticated via time stamps or sequence numbers?

- Are message recipients authenticated by digital certificates?

- Are all messages sent over the Internet first encrypted?

[This page intentionally left blank]

10.0 Training: A Necessary Investment in People

10.1   Introduction to Training

Most employees of an organization could probably offer a fairly accurate description of the term "computer virus". Viruses are, unfortunately, all too commonplace. They are routinely reported on in the major media and, on occasion, are headline stories. But ask those same employees what encryption software is, or suggest effective disk backup procedures, and they may find themselves with little to say. While threats and catastrophes are newsworthy, day-to-day activities that protect information systems are often considered mundane.

When an organization allows television, magazines, and newspapers to be solely responsible for educating its employees, there is no logical reason for it to expect its employees to know how to implement even the most clearly stated information technology security procedures. After all, while employees may have heard a thirty-second newsflash about the latest virus, they will not have been exposed to proper ways of using computer equipment and protecting information.

As mentioned throughout chapters 5.0 - 9.0, all of the technological and procedural precautions in the world will be ineffective if they are not executed properly. But through well-conceived and committed security training programs, employees will be better prepared to avoid problems in the first place, minimize the damage of those problems that do arise, and maximize their contributions to system and information recovery when necessary.

Without appropriate training (and associated reference tools), employees will instead be more likely to actually *contribute* to security risk through accidental but not necessarily malicious behavior. After all, most security problems are the result of unintentional human error. These mistakes will be less likely to occur when a well-intentioned employee has been properly trained.

Because system security demands information security and confidentiality, employee training must incorporate both topics.

10.2   Commonly Asked Questions

Q. If funds are scarce, isn't it better to implement security and postpone training rather than neglect security altogether?
A. Neglecting security altogether is a terrible option. Unfortunately, attempting to implement security without appropriate training is not much better. A more effective approach is to rely on the security priorities that are established in the organization's risk assessment (see chapter 2.0) and then fund as many precautionary measures as can be implemented and trained for based on those priorities. While some vulnerabilities might be left unaddressed, the organization can have the peace of mind of knowing that at least those steps it has taken have a realistic chance of being properly implemented. It can then informally increase vigilance in areas of vulnerability it will not be able to address until additional funds become available.

Q. Can't training sometimes be overdone?
A. Training can surely be overdone, although that is rarely the case in today's world of shrinking and non-existent training budgets. More often, training problems are a result of poor focus and poor timing. A training program should be focused on helping employees do their jobs better. It must be relevant to assigned duties and be presented in an understandable way that encourages employees to make security a part of their everyday routines.

Similarly, training classes should be scheduled at convenient times for participants. If focus and timing are properly handled (i.e., sessions are helpful and convenient), it is much less likely that participants will complain about training being a burden. Training is a prerequisite for order, consistency, and realistic expectations of effective system defense.

Q. How does an organization know if its training program is effective?
A. The most obvious way of measuring the effectiveness of security training is by monitoring the workplace for improved security performance. Scheduled and unscheduled testing of the security system is an excellent way of assessing its condition (see chapter 4.0). Pre- and post-testing employees on training content is also an effective way of measuring improvements in security awareness, while yet another (and even more straightforward) way of evaluating training is to simply ask training participants what they thought of the experience. Since security depends heavily on the attitude and resulting commitment of employees, their opinion of the training, its relevance, and effectiveness is quite probably a good indicator of its success.

10.3   Targeting Training Efforts

Who should receive security training? In a word, everybody! After all, a security breach affects each person in an organization. No matter what task an employee is assigned, his or her role influences, and is influenced by, security policies and procedures. For example, people who clean offices need to know what can and can't be thrown away, and which rooms may or may not be off-limits. All employees need to appreciate the necessity of protecting passwords and monitoring computer activity in their work areas. Supervisors need to understand the importance of policy enforcement. And everyone needs to be aware of proper use of removable media and viruses that can be spread through these media if users fail to exercise due caution.

10.4   How Does Security Affect the Workplace?

Security Area – Affected Activities

- Physical strategies (chapter 5.0) - Housekeeping/custodial, maintenance and operations, weekend/evening activities

- Information/data protection (chapter 6.0) - Public relations releases, research and evaluation reporting, interoffice mail delivery, disposal services

- Software regulations (chapter 7.0) - Administrative/clerical assistance, instructional delivery, library offerings

- Access mechanisms (chapter 8.0) - Access by Board members, contractors, and telecommuters.

- Network/Internet connections (chapter 9.0) - Internet searches, site-to-site transmissions, public access (e.g., company portal/homepage)

Every effort should be made to make security training as relevant as possible to day-to-day activities in the work environment. Exercises in the theoretical are not often well received by busy people. If employees to whom training is directed don't think it is practical, then the training will be seen as an additional burden.

One way to make training sessions meaningful is to customize separate training programs to meet the needs of different types of employee and job groupings. For example, a training session designed to address security issues that affect clerical employees (e.g., software use and system access) has a good chance of being well-received by people who perform clerical duties because it is relevant to their jobs. Those same people might find a more general training session that includes significant periods of time discussing the management of employees in computer labs less applicable to their duties and, consequently, less interesting.

Each organization will be different in terms of the types of job-alike training sessions that it might want to offer, but the following groups are common to many organizations and are logical target audiences for security training.

"Job-alike" training is used to describe a training program in which sessions are designed for specific user groups based on the similarities of their job duties.

An example of Job-Alike training groups:

Group A

- High-level executives
- Middle managers
- IT professionals

Group B

- Clerical employees
- Paraprofessionals
- Non-IT operational employees (i.e., sales, production, shipping, accounting)
- Other support staff

10.5   Training Goals

Even when information security training is customized to meet the needs of specific user groups through a job-alike approach, every session, no matter the target audience, should have the following goals:

Goal 1:   Raise employee awareness of information technology security issues in general.

Goal 2:   Ensure that employees are aware of local, state, and federal laws and regulations governing confidentiality and security.

Goal 3:   Explain organizational security policies and procedures.

Goal 4:   Ensure that employees understand that security is a team effort and that each person has an important role to play in meeting security goals and objectives.

Goal 5:   Train employees to meet the specific security responsibilities of their positions.

Goal 6:   Inform employees that security activities will be monitored.

Goal 7:   Remind employees that security breaches have serious consequences.

Goal 8:   Assure employees that reporting potential and actual security breakdowns and vulnerabilities is responsible and necessary behavior (and not trouble-making).

Goal 9:   Communicate to employees that the goal of creating a "trusted system" is achievable.

Each of the above goals should provide the same types of information to all employees without regard to their job-alike grouping. The significant exception to this point is Goal 5, in which security responsibilities are explained as they specifically relate to participant duties.

In the broader sense of computer use, all employees should learn to:

- Never use a computer as a tool to harm other people;

- Never interfere with other people's computer work;

- Never snoop around in other people's computer files;

- Never use a computer to steal;

- Never use a computer as a tool for misrepresenting information or the company;

- Never use other people's computer resources without their permission; and

- Never lose sight of the social consequences of the work being done with the computer.

While security training focuses on improving the implementation of security procedures, training employees on basic computer use and etiquette also contributes to system security, and is vital.

Ongoing training is essential for keeping employees focused. Distributing handouts, cheat sheets, and other reference materials is an effective way of supporting employees long after a training session is over and everyone is back on the job.

10.6   A Sample Training Outline

Allowing for customizing to meet the requirements of job-alike training, the following outline provides an overview of how a typical security training session could be effectively structured:

I.   Security overview

    A.   What is information security?

    B.   Why does it matter?

II.   Federal laws

III.   State and local laws, regulations, and standards

    A.   Statute, regulation, and standard overview

    B.   Statute, regulation, and standard relevance and application (include specific examples that relate to audience duties)

IV.   The organization's security plan

    A.   Risk assessment findings (assets, threats, and vulnerabilities)

    B.   Organizational security policies, procedures, and regulations (focus on those related to audience duties)

- Physical security regulations
- Information security regulations
- Software security regulations
- User access security regulations
- Network security regulations

    C.   Security administration

- Expectations
- Monitoring activities
- Authorization
- Enforcement and consequences
- Avenues of communication

V.   On-the-job training

    A.   Explanations

- Turning the computer on and off
- Logging in and out
- Changing passwords

    B.   Demonstrations

- Turning the computer on and off
- Logging in and out
- Changing passwords

C.   Testing

- Turning the computer on and off
- Logging in and out
- Changing passwords

D.   Monitoring

- Turning the computer on and off
- Logging in and out
- Changing passwords

One way of illustrating the rationale for security regulations is to have employees look at the vulnerabilities of an unsecured system from the perspective of a potential intruder, and then consider how much more difficult it would be to attack a secured system.

True training entails more than telling employees what they can and cannot do. Simply saying "back up your work because it is a rule" does not educate employees. Instead, rationale for policies and regulations should be explained to employees. This does not require every step of the organization's risk assessment to be rehashed, as much as it means that procedures should be justified and made relevant to the audience's work.

For example, instead of telling employees that they must protect their passwords, an explanation of what a malicious user could do while posing as an employee (through the use of their password) might be more effective. After all, very few people are willing to allow themselves to be made someone else's scapegoat. By describing how security protects users as well as the system and organization, security training can become an effective way of developing staff support and ensuring that policies and regulations are implemented.

Users must be reminded what is at risk if the system is not effectively secured, including:

- Organizational resources and reputation;

- Confidential information that customers trust company employees to protect; and

- Personal work files that need to be recreated, at considerable effort.

An overwhelming three-hour session in which employees learn little is a poor use of time compared with three more manageable *forty-five minute* sessions in which they retain a lot.

10.7   Training Frequency

How often employees should be trained (and when) is an issue that requires significant consideration. A good rule of thumb is that all newly hired employees should undergo general organizational security training as a part of their orientation before they actually assume their duties. Similarly, job-alike or comparable training should be required of all employees (new or old) at the onset of initiating a security program.

After initial training sessions have been offered, it is important to continue to educate employees regularly. Ongoing efforts allow for major points to be reemphasized, while also providing trainers with opportunities to break complex issues into manageable pieces of information that employees can more easily comprehend. For example, the concept of user authentication may be more readily understood by employees if it is broken into separate sessions on in-house login procedures (session one) and remote access (session two).

Training surely demands the dedication of time and resources, but the alternative usually exacts a far higher toll.

10.8   Closing Thoughts on Security Training

Security policies and regulations are "living" concepts. That is, they can change depending on circumstances. If, for example, an improved type of encryption software is released, an organization and its employees might need to learn how to use it. Similarly, if a new data collection is initiated, policymakers will need to evaluate the confidentiality of the information it generates. In both cases (and countless other examples), having a training mechanism in place to inform and educate employees is not only very valuable, but a real necessity--because a staff that is not properly trained limits, and perhaps even negates, the potential effectiveness of even the best devised security strategies.

Shortchanging security training is the equivalent of short-changing security itself. Don't undermine an investment in equipment, software, and policy development by failing to also invest in your people.

10.9   Security Training Checklist

While it may be tempting to simply refer to the following checklist as your security plan, to do so would limit the effectiveness of the recommendations. They are most useful when initiated as part of a larger plan to develop and implement security policy throughout an organization. Other chapters in this document also address ways to customize policy to your organization's specific needs--a concept that should not be ignored if you want to maximize the effectiveness of any given guideline.

Security Training Checklist

- Have decision makers committed to comprehensive training as a necessary part of implementing any information technology security program?

- Is training targeted at everyone in the organization to the degree their activities warrant?

- Are training sessions customized to meet the needs of specific user groups, a concept referred to here as "job-alike" training?

- Is training designed to raise staff awareness of information technology security issues in general?

- Is training designed to make employees aware of local, state, and federal laws and regulations governing information confidentiality and security?

- Is training designed to explain organizational security policies, procedures, and regulations?

- Is training designed to ensure that employees understand that security is a team effort and that each person has an important role to play?

- Is training designed to help employees meet the specific security responsibilities of their positions?

- Is training designed to inform employees that security activities must and will be monitored?

- Is training designed to remind staff that breaches in security have consequences for the individual and the organization?

- Is training designed to encourage staff to report potential and actual security breakdowns and vulnerabilities?

- Is training designed to communicate to employees that the goal of creating a "trusted" system is achievable?

- Has the sample training outline been reviewed as an aid in helping the organization's training planners develop their own program?

- Is the rationale for security policies and regulations explained as a part of training?

- Are all new employees trained before they assume their duties?

- Will staff training be initiated at the onset of implementing any security program?

- Is employee training and related support information provided on an ongoing basis?

- Have decision makers recognized that a security policy is a "living" concept and, therefore, requires frequent reevaluation?

Reference Materials

Computer Crime Research Center – http://www.crime-research.org/.

Computer Ethics Institute (CEI) – http://computerethicsinstitute.org/.

Computer Emergency Response Team (CERT), part of the Software Engineering Institute (SEI) of Carnegie-Mellon University – http://www.cert.org.

ICSAlabs, an independent division of Verizon – http://www.icsalabs.com.

National Institute of Standards and Technology (NIST) Information Technology Laboratory / Computer Security Division / Computer Security Resource Center – http://csrc.nist.gov.

National Security Institute – http://www.nsi.org.[1]

National White Collar Crime Center (NW3C) / Cyber Crime Links – http://www.nw3c.org/services/research/cyber-crime-links/.[2]

SANS Institute – http://www.sans.org.

---

[1] A private entity, not affiliated with the U.S. Government
[2] NW3C is a nonprofit, membership-affiliated organization comprised of state, local, federal, and tribal law enforcement and prosecutorial and regulatory agencies

[This page intentionally left blank]

IT Policies and Procedures

Section 550

Job Descriptions

Section 550
Job Descriptions

Document ID	Title	Print Date
JD0060	**BETA TEST COORDINATOR**	**mm/dd/yyyy**
Revision	Prepared By	Date Prepared
0.0	**Preparer's Name / Title**	**mm/dd/yyyy**
Effective Date	Reviewed By	Date Reviewed
mm/dd/yyyy	**Reviewer's Name / Title**	**mm/dd/yyyy**
	Approved By	Date Approved
	Final Approver's Name / Title	**mm/dd/yyyy**

SUMMARY OF FUNCTIONS

The Beta Test Coordinator oversees all aspects of the beta test program.

ESSENTIAL DUTIES AND RESPONSIBILITIES

- Identify potential problems and risks; establish and maintain a risk management program for beta testing.
- Design, implement, coordinate, and manage the beta testing process.
- Refine existing beta processes in order to more efficiently track and prioritize issues discovered during the process.
- Create beta-test plans for beta testers.
- Work with technical writer(s) to deliver beta feature documentation, and setup/manage resources for internal beta test activities.
- Provide direct support to beta testers by way of accurate, detailed, thorough, and timely support practices.
- Maintain a cordial, helpful demeanor with beta testers; cultivate relationships to encourage ongoing participation; help identify beta testing candidates.
- Monitor, measure, identify, and prioritize issues discovered during beta testing.
- Work with the internal team to prioritize issues; follow up with Engineering for resolution.
- Communicate the program's status to testers periodically and as needed; ensure successful beta testing through effective communication.

ORGANIZATIONAL RELATIONSHIPS

Reports directly to the IT Manager; works with Computer Engineering, Product Management, Technical Support, and other internal and external beta testers.

PROCEDURES

Procedure ID and Name	Policies & Procedures Manual
ITSW107 Software Testing	Computer & Network (IT)
SWD107 Software Testing	Software Development

QUALIFICATIONS

A bachelor's degree in computer science, computer engineering, or a similar discipline is required, as is 5+ years' experience in software development and testing. A master's degree in information management or similar discipline is preferred. Experience in network management, project management will be beneficial, as will tech support experience. Experience with beta test management software a definite plus. Also, prefer industry certifications (e.g., CompTIA Network+).

Excellent communication skills (oral and written) and the ability to work well with people are essential.

PHYSICAL DEMANDS

Ability to communicate orally with customers, vendors, management, and other co-workers is crucial. Regular use of the telephone and e-mail for communication is essential. Sitting for extended periods is common. Hearing and vision within normal ranges is essential for normal conversations, to receive ordinary information and to prepare or inspect documents.

Activities require the ability to remain in a stationary position 50% of the time, occasionally move about inside the office to access files or office equipment, operate a computer and other office productivity machinery, such as a calculator, hand held devices, copy machine, and computer printer, and operate and monitor various medical equipment. Must be able to constantly position self to maintain equipment, including under tables and desks.

No heavy lifting is expected. Exertion of up to 10 lbs. of force occasionally may be required. Good manual dexterity for the use of common office equipment such as computer terminals, calculator, copiers, and FAX machines.

This is primarily a first-shift position, but the candidate must be able to adapt to a changing schedule (i.e., may have to conduct some beta tests during evenings or on weekends).

WORK ENVIRONMENT

The job is performed indoors in a traditional office setting. Activities include extended periods of sitting and extensive work at a computer monitor and phone.

REVISION HISTORY

Revision	Date	Description of Changes	Requested By
0.0	mm/dd/yyyy	Initial Release	

[This page intentionally left blank]

Document ID	Title	Print Date
JD0070	**BOARD MEMBER**	**mm/dd/yyyy**
Revision	Prepared By	Date Prepared
0.0	**Preparer's Name / Title**	**mm/dd/yyyy**
Effective Date	Reviewed By	Date Reviewed
mm/dd/yyyy	**Reviewer's Name / Title**	**mm/dd/yyyy**
	Approved By	Date Approved
	Final Approver's Name / Title	**mm/dd/yyyy**

SUMMARY OF FUNCTIONS

Each Member of the Board of Directors[1] acts in a position of trust for the community and is responsible for the effective governance of the organization.

ESSENTIAL DUTIES AND RESPONSIBILITIES

- Participate primarily in the organization's financial management process.
- Review and cast votes on stock offerings.
- Review and approve/disapprove of the organization's vision and mission statements and set forth the organization's direction.
- Review and vote on the organization's Strategic and Business Plans, as well as subordinate Plans (e.g., Marketing Plan, Technology Plan); ensure that the various Plans are in sync; ensure that the organization's Top Management effectively carries out these Plans.
- Approves the stakeholder analysis, as well as other inputs to the MP1070-1 – MARKETING PLAN, and ensures the Plan's effectiveness.
- Attend Board meetings and makes decisions regarding the Company's operations, as required.
- Authorize the raising of capital through bank loans.
- Oversee investigations into reporting errors; help prepare and submit all financial restatements as required by law and company policy; help prepare press releases about restatements.
- Reviews and accesses foreign exchange risks and policy options, and then sets the Company foreign exchange management policy.
- Reviews and approves all submitted financial reports, FA1000-1 FINANCIAL OBJECTIVES, the Capital Plan and any changes to the Plan, the Company's formal goals and objectives, the Finance department's continuity plan, and the RC1000-1 BUSINESS PLAN.
- Reviews and approves the risk assessment/risk analysis prior to development of a Risk Management Plan (see procedure AC1030 RISK MANAGEMENT).
- Reviews approved related party transactions and sets auditing or monitoring practices according to the requirements of each individual case.

---

[1] Where the organization is not large or complex enough to warrant a Board of Directors, the CEO/President should consider having an informal group of advisors or business consultants.

- Reviews financial analysis and approves corrections or improvements to financial policies, objectives, or activities.
- Review and approve/disapprove of the organization's financial forecasts and forecasted financial statements.

ORGANIZATIONAL RELATIONSHIPS

Reports to the other members of the Board and to shareholders. Works in conjunction with other Board members and the organization's executive staff (President, Chief Finance Officer, etc.).

PROCEDURES

Procedure ID and Name	Policies & Procedures Manual
AC1020 Risk Assessment	Finance
FA1000 Financial Objectives	Finance
FA1020 Continuity Planning	Finance
FA1060 Board of Directors' Meetings	Finance
FS1000 Financial Forecasting	Finance
FS1010 Financial Reporting	Finance
FS1020 Financial Statement Analysis	Finance
FS1030 Financial Management Review	Finance
FS1040 Financial Restatements	Finance
ITAD101 Information Technology Management	Computer & Network (IT)
MP1010 Stakeholder Analysis	Sales and Marketing
MP1020 Vision and Mission	Sales and Marketing
MP1050 Goals and Objectives	Sales and Marketing
RC1000 Business Plan	Finance
RC1010 Capital Plan	Finance
RC1030 Bank Loans	Finance
RC1040 Stock Offerings	Finance
RC1050 Debt & Investment	Finance
TM1030 Related Party Transactions	Finance
TM1040 Foreign Exchange Management	Finance

QUALIFICATIONS

Prefer a candidate who currently holds (or recently held) an executive position with a firm having $2 million or more in revenue in the most recent fiscal year. Requires 10+ years of experience overseeing a company or companies in a related industry. Knowledge of, experience in field of finance is important.

The candidate must have a strong sense of and commitment to ethical behavior; the appearance of unethical or illegal behavior in the past is unacceptable.

Must be committed to the work of the organization. Require knowledge and skills in one or more areas of Board governance (e.g., policy, finance, programs, personnel). Must be willing to serve on at least one committee and actively participate. Require attendance at monthly Board meetings; a time commitment of about 5 hours per month (including Board preparation, meeting, and committee meeting time) is expected. Must also attend the organization's Annual General Meeting.

PHYSICAL DEMANDS

Ability to communicate orally with top management, advisors, and other board members is crucial. Regular use of the telephone and e-mail for communication is essential. Sitting for extended periods is common. Hearing and vision within normal ranges is essential for normal conversations, to receive ordinary information and to prepare or inspect documents.

Activities require the ability to remain in a stationary position 50% of the time, occasionally move about inside the office to access files or office equipment, operate a computer and other office productivity machinery, such as a calculator, hand held devices, copy machine, and computer printer, and operate and monitor various medical equipment.

No heavy lifting is expected. Exertion of up to 10 lbs. of force occasionally may be required. Good manual dexterity for the use of common office equipment such as computer terminals, calculator, copiers, and FAX machines.

WORK ENVIRONMENT

The job is performed indoors in a traditional office setting. Activities include extended periods of sitting and extensive work at an office/conference desk, using a phone or computer.

REVISION HISTORY

Revision	Date	Description of Changes	Requested By
0.0	mm/dd/yyyy	Initial Release	

Document ID **JD0140**	Title **CHIEF EXECUTIVE OFFICER (CEO)**	Print Date **mm/dd/yyyy**
Revision **0.0**	Prepared By **Preparer's Name / Title**	Date Prepared **mm/dd/yyyy**
Effective Date **mm/dd/yyyy**	Reviewed By **Reviewer's Name / Title**	Date Reviewed **mm/dd/yyyy**
	Approved By **Final Approver's Name / Title**	Date Approved **mm/dd/yyyy**

SUMMARY OF FUNCTIONS

The Chief Executive Officer, or CEO, creates and communicates the organization's vision and mission and leads strategy development, implementation, and revision. The CEO also oversees development and implementation of the organization's strategic plan, helping formulate strategic objectives. To that end, the CEO must maintain an awareness of both the external and internal competitive landscape, opportunities for expansion, customers, markets, new industry developments and standards, and so forth.

The CEO leads a group of top executives, or "top management," including but not limited to the chief financial officer, chief operations officer, chief technology officer, and chief sales & marketing officer.

ESSENTIAL DUTIES AND RESPONSIBILITIES

- Actively participates in the financial management process.
- Approves and signs all financial statements, financial reports, and tax returns.
- Approves the Lead Management Plan, the MT1020-2 PUBLIC RELATIONS PLAN, the Advertising Plan, the MP1070-1 MARKETING PLAN, the MT1010-2 INTERNET PLAN.
- Conducts strategic planning and sets the Strategic Objectives for the Company.
- Develops the Company's vision and mission statements, ensures that such statements are communicated to and understood by all employees, reviews the vision and mission statements, and ensures that changes are made to each, as needed.
- Ensures that the goals and objectives are appropriate for the Company, ensures that goals and objectives are communicated to employees, and monitors the Company's progress.
- Ensures the situational analysis is appropriate for developing marketing and sales strategies.
- Gives the final approval of all salary adjustments, changes in job titles, or job responsibilities.
- Oversees investigations into reporting errors, preparing and submitting all financial restatements as required by law and by company policy, and prepares press releases about restatements.
- Reviews and approves the Risk Management Plan, as well as financial forecasts and forecasted financial statements.

- Reviews the market analysis and uses the information to help shape the MP1070-1 MARKETING PLAN.
- Selects a Strategy Team and ensures the Team has the necessary resources to develop/refine strategies.
- Selects a Strategy Team, ensures the Team has the necessary resources, monitors the Team's progress, and presents its findings to the Board of Directors.
- Signs all reported financial statements.

ORGANIZATIONAL RELATIONSHIPS

Reports directly to the organization's Board of Directors.

PROCEDURES

Procedure ID and Name	Policies & Procedures Manual
AC1000 Sarbanes-Oxley Compliance	Finance
AC1030 Risk Management	Finance
DEV105 Performance Appraisals	Human Resources
FS1000 Financial Forecasting	Finance
FS1010 Financial Reporting	Finance
FS1030 Financial Management Review	Finance
FS1040 Financial Restatements	Finance
ITAD101 Information Technology Management	Computer & Network (IT)
MP1000 Strategy Team	Sales & Marketing
MP1010 Stakeholder Analysis	Sales & Marketing
MP1020 Vision and Mission	Sales & Marketing
MP1030 Marketing Research and Analysis	Sales & Marketing
MP1040 Situational Analysis	Sales & Marketing
MP1050 Goals and Objectives	Sales & Marketing
MP1060 Marketing Strategy	Sales & Marketing
MP1070 Marketing Plan	Sales & Marketing
MT1000 Advertising	Sales & Marketing
MT1010 Internet Marketing	Sales & Marketing
MT1020 Public Relations	Sales & Marketing
MT1050 Lead Management	Sales & Marketing

QUALIFICATIONS

A bachelor's degree in business administration, finance, sales & marketing, engineering, or other suitable field is required. 10+ years of experience in an officer's role (e.g., CFO, CMO) with a medium- to large-size company is also required. Must have demonstrated the ability to handle increasing levels of responsibility and to lead effectively.

Exceptional communication skills and the ability to work well with people are essential.

PHYSICAL DEMANDS

Ability to communicate orally with customers, vendors, management, and other co-workers is crucial. Regular use of the telephone and e-mail for communication is essential. Sitting for extended periods is common. Hearing and vision within normal ranges is essential for normal conversations, to receive ordinary information, and to prepare or inspect documents.

Activities require the ability to remain in a stationary position 50% of the time, occasionally move about inside the office to access files or office equipment, operate a computer and other office productivity machinery, such as a calculator, hand held devices, copy machine, and computer printer, and operate and monitor various medical equipment. Must be able to constantly position self to maintain equipment, including under tables and desks.

No heavy lifting is expected, though occasional exertion of up to 10 lbs. of force may be required. Good manual dexterity required for the use of computers, mobile devices, and other productivity technologies.

WORK ENVIRONMENT

The job is performed indoors in a traditional office setting. Extended periods of sitting and extensive work at a computer and phone are normal.

REVISION HISTORY

Revision	Date	Description of Changes	Requested By
0.0	mm/dd/yyyy	Initial Release	

[This page intentionally left blank]

Document ID	Title	Print Date
JD0300	**DIRECTOR OF QUALITY**	**mm/dd/yyyy**
Revision	Prepared By	Date Prepared
0.0	**Preparer's Name / Title**	**mm/dd/yyyy**
Effective Date	Reviewed By	Date Reviewed
mm/dd/yyyy	**Reviewer's Name / Title**	**mm/dd/yyyy**
	Approved By	Date Approved
	Final Approver's Name / Title	**mm/dd/yyyy**

SUMMARY OF FUNCTIONS

The Director of Quality[1] ensures that the organization's products and services are in compliance with the company's quality requirements, in addition to complying with customer and regulatory requirements for quality, safety, and reliability.

ESSENTIAL DUTIES AND RESPONSIBILITIES

- Responsible for the development, implementation and strict adherence to a quality program. Develops and/or reviews standards, policies and procedures for all functions and departments involved with or related to the production of all products. The Director of Quality has the ultimate authority and decision over the shipment of any product or products and accepts the responsibility for products being in compliance with all regulatory and company standards.
- Reviews and resolves quality control problems/concerns with the Quality Control Manager and others including vendors, customers, quality control personnel, and any personnel related to production. Coordinates and assists with vendor inspections.
- Periodically inspects completed quality control checklists, forms, and other documents; randomly inspects and verifies quality control checks for conformance to prescribed standards.
- Schedules and performs quality audits and reports findings to the President, Quality Control Manager and Vice President of Production and Operations; develops corrective action plans and ensures timely resolution of findings.
- Receives and reviews all customer satisfaction surveys and customer contacts and complaints. Reviews complaint trends and product/component failure analysis; reviews corrective actions with appropriate personnel.
- Prepares reports and other documentation required by regulatory agencies and to support the quality function.

ORGANIZATIONAL RELATIONSHIPS

Reports directly to the President. Supervises, trains, and assists all quality control personnel. Directs quality-related activities in conjunction with Manufacturing, Engineering, Purchasing, Customer Service, and any other department/function that affects the quality of the organization's goods or services.

---

[1] May be referred to as the Quality Assurance Manager or Quality Control Manager

PROCEDURES

Procedure ID and Name	Policies & Procedures Manual
AD1000 Document Control	Sales & Marketing
AS1000 Document Control	AS 9100
AS1070 Customer Communication	AS 9100
AS1100 Preproduction Quality and Planning	AS 9100
AS1110 Supplier Evaluation	AS 9100
AS1130 Receiving and Inspection	AS 9100
AS1140 Control of Production-Service Processes	AS 9100
AS1150 Manufacturing	AS 9100
AS1180 Control of Monitoring & Measuring Eqpt.	AS 9100
AS1210 Monitoring-Measurement of Processes	AS 9100
AS1230 Control of Nonconforming Material	AS 9100
AS1240 Data Analysis-Continual Improvement	AS 9100
AS1250 Corrective Action	AS 9100
AS1260 Preventive Action	AS 9100
FS1070 Hazard Analysis	ISO 22000
FS1100 Supplier Evaluation	ISO 22000
FS1120 Manufacturing	ISO 22000
FS1140 Control of Monitoring and Measuring	ISO 22000
FS1150 Control of Potentially Unsafe Food Product	ISO 22000
FS1190 Product Recall	ISO 22000
ITAD110 IT Department Satisfaction	Computer & Network (IT)
ITSW106 Software Documentation	Computer & Network (IT)
ITSW107 Software Testing	Computer & Network (IT)
ITSW109 Software Releases Updates	Computer & Network (IT)
MFG111 Corrective Action	Business Sampler
PM1030 Product Recalls	Sales and Marketing
PUR101 Vendor Selection	Accounting
PUR104 Receiving and Inspection	Accounting
QP1030 Control of Nonconforming Product/Mat'l.	ISO 9001 QMS
QP1120 Vendor Evaluation	ISO 9001 QMS
QP1130 Preproduction Planning	ISO 9001 QMS
QP1140 Manufacturing	ISO 9001 QMS

Procedure ID and Name	Policies & Procedures Manual
QP1150 Identification and Traceability	ISO 9001 QMS
QP1170 Control of Monitoring & Measuring Eqpt.	ISO 9001 QMS
QP1180 Process Monitoring and Measurement	ISO 9001 QMS
QP1200 Data Analysis and Continual Improvement	ISO 9001 QMS
QP1210 Receiving and Inspection	ISO 9001 QMS
QP1220 Purchasing	ISO 9001 QMS
SWD106 Software Documentation	Software Development
SWD107 Software Testing	Software Development
SWD109 Software Releases Updates	Software Development

QUALIFICATIONS

A bachelor's degree in engineering or quality is required, as is 10 years of experience in Quality Assurance/Quality Management. A master's degree in quality or a relevant field of science (e.g., bioengineering degree for a bioengineering company) is preferred.

Must have proven ability to lead a diverse team of technicians. Excellent communication skills and the ability to work well with people at all levels are essential. Must be able to demonstrated strong organizational and managerial skills. Project management experience is a must; prefer someone with strong MS-Project skills.

The ideal candidate is certified in one or more quality-related disciplines (e.g., CQA, CMQ/OE, PMP). Experience with MS-Office and Minitab are extremely helpful.

PHYSICAL DEMANDS

Ability to communicate orally with customers, vendors, management and other co-workers is crucial. Regular use of the telephone and e-mail for communication is essential. Sitting for extended periods is common. Hearing and vision within normal ranges is helpful for normal conversations, to receive ordinary information, and to prepare or inspect documents.

No heavy lifting is expected. Exertion of up to 10 lbs. of force occasionally may be required. Good manual dexterity for the use of common office equipment such as computer terminals, calculator, copiers, and fax machines.

Good reasoning ability is required to solve a wide range of business problems. Able to apply statistical calculations, analysis of variance, correlation techniques, and sampling theory as well as algebra, linear equations, and other analytics as required. Able to understand and utilize Internet server and network reports to conduct business.

WORK ENVIRONMENT

The job is performed indoors in a traditional office setting. Activities include extended periods of sitting and extensive work at a computer.

REVISION HISTORY

Revision	Date	Description of Changes	Requested By
0.0	mm/dd/yyyy	Initial Release	

Document ID **JD0330**	Title **DOCUMENT MANAGER**	Print Date **mm/dd/yyyy**
Revision **0.0**	Prepared By **Preparer's Name / Title**	Date Prepared **mm/dd/yyyy**
Effective Date **mm/dd/yyyy**	Reviewed By **Reviewer's Name / Title**	Date Reviewed **mm/dd/yyyy**
	Approved By **Final Approver's Name / Title**	Date Approved **mm/dd/yyyy**

SUMMARY OF FUNCTIONS

The document manager is responsible for control, security, accessibility, and timeliness of organizational documents that may be used by/useful to more than one employee, such as policies, procedures, guidelines, forms, templates, and training materials.

ESSENTIAL DUTIES AND RESPONSIBILITIES

- Develop the document management plan and update it, as needed.
- Manage organizational documentation through the document life cycle.
- Maintain organizational documents and the document management system.
- Identify and investigate the need for documents of various types.
- Ensure that organizational documents go through a documented and approved review-and-approval process before being stored.
- Ensure that internal controls are in place and are functional.
- Ensure the security, accessibility, and proper distribution of organizational documents.
- Help develop and enforce documentation design, review, and storage guidelines.
- With the IT security manager, assign/approve user privileges.
- Plan and conduct meetings and presentations related to document management.

ORGANIZATIONAL RELATIONSHIPS

Reports directly to the administrative services manager. Assists and works in conjunction with the IT staff to facilitate smooth operation of the document management system.

PROCEDURES

Procedure ID and Name	Policies & Procedures Manual
AD1000 Document Control	Sales and Marketing
AS1000 Document Control	AS 9100
AS1010 Quality Records	AS 9100
AS1090 Design Change	AS 9100
FA1030 Document Control	Finance
FS1000 Document Control	ISO 22000

Procedure ID and Name	Policies & Procedures Manual
ITAD103 IT Document Management	Computer & Network (IT)
QP1000 Document Control	ISO 9001 QMS
QP1010 Record Control	ISO 9001 QMS
QP1110 Design Change	ISO 9001 QMS

QUALIFICATIONS

A bachelor's degree in library science is required; an advanced degree (e.g., MLS, MA) is preferred. Experience in document management and document management systems or content management systems software is preferred. Must have experience conducting meetings and presentations.

PHYSICAL DEMANDS

Ability to communicate well with document users - orally and in writing - is crucial. Regular use of the telephone, email, and other means of communication is part of the job. Sitting for extended periods is common. Hearing and vision within normal ranges is essential for normal conversations, to receive ordinary information, and prepare or inspect documents.

The job mostly entails sitting at a workstation for extended periods, though you will occasionally move about the office to access files or office equipment, operate a computer and other office productivity devices (calculator, hand held devices, copier, printer, or fax), conduct meetings.

No heavy lifting is expected, though occasionally exerting up to 10 lbs. of force (carrying a laptop, tablet, or other device, for instance) may be required. Good manual dexterity (for the use of common office equipment such as computers, calculator, copiers, scanners, and fax machines) is helpful.

WORK ENVIRONMENT

The job is performed indoors in a traditional office setting. Activities include extended periods of sitting and extensive work at a computer, phone, and other mobile communication devices.

REVISION HISTORY

Revision	Date	Description of Changes	Requested By
0.0	mm/dd/yyyy	Initial Release	

[This page intentionally left blank]

Document ID **JD0410**	Title **FINANCIAL MANAGER**	Print Date **mm/dd/yyyy**
Revision **0.0**	Prepared By **Preparer's Name / Title**	Date Prepared **mm/dd/yyyy**
Effective Date **mm/dd/yyyy**	Reviewed By **Reviewer's Name / Title**	Date Reviewed **mm/dd/yyyy**
	Approved By **Final Approver's Name / Title**	Date Approved **mm/dd/yyyy**

SUMMARY

The Financial Manager is responsible for the financial well-being of the organization. They develop strategies and plans for the organization's long-term financial objectives, produce financial reports, and direct investment activities.

ESSENTIAL DUTIES AND RESPONSIBILITIES

- Prepare financial statements, business activity reports, and financial forecasts.
- Ensure that the organization's financial records and recordkeeping methods are in compliance with applicable standards and regulations.
- Manage employees and contractors who are responsible for financial reporting and budgeting.
- Periodically review the organization's financial reports and identify opportunities for cost reduction.
- Analyze data and advise top management on how to maximize profits.
- Analyze market trends and identify opportunities for growth/expansion.
- Oversee organization's investments.
- Give final approval to expenditures greater than (*n* dollars).

ORGANIZATIONAL RELATIONSHIPS

Reports directly to the organization's President.

PROCEDURES

Procedure ID and Name	Policies & Procedures Manual
G&A108 Property Tax Assessments	Accounting
PUR101 Vendor Selection	Accounting
ITAD109 IT Outsourcing	Computer & Network (IT)
ITAM102 IT Asset Management	Computer & Network (IT)
ITAM103 IT Vendor Selection	Computer & Network (IT)
FA1010 Management Responsibility	Finance
FA1040 Record Control	Finance
FS1100 Supplier Evaluation	ISO 22000

QUALIFICATIONS

A bachelor's degree in finance, accounting, economics, or business administration is required. Five or more years' experience as a financial analyst is also required.

Must have demonstrated ability to lead a team of 6 or more. Good communication skills and the ability to work well with people with and without finance/accounting backgrounds are essential. Project management experience a must.

Preference will be given to candidates with Certified Financial Analyst (CFA) designation

PHYSICAL DEMANDS

Ability to communicate orally with top management, and coworkers is crucial. Regular use of phone and email for communication is essential. Hearing and vision correctable to within normal ranges is essential for normal conversations, receiving ordinary information, and preparing or inspecting documents.

The ability to remain in a stationary position roughly 50% of the time, as well as the ability to move about the office occasionally (accessing files/storage, office equipment, computers and other office productivity devices, attending meetings, etc.), is required.

Using a computer while sitting for extended periods is common. Must also be able to position self to maintain equipment, including under tables and desks.

No heavy lifting is expected, though occasional exertion of about 20 lbs. of force (e.g., picking up and carrying binders, laptops) may be required. Good manual dexterity required to use common office equipment (e.g., computers, mobile devices, calculators, copiers, scanners).

WORK ENVIRONMENT

The job is performed indoors in a traditional office setting. Extended periods of sitting while using a computer or other devices are common.

REVISION HISTORY

Revision	Date	Description of changes	Requested By
0.0	mm/dd/yyyy	Initial Release	

Document ID	Title	Print Date
JD0500	**HELP DESK TECHNICIAN**	**mm/dd/yyyy**
Revision	Prepared By	Date Prepared
0.0	**Preparer's Name / Title**	**mm/dd/yyyy**
Effective Date	Reviewed By	Date Reviewed
mm/dd/yyyy	**Reviewer's Name / Title**	**mm/dd/yyyy**
	Approved By	Date Approved
	Final Approver's Name / Title	**mm/dd/yyyy**

SUMMARY

The Help Desk Technician (aka, Computer Support Specialist) provides assistance to any and all employees using computer hardware and software/supports information technology employees within the organization/assists non-IT users (internal and/or external) who are experiencing hardware and/or software problems.

ESSENTIAL DUTIES AND RESPONSIBILITIES

- Test and evaluate computer hardware, software, and/or systems (networks).
- Perform periodic maintenance of the computer network (WAN/LAN, hardware, and software).
- Troubleshoot computer-related problems; develop and implement solutions to those problems in a timely manner.
- Understand and be understood by non-IT employees/customers.
- Work independently and as part of a team of technicians.
- Make decisions quickly and decisively, often with limited information.

ORGANIZATIONAL RELATIONSHIPS

Reports directly to the Information Security Manager/Technical Support Manager/IT Manager.

PROCEDURES

Procedure ID and Name	Policies & Procedures Manual
ITSD108 IT Incident Handling	Computer & Network (IT)

QUALIFICATIONS

A bachelor's degree in computer science/information technology is required. 2+ years of experience in an IT environment (discipline) is also required. Preference will be given to candidates with CompTIA A+ certification.

Excellent communication skills and the ability to work well with IT technicians / specialists and non-IT personnel are essential. Interpersonal skills and listening are crucial. Strong troubleshooting and problem-solving skills are a must.

A year or more of experience in a help desk environment using Remedy is preferred.

PHYSICAL DEMANDS

Ability to communicate orally with customers, vendors, management, and coworkers is crucial. Regular use of phone and email for communication is essential. Hearing and vision correctable to within normal ranges is essential for normal conversations, receiving ordinary information, and preparing or inspecting documents.

The ability to remain in a stationary position roughly 50% of the time, as well as the ability to move about the office occasionally (accessing files/storage, office equipment, computers and other office productivity devices, attending meetings, etc.), is required.

Using a computer while sitting for extended periods is common. Must also be able to position self to maintain equipment, including under tables and desks.

No heavy lifting is expected, though occasional exertion of about 20 lbs. of force (e.g., picking up and carrying binders, laptops) may be required. Good manual dexterity required to use common office equipment (e.g., computers, mobile devices, calculators, copiers, scanners).

WORK ENVIRONMENT

The job is performed indoors in a traditional office setting. Extended periods of sitting while using a computer or other devices are common.

REVISION HISTORY

Revision	Date	Description of Changes	Requested By
0.0	mm/dd/yyyy	Initial Release	

Document ID	Title	Print Date
JD0510	**HUMAN RESOURCES MANAGER**	**mm/dd/yyyy**
Revision	Prepared By	Date Prepared
0.0	**Preparer's Name / Title**	**mm/dd/yyyy**
Effective Date	Reviewed By	Date Reviewed
mm/dd/yyyy	**Reviewer's Name / Title**	**mm/dd/yyyy**
	Approved By	Date Approved
	Final Approver's Name / Title	**mm/dd/yyyy**

SUMMARY OF FUNCTIONS

The Human Resources Manager plans, directs, and coordinates functions related to the organization's employees and contractors. They develop, implement, and maintain human resources[1] policies, procedures, and forms; assist and support department managers and employees regarding personnel issues; and maintain personnel records in accordance with organizational and regulatory requirements.

The HR Manager also oversees recruiting, interviewing, and hiring of employees and contractors. They consult with top management (e.g., President, Finance Manager) on strategic workforce planning and serve as the organization's link between management and employees/contractors.

ESSENTIAL DUTIES AND RESPONSIBILITIES

- Under the direction of the Executive Officers of the company, develops implements and updates personnel policies, procedures and forms. Stays current with laws and regulations affecting personnel issues (Equal employment, employee safety, etc.), employment practices or trends and recommends new or revised policies and procedures as appropriate.
- Assists and supports department managers and all employees regarding personnel issues. Answers employee questions regarding personnel policies, procedures and benefits; researches and disseminates topical or timely information to managers and/or employees on personnel issues.
- Coordinates and assists with employee recruitment, hiring, orientation, and training; determines employee classifications and ensures completion of all appropriate paperwork for new employees.
- Coordinates and assists manager with employee reviews and performance appraisals. Coordinates and participates in completion of terminations and exit interviews.
- Establishes and maintains personnel records and reports; maintains company organization charts and employee directory.
- Prepares and coordinates all accident reports and worker's compensation reports. Handles follow-up insurance and worker's compensation claims. Handles return-to-work and disability slips.
- Performs other related duties as required or as assigned.

---

[1] Also referred to as "talent," "human capital," and "personnel."

ORGANIZATIONAL RELATIONSHIPS

Reports directly to the Vice President of Finance and Administration. Coordinates activities and assists all department managers and employees.

PROCEDURES

Procedure ID and Name	Policies & Procedures Manual
AD1040 Sales Hiring	Sales & Marketing
ADM101 Personnel Records	Human Resources
ADM102 Form Development	Human Resources
ADM107 Separation	Human Resources
ADM108 Workplace Rules & Guidelines	Human Resources
ADM109 Management Responsibility	Human Resources
AS1030 Job Descriptions	AS 9100
AS1040 Competence, Awareness, and Training	AS 9100
CMP101 Workplace Safety	Human Resources
CMP102 Americans with Disabilities	Human Resources
CMP103 Family And Medical Leave	Human Resources
CMP104 Drug Free Workplace	Human Resources
CMP105 Health Insurance Portability Accountability	Human Resources
CMP106 Harassment & Discrimination	Human Resources
CMP107 Federal Posting Requirements rev 1.0	Human Resources
CMP108 Equal Employment Opportunity	Human Resources
COM101 Payroll	Human Resources
COM102 Paid & Unpaid Leave	Human Resources
COM103 Insurance Benefits	Human Resources
COM104 Healthcare Benefits	Human Resources
COM105 Employee Retirement Income Security	Human Resources
COM106 Consolidated Budget Reconciliation	Human Resources
DEV101 Development Management	Human Resources
DEV102 Training Reimbursement	Human Resources
DEV103 Computer User & Staff	Human Resources
DEV104 Internet & E-Mail Acceptable Use	Human Resources
DEV105 Performance Appraisals	Human Resources
DEV106 Employee Discipline	Human Resources
FS1020 Management Responsibility	ISO 22000

Procedure ID and Name	Policies & Procedures Manual
FS1030 Competence, Awareness, and Training	ISO 22000
FS1040 Job Descriptions	ISO 22000
FS1060 Hazard Analysis Preparation	ISO 22000
G&A109 Release of Confidential Information	Accounting
HRG101 Employee Hiring	Human Resources
HRG102 Job Descriptions	Human Resources
HRG103 Employment Applications	Human Resources
HRG104 Interviewing Applicants	Human Resources
HRG105 Background Investigations	Human Resources
ITAD108 Email Policy	Computer & Network (IT)
ITAM101 IT Asset Standards	Computer & Network (IT)
ITSD106 IT Access Control	Computer & Network (IT)
ITSD108 IT Incident Handling	Computer & Network (IT)
ITTS105 IT User-Staff Training Plan	Computer & Network (IT)
QP1070 Competence, Training, and Awareness	ISO 9001 QMS

QUALIFICATIONS

A bachelor's degree in human resources or business administration is required. Must have excellent oral and written communication skills and the ability to work well with people at all levels of the organization. Leadership skills are beneficial. Familiarity with personnel standards and regulations at the federal level is required; knowledge of state regulations, standards, and guidelines is desired. Project management experience is preferred.

SPHR or comparable HR certification is highly desirable. Membership in a professional organization (e.g., SHRM) is beneficial.

PHYSICAL DEMANDS

Occasional travel by airplane and automobile to various worksites for conducting business is necessary (around 10%). Must be able to communicate well orally and in writing with board of directors, top management, legal staff, coworkers, and contractors individually and in groups. Regular use of a telephone, email, or other medium to communicate is essential.

Sitting for extended periods is common. Hearing and vision within normal ranges is essential for normal conversations, to receive ordinary information and to prepare or inspect documents.

No heavy lifting is expected. Exertion of up to 10 lbs. of force occasionally may be required. Good manual dexterity for the use of common office equipment such as computer terminals, calculator, copiers, and FAX machines.

Good reasoning ability, eye for detail are required to solve a wide range of business problems.

WORK ENVIRONMENT

The job is performed indoors in a traditional office setting. Activities include extended periods of sitting and extensive work at a computer or other device.

REVISION HISTORY

Revision	Date	Description of Changes	Requested By
0.0	mm/dd/yyyy	Initial Release	

Document ID	Title	Print Date
JD0560	**INTERNAL AUDIT TEAM LEADER**	**mm/dd/yyyy**
Revision	Prepared By	Date Prepared
0.0	**Preparer's Name / Title**	**mm/dd/yyyy**
Effective Date	Reviewed By	Date Reviewed
mm/dd/yyyy	**Reviewer's Name / Title**	**mm/dd/yyyy**
	Approved By	Date Approved
	Final Approver's Name / Title	**mm/dd/yyyy**

SUMMARY OF FUNCTIONS

The Audit Team Leader oversees a team of auditors for the duration of an internal audit

ESSENTIAL DUTIES AND RESPONSIBILITIES

- Oversee the accounting and financial reporting processes and the audits of the financial statements of the Company.
- Evaluate and select an External Auditor[1].
- Manage the Internal Audit process, develop and manage the Internal Audit schedule (or cycle), supervise Audit Team members, and report the Audit Team's findings to the Audit Committee.
- Review and approve of root cause analysis and investigate material errors in financial statements.
- Review and approve the Internal Audit Department's annual and long-range audit plans and activities, for reviewing significant findings and recommendations by Internal Audit and ensuring the adequacy of management's corrective actions.
- Conduct and supervise the IT Security audit; conduct opening and closing meetings for the audit; prepare and present the final audit report.

ORGANIZATIONAL RELATIONSHIPS

Reports directly to the IT Security Manager or Accounting Manager.

PROCEDURES

Procedure ID and Name	Policies & Procedures Manual
AC1000 Sarbanes-Oxley Compliance	Finance
AC1040 External Auditing	Finance
AC1050 Internal Auditing	Finance
FS1040 Financial Restatements	Finance
ITSD107 IT Security Audits	Computer & Network (IT)

---

[1] Also known as an "independent auditor" or a "third-party auditor"

QUALIFICATIONS

A high school diploma or GED plus 5 or more years of auditing experience is required; a bachelor's degree (in accounting, computer science, or other appropriate field of study) and 2+ years of auditing experience are acceptable, as well.

Good communication skills and the ability to work well with people are essential. 3+ years of experience with appropriate computer applications is beneficial. Project management experience is preferred.

PHYSICAL DEMANDS

Ability to communicate orally with customers, vendors, management, and coworkers is crucial. Regular use of the telephone and email for communication is essential. Sitting for extended periods is common. Hearing and vision within normal ranges is essential for normal conversations, to receive ordinary information and to prepare or inspect documents.

Activities require the ability to remain in a stationary position 50% of the time, occasionally move about inside the office to access files or office equipment, operate a computer and other office productivity machinery, such as a calculator, hand held devices, copy machine, and computer printer, and operate and monitor various medical equipment. Must be able to constantly position self to maintain equipment, including under tables and desks.

No heavy lifting is expected. Exertion of up to 10 lbs. of force occasionally may be required. Good manual dexterity for the use of common office equipment such as computer terminals, calculator, copiers, and FAX machines.

WORK ENVIRONMENT

The job is performed indoors in a traditional office setting. Activities include extended periods of sitting and extensive work at a computer monitor and phone.

REVISION HISTORY

Revision	Date	Description of Changes	Requested By
0.0	mm/dd/yyyy	Initial Release	

Document ID **JD0630**	Title **IT ASSET MANAGER**	Print Date **mm/dd/yyyy**
Revision **0.0**	Prepared By **Preparer's Name / Title**	Date Prepared **mm/dd/yyyy**
Effective Date **mm/dd/yyyy**	Reviewed By **Reviewer's Name / Title**	Date Reviewed **mm/dd/yyyy**
	Approved By **Final Approver's Name / Title**	Date Approved **mm/dd/yyyy**

SUMMARY

The IT Asset Manager manages, controls, and protects the organization's IT assets (i.e., hardware) throughout their life cycle, from acquisition through final disposition. In addition, the IT Asset Manager designs, develops, and implements the organization's asset management strategy.

ESSENTIAL DUTIES AND RESPONSIBILITIES

- Manage IT hardware asset portfolio with respect to risk, cost control, governance, compliance, and performance objectives.
- Develop and maintain company policies and processes.
- Manage a team of IT Asset Analysts.
- Plan and implement IT hardware asset life cycle strategy; advise Procurement and IT Operations in procurement strategies for IT hardware acquisition.
- Serve as IT hardware asset management subject matter expert.
- Optimize usage and cost of IT hardware deployments.
- Manage acquisition, deployment, utilization, tracking, security, and final disposition of IT assets.

ORGANIZATIONAL RELATIONSHIPS

Reports directly to IT Management. Assists and works in conjunction with hardware/ software installers and IT Security.

PROCEDURES

Procedure ID and Name	Policies & Procedures Manual
ITAM101 IT Asset Standards	Computer & Network (IT)
ITAM102 IT Asset Management	Computer & Network (IT)
ITAM103 IT Vendor Selection	Computer & Network (IT)
ITAM104 IT Asset Assessment	Computer & Network (IT)
ITAM105 IT Asset Installation Satisfaction	Computer & Network (IT)

QUALIFICATIONS

A bachelor's degree in business administration or information technology is required, as is 5-7 years' experience in IT asset management. Experience in project management and IT procurement are a plus, as is experience with asset management tools (e.g., Flexera, CA). Understanding of Microsoft Active Directory is very important. Must have professional certification (e.g., CHAMP, ITIL, CITAM) or be able to achieve within six (6) months of hire.

Must be a problem solver and innovator. Must possess strong computer skills – expert in Excel to analyze large volumes of data. Experience with statistical analysis software (e.g., SAS, Minitab) a plus.

Strong interpersonal skills required; leadership skills desirable. Desire demonstrated cross-cultural effectiveness and capability of driving change. Ability to see structure and bring order to undefined (or poorly defined) processes, as well as develop and implement processes, are a necessity. Understanding of ISO 9001 a plus.

Must be comfortable in a fast-paced, dynamic environment, able to handle multiple tasks simultaneously. Must be able to work independently and be self-motivated (personal initiative). Solid project management skills and experience are needed; certification in project management (e.g., PMP) will be helpful.

Must demonstrate strong oral and written communication skills, excellent customer service skills, and be able to handle pressure. Prefer candidates with demonstrated experience in analyzing and presenting data to management.

PHYSICAL DEMANDS

Ability to communicate orally with customers, vendors, management, and coworkers is crucial. Regular use of phone and email for communication is essential. Hearing and vision correctable to within normal ranges is essential for normal conversations, receiving ordinary information, and preparing or inspecting documents.

The ability to remain in a stationary position roughly 50% of the time, as well as the ability to move about the office occasionally (accessing files/storage, office equipment, computers and other office productivity devices, attending meetings, etc.), is required.

Using a computer while sitting for extended periods is common. Must also be able to position self to maintain equipment, including under tables and desks.

Some moderately heavy lifting (of computer monitors, printers, etc.) may be required. Good manual dexterity required to use common office equipment (e.g., computers, mobile devices, calculators, copiers, scanners).

WORK ENVIRONMENT

The job is performed indoors in a traditional office setting. Extended periods of sitting while using a computer or other devices are common.

REVISION HISTORY

Revision	Date	Description of Changes	Requested By
0.0	mm/dd/yyyy	Initial Release	

[This page intentionally left blank]

Document ID	Title	Print Date
JD0640	**IT DISASTER RECOVERY COORDINATOR**	**mm/dd/yyyy**
Revision	Prepared By	Date Prepared
0.0	**Preparer's Name / Title**	**mm/dd/yyyy**
Effective Date	Reviewed By	Date Reviewed
mm/dd/yyyy	**Reviewer's Name / Title**	**mm/dd/yyyy**
	Approved By	Date Approved
	Final Approver's Name / Title	**mm/dd/yyyy**

SUMMARY

The IT Disaster Recovery Coordinator directs IT disaster response/crisis management activities in compliance with the IT emergency plan and helps provide and coordinate disaster preparedness training with respect to the organization's information technologies, helping ensure business continuity.

ESSENTIAL DUTIES AND RESPONSIBILITIES

- Work with Business Continuity management to ensure that the disaster recovery (crisis management) and business continuity plans drive disaster recovery (DR) strategy and procedures.
- Establish and maintain the overall plans for executing all DR procedures and understand their interdependencies.
- Establish and maintain detailed DR communications and command and control plans through a change management process.
- Work with the IT technical staff to ensure that disaster recovery solutions are adequate, in place, maintained, and tested as part of the regular operational life cycle.
- Develop and understand all testing necessary for a successful DR execution.
- Schedule and lead all DR exercises.
- Provide ongoing feedback for risk management, mitigation, and prevention.
- Represent disaster recovery cost requirements in the annual budgeting process.
- Regularly report Disaster Recovery activities to upper management.
- Act as liaison for auditing and examination of disaster recovery processes.
- Help ensure compliance with all applicable federal, state and local laws, regulations, and ordinances.

ORGANIZATIONAL RELATIONSHIPS

Reports directly to IT Security Management. Assists and works in conjunction with IT Security and disaster recovery technicians (specialists) and disaster response and recovery agencies to help facilitate smooth, efficient, and effective IT disaster recovery.

PROCEDURES

Procedure ID and Name	Policies & Procedures Manual
ITSD104 IT Disaster Recovery	Computer & Network (IT)

QUALIFICATIONS

A bachelor's degree in computer science, information systems, information protection (information security), or a related IT field is required. Certification in CBCP or CFCP is preferred; a PMP certification is desired.

Require 10+ years of experience in IT operations implementing and supporting web and middleware solutions in a data center environment. Must have 4+ years of experience dedicated to disaster recovery operations and management in the financial or other similar industry. Need experience managing large projects, using PMI standard methods and tools.

Understanding of current recovery solutions, high availability architectures and mainframe architectures is needed, as is knowledge of crisis communication solutions. Must know elementary IT network principles.

Require excellent oral and written communication skills to convey plans, exercises, and activities. Must be able to interact with technical, non-technical, and management staff.

Familiarity with business continuity program life cycle plans and source deliverables (e.g., risk assessments, bias, continuity planning) is essential.

PHYSICAL DEMANDS

Ability to communicate orally with IT staff and management is crucial. Regular use of phone and email for communication is essential. Hearing and vision correctable to within normal ranges is essential for normal conversations, receiving ordinary information, and preparing or inspecting documents.

The ability to remain in a stationary position roughly 50% of the time, as well as the ability to move about the office occasionally (accessing files/storage, office equipment, computers and other office productivity devices, attending meetings, etc.), is required.

Using a computer while sitting for extended periods is common. Must also be able to position self to maintain equipment, including under tables and desks.

No heavy lifting is expected, though occasional exertion of about 20 lbs. of force (e.g., picking up / carrying laptops) may be required. Good manual dexterity required to use common office equipment (e.g., computers, mobile devices, calculators, copiers, scanners).

WORK ENVIRONMENT

The job is performed indoors in a traditional office setting. Extended periods of sitting while using a computer or other devices are common.

REVISION HISTORY

Revision	Date	Description of Changes	Requested By
0.0	mm/dd/yyyy	Initial Release	

[This page intentionally left blank]

Document ID JD0650	Title **INFORMATION TECHNOLOGY MANAGER**	Print Date mm/dd/yyyy
Revision **0.0**	Prepared By **Preparer's Name / Title**	Date Prepared mm/dd/yyyy
Effective Date mm/dd/yyyy	Reviewed By **Reviewer's Name / Title**	Date Reviewed mm/dd/yyyy
	Approved By **Final Approver's Name / Title**	Date Approved mm/dd/yyyy

SUMMARY

The Information Technology, or IT, Manager plans, coordinates, and directs the organization's computer systems (information systems) and related activities; helps determine the organization's information technology goals/objectives; helps develop, implements, and manages the organization's information technology plan; and identifies and recommends the appropriate technologies needed to meet the goals of IT.

ESSENTIAL DUTIES AND RESPONSIBILITIES

- Analyze/assess the organization's IT requirements (short- and long-term) and recommend acquisitions and/or upgrades to top management.
- Plan and direct the installation (and upgrading, where needed) of hardware and software tools and technologies.
- With IT Security, help ensure the safety and security of the organization's IT network and electronic documents.
- Perform cost/benefit analyses of IT projects, prepare and present analyses (i.e., justify spending) to the organization's top management.
- Continue to learn about new technologies and look for ways to implement them within the organization.
- Organize, coordinate, and direct IT-management-level personnel (e.g., database manager/administrator, IT security manager, network manager).
- Determine short- and long-term personnel and training needs for IT.
- Plan and direct the work of IT professionals, including computer systems analysts, software developers, information security analysts, and computer support specialists.
- Negotiate with technology vendors, contractors to obtain the highest possible level of services for the organization.

ORGANIZATIONAL RELATIONSHIPS

Reports directly to the organization's Board of Directors. Works in conjunction with Accounting, Finance, Operations, Sales/Marketing, and other core departments.

PROCEDURES

Procedure ID and Name	Policies & Procedures Manual
ITAD101 Information Technology Management	Computer & Network (IT)
ITAD102 IT Records Management	Computer & Network (IT)
ITAD103 IT Document Management	Computer & Network (IT)
ITAD108 Email Policy	Computer & Network (IT)
ITAD109 IT Outsourcing	Computer & Network (IT)
ITAM101 IT Asset Standards	Computer & Network (IT)
ITAM102 IT Asset Management	Computer & Network (IT)
ITAM103 IT Vendor Selection	Computer & Network (IT)
ITAM105 IT Asset Installation Satisfaction	Computer & Network (IT)
ITSD101 IT Threat and Risk Assessment	Computer & Network (IT)
ITSD102 IT Security Plan	Computer & Network (IT)
ITSD103 IT Media Storage	Computer & Network (IT)
ITSD106 IT Access Control	Computer & Network (IT)
ITSD107 IT Security Audits	Computer & Network (IT)
ITSD108 IT Incident Handling	Computer & Network (IT)
ITSW101 IT Project Definition	Computer & Network (IT)
ITTS101 IT System Administration	Computer & Network (IT)
ITTS102 IT Support Center	Computer & Network (IT)
ITTS103 IT Server/Network Support	Computer & Network (IT)
ITTS104 IT Troubleshooting	Computer & Network (IT)
ITTS105 IT User/Staff Training Plan	Computer & Network (IT)

QUALIFICATIONS

A bachelor's degree in information technology or computer science is required; a Master's degree in business administration is preferred. 10 years of related work experience, with 3 or more in a management position, is also required.

Must have demonstrated the ability to lead a diverse team of programmers, designers, analysts, technicians, etc. Excellent communication skills and the ability to work well with people at every level and in every department are essential. Project management experience is a must-have. Expertise in preparing RFPs (RFQs) and negotiating with top management, vendors, etc., is essential. Also need someone with SDLC knowledge and experience. Should be able to run meetings effectively and efficiently.

Candidates with certifications in project management (PMP), management (CM), information management (CITM), or a comparable designation will be given preference. Experience with Microsoft Project preferred.

PHYSICAL DEMANDS

Ability to communicate orally with customers, vendors, management, and coworkers is crucial. Regular use of phone and email for communication is essential. Hearing and vision correctable to within normal ranges is essential for normal conversations, receiving ordinary information, and preparing or inspecting documents.

The ability to remain in a stationary position roughly 50% of the time, as well as the ability to move about the office occasionally (accessing files/storage, office equipment, computers and other office productivity devices, attending meetings, etc.), is required.

Using a computer while sitting for extended periods is common. Must also be able to position self to maintain equipment, including under tables and desks.

No heavy lifting is expected, though occasional exertion of 20 lbs. or less of force (e.g., picking up and carrying laptops / tablets) may be required. Good manual dexterity required to use common office equipment (e.g., computers, mobile devices, calculators, copiers, scanners).

WORK ENVIRONMENT

The job is performed indoors in a traditional office setting. Extended periods of sitting while using a computer or other devices are common.

REVISION HISTORY

Revision	Date	Description of Changes	Requested By
0.0	mm/dd/yyyy	Initial Release	

[This page intentionally left blank]

Document ID **JD0660**	Title **IT PROJECT MANAGER**	Print Date **mm/dd/yyyy**
Revision **0.0**	Prepared By **Preparer's Name / Title**	Date Prepared **mm/dd/yyyy**
Effective Date **mm/dd/yyyy**	Reviewed By **Reviewer's Name / Title**	Date Reviewed **mm/dd/yyyy**
	Approved By **Final Approver's Name / Title**	Date Approved **mm/dd/yyyy**

SUMMARY

The IT Project Manager plans, coordinates, and directs individual IT projects.

ESSENTIAL DUTIES AND RESPONSIBILITIES

- Direct teams of software developers, information analysts, technicians, etc., for the duration of IT projects.
- Plan and manage projects, ensuring that requirements (e.g., time, budget, checkpoints, project reporting, testing, capability and effectiveness of deliverables) are met.
- Continue to learn about new technologies and look for ways to implement them within projects.
- Ensure that IT project teams have sufficient resources to complete any given project.
- Adapt IT project plans (and adjust budgets) as needed, to account for problems as they occur.

ORGANIZATIONAL RELATIONSHIPS

Reports directly to IT Management (CTO, IT Manager, etc .).

PROCEDURES

Procedure ID and Name	Policies & Procedures Manual
ITSW101 IT Project Definition	Computer & Network (IT)
ITSW102 IT Project Management	Computer & Network (IT)

QUALIFICATIONS

A bachelor's degree in information technology or computer science is required. 10 years of IT work experience, with 3 or more of those managing IT projects, is also required.

Must have demonstrated ability to lead a team of programmers, designers, analysts, technicians, etc. Excellent communication skills and the ability to work well with people, whether IT or non-IT, are essential. Project management experience is a must. Expertise in analyzing RFPs (RFQs) is essential. Must be able to run project meetings effectively and efficiently. Proven ability to meet deadlines needed. Experience with Microsoft Project is required, as is experience with the entire SDLC.

Candidates with project management certifications (e.g., PMP) will be given preference.

PHYSICAL DEMANDS

Ability to communicate orally with IT staff and end users is crucial. Regular use of phone, email, and messaging systems (IM) for communication is essential. Hearing and vision correctable to within normal ranges is essential for normal conversations, receiving ordinary information, and preparing or inspecting documents.

The ability to remain in a stationary position roughly 50% of the time, as well as the ability to move about the office occasionally (accessing files/storage, office equipment, computers and other office productivity devices, attending meetings, etc.), is required.

Using a computer while sitting for extended periods is common. Must also be able to position self to maintain equipment, including under tables and desks.

No heavy lifting is expected, though occasional exertion of 20 lbs. or less of force (e.g., picking up and carrying laptops / tablets) may be required. Good manual dexterity required to use common office equipment (e.g., computers, mobile devices, calculators, copiers, scanners).

WORK ENVIRONMENT

The job is performed indoors in a traditional office setting. Extended periods of sitting while using a computer or other devices are common.

REVISION HISTORY

Revision	Date	Description of Changes	Requested By
0.0	mm/dd/yyyy	Initial Release	

Document ID **JD0670**	Title **IT SECURITY MANAGER**	Print Date **mm/dd/yyyy**
Revision **0.0**	Prepared By **Preparer's Name / Title**	Date Prepared **mm/dd/yyyy**
Effective Date **mm/dd/yyyy**	Reviewed By **Reviewer's Name / Title**	Date Reviewed **mm/dd/yyyy**
	Approved By **Final Approver's Name / Title**	Date Approved **mm/dd/yyyy**

SUMMARY

The Information Technology Security Manager[1] ensures that the risk to the organization's information posed by a variety of cyberthreats (cyberattacks; theft or corruption from within; etc.) is minimized. The IT Security Manager ensures that when cyberattacks occur or data are stolen or compromised, these incidents are dealt with promptly and effectively and the chance of that particular type of incident recurring is minimized.

ESSENTIAL DUTIES AND RESPONSIBILITIES

- Research the latest information technology security trends.
- Monitor their organization's networks for security breaches and investigate violations when they occurs.
- Help to design, implement, and maintain the organization's cybersecurity plan.
- Develop and direct implementation of security standards and best practices for the organization.
- Direct the installation and use of security tools (e.g., firewalls, data encryption), to protect sensitive information.
- Recommend security enhancements to IT Management.
- Help computer technicians, end users when they need to install or learn about new security products and/or procedures.
- Ensure that IT security audits are conducted periodically or as needed (e.g., when a security breach occurs).

ORGANIZATIONAL RELATIONSHIPS

Reports directly to the IT Manager (IT Director, CTO, etc.). Works in conjunction with organizational functions/departments to ensure employees are aware of cybersecurity issues, are trained in good cybersecurity practices, and are practicing safe/secure data collection, data transfers and storage, and use of social media, mobile devices, and apps, among others.

---

[1] May be referred to as the Information Security Manager or IT Security Manager

PROCEDURES

Procedure ID and Name	Policies & Procedures Manual
ITAD107 Computer and Internet Usage Policy	Computer & Network (IT)
ITAD108 Email Policy	Computer & Network (IT)
ITSD101 IT Threat / Risk Assessment	Computer & Network (IT)
ITSD102 IT Security Plan	Computer & Network (IT)
ITSD104 IT Disaster Recovery	Computer & Network (IT)
ITSD105 Computer Malware	Computer & Network (IT)
ITSD106 IT Access Control	Computer & Network (IT)
ITSD107 IT Security Audits	Computer & Network (IT)
ITSD108 IT Incident Handling	Computer & Network (IT)
ITTS105 IT User/Staff Training Plan	Computer & Network (IT)
ITAD102 IT Records Management	Computer & Network (IT)
ITSD103 IT Media Storage	Computer & Network (IT)
ITSD104 IT Disaster Recovery	Computer & Network (IT)

QUALIFICATIONS

A bachelor's degree in information technology or computer science is required. 10 years of related work experience, with 3 or more in an information security management position, is also required.

Excellent communication skills and the ability to work well with people at every level and in every department are essential. Candidates with certification in information security (CISSP, CSSLP, CCFP, CISM, etc.) or comparable work experience will be given preference. Risk analysis/assessment experience a plus.

Experience with Microsoft Windows Server 2008/Unix server required. Microsoft Project experience preferred.

PHYSICAL DEMANDS

Ability to communicate orally with vendors, management, and coworkers is crucial. Regular use of phone (mobile device) and email for communication is essential. Hearing and vision correctable to within normal ranges is essential for normal conversations, receiving ordinary information, and preparing or inspecting documents.

The ability to remain in a stationary position roughly 50% of the time, as well as the ability to move about the office occasionally (accessing files/storage, office equipment, computers and other office productivity devices, attending meetings, etc.), is required.

Using a computer while sitting for extended periods is common. Must also be able to position self to relocate or maintain equipment, including under tables and desks.

No heavy lifting is expected, though occasional exertion of 20 lbs. or less of force (e.g., picking up and carrying laptops, peripheral / network devices) may be required. Good manual dexterity required to use common office equipment (e.g., computers, mobile devices, calculators, copiers, scanners).

WORK ENVIRONMENT

The job is performed indoors in a traditional office setting. Extended periods of sitting while using a computer or other devices are common.

REVISION HISTORY

Revision	Date	Description of Changes	Requested By
0.0	mm/dd/yyyy	Initial Release	

[This page intentionally left blank]

Document ID JD0680	Title **IT STORAGE LIBRARIAN**	Print Date mm/dd/yyyy
Revision 0.0	Prepared By **Preparer's Name / Title**	Date Prepared mm/dd/yyyy
Effective Date mm/dd/yyyy	Reviewed By **Reviewer's Name / Title**	Date Reviewed mm/dd/yyyy
	Approved By **Final Approver's Name / Title**	Date Approved mm/dd/yyyy

SUMMARY

The IT Storage Librarian implements the organization's data storage plan, organizes and maintains the organization's electronic records (and related activity logs), ensuring that they are backed up and archived, and ensures their final disposition in accordance with applicable regulations and organizational policy.

ESSENTIAL DUTIES AND RESPONSIBILITIES

- Create and maintain accessible computer archives and databases.
- Organize and classify archival records to make it easy to find materials.
- Provide reference services and assistance for users.
- Safeguard records by copying to film, videotape, disk, or computer formats.
- Preserve and maintain documents and records.
- Help set and administer policy concerning record/file access.

ORGANIZATIONAL RELATIONSHIPS

Reports directly to the IT Manager.

PROCEDURES

Procedure ID and Name	Policies & Procedures Manual
ITAD102 IT Records Management	Computer & Network (IT)
ITSD103 IT Media Storage	Computer & Network (IT)
ITSD104 IT Disaster Recovery	Computer & Network (IT)

QUALIFICATIONS

A bachelor's degree in information management or library science is required. 3+ years of experience in database management (preferably with Oracle DBMS) is required.

Good communication skills and the ability to work well with people at all levels are essential. Strong organizational, management, analytical, and math skills needed. Must be customer (user) focused. Project management experience a plus.

Prefer a candidate with database management certification.

PHYSICAL DEMANDS

Ability to communicate orally with customers, vendors, management, and coworkers is crucial. Regular use of phone and email for communication is essential. Hearing and vision correctable to within normal ranges is essential for normal conversations, receiving ordinary information, and preparing or inspecting documents.

The ability to remain in a stationary position roughly 50% of the time, as well as the ability to move about the office occasionally (accessing files/storage, office equipment, computers and other office productivity devices, attending meetings, etc.), is required.

Using a computer while sitting for extended periods is common. Must also be able to position self to maintain equipment, including under tables and desks. No heavy lifting is expected, though occasional exertion of about 20 lbs. of force (e.g., picking up and carrying binders, laptops) may be required. Good manual dexterity required to use common office equipment (e.g., computers, mobile devices, calculators, copiers, scanners).

WORK ENVIRONMENT

The job is performed indoors in a traditional office setting. Extended periods of sitting while using a computer or other devices are common.

REVISION HISTORY

Revision	Date	Description of Changes	Requested By
0.0	mm/dd/yyyy	Initial Release	

Document ID JD0690	Title **IT SUPPORT CENTER MANAGER**	Print Date mm/dd/yyyy
Revision 0.0	Prepared By **Preparer's Name / Title**	Date Prepared mm/dd/yyyy
Effective Date mm/dd/yyyy	Reviewed By **Reviewer's Name / Title**	Date Reviewed mm/dd/yyyy
	Approved By **Final Approver's Name / Title**	Date Approved mm/dd/yyyy

SUMMARY

The Information Technology Support Center Manager, or Tech Support Manager, supervises and motivates a staff of tech support specialists, manages the IT service group (aka, "help desk"), helps prioritize tech support requests, and helps ensure prompt, satisfactory resolution of requests and problems.

ESSENTIAL DUTIES AND RESPONSIBILITIES

- Motivate a team of tech support personnel (hardware/software specialists) via performance assessment and coaching, career planning, and educational goals
- Supervise tech support quality calibration and validation.
- Ensure periodic review, analysis of tech support's performance; identify opportunities for improvement (with respect to tools, methods, etc.).
- Facilitate resolution in the case of escalated support requests and engage appropriate support personnel.
- Ensure appropriate follow-up with external and internal customers
- Make decisions quickly and decisively, often with limited information.

ORGANIZATIONAL RELATIONSHIPS

Reports directly to the IT Manager (CTO, IT Systems Admin, etc.). Assists and works in conjunction with Information Technology staff and end users to facilitate IT support services.

PROCEDURES

Procedure ID and Name	Policies & Procedures Manual
ITAD102 IT Records Management	Computer & Network (IT)
ITAD104 IT Device Naming Conventions	Computer & Network (IT)
ITAD106 Network Infrastructure Standards	Computer & Network (IT)
ITAD110 IT Department Satisfaction	Computer & Network (IT)
ITAM101 IT Asset Standards	Computer & Network (IT)
ITAM102 IT Asset Management	Computer & Network (IT)
ITAM104 IT Asset Assessment	Computer & Network (IT)
ITAM105 IT Asset Installation Satisfaction	Computer & Network (IT)

Procedure ID and Name	Policies & Procedures Manual
ITSD105 Computer Malware	Computer & Network (IT)
ITSD108 IT Incident Handling	Computer & Network (IT)
ITSW112 Software Training	Computer & Network (IT)
ITTS102 IT Support Center	Computer & Network (IT)
ITTS104 IT Troubleshooting	Computer & Network (IT)

QUALIFICATIONS

A bachelor's degree in information technology or equivalent education/experience level is required. Must have tech support experience at operational and managerial levels.

Must have demonstrated ability to lead a diverse team of computer hardware/software support specialists (technicians). Good communication skills and the ability to work well with technical and non-technical people at all levels are essential, as are strong coaching/mentoring skills. Project management experience preferred but not necessary. Need strong customer support skills and experience.

Prefer candidates with one or more recognized industry certifications (e.g., CompTIA A+, Network+; MCTS; CCNA; CISSP). Experience with Remedy Help Desk is required.

PHYSICAL DEMANDS

Ability to communicate orally with customers, vendors, management, and coworkers is crucial. Regular use of phone and email for communication is essential. Hearing and vision correctable to within normal ranges is essential for normal conversations, receiving ordinary information, and preparing or inspecting documents.

The ability to remain in a stationary position roughly 50% of the time, as well as the ability to move about the office occasionally (accessing files/storage, office equipment, computers and other office productivity devices, attending meetings, etc.), is required.

Using a computer while sitting for extended periods is common. Must also be able to position self to install, maintain, or exchange equipment, including under tables and desks.

No heavy lifting is expected, though occasional exertion of about 20 lbs. of force (e.g., picking up and carrying binders, laptops) may be required. Good manual dexterity required to use common office equipment (e.g., computers, mobile devices, calculators, copiers, scanners).

WORK ENVIRONMENT

The job is performed indoors in a traditional office setting. Extended periods of sitting while using a computer or other devices are common.

REVISION HISTORY

Revision	Date	Description of Changes	Requested By
0.0	mm/dd/yyyy	Initial Release	

[This page intentionally left blank]

Document ID **JD0710**	Title **LAN ADMINISTRATOR**	Print Date **mm/dd/yyyy**
Revision **0.0**	Prepared By **Preparer's Name / Title**	Date Prepared **mm/dd/yyyy**
Effective Date **mm/dd/yyyy**	Reviewed By **Reviewer's Name / Title**	Date Reviewed **mm/dd/yyyy**
	Approved By **Final Approver's Name / Title**	Date Approved **mm/dd/yyyy**

SUMMARY

The Local Area Network Administrator, or LAN Administrator, oversees the day-to-day operation of the organization's local area network. The LAN Administrator organizes, supervises, and oversees installation and support of the organization's LAN, including network segments, intranets, and other data communication systems.

ESSENTIAL DUTIES AND RESPONSIBILITIES

- Oversee installation, maintenance, repairs, and upgrading of LAN hardware and software.
- Develop and maintain local area network map(s); maintain LAN inventory (catalog).
- Help Information Security (aka, Info Sec) to ensure LAN security
- Ensure that LAN is in continuous operation.
- Collect and analyze data to evaluate LAN performance and identify opportunities for improvement.
- Help tech support resolve LAN-related problems.
- Solve LAN problems quickly and effectively when a user or an automated monitoring system lets them know about a problem.

ORGANIZATIONAL RELATIONSHIPS

Reports directly to the Network & Computer Systems Administrator. Works in conjunction with IT Admin and Info Sec to ensure proper functioning, utilization, and security of the LAN.

PROCEDURES

Procedure ID and Name	Policies & Procedures Manual
ITAD106 Network Infrastructure Standards	Computer & Network (IT)
ITSD105 Computer Malware	Computer & Network (IT)

QUALIFICATIONS

A bachelor's degree in computer science, computer engineering, or information technology is required; three (3) years' work experience in systems administration is also required. Systems administration certification (e.g., CompTIA, Cisco) is desirable.

Must have demonstrated above-average analytical and problem-solving abilities. Must be capable of leading a team of computer / network technicians. Good oral and written communication skills are a must. Previous LAN management experience is highly desired.

PHYSICAL DEMANDS

Must be able to communicate orally with customers, vendors, management, and technicians. Regular use of phone and email for communication is essential. Hearing and vision correctable to within normal ranges is essential for normal conversations, receiving ordinary information, preparing or inspecting equipment, manuals, and other documents, and some LAN tools.

The ability to remain in a stationary position roughly 50% of the time, as well as the ability to move about the office occasionally (accessing files/storage, office equipment, computers and other office productivity devices, attending meetings, etc.), is required.

Using a computer while sitting for extended periods is common. Must also be able to position self to maintain LAN equipment, including under and behind tables and desks.

Heavy lifting (50+ lbs) may be expected occasionally. Good manual dexterity required to use common office equipment (e.g., computers, mobile devices, calculators) and LAN tools (e.g., network testers, wire strippers, crimpers)

WORK ENVIRONMENT

The job is performed indoors in a traditional office setting. Some extended periods of sitting while using a computer or other device.

REVISION HISTORY

Revision	Date	Description of Changes	Requested By
0.0	mm/dd/yyyy	Initial Release	

Document ID JD0860	Title **NETWORK & COMPUTER SYSTEMS ADMINISTRATOR**	Print Date mm/dd/yyyy
Revision 0.0	Prepared By **Preparer's Name / Title**	Date Prepared mm/dd/yyyy
Effective Date mm/dd/yyyy	Reviewed By **Reviewer's Name / Title**	Date Reviewed mm/dd/yyyy
	Approved By **Final Approver's Name / Title**	Date Approved mm/dd/yyyy

SUMMARY

The Network and Computer Systems Administrator[1] is responsible for the day-to-day operation of the organization's computer networks. They organize, supervise, and oversee installation and support of the organization's computer systems, including local area networks (LANs), wide area networks (WANs), network segments, intranets, and other data communication systems.

ESSENTIAL DUTIES AND RESPONSIBILITIES

- Determine what the organization needs in a network and computer system before building it out.
- Oversee installation of all network hardware and software, as well as necessary systems upgrades and repairs.
- Help maintain network and computer system security and ensure that all systems are operating correctly.
- Collect and analyze data to evaluate network/systems performance and help make the system work better, faster, and with greater accuracy; identify and implement system improvements where needed.
- Prepare training materials and train users on the proper use of hardware and software when necessary.
- Solve problems quickly when a user or an automated monitoring system lets them know about a problem.

ORGANIZATIONAL RELATIONSHIPS

Reports directly to the IT Manager. Assists and works in conjunction with IT Administration and Information Security to help facilitate the proper function, utilization, availability, and security of IT systems and operations.

PROCEDURES

Procedure ID and Name	Policies & Procedures Manual
ITTS101 IT System Administration	Computer & Network (IT)

---

[1] Also referred to as "IT Systems Administrator," "Systems Admin," or "Sys Admin."

Procedure ID and Name	Policies & Procedures Manual
SEC101 Procedural Security	Security Planning
SEC115 Information Security EDP Center	Security Planning

QUALIFICATIONS

A bachelor's degree in computer science, information technology, computer engineering, or a related discipline is required. Five (5) or more years of experience as a systems administrator is also required. Systems administration certification (e.g., IEEE, CompTIA Network+, Cisco) is desirable.

Must have demonstrated analytical and problem-solving abilities. Must be capable of leading a diverse team of computer/network technicians, systems analysts, software developers, and other computer professionals. The position requires someone with exceptional communication skills, both orally and in writing; presentation skills/experience are a definite plus. IT project management experience is a must.

PHYSICAL DEMANDS

Ability to communicate orally with customers, vendors, management, and coworkers is crucial. Regular use of phone and email for communication is essential. Hearing and vision correctable to within normal ranges is essential for normal conversations, receiving ordinary information, and preparing or inspecting documents.

The ability to remain in a stationary position roughly 50% of the time, as well as the ability to move about the office occasionally (accessing files/storage, office equipment, computers and other office productivity devices, attending meetings, etc.), is required.

Using a computer while sitting for extended periods is common. Must also be able to position self to maintain equipment, including under tables and desks.

No heavy lifting is expected; occasional exertion of 20-30 lbs. of force (e.g., carrying laptops, desktops, peripherals) may be required. Good manual dexterity required to use common office equipment (e.g., computers, mobile devices, calculators, copiers, scanners).

WORK ENVIRONMENT

The job is performed indoors in a traditional office setting. Extended periods of sitting while using a computer or other devices are common.

REVISION HISTORY

Revision	Date	Description of Changes	Requested By
0.0	mm/dd/yyyy	Initial Release	

[This page intentionally left blank]

Document ID **JD0930**	Title **PRESIDENT**	Print Date **mm/dd/yyyy**
Revision **0.0**	Prepared By **Preparer's Name / Title**	Date Prepared **mm/dd/yyyy**
Effective Date **mm/dd/yyyy**	Reviewed By **Reviewer's Name / Title**	Date Reviewed **mm/dd/yyyy**
	Approved By **Final Approver's Name / Title**	Date Approved **mm/dd/yyyy**

SUMMARY OF FUNCTIONS

The President is responsible for the overall direction and administration of all company operations, programs, and services.

ESSENTIAL DUTIES AND RESPONSIBILITIES

- To develop and maintain a positive company image and positive relations between the company and key customers, vendors, and regulators.
- To develop in conjunction with the managers of the company, plans for the growth and development of the company and the expansion or improvement of company facilities.
- Monitors and develops the annual budget for approval by the Board of Directors.
- Ensures that company operations comply with all applicable laws and regulations.
- Develops, monitors, approves, and implements policies and procedures appropriate to the operations of the company.
- Serves as the final authority for employee relations and personnel matters; has ultimate authority for all hire/fire decisions, compensation, and disciplinary actions.
- Handles negotiations with outside parties on behalf of the company.
- Oversees all operation areas of the company through supervision of all vice-presidents, directors, and managers.

ORGANIZATIONAL RELATIONSHIPS

Directly accountable to the board of directors for effectively performing all responsibilities. Provides reports on all aspects of company performance as requested by the board. Serves as the chairperson of policy and management teams. Directly supervises the organization's Vice-Presidents (e.g., VP-Finance, VP-Sales).

PROCEDURES

Procedure ID and Name	Policies & Procedures Manual
CSH105 Check Signing Authority	Accounting
FS1020 Management Responsibility	ISO 22000
HRG101 Employee Hiring	HR
ITAD101 Information Technology Management	Computer & Network (IT)

QUALIFICATIONS

A bachelor's degree in business administration or accounting is required; an MBA in Management is preferred. Top management experience at a Fortune 1000 company is preferred. A proven record of leadership (e.g., progression through positions of increasing responsibility) is beneficial. Good communication skills and the ability to work well with people are essential.

PHYSICAL DEMANDS

Occasional travel (by airplane, automobile) in the conduct of business is necessary. Ability to communicate orally with board of directors, customers, vendors, shareholders, management, and other co-workers, both individually and in front of a group is crucial. Regular use of the telephone and e-mail for communication is essential.

Sitting for extended periods is common. Hearing and vision within normal ranges is essential for normal conversations, to receive ordinary information, and to prepare or inspect documents.

No heavy lifting is expected. Exertion of up to 10 lbs. of force occasionally may be required. Good manual dexterity for the use of common office equipment such as computer terminals, calculator, copiers, and FAX machines.

Good reasoning ability is required to solve a wide range of business problems. Able to apply statistical calculations, analysis of variance, correlation techniques, and sampling theory as well as algebra, linear equations, and other analytics as required. Able to understand and utilize financial reports and legal documents to conduct business.

WORK ENVIRONMENT

The job is performed indoors in a traditional office setting. Activities include extended periods of sitting and extensive work at a computer monitor and/or calculator.

REVISION HISTORY

Revision	Date	Description of Changes	Requested By
0.0	mm/dd/yyyy	Initial Release	

Document ID	Title	Print Date
JD0960	**PRODUCT MANAGER**	**mm/dd/yyyy**
Revision	Prepared By	Date Prepared
0.0	**Preparer's Name / Title**	**mm/dd/yyyy**
Effective Date	Reviewed By	Date Reviewed
mm/dd/yyyy	**Reviewer's Name / Title**	**mm/dd/yyyy**
	Approved By	Date Approved
	Final Approver's Name / Title	**mm/dd/yyyy**

SUMMARY

The Product Manager, or PM, leads the organization's efforts to design, develop, prototype, test, and introduce products/services to the marketplace, as well as product refinement/ upgrades. In addition, the Product Manager oversees development and management of the Product Life Cycle Management (LCM) plan. The PM may have responsibility for a line of products (i.e., the "brand") if the organization is large.[1]

ESSENTIAL DUTIES AND RESPONSIBILITIES

- Manages the product design and development process.
- Coordinates and supports product launches with Sales, Marketing, Production, and other departments
- Reviews and analyzes data from within (e.g., sales, accounting numbers), marketplace, competition, customer feedback, social media – use to determine what products/services to develop, what to upgrade/improve, and what to discontinue.
- Selects and manages the members of the product development team.
- Develops and manages Product LCM plan; manages product life cycles.

ORGANIZATIONAL RELATIONSHIPS

Reports directly to the organization's President / chief executive.[2] Works in conjunction with R&D, Sales, Marketing, Production, and other departments.

PROCEDURES

Procedure ID and Name	Policies & Procedures Manual
PM1000 Product Life Cycle Management	Sales and Marketing
PM1010 Product Development	Sales and Marketing
PM1020 Product Launch	Sales and Marketing
SWD102 Project Management	Software Development

---

[1] In large organizations, Product Managers may be Brand Managers, or several Product Managers may report to a Brand Manager.

[2] May report to a Brand Manager, in the case of a large organization.

Procedure ID and Name	Policies & Procedures Manual
ITSW109 Software Releases / Updates	Computer & Network/IT
SWD109 Software Releases / Updates	Software Development
ITSW110 Software Support	Computer & Network/IT
SWD110 Software Support	Software Development

QUALIFICATIONS

A bachelor's degree in accounting, sales/marketing, economics, or finance is required. Two to five (2-5) years of product development or product management experience is needed; prefer someone with product life cycle experience. Good mathematical skills are a necessity – prefer experience with statistical analysis software.

Need a highly motivated self-starter; will be working in a fast-paced environment. Must have experience leading a diverse team. Good communication skills and the ability to work well with people at all levels are essential; group facilitation skills needed.

Candidate also needs strong organizational, time management, and problem-solving skills. Project management experience is a must; project management certification helpful but not required.

PHYSICAL DEMANDS

Ability to communicate orally with customers, management, and coworkers is crucial. Regular use of phone and email for communication is essential. Hearing and vision correctable to within normal ranges is essential for normal conversations, receiving ordinary information, and preparing or inspecting documents.

The ability to remain in a stationary position roughly 50% of the time, as well as the ability to move about the office occasionally (accessing files/storage, office equipment, computers and other office productivity devices, attending meetings, etc.), is required.

Using a computer while sitting for extended periods is common. Must also be able to position self to maintain equipment, including under tables and desks.

No heavy lifting is expected, though occasional exertion of about 20 lbs. of force (e.g., picking up and carrying binders, laptops) may be required. Good manual dexterity required to use common office equipment (e.g., computers, mobile devices, calculators, copiers, scanners).

WORK ENVIRONMENT

The job is performed indoors in a traditional office setting. Extended periods of sitting while using a computer or other devices are common.

REVISION HISTORY

Revision	Date	Description of Changes	Requested By
0.0	mm/dd/yyyy	Initial Release	

[This page intentionally left blank]

Document ID	Title	Print Date
JD0990	**PROJECT MANAGER**	**mm/dd/yyyy**
Revision	Prepared By	Date Prepared
0.0	**Preparer's Name / Title**	**mm/dd/yyyy**
Effective Date	Reviewed By	Date Reviewed
mm/dd/yyyy	**Reviewer's Name / Title**	**mm/dd/yyyy**
	Approved By	Date Approved
	Final Approver's Name / Title	**mm/dd/yyyy**

SUMMARY OF FUNCTIONS

The Project Manager supervises and directs project personnel and processes, to keep projects running smoothly and within budget without compromising safety and quality standards, in addition to meeting customer, statutory/regulatory, and organizational requirements.

ESSENTIAL DUTIES AND RESPONSIBILITIES

- Develops project schedules in conjunction with the Vice President of Production and Operations; plans, directs, and assigns duties for project personnel; schedules and authorizes overtime as necessary to meet project schedules.
- Recruits, hires, and trains employees on relevant functions; conducts orientations and meetings; assures that established policies and procedures are followed.
- Coordinates with Managerial staff for development of manufacturing methods processes, tooling, and molds necessary to produce new products. Reviews and implements engineering change notices as appropriate; updates manufacturing documentation including assembly manuals.
- Oversees and supervise all functions including receiving of components, inventory control, production and interim quality checks and shipping; assures compliance with all regulations and good manufacturing practices.
- Troubleshoots any project problems; assures that machinery, equipment, and facilities are properly maintained for efficient production; reports any process or equipment problems to Vice President of Production and Operations and/or Director of Quality.
- Performs other project duties as required.

ORGANIZATIONAL RELATIONSHIPS

Reports to the Vice President of Operations. Coordinates activities with Engineering, IT, Sales, Customer Service, and other functions, as needed. Supervises all personnel assigned to a given project.

PROCEDURES

Procedure ID and Name	Policies & Procedures Manual
ITSW108 Design Changes During Development	Computer & Network (IT)
PUR103 Purchasing Project	Accounting
QP1090 Project Definition	ISO 9001 QMS
REV108 Progress Billing	Accounting
SWD101 Project Definition	Software Development
SWD102 Project Management	Software Development
SWD108 Design Changes During Development	Software Development

QUALIFICATIONS

A bachelor's degree in business or marketing is required; a master's degree in management is preferred. Good communication skills and the ability to work well with people are essential. Good leadership skills are needed. Experience with project management, spreadsheet applications is required. Desire someone with a record of increasing responsibility and accomplishment.

Project management certification (e.g., PMP) is highly desirable.

PHYSICAL DEMANDS

Ability to communicate orally with management and other co-workers is important. Regular use of the telephone and e-mail for communication is essential. Standing or sitting for extended periods is common. Hearing and vision within normal ranges is important for conversations, to receive ordinary information and to prepare or inspect building plans, blueprints and drawings.

Heavy lifting is not expected. Exertion of up to 10 lbs. of force occasionally is required. Good manual dexterity for the use of common office equipment such as computer terminals, calculator, copiers, and FAX machines or measuring tools is required.

Good math and reasoning ability is essential. Able to apply statistical calculations, analysis of variance, correlation techniques, and sampling theory as well as geometry, trigonometry, algebra, linear equations, and other analytics as required. Able to understand and utilize architectural or engineering drawings, utilize financial reports and legal documents to conduct business.

WORK ENVIRONMENT

The job is performed indoors in a variety of settings, including the office, manufacturing floor, and warehouse. Exposure to loud noises, dust, dirt, and smoke may occur. Protective safety clothing/gear (including appropriate clothing, shoes, gloves, hardhat, and goggles) are occasionally required. Activities include extended periods of standing or sitting and extensive work with measuring devices and other machinery.

REVISION HISTORY

Revision	Date	Description of Changes	Requested By
0.0	mm/dd/yyyy	Initial Release	

[This page intentionally left blank]

Document ID	Title	Print Date
JD1020	**PURCHASING MANAGER**	**mm/dd/yyyy**
Revision	Prepared By	Date Prepared
0.0	**Preparer's Name / Title**	**mm/dd/yyyy**
Effective Date	Reviewed By	Date Reviewed
mm/dd/yyyy	**Reviewer's Name / Title**	**mm/dd/yyyy**
	Approved By	Date Approved
	Final Approver's Name / Title	**mm/dd/yyyy**

SUMMARY OF FUNCTIONS

The Purchasing Manager is responsible for overseeing all inventory, supplies, and capital goods purchases for the organization. They evaluate and recommend vendors and determine the most cost-effective inventory and reorder levels. Negotiating price, delivery, and credit terms are among their responsibilities.

ESSENTIAL DUTIES AND RESPONSIBILITIES

- Responsible for efficient purchasing of inventory, supplies, and capital equipment. Receives purchase requisitions and verifies for accuracy and authorization(s). Periodically evaluates vendors/suppliers and advises Controller and Operations Manager when vendors are not meeting requirements. Evaluates and recommends new/substitute vendors, when necessary.
- Prepares and issues purchase orders; determines and negotiates prices, delivery and credit terms; buys according to established company policies and procedures; maintains accurate purchasing records.
- Responsible for evaluating, assessing and selecting vendors based on capabilities, performance, and consistent quality. Maintains rapport and good working relationships with vendors; keeps accurate vendor records.
- Evaluates inventory reorder levels and quantity price breaks to determine most economical purchasing of inventory and supplies in relationship to company's cost of capital. Prepares monthly reports and reviews forecast of purchasing commitments with Vice President of Finance.
- Expedites purchase orders as necessary and ensures delivery of purchased items for uninterrupted manufacturing flow.
- Performs other purchasing or inventory control duties as necessary or as requested.

ORGANIZATIONAL RELATIONSHIPS

Reports to the Controller. Coordinates activities with all departments, especially Manufacturing, Accounts Payable, and Receiving. Works with the Quality Assurance Manager to ensure quality of purchased materials.

Supervises a team of Purchasing agents.

PROCEDURES

Procedure ID and Name	Policies & Procedures Manual
AS1180 Control of Monitoring & Measuring Equipment	AS 9100
FS1090 Purchasing	ISO 22000
FS1100 Supplier Evaluation	ISO 22000
FS1140 Control of Monitoring and Measuring	ISO 22000
INV101 Inventory Control	Accounting
INV102 Inventory Counts	Accounting
INV104 Customer Property	Accounting
ITAM102 IT Asset Management	Computer & Network (IT)
PUR101 Vendor Selection	Accounting
PUR102 Purchasing General	Accounting
PUR103 Purchasing Project	Accounting
PUR104 Receiving and Inspection	Accounting
PUR105 Shipping and Freight Claims	Accounting
PUR106 Accounts Payable and Cash Disbursement	Accounting
QP1170 Control of Monitoring & Measuring Equipment	ISO 9001 QMS
SEC118 Inventory Delivery Receiving Controls	Security Planning

QUALIFICATIONS

A bachelor's degree majoring in business administration or accounting is required; preferred. Good communication skills and the ability to work well with people are essential. Good leadership skills are beneficial. Familiarity with accounting, purchasing, and spreadsheet applications is required.

PHYSICAL DEMANDS

Ability to communicate orally with vendors, management, and other co-workers, both individually and in front of a group is crucial. Regular use of the telephone and e-mail for communication is essential.

Sitting for extended periods is common. Hearing and vision within normal ranges is essential for normal conversations, to receive ordinary information and to prepare or inspect documents.

No heavy lifting is expected. Exertion of up to 10 lbs. of force occasionally may be required. Good manual dexterity for the use of common office equipment such as computer terminals, calculator, copiers, and FAX machines.

Good reasoning ability is required to solve a wide range of business problems. Must be able to apply knowledge of statistical tools to quality assurance. Must also be able to understand and utilize financial reports and legal documents to conduct business.

WORK ENVIRONMENT

The job is performed indoors in a traditional office setting. Activities include extended periods of sitting and extensive work at a computer.

REVISION HISTORY

Revision	Date	Description of Changes	Requested By
0.0	mm/dd/yyyy	Initial Release	

[This page intentionally left blank]

Document ID **JD1040**	Title **QUALITY MANAGER**	Print Date **mm/dd/yyyy**
Revision **0.0**	Prepared By **Preparer's Name / Title**	Date Prepared **mm/dd/yyyy**
Effective Date **mm/dd/yyyy**	Reviewed By **Reviewer's Name / Title**	Date Reviewed **mm/dd/yyyy**
	Approved By **Final Approver's Name / Title**	Date Approved **mm/dd/yyyy**

SUMMARY

The Quality Manager[1] is responsible for overall development, implementation, and maintenance of the organization's Quality Management System (QMS).

ESSENTIAL DUTIES AND RESPONSIBILITIES

- Ensure that the organization's Quality Management System conforms to customer, internal, ISO 9001, and regulatory/legal requirements.
- Ensure evaluation of, and reporting on, vendor quality systems.
- Oversee inspection (examination) of incoming materials, ensuring that they meet requirements.
- Manage the monitoring, measurement, and review of internal processes, especially those that affect the quality of the organization's products[2].
- Lead a team of Quality engineers, inspectors, auditors, analysts, and technicians
- Work with customers, employees, contractors, and outsourcing firms to develop product requirements.
- Report to top management on the performance of the QMS (e.g., results of quality audits, corrective actions), including the need for improvement.
- Conduct periodic management review meetings.
- Oversee product recalls.
- Responsible for accuracy and timely inspection/calibration of monitoring and measuring devices.
- Keep up on standards, regulations/laws, issues, and news with respect to product (service) quality.

ORGANIZATIONAL RELATIONSHIPS

Reports directly to the Director of Quality. Works in conjunction with Procurement, Production, and any other department that has an effect on the quality of the organization's products.

---

[1] May be referred to in some cases as the Quality Assurance or Quality Control Manager.

[2] The term "product" refers to what the organization sells or leases, whether goods or services.

PROCEDURES

Procedure ID and Name	Policies & Procedures Manual
AD1000 Document Control	Sales and Marketing
AS1000 Document Control	AS 9100
AS1020 Management Responsibility	AS 9100
AS1070 Customer Communication	AS 9100
AS1100 Preproduction Quality and Planning	AS 9100
AS1110 Supplier Evaluation	AS 9100
AS1130 Receiving and Inspection	AS 9100
AS1140 Control of Production-Service Processes	AS 9100
AS1150 Manufacturing	AS 9100
AS1170 Customer Property	AS 9100
AS1180 Control of Monitoring and Measuring Equipment	AS 9100
AS1210 Monitoring-Measurement of Processes	AS 9100
AS1230 Control of Nonconforming Material	AS 9100
AS1240 Data Analysis-Continual Improvement	AS 9100
AS1250 Corrective Action	AS 9100
AS1260 Preventive Action	AS 9100
FS1070 Hazard Analysis	ISO 22000
FS1100 Supplier Evaluation	ISO 22000
FS1120 Manufacturing	ISO 22000
FS1140 Control of Monitoring and Measuring	ISO 22000
FS1150 Control of Potentially Unsafe Food Product	ISO 22000
FS1190 Product Recall	ISO 22000
ITAD110 IT Department Satisfaction	Computer & Network (IT)
ITAM103 IT Vendor Selection	Computer & Network (IT)
ITSW106 Software Documentation	Computer & Network (IT)
ITSW107 Software Testing	Computer & Network (IT)
ITSW109 Software Releases Updates	Computer & Network (IT)
MFG111 Corrective Action	Business Sampler
PM1030 Product Recalls	Sales and Marketing
PM1030 Product Recalls	Sales and Marketing
PUR101 Vendor Selection	Accounting

Procedure ID and Name	Policies & Procedures Manual
PUR104 Receiving and Inspection	Accounting
QP1000 Document Control	ISO 9001 QMS
QP1030 Control of Nonconforming Product / Material	ISO 9001 QMS
QP1040 Corrective Action	ISO 9001 QMS
QP1050 Preventive Action	ISO 9001 QMS
QP1060 Management Reviews	ISO 9001 QMS
QP1120 Vendor Evaluation	ISO 9001 QMS
QP1130 Preproduction Planning	ISO 9001 QMS
QP1140 Manufacturing	ISO 9001 QMS
QP1150 Identification and Traceability	ISO 9001 QMS
QP1170 Control of Monitoring & Measuring Equipment	ISO 9001 QMS
QP1180 Process Monitoring and Measurement	ISO 9001 QMS
QP1200 Data Analysis & Continual Improvement	ISO 9001 QMS
QP1210 Receiving and Inspection	ISO 9001 QMS
QP1220 Purchasing	ISO 9001 QMS
SWD106 Software Documentation	Software Development
SWD107 Software Testing	Software Development
SWD109 Software Releases Updates	Software Development

QUALIFICATIONS

A bachelor's degree in engineering or quality is required, as is 10 years of experience in Quality Assurance/Quality Control. Current CQA or similar certification is required.

Must have proven ability to lead a diverse team of technicians. Excellent communication skills and the ability to work well with people at all levels are essential. Must have strong organizational, analytical, problem solving, and management skills. Experience with MS-Office (especially Excel, Word) is needed. Project management experience is a plus.

PHYSICAL DEMANDS

Ability to communicate orally with customers, vendors, management, and coworkers is crucial. Regular use of phone and email for communication is essential. Hearing and vision correctable to within normal ranges is essential for normal conversations, receiving ordinary information, and preparing or inspecting documents.

The ability to remain in a stationary position roughly 50% of the time, as well as the ability to move about the office occasionally (accessing files/storage, office equipment, computers and other office productivity devices, attending meetings, etc.), is required.

Using a computer while sitting for extended periods is common. Must also be able to position self to maintain equipment, including under tables and desks.

No heavy lifting is expected, though occasional exertion of 10-20 lbs. of force (e.g., carrying a laptop, binder, or both) is required. Good manual dexterity required to use common office equipment (e.g., computers, mobile devices, calculators, copiers, scanners).

WORK ENVIRONMENT

The job is normally performed indoors, in a traditional office setting. Extended periods of sitting while using a computer or other devices are common. Occasional travel to vendor sites (10-15%) for audits, inspections, etc., may be required.

REVISION HISTORY

Revision	Date	Description of Changes	Requested By
0.0	mm/dd/yyyy	Initial Release	

Document ID **JD1210**	Title **SHIPPING / RECEIVING CLERK**	Print Date **mm/dd/yyyy**
Revision **0.0**	Prepared By **Preparer's Name / Title**	Date Prepared **mm/dd/yyyy**
Effective Date **mm/dd/yyyy**	Reviewed By **Reviewer's Name / Title**	Date Reviewed **mm/dd/yyyy**
	Approved By **Final Approver's Name / Title**	Date Approved **mm/dd/yyyy**

SUMMARY OF FUNCTIONS

The Shipping/Receiving Clerk pulls orders and packs and prepares them for shipment. They carry out (and occasionally supervise) shipping and receiving functions and work with parcel and LTL carriers.

ESSENTIAL DUTIES AND RESPONSIBILITIES

- Responsible for routing outbound freight to assure delivery as required; monitors carriers performance and tariff charges and determines best carriers for the most cost-effective and reliable delivery within established standards.
- Maintains shipping and receiving logs and maintains files of shipping records. Processes loss freight or shipping damages claims. Verifies freight bills with accounting and resolves errors with carriers.
- Takes finished orders after final quality control inspection and wraps and packs in containers as per required standards. Determines most cost efficient bundling of items (e.g., palletizing or individual packages). Prepares packing lists, bills of lading, and other shipping documentation as necessary.
- Supervises loading and unloading of all delivery trucks. Assures compliance with workplace safety procedures. Limits access to loading docks by unauthorized individuals.
- Receives and inspects external packaging of all incoming shipments. Notifies delivery personnel of any apparent shipping damage and proceeds accordingly. Reviews incoming packing lists and logs and routes to receiving inspection area.
- Receives and process returned goods shipments; completes and forwards return goods authorization (RGA) paperwork. Routes service/repair shipments to Customer Service.
- Performs other shipping/receiving duties, as requested.

ORGANIZATIONAL RELATIONSHIPS

Reports to the Production Manager. Works with Sales and Customer Service.

PROCEDURES

Procedure ID and Name	Policies & Procedures Manual
ITAM102 IT Asset Management	Computer & Network (IT)

QUALIFICATIONS

A high school diploma or GED is required. Good math and communication skills and the ability to work well with people are essential. Familiarity with shipping manifest applications is beneficial.

PHYSICAL DEMANDS

Ability to communicate orally with management and other co-workers is crucial. Regular use of the telephone and e-mail for communication is essential. Sitting or standing for an extended period is common. Hearing and vision within normal ranges is essential for normal conversations, to receive ordinary information, and to prepare or inspect documents.

Heavy lifting may be expected. Exertion of up to 50 lbs. of force occasionally may be required moving boxes and other goods. Good manual dexterity for the use of common office equipment such as computer terminals, calculator, and FAX machines.

Good reasoning ability is required to solve a wide range of business problems. Able to apply algebra or other analytics as required. Able to understand and utilize management reports, memos, and other documents to conduct business.

WORK ENVIRONMENT

The job is performed indoors in a traditional warehouse setting. Exposure to common dust, dirt, and noise is expected. Activities include extended periods of sitting or standing and extensive work at a computer and/or loading dock or warehouse.

REVISION HISTORY

Revision	Date	Description of Changes	Requested By
0.0	mm/dd/yyyy	Initial Release	

Document ID **JD1230**	Title **SOFTWARE DESIGNER**	Print Date **mm/dd/yyyy**
Revision **0.0**	Prepared By **Preparer's Name / Title**	Date Prepared **mm/dd/yyyy**
Effective Date **mm/dd/yyyy**	Reviewed By **Reviewer's Name / Title**	Date Reviewed **mm/dd/yyyy**
	Approved By **Final Approver's Name / Title**	Date Approved **mm/dd/yyyy**

SUMMARY

The Software Designer helps transform a set of requirements – customer[1], IT, industry, and legal/regulatory – into software solutions.

ESSENTIAL DUTIES AND RESPONSIBILITIES

- Analyze customer needs (RFQs) and develop replies (SOWs); negotiate with customers.
- Communicate overall design and approach to a team of programmers; create flowcharts, diagrams, other models, and programming instructions to guide programming team.
- Review requirement and design changes, determine what parts of software are affected, and direct programming to meet requirements; determine specific components of ?
- Develop test scenarios and test cases; review results of test cases and make adjustments, as needed, to meet requirements.
- Document all aspects of software, for ongoing maintenance and revisions.
- Collaborate with other IT specialists, technicians, etc., to deliver software solutions.
- Perform other job-related duties, as needed.

ORGANIZATIONAL RELATIONSHIPS

Reports directly to a Systems Analyst. Works in conjunction with internal or external customers and other IT staff (designers, developers, administrators, managers, etc.) to facilitate software design, development, testing, and implementation.

PROCEDURES

Procedure ID and Name	Policies & Procedures Manual
ITSW104 Software Design	Computer & Network (IT)
ITSW105 Software Programming	Computer & Network (IT)
ITSW107 Software Testing	Computer & Network (IT)

---

[1] The "customer" (a.k.a., end user) may be internal or external.

Procedure ID and Name	Policies & Procedures Manual
ITSW108 Design Changes During Development	Computer & Network (IT)
ITSW109 Software Releases Updates	Computer & Network (IT)
SWD104 Software Design	Software Development
SWD105 Software Programming	Software Development
SWD107 Software Testing	Software Development
SWD108 Design Changes During Development	Software Development
SWD109 Software Releases Updates	Software Development

QUALIFICATIONS

A bachelor's degree in mathematics, computer science, software engineering, or a related discipline is required; a master's degree in IT administration or related field of study is preferred. 5+ years of Java or C# programming experience is required.

Must have demonstrated ability to lead a diverse team of programmers/technicians. Good communication skills and the ability to work well with people at all levels are essential. Must be detail oriented, yet creative. Strong math, analytical, and problem-solving skills needed. Project management experience preferred; PMP certification helpful.

Software designer/developer certification is desired.

PHYSICAL DEMANDS

Ability to communicate orally with customers, IT personnel, other coworkers, and management is crucial. Regular use of phone and email for communication is essential. Hearing and vision correctable to within normal ranges is essential for normal conversations, receiving ordinary information, and preparing or inspecting documents.

The ability to remain in a stationary position roughly 75% of the time, as well as the ability to move about the office occasionally (accessing files/storage, office equipment, computers and other office productivity devices, attending meetings, etc.), is required.

Using a computer while sitting for extended periods is the norm. May occasionally need to position self to install or maintain equipment, including under tables and desks.

No heavy lifting is expected; occasional exertion of about 20 lbs. of force (e.g., carrying binders, reports, laptops) is required. Good manual dexterity required to use common office equipment (e.g., computers, mobile devices).

WORK ENVIRONMENT

The job is performed indoors in a traditional office setting. Extended periods of sitting while using a computer and/or other device (smartphone, etc.) are common.

REVISION HISTORY

Revision	Date	Description of Changes	Requested By
0.0	mm/dd/yyyy	Initial Release	

[This page intentionally left blank]

Document ID JD1240	Title SOFTWARE SUPPORT ANALYST	Print Date mm/dd/yyyy
Revision 0.0	Prepared By Preparer's Name / Title	Date Prepared mm/dd/yyyy
Effective Date mm/dd/yyyy	Reviewed By Reviewer's Name / Title	Date Reviewed mm/dd/yyyy
	Approved By Final Approver's Name / Title	Date Approved mm/dd/yyyy

SUMMARY

The Software Support Analyst provides assistance, advice, and solutions for computer software problems (e.g., operating systems, application malfunctions), investigating problems, identifying their root causes, and suggesting solutions and/or pathways to them.

ESSENTIAL DUTIES AND RESPONSIBILITIES

- Handle software-related requests for assistance with problems.
- Troubleshoot software and identify root causes of software problems.
- Analyze software related issues and propose solutions.
- Fix software problems and test solutions prior to implementing them.
- Obtain and log customer feedback for the purpose of process improvement.
- Document software support activities thoroughly, accurately, and in a timely manner.
- Make decisions quickly, sometimes with limited information.
- Review work log, customer feedback periodically with supervisor and other analysts and technicians, to identify and act on opportunities for improvement.

ORGANIZATIONAL RELATIONSHIPS

Reports directly to the Technical Support Manager (Tech Support Manager). Works in conjunction with Software Development staff, Tech Support staff, and end users to develop quick, effective solutions to software problems.

PROCEDURES

Procedure ID and Name	Policies & Procedures Manual
ITSW110 Software Support	Computer & Network (IT)
SWD110 Software Support	Software Development

QUALIFICATIONS

A bachelor's degree in computer science or computer engineering is required, as is 5+ years of experience in software design, testing, and/or troubleshooting. The ideal candidate will have a certified software quality analyst, certified software tester, or similar designation. One year or more of experience with Remedy is required.

Must work well independently or as part of a team of software analysts and support technicians. Good communication skills (esp. listening) and the ability to work well with people at all levels (technical, non-technical, etc.) are essential. Strong analytical and problem solving skills are a must.

PHYSICAL DEMANDS

Ability to communicate orally with end users, vendors, management, and coworkers is crucial. Regular use of phone and email for communication is essential. Hearing and vision correctable to within normal ranges is essential for normal conversations, receiving ordinary information, and preparing or inspecting documents.

The ability to remain in a stationary position roughly 50% of the time, as well as the ability to move about the office occasionally (accessing files/storage, office equipment, computers and other office productivity devices, attending meetings, etc.), is required.

Using a computer while sitting for extended periods is common. Must also be able to position self to maintain equipment, including under tables and desks.

No heavy lifting is expected, though occasional exertion of about 20 lbs. of force (e.g., picking up and carrying binders, laptops) may be required. Good manual dexterity required to use common office equipment (e.g., computers, mobile devices, calculators, copiers, scanners).

WORK ENVIRONMENT

The job is performed indoors in a traditional office setting. Extended periods of sitting while using a computer or other devices are common.

REVISION HISTORY

Revision	Date	Description of Changes	Requested By
0.0	mm/dd/yyyy	Initial Release	

Document ID **JD1260**	Title **SOFTWARE TRAINER**	Print Date **mm/dd/yyyy**
Revision **0.0**	Prepared By **Preparer's Name / Title**	Date Prepared **mm/dd/yyyy**
Effective Date **mm/dd/yyyy**	Reviewed By **Reviewer's Name / Title**	Date Reviewed **mm/dd/yyyy**
	Approved By **Final Approver's Name / Title**	Date Approved **mm/dd/yyyy**

SUMMARY

The Software Trainer (training specialist) develops and executes training plans, training materials, and classes, schedules classes into facilities, and provides software instruction to the organization's employees. They also review results and trainee feedback to improve materials and classes, as well as identify and develop additional software training opportunities.

ESSENTIAL DUTIES AND RESPONSIBILITIES

- Assess individual and group training needs; maintain individual and group training records.
- Plan, prepare, and research lessons.
- Organize and promote courses.
- Develop and deliver programs of learning activities.
- Prepare teaching/course materials.
- Instruct users on an individual or group basis.
- Proctor course examinations.
- Check and assess (grade) users' work and deliver feedback with course grades.
- Apply new technologies to deliver courses and improve the learning experience for users (e.g., distance learning, interactive CBT, blended training).
- Keep personal IT skills and knowledge up to date.

ORGANIZATIONAL RELATIONSHIPS

Reports directly to the Software Support Manager. Works with IT Management, software development/procurement, and user groups.

PROCEDURES

Procedure ID and Name	Policies & Procedures Manual
ITSW110 Software Support	Computer & Network (IT)
ITSW112 Software Training	Computer & Network (IT)
SWD110 Software Support	Software Development
SWD112 Software Training	Software Development

QUALIFICATIONS

A bachelor's degree is required; a degree in adult education, communications, or computer science is preferred. Prior experience as a post-secondary or workplace trainer/instructor is also required.

Exceptional communication skills and the ability to work well with people at all levels are essential. Strong organizational, planning, and motivational skills are desired. Ability to quickly set up and use audiovisual equipment is a plus, though not required. Knowledge of, experience with educational, presentation software is necessary. Experience with PowerPoint, Visio is desirable.

Teacher or trainer certification (e.g., MCT) is preferred; software design/development experience would be a plus.

PHYSICAL DEMANDS

Ability to communicate orally with software designers/vendors, IT management, and software users (esp. nontechnical users) is crucial. Regular use of phone and email for communication is essential. Hearing and vision correctable to within normal ranges is essential for normal conversations, receiving ordinary information, and preparing or inspecting documents.

The ability to remain in a stationary position roughly 50% of the time, as well as the ability to move about the office occasionally (accessing files/storage, office equipment, computers and other office productivity devices, attending meetings, etc.), is required.

Using a computer while sitting for extended periods is common. Must also be able to position self to maintain equipment, including under tables and desks.

Occasional heavy lifting (e.g., 15+ lbs. of course materials, binders) can be expected; lighter loads (5-10 lbs.) is more commonplace. Good manual dexterity required to use common office equipment (e.g., computers, mobile devices, calculators, copiers, scanners).

WORK ENVIRONMENT

The job is performed indoors in a traditional office setting. Extended periods of sitting while using a computer or other devices are common.

REVISION HISTORY

Revision	Date	Description of Changes	Requested By
0.0	mm/dd/yyyy	Initial Release	

[This page intentionally left blank]

Document ID **JD1290**	Title **SYSTEMS ANALYST**	Print Date **mm/dd/yyyy**
Revision **0.0**	Prepared By **Preparer's Name / Title**	Date Prepared **mm/dd/yyyy**
Effective Date **mm/dd/yyyy**	Reviewed By **Reviewer's Name / Title**	Date Reviewed **mm/dd/yyyy**
	Approved By **Final Approver's Name / Title**	Date Approved **mm/dd/yyyy**

SUMMARY

The Systems Analyst studies the organization's current computer systems and procedures and recommends changes to programs, systems, and planning, to help information technology (IT) operate more efficiently and effectively and meet customer, organizational, and other requirements. They bring business and IT together by understanding – and helping them understand – their needs, capabilities, and limitations.

ESSENTIAL DUTIES AND RESPONSIBILITIES

- Consult with business managers to determine how best to meet customers – and the organization's – requirements.
- Lead a team of software designers, software testers, and technical writers; demonstrate leadership qualities.
- Design and develop system and program requirements; develop and communicate overall design approach.
- Determine how existing systems might meet emerging requirements.
- Create software test plans, test scenarios, and test cases.
- Review design changes, update program/system requirements as needed.
- Explain programs and systems to technical writers, for development of technical and/or end-user documentation.
- Stay informed of emerging technologies; determine how they might be useful to the organization.

ORGANIZATIONAL RELATIONSHIPS

Reports directly to the IT Manager; works with business managers and technical staff to facilitate software development.

PROCEDURES

Procedure ID and Name	Policies & Procedures Manual
ITSW103 Systems Analysis	Computer & Network (IT)
ITSW106 Software Documentation	Computer & Network (IT)
ITSW107 Software Testing	Computer & Network (IT)
ITSW108 Design Changes During Development	Computer & Network (IT)

Procedure ID and Name	Policies & Procedures Manual
SWD103 Systems Analysis	Software Development
SWD106 Software Documentation	Software Development
SWD107 Software Testing	Software Development
SWD108 Design Changes During Development	Software Development

QUALIFICATIONS

A bachelor's degree in computer science/IT is required; an MBA (information management) is preferred. 5+ years of experience in software development is required. 1+ years' experience managing software developers also required; must have demonstrated ability to lead a diverse team of technicians. Knowledge of SDLC a necessity.

Good communication skills and the ability to work well with people at all levels are essential. Require strong math, technical, organizational, and management skills. Prior project management experience is preferred.

Prefer candidates with systems analysis certification. Need Java programming experience. Experience with UML (Rational) is a definite plus.

PHYSICAL DEMANDS

Ability to communicate orally with customers, vendors, management, and coworkers is crucial. Regular use of phone and email for communication is essential. Hearing and vision correctable to within normal ranges is essential for normal conversations, receiving ordinary information, and preparing or inspecting documents.

The ability to remain in a stationary position roughly 50% of the time, as well as the ability to move about the office occasionally (accessing files/storage, office equipment, computers and other office productivity devices, attending meetings, etc.), is required.

Using a computer while sitting for extended periods is common. No heavy lifting is expected, though occasional exertion of about 20 lbs. of force (e.g., picking up and carrying binders, laptops) may be required. Good manual dexterity required to use common office equipment (e.g., computers, mobile devices, calculators, copiers, scanners).

WORK ENVIRONMENT

The job is performed indoors in a traditional office setting. Extended periods of sitting while using a computer or other devices are common.

REVISION HISTORY

Revision	Date	Description of Changes	Requested By
0.0	mm/dd/yyyy	Initial Release	

[This page intentionally left blank]

Document ID	Title	Print Date
JD1300	**TECHNICAL SUPPORT MANAGER**	**mm/dd/yyyy**
Revision	Prepared By	Date Prepared
0.0	**Preparer's Name / Title**	**mm/dd/yyyy**
Effective Date	Reviewed By	Date Reviewed
mm/dd/yyyy	**Reviewer's Name / Title**	**mm/dd/yyyy**
	Approved By	Date Approved
	Final Approver's Name / Title	**mm/dd/yyyy**

SUMMARY

The Technical Support Manager[1] is responsible for the day-to-day operation of the organization's computer systems and network, ensuring 24/7 operation of systems and when problems arise, effecting quick and permanent solutions.

ESSENTIAL DUTIES AND RESPONSIBILITIES

- Direct and coordinate a team of tech support specialists / help desk technicians.
- Prioritize IT-related problems as they come in to Help Desk and escalate when necessary.
- Assign problems/tasks to tech support specialists.
- Regularly analyze and review logs to determine if problems are imminent and develop solutions before they occur.
- Analyze situations and determine resources needed to solve them.
- Make decisions quickly, often with limited information.
- Follow up with customers to gauge their satisfaction with problem resolution; identify tech support problem areas (i.e., negative trends) and, if warranted, implement corrective actions.
- Ensure ongoing training for tech support staff; advise tech support staff on career planning; maintain and analyze training records.

ORGANIZATIONAL RELATIONSHIPS

Reports directly to the Computer & Network Systems Administrator. Works with other IT staff to effect rapid corrections and, more importantly, corrective and preventive actions to prevent the occurrence or recurrence of problems.

PROCEDURES

Procedure ID and Name	Policies & Procedures Manual
ITAD102 IT Records Management	Computer & Network (IT)
ITAD104 IT Device Naming Conventions	Computer & Network (IT)
ITAD106 Network Infrastructure Standards	Computer & Network (IT)

---

[1] May be called the Tech Support Manager, IT Support Center Manager, or Help Desk Manager.

Procedure ID and Name	Policies & Procedures Manual
ITAD110 IT Department Satisfaction	Computer & Network (IT)
ITAM101 IT Asset Standards	Computer & Network (IT)
ITAM102 IT Asset Management	Computer & Network (IT)
ITAM104 IT Asset Assessment	Computer & Network (IT)
ITAM105 IT Asset Installation Satisfaction	Computer & Network (IT)
ITSD105 Computer Malware	Computer & Network (IT)
ITSW112 Software Training	Computer & Network (IT)
ITTS102 IT Support Center	Computer & Network (IT)
ITTS104 IT Troubleshooting	Computer & Network (IT)

QUALIFICATIONS

A bachelor's degree in computer science or electrical engineering is required; an MBA in information management is desirable. 5+ years of experience in technical support (help desk) is desired, though a similar amount of experience in a customer support role would be very helpful.

Experience as a team leader in any area of IT will be considered. Good communication skills and the ability to work well with people at all levels are essential; must be customer focused. Strong computer, analytical, organizational skills. Must be able to work quickly and methodically. Need a problem solver. Want someone with a positive, take-charge attitude. Prefer someone with appropriate project management and/or tech support management certification.

Experience using Remedy is important – experience managing with Remedy ITSM even better.

PHYSICAL DEMANDS

Ability to communicate well orally and in writing with customers, vendors, management, and coworkers is crucial. Regular use of phone and email for communication is essential. Hearing and vision correctable to within normal ranges is essential for normal conversations, receiving ordinary information, and preparing or inspecting documents.

The ability to remain in a stationary position roughly 50% of the time, as well as the ability to move about the office occasionally (accessing files/storage, office equipment, computers and other office productivity devices, attending meetings, etc.), is required.

Using a computer while sitting for extended periods is common. Must also be able to position self to maintain equipment, including under tables and desks.

No heavy lifting is expected, though occasional exertion of about 20 lbs. of force (e.g., picking up and carrying binders, laptops) may be required. Good manual dexterity required to use common office equipment (e.g., computers, mobile devices, calculators, copiers, scanners).

WORK ENVIRONMENT

The job is performed indoors in a traditional office setting. Extended periods of sitting while using a computer or other devices are common.

REVISION HISTORY

Revision	Date	Description of Changes	Requested By
0.0	mm/dd/yyyy	Initial Release	

[This page intentionally left blank]

Document ID **JD1310**	Title **TECHNICAL SUPPORT SPECIALIST**	Print Date **mm/dd/yyyy**
Revision **0.0**	Prepared By **Preparer's Name / Title**	Date Prepared **mm/dd/yyyy**
Effective Date **mm/dd/yyyy**	Reviewed By **Reviewer's Name / Title**	Date Reviewed **mm/dd/yyyy**
	Approved By **Final Approver's Name / Title**	Date Approved **mm/dd/yyyy**

SUMMARY

The Technical Support Specialist[1] provides help and advice to people and organizations using computer software or equipment. They support information technology (IT) employees within the organization and assist non-IT users who are having computer or application problems.

ESSENTIAL DUTIES AND RESPONSIBILITIES

- Test and evaluate existing network systems.
- Perform regular maintenance to ensure that networks operate correctly.
- Troubleshoot local area networks (LANs), wide area networks (WANs), and Internet systems.
- Responsible for a variety of recovery tasks (e.g., installing and testing replacement hardware and software, keeping customer apprised of work status).
- Solve technical problems quickly and effectively.
- Work often as part of a team of technicians to resolve high-priority situations; work independently on routine (lower-priority) problems.
- Work well in high-pressure situations (e.g., computer or system shutdowns).
- Make decisions quickly, often with limited information.
- Train users how to use new hardware, software; use new features of existing software; etc.

ORGANIZATIONAL RELATIONSHIPS

Reports directly to the Tech Support Manager. Assists IT users and works in conjunction with other Tech Support Specialists to facilitate turnaround time and deliver solutions.

PROCEDURES

Procedure ID and Name	Policies & Procedures Manual
ITSD104 IT Disaster Recovery	Computer & Network (IT)

---

[1] May be called Tech Support Specialist, Tech Support Rep, or Help Desk technician

QUALIFICATIONS

A bachelor's degree is required. One or more years of tech support experience is preferable, though we will train the right candidate.

Good communication skills and the ability to work well with people at all levels are essential; job requires an excellent listener and very strong interpersonal skills. Need a great eye for detail and strong problem-solving ability. Experience with Remedy is a plus, as is Tech Support/Help Desk certification.

PHYSICAL DEMANDS

Ability to communicate orally with customers, vendors, management, and coworkers is crucial. Regular use of phone and email for communication is essential. Hearing and vision correctable to within normal ranges is essential for normal conversations, receiving ordinary information, and preparing or inspecting documents.

The ability to remain in a stationary position roughly 50% of the time, as well as the ability to move about the office occasionally (install and test hardware/software, etc.), is required.

Using a computer while sitting for extended periods is common. Must also be able to position self to install/maintain equipment, including under tables and desks.

No heavy lifting is expected, though occasional exertion of about 20 lbs. of force (e.g., picking up and carrying IT equipment) may be required. Good manual dexterity required to use common office equipment (e.g., computers, mobile devices, testing equipment).

WORK ENVIRONMENT

The job is performed indoors in a traditional office setting. Extended periods of sitting while using a computer or other devices are common.

REVISION HISTORY

Revision	Date	Description of Changes	Requested By
0.0	mm/dd/yyyy	Initial Release	

Document ID	Title	Print Date
JD1320	**TECHNICAL WRITER**	**mm/dd/yyyy**
Revision	Prepared By	Date Prepared
0.0	**Preparer's Name / Title**	**mm/dd/yyyy**
Effective Date	Reviewed By	Date Reviewed
mm/dd/yyyy	**Reviewer's Name / Title**	**mm/dd/yyyy**
	Approved By	Date Approved
	Final Approver's Name / Title	**mm/dd/yyyy**

SUMMARY

The Technical Writer[1] produces instruction manuals and other supporting documents to communicate complex and technical information more easily. They also develop, gather, verify, and disseminate technical information among customers, designers, and manufacturers.

ESSENTIAL DUTIES AND RESPONSIBILITIES

- Determine requirements and preferences of technical documentation users.
- Study product samples and discuss with Design & Development.
- Assist technical staff in making products easy to use (and make procedures and work instructions less complex, easier to follow).
- Design and develop supporting documentation for products (e.g., user manuals).
- Identify and use photos, drawings, diagrams, and charts to increase user understanding.
- Understand and translate complex information for users of varying backgrounds, experiences.
- Test documents on designers and users and gather feedback on their usefulness (usability studies).
- Periodically review all documentation for timeliness, accuracy, and usefulness; make corrections/updates as needed.
- Manage the document review and approval process.
- Develop documentation for a variety of media (print, PowerPoint, video, etc.).

ORGANIZATIONAL RELATIONSHIPS

Reports directly to the Training Manager. Works with a variety of designers, developers, technicians, and support staff to develop technical or end user documentation, typically used for training and reference.

---

[1] May be called a Content Developer or Technical Communicator, as well.

PROCEDURES

Procedure ID and Name	Policies & Procedures Manual
ITSW106 Software Documentation	Computer & Network (IT)
SWD106 Software Documentation	Software Development

QUALIFICATIONS

A bachelor's degree in journalism or communications is preferred, though 3+ years of experience as a technical writer may be considered in lieu of a degree. required.

Exceptional communication skills and the ability to work well with people at all levels are essential. Would like someone with presentation skills, who is comfortable speaking to groups of 6 or more people.

Experience with MS-Word, PowerPoint, SharePoint, and Visio is required. Candidate should be experienced in Framemaker and wiki development. Experience with PhotoShop, RoboHelp, DreamWeaver, and/or HTML is helpful.

PHYSICAL DEMANDS

Ability to communicate orally with customers, vendors, management, and coworkers is crucial. Regular use of phone and email for communication is essential. Hearing and vision correctable to within normal ranges is essential for normal conversations, receiving ordinary information, and preparing or inspecting documents.

The ability to remain in a stationary position roughly 50% of the time, as well as the ability to move about the office occasionally (accessing files/storage, office equipment, computers and other office productivity devices, attending meetings, etc.), is required.

Using a computer while sitting for extended periods is common. Must also be able to position self to maintain equipment, including under tables and desks.

No heavy lifting is expected, though occasional exertion of about 20 lbs. of force (e.g., picking up and carrying binders, laptops) may be required. Good manual dexterity required to use common office equipment (e.g., computers, mobile devices, calculators, copiers, scanners).

WORK ENVIRONMENT

The job is performed indoors in a traditional office setting. Extended periods of sitting while using a computer or other devices are common.

REVISION HISTORY

Revision	Date	Description of Changes	Requested By
0.0	mm/dd/yyyy	Initial Release	

[This page intentionally left blank]

Document ID **JD1330**	Title **TELECOMMUNICATIONS MANAGER**	Print Date **mm/dd/yyyy**
Revision **0.0**	Prepared By **Preparer's Name / Title**	Date Prepared **mm/dd/yyyy**
Effective Date **mm/dd/yyyy**	Reviewed By **Reviewer's Name / Title**	Date Reviewed **mm/dd/yyyy**
	Approved By **Final Approver's Name / Title**	Date Approved **mm/dd/yyyy**

SUMMARY

The Telecommunications (Telecomm) Manager oversees the configuration, installation, and maintenance of – as well as updates to – the organization's WAN and LAN systems, including network hardware and software. This includes the organization's voice, fax, and A/V systems (e.g., teleconferencing).

ESSENTIAL DUTIES AND RESPONSIBILITIES

- Manage configuration and installation of network hardware and software, as well as network repairs and upgrades.
- Ensure network and computer system security.
- Collect network data for evaluation, with an eye to continual improvement.
- Help identify and implement improvements where needed.
- Help to quickly identify and resolve network issues.

ORGANIZATIONAL RELATIONSHIPS

Reports directly to the Network and Computer Systems Administrator. Works with support technicians and service advisors to ensure optimal network performance and minimal, if any, downtime.

PROCEDURES

Procedure ID and Name	Policies & Procedures Manual
ITAD106 Network Infrastructure Standards	Computer & Network (IT)

QUALIFICATIONS

A bachelor's degree in computer science, information technology, computer engineering, or a related discipline is required. 3+ years of experience as a network technician (troubleshooter) is also required. Computer network certification (e.g., CompTIA Network+, Cisco, Microsoft) is desirable.

Must be able to demonstrate analytical and problem-solving abilities. Must have experience leading a team of 2 or more network technicians. Must possess good communication skills, both orally and in writing. IT project management experience is desired.

PHYSICAL DEMANDS

Ability to communicate orally with customers, vendors, and IT management is crucial. Regular use of phone and email for communication is essential. Hearing and vision correctable to within normal ranges is essential for normal conversations, receiving ordinary information, and preparing or inspecting documents.

The ability to remain in a stationary position roughly 50% of the time, as well as the ability to move about the office (e.g., to access office equipment, install or repair computers and other office productivity devices), is required.

Using a computer while sitting for extended periods is common. Must also be able to position self to install and maintain LAN/WAN equipment, including under tables and desks.

Occasional lifting of 20-30 lbs. (e.g., cables, routers, storage devices) is expected. Good manual dexterity required to use common office equipment (e.g., computers, mobile devices), installation and repair tools, etc.

WORK ENVIRONMENT

The job is performed indoors in a traditional office setting. Periods of sitting while using a computer or other device (roughly 50%) are interspersed with moving about the facilities to install, repair, or maintain network devices.

REVISION HISTORY

Revision	Date	Description of Changes	Requested By
0.0	mm/dd/yyyy	Initial Release	

Document ID JD1370	Title **TRAINING MANAGER**	Print Date mm/dd/yyyy
Revision 0.0	Prepared By **Preparer's Name / Title**	Date Prepared mm/dd/yyyy
Effective Date mm/dd/yyyy	Reviewed By **Reviewer's Name / Title**	Date Reviewed mm/dd/yyyy
	Approved By **Final Approver's Name / Title**	Date Approved mm/dd/yyyy

SUMMARY

The Training Manager[1] plans, directs, and coordinates programs for the purpose of enhancing the knowledge and skills of the organization's employees. They also oversee a staff of training and development specialists.

ESSENTIAL DUTIES AND RESPONSIBILITIES

- Review training records periodically (or as needed) and evaluate employees' training requirements; confer with department managers to determine training requirements.
- Align training and development with organizational strategy.
- Create a training budget and keep training & development operations within budget.
- Develop or update training programs to ensure that they are current.
- Oversee the creation of training manuals, online learning modules, and other educational materials for employees.
- Review training materials from a variety of vendors and select materials with appropriate content.
- Teach training methods and skills to instructors and supervisors (i.e., "train the trainer").
- Evaluate effectiveness of training programs and instructors; review course evaluations and recommend course revisions/updates.

ORGANIZATIONAL RELATIONSHIPS

Reports directly to the Human Resources Manager. Works in conjunction with HR staff, department managers to ensure all employees are adequately trained to perform their duties.

PROCEDURES

Procedure ID and Name	Policies & Procedures Manual
ITSW112 Software Training	Computer & Network (IT)
SWD112 Software Training	Software Development

---

[1] May be the Training & Development Manager in some organizations.

QUALIFICATIONS

A bachelor's degree in education, business administration, or liberal arts or at least five years of teaching equivalent is required. Requires 2+ years of experience in a corporate or business setting, preferably in human resources, personnel, or administration; training experience in a business setting is preferred.

Proven ability to lead by example and foster mentoring relationships is a must. Outstanding oral, written, multitasking, and presentation skills are crucial, as is the ability to create momentum and foster organizational change.

Experience with Adobe Presenter, Microsoft Office preferred.

PHYSICAL DEMANDS

Ability to communicate orally with trainees, department and senior management, training vendors, and coworkers is crucial. Regular use of phone and email for communication is essential. Hearing and vision correctable to within normal ranges is essential for normal conversations, receiving ordinary information, and preparing or inspecting documents.

The ability to remain in a stationary position roughly 50% of the time, as well as the ability to move about the office occasionally (accessing files/storage, office equipment, computers and other office productivity devices, attending meetings, etc.), is required. Using a computer while sitting for extended periods is common. Must also be able to position self to set up and utilize multimedia equipment, including under tables and desks.

No heavy lifting is expected, though occasional exertion of 20+ lbs. of force (e.g., moving and setting up presentation equipment) may be required. Good manual dexterity required to use common office equipment (e.g., computers, mobile devices, calculators, copiers, scanners).

WORK ENVIRONMENT

The job is performed indoors in a traditional office setting. Extended periods of sitting while using a computer or other devices are common.

REVISION HISTORY

Revision	Date	Description of Changes	Requested By
0.0	mm/dd/yyyy	Initial Release	

bizmanualz

IT Policies and Procedures

Section 600

Index

Section 600

Index

INDEX   <u>SECTION/ID</u>   <u>Page</u>

-

INDEX   **SECTION/ID**   **Page**

D

INDEX   **SECTION/ID**   **Page**

INDEX   **SECTION/ID**   **Page**

INDEX   **SECTION/ID**   **Page**

J

K

INDEX   **SECTION/ID**   **Page**

P

S

INDEX   **SECTION/ID**   **Page**

INDEX   **SECTION/ID**   **Page**

T

U

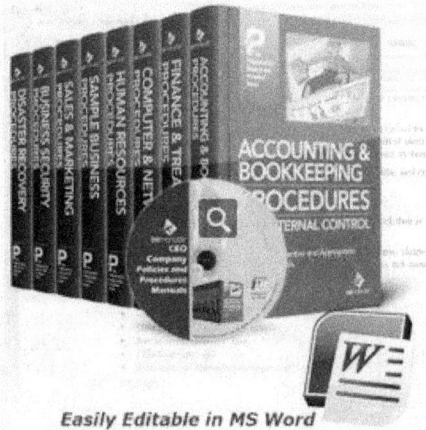

Policies and Procedures Manuals from Bizmanualz

Product details at www.bizmanualz.com

Free samples at www.bizmanualz.com/sample-policies-procedures

Prewritten policies and procedures help you document your processes faster. No need to start from scratch! Our experts have done the research and writing, saving you time, money, and aggravation. Each manual contains a set of easily-**editable Microsoft Word** documents (available for download or on CD).

ABR31 Accounting Policies and Procedures

Protect your business assets with easily editable internal controls, policies, and procedures.

Includes over 3 dozen Accounting procedures for cash, inventory & assets, purchasing, revenue, and administration. Also contains an Accounting Policy Manual and Embezzlement Prevention guide.

ABR42 Finance Policies and Procedures

Quickly create a financial management system to manage risk, optimize returns, and establish effective internal controls.

Includes dozens of Finance procedures for administration, financial statements, internal controls, raising capital, and treasury management. Also includes a Finance Policy Manual and a business management guide.

ABR34 Computer & IT Policies and Procedures

Protect and control your IT assets with easily editable information technology policies and procedures.

Includes 40 procedures for IT administration, IT training and support, IT asset management, IT security and disaster recovery, and software development. Also includes an IT Policy Manual and IT security guide.

ABR44 Sales & Marketing Policies and Procedures

Drive customer satisfaction with improved strategies and tactics.

Includes over 30 Sales and Marketing procedures for planning and strategy, tactics, sales, administration, and product management. Also contains a Sales & Marketing Policy Manual and Internet Marketing guide.

ABR211 ISO 9001 QMS Policies and Procedures

Quickly create your own ISO 9001 quality management system with easily editable quality policies and procedures. Includes 30 quality procedures and a sample Quality Manual.

ABR41 Human Resources Policies and Procedures

Reduce exposure to employee liability issues with easily editable HR policies and procedures.

Includes 35 HR procedures for administration, hiring, compensation, payroll, development, and compliance. Also includes sample job descriptions, an HR Policy Manual, and an Employee Handbook.

A490 Business Policies and Procedures Sampler

Quickly create a total system of internal controls for key departments in your organization.

111 easily editable policies and procedures for a variety of everyday functional areas.

More Procedure Manuals from Bizmanualz

- Security Planning Policies & Procedures
- Disaster Recovery Policies & Procedures
- ISO22000 Food Safety Policies & Procedures
- AS9100 Aerospace Policies & Procedures
- Medical Office Policies & Procedures
- Banking Policies & Procedures
- Non-Profit Policies & Procedures
- Construction Policies & Procedures
- Software Development Policies & Procedures

Buy a Bundle, Save a Bundle!

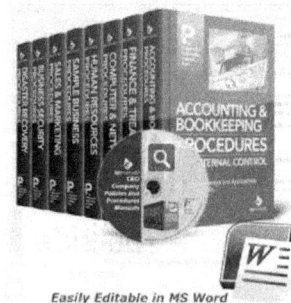

Easily Editable in MS Word

Buy the 9-manual "CEO Management Procedures Series" or the 5-manual "CFO Management Series" and save *up to 40 percent!*

www.ingramcontent.com/pod-product-compliance
Lightning Source LLC
Chambersburg PA
CBHW062009190326
41458CB00009B/3021